T0180402

Lecture Notes in Computer Science 12234

More information about this series at http://www.springer.com/series/7408

António Casimiro · Frank Ortmeier ·
Friedemann Bitsch · Pedro Ferreira (Eds.)

Computer Safety, Reliability, and Security

39th International Conference, SAFECOMP 2020
Lisbon, Portugal, September 16–18, 2020
Proceedings

 Springer

Editors
António Casimiro ⓘ
University of Lisbon
Lisbon, Portugal

Frank Ortmeier ⓘ
Otto-von-Guericke University
Magdeburg, Germany

Friedemann Bitsch ⓘ
Thales Deutschland GmbH
Ditzingen, Germany

Pedro Ferreira ⓘ
University of Lisbon
Lisbon, Portugal

ISSN 0302-9743   ISSN 1611-3349 (electronic)
Lecture Notes in Computer Science
ISBN 978-3-030-54548-2   ISBN 978-3-030-54549-9 (eBook)
https://doi.org/10.1007/978-3-030-54549-9

LNCS Sublibrary: SL2 – Programming and Software Engineering

This Springer imprint is published by the registered company Springer Nature Switzerland AG
The registered company address is: Gewerbestrasse 11, 6330 Cham, Switzerland

Preface

This volume (12234) contains the proceedings of the 39th International Conference on Computer Safety, Reliability and Security (SAFECOMP 2020) held in September 2020. Due to the COVID-19 pandemic, SAFECOMP took place, for the first time, as a virtual conference on the Web, instead of being held in Lisbon, Portugal, as planned. Since 1979, when the conference was established by the European Workshop on Industrial Computer Systems, Technical Committee 7 on Reliability, Safety and Security (EWICS TC7), it has contributed to the state of the art through the knowledge dissemination and discussions of important aspects of computer systems of our everyday life. With the proliferation of embedded systems, the omnipresence of the Internet of Things and commodity of advanced real-time control systems, our dependence on the safe and correct behavior is ever increasing. Currently, we are witnessing the beginning of truly autonomous systems, perhaps with driver-less cars (the most well-known to the non-specialist), where the safety and correctness of their computer systems are already being discussed in the main-stream media. In this context, it is clear that the relevance of the SAFECOMP conference series is increasing.

The International Program Committee, consisting of 57 members from 14 countries, received 116 papers from 29 nations. Of these, 29 papers were selected to be published in the SAFECOMP 2020 proceedings and presented at the conference, resulting in an acceptance rate of 25%. The review process was thorough with each paper receiving at least three reviews. The reviewers had ensured independence, preliminary online discussions, and a final discussion and selection phase, which took place during the IPC meeting (held by video conference in April 2020) and was attended by more than 40 IPC members. Our warm thanks go to reviewers who offered their time and competence to ensure a high-quality program.

The conference featured three keynotes: "Towards AI trustworthiness" by Guillaume Soudain, Software and Airborne Electronic Hardware Expert in the Certification Directorate of the European Aviation Safety Agency (EASA); "Safe Perception and AI for Autonomous Driving" by Jonas Nilsson, Senior System Safety Architect at NVIDIA; "ISO TR 4804: Safety and Cybersecurity for Automated Driving Systems" by Simon Fürst, Principal Expert of Autonomous Driving Technologies at BMW Group.

Despite being organized as an on-line event, SAFECOMP 2020 kept a single-track format. This fostered academic exchange and discussions, providing opportunities for participants to interact with presenters, and with each other, through discussion forums. The conference also included a position papers session, giving the opportunity for new ideas and work in progress to be presented and for the collection of valuable feedback from the audience. The position papers proceedings are published in the HAL repository.

As it has been the tradition for many years, the day before the main conference was dedicated to workshops. This year there were four workshops: DECSoS – 15th International Workshop on Dependable Smart Embedded Cyber-Physical Systems and

Systems-of-Systems; WAISE – Third International Workshop on Artificial Intelligence Safety Engineering; DepDevOps – First International workshop on Dependable Development-Operation Continuum Methods for Dependable Cyber-Physical Systems; and USDAI – Underpinnings for Safe Distributed AI, of which the last two were new workshops co-located with SAFECOMP. Papers from these are published in a separate LNCS volume (12235).

We would like to express our gratitude to the many who contributed to make this conference possible: the authors of submitted papers and the invited speakers; the Program Committee members and external reviewers; EWICS TC7 headed by Francesca Saglietti; the supporting and sponsoring organizations; Friedemann Bitsch and Pedro Ferreira as publication co-chairs; Erwin Schoitsch as workshop chair; Jérémie Guiochet as position papers chair; Bernardo Ferreira as publicity chair; and the local Organization Committee, led by Ibéria Medeiros, who took care of the arrangements that made it possible to run the conference as a virtual event.

We hope that the reader will find these proceedings interesting and hope that SAFECOMP 2021 will be once again a physical conference with possibly additional virtual channels to reach an even greater audience.

June 2020   António Casimiro
                                                                        Frank Ortmeier

Organization

Committees

EWICS TC7 Chair

Francesca Saglietti — University of Erlangen-Nuremberg, Germany

General Chair

António Casimiro — University of Lisbon, Portugal

Program Co-chairs

António Casimiro — University of Lisbon, Portugal
Frank Ortmeier — Otto-von-Guericke University, Germany

General Workshop Chair

Erwin Schoitsch — AIT Austrian Institute of Technology, Austria

Publication Chairs

Friedemann Bitsch — Thales Deutschland GmbH, Germany
Pedro Ferreira — University of Lisbon, Portugal

Position Papers Chair

Jérémie Guiochet — University of Toulouse III, France

Publicity Chair

Bernardo Ferreira — University of Lisbon, Portugal

Local Organizing Committee

António Casimiro — University of Lisbon, Portugal
Pedro Ferreira — University of Lisbon, Portugal
Ibéria Medeiros — University of Lisbon, Portugal

International Program Committee

Uwe Becker — Draeger Medical GmbH, Germany
Peter G. Bishop — Adelard, UK
Friedemann Bitsch — Thales Deutschland GmbH, Germany
Sandro Bologna — Associazione Italiana Esperti Infrastrutture Critiche, Italy
Andrea Bondavalli — University of Florence, Italy

Jens Braband	Siemens AG, Germany
Simon Burton	Robert Bosch GmbH, Germany
Peter Daniel	EWICS TC7, UK
Ewen Denney	SGT, NASA Ames Research Center, USA
Felicita Di Giandomenico	ISTI-CNR, Italy
Wolfgang Ehrenberger	University of Applied Science Fulda, Germany
John Favaro	Intecs, Italy
Francesco Flammini	Mälardalen University, Sweden
Simon Fuerst	BMW Group, Germany
Barbara Gallina	Mälardalen University, Sweden
Ilir Gashi	CSR, City University London, UK
Bruno Gonçalves	GMVIS Skysoft SA, Portugal
Janusz Górski	Gdańsk University of Technology, Poland
Jérémie Guiochet	LAAS-CNRS, France
Ibrahim Habli	University of York, UK
Hans Hansson	Mälardalen University, Sweden
Maritta Heisel	University of Duisburg-Essen, Germany
Chris Johnson	University of Glasgow, UK
Rajeev Joshi	Automated Reasoning Group, Amazon Web Services, USA
Joost-Pieter Katoen	RWTH Aachen University, Germany
Phil Koopman	Carnegie-Mellon University, USA
Timo Latvala	Space Systems Finland Ltd., Finland
John McDermid	University of York, UK
Simin Nadjm-Tehrani	Linköping University, Sweden
Mattias Nyberg	KTH Royal Institute of Technology, Sweden
Philippe Palanque	ICS-IRIT, University Toulouse, France
Michael Paulitsch	Intel, Austria
Holger Pfeifer	Technical University of Munich, Germany
Luís Miguel Pinho	CISTER Research Centre, ISEP, Portugal
Peter Popov	City University London, UK
Alexander Romanovsky	Newcastle University, UK
Matteo Rossi	Politecnico di Milano, Italy
Francesca Saglietti	University of Erlangen-Nuremberg, Germany
Christoph Schmitz	Zühlke Engineering AG, Switzerland
Erwin Schoitsch	AIT Austrian Institute of Technology, Austria
Christel Seguin	Office National d'Etudes et Recherches Aérospatiales, France
Frank Singhof	Lab-STICC, Université de Bretagne Occidentale, France
Håkan Sivencrona	ZENUITY, Sweden
Oleg Sokolsky	University of Pennsylvania, USA
Wilfried Steiner	TTTech Computertechnik AG, Austria
Mark Sujan	University of Warwick, UK
Kenji Taguchi	CAV Technologies Co., Ltd., Japan
Stefano Tonetta	Fondazione Bruno Kessler, Italy

Martin Törngren	KTH Royal Institute of Technology, Sweden
Mario Trapp	Fraunhofer Institute for Cognitive Systems IKS, Germany
Elena Troubitsyna (FI)	KTH Royal Institute of Technology, Sweden
Tullio Vardanega	University of Padua, Italy
Marcel Verhoef	European Space Agency, The Netherlands
Marco Vieira	University of Coimbra, Portugal
Jonny Vinter	RISE Research Institutes of Sweden, Sweden
Marcus Völp	SnT, University of Luxembourg, Luxembourg
Hélène Waeselynck	LAAS-CNRS, France

Sub-reviewers

Haris Aftab	University of York, UK
Nuno Antunes	University of Coimbra, Portugal
Erfan Asaadi	SGT, NASA Ames Research Center, USA
Mehrnoosh Askarpour	Politecnico di Milano, Italy
Ill-Ham Atchadam	Lab-STICC, Université de Bretagne Occidentale, France
Andrea Baldovin	Intel, Austria
Angela Borchert	University of Duisburg-Essen, Germany
Alessio Bucaioni	Mälardalen University, Sweden
Alexandre Canny	ICS-IRIT, University Toulouse, France
Andrea Ceccarelli	University of Florence, Italy
Matthew Cleaveland	University of Pennsylvania, USA
Joao Cunha	University of Coimbra, Portugal
Mirko D'Angelo	Linnaeus University, Sweden
Marvin Damschen	RISE Research Institutes of Sweden, Sweden
Mourad Dridi	Lab-STICC, Université de Bretagne Occidentale, France
Nicolás Díaz Ferreyra	University of Duisburg-Essen, Germany
Eduard Paul Enoiu	Mälardalen University, Sweden
Raul Ferreira	LAAS-CNRS, France
Peter Folkesson	RISE Research Institutes of Sweden, Sweden
Jose Fonseca	University of Coimbra, Portugal
José M. Gaspar Sánchez	KTH Royal Institute of Technology, Sweden
Mohammad Gharib	University of Florence, Italy
Magnus Gyllenhammar	ZENUITY, Sweden
Richard Hawkins	University of York, UK
Hoyer Patrik	Huld, Finland
Dubravka Ilic	Huld, Finland
Radoslav Ivanov	University of Pennsylvania, USA
Marcus Jägemar	Mälardalen University, Sweden
Nils Jörgensen	KTH Royal Institute of Technology, Sweden
Stefan Kaalen	KTH Royal Institute of Technology, Sweden
Ramneet Kaur	University of Pennsylvania, USA

Shahid Khan   RWTH Aachen University, Germany
Pierre Kleberger   RISE Research Institutes of Sweden, Sweden
Ryo Kurachi   Nagoya University, Japan
Livia Lestingi   Politecnico di Milano, Italy
Elena Lisova   Mälardalen University, Sweden
Nuno Lourenco   University of Coimbra, Portugal
Giulio Masetti   ISTI-CNR, Italy
Yutaka Matsuno   Nihon University, Japan
Joshua Moerman   RWTH Aachen University, Germany
Naveen Mohan   KTH Royal Institute of Technology, Sweden
Damir Nesic   KTH Royal Institute of Technology, Sweden
Thomas Noll   RWTH Aachen University, Germany
Fabian Oboril   Intel, Austria
Takao Okubo   Institute of Information Security, Japan
Lorenzo Pagliari   Linnaeus University, Sweden
Ganesh Pai   SGT, NASA Ames Research Center, USA
Masoumeh Parseh   KTH Royal Institute of Technology, Sweden
Colin Paterson   University of York, UK
Chiara Picardi   University of York, UK
Rita Pimentel   RISE SICS Västerås, Sweden
Inês Pinto Gouveia   SnT, University of Luxembourg, Luxembourg
Viorel Preoteasa   Space Systems Finland Ltd., Finland
Yuliya Prokhorova   Huld, Finland
Anne Remke   Universität Münster, Germany
Mehdi Saman Azari   Linnaeus University, Sweden
Behrooz Sangchoolie   RISE Research Institutes of Sweden, Sweden
Thomas Santen   TU Berlin, Germany
Ricardo Severino   CISTER Research Centre, ISEP, Portugal
Prasannjeet Singh   Linnaeus University, Sweden
Martin Skoglund   RISE Research Institutes of Sweden, Sweden
Lars Svensson   KTH Royal Institute of Technology, Sweden
Henrik Thane   Mälardalen University, Sweden
Hai Nam Tran   Lab-STICC, Université de Bretagne Occidentale,
                             France
Kimmo Varpaaniemi   Space Systems Finland Ltd., Finland
Matthias Volk   RWTH Aachen University, Germany
Andrzej Wardziński   Gdańsk University of Technology, Poland
Fredrik Warg   RISE Research Institutes of Sweden, Sweden
Roman Wirtz   University of Duisburg-Essen, Germany
Ning Xiong   Mälardalen University, Sweden
Tommaso Zoppi   University of Florence, Italy

Gold Sponsor

Intel

Silver Sponsor

Edge Case Research

EDGE CASE RESEARCH

Supporting Institutions

European Workshop on
Industrial Computer Systems –
Reliability, Safety and Security

Faculdade de Ciências da
Universidade de Lisboa

LASIGE Research Unit

AG Software Engineering,
Otto-von-Guericke-Universität
Magdeburg

Austrian Institute of Technology

Thales Deutschland GmbH

Lecture Notes in Computer Science (LNCS),
Springer Science + Business Media

European Network of Clubs for Reliability
and Safety of Software-Intensive Systems

German Computer Society

Informationstechnische Gesellschaft

Electronic Components and Systems
for European Leadership - Austria

ARTEMIS Industry Association

Verband österreichischer
Software Industrie

Austrian Computer Society

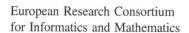

European Research Consortium
for Informatics and Mathematics

Invited Talks

Towards AI Trustworthiness

Guillaume Soudain

Certification Directorate European Union Aviation Safety Agency, Germany
guillaume.soudain@easa.europa.eu

Abstract. Deep learning opens up promising prospects for aviation as in many other fields. However, it raises the crucial question of the level of confidence that can be placed in these techniques when used in safety-critical applications and of their compatibility with strict certification requirements.

EASA has published its Artificial Intelligence Roadmap at the beginning of 2020, with a view to enabling the approval of AI-based solutions and with an initial focus on machine learning techniques. Guillaume Soudain, Software Senior Expert and AI project leader at EASA, will present the perspectives of this roadmap.

The key questions we are trying to answer are: how to build public confidence in artificial intelligence? How to prepare the certification of machine learning solutions? And how to prepare the future of this rapidly evolving field of computer science?

Safe Perception and AI for Autonomous Driving

Jonas Nilsson

NVIDIA, Sweden
jonasn@nvidia.com

Abstract. Commercializing autonomous driving requires technical advancements in many areas. To solve the technical challenges, these systems are becoming more complex and are increasingly adopting AI technology. The growing complexity of these designs poses many new challenges in assuring safety. This talk will focus on approaches and challenges for designing and validating safety-critical autonomous systems, with focus on perception and AI.

ISO TR 4804: Safety and Cybersecurity for Automated Driving Systems

Simon Fürst

BMW, Germany
Simon.Fuerst@bmw.de

Abstract. The standard ISO TR 4804 will be newly released in Q3/20. It provides an overview and guidance of the generic steps for developing and validating a safe and secure automated driving system with the goal of achieving a positive risk balance and the avoidance of unreasonable risk. This is derived from basic principles of relevant worldwide publications. It considers safety by design, verification, and validation methods for automated driving, focusing on SAE level 3 and level 4 automation features of automated vehicles. In addition, it outlines cybersecurity considerations in conjunction with safety aspects.

This new standard describes a framework for a harmonized safety design by systematically breaking down safety principles into safety by design capabilities, elements, and architectures. This generic methodology can be applied by vehicle manufacturers and suppliers worldwide. The standard aims to support a harmonization of different, currently already applicable industry approaches of automated driving systems.

Additionally, the document gives guidance to system developers with a dedicated safety lifecycle for DNNs used for automated driving systems. It includes all relevant steps, such as definition and selection of data, architecture of DNNs, their development and evaluation, and finally the monitoring and deployment.

Contents

Threat Analysis and Risk Mitigation

Cyber-Physical Systems Security

Fault Injection and Fault Tolerance

Safety Cases and Argumentation

Engineering of Runtime Safety Monitors for Cyber-Physical Systems with Digital Dependability Identities

Jan Reich[1]([✉]), Daniel Schneider[1], Ioannis Sorokos[1], Yiannis Papadopoulos[2], Tim Kelly[3], Ran Wei[3], Eric Armengaud[4], and Cem Kaypmaz[5]

[1] Fraunhofer IESE, Kaiserslautern, Germany
{jan.reich,daniel.schneider,ioannis.sorokos}@iese.fraunhofer.de
[2] University of Hull, Kingston upon Hull, UK
y.i.papadopoulos@hull.ac.uk
[3] University of York, York, UK
{tim.kelly,ran.wei}@york.ac.uk
[4] AVL List GmbH, Graz, Austria
eric.armengaud@avl.com
[5] AVL Turkey, Istanbul, Turkey
cem.kaypmaz@avl.com

Abstract. Cyber-Physical Systems (CPS) harbor the enormous potential for societal improvement in terms of safety, comfort and economic efficiency. However, these benefits will only be unlocked if the safety of these systems can be assured with a sufficient level of confidence. Traditional safety engineering and assurance approaches alone cannot address the CPS-inherent uncertainties and unknowns induced by openness and adaptivity. Runtime safety assurance approaches such as *Conditional Safety Certificates* (ConSerts) represent novel means to cope with CPS assurance challenges by introducing modular and formalized safety arguments with variant support, thereby shifting the final safety certification step to runtime. However, the systematic engineering of ConSerts at design-time is a complex task which, up to now, has not been sufficiently addressed. Without systematic safety assurance at *both* design-time and runtime, CPS will hardly be assurable with acceptable confidence given the uncertainties and unknowns. In this paper, we present an engineering method for synthesizing ConSerts based on *Digital Dependability Identities* (DDI). The approach is demonstrated for a cooperative vehicle platooning function (CACC) from an industrial case study.

Keywords: Dynamic risk management · Runtime certification · Runtime safety monitor · Model-based safety engineering

1 Introduction

CPS Safety. Cooperative Cyber-Physical Systems (CPS) harbor enormous potential for societal improvement in terms of safety, comfort and economic efficiency. However, CPS

© Springer Nature Switzerland AG 2020
A. Casimiro et al. (Eds.): SAFECOMP 2020, LNCS 12234, pp. 3–17, 2020.
https://doi.org/10.1007/978-3-030-54549-9_1

functions will only be accepted by society if their safety is confidently assured. Justified belief that systems are free from posing an unacceptable risk to their environment must be created. Therefore, we need a safety argument, conveying a convincing story about why evidence, in the form of safety analyses, design measures and verification/validation results, supports the safety claim.

CPS Safety-related Uncertainties and Unknowns. Traditional safety assurance approaches, e.g. the automotive functional safety standard ISO 26262, assume that the complete set of evidence for supporting the safety claim can be generated at design-time. The CPS-inherent characteristics of openness and adaptivity pose a significant problem for traditional approaches because the amount of safety-relevant CPS context changes can hardly be anticipated completely at development time. These changes include CPS capability changes, triggered by e.g. sensor failure or changing cooperation partner capabilities, and environmental changes, such as vision range restriction or road friction changes due to weather. Thus, CPS complexity renders safety certification at development time with acceptable performance much harder.

Safety@Runtime. Runtime safety assurance approaches such as Conditional Safety Certificates (*ConSerts*) [1] represent novel means to cope with the CPS assurance challenges by shifting parts of the safety assurance process to the runtime, when all relevant uncertainties and unknowns can be resolved. Specifically, ConSerts allow the definition of modular safety concepts describing CPS cooperation variants. By making the guaranteed and demanded safety interface to other CPS systems and the environment explicit, these modular safety concepts are certifiable at design-time. At runtime, CPS constituents resolve those open ends by checking the compatibility of the safety interface and by monitoring runtime evidence required for safe operation.

Problem. ConSerts rely on solid design-time safety engineering and only shift the minimum necessary safety activities to runtime, i.e. safety interface matching and runtime evidence monitoring. Only limited research has yet examined this design-time engineering backbone; requirements for a concrete ConSerts-based engineering method remain an open research topic. Key aspects of such a method are a) a comprehensive assurance argument combining development time safety assurance with runtime safety assurance and b) a systematic design of ConSerts out of established development time safety artifacts.

Solution. *Digital Dependability Identities* (DDI) are an overarching solution framework for engineering dependable CPS, developed in the H2020 DEIS project. In this paper, we demonstrate the application of the DDI framework for an industrial case study of a cooperative platooning function, specifically focusing on the transition from design-time safety models (*Design-time DDIs*) to runtime safety models (*ConSerts*, which serve as *Runtime DDIs*). To that end, in Sect. 2, we introduce the overall idea of the DDI engineering framework for design-time and runtime DDIs. In Sect. 3, the framework is applied and discussed for a CPS-based platooning function. Section 4 discusses related work and Sect. 5 concludes the paper's scientific contribution.

2 Runtime DDI Engineering Approach Overview

This section introduces the DDI engineering approach for seamless dependability engineering of CPS functions by creating design-time DDIs and transforming them into runtime DDIs that are used to dynamically assure CPS safety at runtime.

2.1 What Are Digital Dependability Identities (DDI)?

DDI Definition. A fundamental problem of current dependability engineering processes hampering effective assurance lies in the fact that safety argument models are not formally related to the evidence models supporting the claim. Such evidence models include hazard and safety analysis models and dependability process execution documentation. As such artifacts refer to the same system and therefore are naturally interrelated with each other, we claim this should also be the case for the system's model-based reflection: The *Digital Dependability Identity* (DDI) [2]. By establishing this kind of traceability, DDIs represent an integrated set of dependability data models (i.e. evidence), generated by engineers and reasoned upon in dependability arguments (i.e. how are claims supported by evidence). A DDI is, therefore, an evolution of classical modular dependability assurance models, allowing for comprehensive dependability reasoning by formally integrating several separately defined dependability aspect models. DDIs are produced during design, certified on system/component release, and then maintained over the system/component lifetime.

DDI Contents. A DDI contains information that uniquely describes the dependability characteristics of a system or component. DDIs are formed as modular assurance cases, are composable and can be synthesized to create more complex DDIs from the DDIs of constituent systems and system components. The DDI of a system contains a) claims about the dependability guarantees given by a system to other systems b) supporting evidence for the claims in the form of various models and analyses and c) demands from other connected systems being necessary to support the claims.

Previous Work on DDIs. In the first phase of the DEIS project, the focus has been to integrate various state-of-the-art design-time safety and security engineering aspects together into an exchange format, the *Open Dependability Exchange* Meta-Model (ODE), used as the blueprint for DDIs. Accompanying engineering methods and tools have been developed to enable distributed dependability engineering in multi-tier integrator-supplier scenarios [3]. In [4], we showed, for an industrial railway use case, how to use design-time DDIs to automatically verify safety requirements with component fault trees and model-based evidence lifecycle documentation.

Runtime DDIs. To cope with the openness and adaptivity CPS challenges safely, systems can be engineered in a way that enables them to assure dependability at runtime on their own. Consequently, runtime DDIs need to be developed with appropriate model contents and runtime mechanisms to enable dependable integration and cooperation at runtime. The upcoming sections take the approach outlined in [4] to engineer design-time DDIs as a basis and add on top the aspect of how to address openess and adaptivity challenges. Therefore, the specific content additions of runtime DDIs are explained, exemplified for a cooperative platooning application and a process for their systematic derivation is proposed.

2.2 Runtime DDI Engineering Approach

Being equipped with knowledge about high-level DDI contents, this section describes from a bird's eye view, how the DDI Dependability Engineering Framework bridges the gap between a CPS use case description and its dependable operation at runtime. Figure 1 visualizes the principal building blocks of CPS dependability assurance.

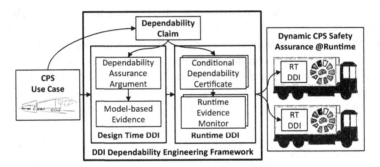

Fig. 1. DDI dependability engineering framework overview.

CPS Functionality. The starting point for all dependability assurance activities is the description and planning of the functionality that the CPS shall render for its stakeholders, which may be either direct system users, companies or even the society. An essential property of a CPS function is that it is executed on multiple independent systems leading to a required distribution of dependability assurance over multiple system manufacturers. For example, a platooning CPS function is executed on multiple trucks of potentially different manufacturers. Enabling cooperative function execution while still allowing decoupled development is only possible by making development and runtime execution interfaces explicit for both functional and quality aspects. Concretely, structural and behavioral aspects of the intended CPS function must be made explicit along with assured constraints regarding their quality bounds.

Dependability Claim. DDIs are concerned with the comprehensive and transparent assurance of dependability claims. Each assurance activity and each artifact contained in a DDI is motivated by a root dependability claim defining risk reduction for a dependability property such as safety, security, availability or reliability. The definition of *acceptable risk reduction* is typically derived from domain-specific risk management standards targeting different risk causes such as functional safety causes (e.g. ISO 26262), causes related to functional insufficiencies and foreseeable misuse (e.g. SOTIF PAS 21448) or causes due to cyber-security threats (e.g. ISO/SAE 21434). These standards contain requirements for assessing risk criticality and reducing risks to an acceptable level. Note that existing standards do not specifically consider CPS challenges as of now. However, the DDI framework has been defined generally enough to be open for structured extension with contents from future risk management standards specific for CPS assurance challenges.

Design-Time Dependability Assurance. Having a dependability claim to be assured for the CPS function, risk management activities must then be systematically planned. These activities create necessary evidence for supporting the system engineers' reasoning that the dependability claim holds for the developed system/CPS. For both risk management planning and dependability assessment purposes, an explicit argument inductively relates created evidence to the top-level claim through layers of argumentation. While the performed activities and produced artifacts vary depending on the kind of risk that is being managed, argumentation supported by evidence is mandatory for all risks. DDIs deal with dependability risks, thus the currently supported design-time DDI assurance activities and evidence focus on well-established dependability methods such as hazard and risk analysis, safety and security analyses, safety design concepts, validation, and verification. These activities are effective in demonstrating dependability of closed embedded systems, unrelated to the CPS challenges. In addition, reliance on model-based approaches already compensates for the increasing complexity of closed systems. Thus, we believe model-based development is also necessary for assuring CPS.

Runtime Dependability Assurance. The open and adaptive nature of CPS, combined with their increased need for environmental operational awareness to render optimal functionality, increases their complexity tremendously. To assure with sufficient confidence that CPS behavior is dependable in all situations, dependability assessment of those situations is mandatory. A common way to simplify this process is to build the system using worst-case assumptions about the environment, specific for the managed risk. Thus, we only look at the most critical situations and constrain system behavior to be dependable in those situations. The problem with this strategy is that worst-case assumptions lead to performance loss. An alternative to unacceptable performance due to design-time worst-case assumptions is to enable the CPS to reason about dependability at runtime. This alternative involves determining the worst case of the *current* operational situation instead of acting according to the worst case of *all possible* situations. This approach avoids the commonly known state-space explosion problem but demands engineering dependability intelligence into the CPS. Such dependability intelligence builds upon the design-time assurance case by equipping a system with pre-certified knowledge about dependability guarantees it can offer and dependability demands it needs from other systems or the environment to render those guarantees. Additionally, the dependability intelligence needs to monitor both CPS and environment for changes (*Runtime Evidences*) that affect dependability. Based on such changes, it can reason about possible CPS configurations leading to dependable CPS behavior in different situations. Summarizing, runtime DDIs are a reduced form of pre-certified design-time dependability assurance cases, containing only those dependability artifacts and reasoning intelligence required for monitoring dependability-relevant context changes and reacting to them in a dependable way.

Runtime DDI Engineering. Regarding the engineering of concrete runtime DDIs, the DEIS consortium focuses on the usage of *Conditional Safety Certificates* (ConSerts) [1] for expressing modular, variable and fully formalized safety concepts including required runtime evidences enabling safety guarantee-demand matching and thus a basic form of dependability reasoning at runtime. For monitoring CPS state and environment, the consortium explored state-based probabilistic methods such as Bayesian Networks [5]. In Sect. 3, we focus on explaining concretely for the platooning use case, how its design-time DDI looks like and how the ConSert part of runtime DDIs is systematically synthesized. Note that although Sect. 3 demonstrates the usage of DDIs for assuring a *safety* claim, the overall engineering procedure is similar for other dependability properties.

3   Runtime DDI Engineering for Platooning

This section exemplifies the runtime DDI engineering activities and artifacts needed to fulfill the safety claim for a platooning function executed on a CPS.

3.1   Platooning Use Case Description

Function and Constraints. The goal of truck platooning or more general cooperative adaptive cruise control (CACC) is to reduce fuel consumption of all involved vehicles by maintaining reduced air drag at small inter-vehicular distances. Platooning is particularly relevant for heavy-duty trucks due to their high air resistance area and thus hold high potential for fuel economy. Since humans have limited reaction capabilities compared to automated systems, they cannot safely drive at distances where air drag is reduced through slipstream. The example in this paper is limited to automated longitudinal control of a two-vehicle platoon. The platoon's leader truck is assumed to be driven by a human and the follower truck's longitudinal motion is controlled by the platooning system, which is executed in a distributed CPS fashion on both vehicles.

Safe Nominal Behavior. For human-driven vehicles or ADAS, it is often the correct realization of the driver's intent that defines safe behavior for control software. For highly and fully automated systems, this is more complex due to many aspects of the environment that have to be considered in the safe nominal behavior specification. The currently most comprehensive safe nominal behavior definition for highly automated vehicles has been published by Intel/Mobileye in 2017 coined *Responsibility Sensitive Safety (RSS)* [6]. In this paper, we use the RSS formalization of a longitudinal safe distance as safe nominal behavior definition (see Eq. (1)).

$$d_{safe} = \left[v_F \rho + \frac{1}{2} a_{max,acc,F} \rho^2 + \frac{\left(v_F + \rho a_{max,acc,F} \right)^2}{2 a_{min,brake,F}} - \frac{v_L^2}{2 a_{max,brake,L}} \right]_+ \quad (1)$$

Effectively, the first three terms together represent the stopping distance of the follower vehicle considering a) a reaction distance (v_F: follower speed, ρ: reaction time), b) an acceleration distance if the follower constantly accelerates with $a_{max,acc,F}$ during reaction time and c) the follower braking distance, when the follower constantly brakes with deceleration $a_{min,brake,F}$. To compute the safe distance, we subtract the leader braking distance with leader speed v_L and constant leader deceleration $a_{max,brake,L}$ from the follower stop distance. Note that the leader vehicle driver's reaction time is not factored in, because, in this time span, the motion state of the platoon does not change and is therefore irrelevant for safety assurance.

Influences on Safe Distance. By looking at Eq. (1), we observe that the safe distance is dynamic, as it depends on the right-hand-side variables. Within the platoon context, such changes can either be triggered in the environment, e.g. road surface conditions may affect the minimum and maximum deceleration capabilities of both trucks. Alternatively, the Wi-Fi communication quality is affected by weather conditions such as precipitation influencing follower reaction time. In contrast, the safe distance may be affected by CPS-internal states such as vehicle mass (very dynamic specifically for trucks) or quality of vehicle speed determination. In summary, the CPS function description together with a safe nominal behavior specification provide sufficient information to start DDI-driven safety assurance.

3.2 Design-Time Safety Engineering with DDIs

This section describes how a platooning system safety assurance case is synthesized for the platooning function and finally captured in a design-time DDI.

CPS Safety. The design-time DDI depicted in Fig. 2 by definition contains a top-level safety claim, for which a safety assurance argument is developed. The argument associates all safety-related activities and their evidence with each other to create justified belief in the validity of the safety claim. Since safety is a system property, the design-time DDI necessarily spans *the whole collaboration space* on which the CPS function is executed (i.e. leader and follower roles). Note that we refer to roles instead of systems here to highlight the fact that at this point, we are dealing with functional entities and not with concrete constituent systems realizing these functional entities. Conceptually, one truck can have the main responsibility for achieving safety in the end, but the top-level safety claim has to be necessarily defined and analyzed for the entire CPS. To illustrate this point, we note that the inter-truck distance as the main safety property to be assured cannot be interpreted for a single truck alone. Rather, a distance can only be defined between multiple objects and therefore is necessarily a property of the object *group* or in the platooning context, the whole platoon. The goal of CPS safety engineering is thus to decompose a CPS safety claim into a set of safety requirements for each cooperation role that allows the cooperative fulfillment of the safety claim.

Hazard and Risk Assessment (HARA). Following the RSS definition of a safe distance, the CPS state that poses safety risk (hazard) is existent if the actual distance is lower than the safe distance. This observation is straight-forward for the hazard in a longitudinal direction. In general, a more systematic hazard and risk assessment (HARA) should be performed for all potential CPS behaviors in the intended operational environment. Given a safe nominal behavior specification, conventional HARA methods are applicable for

CPS. For determining the worst-case criticality of the hazard in all situations, we adopt the ASIL classification from ISO 26262, which yields an ASIL D criticality. Thus, the platoon's safety goal is specified as *"Safe Truck Distance is not violated during platoon driving (ASIL D)"*.

Functional Architecture. After HARA, functional cause-effect relationships that lead to a violation of the safety goal must be analyzed. To obtain sufficient completeness regarding potential violation causes, requires systematic safety analysis using a functional network linking functional blocks and their cause-effect relations. Conventionally, functional models contain data and information flow connectors between sensing, control and actuation functions. In [7], an approach for the service-oriented definition of cause-effect relationships has been presented, which better supports the derivation of modular failure mode interfaces than purely dataflow-oriented models. As we will see, modularity is a necessary property for the derivation of runtime DDIs. Therefore, service-oriented functional networks (e.g. expressed in languages such as SysML) are a suitable basis for CPS safety analysis. The application service of a platoon is *"Safe Platoon Driving with defined performance"*, which uses actuation services like *"Truck Distance Realization"* or functional services such as *"Follower Brake Distance Computation"*, which use sensing services such as *"Follower Speed Provision"*.

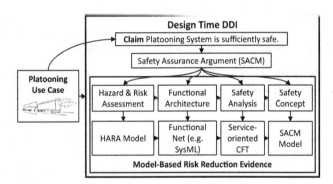

Fig. 2. Contents of a design-time DDI.

Safety Analysis. Starting from a CPS-level hazard, causes leading to this hazard should be systematically identified deductively or inductively. There are several different types of causes to be analyzed, e.g. causes related to a) systematic software faults and random hardware failures, b) functional insufficiencies or foreseeable misuse or c) malicious cyber-security threats. For each cause type, there are specific analysis techniques, e.g. fault trees, failure mode and effect analysis (FMEA), Markov chains or Systems Theoretic Process Analysis (STPA). For platooning safety analysis, we used an extension of component fault trees coined *Service-Oriented Component Fault Trees* (SCFT) [8]. Unlike dataflow-oriented deductive safety analyses starting at the actuators, SCFT analysis starts at the entity with the application context knowledge enabling a derivation of modular interface failure modes. SCFTs build on a stepwise deductive HAZOP guideword interpretation for functional service hierarchies. Example failure modes for a first analysis step in the context of the platooning safety goal are *"Too Low Computed {reaction, acceleration, braking} Distance"* as these can lead to a violation of the safety goal.

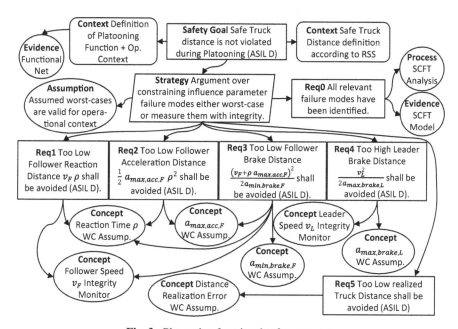

Fig. 3. Platooning functional safety concept.

Safety Concept. After the identification of all functional failure modes, the next step is the creation of a functional safety concept mitigating the propagation from causes to safety goal violation. Figure 3 presents the safety concept documented in an adapted notation based on the Goal Structuring Notation (GSN) [9]. In general, a safety concept provides the rationale for safety measures (depicted as *Concepts*), which add additional design elements for mitigating critical failure modes, i.e. lowering their occurrence probability by failure detection and appropriate transition to a safe state. Note that the *Concept* elements are placeholders for safety argument fragments arguing the requirement satisfaction either through the appropriate choice of worst-case assumptions or dynamic monitoring of measurement integrity. The integrity of safety measure implementation is dependent on the risk criticality of the hazardous event, which originates from the HARA (in our case ASIL D). The safety concept should give a comprehensive argument along with evidence about why a safety goal cannot be violated given the chosen safety measures. In the DDI engineering approach, this evidence is explicit by linking all artifacts such as functional net, the SCFT model along with its analysis results, the definition of the safe nominal behavior and the operational context to the assurance claims they should fulfill (e.g. *Req0*). Together with the evidence artifacts, the safety concept is expressed in a comprehensive safety case representing the design-time DDI's backbone. The DDI formalism for expressing assurance cases is the *Structured Assurance Case Metamodel*

(SACM) [10], which is a successor of GSN and has been recently standardized by the *Object Management Group* (OMG).

CPS Hazard Mitigation Strategies. To derive concrete safety measures to adequately mitigate platooning failure modes (see requirements *Req1–Req5* in Fig. 3) there are two potential strategies: On the one hand, we can postulate and use worst-case assumptions, which must be valid for the intended operational context. For instance, if we assume the maximum leader deceleration to be bound by 9,81 m/s^2 (=1 g), we have to provide an additional argument that justifies the assumption's validity, e.g. through physics reasoning. Worst-case assumptions are a classical means to simplify safety assurance at the cost of under-performance in non-worst cases. For instance, we can consider the larger-than-necessary controlled truck distance for the majority of operation time the lead driver does not perform emergency braking. On the other hand, we can monitor the variables of interest at runtime to replace the worst-case value with the actual runtime value (see Fig. 4, left). For instance, a common established measure in vehicles is speed integrity monitoring. In order to use runtime monitors safely, we have to design them with the same integrity as the hazard they should mitigate. This means, that an assurance argument has to be developed for the correct provision of a "situation-specific worst-case speed value bound", which effectively means that the speed provision error is constrained by employing adequate redundancy mechanisms developed with appropriate safety processes.

In summary, this section led through the systematic engineering of a design-time DDI for the platooning function leading to a justified functional safety concept. The next step is to modularize and abstract this safety concept into runtime DDIs that can be deployed to concrete trucks, enabling dynamic safety assurance for a platoon.

3.3   Runtime Safety Model Derivation

In this section, CPS assurance challenges and potential solutions principles are presented first. Afterward, the design-time DDI of the CPS-based platooning function is systematically transformed into ConSerts, which build the fundamental basis of a runtime DDI suitable for dynamic safety assurance of a CPS at runtime.

CPS Assurance Challenges. The major challenge of safety assurance of CPS functionality is complexity. More specifically, this comparative increase in complexity stems from two CPS-inherent characteristics: open context and adaptivity. *Open context* means that CPS constituent systems are typically developed independently, but should, in the end, provide a common functionality at runtime. Thus, the concrete nature of potential cooperation partners is intentionally left open for the sake of flexibility. In contrast, *adaptivity* means that CPS need to adapt themselves to changing context conditions safely. Although adaptivity was already required for partly automated systems, the amount of required situational awareness has tremendously increased for fully automated CPS functionality. For *safety* assurance, both open context and adaptivity are hard problems, because safety as a property of the entire CPS system *group* needs to be decomposed onto independently developed constituent systems, which finally need to collaboratively adapt safely to changing context.

Open Context Solution. Complexity is not a new phenomenon in the domain of systems and software engineering: A proven solution principle for tackling system-level complexity is *Divide-and-Conquer* (D&C). The idea behind D&C is to iteratively identify a service interface and decompose the solution across its boundary. If such an interface exists, both user and provider of the interface can be developed independently, thereby promoting *design-time modularity* and *runtime compatibility*. To apply D&C to the CPS' open context, we need an explicit and semantically complete interface definition a) for functionality aka *services* being provided or required at that interface and b) for safety guarantees and demands associated to the service interface. In Fig. 3, the mentioned service and safety interfaces emerge immediately as the *Concepts* are deployed to our envisioned systems *Leader Truck* and *Follower Truck* (see Fig. 4, right). The deployment of safety measures is a critical decision with impact, as it determines a) the system role that is finally responsible for achieving the CPS safety at runtime and b) the safety guarantee/demand interface required between trucks, which is directly related to the effort for defining the interface. We found in past projects that minimizing the number of required services and associated safety demands is a good rule of thumb for deployment. In our platoon, the follower truck gets the overall safety responsibility, mainly because it is the only vehicle that can transition the platoon to a safe state in case the communication link is down. We cannot rely on the leader truck's human driver in this regard. In contrast, the leader truck can provide the leader's current speed with much better quality from its internal sensors than measuring it remotely in the follower. In summary, by employing the D&C principle on the design-time DDI, safety concepts can be modularized by deploying the safety measures to the CPS cooperation roles to be implemented by specific systems.

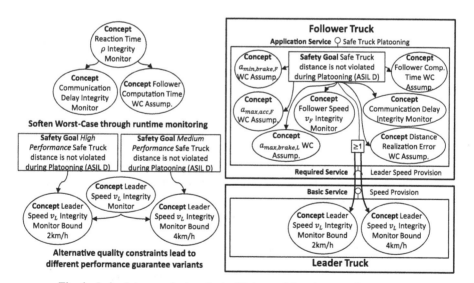

Fig. 4. *Left*: platoon variant analysis, *Right*: modular platoon safety concept.

Context Adaptivity Solution. Cooperation-partner diversity and context-dependent optimal performance necessitates context adaptivity. For instance, different truck models from different brands may have different functional capabilities for sensing and actuating with different safety guarantees for these capabilities. Further, CPS must adapt to changing risk levels as the environment changes. Different risks lead to situation-dependent safety requirements and situation-dependent optimization potential. Without context adaptivity, there would be *exactly* one possibility to cooperate safely. Regarding the environment, this would need to be the set of worst-case conditions for all properties, while for the truck interface exactly one configuration of leader capabilities would be allowed by the follower. Therefore, variants need to be factored into both service/safety interface and safety concept that a) increase chances of interface compatibility and b) enable situation-dependent optimal performance while still maintaining safety. Two types of variants are depicted in Fig. 4, left: The top variant decomposes the reaction time worst-case assumption into another worst-case assumption about follower computation time, but makes the communication delay *dynamic* so that the platoon can adapt to different situations. The other example induces variants on the safety demand bound for the provided leader speed leading to different *performance* guarantees for the overall platoon since the safe distance computation still considers the situation-specific worst-case.

Information Abstraction. The last property that distinguishes a design-time DDI from a runtime DDI is the amount of incorporated information. After modularizing the CPS safety concept into black-box system safety concepts with defined interfaces, each truck manufacturer can certify their implementation including all pre-engineered variants *conditionally* at design-time. Thus, runtime DDIs contain only the information required to reason about variable safety conditions dynamically at runtime. These conditions are a) a representation of the service interface with its safety guarantees and demands, b) a system-internal mapping of safety guarantees and their required safety demands, and c) context variable requirements for monitoring regarding their concrete equivalence classes. In addition to the above, a runtime DDI also requires mechanisms for safety interface matching, variant resolution, and runtime context monitoring.

ConSerts. *Conditional Safety Certificates* (ConSerts) [1] is a concrete instance of a runtime safety assurance approach that unifies all above explained solution building blocks for CPS safety assurance. ConSerts support *open context* in that they use a black-box service architecture to achieve modularity. Through ConSerts, provided and required functional services are enriched with safety guarantees and safety demands defining a) formalized failure modes along with variable bounds to be assured for them, b) context-specific constraints such as situation, for which these bounds have to be valid and c) an integrity statement indicating the confidence required for the assurance of the bounds. ConSerts support *adaptivity* in that they allow to define a) different safety guarantees and demands for a single service and b) monitored context properties to provide *runtime evidences*. ConSerts support *information abstraction* through the usage of Boolean logic for expressing safety guarantee/demand and runtime evidence relationships thus abstracting the design-time safety concept to the mere dependency logic being relevant at runtime.

Platooning Runtime DDIs. Figure 5 shows runtime DDIs for the leader and follower platoon trucks. They contain the service interface, its safety guarantees (SG), safety demands (SD) and required runtime evidences (RtE). The *"Safe Truck Platooning"* service can be guaranteed by the follower truck with high quality (=small truck distance, SG1), if the communication delay does not exceed a certain quality bound and the follower speed can be determined with the required confidence (RtE1,2). In addition, deviations of the provided leader speed bound to max 2 km/h are demanded from the leader truck to fulfill SG1. One potential realization of SG4 is to employ diverse redundancy regarding the measurement principle of the leader's speed (RtE3,4). If RtE 3 cannot be provided anymore due to e.g. ESP system failure, graceful degradation is triggered through ConSert evaluation in that only SG2 can be guaranteed given that RtEs 1, 2 and 4 are still existent. This leads to a softer safety demand to the leader (SD2) yet still better performance than deactivation of the cooperation. In this way, ConSerts allow the definition and dynamic negotiation of arbitrary degradation level variants between the maximum (SG1) and no performance (SG3,6), while always guaranteeing CPS safety in a modular fashion during CPS cooperation.

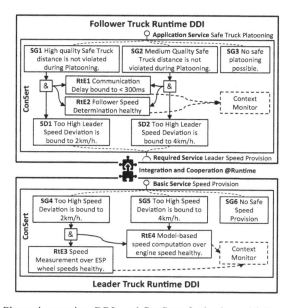

Fig. 5. Platooning runtime DDIs and ConSerts for leader and follower trucks.

4   Related Work

In the SPES projects [11], the Open Safety Metamodel (OSM) enables modular, cross-tool and cross-company safety certification. The OSM had a major influence on the evidence formalization in design-time DDIs. The AMASS project focusses on organizing safety cases, formalized in the Common Assurance and Certification Metamodel

(CACM) [12]. The CACM is an extension of the DDI's Structured Assurance Case Metamodel (SACM), in that it adds capabilities to model risk management standard terminology. Integrating CACM in the DDI is ongoing work to extend the latter with further formalization capabilities regarding concepts and terminology from dependability standards as well as evidence management processes. In contrast, there are pure runtime safety monitor approaches such as [13], which dynamically assess risk at runtime and react appropriately. The DDI improves upon these works by seamlessly integrating design-time safety assurance and runtime monitoring.

5 Conclusion and Future Work

In this paper, we described a continuous engineering method for safety assurance of CPS-based functionality via ConSerts. Our method seamlessly integrates development time and runtime assurance to provide safety claim confidence. The DDI dependability-engineering framework in Sect. 2 unifies development time and runtime assurance artifacts in an integrated data store, the DDI. In Sect. 3, we executed the DDI engineering workflow for a CPS-based platooning function, from use case description over integrated development time assurance (HARA, functional analysis, safety analysis, safety concept) to the derivation of modular safety concepts and ConSerts as fully formal runtime safety models. The demonstration suggests that the DDI framework can bridge the gap between established development time assurance practice and innovative runtime assurance concepts for tackling uncertainties and unknowns of CPS at runtime. In the future, we look to enrich runtime DDIs with probabilistic reasoning schemes to account for uncertain perception at runtime. *Dynamic Safety Management* [14] is a promising conceptual framework for runtime safety assurance, which we see as a roadmap for the evolution of DDIs.

Acknowledgment. This work was funded by the DEIS Project (EC Grant 732242).

References

1. Schneider, D.: Conditional safety certification for open adaptive systems. Dissertation, Technical University of Kaiserslautern, Germany (2014). ISBN 978-3-8396-0690-2
2. Schneider, D., et al.: WAP: digital dependability identities. In: Proceeding of IEEE International Symposium on Software Reliability Engineering (ISSRE), pp. 324–329 (2015)
3. DEIS Consortium: Dependability engineering innovation for cyber-physical systems project dissemination. http://www.deis-project.eu/dissemination/. Accessed 21 May 2019
4. Reich, J., Zeller, M., Schneider, D.: Automated evidence analysis of safety arguments using digital dependability identities. In: Romanovsky, A., Troubitsyna, E., Bitsch, F. (eds.) SAFE-COMP 2019. LNCS, vol. 11698, pp. 254–268. Springer, Cham (2019). https://doi.org/10.1007/978-3-030-26601-1_18
5. Kabir, S., et al.: A runtime safety analysis concept for open adaptive systems. In: Papadopoulos, Y., Aslansefat, K., Katsaros, P., Bozzano, M. (eds.) IMBSA 2019. LNCS, vol. 11842, pp. 332–346. Springer, Cham (2019). https://doi.org/10.1007/978-3-030-32872-6_22
6. Shalev-Shwartz, S., Shammah, S., Shashua, A.: On a formal model of safe and scalable self-driving cars. Intel/Mobileye (2017). http://arxiv.org/pdf/1708.06374v5

7. Reich, J., Schneider, D.: Towards (semi-)automated synthesis of runtime safety models: a safety-oriented design approach for service architectures of cooperative autonomous systems. In: Proceeding of 13th International Workshop on Dependable Smart Embedded and Cyber-physical Systems and Systems-of-Systems (DECSOS), Västerås, Sweden (2018)
8. Adler, R., Schneider, D., Höfig, K.: Evolution of fault trees from hardware safety analysis to integrated analysis of software-intensive control systems. In: Proceeding of 27th European Safety and Reliability Conference (ESREL), Portoroz, Slovenia (2017)
9. Kelly, T., Weaver, R.: The goal structuring notation - a safety argument notation. In: Proceeding of the Dependable Systems and Networks Workshop (2004)
10. Wei, R., Kelly, T.P., Dai, X., Zhao, S., Hawkins, R.: Model-based system assurance using the structured assurance case metamodel. J. Syst. Softw. **154**, 211–233 (2019). https://doi.org/10.1016/j.jss.2019.05.013
11. Pohl, K., Hönninger, H., Achatz, R., Broy, M. (eds.): Model-Based Engineering of Embedded Systems – The SPES 2020 Methodology. Springer, Heidelberg (2012). https://doi.org/10.1007/978-3-642-34614-9
12. de la Vara, J.L., et al.: Model-based specification of safety compliance needs for critical systems: a holistic generic metamodel. Inf. Softw. Technol. **72**, 16–30 (2016)
13. Eggert, J.: Predictive risk estimation for intelligent ADAS functions. In: IEEE 17th International Conference on Intelligent Transportation Systems (ITSC), Qingdao, China (2014)
14. Trapp, M., Schneider, D., Weiss, G.: Towards safety-awareness and dynamic safety management. In: 14th European Dependable Computing Conference (EDCC), Iasi, Romania (2018)

Systematic Evaluation of (Safety) Assurance Cases

Thomas Chowdhury$^{(\boxtimes)}$, Alan Wassyng, Richard F. Paige, and Mark Lawford

McMaster Centre for Software Certification, McMaster University, Hamilton, Canada
{chowdt2,wassyng,paigeri,lawford}@mcmaster.ca

Abstract. An Assurance Case (AC) documents an argument that supports a claim made about a system. An *effective* Assurance Case provides adequate belief to stakeholders that the system under consideration adequately embodies specific critical properties, for example safety and security. Comprehensive evaluation of an AC is a necessary step in building this belief. This involves measuring confidence in the assurance case argument, but also includes an overall quality assessment of the AC. This paper describes essential components of a (safety) AC evaluation process using previously defined evaluation criteria. These criteria were classified as applying to either *structure* or *content* of the (safety) AC. Two example (safety) ACs are used to demonstrate the approach, and for brevity, we illustrate the examples using purely *Goal Structuring Notation (GSN)* and in a second example, a *GSN*-like notation.

Keywords: Assurance case · Safety · GSN · Traceability

1 Introduction

An Assurance Case (AC) is a generalization of a safety case for a particular system. It is a living document that provides arguments that assure critical properties the system is required to embody. For demonstration purposes within the restrictions of this paper, we focus on safety as the critical property to be assured. One of the main objectives of an AC evaluation is to ensure that arguments in the AC are valid and sound. However, sound argumentation is not enough. The AC must be understandable by all stakeholders. It must also be of sufficient quality to engender trust that sufficient care was taken in its construction. Any weakness in claims, arguments or evidence potentially degrades the quality of an AC. The objective of our work is to assess the *overall quality* of an AC. This paper describes essential elements of a systematic and comprehensive evaluation process guided by previously defined evaluation criteria [4].

There are many notations used to document ACs. Goal Structuring Notation (GSN) [7] has gained considerable popularity in academia and is making inroads in industry. Thus, we use GSN examples to illustrate our evaluation process.

© Springer Nature Switzerland AG 2020
A. Casimiro et al. (Eds.): SAFECOMP 2020, LNCS 12234, pp. 18–33, 2020.
https://doi.org/10.1007/978-3-030-54549-9_2

1.1 Contribution

The contribution of this work is the definition of a systematic approach to the comprehensive evaluation of ACs. In this paper:

- we present pertinent aspects of our approach, supplemented by high-level, semi-formal models of the evaluation process and its outcomes;
- we provide sufficient detail to illustrate our approach on three criteria from [4] – two that apply to content, and another one that applies to structure of an AC;
- we evaluate our approach using two example ACs. The one AC is documented in GSN, the other is documented using a GSN-like notation.

2 Preliminaries

This section briefly introduces assurance cases, GSN, and recaps the evaluation criteria we presented in [4].

2.1 Assurance Cases

According to Bloomfield et al., "An Assurance Case is a documented body of evidence that provides a convincing and valid argument that a specified set of critical claims about a system's properties are adequately justified for a given application in a given environment" [3]. In general, an AC starts with a top-level claim regarding critical properties of a system, which is then supported by sub-claims. Terminal claims are grounded in evidence from the development of the system. There are many notations used to document ACs. Some of them are largely textual, and others are largely graphical with extensive references to textual documents produced during system development. The primary reason to develop a (safety) AC is to present explicit, understandable reasoning as to why we should believe that the system of interest is adequately safe.

2.2 Goal Structuring Notation

Goal Structuring Notation (GSN) was developed by Tim Kelly [7], motivated by Toulmin's work on argumentation [11]. The main body of a GSN diagram consists of *goals* representing claims and sub-claims, optional *strategies* that describe how goals are decomposed into sub-goals as representative of an argument, and *solutions* representing evidence that supports terminal goals. In addition, the AC developer can include supplementary information by adding *assumptions*, *context*, and *justifications*.

2.3   Recap of Our Evaluation Criteria in [4]

In [4] we defined criteria for the evaluation of an AC. We categorized the criteria
into two groups, one for the structure of an AC and another for the content of an
AC. Furthermore, we defined them from two different evaluation perspectives:
i) the AC developer's perspective; and ii) the external reviewer's perspective.
Table 1 presents all the criteria. We have added a little extra discussion for
three of these criteria below the table. These three criteria are the same criteria
for which details of the evaluation process are described in Sect. 4.

Table 1. A list of evaluation criteria and their rationale (from [4]).

Evaluation criteria for structure		Evaluation criteria for content	
Criterion	Rationale	Criterion	Rationale
Syntax check	Difficult to navigate and understand if syntax is not well-defined	Convincing basis	A feasible top-level claim is essential. Reasoning needs to be explicit so that it can be reviewed. Confirmation bias can adversely affect reasoning and the acceptance of evidence
Traceability	Necessary for understanding and maintenance	Rigour of argument	Rigour is important in making the reasoning less subjective and more repeatable
Robustness	Essential to achieving incremental assurance	Quality of hazard analysis	Hazard identification and mitigation is a critical aspect in assuring safety
Understandability	Need to facilitate understanding through structure	Arguing completeness	Deficiencies in completeness are a common source of error
Efficiency	Need to facilitate the ease with which ACs can be evaluated through structure and notation	Repeated arguments	A source of error if they are used where not completely appropriate
		ALARP	ALARP and associated principles are essential in demonstrating cost-benefit considerations and due diligence
		Confidence	An essential measure of trust in the reasoning and associated evidence. Not dealt with in detail in this paper because of the abundance of publications on this topic

- *Structure Evaluation-Syntax Check:* In addition to affecting understand-ability, syntax errors in the AC may indicate a lack of care taken in its con-struction and thus adversely affect the perceived quality of the AC.
- *Content Evaluation-Convincing Basis:* As with any complex document, the overview presented to readers is crucially important. The overview in an AC is represented by the top-level of the argument – the top claim and its immediate supporting sub-claims and their associated assumptions and context. Throughout the AC, the argument that supports upper-level claims should be explicit. It may be described in natural language, a logic of some kind, or a combination of these. The important point is that for every (sub)claim, there needs to be some reasoning that shows why, if its premises are true, then the parent claim is true. "Confirmation bias" [8] is another challenge in ACs. A simple example is when people look for specific evidence that supports a claim without considering counter-evidence. Apparent confirmation bias degrades confidence in an AC.
- *Content Evaluation-Rigour of the argument:* Explicit argumentation is an important characteristic of an AC. Evaluation of rigour of the argument is complementary to evaluating the convincing basis. Presentation of the argument in natural language is not as convincing as semi-formal notations or rigorous application of reasoning patterns.

3   Related Work

Reference [4] included a thorough literature review on the evaluation of an AC in the context of defining evaluation criteria. We have added some additional publications that specifically deal with the process of evaluating ACs. In [10], the author uses problem focused guide words (incorrectly phrased, relevance, directness, deductively invalid, undercutting evidence, rebutting evidence, low inductive strength, high inductive strength, coverage, replicability) to structure the evaluation process, followed by suggestions on how these often can be fixed. In [9], the assessment process consists of four steps (preparation, logic and structure validation, quality evaluation, record and feedback) performed by a safety assessor, who makes recommendations that are then implemented by the safety case developer. In [6], the Health and Safety Executive (HSE) defines 36 principles categorized into 10 groups that are used to assess safety cases.

A key part of evaluating ACs is assessing confidence; there has been much work published on this (much of which is reviewed in [4]). A relatively recent publication [2] has been added to the literature on AC confidence. It introduces a confidence measure technique 'INCIDENCE', which considers both design time and run time evidence and uses GSN as an example.

4   Evaluation of an Assurance Case

This section presents details of our systematic evaluation of ACs. To put this on a well-structured footing, we started by modelling the evaluation process and its

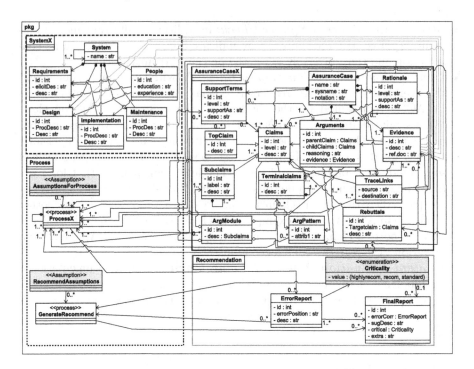

Fig. 1. The generic model of the AC evaluation process.

relevant data, including all primary components of an AC as well as development artefacts from the system of interest. This generic model is shown in Fig. 1. The generic model shows explicitly process, recommendation, AC data and system development data with associations and data flows required for the systematic evaluation. The model serves as a guide to the evaluation as well as a check on it consistency. The main components are (colours are not shown in this paper):

- The Process for evaluating the AC (represented by Green rectangles);
- The Recommendation arising from the evaluation (Blue rectangles);
- AC data that is the subject of the evaluation (Yellow rectangles);
- System development data that is referred to in the AC (Orange rectangles).

In addition,

- Black arrows/lines are used for input and output and associations;
- Red arrows/lines are used to highlight links between the AC and system development artefacts.

Figure 1 contains all essential links for refinement of all 12 criteria. In this paper, we had space to focus on only 3 criteria. The generic model must be refined and instantiated for specific evaluation criteria. The generic model systematizes the process of defining an evaluation process for arbitrary AC criteria, making AC evaluation more repeatable and less error prone, as we can rely on the model to guide us as to how to carry out the instantiation. Refinement will involve precisely modeling inputs and outputs of individual steps in an evaluation process. Instantiation will involve adding textual descriptions for process stages, which can be checked for conformance with the components of the model.

To illustrate refinement and instantiation of our model we chose one content criterion and one structural criterion as examples for instantiation. The content criterion we selected was "Convincing basis for the AC" and we have included the refined version of the model for *Convincing basis* in Fig. 2, and the instantiated process in Sect. 4.1:1. We also include a much briefer discussion on another content criterion, "Rigour of the argument" in Sect. 4.1:2. The structural criterion we selected to include in this paper was "Syntax check". In this case we show the instantiated process in Sect. 4.2, but there is no space to include another figure showing the refined model. (Actually, we wanted to include "Traceability" as the structural criterion, but it is too complex to show in the space available).

We conducted a self-validation of our AC evaluation processes as a first step in evaluating our approach. A full-scale evaluation of the process is very difficult to arrange at this stage of development. The result of our self-validation of the process for *Convincing basis* is documented in Sect. 5.1; for *Rigour of the argument* in Sect. 5.2; and for *Syntax check* in Sect. 5.3.

4.1 Evaluating Content of an Assurance Case

We can now describe how we refined the high-level model for each of the evaluation criteria. We start with criteria related to content of the AC, and will show the major steps in evaluating *the convincing basis for the AC*.

1. *Convincing basis for the AC:* Figure 2 shows the relevant aspects of a refinement of the model in Fig. 1. We did not include the documentation resulting from the development of the system, since that part of the model does not change depending on the specific criterion being evaluated, and the links to that data are obvious.

   One of the main intentions of *convincing basis* is to check explicitness of claims, arguments, supporting terms and evidence. In addition to this, a convincing basis looks for a complete top-level claim description, and compliance of evidence with acceptance criteria to avoid confirmation bias highlighted by Leveson [8].

   The refinement shows that "ProcessX" now consists of 4 main steps (reading bottom to top):

   - TopLevelClaimCheck – a review of the top level claim. Inputs to this process are the AC data items of the TopClaim itself, and TopClaimSupp.Terms. Output is simply to the ErrorReport. These links make it reasonably clear that the focus of this check is the wording of the top-level claim. Assumptions and criteria for this check are found in TopLevelAssumptions.

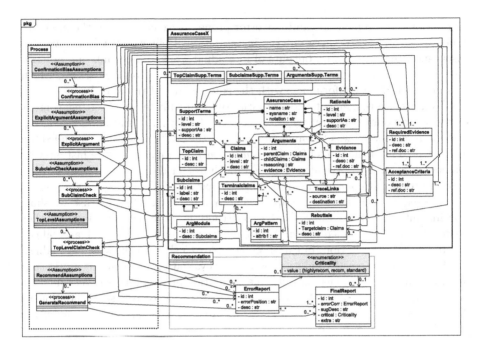

Fig. 2. The evaluation process for *Convincing basis for the AC.*

- SubClaimCheck – a review of all subclaims. Inputs to this process are Subclaims, SubclaimsSupp.Terms, Rationale, TerminalClaims, AcceptanceCriteria and the RequiredEvidence. Output is again to the ErrorReport. The focus of this check is on the wording and rationale for the decomposition of the argument, and also on whether or not the evidence required to support terminal claims makes sense. Assumptions and criteria for this check are to be found in SubclaimCheckAssumptions.
- ExplicitArgument – a review that evaluates how explicit the argument is, in general. Inputs to this process are ArgumentsSupp.Terms, Arguments and Rationale. Indirect inputs are Claims, Evidence, Rebuttals, ArgPatterns and ArgModules. Output is again to the ErrorReport. The focus of this check is on whether the argument, i.e., reasoning, is made visible explicitly in the AC.
- ConfirmationBias – a review that evaluates how susceptible the argument is to confirmation bias. Inputs to this process are Rebuttals, RequiredEvidence and AcceptanceCriteria. Output is again to the ErrorReport. The focus of this check is to ensure that the AC has specific safeguards against confirmation bias.

Instantiated Evaluation Process: We can now instantiate the model. We do this by describing the major steps in each of the 4 sub-processes. We can then check these steps to see that they conform to the model.

- *TopLevelClaimCheck:*

(1) Top-level claim should consist of two parts: subject and predicate. The subject should represent a system or a component or subsystem of a system and the predicate should represent critical properties of that system to assure, contextual, environmental and operational information.
(2) The meaning of a top-level claim shall be clear and not create any ambiguity.
(3) All critical terms mentioned in a top-level claim shall be clarified.
(4) Necessary assumptions shall be stated explicitly.

- *SubClaimCheck:*

(1) The meaning of a claim shall be clear and not create any ambiguity.
(2) All critical terms mentioned in a claim shall be clarified.
(3) Claims related to process or product or people shall be clarified to support upper-level claims.
(4) Necessary assumptions to support claims related to process or product or people shall be stated explicitly.
(5) Terminal claims shall be supported by proper evidence and acceptance criteria for evidence shall be clarified.

- *(Review)ExplicitArgument:*

(1) The reasoning of how an upper-level claim is decomposed into supporting claims and/or evidence and how lower-level claims and/or evidence together support an upper-level claim shall be documented explicitly. The latter is more important than the former one.
(2) The rationale for reasoning shall be documented if it is necessary.
(3) All key terms mentioned in reasoning shall be clarified.
(4) Necessary assumptions in reasoning shall be clarified.

- *(Review)ConfirmationBias:*

(1) Rebuttals shall be documented and resulting violation of a claim shall be documented.
(2) Evidence to support rebuttals shall be clarified.
(3) Evidence description shall comply with acceptance criteria for that specific evidence.

- *GenerateRecommend:*

(1) For any error found in an AC, a recommendation shall be made with appropriate criticality (e.g. highly recommended, recommended, standard).

This process guides AC developers and external reviewers as follows:

- *AC Developer:* AC developers use the evaluation process from the beginning of an AC development. For example, AC developers may provide guidelines to system developers for defining boundary values for system functionalities, etc. It also guides AC developers to use rebuttals and thus avoid "confirmation bias", and to check that evidence complies with its acceptance criteria.

- *External Reviewer:* External reviewers are guided as to how to check claims, arguments and evidence using proposed procedures, and especially to examine claims for ambiguity. Furthermore, external reviewers are reminded to check for rebuttals, and judge whether or not they are adequately resolved.

2. **Rigour of the Argument:** We briefly describe another instantiated process for the content criterion – *rigour of the argument*. In this case, due to space limitations, we have not shown the refined model for this process.

Instantiated Evaluation Process: This criterion focuses on rigorous argument structure. Pattern instantiation may guide in achieving this, or a thorough description of argument may help in acquiring a rigorous argument. Such a description may be a deductive or inductive proof in an argument. The evaluation process "ProcessX" is refined in four checks: "CheckFormalArgument," "CheckInformalArgument," "CheckClaimForValidity" and "CheckRationaleForValidity". The rules for each check are as follows:

- *CheckFormalArgument:*

(1) A formal argument shall be valid with necessary assumptions.
(2) Rationale to support the formal argument shall be clarified.
(3) All terms supporting the formal argument shall be valid.
(4) Rebuttals in a formal argument shall be clarified, and they shall be complete and consistent. (if it is found)
(5) Mitigation of rebuttals in a formal argument shall be clarified, and they shall be complete and consistent.(if rebuttals exist)
(6) An argument branch in an AC complying with an argument pattern shall thoroughly follow the pattern.

- *CheckInformalArgument:*

(1) An informal argument shall be defined inductively, and the steps shall be complete and consistent.
(2) Rationale to support the informal argument shall be clarified.
(3) All terms supporting the informal argument shall be complete and consistent.
(4) Rebuttals in an informal argument shall be clarified, and they shall be consistent. (if it is found)
(5) Mitigation of rebuttals in an informal argument shall be clarified, and they shall be consistent. (if rebuttals exist)
(6) An argument branch in an AC complying with an argument pattern shall thoroughly follow the pattern.

- *CheckClaimForValidity:*

(1) Claim shall be valid (by reviewing proofs-deductive or inductive), complete and consistent

(2) Rebuttals shall be valid (by reviewing proofs-deductive or inductive) and complete (if it is found)

- *CheckRationaleForValidity:*

(1) Rationale shall be supported by deductive or inductive proofs.(if it is necessary).

- *GenerateRecommend:*

(1) For any error found in an AC, a recommendation should be made with criticality (e.g. highly recommended, recommended, standard).

This process guides AC developers and external reviewers as follows:

- *AC Developer:* AC developers are guided to use more rigorous approaches to their arguments. Based on these checks, they are more likely to find and fix gaps/fallacies in arguments. They are reminded that there should be explicit reasoning to show how child claims support a parent claim. The AC developers may also find it worthwhile to provide documentation to external reviewers that aid them in understanding the arguments.
- *External Reviewer:* External reviewers have a basic check list that guides them in evaluating the rigour of the argument. It provides context for them in deciding whether or not the argumentation is defined with adequate rigour – and it does not have to be formal.

4.2   Evaluating the Structure of an Assurance Case

An AC must be evaluated in terms of its structure and content. In this section, we illustrate the instantiation of the evaluation model with one criterion for structure, more specifically for the "Syntax Check" criterion. We use a GSN example to show the approach and also describe how developers and external reviewers utilize the instantiated process.

Syntax check:

- *Instantiated evaluation process:* The "Syntax check" is an early but important stage of the evaluation process: without valid syntax, an AC is unusable in more sophisticated stages of evaluation. A syntax check can be performed with or without tool support. If a tool is used for syntax checking, experts should still review the syntax of an AC to avoid tool failures. In this illustration, we consider syntax checking of a graphical notation for ACs only for syntax checking as our example is documented using GSN; nevertheless we have defined rules for both graphical and textual syntax.
- *CheckGraphSyntax:*

(1) Check what type of notation is defined. If it is a user-defined notation, obtain the documentation. Otherwise, a standard for a particular notation should be followed;

(2) Shapes of nodes shall be compliant with recommended shapes;

(3) There shall be one and only one association between any two nodes;

(4) Only valid associations shall exist between any two nodes;

(5) The only terminal nodes in the AC are those that in the defined syntax have no outgoing associated nodes;

(6) Label/identifier of a claim/argument/evidence should be defined in an acceptable format;

- *CheckTextSyntax:*

(1) Check what type of notation is defined. If it is a user-defined notation, then one should look for the documentation;

(2) All artefacts of an AC shall comply with notation mentioned in the documentation.

(3) Label/identifier of a claim/argument/evidence should be defined in an acceptable format;

- *GenerateRecommend:*

(1) For any error found in an AC, a recommendation should be made with criticality (e.g. highly recommended, recommended, standard).

This process guides AC developers and external reviewers as follows:

- *AC Developer:* AC Developers can evaluate the syntax of an AC with or without tool support. If developers evaluate manually, then they use rules to evaluate the AC. For instance, developers may generate a report if they encounter an error, e.g. shapes not complying with GSN community standard 2.0 [5] for an AC documented by GSN. This report can help developers to fix an AC before final submission to external reviewers. They should start the process as soon as the development of an AC starts. Developers should validate the tool in use. This evaluation should produce qualitative results instead of only boolean values (e.g. 'yes' or 'no'). AC developers can perform their evaluation without tool support as well. This is clearly more time consuming and probably more error prone. It is also more likely for "home grown" AC notations as compared with using a standard/commercially available technique. A simple notation that the AC has been checked for appropriate syntax may be welcomed by the external reviewer.

- *External Reviewer:* The procedure provides specific rules for syntax checking. External reviewers should also use tools when available. Syntax checks are relatively easy to define when the AC developers have provided adequate guidance as to what notation has been used.

5   Validation of the Evaluation Processes

This section presents a self-validation: applying the Evaluation Processes to example ACs.

5.1 Validation of "Convincing Basis for the AC" (A Content Criterion)

We use an excerpt of a GSN-like example of a coffee cup to illustrate the *Convincing basis* check. The top-level claim (represented by a rectangle) of the AC is labelled as 'TopClaim, C', contexts (represented by rounded rectangles) are labelled as 'K1', 'K2', 'K3' and 'K4', assumptions (represented by ovals) are labelled as 'A1' and 'A2', an argument (represented by a parallelogram) is labelled as 'R' and sub-claims (represented by rectangles) supporting the top-level claim are labelled as 'CR', 'CI', 'CPM' and 'CA'.

We use the AC for a coffee cup shown in Fig. 3. Four checks have defined rules that we use to perform an evaluation.

'TopLevelClaimCheck': evaluates the top-level claim in Fig. 3. Concerning rule (1), we find that top-level claim, "TopClaim, C" consists of two parts: the subject "The coffee cup $< X >$" specifies the system and the predicate "is safe in its intended environment, and its intended uses" specifies the critical

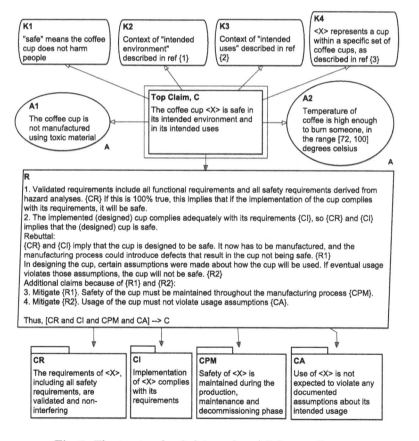

Fig. 3. The top two level claims of an AC for a coffee cup.

property 'safe', with environmental and operational conditions in the description. Concerning rule (2), we find that the meaning of the top-level claim is clear and does not create any ambiguity. Concerning rule (3), we find clarification of all terms (e.g. 'safe,' "intended environment," "intended uses," "coffee cup specification"). Concerning rule (4), we find that necessary assumptions (e.g. non-toxic material for a coffee cup and tolerable temperature) are clarified.

'SubClaimCheck': checks the second level claims of Fig. 3. The sub-claims 'CR,' 'CI,' 'CPM' and 'CA' are represented by modules as they contain implicit argument branches. Page restrictions prevent us from including them. Concerning rule (1), the meaning of all sub-claims is clear and does not create any ambiguity. Claim 'CR2.2.1.1.1.2.2' assures the competency of people in performing 'FTA' in Fig. 4.

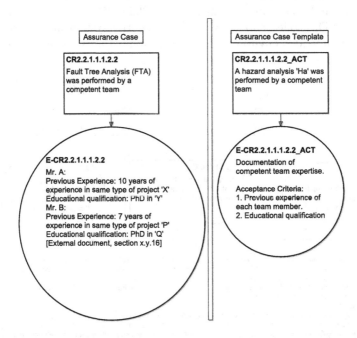

Fig. 4. An excerpt of evidence complying with acceptance criteria for a coffee cup example.

Concerning rule (2), we do not find any clarification for any term mentioned in the claims. Concerning rule (3), we find that claims 'CI' clarifies assuring implementation complies with requirements. Other claims ('CR', 'CPM' and 'CA') explain assuring valid and non-interfering requirements, ensuring safety during production, maintenance and decommissioning and operational assumptions. Concerning rule (4), we find no assumptions. Concerning rule (5), we find that terminal claim 'CR2.2.1.1.1.2.2' is supported by evidence 'E-CR2.2.1.1.1.2.2' and claim 'CR2.2.1.1.1.2.2_ACT' and acceptance criteria

'E-CR2.2.1.1.1.2.2_ACT' from an assurance case template are clarified. We use '(Review)ExplicitArgument' to evaluate the explicitness of an argument. Concerning rule (1), we find that argument 'R' describes explicit reasoning of how subclaims ('CR,' 'CI', 'CPM' and 'CA') support top-level claim 'C.' Argument 'R' demonstrates reasoning adequately along with rebuttals and mitigation of these rebuttals. Concerning rules (2), (3) and (4), we do not find any justification, context or assumption.

'(Review)ConfirmationBias': reviews confirmation bias. Concerning rule (1), we find that argument 'R' demonstrates rebuttals with possible counters explicitly. Concerning rules (2), we do not find any evidence to support those rebuttals. Concerning rule (3), Fig. 4 shows terminal claim 'CR2.2.1.1.1.2.2' is supported by evidence 'E-CR2.2.1.1.1.2.2' and evidence complies with acceptance criteria 'E-CR2.2.1.1.1.2.2'.

'GenerateRecommend' generates the following: a) It is recommended to clarify key terms, e.g. context of "documented assumption" mentioned in claim 'CA.' should be clarified. b) It is highly recommended to state necessary assumptions. c) It is recommended to state assumptions, justifications in reasoning 'R' e.g. justification for 'R' should be clarified. d) It is recommended to clarify evidence to support rebuttals.

5.2 Validation of "Rigour of the Argument" (A Content Criterion)

We use the same example in Fig. 3 to illustrate the rigour of the argument evaluation. The argument is informal so we use 'CheckInformalArgument.' We also perform 'CheckClaimForValidity' and 'CheckRationaleForValidity'.

'CheckInformalArgument': concerning rule (1), we find that the arguments are defined inductively with adequate steps, including rebuttals to support the upper-level claims, and they are complete and consistent. For instance, argument 'R' has four steps of reasoning. Concerning rule (2), we do not find any rationale for the argument, since 'R' is not supported by a justification. Concerning rule (3), we do not find any context or assumption to support the argument. Concerning rule (4), we find that some arguments do use rebuttals, e.g., 'R' uses two rebuttals, 'R1' and 'R2'. Rebuttals mentioned in the argument 'R' are consistent. Concerning rule (5), we find that the mitigation of each rebuttal is demonstrated. For instance, mitigations 'CPM' and 'CA' in argument 'R' resolve the rebuttals, 'R1' and 'R2'. Concerning rule (6), we find that an argument branch considers different phases of the development process.

'CheckClaimForValidity': concerning rule (1), we find that the sub-claims are valid, complete and consistent because arguments are valid and evidence complying with acceptance criteria support terminal claims. Sub-claims ('CR', 'CI,' 'CPM' and 'CA' are represented by modules, details of which are not included in this paper) are complete and consistent and valid supported by arguments. Concerning rule (2), we find that arguments have defined rebuttals and mitigations. Rebuttals are complete (shown earlier), but there is no proof to check the validity of those rebuttals.

'CheckRationaleForValidity': concerning rule (1) we find that no justification exists to support the argument.

'GenerateRecommend' produces the following: a) It is recommended that rationale should exist to support argument 'R.' b) It is recommended that for environmental or operational conditions during production, details of the maintenance stage should be clarified.

5.3 Validation of "Syntax Check" (A Structure Criterion)

To illustrate our syntax check process, we use AFI RVSM Pre-Implementation Safety Case [1] as an example. It uses GSN for documentation. The safety case shows safety arguments of RVSM (Reduced Vertical Separation Minimum) implementation and maintenance to reduce the vertical separation between Flight Levels 290 and 410 (inclusive) from 600 m to 300 m in AFI airspace. We apply the rules for syntax check to an assurance case of type GSN.

'CheckGraphSyntax': concerning rule (1), we consider the GSN community Standard 2.0 [5] as a reference. Concerning rule (2), by review we note that shapes of goal and strategy comply with the standard. However, the example refers to a solution as *evidence,* and they used a rounded rectangle for evidence instead of a circle. They used one context and did not use any assumption or justification in their safety case, though mentioned those terms in their example safety case, and they otherwise comply with the standard. However, the shape of the context used in the safety case does not comply with the standard. Concerning rule (3) and (4), there is one and only one valid association ('SupportedBy') that exists between any two nodes. For rule (5), the terminal nodes (in some pages, terminal nodes are goals, and in some pages, terminal nodes are evidence) have no outgoing association with other goals. With rule (6), the label of goals, strategies and evidence follows a hierarchy. Thus, with rule (2), one shape (context) does not comply with the standard.

'GenerateRecommend' generates that it is highly recommended to fix the shape to comply with the standard, or to explicitly document how and why it deviates from the standard.

6 Conclusion

Our proposed approach incorporates rules to identify known weaknesses in an AC. These weaknesses can be associated with specific, previously published evaluation criteria, and the evaluation process made more structured and systematic by using these criteria to drive the evaluation process. We illustrated the application of these evaluation rules, via refinement and instantiation of a generic evaluation process, for two criteria related to content of the AC, and one criterion related to structure of the AC. These three processes were then self-validated using one *GSN* example and another *GSN*-like example. We have thus shown that systematic and comprehensive evaluation of ACs is feasible.

References

1. ALTRAN-ATM Division, National Aerospace Laboratory NLR and AFI RVSM Project Management Team: AFI RVMS Pre-Implementation Safety Case, final edn., February 2008
2. Belle, A.B., Lethbridge, T.C., Kpodjedo, S., Adesina, O.O., Garzón, M.A.: A novel approach to measure confidence and uncertainty in assurance cases. In: 2019 IEEE 27th International Requirements Engineering Conference Workshops (REW), pp. 24–33. IEEE (2019)
3. Bloomfield, R., Bishop, P., Jones, C., Froome, P.: ASCAD. Adelard Safety Case Development Manual. Adelard **5** (1998)
4. Chowdhury, T., Wassyng, A., Paige, R., Lawford, M.: Criteria to systematically evaluate (safety) assurance cases. In: 30th International Symposium on Software Reliability Engineering (ISSRE), pp. 380–390. IEEE (2019)
5. Group, A.C.W., et al.: Goal structuring notation community standard (version 2) (2018)
6. Hse, M.: Assessment Principles for Offshore Safety Cases (APOSC) (2006)
7. Kelly, T.P.: Arguing Safety–A Systematic Approach to Safety Case Management. The University of York, Department of Computer Science (1998)
8. Leveson, N.: Cost-effective safety certification of software-intensive systems. Seventh Software Certification Consortium (SCC), Annapolis, May 2011
9. Luo, Y., van den Brand, M., Li, Z., Saberi, A.K.: A systematic approach and tool support for GSN-based safety case assessment. J. Syst. Archit. **76**, 1–16 (2017)
10. Mayo, P.: Structured safety case evaluation: a systematic approach to safety case review. In: Proceedings of the First IET International Conference on System Safety, pp. 164–173 (2006)
11. Toulmin, S.E.: The Uses of Argument. Cambridge University Press, Cambridge (2003)

Just Enough Formality in Assurance Argument Structures

Torin Viger[1](✉), Rick Salay[2], Gehan Selim[1], and Marsha Chechik[1]

[1] Department of Computer Science, University of Toronto, Toronto, Canada
{torinviger,gehan.selim,chechik}@cs.toronto.edu
[2] Department of Electrical and Computer Engineering, University of Waterloo,
Waterloo, Canada
rsalay@gsd.uwaterloo.ca

Abstract. *Safety assurance cases (ACs)* are structured arguments that assert the safety of cyber-physical systems. ACs use reasoning steps, or *strategies*, to show how a safety claim is decomposed into subclaims which are then supported by *evidence*. In practice, ACs are informal, and thus it is difficult to check whether these decompositions are valid and no subclaims are missed. This may lead to the approval of fallacious safety arguments and thus the deployment of unsafe systems. Fully formalizing ACs to facilitate rigorous evaluation is not realistic due to the complexity of creating and comprehending such ACs. We take an intermediate approach by formalizing several types of decomposition strategies, proving the conditions under which they are deductive, and applying them as templates that guard against common errors in ACs. We demonstrate our approach on two scenarios: creation of ACs with deductive reasoning steps and evaluation and improvement of existing ACs.

Keywords: Assurance cases · Goal Structuring Notation (GSN) · Safety arguments · Argument decomposition · Strategies · Formalization · Deductive reasoning · Fallacies · Argument templates

1 Introduction

Cyber-physical systems have become deeply ingrained in many aspects of our daily life. With an increased usage of these systems in safety-critical domains (e.g., automotive and aerospace), the need to ensure that they function correctly and safely has increased as well. In response to that need, several industry-specific standards have been built with the aim of providing guidance on developing *safe* systems. For example, ISO 26262 [18] is the de facto functional safety standard in the automotive industry. At a high level, the standard specifies a framework of activities aimed to manage functional safety during automotive product development, where each of these activities results in one or more work products. Part 2 of the standard then requires compiling these work products into *assurance cases* [18]. Safety assurance cases (*ACs*) are structured arguments used to argue that systems are safe for use in their target operational environments.

© Springer Nature Switzerland AG 2020
A. Casimiro et al. (Eds.): SAFECOMP 2020, LNCS 12234, pp. 34–49, 2020.
https://doi.org/10.1007/978-3-030-54549-9_3

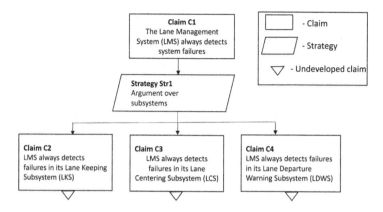

Fig. 1. Fragment of an assurance case (AC) for the LMS system.

Modern safety ACs usually take the form of tree-like structures, where the root of the tree contains the system's safety claim(s), and the remainder of the tree hierarchically develops an argument that supports the top-level safety claim(s), based on *evidence*. There are several notations that can be used to describe ACs (e.g., *Goal Structuring Notation (GSN)* [16], *Claim-Argument-Evidence (CAE)* [3]), and ACs can be represented by metamodels such as *Structured Assurance Case Metamodel (SACM)* [28]. In this paper, we focus on ACs represented in GSN.

Motivating Example. Figure 1 shows a fragment of an informal GSN AC for a vehicle's *Lane Management System (LMS)*. The LMS is an automated vehicle safety feature which ensures that vehicles maintain a safe position in their lanes [20]. GSN ACs contain claims which assert that certain system properties hold, and argument steps or *strategies* which decompose claims into more refined subclaims that support their parent claims. These subclaims are further decomposed until they can be linked to *solution* nodes which support their corresponding claims through *evidence*. A *justification* node can be linked to a strategy to argue that the decomposition is appropriate for its claim. In this fragment, claim *C1* asserts that the LMS always detects any system failures. It is decomposed by strategy *Str1* into subclaims which assert that the LMS always detects failures in each of its subsystems. However, the content of *C1* is informal, and thus it is difficult to evaluate whether this decomposition strategy is sufficient to produce a sound argument, i.e., whether the validity of *C2-C4* is sufficient to imply *C1*. Are the subsystems in *C2-C4* the only ones that can fail? Can a failure be caused by an improper interaction between two correctly functioning systems? These questions are not explicitly addressed in the argument.

The former example demonstrates only a subset of possible AC fallacies that have been identified in the literature, e.g., [14,15]. Approval of fallacious ACs can result in the deployment of unsafe systems, e.g., the crash of the RAF Nimrod aircraft in 2006 [17], yielding severe real-world consequences. Yet human-based assessment of ACs has been found to be inconsistent [15] (i.e., different reviewers can find different fallacies in the same AC); it should be augmented with a degree of automation, based on rigour and formality.

Two main approaches have been investigated in the literature to facilitate rigorous AC evaluation. The first, e.g., [1,2,4,32], involves fully formalizing ACs. We believe that this is not realistic due to the reduced understandability of fully formalized ACs, which complicates their development and limits the reviewability [14]. The second approach, which we adopt here, is to formalize ACs partially, to maintain their accessibility while enabling analysis. This approach is promoted by Rushby [29,30] who suggested that while AC aspects relevant to our knowledge of the assured system (e.g., its environment and hazards) require human assessment, reasoning about the system design can be automated. This approach has been implemented in the AdvoCATE tool [11,24] which has a feature that takes claims supported by theorem-proving evidence and decomposes them into sub-arguments based on the theorem prover's internal logic. Template-based approaches to AC development such as [33] have proven to be effective in mitigating common developer errors; however, we are not aware of an existing set of AC strategy templates which are provably *deductive* (i.e., strategy templates in which the parent claim is a logical consequence of the child claims).

Contributions. In this paper, we aim to take a step towards improving the safety assurance of cyber-physical systems by facilitating the rigorous evaluation of their ACs. Specifically, we formalize several types of decomposition strategies, identifying the conditions under which each of these strategies yields a deductive argument, and applying them as templates that guard against particular types of AC errors. Our approach can be leveraged in two scenarios: (i) creating ACs with deductive reasoning steps; and (ii) evaluating existing ACs by mapping their strategies to these provably deductive strategies and assessing whether any of the necessary AC components are missing or are in the wrong form. This is complementary to the approach implemented in AdvoCATE [11,24], which formally decomposes claims that are supported by evidence from theorem provers. We demonstrate scenarios (i) and (ii) by creating AC fragments for a simple floor-cleaning system (FCS) (introduced in Sect. 2) and by applying a strategy template to an informal fragment of the LMS AC, respectively.

Organization. The rest of this paper is organized as follows: Sect. 2 formalizes AC claims and demonstrates them on the FCS example. Section 3 uses the formal notion of AC claims to characterize different classes of strategies, and identifies the conditions under which these strategies are provably correct. In Sect. 4 we show how these strategies can be used to construct an AC with provably deductive reasoning steps on the FCS example, and we demonstrate how to rigorously assess and augment existing ACs (i.e., the LMS AC) using these formal strategies. Section 5 discusses related work and Sect. 6 concludes with future work.

2   Preliminaries

After introducing the FCS running example, we define concepts of *executions*, *properties* and *AC claims*.

2.1   Running Example: Floor-Cleaning System

The FCS is an automated system which operates over a grid of $n \times n$ floor tiles. It is designed to vacuum all tiles that contain objects and to clean all grimy tiles without becoming damaged. It can do so by executing sequences of the following actions: `moveTile`(dir) moves the FCS to the adjacent floor tile in the specified direction (where $dir \in \{(1,0),(0,1),(-1,0),(0,-1)\}$), `cleanTile` cleans the floor tile at its current position, `vacuumTile` vacuums the floor tile at its current position, and `idle` tells the system to remain stationary.

The Boolean variables $\{G_{ij}, O_{ij}, H_{ij}\}$ describe a tile's state at position (i,j), where G_{ij} denotes whether the tile is grimy, O_{ij} denotes whether the tile contains objects, and H_{ij} denotes whether the tile is hazardous. Environment actions may cause the states of tiles to change. Specifically, actions `dirtyTile`(i,j), `addObject`(i,j), and `addHazard`(i,j) set G_{ij}, O_{ij} and H_{ij}, respectively, to *True*. The FCS may be damaged if it moves to a hazardous tile (i.e., $H_{ij} = True$) or if it attempts to clean a tile containing an object (i.e., $O_{ij} = True$) before vacuuming it.

Any environment state is defined by the states of its n^2 tiles. A system state is described by a predicate *Damaged* indicating if the system is damaged, and a variable $pos = (x,y) \in \{1,2,\ldots,n\} \times \{1,2,\ldots,n\}$ indicating its current position in the grid. Any *world state* (i.e., a system state joint with an environment state) can be represented as $\{Damaged, pos, (G_{11}, O_{11}, H_{11}), \ldots (G_{nn}, O_{nn}, H_{nn})\}$. Let S_{FCS} denote all world states, let A_{FCS} denote the set of all system and environment actions, and let $\Delta_{FCS} \subseteq S \times A \times S$ denote all valid state-action-state transitions (i.e., $(s,a,s') \in \Delta_{FCS}$ iff applying action a in state s causes a transition to state s'). The FCS and its environment are described by a Labeled Transition System *(LTS)* $M_{FCS} = (S_{FCS}, A_{FCS}, \Delta_{FCS})$ [19].

2.2   AC Claims as Properties over Executions

An AC claim asserts that a property holds for a system over a set of its possible executions. We formally define properties and executions in terms of LTS models; however, these definitions generalize to all models representing system states and transitions between them. Executions represent paths through the operation of a system. Properties are statements which make assertions over executions.

Definition 1 (Execution). *Given an LTS $M = (S, A, \Delta)$, an execution $\{s_0, (a_1, s_1), (a_2, s_2) \ldots\}$ is an initial state $s_0 \in S$ and a sequence of action-state pairs (a_i, s_i), where each action $a_i \in A$, each state $s_i \in S$, and each state-action-state transition $(s_{i-1}, a_i, s_i) \in \Delta$. The set of all executions of M is a set X consisting of each execution $x = \{s_0, (a_1, s_1), \ldots\}$, where every transition (s_{i-1}, a_i, s_i) is valid (i.e. $(s_{i-1}, a_i, s_i) \in \Delta$).*

In M_{FCS}, let s_0 denote a non-damaged system state at position $(1, 2)$ on a 3×3 grid, where all tiles are clean, nonhazardous, and contain no object (i.e., G_{ij}, O_{ij}, and H_{ij} are *False* for each i, j). One possible execution is given by $\{s_0, (\texttt{addObject}(1, 1), s_1), (\texttt{moveTile}(0, -1), s_2), (\texttt{vacuumTile}, s_3)\}$, where each state s_i (for $i = 1, 2, 3$) results from applying action a_i to state s_{i-1}.

Definition 2 (Property). *A property $\mathbb{P}: S \times (A \times S)^* \longrightarrow \{\text{True}, \text{False}\}$ is a statement which can be evaluated for any execution $x = \{s_0, (a_1, s_1), (a_2, s_2) \ldots\}$.*

A possible property of M_{FCS} is $\mathbb{P}_0$: "The system never reaches a hazardous tile". Consider an execution $x_0 = \{s_0, (a_1, s_1), (a_2, s_2), \ldots\}$. If (i_n, j_n) denotes the position of the FCS in state s_n, then the environment variable $H_{i_n j_n}$ indicates whether the system is on a hazardous tile in state s_n. The property $\mathbb{P}_0(x_0)$ holds if and only if $H_{i_n j_n}$ is *False* for all n.

We can now express the notion of AC claims.

Definition 3 (Claim). *Let $M = (S, A, \Delta)$ be an LTS, let X denote a subset of all executions of M, and let $\mathbb{P}$ be a property. The claim $C(\mathbb{P}, M, X)$ denotes the statement $\forall x \in X$, $\mathbb{P}(x)$, i.e., "Property $\mathbb{P}$ holds for every execution $x \in X$".*

For M_{FCS} and property $\mathbb{P}_0$ as above, let X_0 be the set of executions where M_{FCS} starts on a nonhazardous tile. The claim $C(\mathbb{P}_0, M_{FCS}, X_0)$ asserts that the system will never reach a hazardous tile in any execution where it begins on a nonhazardous tile, or, formally, $\forall x = \{s_0, (a_1, s_1), \ldots\} \in X_0, \forall i \in \{0, 1, \ldots, \}$, $Damaged(s_i) = False$.

3   Formal Strategies

In this section, we categorize strategies based on how the properties and executions of parent claims relate to those of subclaims. Specifically, we define and formalize two common strategies (domain and property decomposition strategies), identify their needed components, and prove that the resulting decompositions are *deductive*, i.e., the parent claim is logically inferred from the child claims.

Definition 4 (Deductive Decomposition Strategy). *Let strategy Str decompose claim C into subclaims C1, ..., Cn. Str is deductive iff $(C1 \wedge \ldots \wedge Cn) \Rightarrow C$.*

3.1   Domain Decomposition Strategies

Domain decomposition strategies are similar to *proofs by cases* which divide a proposition into a set of cases, with each case covering a set of instances where the proposition may/not hold. A *domain decomposition strategy* takes a claim that some property $\mathbb{P}$ holds for a set of executions, and decomposes it into subclaims which assert that $\mathbb{P}$ holds over a subset of these executions. It does so by choosing a domain of values that each execution can be mapped onto, partitioning the domain into subsets, and arguing separately over the executions mapped to each subset. For example, any execution of the FCS can be mapped onto the domain of natural numbers based on the number of tiles cleaned by the FCS, and thus, these executions can be partitioned into subsets by a partition of natural numbers.

Definition 5 (Domain Decomposition Strategy, Justification, Completeness). *Given an LTS $M = (S, A, \Delta)$ and a set of executions X of M, let D be a domain of values and let f be a relation which maps executions in X to values in D. Let $\mathscr{D} = \{D_1, D_2, \ldots, D_n\}$ be a set of subdomains of D, i.e., $\forall i \in \{1, \ldots, n\}$, $D_i \subseteq D$. Given a property $\mathbb{P}$ and the claim $C(\mathbb{P}, M, X)$, a domain decomposition strategy $(C(\mathbb{P}, M, X), D, \mathscr{D}, f)$ decomposes $C(\mathbb{P}, M, X)$ into n subclaims of the form $C(\mathbb{P}, M, X_i)$, where $X_i = \{x \in X \mid f(x) \in D_i\}$ for $i \in \{1, \ldots n\}$. This strategy is* justified *if the relation f is a function (i.e., f maps every every execution $x \in X$ to a value $d \in D$), and it is* complete *if $D = (D_1 \cup D_2 \ldots \cup D_n)$.*

Theorem 1. *If a domain decomposition strategy $(C(\mathbb{P}, M, X), D, \mathscr{D}, f)$ is justified and complete, then it is deductive.*

Proof. Consider a domain decomposition strategy $(C(\mathbb{P}, M, X), D, \mathscr{D}, f)$, which decomposes a claim $C(\mathbb{P}, M, X)$ into subclaims of the form $C(\mathbb{P}, M, X_1)$, $\ldots, C(\mathbb{P}, M, X_n)$, where each X_i is defined as in Definition 5. Suppose that this strategy is justified and complete, and that each subclaim $C(\mathbb{P}, M, X_i)$ holds $\forall i \in \{1, 2, \ldots, n\}$. We proceed by showing that for each execution $x \in X$, $\mathbb{P}(x)$ holds.

Consider any execution $x \in X$. Since this strategy is justified, we have $f(x) = d$ for some $d \in D$. From completeness we have that $D = (D_1 \cup \ldots \cup D_n)$. Therefore, $\exists i \in \{1, 2, \ldots, n\}$ such that $f(x) \in D_i$. Fix this value of i. The claim $C(\mathbb{P}, M, X_i)$ states that $\forall x_i \in X_i$, $\mathbb{P}(x_i)$, where $X_i = \{x' \in X \mid f(x') \in D_i\}$. Since $f(x) \in D_i$, we have that $x \in X_i$, and thus $C(\mathbb{P}, M, X_i) \Longrightarrow \mathbb{P}(x)$. The claim $C(\mathbb{P}, M, X_i)$ holds by assumption; thus, $\mathbb{P}(x)$ holds. Since x is an arbitrary execution in X, $\mathbb{P}(x)$ holds for every $x \in X$. Therefore, $(C(\mathbb{P}, M, X_1) \wedge \ldots \wedge C(\mathbb{P}, M, X_n)) \Longrightarrow C(\mathbb{P}, M, X))$ if the domain decomposition strategy is justified and complete. ☐

Figure 2 shows a template for justified and complete domain decomposition strategies as per Definition 5. Examples of using domain decomposition strategies to decompose claims are shown in Sect. 4 by *Str2* and *Str3*.

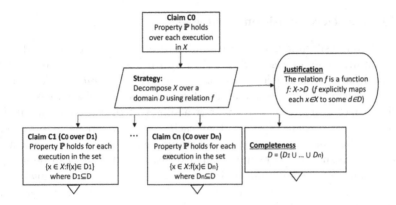

Fig. 2. Template for a justified, complete domain decomposition strategy.

3.2   Property Decomposition Strategies

Property decomposition strategies decompose a claim that a property holds over a set of executions into subclaims, each of which asserts that a *different* property holds over the *same* set of executions. Given an LTS M, an execution set X, and properties $\mathbb{P}, \mathbb{P}_1, \mathbb{P}_2, \ldots \mathbb{P}_n$, consider decomposing the claim $C(\mathbb{P}, M, X)$ into subclaims $C(\mathbb{P}_i, M, X)$ for $i = 1..n$. A *property decomposition* proves that these subclaims imply the parent claim by asserting that the set of executions which satisfy $\mathbb{P}_1, \ldots \mathbb{P}_n$ is a subset of the executions which satisfy $\mathbb{P}$.

Definition 6 (Property Decomposition Strategy and Justification).   *Given a set of executions X of an LTS M, a property $\mathbb{P}$, and a set of properties $\mathscr{P} = \{\mathbb{P}_1, \ldots, \mathbb{P}_n\}$, $(C(\mathbb{P}, M, W), \mathscr{P})$ is a* property decomposition strategy *that decomposes the claim $C(\mathbb{P}, M, X)$ into n subclaims of the form $C(\mathbb{P}_i, M, X)$ for $i \in \{1, 2, \ldots n\}$.*
    Consider the execution sets $X_\mathbb{P}, X_{\mathbb{P}_1} \ldots X_{\mathbb{P}_n}$, where $X_\mathbb{P} = \{x \mid \mathbb{P}(x)\}$ and $X_{\mathbb{P}_i} = \{x \mid \mathbb{P}_i(x)\}, \forall i \in \{1, 2, \ldots, n\}$. A property decomposition strategy is justified if $X_\mathbb{P} \supseteq (X_{\mathbb{P}_1} \cap X_{\mathbb{P}_2} \cap \ldots \cap X_{\mathbb{P}_n})$. Note that $X_\mathbb{P}$ denotes the set of all executions which satisfy property $\mathbb{P}$, whereas X denotes only the executions covered by the strategy's parent claim.

Theorem 2. *If a property decomposition strategy* $(C(\mathbb{P}, M, X), \mathscr{P})$ *is justified, then it is deductive.*

Proof. Consider a property decomposition strategy $(C(\mathbb{P}, M, X), \mathscr{P})$ which decomposes a claim $C(\mathbb{P}, M, X)$ into subclaims $C(\mathbb{P}_1, M, X), \ldots, C(\mathbb{P}_n, M, X)$. Suppose that this strategy is justified, and that $\forall i = 1..n$, each subclaim $C(\mathbb{P}_i, M, X)$ holds. We proceed by showing that for any execution $x \in X$, $\mathbb{P}(x)$ holds.
    Consider an execution $x \in X$. By assumption, properties $\mathbb{P}_1(x), \ldots, \mathbb{P}_n(x)$ hold; therefore, $x \in X_{\mathbb{P}_1} \cap X_{\mathbb{P}_2} \cap \ldots \cap X_{\mathbb{P}_n}$ (where each set $X_{\mathbb{P}_1}$ is defined as in Definition 6). Since this strategy is justified, $X_\mathbb{P} \supseteq (X_{\mathbb{P}_1} \cap X_{\mathbb{P}_1} \cap \ldots \cap X_{\mathbb{P}_n})$ and thus $x \in X_\mathbb{P}$. By the definition of $X_\mathbb{P}$, $\mathbb{P}(x)$ holds. Since x is an arbitrary

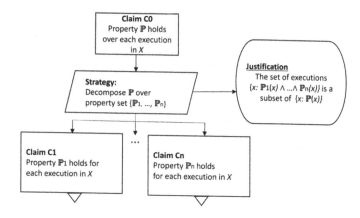

Fig. 3. A template for a justified property decomposition strategy.

element of X, $\mathbb{P}(x)$ holds for every $x \in X$. Therefore, $(C(\mathbb{P}_1, M, X) \wedge \ldots \wedge C(\mathbb{P}_n, M, X)) \Longrightarrow C(\mathbb{P}, M, X)$ when the property decomposition strategy is justified. $\square$

Figure 3 shows a general template for justified property decomposition strategies, however the exact form of the justification of these strategies depends on the relationship between properties $\mathbb{P}$ and $\{\mathbb{P}_1, \ldots, \mathbb{P}_n\}$. We identify several strategy subtypes based on the form of these properties, and show the methods of justification used to give a deductive argument in each case.

Property Decomposition Strategies as Proof by Cases. When a property $\mathbb{P}$ is expressed as the conjunction of a set of properties $\mathbb{P}_1, \ldots, \mathbb{P}_n$, the property decomposition strategy $(C(\mathbb{P}, M, X), \{\mathbb{P}_1, \ldots, \mathbb{P}_n\})$ (which decomposes $C(\mathbb{P}, M, X)$ into $C(\mathbb{P}_1, M, X), \ldots, C(\mathbb{P}_n, M, X))$ is analogous to a proof by cases. Justification of these strategies is trivial, as every execution which satisfies all of $\mathbb{P}_1, \ldots, \mathbb{P}_n$ clearly satisfies $(\mathbb{P}_1 \wedge \ldots \wedge \mathbb{P}_n)$.

Property Decomposition Strategies by Contrapositive. Given a set of properties $\{\mathbb{P}_{H1}, \ldots, \mathbb{P}_{Hn}\}$, suppose $\mathbb{P}$ is a property where, for any execution x, $\neg \mathbb{P}(x) \Rightarrow (\mathbb{P}_{H1}(x) \vee \ldots \vee \mathbb{P}_{Hn}(x))$ (i.e., if $\mathbb{P}(x)$ does *not* hold, then some $\mathbb{P}_{Hi}$ must hold). By contrapositive, this is logically equivalent to the expression $(\neg \mathbb{P}_{H1}(x) \wedge \ldots \wedge \neg \mathbb{P}_{Hn}(x)) \Rightarrow \mathbb{P}(x)$. Thus, if $\neg \mathbb{P}_{Hi}(x)$ holds $\forall i = 1..n$, then $\mathbb{P}(x)$ holds. Therefore, the property decomposition $(C(\mathbb{P}, M, X), \{\neg \mathbb{P}_{H1}, \ldots, \neg \mathbb{P}_{Hn}\})$ is justified by contrapositive.

Property decompositions by contrapositive are used frequently in practice to assert that a system is safe by arguing that all ways in which the system may not be safe (i.e., all the *hazards*) have been mitigated. An example of a property decomposition strategy by contrapositive is given by *Str4* in Sect. 4.

Property Decomposition Strategies by Induction. Given a set of executions X of an LTS $M = (S, A, \Delta)$, let $\mathbb{P}_{state}$ be a property that can be evaluated for individual execution states (i.e., $\mathbb{P}_{state} \colon S \to \{\text{True}, \text{False}\}$). For any $x = \{s_0, (a_1, s_1) \ldots\} \in X$, define the following properties:

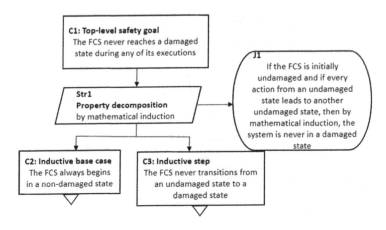

Fig. 4. Strategy *Str1* of an FCS AC.

$$\mathbb{P}_{init}(x) = \mathbb{P}_{state}(s_0)$$
$$\mathbb{P}_{ind}(x) = \forall i \in \mathbb{N}, \mathbb{P}_{state}(s_{i-1}) \implies \mathbb{P}_{state}(s_i)$$
$$\mathbb{P}(x) = \forall i \in \mathbb{N}, \mathbb{P}_{state}(s_i)$$

A decomposition of the form $(C(\mathbb{P}, M, X), \{\mathbb{P}_{init}, \mathbb{P}_{ind}\})$ is a *property decomposition by induction*. By induction, if $\mathbb{P}_{state}$ holds for all possible initial states and if for any transition $(s, (a, s'))$, $\mathbb{P}_{state}(s) \Rightarrow \mathbb{P}_{state}(s')$, then $\mathbb{P}_{state}$ holds for all states. Thus, any execution that satisfies $\mathbb{P}_{init}$ and $\mathbb{P}_{ind}$ also satisfies $\mathbb{P}$. Decompositions of this type are therefore justified as per Definition 6.

The subclaim $C(\mathbb{P}_{ind}, M, X)$ holds if and only if $\mathbb{P}_{ind}$ holds for every transition $\{s_{i-1}, (a_i, s_i)\}$ contained within some execution in X. Thus, if we define X_{ind} to be the set of all such executions (i.e., X_{ind}: $\{\{s, (a, s')\} : \exists x \in X, (s, (a, s')) \subseteq x\}$, the claims $C(\mathbb{P}_{ind}, M, X)$ and $C(\mathbb{P}_{ind}, M, X_{ind})$ are logically equivalent. The form $C(\mathbb{P}_{ind}, M, X_{ind})$ may be preferred, as the executions $\{s, (a, s')\}$ of X_{ind} can be partitioned based on the properties of the individual states/actions s, a, and s', which facilitates further decomposition using domain decomposition strategies over these partitions.

An example of a property decomposition strategy by induction is shown in Sect. 4 by *Str1* (Fig. 4).

4   Applications

In this section, we demonstrate two ways to apply our formal strategies (Sect. 3): (i) to create deductive AC arguments; and (ii) to augment existing AC strategies by evaluating them against deductive strategies.

4.1   Creating Deductive ACs

Consider claim *C1*: "The FCS never reaches a damaged state". *C1* can be formalized as $C(\mathbb{P}_{C1}, M_{FCS}, X_{FCS})$, where M_{FCS} is the FCS LTS model,

X_{FCS} is the set of all possible executions of M_{FCS}, and $\mathbb{P}_{C1}$ is defined by $\mathbb{P}_{C1}(x) : \forall s_i \in x, \neg Damaged(s_i))$. We apply a sequence of strategies from Sect. 3 to $C1$ in order to develop an AC for the FCS with deductive reasoning steps.

Str1: Property Decomposition by Induction of C1. By defining $\mathbb{P}_{state}(s)$: $\neg Damaged(s)$, the property $\mathbb{P}_{C1}(x)$ is representable in the form $\forall s \in x, \mathbb{P}_{state}(s)$. Thus, we may decompose $C(\mathbb{P}_{C1}, M_{FCS}, X_{FCS})$ using the property decomposition strategy by induction $Str1 = (C(\mathbb{P}_{C1}, M_{FCS}, X_{FCS}), \{\mathbb{P}_{init}, \mathbb{P}_{ind}\})$. Here, $\mathbb{P}_{init}$ asserts that the FCS begins in a non-damaged state, and $\mathbb{P}_{ind}$ asserts the FCS never transitions from an undamaged state to a damaged state. These terms are formalized as:

$\mathbb{P}_{init}(\{s_0, (a_1, s_1)\ldots\}) = \neg Damaged(s_0)$

$\mathbb{P}_{ind}(\{s_0, (a_1, s_1)\ldots\}) = \forall i \in \mathbb{N}, \neg Damaged(s_{i-1}) \Rightarrow \neg Damaged(s_i)$

Applying $Str1$ to $C1$ generates the two subclaims $C(\mathbb{P}_{init}, M_{FCS}, X_{FCS})$ and $C(\mathbb{P}_{ind}, M_{FCS}, X_{FCS})$. As $Str1$ is justified by induction, Theorem 2 shows that it is deductive. This decomposition of $C1$ is shown in Fig. 1, and the claims $C(\mathbb{P}_{init}, M_{FCS}, X_{FCS})$ and $C(\mathbb{P}_{ind}, M_{FCS}, X_{FCS})$ are represented as $C2$ and $C3$, respectively.

Section 3.2 shows that $C(\mathbb{P}_{ind}, M_{FCS}, X_{FCS})$ is logically equivalent to the claim $C(\mathbb{P}_{ind}, M_{FCS}, X_{ind})$, where X_{ind} is the set of all state-action-state transitions of executions in X_{FCS} (i.e., X_{ind}: $\{\{s, (a, s')\} : \exists x \in X_{FCS}, (s, (a, s')) \subseteq x\}$). We represent $C3$ in this equivalent form $C(\mathbb{P}_{ind}, M_{FCS}, X_{ind})$ in order to further decompose it using a domain decomposition over system actions.

Str2: Domain Decomposition of C3 over Action Types. The set of FCS actions A_{FCS} consists of system actions (A_{SYS}) and environment actions (A_{ENV}). By partitioning A_{FCS} into subsets A_{SYS} and A_{ENV} and mapping each transition (s, a, s') to the action a, we decompose $C3$ using the domain decomposition strategy $Str2 = (C(\mathbb{P}_{ind}, M_{FCS}, X_{ind}), D_{Str2}, \mathscr{D}_{Str2}, f_{Str2})$ as per Definition 5, with terms defined as follows:

$D_{Str2} = A_{FCS}$ (all FCS actions)

$\mathscr{D}_{Str2} = \{A_{SYS}, A_{ENV}\}$

$f_{Str2}(S \times (A \times S)) \longrightarrow D_{Str2} : f_{Str2}(s, (a, s')) = a.$

$Str2$ is justified, as $\forall (s, (a, s')) \in X_{ind}, f_{Str2}(s, (a, s')) \in D_{Str2}$. It is also complete, as $D_{Str2} = \mathscr{D}_{Str2}[0] \cup \mathscr{D}_{Str2}[1]$ (i.e., $A_{SYS} \cup A_{ENV}$). Therefore, $Str2$ is deductive. Figure 5 shows $Str2$ with subclaims $C4$ and $C5$, as well as explicit completeness and justification claims.

Strategy $Str3$ decomposes $C5$ using a similar decomposition to $Str2$ over individual FCS actions. This generates subclaims $C6$-$C9$, each of which argues over all state-action-state transitions of a particular FCS action in X_{ind}. For example, $C9$ has the form $C(\mathbb{P}_{ind}, M_{FCS}, X_{clean})$, where $X_{clean} = \{(s, (a, s') \in X_{ind}: a = \texttt{cleanTile}\}$.

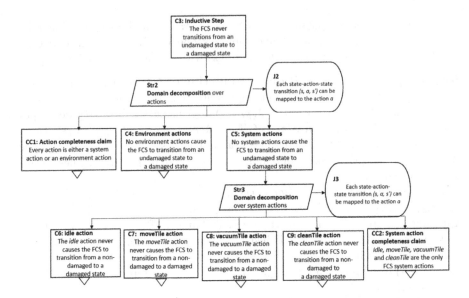

Fig. 5. Strategies *Str2* and *Str3* of an AC for the FCS system.

***Str4*: Property Decomposition of *C9* by Contrapositive.** Consider the properties $\mathbb{P}_{haz}(s,(a,s'))$ and $\mathbb{P}_{obj}(s,(a,s'))$ given by $\mathbb{P}_{haz}(s,(a,s'))$: "The system is on a hazardous tile in state s" and $\mathbb{P}_{obj}(s,(a,s'))$: "The system is on a tile containing an object in state s". As described in Sect. 2.1, the `cleanTile` action can only damage the FCS if it is performed on a hazardous tile or on a tile containing an object. Therefore, for any $x \in X_{clean}$, $\neg\mathbb{P}_{ind}(x) \Rightarrow (\mathbb{P}_{haz}(x)\vee\mathbb{P}_{obj}(x))$. By contrapositive, $(\neg\,\mathbb{P}_{haz}(x) \wedge \neg\,\mathbb{P}_{obj}(x)) \Rightarrow \mathbb{P}_{ind}(x)$, thus the property decomposition $Str4 = (C(\mathbb{P}_{ind}, M_{FCS}, X_{clean}), \{\neg\mathbb{P}_{haz}, \neg\mathbb{P}_{obj}\})$ is justified by contrapositive, and, by Theorem 2, is deductive. Figure 6 shows *Str4*.

By decomposing claims using the provably deductive strategies in Sect. 3, we generate an AC with reasoning steps that are not susceptible to uncertainty or fallacies. These deductive strategies ensure that each strategy's parent claim holds provided that all of its subclaims hold. To evaluate whether the AC's top-level claim holds, reviewers only need to assess the remaining unformalized AC artifacts (e.g. the evidence used to support decomposed claims).

4.2   Evaluating Existing ACs

We now evaluate the LMS AC fragment in Fig. 1 by comparing it to a deductive domain decomposition, and augment the argument accordingly to produce a deductive reasoning step.

In Fig. 1, *C1* asserts that the property $\mathbb{P}_{C1}$: "When a failure is detected, the system notifies the driver" holds over the set X_{C1} of all executions in which a failure occurs. *C1* is then decomposed over the domain D_{Str1} of LMS subsystems,

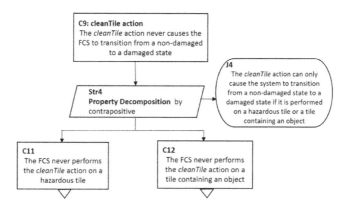

Fig. 6. Strategy *Str4* of an FCS AC.

and the relation f_{C1} maps executions in X_{C1} to the corresponding subsystem which failed. However, this decomposition is not justified as per Definition 5, since any execution in which a failure occurs due to *interactions between multiple subsystems* is not mapped to D_{Str1} by f_{C1}. Furthermore, there is no completeness claim to assert that all subsystems are covered by subclaims in this decomposition.

To address these fallacies, we augment the LMS AC fragment to match the form of a deductive domain decomposition strategy (see Fig. 7). We extend the domain of decomposition D_{Str1} from LMS subsystems to all possible LMS failure cases, and introduce a new child claim *C5* to cover additional failures which result from the interactions between subsystems. The completeness claim *C6* is then added to assert that the subsystems identified in *C2*, *C3* and *C4* are the only subsystems, and that every possible failure case is a subsystem failure or a failure in the interaction between subsystems. Finally, a justification node *J1* is introduced to define a complete mapping from the set X_{C1} to the set of LMS failure cases (i.e., by mapping each execution where the system fails to its corresponding failure case). This strategy now has the exact form of a domain decomposition strategy (see Definition 5), and thus, by Theorem 1, is deductive.

While completeness or justification of an argument may appear obvious in some scenarios, others may require a more careful consideration. In this example, by explicitly considering the mapping between executions and domain values, we found that not all executions were mapped onto the strategy's domain and thus the argument was not valid. Rather than leaving argument completeness and justification as implicit assumptions (as is often done in practice), our approach explicitly addresses these questions and gives AC reviewers an argument artifact to assess. Furthermore, the logic of these decompositions is independent of how the system and its executions are modeled.

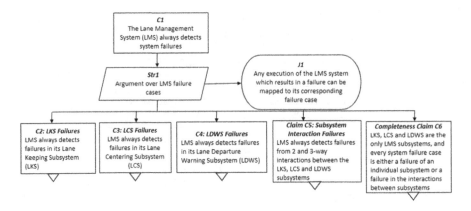

Fig. 7. An augmented version of the LMS AC fragment.

5   Related Work

Several tools semi-automate the workflow of AC development by integrating formal and informal reasoning. For example, NASA's *AdvoCATE* toolset [11,24] allows manually building AC fragments, and merging these fragments with (i) fragments generated by formal verification tools; and (ii) information from requirements and hazards tables [8]. *D-Case Editor* [21] is an Eclipse-based tool that supports building *dependability* ACs, or *D-cases*, using a typed variant of GSN [22,31]. The *Evidential Tool Bus (ETB)* [6] uses a Datalog variant to represent AC nodes and inference rules. Finally, the *Isabelle/SACM* [25] framework translates SACM [28] ACs into Isabelle [26], to enable formal verification of ACs. External tools can be integrated into the aforementioned frameworks. Thus, our decomposition strategies can be *plugged in* as additional features to these tools.

Some of the aforementioned tools support parametrized patterns that are comparable to our decomposition strategies. For example, AdvoCATE allows building AC patterns, with semantics defined in terms of the possible pattern instantiations [9,11]. This formalization was used to demonstrate allowable recursion and restrictions on pattern usage. D-Case Editor supports parametrized patterns [22,23] which were formally defined, together with their scoping rules. The D-Case/Agda extension [31] can be used to formalize and verify D-Case patterns using the Agda functional programming language [27]. Our work is similar to the former pattern-formalization approaches in that we formally define AC patterns or templates, to facilitate their verification. An additional contribution in our work is that our decomposition strategies and their templates are provably deductive, and thus are not vulnerable to logical reasoning fallacies.

AdvoCATE also facilitates building hierarchical [12] and modular [10] ACs, where both concepts were formalized together with their allowable operations and desirable properties (e.g., well-formedness). D-Case Editor supports building modules [22] which can be formalized and verified using D-Case/Agda [31].

AdvoCATE also supports querying ACs [7], with formalized underlying syntax and semantics of queries and their resulting views. The formalization of AC hierarchies, modules, and querying operations are complementary to our work.

6   Conclusion and Future Work

In this paper, we have formalized the semantics for a set of provably deductive AC decomposition strategies that guard against logical reasoning fallacies. We demonstrated the usefulness of these strategies by leveraging them as *templates* in two scenarios. First, we used our strategy templates to build deductive arguments for a simple floor-cleaning system (FCS) example. Second, we used our templates to evaluate a fragment of an AC for an automotive lane management system (LMS). This application identified fallacies in the AC, which we then addressed. Our work adds to the literature by identifying strategy templates (or patterns) that are *provably deductive*, and hence are invulnerable to logical reasoning AC faults, by construction.

The next step is to provide tool support for our strategy templates, implementing them on top of our AC tool MMINT-A [13], and working with our industrial partner to evaluate the approach on large ACs. While Sect. 4 shows how our approach can be used to create deductive ACs and evaluate existing ones *manually*, automated tool support can facilitate the use of our strategies in practice. Our aim is to generate deductive decompositions by prompting users to describe the defining characteristics of the decomposition (e.g., decomposition property, domain of decomposition), and producing strategies based on these characteristics and our deductive templates. Such automation will enable AC developers to create deductive assurance arguments without requiring them to fully understand all aspects of the formalization of our strategies. We also aim to expand the library of patterns, e.g., to address a range of AC uncertainties [5].

References

1. Basir, N., Denney, E., Fischer, B.: Deriving safety cases from automatically constructed proofs. In: Proceedings of International Conference on Systems Safety (2009)
2. Basir, N., Denney, E., Fischer, B.: Deriving safety cases for hierarchical structure in model-based development. In: Schoitsch, E. (ed.) SAFECOMP 2010. LNCS, vol. 6351, pp. 68–81. Springer, Heidelberg (2010). https://doi.org/10.1007/978-3-642-15651-9_6
3. Bloomfield, R., Bishop, P., Jones, C., Froome, P.: ASCAD: Adelard Safety Case Development Manual, London, UK (1998). Accessed 28 Jan 2020
4. Brunel, J., Cazin, J.: Formal verification of a safety argumentation and application to a complex UAV system. In: Proceedings of SafeComp 2012, pp. 307–318 (2012)
5. Chechik, M., Salay, R., Viger, T., Kokaly, S., Rahimi, M.: Software assurance in an uncertain world. In: Hähnle, R., van der Aalst, W. (eds.) FASE 2019. LNCS, vol. 11424, pp. 3–21. Springer, Cham (2019). https://doi.org/10.1007/978-3-030-16722-6_1

6. Cruanes, S., Hamon, G., Owre, S., Shankar, N.: Tool integration with the evidential tool bus. In: Giacobazzi, R., Berdine, J., Mastroeni, I. (eds.) VMCAI 2013. LNCS, vol. 7737, pp. 275–294. Springer, Heidelberg (2013). https://doi.org/10.1007/978-3-642-35873-9_18

7. Denney, E., Naylor, D., Pai, G.: Querying safety cases. In: Bondavalli, A., Di Giandomenico, F. (eds.) SAFECOMP 2014. LNCS, vol. 8666, pp. 294–309. Springer, Cham (2014). https://doi.org/10.1007/978-3-319-10506-2_20

8. Denney, E., Pai, G.: A lightweight methodology for safety case assembly. In: Ortmeier, F., Daniel, P. (eds.) SAFECOMP 2012. LNCS, vol. 7612, pp. 1–12. Springer, Heidelberg (2012). https://doi.org/10.1007/978-3-642-33678-2_1

9. Denney, E., Pai, G.: A formal basis for safety case patterns. In: Bitsch, F., Guiochet, J., Kaâniche, M. (eds.) SAFECOMP 2013. LNCS, vol. 8153, pp. 21–32. Springer, Heidelberg (2013). https://doi.org/10.1007/978-3-642-40793-2_3

10. Denney, E., Pai, G.: Towards a formal basis for modular safety cases. In: Koornneef, F., van Gulijk, C. (eds.) SAFECOMP 2015. LNCS, vol. 9337, pp. 328–343. Springer, Cham (2015). https://doi.org/10.1007/978-3-319-24255-2_24

11. Denney, E., Pai, G.: Tool support for assurance case development. J. Automated Soft. Eng. **25**(3), 435–499 (2018)

12. Denney, E., Pai, G., Whiteside, I.: Formal foundations for hierarchical safety cases. In: Proceedings of HASE 2015, pp. 52–59. IEEE (2015)

13. Fung, N.L.S., Kokaly, S., Di Sandro, A., Salay, R., Chechik, M.: MMINT-A: a tool for automated change impact assessment on assurance cases. In: Gallina, B., Skavhaug, A., Schoitsch, E., Bitsch, F. (eds.) SAFECOMP 2018. LNCS, vol. 11094, pp. 60–70. Springer, Cham (2018). https://doi.org/10.1007/978-3-319-99229-7_7

14. Graydon, P.J.: Formal assurance arguments: a solution in search of a problem? In: Proceedings of ICDSN 2015, pp. 517–528. IEEE (2015)

15. Greenwell, W.S., Knight, J.C., Holloway, C.M., Pease, J.J.: A taxonomy of fallacies in system safety arguments. In: Proceedings of ISSC 2006 (2006)

16. GSN Working Group: GSN Community Standard Version 2, York, UK (2011). http://www.goalstructuringnotation.info/. Accessed 28 Jan 2020

17. Haddon-Cave, C.: The Nimrod Review: An Independent Review into the Broader Issues Surrounding the Loss of the RAF Nimrod MR2 Aircraft XV230 (2009)

18. ISO: ISO 26262: Road Vehicles - Functional Safety, International Organization for Standardization (ISO) (2011)

19. Keller, R.M.: Formal verification of parallel programs. Commun. ACM **19**(7), 371–384 (1976)

20. Kokaly, S.: Managing Assurance Cases in Model Based Software Systems. Ph.D. thesis, McMaster University (2019)

21. Matsuno, Y.: D-Case Editor: A Typed Assurance Case Editor. University of Tokyo (2011)

22. Matsuno, Y.: A design and implementation of an assurance case language. In: Proceedings of ICDSN 2014, pp. 630–641. IEEE (2014)

23. Matsuno, Y., Taguchi, K.: Parameterised argument structure for GSN patterns. In: Proceedings of ICQS 2011, pp. 96–101. IEEE (2011)

24. NASA: AdvoCATE Tool Webpage (2019). https://ti.arc.nasa.gov/tech/rse/research/advocate/. Accessed 28 Jan 2020

25. Nemouchi, Y., Foster, S., Gleirscher, M., Kelly, T.: Isabelle/SACM: computer-assisted assurance cases with integrated formal methods. In: Ahrendt, W., Tapia Tarifa, S.L. (eds.) IFM 2019. LNCS, vol. 11918, pp. 379–398. Springer, Cham (2019). https://doi.org/10.1007/978-3-030-34968-4_21

26. Nipkow, T., Paulson, L.C., Wenzel, M.: Isabelle/HOL: A Proof Assistant for Higher-Order Logic, LNCS, vol. 2283. Springer, Heidelberg (2002). https://doi.org/10.1007/3-540-45949-9

27. Norell, U., Danielsson, N.A., Abel, A.: Agda Wiki Page (2020). https://wiki.portal.chalmers.se/agda/pmwiki.php. Accessed 28 Feb 2020

28. Object Management Group (OMG): Structured Assurance Case Metamodel (SACM). http://www.omg.org/spec/SACM/. Accessed 22 Feb 2020

29. Rushby, J.: Formalism in safety cases. In: Dale, C., Anderson, T. (eds.) Proceedings of SSS 2010, pp. 3–17. Springer, London (2010). https://doi.org/10.1007/978-1-84996-086-1_1

30. Rushby, J.: Logic and epistemology in safety cases. In: Bitsch, F., Guiochet, J., Kaâniche, M. (eds.) SAFECOMP 2013. LNCS, vol. 8153, pp. 1–7. Springer, Heidelberg (2013). https://doi.org/10.1007/978-3-642-40793-2_1

31. Takeyama, M.: "D-Case in Agda" Verification Tool (D-Case/Agda). https://wiki.portal.chalmers.se/agda/pmwiki.php?n=D-Case-Agda.D-Case-Agda. Accessed 25 Feb 2020

32. Yamamoto, S.: Argument algebra: a formalization of assurance case development. In: Kravets, A., Shcherbakov, M., Kultsova, M., Iijima, T. (eds.) JCKBSE 2014. CCIS, vol. 466, pp. 717–725. Springer, Cham (2014). https://doi.org/10.1007/978-3-319-11854-3_62

33. Yamamoto, S., Matsuno, Y.: An evaluation of argument patterns to reduce pitfalls of applying assurance case. In: 2013 1st International Workshop on Assurance Cases for Software-Intensive Systems (ASSURE), pp. 12–17. IEEE (2013)

Towards Recertification of Modular Updates in Integrated Maritime Systems of Systems

Georg Hake[1]([⊠]), Sebastian Feuerstack[2], and Axel Hahn[1]

[1] University of Oldenburg, Oldenburg, Germany
{georg.hake,axel.hahn}@uol.de
[2] OFFIS - Institute for Information Technology, Oldenburg, Germany
sebastian.feuerstack@offis.de

Abstract. The transformation of maritime navigation and control systems into an integrated System of Systems (SoS) consisting of a heterogeneous mixture of individual software-intense and safety-critical subsystems poses new challenges for the verification and validation of the overall system composition. Other than in traditional maritime architectures, the software-reliant structure of a SoS can be subject to change while already in operation, as features can be updated, errors can be fixed, or processes can be optimized. Thus, the alteration of a module on the system level necessitates the reassessment of compliance with the corresponding certification records. In this work, we present an approach on how the modules of a SoS can be associated through extended safety contracts with the corresponding safety case specification to verify the impact of a modification before deployment. Moreover, for each type of update (perfective, corrective, adaptive), the elements that need to be reassessed on the associated safety case are identified. Finally, the concept is established on a safety-critical module of the Maritime Traffic Alert and Collision Avoidance System (MTCAS) in order to assess the applicability of the developed approach.

Keywords: System of Systems · Updates · Contracts · Certification

1 Introduction

Traditional ship-side and vessel traffic service (VTS) architectures undergo a change, shifting away from manually controlled, mechanical and electrical dominated architectures towards software-intense System of Systems (SoS) consisting of a heterogeneous network of safety-critical subsystems providing navigational support or (semi-) autonomous control structures up to fully autonomous Maritime Autonomous Surface Ships (MASS). Different to traditional shipboard control systems, their functionality relies intensively on software-based navigation and steering systems. This enables the system owner or the supplier of a containing module to apply changes to a system that has been handed over to the customer and is already in full service. Moreover, updates of individual system modules can be supplied remotely and in form of a new feature demanded by the customer (adaptive update), a safety-critical fix of a malfunctioning module (corrective update) or in form of performance improvements (perfective update).

© Springer Nature Switzerland AG 2020
A. Casimiro et al. (Eds.): SAFECOMP 2020, LNCS 12234, pp. 50–63, 2020.
https://doi.org/10.1007/978-3-030-54549-9_4

Hence, for the certification and classification societies responsible to verify the adherence of safety standards and rules for maritime systems, the traditional way of certifying, in which an extensive set of documents is compiled once for a fixed system configuration, will no longer be sufficient. To detect whether a given certification remains valid after being altered, it becomes necessary to trace the impact of the change to its safety case by monitoring, testing, or formally verifying and validating changed modules and their effects on the encompassed SoS [1]. With certification costs estimated around 30% of the lifecycle costs in the aerospace domain [2], as well as 25–75% of the development costs of a product [3], the reduction of the recertification overhead after an update becomes a valuable goal [4].

In recent years attempts to improve the maintainability of safety cases by applying safety contracts to the software modules have been proposed [5]. Safety contracts allow the safety-related properties of a system or its subsystems to be formalized in modular form on the basis of assumptions and guarantees. We extend those approaches by creating a mapping between the modules of the system and the corresponding modular safety argument by extending the systems safety contracts with information about the corresponding safety case elements. Based on the established linkage between the system and safety case modules, the impact of change for each update type is demonstrated. In doing so, we provide support for certification authorities and system owners to identify the parts of the safety argument impacted by a change.

Our work is structured as follows: In Sect. 3, the concepts of modern maritime bridge architectures and the current maritime certification processes are introduced. Subsequently, Sect. 4 outlines the correspondence between system architecture modules and their related safety case elements along the development process. By enhancing the associated safety contracts, we enable a bidirectional relation between system and safety modules. Based on the identified dependencies, for each type of update the required transformation on the safety case is shown. The result is a mapping from the module of the system that is changed to the relevant and dependent parts of the corresponding safety case. Finally, we illustrate our approach on the Maritime Traffic Alert and Collision Avoidance System (MTCAS) as one of the building blocks of the modularized bridge system architecture and the capabilities and limits are evaluated. With this threefold approach [4] we align a systematic analysis of existing concepts, the integration of selected methods into a conceptual model and an evaluation based on an existing safety-critical system from the maritime domain.

2 Related Work

The management of change in software systems and its relation to the related assurance cases based on assume-guarantee contracts has been intensively explored by the research group around Jaradat, Bate and Kelly [5, 6]. The authors present methods to identify the parts of the system most sensitive to a change and use contracts to guide the maintenance process. The approaches are closely aligned with the Modular Software Safety Case (MSSC) process developed by the Industrial Avionics Working Group's (IAWG), which aligns the software implementation with the safety argument by applying two types of contract relationships for the modules of the system as well as their interdependencies [7, 8]. Similarly, [9] considers eight categories of change in an ARINC 653 based

Integrated Modular System (IMS) for the aviation domain. Likewise in the automotive domain, [10] presents an approach for AUTOSAR embedded applications. Salameh and Jaradat [11] embedded the aforementioned contract-based maintenance methods into an encompassing change management framework. Furthermore, [12, 13] demonstrate a tracing approach based on Digital Dependability Identities (DDI) that provide tracing measures for a system or its modules along its lifetime. From a structural perspective, the authors in [14] provide an overview of the design and argument patterns used in various domains. Finally, [15] present assurance case reuse approaches for evolutionary systems by applying evolutionary assurance case modeling processes. We built upon these approaches by establishing an adapted bidirectional dependency relationship between the requirements of integrated maritime bridge systems and a modular classification process to identify the elements that need to be re-evaluated after an update. In the following, we highlight the requirements unique for the maritime domain.

3 Background and Motivation

3.1 Integrated Bridge Systems

Today's ship systems are equipped with a combination of sensors, actuators, workstations and communication systems. The heterogeneous system landscape of safety-critical systems on modern vessels range from (i) real-time to non-real time systems, (ii) mixed criticality states and (iii) single- to multi-core hardware that is connected either (iv) directly or through a redundant bus-network [16]. Moreover, the systems differ in terms of criticality and the certification specification. While in the past the overall system functionality has been developed and implemented independently, today interdependent systems are unified into an Integrated Bridge System (IBS), which is defined by the International Maritime Organization (IMO) as "a combination of systems which are interconnected in order to allow centralized access to sensor information or command/control from workstations, with the aim of increasing safe and efficient ship's management by suitably qualified personnel" [17]. IBS thus offer monitoring and control functions that converge on the ship's bridge and are visualized and made available at a central location. The realization of individual functional concepts supporting manned or unmanned ship operation are depicted from the environmental perception towards the provided system functionality in Fig. 1.

For example, a typical system functionality of an IBS are navigational support features (depicted on the left), which rely on sensors like GPS, Radar and AIS (as depicted on the right), process the situation on one or more workstations (e.g. industrial PCs) through the modules of the system such as Route Planning, Traffic Surveillance and display the sea-chart on an Electronic Chart Display and Information System (ECDIS) (depicted in the middle) [18].

A module M in an IBS describes a subsystem from a SoS perspective and will be used in the following to describe the unit of exchange in this work. The modules in turn, rely on sensors, communication systems, actuators and environmental information. By selecting a set of modules in combination enables the defined feature set of a SoS composition.

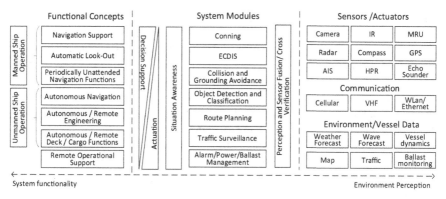

Fig. 1. Realization of the functional scope of a ship's bridge system based on [19, 20]

3.2 Software Maintenance Processes on Maritime Software Systems

To enable a software-oriented maintenance process based on the IMO guidance for updating shipborne equipment [21] and ISO standard 14764 [22] on software maintenance, an industry standard has been established by a joint working group comprising international maritime electronics suppliers [23], as well as recommendations by the International Association of Classification Societies (IACS) [24].

The proposed maintenance processes can occur at different phases of the lifecycle of the product, such as design time, development time, during the testing and verification stages, or when the vessel is already in operation. During all these phases, the updated modules can be integrated into the existing system as part of an onboard maintenance process, during onshore maintenance or as remote maintenance process.

The maintenance activities are triggered by the time and place, operational mode, the criticality of the modules and the category of maintenance that was detected. Finally, different stakeholders have to be addressed during the update phases, including manufacturers, shipowners or classification societies [23].

3.3 Maritime Safety Assessment and Goal-Based System Certification

Shipping companies, shipbuilders and suppliers have to document safety-relevant requirements, design decisions and results of the validation of the ship's system extensively in order to obtain the operating license from a certification authority (e.g. DNV GL, Bureau Veritas). To obtain such a release, shipbuilders have so far followed a rigid set of rules and design standards [25]. The safeguarding of maritime systems is characterized by global and local guidelines, which are derived primarily from historical experience. For the most part, prescriptive rules have to be followed rigidly, which has been sufficient for a traditional shipbuilding process, but reached its limits with software-intense IBSs. Up until now, the IMO provides two types of safety analysis: Formal Safety Assessment (FSA) and Goal-based Standards (GBS). Both FSA and GBS are risk-based approaches that classify a system as safe as long as the calculated risk of the system does not exceed an acceptable threshold [25]. However, in case of an update, the system owner has to prove to the certification authority that the system stayed within the risk threshold that has been classified beforehand [26]. In both cases, the system developer must demonstrate in the burden of proof that his system meets its safety requirements. To this end, he must combine the collected evidence and tests and structure them in such a way that he can provide the certifier with credible and structured evidence that the specified objectives are met and hazards can be ruled out.

In order to structure the evidence and to put the collected evidence into context with the goals and requirements to be achieved, the documents can consist of prose, tables or a graphical notation, such as the Claims Argument Evidence or the Goal Structuring Notation (GSN) [5]. In this work, GSN is used to derive a modular Safety Argument and track changes in the model accordingly. GSN uses a tree-like model, as depicted on the right side of Fig. 3 and Fig. 5, that is made up of a Top-Goal (rectangles) which is solved by a structure of underlying Strategy (parallelograms) and Sub-Goal (rectangles) Elements, which in turn are supported by Solution (circles) and Context (squashed rectangles) Elements.

4   Modular Updates in Integrated Maritime SoS

4.1   Structural Augmentation of IBS for Change Management

To lay the foundation for a certifiable update process, the SoS architecture of an IBS needs to be adapted to establish traceability. When updating one of the systems modules, two scenarios can be assumed: Either an existing legacy system is altered or an upcoming system composition is planned with regard for future maintenance. In both scenarios, the system owner and/or the supplier of one module either have restricted knowledge about the underlying system architecture and/or about internals of any module other than their own (equally to a Safety Element out of Context (SEooC) according to ISO 26262 in the automotive domain [27]).

To achieve exchangeability and control the impact of the change, a service-oriented approach for the modules is proposed, similar to Software Components (SWC) in AUTOSAR [10]. Each module fulfills a well-defined set of services and interacts with its environment through controlled interfaces. The composition of individual modules M_1 and M_2 into an encompassing SoS linked at their interfaces via connection a, b and c and annotated with module contracts is depicted in Fig. 2 from the perspective of the logical model.

In order to formally describe the behavior of the system's modules and to anchor them within the GSN model, the respective modules are annotated with assume-guarantee (A/G) contracts. A/G contracts describe the properties of its associated module by guaranteeing a defined behavior as long as the assumptions made about its environment remain valid.

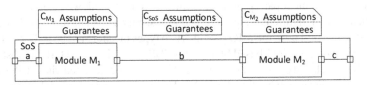

Fig. 2. Logical system perspective of a SoS, its modules and the attached A/G-contracts

Annotated System and safety case modules provide formal methods on refinement, conjunction, and composition of individual modules, denoted respectively by the symbols $\preccurlyeq$, $\wedge$ and $\otimes$ [28, 29].

A contract can be represented as a tuple $C = (A, G)$ with A depicting the assumption about the working environment of a module M and G the properties, which M pledges to fulfill assuming A to be true [29]. For the contracts $C_{M_1} = \left(A_{M_1}, G_{M_1}\right)$ and $C_{M_2} = \left(A_{M_2}, G_{M_2}\right)$ the composition of contracts $C_{SoS} = C_{M_1} \otimes C_{M_2}$ is given by [28]:

$$A_{C_{M_1} \otimes C_{M_2}} = \text{weakest} \left\{ A \left| \begin{array}{c} A \wedge G_{M_2} \Rightarrow A_{M_1} \\ \text{and} \\ A \wedge G_{M_1} \Rightarrow A_{M_2} \end{array} \right. \right\} \tag{1}$$

$$G_{C_{M_1} \otimes C_{M_2}} = G_{M_1} \wedge G_{M_2} \tag{2}$$

The assumption $A_{C_{M_1} \otimes C_{M_2}}$ is defined by the weakest Assumption A for that $A \wedge G_{M_2} \Rightarrow A_{M_1}$ and $A \wedge G_{M_1} \Rightarrow A_{M_2}$ holds. The guarantee $G_{C_{M_1} \otimes C_{M_2}}$ is described by the conjunction of $G_{M_1} \wedge G_{M_2}$. The aforementioned specifications allow for a modularized system design, which eases the exchange of a module and track its impact, as it induces properties such as high cohesion, low coupling, well-defined interfaces and information hiding [8].

4.2 Contract-Based Link of System Level and Safety Level Contracts

The contract-based system model enables the system owner to compose a complete bridge architecture from its modules and verify the compatibility on the contract level through Virtual Integration Testing (VIT). In our minimal example in Fig. 2, for the contract based refinement of modules into a SoS denoted as $C_{M_1} \otimes C_{M_2} \preccurlyeq C_{SoS}$ the following integration conditions need to hold [30]:

For contracts $C_{SoS} = (A, G)$, $C_{M_1} = \left(A_{M_1}, G_{M_1}\right)$ and $C_{M_2} = \left(A_{M_2}, G_{M_2}\right)$ the integration $C_{M_1} \otimes C_{M_2} \preccurlyeq C_{SoS}$ holds if and only if $A \wedge G_{M_1} \Rightarrow A_{M_2}$ and $A \wedge G_{M_2} \Rightarrow A_{M_1}$ and $G_{M_1} \wedge G_{M_2} \Rightarrow G$.

A system owner can utilize the contracts to check from a top-down perspective whether his system composition remains valid after an update. Hence, the ambition for an update of a previously certified model would be the traceability of the overall impact of the change for each type of update. Similar to [6], the aim of this work is the realization of module and evidence traceability. Module level traceability denotes the traceability from the safety argument to the module of the system, while evidence traceability describes the traceability of safety evidence across system artefacts [5]. We argue that even in only partially formalized and integrated system contexts, as often present in testing scenarios, the attribution of a module with contracts can support its impact analysis in narrowing down the cause of contract breach.

Our approach is depicted in Fig. 3 and shows the relation between different phases (Design, Safety Analysis, Development and the Safety Case) in the assurance process.

Beginning with the functional model, the functional requirements are derived and subsequently translated into functional contracts. Similarly, the logical model is designed

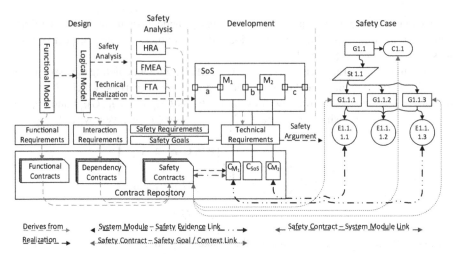

Fig. 3. Linking safety analysis, system development and the safety case via assume/guarantee-contracts

and the interactions between modules become apparent. From this perspective, relationships between the individual modules can be defined and formalized within dependency contracts. In the safety analysis phase, the safety requirements are obtained (e.g. through Hazard and Risk Assessment (HRA)) and transformed into safety contracts. The contracts of each phase overlap in their description of the module functions and complement each other. Thus, the provided functional scope of performance of one module can serve as necessary environmental behavior of another module. Such a dependency must at that point be mapped on the logical level and the safety analysis.

The contracts from the design phase (functional and logical model) as well as the safety contracts derived from the safety analysis are merged and integrated within a contract repository. With a module being developed, the requirements from the contracts are realized and extended by technical contracts (e.g. C_{SoS}, C_{M_1}, C_{M_2}) that define the interaction of modules on a technical level.

As different forms of contracts are derived from the individual phases of the development process, our goal in this work is to enable top-down and bottom-up analysis by extending the safety contracts. For this reason, we supplement the safety contract with direct relations to the safety goals (e.g. $G_{1.1.1}$, $G_{1.1.3}$) and context elements (e.g. $C_{1.1}$) depicted in Fig. 3 as single dotted line. Furthermore, a relation between safety evidence (e.g. $E_{1.1.1.1}$, $E_{1.1.1.3}$) to the module contracts (e.g. C_{SoS}, C_{M_1}, C_{M_2}) is implicit and indicated as double dotted and dashed line. Finally, the dependency between the module contracts and the safety contracts is illustrated as single dotted and dashed line. This results in a bidirectional relationship of the safety arguments, the safety evidence, and the system's modules through the safety contracts as intermediary. The connections between the individual parts are described further in the following.

Safety Contract to Safety Goal: The safety contract derives from the safety analysis as well as the functional and dependency contracts. We extend the safety contracts with additional reference to the module contracts and the (sub-)goals of the safety case.

Hence, when updating a module on the system level, the safety contracts touched can be identified automatically.

Furthermore, the reference to the safety-goals derives naturally as they represent a formalization of the latter. However, there isn't a one-to-one dependency between a safety contract and the safety case, as safety goals can be established by the safety analysis as well as stipulated by the classification guidelines.

Safety Contracts to Module Contract to Safety Evidence: The module contracts are realizations of the safety contracts. Thus, a many-to-many mapping between the two contract-types can be implicit. When exchanging a module on the system level, a number of the technical module contracts is touched, which in turn are related to one or many safety contracts. When knowing which safety contracts and module contracts become invalid after an update, it is possible to identify which of the supporting evidence (e.g. VIT, module or system tests) contains the individual modules and may have to be repeated.

The development phase and the safety analysis phase can take place in parallel or consecutively. In principle, however, both phases complement each other. As described beforehand, in our modular approach the unit of exchange is defined as one module (e.g. M_1, M_2). Though, based on the design process, a module realized in a system composition can have different granularities and relationships to its logical model due to external factors in the technical realization. Moreover, the safety case structure does not necessarily correlate in a one-to-one mapping with the system elements [6].

The system designer and developer need to incorporate both, a top-down as well as a bottom-up analysis in case of a change. A top-down analysis traces the changes from the system-domain to the safety argument, while a bottom-up analysis follows the impacted safety-argument elements to their related evidence [5, 11]. The linkage between safety contracts to module contracts and the safety goals and evidence on the safety allows a bidirectional traceability from the system level to the certification side and vice versa. To demonstrate the bidirectional dependency, in the following the different kind of updates and their impact on the safety case will be shown along these connections.

4.3 Impact of Different Update Types

In the following, we will show how the three different kind of update types, namely adaptive, corrective, and perfective updates, can be applied to one of the modules of the SoS. It can be differentiated between the before- and after-state of a module once it has been updated. In detail, any kind of change to a service-oriented module can affect a combination of either (i) an interface change, (ii) a change in the implementation and/or (iii) a contract change (as highlighted for each update type in Fig. 5). For an interface change, one or more of the interfaces of the module can be altered, new interfaces can be added or existing ones can be removed. In case of an implementation change, the behavioral model is reformed or the architectural structure of the system composition will be altered. A contract change, on the other hand, includes the modification of existing contracts or the introduction of new contracts [31]. The system owner can identify the faulty behavior, either by testing or monitoring the contract compliance of the module or system. A faulty system composition arises if the *independent implementability* property as defined in [28, 29] of the contract composition has been violated:

For all contracts C_1, C_2, C_1' and C_2', if C_1 is compatible with C_2 and $C_1' \preccurlyeq C_1$ and $C_2' \preccurlyeq C_2$ hold, then C_1' is compatible with C_2' and $C_1' \otimes C_2' \preccurlyeq C_1 \otimes C_2$.

A contract is *compatible* if and only if $A \neq \emptyset$. Two contracts are compatible if $C_1 \otimes C_2$ is defined and compatible. Hence the property is violated when an updated module iii$_a$) C_1' is not compatible with C_2 or iii$_b$) does not refine C_1. Moreover, the contract can become iii$_c$) *inconsistent* after the update, when its guarantee remains always unfulfilled. In the following we differentiate the changes for the individual types of updates [29].

Corrective Update. A corrective update fixes an error in the system code and by that, can cause changes to the assumptions and guarantees of the module contract. Due to a corrective update the module interfaces need to be added or be removed, the assumptions and guarantees of the contract can change, as well as the implementation within the module. Therefore, C_1' can become incompatible, inconsistent and and/or not a refinement of C_1 anymore. Thus, it has to be established which of the extended safety contracts are referencing to the modules of the system and ensured that the change does not violate either the guarantees from a safety perspective or the contractually secured safety objectives. In addition, it is possible to determine at system level which dependencies the exchanged module has. For this purpose, the extent of the changes must be checked on the basis of the displacements and the neighboring modules to which it is transferred. The module contracts enable VIT to detect ripple effects before deployment [29]. In the worst case, all modules are functionally dependent, so that the entire system must be conservatively re-tested.

Perfective Update. In case of a perfective update, after the replacement of a module its services provided and its interfaces stay the same from the functional and logical perspective. For, the contracts it can be assumed that $C_1' \preccurlyeq C_1$ and the independent implementability property has not been violated. However, performance measures for the services at the module interfaces are improved and need to be tested first. Furthermore, the updated module might promises to deliver a better performance, but lack the same reliability as before. Hence, the authority responsible for (re-)certifying the system composition needs to assure the performance improvement, or at minimum, reassuring the compliance with the guaranteed boundaries defined in the contract. Hence, from a safety case perspective, only the evidence level is affected and needs to be updated to support the safety arguments.

Adaptive Update. An adaptive update adds an additional function to the module or system. Hence, either a further module is added to the overall system or a module is extended and, thereby, its contracts. It is therefore necessary to determine the extent of the functional addition and which modules the exchange will affect. In our process in Fig. 3, each of the individual phases need to be extended by an adaptive update. First the functional and logical model are extended, which results in an adaptation to the existing safety analysis in relation to the safety case. In the best case, the addition of new modules only requires an addition to the safety analysis and the safety case, in the worst case a structural adjustment of the entire system analysis. By isolating the modules, however, the extent of the structural change can be contained. For this purpose, it is necessary to determine which system requirements the module needs and to what extent the offered and required services at the interfaces integrate with the other modules in the overall system.

5   Evaluation

5.1   Modular System Composition of 'MTCAS'

To demonstrate the link between a module on the system level and the safety case, we apply the developed concept to the safety-critical Maritime Traffic Alert and Collision Avoidance System 'MTCAS'. In particular we demonstrate its modularized structure and technical realization.

MTCAS was developed as pro-active maritime collision avoidance system providing context-sensitive vessel behavior prediction and collision avoidance techniques. Other than traditional collision avoidance systems, MTCAS aims at reducing the number of false alarms by intelligently predicting the route taken by its own-ship and the target-ships, providing conflict assessment, offer resolution suggestions and supporting the navigators during the maneuver negotiation [32].

Based on the spectrum of system configurations presented in Sect. 3.1, MTCAS can be categorized as safety-critical system with soft real-time demands that runs on multi-core platforms and is connected to the vessel via network. For a technical realization, a hypervisor concept has been applied and a functional decomposition based on MTCAS feature set has been realized as depicted in Fig. 4. Each feature of MTCAS is encapsulated within a partition for which a hypervisor enables temporal and spatial isolation and contractual obligations could be expressed.

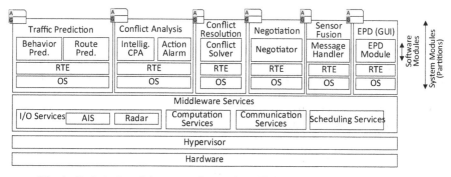

Fig. 4. Technical module perspective on the collision avoidance system MTCAS

5.2 Impact of Update Types on MTCAS

In the following, we will show how the three different kind of update types, namely adaptive, corrective, and perfective updates, can be applied to one of the modules of MTCAS. In particular, we chose the Conflict Analysis module to be exchanged as depicted in Fig. 5. The Conflict Analysis module is further composed out of two software modules: The Closest Point of Approach (CPA) and the Ultimate Action Alarm module.

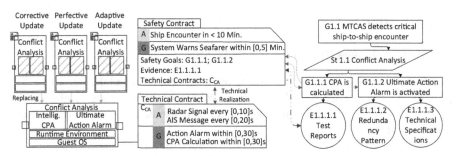

Fig. 5. Bidirectional dependency of conflict analysis module, safety contract and safety case

For the purpose of this demonstration we assume, the ultimate action alarm to be activated too late, meaning the approaching vessels are less than 30 s and within a distance of 1 nm away from a critical ship pose (CSP). In this situation, the conflict analyzer needs to forward the alarm to the conflict resolution module in order for MTCAS to calculate a last-minute maneuver such that the navigator of the vessel can take action until a collision becomes unavoidable. For each of the update types of the conflict analysis module, the parts of the module that change are highlighted in the illustration with cross stripes. Furthermore, the mapping between the safety contract of the Conflict Analysis Module, its technical contract C_{CA}, as well as the safety case elements is depicted.

Corrective Update. In a corrective update scenario, the module *Conflict Analysis* is not alarming the *Conflict Resolution* module within a timeframe of $[0, 30]$ s and therefore breaching the guarantees of its technical contract C_{CA}. A corrective update of the *Conflict Analysis* module would cause an implementation, contract and interface change. As C_{CA} is referred in the safety contract, it becomes apparent that for a renewal of the certification the safety goals $G1.1.1$ and $G1.1.2$ and the evidence $E1.1.1.1$ have to be rechecked.

Perfective Update. A perfective update of the conflict analysis would improve the time the Action Alarm or the CPA calculation are performed. Therefore, the implementation of the conflict analysis would be optimized and the guarantees of the module contract would be narrowed (e.g. Action Alarm within $[0, 20]$ s). Therefore, the independent implementability property has not been violated as $C_1' \preccurlyeq C_1$. Since the perfective update neither violates the safety contract nor the safety case, only the contract module has to be adapted in the example. Though, the technical specification has not been violated, the evidence $E1.1.1.1$ still needs to be renewed to support its sub-goal.

Adaptive Update. In the case of an adaptive update, a functional extension is made, or the module must follow regulatory adjustments, so that the structure of the *Conflict Analysis* module changes. Similar to a corrective update, the implementation, contract and interfaces change. If one were to assume that a regulatory requirement stipulates that the redundancy principle should be incorporated into the *Conflict Analysis* module, then the module must be available twice. This would result in a new system composition $C_1 \otimes C_2 \otimes C_3$ for that the compatibility and consistency has to be tested, a new safety goal module such as $G1.1.3$, which integrates the redundancy principle has to be integrated. Finally, the safety contract must be extended and the module must be divided into redundant modules so that the fail-safe feature of one module is ensured.

6   Discussion

With maritime navigation and control systems becoming tightly interconnected and intensively based on software systems, a new approach for safety assurances and reliability becomes apparent and raises the question how to control integration process and the change management. Our work demonstrates how a maintenance process can be enhanced by formal methods and linked to the respective parts of the safety case.

However, today's operating safety-critical systems in domains like aviation, maritime, railway, automotive or within the industry, have been grown historically, lack formal specifications, performance measures, standardized interfaces and can be outdated. Therefore, the biggest challenge for future work will be support of the transition phase and gain momentum for a general acceptance in the industry.

Furthermore, though one may naively assume it at first, safety-critical systems composed of independent modules can be expected to be comprehensively declared safe by composing the safety arguments of its individual modules. The presented approach can point to the relevant parts of the safety case, but still requires expert knowledge when examining the effect of an update on the system.

Hence, we raise no claim to completeness, especially in the areas of timing behavior and impact analysis. In future works the guarantees for timing and resource allocation in IBS need to be narrowed across all layers of the system. Furthermore, the impact of the change needs to be contained, identified and measured along the network of dependent modules. This work provides a first step in both directions by using contract specifications and modularization techniques.

Finally, while the presented technique does support a certification agency in re-evaluating a safety case for a SoS, it does not attempt to automatically recertify the system at hand. Forthcoming approaches have to include monitoring capabilities, parallel running feature updates and mode management methods to support safety arguments with increased and more targeted safety evidence. We will extend our approach with dependability analysis techniques embedded in a comprehensive verification and validation infrastructure to support external auditors and technical reviewers with a broader set of information about the impact of a change.

Acknowledgement. This work has been funded by the German Federal Ministry of Education and Research (BMBF) in the project Step-Up!CPS (Funding reference number: 01IS18080D). The responsibility for the content remains with the authors.

References

1. Denney, E., Pai, G., Habli, I.: Dynamic safety cases for through-life safety assurance. In: 2015 IEEE/ACM 37th IEEE International Conference on Software Engineering, Florence, Italy, pp. 587–590. IEEE (2015)
2. Cleaveland, R.: Formal certification of aerospace embedded software. In: National Workshop on Aviation Software Systems: Design for Certifiably Dependable Systems (2006)
3. Storey, N.R.: Safety Critical Computer Systems. Addison-Wesley Longman Publishing Co. Inc., Boston (1996)
4. Bate, I., Hansson, H., Punnekkat, S.: Better, faster, cheaper, and safer too—is this really possible?. In: Proceedings of 2012 IEEE 17th International Conference on Emerging Technologies Factory Automation (ETFA 2012), pp. 1–4 (2012)
5. Jaradat, O.: Contracts-Based Maintenance of Safety Cases. Mälardalen University Press, Västerås (2018)
6. Jaradat, O., Bate, I., Punnekkat, S.: Facilitating the maintenance of safety cases. In: Kumar, U., Ahmadi, A., Verma, A.K., Varde, P. (eds.) Current Trends in Reliability, Availability, Maintainability and Safety. LNME, pp. 349–371. Springer, Cham (2016). https://doi.org/10.1007/978-3-319-23597-4_25
7. Industrial Avionics Working Group: Modular Software Safety Case Process Overview (2012)
8. Fenn, J.L., Hawkins, R.D., Williams, P.J., Kelly, T.P., Banner, M.G., Oakshott, Y.: The who, where, how, why and when of modular and incremental certification. In: 2nd IET International Conference on System Safety 2007, London, pp. 135–140. IEEE (2007)
9. Nicholson, M., Conmy, P., Bate, I., McDermid, J.: Generating and maintaining a safety argument for integrated modular systems. In: 5th Australian Workshop on Industrial Experience with Safety Critical Systems and Software, Melbourne, Australia, pp. 31–41 (2000)
10. Martorell, H., Fabre, J.-C., Lauer, M., Roy, M., Valentin, R.: Partial updates of AUTOSAR embedded applications - to what extent? In: 11th European Dependable Computing Conference (EDCC), Paris, pp. 73–84. IEEE (2015)
11. Salameh, A., Jaradat, O.: A safety-centric change management framework by tailoring agile and V-Model processes. In: Presented at the 36th International System Safety Conference, ISSC 2018 (2018)
12. Reich, J., Zeller, M., Schneider, D.: Automated evidence analysis of safety arguments using digital dependability identities. In: Romanovsky, A., Troubitsyna, E., Bitsch, F. (eds.) SAFECOMP 2019. LNCS, vol. 11698, pp. 254–268. Springer, Cham (2019). https://doi.org/10.1007/978-3-030-26601-1_18
13. Schneider, D., Trapp, M., Papadopoulos, Y., Armengaud, E., Zeller, M., Höfig, K.: WAP: digital dependability identities. In: 2015 IEEE 26th International Symposium on Software Reliability Engineering (ISSRE), pp. 324–329. IEEE (2015)
14. Gleirscher, M., Kugele, S.: Assurance of System Safety: A Survey of Design and Argument Patterns. Unpublished Working Paper (2019)
15. Kokaly, S., Salay, R., Cassano, V., Maibaum, T., Chechik, M.: A model management approach for assurance case reuse due to system evolution. In: Proceedings of the 19th International Conference on Model Driven Engineering Languages and Systems - MODELS 2016, Saint-Malo, France, pp. 196–206. ACM Press (2016)
16. Saidi, S., Ernst, R., Uhrig, S., Theiling, H., de Dinechin, B.D.: The shift to multicores in real-time and safety-critical systems. In: 2015 International Conference on Hardware/Software Codesign and System Synthesis (CODES+ISSS), Amsterdam, pp. 220–229. IEEE (2015)
17. International Maritime Organization (IMO): Integrated bridge system (IBS). http://www.imo.org/en/OurWork/Safety/SafetyTopics/Pages/IntegratedBridgeSystems.aspx. Accessed 3 Mar 2020

18. Lund, M.S., Gulland, J.E., Hareide, O.S., Josok, O., Weum, K.O.C.: Integrity of integrated navigation systems. In: 2018 IEEE Conference on Communications and Network Security (CNS), Beijing, pp. 1–5. IEEE (2018)
19. Brandsæter, A., Knutsen, K.E.: Towards a framework for assurance of autonomous navigation systems in the maritime industry. In: Safety Reliability Societies in a Changing World, pp. 449–457. Taylor & Francis, Abingdon (2018)
20. DNV GL: Class guideline - DNVGL-CG-0264 Autonomous and remotely operated ships. DNV GL (2018)
21. International Maritime Organization: Guidance on procedures for updating shipborne navigation and communication equipment (2010)
22. International Organization for Standardization: ISO/IEC 14764:2006 (2006)
23. CIRM/BIMCO Joint Working Group: Industry Standard on Software Maintenance of Shipboard Equipment v1.0 (2017)
24. IACS: Recommended procedures for software maintenance of computer based systems on board (2018)
25. Montewka, J., Wróbel, K., Heikkilä, E., Valdez Banda, O.A., Goerlandt, F., Haugen, S.: Challenges, solution proposals and research directions in safety and risk assessment of autonomous shipping. In: 14th PSAM Conference Probabilistic Safety Assessment and Management (2018)
26. Heikkilä, E., Tuominen, R., Tiusanen, R., Montewka, J., Kujala, P.: Safety qualification process for an autonomous ship prototype – a goal-based safety case approach. In: Marine Navigation, Gdynia, pp. 365–370. CRC Press (2017)
27. International Organization for Standardization: ISO 26262-1:2018 (2018)
28. Benveniste, A., et al.: Contracts for system design. Found. Trends Electron. Des. Autom. **12**, 124–400 (2018)
29. Bebawy, Y., et al.: Step-UP!CPS Deliverable 3.1 - Formal Foundations for Modular Updates Version 1 (2019)
30. Stierand, I., Reinkemeier, P., Bhaduri, P.: Virtual integration of real-time systems based on resource segregation abstraction. In: Legay, A., Bozga, M. (eds.) FORMATS 2014. LNCS, vol. 8711, pp. 206–221. Springer, Cham (2014). https://doi.org/10.1007/978-3-319-10512-3_15
31. Bebawy, Y., et al.: Step-UP!CPS Deliverable 4.1 - Process Support and Technologies for the Validation of Modular Updates - Version 1 (2020)
32. Steidel, M., Hahn, A.: MTCAS – an assistance system for collision avoidance at sea. In: Presented at the 18th International Conference on Computer and IT Applications in the Maritime Industries, Tullamore (2019)

Formal Verification and Analysis

A Functional Verification Methodology for Highly Parametrizable, Continuously Operating Safety-Critical FPGA Designs: Applied to the CERN RadiatiOn Monitoring Electronics (CROME)

Katharina Ceesay-Seitz$^{(\boxtimes)}$ ⬥, Hamza Boukabache, and Daniel Perrin ⬥

CERN, European Organisation for Nuclear Research, 1211 Geneva 23, Meyrin,
Switzerland
{katharina.ceesay-seitz,hamza.boukabache,daniel.perrin}@cern.ch
https://home.cern/

Abstract. Electronic systems that are related to human safety need to comply to strict international standards such as the IEC 61508. We present a functional verification methodology for highly parametrizable, continuously operating, safety-critical real-time systems implemented in FPGAs. It is compliant to IEC 61508 and extends it in several ways. We focus on independence between design and verification. Natural language properties and the functional coverage model build the connection between system safety requirements and verification results, providing forward and backward traceability. Our main verification method is Formal Property Verification (FPV), even for Safety Integrity Level 1 and 2. Further, we use constrained-random simulation in SystemVerilog with the Universal Verification Methodology and a design independent C reference model. When faults are discovered, the coverage model is extended to avoid regressions. Automation allows the reproduction of results and the reuse of verification code. We evaluate our methodology on a subset of the newly developed CERN RadiatiOn Monitoring Electronics (CROME). We present the challenges we faced and propose solutions. Although it is impossible to simulate the full design exhaustively, several formal properties have been fully proven. With FPV we found some safety-critical faults that would have been extremely hard to find in simulation.

Keywords: Functional verification · Safety · Formal Property Verification · Constrained-random simulation · Natural language properties · Functional coverage · Regression coverage

1 Introduction

When electronic systems are related to human safety, their whole life cycle needs to comply with strict domain-specific standards [1–4]. The general standard for

© Springer Nature Switzerland AG 2020
A. Casimiro et al. (Eds.): SAFECOMP 2020, LNCS 12234, pp. 67–81, 2020.
https://doi.org/10.1007/978-3-030-54549-9_5

functional safety of electrical/electronic/programmable electronic safety-related systems is the IEC 61508 [5]. Its latest version dates back to 2010. The ISO 26262 automotive standard is the most modern one. Its latest version is from 2018 [1]. One very strict, but also quite old standard for safety-critical hardware is the DO-254 from 2000 [2]. The IEC 60532 standard for radiation protection instrumentation assigns Safety Integrity Levels (SILs) to certain radiation protection functions [3]. These SILs and corresponding requirements for the design and verification of safety-related electronic systems are defined in the IEC 61508 [5]. Since 2010, verification methodologies and electronic design automation tools for digital design verification have progressed at a rapid pace. Our methodology adds modern verification techniques to the IEC 61508's V-model flow.

The most common technique for functionally verifying the Hardware Description Language (HDL) code for Field Programmable Gate Arrays (FPGAs) is still simulation with directed tests [6]. Stimuli are applied to the inputs of the Design Under Verification (DUV) and the values at the outputs are examined. For highly parametrizable systems that have many input parameters of large bit-widths it would be extremely time consuming to manually specify all interesting combinations and calculate the expected output values. More flexible techniques like constrained-random simulation are available [7]. But even with this method it can be infeasible to simulate all possibilities for certain designs. Let's imagine we could simulate one combination at each CPU clock cycle of the workstation which executes the simulation tool. It would take roughly 146 years to simulate each of the possible input combinations of a single 64-bit vector. In reality, many CPU clock cycles will pass until the simulator applies a new stimulus. While in many cases it might be sufficient to simulate only representative values, it is often hard to tell which value ranges are representative enough to catch all corner cases. These might be rare inputs or combinations of extreme values of mathematical functions or boundary values [8]. Furthermore, for some input values it might be necessary to verify all possible combinations. Therefore, additional verification techniques need to be applied.

We propose a functional verification methodology that combines the state-of-the-art verification techniques of the semiconductor industry: Formal Property Verification (FPV) and constrained-random simulation using the Universal Verification Methodology (UVM) [9], both with functional and structural coverage collection, while complying to IEC 61508. We evaluate them for a highly parametrizable, continuously operating safety-critical real-time system. We propose a workflow that extends the verification process required by IEC 61508 with the following concepts (see also Table 1):

- Independence between design and verification engineers
- Semi-formal methods during verification planning and requirements review
- Formal methods as main verification method even for SIL 1 and SIL 2.
- Constrained-random inputs for (expanded) functional black-box testing
- Coverage for regression test cases
- Traceability from requirements over coverage model and Natural Language Properties (NLPs) to verification results and backwards
- Repeatability of the results

Section 2 summarises related work and background. Section 3 provides an overview of our methodology. Section 4 is an in-depth case study of applying our methodology to the CERN RadiatiOn Monitoring Electronics (CROME). Section 5 concludes the paper.

2   Related Work and Background

Independence between verification and design is very important in our methodology. Engineers are more likely to find faults in code written by other people than in their own [10]. The IEC 61508 does not mandate it, it only refers to application specific standards [5]. It is required e.g. by the DO-254 [2].

Formal Property Verification (FPV), also called assertion-based verification, can exhaustively proof that a property holds on a design. Many engineers still hesitate to use formal verification because of its perceived complexity [6,11]. A campaign was launched at Intel to convince engineers of its benefits [11]. As we will also demonstrate, additional faults can be found with FPV in designs that had already been verified by simulation [11,12]. Often it is only used for simple designs or control paths [8,13]. In [14], each design was first classified as suitable or not for FPV. A design with our characteristics would not be suitable according to their criteria. Opposed to that we decided to use FPV as main verification method for a complex continuously operating safety-critical design and got indispensable results. Our methodology shows how to integrate it into a safety-standard compliant process.

Requirements-based testing is required by e.g. DO-254 [2] and ISO 26262 [1]. In [15], this method was extended with constrained-random simulation for robustness testing, or in IEC 61508 terms "expanded functional testing" [5]. Researchers in [11] mentioned the difficulty of tracking verification progress in FPV. We use the functional coverage model and Natural Language Properties (NLPs) [16] as connection between system safety requirements and test results. The methodology in [14] uses templates instead of NLPs that are automatically translated into SystemVerilog Assertions (SVA) by a proprietary tool. The importance of a consistent translation from properties in easily reviewable form to formal languages was also shown in [17]. The lack of such methods can lead to incorrect translations and additional iterations. In [18], each requirement was related to a test case and coverage model item. Encountered faults were added to a fault database, related to requirements and if necessary, the coverage model was extended. We call the extension of the coverage model "regression coverage". Our approach (detailed in Sect. 3.2) was prior to that described in [19].

An advantage of FPV with SVA is that properties are proven directly on the HDL code. Several formal verification methodologies for FPGAs exist that require a translation from HDL to a formal model in a tool-specific language [13, 20]. To comply to safety standards, it would be necessary to derive this model from the HDL code [17]. Any used tools need to be qualified [5]. We decided for SVA, for which several qualified tools are available [17].

Constrained-random simulation is very useful for highly parametrizable systems. A large number of stimuli can be applied without the need to explicitly specifying them. Weighted constraints can be used to guide the randomization in order to increase chances of generating scenarios of interest while also testing unusual input combinations. This technique typically finds more faults than directed testing [8,15]. SystemVerilog provides many features to ease the development of flexible testbenches as well as properties and sequences which can be used both in simulation and FPV [7]. The SystemVerilog UVM library facilitates abstraction into transactions and verification code reuse. UVM was released in 2011, after the publication of the IEC 61508. It has been standardized in 2017 [9].

It can be distinguished between functional and structural coverage. The functional coverage model states which scenarios are of verification interest. It is defined by the verification engineers. Structural coverage measures how many percentage of the Hardware Description Language (HDL) code have been covered [8]. A very effective coverage metric is Modified Condition/Decision Coverage (MC/DC), where each condition has to affect the condition outcome at least once. It is required by the DO-178 standard for software in avionics industry [4]. Simulation tools provide this metric as well for HDL code [15]. SystemVerilog covergroups, cover properties or assertions could also be added by the designers to ensure that simulation test benches cover important implementation details [8,12]. This would not violate the concept of independence [12].

In this article we solely focus on functional verification. Measures for avoiding failures due to random hardware faults need to be considered additionally for any safety-critical design [5].

3   Our Functional Verification Methodology

IEC 61508 lists several techniques that can be chosen for verifying FPGAs. Table 1 lists the techniques that we chose plus some techniques that we added (A). The last 4 columns show the level of recommendation by IEC 61508 per SIL. Due to the large number of inputs (~200) of our design and our positive experience with FPV that we will highlight in later sections, we decided to use it as main verification method. We complement it with constrained-random simulation using the UVM. For software, the IEC 61508 requires traceability from system safety requirements to verification results and vice versa, as well as repeatability of the verification activities. We adopt these points for FPGAs.

3.1   Verification Planning

Our workflow, detailed in Fig. 1, starts based on the system safety requirements, design requirements and the specification. Consistency between the first and the last two needs to be verified [5]. Each verification requirements is related to at least one system requirement. If we encounter undocumented design decisions during verification, we report them first to the requirements engineers rather

Table 1. E/E/EP system verification requirements and techniques

Sections in IEC 61508:2010 - Part 2	Techniques	Required by			
		SIL 1	SIL 2	SIL 3	SIL 4
7.9.2.1-4 Verification planning	Semi-formal methods	A	A	A	A
7.9.2.5 Conformance to safety requirements	Requirements traceability	A	A	A	A
7.9.2.7, Table B.1 Verification of system design requirements	Inspection of specification	–	HR	HR	HR
	Semi-formal methods	R	R	HR	HR
7.9.2.8, Table B.2, Table B.5, Table F.2 Verification of the system design and development	Simulation	–	R	R	R
	Formal methods	–	–	R	R
	Functional testing on module level	HR	HR	HR	HR
	Expanded functional testing	–	HR	HR	HR
	Black-box testing	R	R	R	R
	Constrained-random input	A	A	A	A
	Coverage of the verification scenarios	R	R	HR	HR
	Coverage for regression testing	A	A	A	A
7.9.2.6, 7.9.2.10 Verification results documentation	Requirements traceability	A	A	A	A

A ... Additionally added to our methodology, - ... No recommendation for or against the method by the standard, R ... Recommended, HR ... Highly recommended

than the designers, to keep independence high. After consensus, requirements, specification and verification items are updated by the responsible persons.

In our methodology, the functional coverage model builds the connection between the verification requirements and the results. Each verification requirement needs to be described by at least one SystemVerilog covergroup or cover property for simulation or by at least one NLP [16]. Within each method the Mutually Exclusive and Collectively Exhaustive (MECE) principle should be followed [21]. For our kind of design we identified the following grouping inspired by [21] as useful: use cases, interesting scenarios, temporal relations, value ranges, stress tests, negated requirements. Input values should only be covered if they had an effect and verification passes [8].

The analysis of uncovered items might reveal internal design details. In order to keep independence high, we suggest that the design engineers should analyse the structural coverage reports and disclose as little information as possible to the verification engineers. The goal should be 100% functional and structural coverage. If it can not be reached, an analysis should be performed and it should be justified why less than 100% are acceptable [15].

Natural Language Properties (NLPs) [16] are our coverage model items for FPV. They are a semi-formal notation where natural language snippets are translated into SystemVerilog property snippets with a fixed N:1 mapping. E.g. one can use different natural language expressions to describe the same formal statement. *"Expr implies that Seq"* and *"Every time when Expr: Seq"* can be both translated into and implication *"Expr |->Seq"*. Technical details can be hidden by application specific NLPs, e.g. *"Cycle is the start of a measurement cycle"* is translated into *"($rose(mtValidxDI))"*. That way an unambiguous connection

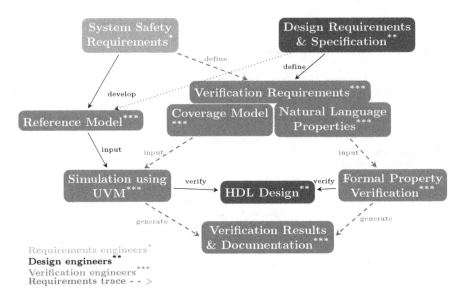

Fig. 1. Verification workflow

between a NLP and a formal property is established. The NLPs can be easily reviewed by requirements engineers unfamiliar with SVA. We use this review step to increase independence between design and verification.

For formal verification we calculate functional coverage as follows:

$$Functional\ coverage[\%] = \frac{Nr.\ of\ proven\ properties}{Nr.\ of\ properties} * 100.00 \tag{1}$$

Or with weights, similar to SystemVerilog covergroup coverage [7]:

$$Weighted\ functional\ coverage[\%] = \frac{\sum_i (w_i * p_i)}{\sum_i w_i} * 100.00 \tag{2}$$

$w_i = weight\ per\ property, p_i = 1\ if\ property\ was\ proven,\ 0\ otherwise$

3.2   Automated Verification

Formal Property Verification (FPV). Our main verification method is FPV with SVA [22]. We use as little formal assumptions, i.e. constraints, as possible, therefore even allowing scenarios that are outside the current specification. When the specification changes, the same properties can be reused for verification. This reduces the logic in the Cone-of-Influence of the formal properties, which makes it easier for formal tools to conclude. The properties can be validated in simulation by including the SystemVerilog file that contains the properties inside the SystemVerilog DUV interface.

The number of states of continuously operating designs grows exponentially with the number of input bits and necessary clock cycles for a proof. We model complex calculations with 64-bit operands in auxiliary code and use properties to proof the equivalence of the DUV's outputs with the modelled calculations.

We start with black-box verification, which means that we do not modify or access internal signals and describe properties only in terms of input and output relations. If these properties are inconclusive, we apply abstraction techniques like inserting cut points on internal registers. That means that logic which drives these registers is cut away. This reduces the complexity of the proof calculation and therefore it is easier for the formal tool to conclude. A proof is valid for all values that are possible within the bit-widths of these registers. This includes the values that can be generated by the logic which is cut off. Therefore it is a logically safe transformation that might introduce false negatives, but never false positives [22]. Such techniques require the verification engineer to gain knowledge about the code, thus violating the principle of independence. Therefore, we apply these methods only after all independent black-box verification activities have been completed.

Constrained-Random Simulation. We use constrained-random simulation with the SystemVerilog UVM library whenever formal tools can't deliver results within reasonable time. Verification engineers develop a reference model based on the requirements, independent from the design engineers. SystemVerilog can communicate with a C or C++ model through its Direct Programming Interface (DPI). The test bench simultaneously sends UVM transaction to the Design Under Verification (DUV) and the reference model and compares the outputs.

Regression Coverage. Whenever a fault is found with simulation-based or formal verification that occurs in a scenario that is not yet part of the coverage model for simulation, we add it in the following way:

1. Identify input and output signal traces and their relationships that revealed the fault. Add a new covergroup, coverpoint or coverpoint bin. If a sequence of stimuli is needed to uniquely identify the scenario, use e.g. value transition or expression coverpoint bins or cover properties. Internal signals can be used if provided by the design engineer. We call these "regression covergroups/-bins".
2. Rerun the failing test and check that the new regression bin is covered in the same simulation time step in which the test failed.
3. Rerun all other test cases and check that the new coverage item is not covered by any other test that passes. If it is, the coverage item does not model a unique scenario. Either add step 6 or modify the coverage item and start at step 1.
4. The design engineer removes the fault of the DUV.
5. Rerun the failing test with the updated DUV. Check that the bin is still covered in the same simulation time step. Check that the verification passes.
6. Optionally: Copy the failing UVM test and UVM sequence class. Rename them to match the regression coverpoint bin and implement a stop condition. The test can stop when it has covered its corresponding bin. Add this test case to the regression test suite and do not modify it anymore.

Regarding point 3: In a continuously operating system, a unique scenario that leads to a fault might have to be described by long and complex signal traces and their relationships. Sometimes it can be more efficient in terms of engineering time to describe a signal relationship with a higher level of abstraction, which is not uniquely identifying the faulty scenario, but which includes it.

Regarding point 6: As long as the calls to randomisation functions in the regression test case are not altered, it can be used to reproduce the same scenario. SystemVerilog provides random stability as long as the order of new requests for random values is not altered within a thread [7].

Documentation, Traceability and Reproducibility. Forward tracing as shown by the arrows in Fig. 1 and backward tracing (by following the arrows in reversed direction) of verification items is used to measure verification progress and to provide verification evidence. All verification activities are documented in a version control system and can be reconstructed and reproduced.

4 Application to the CERN RadiatiOn Monitoring Electronics (CROME)

4.1 CERN RadiatiOn Monitoring Electronics (CROME)

CERN, the European Organisation for Nuclear Research, operates the world's most powerful particle accelerators. Particle collisions produce ionizing radiation. The radiation protection group is responsible for protecting humans from any unjustified radiation exposure. The CERN RadiatiOn Monitoring Electronics (CROME) are the new generation of instruments used for measuring ionizing radiation levels and triggering alarms and machine interlocks based on these measurements [23]. Several hundred units will be installed.

The CROME Measuring and Processing Unit consists of a radiation detector and an electronic system for data communication and storage, signal processing and safety-related decision taking. The latter contains a heterogeneous Zynq-7000 System-on-Chip (SoC) consisting of an ARM core and an FPGA. The ARM core executes an embedded Linux and an application that receives around 100 parameters with ranges up to 64 bit over the network, which it transfers to the FPGA. The FPGA performs the radiation dose and dose rate calculations. Based on that, it autonomously triggers alarms and machine interlocks. It contains all safety-critical code, implemented in VHDL. Triple Modular Redundancy and Soft Error Mitigation are used for detecting random hardware faults [24].

The devices can be used in areas with very different radiation levels, e.g. in service caverns close to the particle detectors as well as at the fences of the CERN site. To that end they were kept very generic and parametrizable. Periods of uninterrupted operation can last several months or years. These system attributes lead to high numbers of possible input values and deep internal states that are challenging for verification.

The *calculation of the radiation dose* consists of 3 additions with 64-bit operands, 1 multiplication with 32-bit operands and logic for rounding. It is calculated from the measured input current (fA - nA) and it is the base for one of the system's alarms. The dose is accumulated over a configurable period, which can last several years. Internal registers track the state. The calculation can be influenced at run-time by sending 6 parameters of up to 64 bit length from the CERN control room to a CROME device. The dose alarm decision is based on the outcome of 7 conditions, sampled on 2 real-time measurement cycles that can be thousands of clock cycles apart.

The *alarm and interlock matrix* block implements a complex configurable logical formula which drive the safety-critical outputs of the system. These outputs are connected to the alarm units, which provide visual and audible alarms and to the machine interlocks, which stop the particle accelerators in case of a too high radiation level. The formula can be configured by 200 2-bit wide parameters. In total the block has 2^{451} possible input values. Some of its outputs are fed back to the logical formula as input. Apart from that the block does not store an internal state and therefore results are available after a few clock cycles.

4.2   Verification Planning

We derived 76 verification requirements for the radiation dose calculation from only 26 system-level requirements, which were written with a very high level of abstraction and some ambiguities. The latter were discussed directly with the requirements engineers for increasing independence. 8 statements that were added and 10 statements that were only partially contained in the design specification lead to further verification requirements. The analysis lead to 12 updates of either requirements, specification or verification code. Verification planning lead to a more complete documentation of the whole project, which is very important to comply with safety standards [5]. We specified 52 cover properties and 4 covergroups that contained 56 coverpoints, as well as 30 NLPs.

During the review of the NLPs we discovered one very critical misunderstanding regarding the triggering of the radiation dose alarm. The design and verification engineers interpreted a requirement in the same way, but differently than the requirements engineers. This could not have been discovered with any automated verification technique. It shows the importance of independence and reviews. The detailed example has been reported in [16].

4.3   Automated Verification

Simulation and FPV were executed on a CentOS 7 workstation with 4 GHz CPU and 32 GB RAM. The single-threaded Questa Sim simulator, version 10.7, was used for simulation. Questa PropCheck, version 10.7c, was used for FPV with 8 hardware threads on 4 processor cores.

Formal Property Verification

Radiation Ambient Equivalent Dose Calculation. The dose calculation was modelled with auxiliary code. Properties compare the outputs of both models. So far, the dose calculation could be proven with the following constraints:

- 101 different calculation period lengths from 0 to 100, where 0 stands for an unlimited period
- Operands of additions restricted to 8 possible values or calculation period restricted to 2 real-time measurement cycles
- Time counting register restricted to 13.6 years in 100 ms unity, which therefore also limits the maximum period length to 13.6 years.

We allowed arbitrary values in the reset state by using a netlist constraint that sets the initial values of input ports to X. That means proofs cover every possible starting state, which includes the actual reset state.

A cutpoint was inserted at the register *etxDN* that normally loads the time counting register *etxDP* with a new calculated value. That means that the formal tool treats *etxDN* as an input and generates a proof for all possible values. If cutpoints are enabled, the auxiliary code also uses *etxDP*. That ensures that the formal tool uses the same value inside the DUV and the auxiliary model during one round of calculation. *etxDN* cannot be used in the model, as its value can be arbitrary in any clock cycles. The DUV and the model can perform their calculations in different clock cycles. The properties proof that, after a defined number of clock cycles following the start of one round, the outputs of both models are equivalent.

This way the unlimited number of consecutive calculations that keep track of an internal state is reduced to a smaller sequence of recurring operations. The elapsed time tracking register needs to be verified in a separate proof.

Proven: 8 properties could be fully proven, without any constraints on parameter values. Most importantly they include the proof of correct triggering of radiation dose alarms. The triggering is decided by 7 conditions at 2 consecutive real-time cycles with configurable distance.

Undocumented Design Decision Found: One fault happened only with very specific input bit combinations when an internal calculation result was negative and rounded. Even though thousands of inputs had already been simulated, this scenario had not been covered. To cover it, very tightly constrained simulation test cases were needed. The rounding mechanism was not documented. The coverage model had to be updated.

Fault that Happens After 7 years of Continuous Device Operation: In the division of the elapsed time value, one of the operands was treated as a signed value. The calculation was only wrong, when the most significant bit had value '1'. This fault could have never been found by black-box simulation because it would have required to simulate 7 years of device operation to discover it. For environmental radiation monitors it is a realistic scenario to operate continuously for such a long time. FPV revealed the fault within 1 s.

Alarm and Interlock Matrix. The logical formulas of the matrix were modelled with auxiliary code. Properties were used to prove the equivalence of the calculated values with the DUV's outpus.

Proven: The alarm and interlock matrix was fully proven with 46 properties.

Fault in Radiation Dose Alert: In one very specific input combination, the radiation dose alert was not triggered due to a wrongly specified range of a partially used VHDL vector. Many stimuli had already been simulated by the designer and user tests with the programmed FPGA had passed. Only FPV revealed the fault.

Output not in Safe State in Case of Invalid Inputs: The system requirements allowed 3 different values for certain inputs that were stored as 2 bits. The 4th possible value is illegal and not expected. No specific measures were implemented to handle that case, so the outputs would have been in inconsistent states and not in their safe state.

Constrained-Random Simulation

Table 2. Functional coverage of the radiation dose calculation

Cover type	Covered - all tests	Covered - passed tests	Nr. of coverpoints	Nr. of bins	Nr. of stimuli applied
Cover properties	100.00%	100.00%	–	–	16355
cgIntConditions	100.00%	93.98%	28	466	324647
cgIntRegression	100.00%	100.00%	3	3	250
cgIntValueRanges	91.95%	73.02%	17	656	249327
cgIntRobustness	7.15%	6.02%	8	392	280977
Total	79.82%	74.60%	56	1517	454200

Radiation Ambient Equivalent Dose Calculation. Table 2 shows the number of stimuli that were applied to reach ca. 80% of coverage with constrained-random inputs. The goal was not to find the minimum number of stimuli necessary to reach full coverage, but rather to simulate large numbers of stimuli in the proximity of interesting scenarios and corner cases in order to increase the chances of finding faults in operation conditions that have not even been considered.

A coverage bin can be a value, value range, value transition or a condition outcome. An additional condition for coverage sampling can be specified. E.g. sampling a value for radiation dose calculation period is only valid, when the whole period has been simulated. It is not meaningful to sample it already when it has been applied to the input. The period can span thousands of clock cycles or in real-time: days, months or years. Some faults only appear after a long sequence of applied inputs and internal state changes, like e.g. the fault that would have happened after 7 years of operation that we found with formal verification.

We did not reach 100% functional coverage for all covergroups. This shows the shortcomings of simulation for continuously operating devices. The last two groups contain values and expressions that are related to the radiation dose calculation period. Since simulation is even slower than real time, it is impossible to simulate these scenarios with purely design independent black-box techniques. Code coverage confirmed that the only bits that were never toggled were the higher-order bits of registers that store time values. Toggle coverage reached only 78%. The rest was fully covered.

It is possible to access any internal signals from within the SystemVerilog testbench. The internal state, e.g. the elapsed time register, could be manipulated to simulate different real time values and reach full coverage. As discussed for cutpoints, to keep independence high, this technique should only be applied after independent black-box verification has reached its limits.

In a first attempt the simulation that created the coverage shown in Table 2 ran nearly 40 h. The cause for that long runtime were the cover properties. They contained many sequences that spanned over a large number of clock cycles, using SystemVerilog constructs like ##[1:$], which means that something happens after 1 or an arbitrary number of clock cycles. As long as a property or sequence is not yet covered, the simulator has to create a new instance of it at each clock cycle and check in each following clock cycle whether it has been covered. This construct is very useful to intersect different sequences at arbitrary times, but it comes with the cost of runtime increase. A more efficient alternative turned out to be covergroups that use expression coverage with value transition bins. The covergroup sampling did not add any significant overhead.

We tracked the test cases that actually contributed to the coverage of the cover properties. We ran each of them until its contribution to coverage of cover properties stagnated. Once all properties were covered, we executed the rest of the test suite with cover properties disabled. This approach led to a total simulation runtime of 3 h.

Table 3. Verification findings - radiation dose calculation

Found by	Update of specification	Update of implementation	Update of verification code	Total found by method
Review of requirements	4	5	6	9
Natural Language Properties	1	1	1	1
Review of design specification	1	2	0	2
Constrained-random simulation	5	9	2	15
Formal Property Verification	4	3	4	11
Total	15	20	13	38

4.4   Results Summary

Table 3 shows the faults that we found in the radiation dose calculation. Some findings caused updates of multiple artefacts. The total numbers per method should not be compared, because faults that had already been found with one verification technique had been removed and could have therefore not been found anymore with the other techniques. The results show that each described method contributes to the discovery of faults. Table 4 shows how long it would minimum take to apply each input combination that has been covered by formal proofs if we could simulate one stimulus at each CPU clock cycle. Many more simulation cycles would have to be added to cover all different traces of continuous operation, like e.g. different dose calculation periods. The fault that would have happened after 7 years of operation clearly shows this need. The fault that was not covered because it was hidden behind an undocumented design decision and the fault in the radiation dose alert show that testing only a few values per equivalent class is not always sufficient.

Table 4. Estimated minimum simulation time for the proven bits, compared to actual formal verification run time.

	Radiation dose calculation	Alarm & interlock matrix
Nr. input bits covered by proofs	70	451
Nr. proven properties	8	46
Estimated min. simulation time	9359 years	$7.99 * 10^{137}$ years
Runtime formal verification for all proofs	1.46 h	33 s

Documentation, Traceability and Reproducibility. We use the version control system Git to communicate design and verification artefact updates. It can be easily forgotten to update a version number inside the DUV or verification code. Git generates unique hashes for each commit. We used these hashes to track the faulty and updated versions, log files, planning and results documentation. Any state of the test bench can be checked out and results can be reproduced.

5   Conclusion and Future Work

We presented a functional verification methodology for highly parametrizable, continuously operating, safety-critical real-time systems implemented in FPGAs. The methodology can also be applied to digital Application Specific Integrated Circuits (ASICs). We started with a discussion of our methodology in comparison to the requirements of the IEC 61508 and related work. We defined a workflow that starts with the system safety requirements as input and verification results as output. Forward and backward traceability between these artefacts is provided via functional coverage items. We applied our technique of NLPs [16] to aid the requirements review. Our main verification method is Formal Property Verification (FPV). This decision was supported by the discovery of several interesting faults and successful proofs. Additionally we apply constrained-random simulation with the UVM. For both methods we use functional and structural coverage as a metric for progress tracking.

The methodology was demonstrated on a subset of the CERN RadiatiOn Monitoring Electronics (CROME). We will further apply it to that system and use it for future FPGA or ASIC projects. There is still potential for further automation and usage of the UVM's concepts for reusability from block to FPGA system level. Fault injection will have to be added to address random hardware faults. Then we intend to extend the methodology to include SoC system level verification that also includes the software running on the ARM core. We are also working on unifying the reference model for simulation with the auxiliary code for formal verification to reduce effort.

References

1. ISO 26262: Road vehicles - Functional safety, International Organisation for Standardisation (ISO) (2018)
2. DO-254 - Design Assurance Guidance for Airborne Electronic Hardware, Radio Technical Commission for Aeronautics, Washington, USA (2011)
3. IEC 60532: Radiation protection instrumentation, International Electrotechnical Commission (IEC), Geneva, Switzerland (2010)
4. DO-178 - Software considerations in airborne systems and equipment certification, Radio Technical Commission for Aeronautics, Washington, USA (2000)
5. IEC 61508: Functional safety of electrical/electronic/programmable electronic safety-related systems. The International Electrotechnical Commission (2010)
6. Foster, H.D.: 2018 FPGA functional verification trends. In: Proceedings of 2018 19th International Workshop on Microprocessor and SOC Test, Security and Verification (MTV), Austin, TX, USA (2019). https://doi.org/10.1109/MTV.2018.00018
7. IEEE Std 1800–2017: IEEE Standard for SystemVerilog - Unified Hardware Design, Specification and Verification Language. IEEE Computer Society (2018)
8. Bergeron, J., Cerny, E., Nightingale, A.: Verification Methodology Manual for System Verilog. Springer, Boston (2005). https://doi.org/10.1007/b135575
9. IEEE Std 1800.2-2017: IEEE Standard for Universal Verification Methodology Language Reference Manual. IEEE (2017)
10. Arthur, J.D., Groner, M.K., Hayhurst, K.J., Holloway, C.M.: Evaluating the effectiveness of independent verification and validation. Computer 32(10), 79–83 (1999). https://doi.org/10.1109/2.796141
11. Achutha KiranKumar, M.V., Bindumadhava, S.S., Abhijith Bharadwaj, A.: Making formal property verification mainstream: an intel graphics experience. In: Proceedings of Design and Verification Conference and Exhibition United States, DVCon United States, San Jose, CA, USA (2017)
12. Butka, B.: Advanced verification methods and safety critical hardware. In: 2012 Integrated Communications, Navigation and Surveillance Conference, Herndon, VA, pp. K3-1–K3-9. IEEE (2012)

13. Grimm, T., Lettnin, D., Huebner, M.: A survey on formal verification techniques for safety-critical systems-on-chip. Electronics **7**(6), 81 (2018)
14. Devarajegowda, K., Servadei, L., Han, Z., Werner, M., Ecker, W.: Formal verification methodology in an industrial setup. In: 22nd Euromicro Conference on Digital System Design (DSD), Greece, pp. 610–614. IEEE (2019). https://doi.org/10.1109/DSD.2019.00094
15. Butka, B.: Is the current DO-254 verification process adequate for the future? In: 2012 IEEE/AIAA 31st Digital Avionics Systems Conference (DASC), Williamsburg, VA, pp. 6A6-1-6A6-11. IEEE (2012). https://doi.org/10.1109/DASC.2012.6382383
16. Ceesay-Seitz, K., Boukabache, H., Perrin, D.: Semi-formal reformulation of requirements for formal property verification. In: Proceedings of Design and Verification Conference and Exhibition Europe, DVCon Europe, Munich (2019)
17. John, A.K., Bhattacharjee, A.K.: Qualification of hardware description language designs for safety critical applications in nuclear power plants. IEEE Trans. Nucl. Sci. **67**(3), 502–507 (2020). https://doi.org/10.1109/TNS.2020.2972903
18. Carter, H., Williams, P., Fitzpatrick, T.: Foliations of coverage: introducing functional coverage to DO-254 verification projects. In: Proceedings of 2019 IEEE Aerospace Conference, Big Sky, MT, USA (2019). https://doi.org/10.1109/AERO.2019.8741814
19. Ceesay-Seitz, K.: Automated verification of a system-on-chip for radiation protection fulfilling Safety Integrity Level 2. CERN-THESIS-2019-022, Geneva, CERN (2019). https://cds.cern.ch/record/2672187/
20. Jabeen, S., Srinivasan, S., Shuja, S.: Formal verification methodology for real-time field programmable gate array. IET Comput. Digit. Tech. **11**(5), 197–203 (2017)
21. Sprott, J., Marriott, P., Graham, M.: Navigating the functional coverage black hole: be more effective at functional coverage modeling. In: Proceedings of Design and Verification Conference and Exhibition United States, DVCon United States, San Jose, CA, USA (2015)
22. Seligman, E., Schubert, T., Achutha KiranKumar, M.: Formal Verification an Essential Toolkit for Modern VLSI Design. Elsevier Inc., Amsterdam (2015)
23. Boukabache, H., et al.: Towards a novel modular architecture for cern radiation monitoring. Radiat. Prot. Dosimetry. **173**(1–3), 240–244 (2016). https://doi.org/10.1093/rpd/ncw308
24. Toner, C., et al.: Fault resilient FPGA design for 28 nm ZYNQ system-on-chip based radiation monitoring system at CERN. Microelectron. Reliab. **100**, 113492 (2019). https://doi.org/10.1016/j.microrel.2019.113492

A Compositional Semantics
for Repairable BDMPs

Shahid Khan[1]([⊠]) [iD], Joost-Pieter Katoen[1] [iD], and Marc Bouissou[2]

[1] Software Modeling and Verification, RWTH Aachen University, Aachen, Germany
{shahid.khan,katoen}@cs.rwth-aachen.de
[2] EDF-R&D, Electricité de France, Palaiseau, France
marc.bouissou@edf.fr

Abstract. Boolean-logic Driven Markov Processes (BDMPs) is a graphical language for reliability analysis of dynamic repairable systems. Simulation and trace-based analysis tools for BDMPs exist and have been used to analyze reliability, safety and security aspects of industrially relevant case studies. To enable a model-based analysis of BDMPs, such as probabilistic model checking, formal semantics is indispensable. This paper presents a rigorous semantics to repairable BDMPs using Markov automata (MA), a variant of continuous-time Markov chains (CTMCs) with action transitions. The semantics is modular: an MA is associated with each BDMP element and these are combined to obtain an automaton for the entire BDMP. By ignoring the actions that are used to "glue" the MA of BDMP elements, a CTMC is obtained that is amenable to analysis by e.g., model checking. We report on a prototypical implementation and experimentally show that our semantics corresponds to the BDMP interpretation by the tool Yet Another Monte Carlo Simulation.

Keywords: Reliability · Dependability · Formal methods ·
Probabilistic model checking · Monte-Carlo simulation · Compositional
analysis

1 Introduction

Static Fault Trees. Fault trees [18] are used for safety and reliability engineering in many application areas. *Static Fault Trees* (SFTs) are the simplest; their leaves, called *basic events* (BEs), model individual component failures or human errors. The failure times are governed by continuous probability distributions. Internal nodes, called *gates*, model how component failures lead to system failures. Gates are like logic circuit elements such as AND and OR, both instances of the voting (VOT) gate. Fault tree analysis amounts to determine the failure probability of the root of the fault tree, called the top event. SFTs are simple; the ordering of failures is irrelevant and repairs are excluded.

S. Khan—Supported by a HEC-DAAD Scholarship.

A. Casimiro et al. (Eds.): SAFECOMP 2020, LNCS 12234, pp. 82–98, 2020.
https://doi.org/10.1007/978-3-030-54549-9_6

Extensions. SFTs have been extended in numerous ways, e.g., with priority-AND PAND gates [20], by dynamic fault trees (DFTs) [9] possibly extended with repairs [6,11], state-event fault trees (SEFTs) [14], component fault trees (CFTs) [15], Boolean logic Driven Markov Processes (BDMPs) [5] and a generalisation thereof [17]. These extensions are driven by the need to model e.g., (a) the replacement of failed components by spare ones, (b) hot and cold redundancies, (c) complex failure orderings, (d) repairs and maintenance strategies, or (e) the failure of a component by going through several degraded modes.

The Need for Semantics. The added expressive power leads to more modeling flexibility but comes at a price: the interpretation of these graphical fault tree languages becomes involved. (Also the analysis is more complex; e.g., maximal cut set computations—the main technique for SFTs—no longer suffice.) The interpretation of fault trees is not just of theoretical interest. Slightly different interpretations may lead to significantly divergent reliability measures and give rise to distinct underlying stochastic (decision) processes. This issue is discussed in detail for DFTs in [13]. Moreover, a rigorous semantics is a prerequisite to enable the analysis of fault trees using multiple tools. Our overall aim is to analyze Bouissou's BDMPs [5] by means of probabilistic model checking [1]. It has been shown in the last years that such an approach is quite successful for analyzing DFTs [11,19]. This paper, therefore, focuses on *providing a rigorous model-based semantics to BDMPs.*

BDMPs in a Nutshell. BDMPs are used in the probabilistic safety assessment of nuclear power plants. Two major mechanisms in BDMPs are *triggers* and *triggered Markov processes.* The triggers model *activation*: if the source of a trigger fails, then the target of the trigger is activated, i.e., woken from a stand-by mode, provided at least one of its parents is activated. Triggered Markov processes are pairs of Markov chains associated with BEs: one describes the behavior when being activated while the other considers the case when de-activated. BE can thus be in four states: working or failed in standby, or working or failed in the activated mode. BDMPs facilitate repairs by transiting from a failed to a working state. BDMPs allow modeling state-dependent failures, an aspect that is not supported by SFTs. BDMPs can be analyzed by the discrete-event simulator YAMS and the trace-based analysis tool FIGSEQ [4].

Contributions of This Paper. The main contribution is a *formal semantics* of BMDPs. The semantics is operational: we map each BDMP onto a *Markov automaton* [10]. This semantics assumes all continuous failure distributions to be negative exponentials. It covers two versions of triggers and takes triggered Markov processes as basic events. It thus includes repairs. This complicates matters a bit, as—in contrast to SFTs and classical (non-repairable) DFTs—the property is lost that once a sub-tree has failed it remains to do so. Many existing semantics of extensions of SFTs do not contain repairs; a notable exception is recent work on rare event simulation of DFTs with repairs [6]. Our semantics is *modular*, following the compositional approach for DFTs in [3]. This entails that each BDMP construct, i.e., basic event, gate (such as VOT and priority AND), triggers, etc. are mapped onto a single Markov automaton (MA). The MA for the entire BMDP is obtained by composing the constituting MA together. In order to enable this composition, the MAs for the BDMP elements are equipped with extra signals (a.k.a. *actions*). Once the entire MA of a BDMP is obtained, the actions are not of any further use and are abstracted away.

A prototypical implementation of the semantics has been made. It constructs the MA in a modular way as defined in this paper using the tool moconv[1] and uses the probabilistic model checker STORM [8] for reliability and availability analysis. Our semantics is validated by comparing the analysis results of our prototype with the simulation results of the BDMP analysis tool YAMS [4]. (In the absence of any other formal semantics of BDMPs, this is the best we can hope for.) We stress that the focus of this work has not been to define a memory-efficient semantics—the peak memory consumption of a compositional approach can be substantial [19]. The modular approach, however, is conceptually simple, easily reveals the intricacies of some of the individual BMDP elements and can easily be extended with new types of gates. We, therefore, believe that our semantics increases the understanding of BDMPs and can provide the basis for more efficient state-space generation techniques for BDMPs, e.g., our semantics is amenable to partial-order reduction techniques for MA. The main contributions of this paper are:

1. A compositional, operational semantics of repairable BDMPs.
2. A prototypical implementation of this semantics.
3. An experimental validation of the semantics by comparing analysis results.

Organization of the Paper. Section 2 discusses the formal model, Markov Automata (MA). The components of BDMPs and their semantics are detailed in Sect. 3. The proposed prototypical implementation along with experimental results are discussed in Sect. 4. Section 5 concludes the paper and discusses some future work.

2   Markov Automata

Markov automata are a mathematical model that support discrete probability distributions, exponential delays, non-determinism among choices, and parallel composition. MA subsume DTMCs, CTMCs, CTMDPs and PAs as detailed by [12]. Here we outline the theory of MA necessary to understand the present work. We use $\mathbb{R}$ for the set of real numbers, μ for a distribution over the set S $\mu: S \to [0,1]$ such that $\sum_{s \in S} \mu(s) = 1$, $Dist(S)$ for the set of discrete probability distributions over the set S, $supp(Dist)$ for the support of distribution function $Dist$, and $\perp$ ($\top$) for FALSE (TRUE). Syntactically, a Markov automaton $\mathcal{M}$ is a tuple $(S, Act, \to, \dashrightarrow, s_0)$ where S is a finite set of states, Act is a finite set of actions, $\to \subseteq S \times Act \times Dist(S)$ is a set of action transitions, $\dashrightarrow \subseteq S \times \mathbb{R}_{>0} \times S$

---

[1] The Modest Toolset: http://www.modestchecker.net/.

is a set of Markovian transitions, and $s_0 \in S$ is an initial state. Semantically speaking, if an action a can be performed from a state s such that $(s, a, \mu) \in \rightarrow$ (we write $s \xrightarrow{a} \mu$), then the probability of moving to state $s' \in S$ from state s is $\mu(s')$. Moreover, in case of a Markovian transition $s \overset{\lambda}{\dashrightarrow} s'$, this transition can be performed within time t with a probability which is exponentially distributed with rate λ, i.e., $(1 - e^{-\lambda \cdot t})$. The states of MA are called *Markovian* (iff having only Markovian outgoing transitions), *interactive* (iff having only probabilistic outgoing transitions), *deadlock* (iff having no outgoing transition), or *hybrid* (otherwise). The *exit* rate of a *Markovian* state s is computed as $E(s) = \sum_{s' \in S} R(s, s')$, where $R(s, s') = \sum\{\lambda | s \overset{\lambda}{\dashrightarrow} s'\}$ is the *rate* between state s and s'. The probability of leaving s is $1 - e^{-E(s) \cdot t}$. If s has more than one successor state, then there exists a race between such states after leaving state s; the probability of s' winning the race equals $P(s, s') = \frac{R(s, s')}{E(s)}$.

The parallel composition (denoted $\|$) of two MA $\mathcal{M}_i = (S_i, Act_i, \rightarrow_i, \dashrightarrow_i, s_{0,i})$, where $i \in \{1, 2\}$ w.r.t. $A = Act_1 \cap Act_2$ can be formally defined as the MA $\mathcal{M}_1 \| \mathcal{M}_2 = (S_1 \times S_2, Act_1 \uplus Act_2, \rightarrow, \dashrightarrow, (s_{0,1}, s_{0,2}))$, where $\rightarrow$ and $\dashrightarrow$ are defined as the smallest relations satisfying the following six rules (R_1 through R_6):

$$\frac{s_1 \xrightarrow{\alpha}_1 \mu_1 \quad \alpha \notin A}{(s_1, s_2) \xrightarrow{\alpha} \mu_1 \cdot \{s_2 \mapsto 1\}} R_1 \quad \frac{s_2 \xrightarrow{\alpha}_2 \mu_2 \quad \alpha \notin A}{(s_1, s_2) \xrightarrow{\alpha} \{s_1 \mapsto 1\} \cdot \mu_2} R_2 \quad \frac{s_1 \xrightarrow{\alpha}_1 \mu_1 \quad s_2 \xrightarrow{\alpha}_2 \mu_2 \quad \alpha \in A}{(s_1, s_2) \xrightarrow{\alpha} \mu_1 \cdot \mu_2} R_3$$

$$\frac{s_1 \overset{\lambda}{\dashrightarrow}_1 s_1' \quad s_1 \neq s_1'}{(s_1, s_2) \overset{\lambda}{\dashrightarrow} (s_1', s_2)} R_4 \quad \frac{s_2 \overset{\lambda}{\dashrightarrow}_2 s_2' \quad s_2 \neq s_2'}{(s_1, s_2) \overset{\lambda}{\dashrightarrow} (s_1, s_2')} R_5 \quad \frac{s_1 \overset{\lambda_1}{\dashrightarrow}_1 s_1 \quad s_2 \overset{\lambda_2}{\dashrightarrow}_2 s_2}{(s_1, s_2) \overset{\lambda_1 + \lambda_2}{\dashrightarrow} (s_1, s_2)} R_6$$

In natural language, rules R_1 and R_2 state that an MA can independently take any action not in the common action set. Rule R_3 states that both MA must progress synchronously on the common action α. Rule R_4 and R_5 define that no synchronization takes place on Markovian transitions. The last rule R_6 defines that the rates of self-loops are added in parallel states. The composition operator ($\|$) for MA is commutative and associative. Thus, the order of composition among n MA does not matter. MA is called *open* if it can be composed with another MA. Once all composition is done, the MA is called *closed*. This paper takes a state-based view of Markov automata for model checking and actions are only required for parallel composition. This implies that all actions in *closed* MA are turned into *invisible* actions (τ) and *maximal progress* assumption can be applied thereafter. The *maximal progress* property states that if Markovian and action-based transitions are enabled simultaneously in a state, then the MA will always follow the latter and the former can be removed from the MA.

We do not have input and output actions (as adopted by [3]) in our framework. The composition is done over common *alphabets* as per rule R_3 using synchronization vectors of the form $\langle a, a \rangle \mapsto a$ (both MA must synchronize on action a and this action will behave as a in resultant composed MA) as detailed in [12]. This rule can be extended to an arbitrary number of MA and intuitively speaking, all MA having a shared action must synchronize to perform this action.

In order to enable model checking on Markov automata, we equip states with *atomic propositions* and introduce *variables* in the MA. The *variable expressions*, defined on top of these *variables*, represent visible aspects of the system and can be considered as *labeling* functions returning *atomic propositions* of each state. The action transitions can be equipped with *guards* (predicates over the *variables*) and *updates* (*variable* assignments).

Example 1. These con-
cepts are summarized in
Fig. 1 by parallel compo-
sition of two MA; (a)
and (b). Where (a) has
one transition guarded
by when($\bot$), this guard
makes the transition impossible (we use gray color to

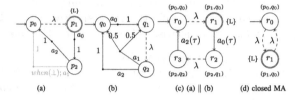

Fig. 1. MA example

highlight impossible transitions). This guard also makes the a_1 labeled action transition of MA (b) impossible which was supposed to synchronize with this impossible transition of (a). We associate one *atomic proposition* L with state p_1 of (a) (double circle is used to distinguish this state from the other states). The treatment of L through different stages of parallel composition can be followed. As a convention, we drop the distribution part of the transition whenever there is only one reachable state after an action, i.e., $supp(Dist(S)) = 1$. Consequently, we have dropped the probabilistic part for both actions a_0 and a_2 in (a) $\|$ (b), see Fig. 1(c). Conversion to invisible labels (τ) is shown in Fig. 1(c) and *closed* MA after removing all action-labeled transitions is shown in Fig. 1(d). The selection of Markovian transition rate λ was deliberate to highlight the application of rules R_4 and R_5.

3   BDMPs and Their Semantics

BDMPs [5] syntactically extend SFTs by
one new element called *trigger* (Trig). The
syntax of this formalism is very flexible.
The triggers can have any type of node as
their source and target. There are three
syntactic restrictions: (1) trigger source
and origin cannot be the same, i.e., trigger loops are not allowed; (2) Top cannot
be the target of a trigger; (3) two triggers
cannot target the same node. However,
the semantics of this language is quite
involved. For instance, there are four variants of *triggers* available in BDMPs. The
name "logic-driven" stems from the fact

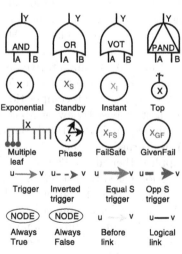

Fig. 2. BDMP elements

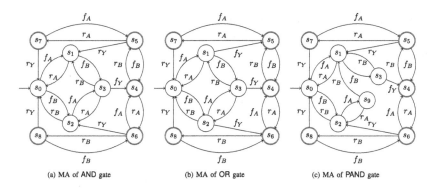

(a) MA of AND gate (b) MA of OR gate (c) MA of PAND gate

Fig. 3. MA of the BDMP gates

that predicates are used to switch between the BE modes, e.g., from *standby* to *active* mode. The structure-function SF and activation-function AF are used to control the failure and activation mechanisms in a BDMP. In the original paper [5], a predicate (*trimming*) was used to do computational optimization and to incorporate don't-care propagation assumption. The don't-care propagation assumption is based on the view that the components of an already failed subsystem can not fail while the system is being repaired. This assumption drastically reduces the state space explosion and is close to reality. For the sake of understandability, in this paper, we only focus on the activation behavior of BDMPs and do not consider this trimming and any other optimizations for BDMPs [5].

Compositional Semantics. In our compositional approach, we use actions to model the failure and mode switching mechanism of BDMPs. We introduce four actions namely active (a), de-active (d), fail (f) and repaired (r) to inform the rest of the system when a component is *active, standby, failed* or *repaired*, respectively. These four actions are enough to model BDMP elements. We define two MA for each BDMP element corresponding to *activation* and *failure*. We have defined different templates for each BDMP element and depending upon the position and the configuration of an element in a BDMP we invoke the corresponding template. These templates correspond to the semantics of each element. The approach is modular therefore it is easy to add more templates if, for instance, other elements are considered in the future. An exhaustive list of BDMP elements is presented in Fig. 2. We segregate these elements into four categories; the first row of Fig. 2 defines *gates*, the second and third row define *leaves*, the fourth row defines *triggers*, and the fifth row defines *others*. We discuss the proposed semantics under each category:

Gates: BDMPs have four types of gates; AND, OR, VOTing and PAND as shown in the first row of Fig. 2. The AND, OR and VOT are inherited from SFTs. PAND is a *dynamic* gate, i.e., its behavior depends on the order of input failures.

All gates shown in Fig. 2 have two inputs (A, B) and one output (Y). We use subscripts to denote actions of a particular BDMP element, e.g., the failure of input A is denoted by f_A. Any n input gate can be represented by a cascade of $n - 1$ two-input gates (a.k.a: binary gates). Therefore it suffices to provide semantics of binary AND, OR and PAND gates. The structure function of AND is true when SF of both inputs A and B is true, i.e., $SF(Y) = SF(A) \wedge SF(B)$.

The failure of an AND is captured by the $s_3 \to s_4$ transition in the MA of Fig. 3(a). The gate is considered repaired if either one or both of its inputs get repaired. Therefore, we have two repair action transitions ($s_5 \to s_1$ and $s_6 \to s_2$) for single input repairs and two repair transitions ($s_7 \to s_0$ and $s_8 \to s_0$) for the repair of both inputs. The states representing the failure of the gate output are double circled. Note that the gate can only leave the double circled states by means of r_Y-labeled transitions.

The structure function of OR is true when SF of any of its inputs is true, i.e., $SF(Y) = SF(A) \vee SF(B)$. This behavior is captured in the MA of Fig. 3(b) by introducing two fail transitions ($s_1 \to s_5$ and $s_2 \to s_6$).

The PAND in BDMPs follows an *exclusive-PAND* semantics, i.e., simultaneous input failures do not cause output failure. The structure-function of PAND is true only when f_A occurs strictly before f_B. The precise semantics are depicted in Fig. 3(c) where intricacies of repair orders can be followed. It is remarked that *exclusive-PAND*, in-general, cannot capture the behavior where both inputs are INST (introduced in the next paragraphs) and both fail simultaneously.

Strictly speaking, the failure behavior of a *gate* does not depend on its activation status. Therefore we did not have any activation transition in the MA of *gates*. This is different for *leaves* as we discuss next. Although the behavior of a gate is independent of the activation, the gates are involved in propagating the activation

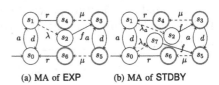

(a) MA of EXP   (b) MA of STDBY

Fig. 4. MA of EXP and STDBY

behavior towards the leaves. Therefore we also define the activation MA for *gates*. (In-fact activation MA templates, in general, only depend on the type of trigger pointing to a node and the number of parents inheriting this nodes.)

Leaves: There are eight types of leaves in BDMPs as shown in the second and third row of Fig. 2. The EXP represents component failures which follow an exponential probability distribution with rate $\lambda \in \mathbb{R}_{>0}$. The EXP can fail upon activation as depicted in Fig. 4(a). The *repair rate* for this BE is μ and it is unaffected by the activation status of EXP. The STDBY is used to model components which can fail in *standby* mode. Hence, two failure rates are relevant: the standby failure rate λ_s and the active failure rate λ_a. If we remove the standby failure behavior of a STDBY, then it behaves as EXP. This can also be observed in Fig. 4(b), i.e., if we remove the Markovian transition ($s_0 \dashrightarrow s_7$) and the then unreachable state s_7, the resulting automaton is identical to Fig. 4(a).

The MULTI element represents a batch of independent and identical EXP components. MULTI with parameters n and m can be modeled as n EXPs inherited by a VOT gate where $K = m$ and $N = n$. The structure function of MULTI becomes true after $N - K$ of these identical units have failed. The semantics of MULTI with $K = 2$ and $N = 3$ are presented in Fig. 5. Notice that the automaton structure of Fig. 5 can be easily extended to other values of K and N. Since the functionality of a VOT is hidden in MULTI, the MA of

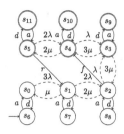

Fig. 5. MA of MULTI

VOT is also hidden in MA of MULTI. If we remove all a and d labeled action-transitions from the MA of MULTI, we get the MA of a VOT gate with three EXPs having identical failure rates (λ) and repair rates (μ).

BDMPs model on-demand failures using INST BEs. The SF of this element (upon activation) becomes one with probability γ or remains zero with probability $1 - \gamma$ as depicted in state s_1 of Fig. 6. The failing mechanism of this BE is quite straightforward but its repair mechanism is not obvious. INST is receptive to activation and deactivation actions even when it is failed. The INST will keep track of the activation requests and if it has a valid activation request at the time of repair, then INST will be checked again.

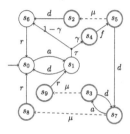

Fig. 6. MA of INST

The structure function of PHASE becomes immediately true upon an activation request and once true it switches to false upon the occurrence of a Markovian transition governed by rate μ, see Fig. 7(a). Notice that action names like *start-phase* and *end-phase* are not used because they are just

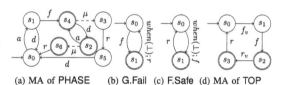

(a) MA of PHASE   (b) G.Fail (c) F.Safe (d) MA of TOP

Fig. 7. MA of other BDMP leaves

aliases of failure and repairing actions, respectively. The SF of G.Fail (F.Safe) becomes true (false) at the start of BDMP analysis and remains true (false) thereafter. This behavior is achieved by adding a $when(\bot)$ guard in the repair (fail) action transition of Fig. 7(b) (Fig. 7(c)). BDMPs achieve the G.Fail (F.Safe) feature by associating a flag $FailF\_Frozen$ to BEs. Setting this flag to true forces the BE to keep its failure state set by the user during modeling. The user can set the failure state through another flag called $FailF$. BDMPs (like other fault tree formalisms) analyze how BEs contribute towards the occurrence of an undesired top-level event (called TOP in BDMPs). It can inherit only one child v and follows failure f_v and repair r_v transitions of this child, see Fig. 7(d).

BDMP Modularization: Before presenting the activation semantics we discuss modularization; an important concept for our approach. A *module* is a subset of BDMP elements disjoint (from activation point of view) from other elements and having the same activation behavior. The modularization creates a partition of BDMP elements. In order to modularize, we traverse the BDMP and identify the nodes that are target of triggers. We call these nodes the *module representatives*. The *module-representative* is the element which

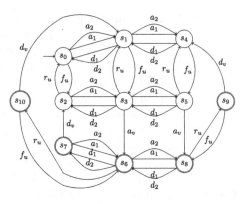

Fig. 8. MA of Trig and two parents

interacts with other parts of the BDMP and decides the activation status of the module it is representing. The activation/deactivation mechanism of all *module-members* are tethered to activation and deactivation of *module-representative*. It becomes apparent that BDMP can be segregated in modules and cardinality of these modules can range from one (imagine module consist of single BE) to the size of entire BDMP (when BDMP is a simple SFT).

Triggers: There are four types of triggers in BDMPs: *trigger* Trig, *inverted trigger* InvTrig, *equal separating trigger* EqSTrig, and *opposite separating trigger* OppSTrig. The Trig link connecting nodes u and v means that, $AF(v)$ is true when $SF(u)$ is true and v is input of some gates $g_1, g_2, \ldots, g_k$ and AF of at least one of these k gates is true. The semantics of Trig for the case where v is inherited by two gates (a.k.a.: nodes) are shown in Fig. 8, where we perform activation action a_v after reception of two actions; failure of u (f_u) and activation of gate 1 or 2 (a_1 or a_2 respectively). Here, we only presented MA for the case where Trig target v is input of two gates but the pattern in this automaton can be extended by adding states and transitions capturing activation, deactivation of more gates (if added). We double circle the states where v is active to distinguish them from the other states.

The InvTrig provides complementary behavior to Trig. Here $AF(v)$ is false when either $SF(u)$ is true, or $SF(u)$ is false and v is the input of some gates $g_1, g_2, \ldots, g_k$ and AF of all of these gates is false. The automata-based view for target v of InvTrig inherited by one gate is shown in Fig. 9(a). Notice that the deactivation action is performed as soon as parent is deactivated or trigger origin u in repaired. The OppSTrig isolates the activation behavior of the target node v from its parents. The semantics of this link is presented in Fig. 9(b). Informally speaking, v is activated at the start of BDMP analysis and it is deactivated as soon as OppSTrig origin u performs a fail action. The EqSTrig achieves complementary behavior of the OppSTrig. The target v of EqSTrig is activated upon failure of the trigger origin, i.e., u. The deactivation of v is performed upon repair of u, see Fig. 9(c).

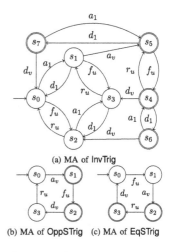

(a) MA of InvTrig

(b) MA of OppSTrig   (c) MA of EqSTrig

Fig. 9. MA of other *triggers*

The aforementioned activation semantics captures the behavior of all BDMP elements except PHASE, which is treated differently. In BDMPs, a flag $In\_progress$ is associated to PHASE. If this flag is set to true, then the acti-

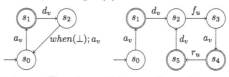

(a) *In_prog.*=⊤,no trigger   (b) *In_prog.*=⊤, one trigger

Fig. 10. MA of PHASE activation

vation action has to be performed at the start of the BDMP analysis. The $In\_progress$ flag of only one phase element should be set to true so that we can clearly identify the first phase of the phased-mission profile. This flag is effective at the beginning of the BDMP analysis. Subsequent activation is conditioned to the fact whether PHASE is the target of a trigger or not. If it is not the target of a trigger, then PHASE can not be activated afterward, see Fig. 10(a).

On the other hand, if PHASE is the target of the trigger then it will get activated on the failure of trigger origin u. This activation mechanism is similar to EqSTrig MA of Fig. 9(c) and we only need to add an activation action at the start provided $In\_progress$ flag is true, see Fig. 10(b). We remark that BDMPs are *multi-top* trees and each top module is activated at the start of the analysis. We assign a different number to each top module because the top element can be the target of the trigger.

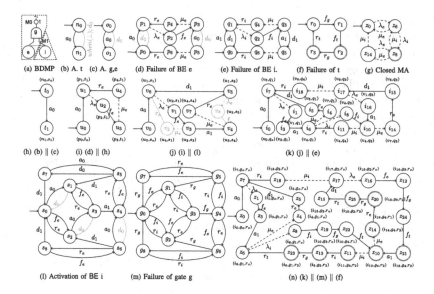

Fig. 11. Composition example

Others: This includes node activation flags (AlwaysFalse, AlwaysTrue), BeforeLink, and LogicLink. The AlwaysTrue (AlwaysFalse) flags can be associated to any node of the BDMP. If this flag is true, then that node and associated

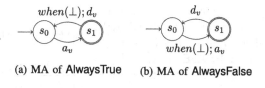

(a) MA of AlwaysTrue   (b) MA of AlwaysFalse

Fig. 12. MA of AlwaysTure and AlwaysFalse

module will remain active (de-active) throughout the analysis of the BDMP as indicated by the MA of Fig. 12(a) (Fig. 12(b)). The BeforeLink connecting two INST type nodes u and v enforces an order in checking the Bernoulli distribution associated to the INST. That is, v is checked only after checking u. The Before-Link were proposed later in BDMPs as an optimization. They are mentioned here for the sake of completeness and we did neither outline its precise semantics nor discuss it further because we do not consider optimizations. The last element we mention is the LogicLink. The semantics of LogicLink are quite subtle. When we syntactically say node B is child of node A, we are semantically implying that the actions of the MA corresponding to B and A are visible to each other.

Composition Example. Let us explain our compositional semantics on a BDMP example. The example BDMP, depicted in Fig. 11(a), has two modules (0 and 1) as there is only one Trig. The BDMP consists of four elements; therefore we need eight automata to construct the complete state-space of the BDMP. The automata and their relevant compositions are:

$$MA_{F_{bdmp}} = \underbrace{MA_{F_t}}_{Fig.(n)} \| \underbrace{MA_{A_t}}_{Fig.(f)} \| \underbrace{MA_{F_g}}_{Fig.(b)} \| \underbrace{MA_{A_g}}_{Fig.(m)} \| \underbrace{MA_{F_e}}_{Fig.(c)} \| \underbrace{MA_{A_e}}_{Fig.(d)} \| \underbrace{MA_{F_i}}_{Fig.(c)} \| \underbrace{MA_{A_i}}_{Fig.(e)}$$
$$\phantom{MA_{F_{bdmp}} = MA_{F_t} \| MA_{A_t} \| MA_{F_g} \| MA_{A_g} \| MA_{F_e} \| MA_{A_e} \| MA_{F_i} \|} \underbrace{\phantom{MA_{A_i}}}_{Fig.(l)}$$

The final MA (see Fig. 11(g)) of the BDMP is obtained by turning all actions into internal actions and applying maximal progress (as described in Sect. 2).

The activation mechanism of t (TOP) is shown in Fig. 11(b) with an impossible deactivation transition. Since all other components of the *primary module* will follow that behavior, the deactivation transition of their MA is colored gray to indicate this impossibility, see Fig. 11(c). The same approach is followed in Fig. 11(d) to indicate that e cannot be deactivated once activated. All states corresponding to the failure of TOP are double circled. Notice in Fig. 11(n) that some states after the Markovian transition from z_{10} are still tagged as fail states but no time is spent in these states because they all have only outgoing action transitions. Another important observation on some paths, e.g., $z_{11} \rightarrow z_{13} \rightarrow z_{23} \rightarrow z_6$ is that there is an interleaving behavior but since all interleavings of action transitions lead to the same end result, we do not draw all possible paths. A similar phenomenon occurs in Fig. 11(j). The transitions to v_2 and v_8 are highlighted as impossible transitions because they are paralleled by immediate (action-based) transitions a_1 and d_1, respectively. Each state is annotated with the state identifiers from the composing automata for the sake of clarity. State identifiers are neither required for composition nor for model checking.

Non-determinism. Due to the compositional nature of semantics, non-determinism can occur. That is to say, the *closed* MA of a BDMP may contain states that have more than one outgoing action-transition. These scenarios occur if there are several possible ways in which failures, activation, and de-activation are propagated through the BDMP. As our semantics is modular, these propagations are initiated locally, though their effect is global. Let us illustrate this by an example, see the BDMP in Fig. 13(a).

Our semantics obtains a choice between the activation and deactivation actions of INST I_A. This can be seen as follows. Consider the *closed* MA in Fig. 13(b) of the BDMP obtained after applying maximal progress. The transitions are labeled with actions (instead of the invisible action τ) for the sake of clarity. Note

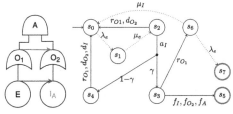

(a) BDMP   (b) Automaton for reachability property

Fig. 13. Non-determinism example

that transition $s_4 \rightarrow s_0$ has three labels indicating that these transitions can be arbitrarily permuted. Their order, however, does not matter and we will finally reach state s_0, regardless of which order is taken. Consider the execution trace of the BDMP in Fig. 13(a), initiated by a repair of E: $r_E \rightarrow r_{O_1} \rightarrow d_{O_2}$. This trace does not activate I_A. However, this propagation of E's repair resulting in O_2's de-activation is not atomic. Therefore, the activation action of I_A can interleave with this trace. This is reflected by state s_2 in the MA which also has an outgoing a_I-action transition. Another non-deterministic choice exists at state s_3. This is due to the two possible execution traces initiated by E's repair: $r_E \rightarrow a_I \rightarrow f_I$ and $r_E \rightarrow a_I \rightarrow r_{O_1} \rightarrow f_I$. The first trace will directly lead to failure. But the second trace repairs O_1 (r_{O_1}) before performing f_I; failure state S_7 will be reached only after E's next failure. In the meantime, I could be repaired leading to a return to the initial state. This behavior is captured through the Markovian transitions from state s_6. These subtle non-deterministic scenarios are mainly due to the instantaneous behavior of the INST element.

4   Prototypical Implementation and Experimentation

Our compositional BDMP semantics has been implemented in a software prototype. The overall setup of our implementation is presented in Fig. 14. We describe each block:

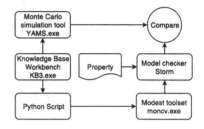

Fig. 14. Prototypical tool

KB3.exe: The *Knowledge Base Workbench* [4] is a GUI based tool used to create, simulate, and export the BDMP as Figaro definition. Figaro is a domain-specific object-oriented probabilistic modeling language defined to carry out operation safety studies [4]. It generalizes various reliability models, e.g., reliability block diagrams and can cast generic models in *knowledge bases* KB. In fact, BDMPs are originally defined as a *knowledge base* in Figaro.

Python Script: This constitutes the core of our implementation. The script takes a BDMP description as Figaro definition and generates a process-algebraic description of its MA using the Modest language [2]. In order to do so, the following five steps are performed;

1. ReadFI: we read the English or French version of BDMP and populate it into a dictionary-based data structure.
2. ModularizeBDMP: the structure of the parsed BDMP is analyzed and segregated into *modules*. We use a depth-first search on the underlying graph to identify *module-representatives*. Whenever we encounter a node having different activation behavior, i.e., the node is either target of Trig, InvTrig, OppSTrig, EqSTrig, tagged as AlwaysTrue or AlwaysFalse, or inherited by more than one *module*, then we consider this node as a *module-representative*. As stated earlier, *modules* create a partition of a BDMP and from an activation point of view we only need to create interaction between partitions. We remark that a module having TOP as *module-representative* is called *primary module* and INST in *primary modules* of BDMPs as originally conceived in [5] have no semantics, i.e., they are never tested.

3. RemoveVOT: converts a VOT gate into a cascade of AND and OR gates.
4. BinarizeGates: This step turns any gate into a cascade of binary gates.
5. WriteModestDefinitions: This step generates a process-algebraic description for each component present in the BDMP under consideration.

monovonv.exe: This component of the Modest tool-set converts a Modest file to a JANI file. JANI is an intermediate language originally designed to exchange models between different formal analysis tools [7]. The model checker STORM has direct support for the JANI format.

Property: We use probabilistic temporal logic to encode the properties of interest, i.e., the *unreliability* and the *unavailability*. In a repairable BDMP, there is no "permanent failure". What we are interested in is an entry in a tangible fail-labeled state. Note that *unreliability* is a simple reachability property and mostly a partial state-space suffices for this property. However, we need complete state-space to compute the *unavailability*.

STORM: We feed the JANI file to STORM along with the property of interest and STORM computes and returns the numerical value for the desired metric. STORM [8] is a state-of-the-art probabilistic model checker. It is an open-source and freely available tool. Recently, STORM participated in the QComp 2019[2] competition and outperformed all competitors on most of the benchmarks. It uses numerical and symbolic methods.

YAMS.exe: YAMS is a freely available Monte-Carlo based simulation tool for BDMPs [4]. YAMS uses a standard event-driven Monte-Carlo simulation method. It can report the mean value of an indicator function along with its standard deviation, i.e., the range of uncertainty against a given confidence level. YAMS can be configured to compute different reliability metrics, e.g., *mean-time-to-failure* (MTTF), *unreliability* and *unavailability*, etc. The simulation time increases with increasing precision requirement, e.g., approximately $\mathcal{O}(10^k)$ simulations are required to obtain a (low) probability of 10^{-k} with a 10% confidence interval.

Results of Test-Cases. The test cases considered along with detailed documentation are available online[3]. These test cases range from simple interactions, e.g., mutual exclusion to literature benchmarks. For each test case, we compare STORM generated results with those of YAMS. YAMS reports results for different confidence bounds and we benchmark, as tolerance, 99% *confidence level* for our comparison. STORM was run for the precision of 10^{-8}. YAMS is a Windows-based tool, whereas STORM was run on a Linux-based machine having 5x: 2 Intel® Xeon® Platinum 8160, 48 threads 2.1 GHz, 384 GB RAM. The symbolic engine of STORM, i.e., *sylvan* was restricted to 8 threads with maximum allocated memory of 40 GB. We build complete state-spaces symbolically and MAs reported here are *sparse* models build from the symbolic models

---

[2] HTTP://qcomp.org/competition/2019/.
[3] HTTP://sourceforge.net/projects/visualFigaro/files/Doc_and_examples/Francais/.

Table 1. Indicative statistics for test-cases

Test case	#elements stat	#elements dyn	Mission Time	YAMS Unrel.	Tol.	Unavl.	Tol.	STORM Complete MA #state	#trans.	Reduced MA #state	#trans.	CTMC #state	#trans.	Comparison Absolute Error Δ_{Unr}	Δ_{Unavl}
1	10	2	10	0.7872	0.0011	0.5157	0.0013	987	1889	313	1299	172	984	0.0000	0.0002
4	19	2	10	0.9101	0.0074	0.6864	0.0120	34336	99002	20027	86719	3105	26436	0.0001	0.0005
17	24	4	10	0.8562	0.0009	0.5978	0.0126	1793667	4630531	511752	3593876	207744	2845056	0.0001	0.0018
23	23	3	20	0.8690	0.0275	0.4950	0.0407	16110	40220	5677	29787	2048	22528	0.0017	0.0096
39	34	6	10	0.7712	0.0034	0.5620	0.0040	144483	336048	50436	242001	12288	157120	0.0008	0.0003
49	13	3	10	0.8811	0.0026	0.6148	0.0040	934	2109	574	1739	117	548	0.0011	0.0010
53	14	5	10	0.6770	0.0038	0.4042	0.0040	101761	220941	36712	166196	10840	104420	0.0015	0.0017

after application of the *maximal progress*. We only look into the accuracy of results and disregard computation requirements in terms of memory and verification time because the implementation is only a sanity check of semantics. The results for six test-cases are reproduced in Table 1. Detailed results along with the python script can be accessed at[4]. The last two columns of Table 1 report the absolute errors of the unreliability (Δ_{Unr}) and unavailability (Δ_{Unavl}). Where $\Delta_{Unr} = |Unrel_{YAMS} - Unrel_{STORM}|$ and $\Delta_{Unavl} = |Unavl_{YAMS} - Unavl_{STORM}|$. We do not reproduce STORM calculated values as they can be easily reproduced from the absolute errors. It is clearly visible (in the last two columns of Table 1) that the *unreliability* and the *unavailability* values computed by STORM are always within YAMS-computed range. The size of the complete MA, the reduced MA (after application of maximal progress), and CTMC (after removal of spurious non-determinism) are also provided.

Non-determinism. As described earlier, the compositional semantics may lead to non-determinism. This occurred in eight test cases. The non-determinism is primarily due to the instantaneous character of INST elements. After delaying the INST activation actions by a very high rate Markovian transition, i.e., 10^5, and applying maximal progress, the minimal and maximal values obtained by STORM coincide. That is, all remaining non-determinism is spurious. Our analysis with STORM yields the same values as the simulation tool YAMS. The usage of high-rate Markovian transitions increases the *stiffness* of the underlying Markov chain and it results in an increased analysis time as convergence is slower.

5   Conclusion

We presented a formal, compositional semantics for repairable BDMPs. Its modularity provides insight into the subtleties of BDMPs and yields a comprehensible semantics that is amenable to model-based analysis such as probabilistic model checking. Experimental evaluations using a prototypical implementation reveal that our semantics coincides with the BDMP interpretation of the simulation tool YAMS. Future work includes reducing the peak memory consumption by leveraging partial-order reduction, bi-simulation, and symmetry reduction as shown to be successful for dynamic fault trees [19]. The challenge is to adapt these techniques to repairs. It would also be interesting to extend our semantics

---

[4] HTTP://github.com/moves-rwth/dft-bdmp/.

to generalized BDMPs [17], and to exploit priorities in GSPNs [16] to obtain a fully deterministic compositional semantics as in [13] for DFTs.

References

1. Baier, C., de Alfaro, L., Forejt, V., Kwiatkowska, M.: Model checking probabilistic systems. In: Clarke, E., Henzinger, T., Veith, H., Bloem, R. (eds.) Handbook of Model Checking, pp. 963–999. Springer, Cham (2018). https://doi.org/10.1007/978-3-319-10575-8_28
2. Bohnenkamp, H.C., D'Argenio, P.R., Hermanns, H., Katoen, J.P.: MODEST: a compositional modeling formalism for hard and softly timed systems. IEEE TSE **32**(10), 812–830 (2006)
3. Boudali, H., Crouzen, P., Stoelinga, M.: A rigorous, compositional, and extensible framework for dynamic fault tree analysis. IEEE TDSC **7**(2), 128–143 (2009)
4. Bouissou, M.: Automated dependability analysis of complex systems with the KB3 workbench: the experience of EDF R&D. In: ICEE. CIEM (2005)
5. Bouissou, M., Bon, J.L.: A new formalism that combines advantages of fault-trees and Markov models: Boolean logic driven Markov processes. Rel. Eng. Sys. Safety **82**(2), 149–163 (2003)
6. Budde, C.E., Biagi, M., Monti, R.E., D'Argenio, P.R., Stoelinga, M.: Rare event simulation for non-Markovian repairable Fault Trees. TACAS 2020. LNCS, vol. 12078, pp. 463–482. Springer, Cham (2020). https://doi.org/10.1007/978-3-030-45190-5_26
7. Budde, C.E., Dehnert, C., Hahn, E.M., Hartmanns, A., Junges, S., Turrini, A.: JANI: quantitative model and tool interaction. In: Legay, A., Margaria, T. (eds.) TACAS 2017. LNCS, vol. 10206, pp. 151–168. Springer, Heidelberg (2017). https://doi.org/10.1007/978-3-662-54580-5_9
8. Dehnert, C., Junges, S., Katoen, J.-P., Volk, M.: A STORM is coming: a modern probabilistic model checker. In: Majumdar, R., Kunčak, V. (eds.) CAV 2017, Part II. LNCS, vol. 10427, pp. 592–600. Springer, Cham (2017). https://doi.org/10.1007/978-3-319-63390-9_31
9. Dugan, J.B., Bavuso, S.J., Boyd, M.A.: Dynamic fault-tree models for fault-tolerant computer systems. IEEE Trans. Reliab. **41**(3), 363–377 (1992)
10. Eisentraut, C., Hermanns, H., Zhang, L.: On probabilistic automata in continuous time. In: LICS, pp. 342–351. IEEE Computer Society (2010)
11. Guck, D., Spel, J., Stoelinga, M.: DFTCalc: reliability centered maintenance via fault tree analysis (tool paper). In: Butler, M., Conchon, S., Zaïdi, F. (eds.) ICFEM 2015. LNCS, vol. 9407, pp. 304–311. Springer, Cham (2015). https://doi.org/10.1007/978-3-319-25423-4_19
12. Hartmanns, A., Hermanns, H.: A modest Markov automata tutorial. In: Krötzsch, M., Stepanova, D. (eds.) Reasoning Web. Explainable Artificial Intelligence. LNCS, vol. 11810, pp. 250–276. Springer, Cham (2019). https://doi.org/10.1007/978-3-030-31423-1_8
13. Junges, S., Katoen, J.-P., Stoelinga, M., Volk, M.: One net fits all: a unifying semantics of Dynamic Fault Trees using GSPNs. In: Khomenko, V., Roux, O.H. (eds.) PETRI NETS 2018. LNCS, vol. 10877, pp. 272–293. Springer, Cham (2018). https://doi.org/10.1007/978-3-319-91268-4_14
14. Kaiser, B., Gramlich, C., Förster, M.: State/event fault trees - a safety analysis model for software-controlled systems. Rel. Eng. Sys. Safety **92**, 1521–1537 (2007)

15. Kaiser, B., Liggesmeyer, P., Mäckel, O.: A new component concept for fault trees. In: SCS. CRPIT, vol. 33, pp. 37–46. Australian Computer Society (2003)
16. Marsan, M.A., Balbo, G., Conte, G., Donatelli, S., Franceschinis, G.: Modelling with Generalized Stochastic Petri Nets, vol. 292. Wiley, New York (1995)
17. Piriou, P.Y., Faure, J.M., Lesage, J.J.: Generalized Boolean logic Driven Markov Processes: a powerful modeling framework for model-based safety analysis of dynamic repairable and reconfigurable systems. Rel. Eng. Sys. Safety **163**, 57–68 (2017)
18. Ruijters, E., Stoelinga, M.: Fault tree analysis: a survey of the state-of-the-art in modeling, analysis and tools. Comput. Sci. Rev. **15**, 29–62 (2015)
19. Volk, M., Junges, S., Katoen, J.P.: Fast dynamic fault tree analysis by model checking techniques. IEEE Trans. Ind. Inform. **14**(1), 370–379 (2018)
20. Walker, M., Papadopoulos, Y.: Synthesis and analysis of temporal fault trees with PANDORA: the time of priority AND gates. Nonlinear Anal. Hybri. Syst. **2**(2), 368–382 (2008)

Model-Based Safety Analysis of Mode Transitions

Marco Bozzano[1], Peter Munk[2], Markus Schweizer[2], Stefano Tonetta[1], and Viktória Vozárová[1(✉)]

[1] Fondazione Bruno Kessler, Trento, Italy
{bozzano,tonettas,vvozarova}@fbk.eu
[2] Robert Bosch GmbH, Research and Advance Engineering, Renningen, Germany
{Peter.Munk,Markus.Schweizer}@de.bosch.com

Abstract. The verification of safety requirements is fundamental in many safety-critical domains. In order to reach the highest level of required safety assurance, system engineers design components with a variety of safety mechanisms. The resulting potential combination and sequence of operational modes may become very complex and requires automated analysis support.

In this paper, we propose new formal methods, based on minimal cut sets, to generate explanations for operational mode transitions, in terms of causes defined as combinations of basic events, namely faults and recovery actions. The problem is quite subtle, as it requires to consider events occurring before, and in between, the source and target operational modes, identifying those that are necessary to bring the system into the source mode. We implemented the approach on top of the xSAP safety analysis platform, and evaluated it on an industrial design, namely an electronic control unit of a power steering system with redundancy and multiple safety mechanisms.

1 Introduction

The increasing level of autonomy and complexity of networked systems and system of systems in automotive as well as in other safety-critical domains augments the required level of functional safety and reliability of Electronic Components and Systems (ECS) [8]. In turn, the growing requirements in terms of functional safety and reliability push the development of new design technologies to analyze the safety of ECS. Fail-operational architectures include various safety mechanisms such as redundancies and fault detection components inside a single control unit. The interplay of multiple faults and mechanisms for fault masking and fault recovery may become very complex and requires automated methods and tools for its analysis.

In this paper we tackle the problem of analyzing the various faults, or in general events, that may lead a system from an operational mode to another. The system usually runs in nominal mode and switches to different backup or degraded modes upon the occurrence of faults or recovery actions. Due to the

© Springer Nature Switzerland AG 2020
A. Casimiro et al. (Eds.): SAFECOMP 2020, LNCS 12234, pp. 99–114, 2020.
https://doi.org/10.1007/978-3-030-54549-9_7

presence of different components and overlay of various redundancies and monitors, the system can switch to an operational mode for various reasons. We propose a model-based approach to the analysis of these mode transitions building on symbolic model-based safety analysis techniques for minimal cut sets and fault-tree generation [4].

The problem is quite subtle because the transition from mode m_1 to mode m_2 can be caused by events that occurred before m_1 but due to some propagation have effect with some delay or the effect is enabled by the new operational mode m_1. At the same time, we should not consider the events before m_1 that caused the system to go to m_1. We propose a formulation that takes into account these aspects and reduce the problem to parameter synthesis for temporal logic [6].

We implemented the approach on top of the xSAP tool [2] and evaluated the results on the architecture of an automotive Electronic Control Unit. This includes a dynamically redundant dual channel, each channel with a dual failsafe core, extended with a watchdog that may trigger the recovery of a passive channel. The results are very useful to understand the interplay of events that cause the mode transitions and show the scalability of the approach.

The rest of this paper is structured as follows. In Sect. 2 we discuss related work. We describe the case study in Sect. 3. In Sect. 4 we discuss some background notions. In Sect. 5 we discuss our formal approach. The experimental evaluation is presented in Sect. 6. Finally, we conclude and discuss future work in Sect. 7.

2   Related Work

The problem addressed in this paper builds upon, and extends previous work on Fault Tree Analysis (FTA), namely generation of minimal cut sets (MCSs) for a given top level event (TLE). The semantics of MCSs is given in terms of fault events occurring on a trace reaching the TLE [4,13]. The problem of computing the cut sets can be reduced to reachability analysis and solved using Binary Decision Diagrams as in [4], or using satisfiability (SAT)-based techniques for parameter synthesis [6]. The region of cut sets can be minimized to obtain the MCSs using classical routines for minimization of Boolean functions [7]. In [3] the SAT-based approach is extended with several enhancements based on the specific features of the problem, such as on-the-fly minimization and layered computation of the MCSs for increasing cardinality.

In this work, the trace-based semantics for MCSs is extended to encompass the case of generic (fault and recovery) events that explain the transitions between different system modes, rather than a TLE. The problem is reduced to parameter synthesis on a property expressed in LTL, and solved using techniques that build upon those in [3].

A qualitative analysis of the EPS case study has been carried out in [1] using FTA. The author performed the analysis by manually inspecting all possible states and transitions, and demonstrated that the order of events causing the mode transitions can be neglected. However, manual analysis is error-prone and

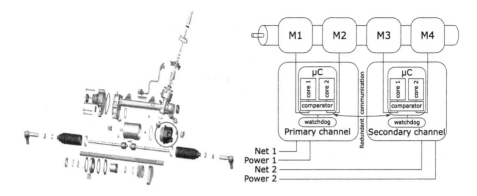

Fig. 1. EPS case study: assembly view with the electronic control unit (ECU) circled in red (left) and schematic overview (right). (Color figure online)

does not scale up when additional channels or states are considered. In this paper, we give a formal definition of the problem and solve it using a formal approach, based on model-checking.

In [10] a methodology is presented, based on Hip-Hops, to construct fault trees structured in terms of a set of (critical and non-critical) modes organized into a mode chart. The methodology is focused on the investigation of failure propagation, based on the annotation of system components with their (dynamic) mode-based behavior. In our case, instead, we are interested in synthesizing the mode-based (failure propagation) behavior automatically from a given behavioral model of the system.

The concept of events triggering mode transitions is related with the notions of causality as given, e.g., in the theory of counterfactual causality [9]. The latter is defined using structural equations, but can be readily re-formulated for transition systems [5]. However, the notion of causality is more fine-grained, in that it aims at distinguishing the notions of causality and temporal correlation, and addresses concepts such as responsibility and blame. Moreover, we are interested in sets of events that are necessary to explain a mode transition in all possible scenarios, whereas classical causality focuses on identifying such causes in a given scenario of interest. Finally, in our setting a cause may not be sufficient to trigger a mode transition – an additional side condition, a *contingency* in causality terminology, may be needed to make it sufficient.

3   Motivating Case Study

As case study, we selected an electronic power steering (EPS) system designed for highly-automated driving vehicles, as shown in Fig. 1. The system is not only able to support the driver in steering, but also to steer the vehicle without any input from the driver, by receiving steering commands from a redundant vehicle bus. Hence, the EPS system has high safety, reliability, and availability requirements.

3.1   ECU Design

In this case study, we focus only on the electronic control unit (ECU) of the EPS system, circled in red in Fig. 1 (left). A schematic overview of the EPS ECU is given in Fig. 1 (right). The ECU includes two separate channels, named *primary* and *secondary* channel in the following. Each channel has its own and independent power supply and connection to an individual vehicle bus. Both channels can communicate with each other by redundant intra-ECU communication channels. Each channel contains a lock-stepped microcontroller with an external watchdog and is able to drive 2 electric motors. The lock-stepped microcontroller contains two cores that compute the same instructions in parallel. At each cycle, a comparator circuit inside the controller compares the state of both cores. The microcontroller shows fail-silent behavior, so in case the two core states are not equal no result is forwarded. In order to check whether the comparator is working correctly, an external watchdog sends challenges to the comparator and checks the correctness of the response. If the challenge is answered incorrectly or if a timeout error occurs, the entire microcontroller is reset.

3.2   System Modes

Each channel is either in mode *master*, *slave*, or *passive*. In master mode, the channel calculates the torque for its two motors and sends a request to the other channel in slave mode to set the same torque to its connected motors, so all four motors provide the same torque. In slave mode, the channel awaits the torque requests from the other channel and sets the torque as described before. If the torque request is not received, the channel in slave mode has to assume that the other channel has failed silently, hence it becomes master and calculates the required torque itself. Since one channel and its directly connected two motors are sufficient to steer the vehicle, the EPS system is still available even if one channel fails.

3.3   Expected Faults and Their Effects

A channel has fail-silent behavior, therefore it enters the passive state only when an internal error occurs and it is detected, e.g. by the lock-step comparator or the watchdog. In passive state, the channel does not send any torque to its two motors anymore. A fault in the power supply of a channel leads to it entering the passive mode. When an erroneous or missing message is received from the vehicle bus connected to a channel, the channel switches or stays in slave mode, relying on the torque requests from the other channel in master mode. A fault in the communication between the channels is critical, as the torque requests cannot be exchanged anymore. For this reason, this intra-ECU inter-channel communication is implemented by heterogeneously redundant links. A fault in the microcontroller and its core, respectively, is very likely to be detected by the comparator circuit. A fault in the comparator itself is critical, for this reason it is implemented in hardware directly. In order to ensure the correct functionality of the comparator circuit, a watchdog, which is external to the microcontroller, monitors it by a challenge-response protocol. In case the comparator does not provide the correct response in time, the entire microcontroller is reset by the watchdog. A fault in the watchdog itself is critical again, as it potentially resets the microcontroller.

The individual faults have different occurrence probabilities, depending e.g. on the complexity of the hardware or the employed level of redundancy. In order to argue the safety of the entire EPS system and its ECU specifically, it is indispensable to analyze the combination and probability of faults that lead to unwanted behavior of the system. In general, the EPS system can exhibit unwanted behavior whenever no channel is in master mode and one of them is in slave mode. Given three modes per channel, overall nine modes exist in the system. Not all nine system modes are equally critical, e.g. one channel being in master mode and the other channel being in passive mode is acceptable for a specific duration. On the contrary, both channels being in master mode and potentially calculating opposite torque request is very critical and it potentially leads to steering in the wrong direction and even hinders the driver to overrule the system.

4   Background

In this section we present some background, in particular we introduce transitions system, temporal logic, model checking, parameter synthesis, and minimal cut sets.

4.1   Symbolic Transition Systems

The system under analysis is a reactive system, whose behavior is characterized by a (possibly infinite) sequence of state changes triggered by events. In this paper, we adopt a standard symbolic representation of the system, where the system states are represented by a finite set V of variables and the state transitions by symbolic formulas that specify how the values of V change [12]. This is usually obtained by using a copy v' of each variable $v \in V$ to represent the next value of v after a transition. We denote by V' the set of next versions v' of the variables in V. We also use a finite set E of event variables to label the transitions and represent the events that triggered a state change. For simplicity, we assume that the variables have all a Boolean domain, but this can be easily lifted and the tool implementation of the approach considers also more complex and infinite-domain variables.

Formally, a Transition System (TS) is a tuple $S = \langle V, E, I, T \rangle$ where:

- V is a set of state variables;
- E is a set of event variables;
- I is a formula over V, representing the initial states;

– T is a formula over $V \cup E \cup V'$, representing the transitions.

A state of S is an assignment to the variables in V. Similarly, an event is an assignment to the variables in E. A trace of S is an infinite sequence $\sigma = s_0, e_0, s_1, e_1, \ldots$ of states and events such that $s_0 \models I$ and $s_i, e_i, s_{i+1} \models T$ for every $i \geq 0$.

4.2   LTL Model Checking

We use Linear-time Temporal Logic (LTL) [14] with future and past operators (see for example [11]) to represent sets of traces. Given a TS $S = \langle V, E, I, T \rangle$, the set of Linear Temporal Logic (LTL) formulas is inductively defined as

$$\varphi ::= p \mid \neg\varphi \mid \varphi \vee \varphi \mid \mathbf{X}\varphi \mid \varphi\,\mathbf{U}\,\varphi \mid \mathbf{Y}\varphi \mid \varphi\,\mathbf{S}\,\varphi$$

with $p \in V \cup E$. Here $\mathbf{X}$ stands for *next*, $\mathbf{U}$ for *until*, $\mathbf{Y}$ for *previous*, and $\mathbf{S}$ for *since*. Other logical constants and operators like $\top$, $\bot$, $\wedge$, $\rightarrow$ and $\leftrightarrow$ are used as syntactic sugar with the standard meaning. The following abbreviations for temporal operators are also used: $\mathbf{F}\,\varphi := \top\mathbf{U}\,\varphi$, $\mathbf{G}\,\varphi := \neg\mathbf{F}\,\neg\varphi$, $\mathbf{O}\,\varphi := \top\mathbf{S}\,\varphi$, $\mathbf{H}\,\varphi := \neg\mathbf{O}\,\neg\varphi$, $\mathbf{Z}\varphi := \neg\mathbf{Y}\neg\varphi$.

Given a trace $\sigma = s_0, e_0, s_1, e_1, \ldots$ of S and $i \geq 0$, we define the relation $\sigma, i \models \varphi$ as follows:

– if $\varphi = p \in V$, then $\sigma, i \models \varphi$ iff $s_i \models p$
– if $\varphi = p \in E$, then $\sigma, i \models \varphi$ iff $e_i \models p$
– if $\varphi = \neg\phi$, then $\sigma, i \models \varphi$ iff $\sigma, i \not\models \phi$
– if $\varphi = \phi \vee \psi$, then $\sigma, i \models \varphi$ iff $\sigma, i \models \phi$ or $\sigma, i \models \psi$
– if $\varphi = \mathbf{X}\phi$, then $\sigma, i \models \varphi$ iff $\sigma, i+1 \models \phi$
– if $\varphi = \phi\mathbf{U}\psi$, then $\sigma, i \models \varphi$ iff for some $j \geq i$, $\sigma, j \models \psi$ and for all $i \leq k < j$, $\sigma, k \models \phi$.
– if $\varphi = \mathbf{Y}\phi$, then $\sigma, i \models \varphi$ iff $i > 0$ and $\sigma, i - 1 \models \phi$
– if $\varphi = \phi\mathbf{S}\psi$, then $\sigma, i \models \varphi$ iff for some j, $0 \leq j \leq i$, $\sigma, j \models \psi$ and for all $j < k \leq i$, $\sigma, k \models \phi$.

The (universal) model checking problem is the problem to check if $\sigma, 0 \models \varphi$ holds for every trace σ of S (denoted by $S \models_\forall \varphi$ or simply $S \models \varphi$). The existential model checking problem is the dual problem of checking if $\sigma, 0 \models \varphi$ holds for some trace σ of S (denoted by $S \models_\exists \varphi$). Note that $S \models_\exists \phi$ iff $S \not\models \neg\phi$.

4.3   Parameter Synthesis

In parametric systems, formulas can include also *parameters*, which are rigid symbols whose value does not change along the execution of the system [6]. Let U be the set of parameters. A *parameter valuation* is an assignment to the parameters. Given a propositional or an LTL formula ϕ and a parameter valuation γ, we denote by $\gamma(\phi)$ the formula obtained from ϕ by replacing each parameter in U with the assignment given by γ.

A *parametric transition system* S is a tuple $S = \langle U, V, E, I, T \rangle$ where U is the set of parameters, V is the set of state variables, E is the set of event variables, $I(U, V)$ is the initial formula, and $T(U, V, E, V')$ is the transition formula. Each parameter valuation γ induces a transition system $S_\gamma = \langle V, E, \gamma(I), \gamma(T) \rangle$.

In the scope of this paper, we are interested in the parameter synthesis for LTL existential model checking, i.e., given an LTL formula φ over $U \cup V \cup E$, the problem of finding all parameter valuations γ such that $S_\gamma \models_\exists \gamma(\varphi)$. We denote by $\rho(U, S, \varphi)$ the set of all such parameter evaluations. This set can be computed effectively with a sequence of incremental model checking problems [6].

4.4   Minimal Cut Sets

Minimal Cut Sets (MCS) analysis produces all possible configurations of system faults (called *fault configurations*) that cause the reachability of an unwanted condition, called the Top Level Event (TLE). More formally, given a transition system $\langle V, E, I, T \rangle$ and a set of faults represented as event variables $\mathcal{F} \subseteq E$, we call *fault configuration* a subset $FC \subseteq \mathcal{F}$.

A *cut set* represents a fault configuration that may cause the top event. Formally, we generalize the definition in [4] as follows. Let $S = \langle V, E, I, T \rangle$ be a TS and let *TLE* be a propositional formula over V. We say that FC is a cut set of *TLE* in S, written $FC \in CS(S, TLE, \mathcal{F})$, iff there exists a trace σ of S such that:

1. $\sigma, j \models TLE$ for some $j \geq 0$;
2. $FC \subseteq \mathcal{F}$ and for all $f \in FC$ there exists i, $0 \leq i < j$ such that $\sigma, i \models f$.

Intuitively, a cut set corresponds to the set of faults that occur along a trace reaching the *TLE*. *Minimal cut sets* (MCSs), written $MCS(S, TLE, \mathcal{F})$, are those that are minimal in terms of faults: $MCS(S, TLE, \mathcal{F}) = \{cs \in CS(S, TLE, \mathcal{F}) \mid \forall cs' \in CS(S, TLE, \mathcal{F}) \ (cs' \subseteq cs \rightarrow cs' = cs)\}$. When S and $\mathcal{F}$ are clear from the context, we just use the notation $CS(TLE)$ and $MCS(TLE)$.

In practice, MCS are of interest since they represent the simpler (and more probable) explanations for a given TLE. The *monotonicity assumption* (i.e, if cs is a cut set, then any superset $cs' \supseteq cs$ is also a cut set) is commonly adopted, since most systems are monotonic and for non-monotonic systems, the assumption leads to a conservative (and accurate) over-approximation of the unreliability of the TLE. Non-monotonic analysis can be addressed by generalizing the concept of MCS to the one of *prime implicant* [7].

4.5   Computing MCSs Using Parameter Synthesis

Given a transition system $S = \langle V, E, I, T \rangle$ and a set of event variables $\mathcal{F} \subseteq E$, the region of cut sets can be computed via parameter synthesis [3]. Let us consider a parameter p_e for every event $e \in \mathcal{F}$ and the LTL formula $\Psi_{TLE} := (\bigwedge_{e \in \mathcal{F}} (e \rightarrow p_e))\mathbf{U} \ TLE$ (see also similar approach in [13]). Then the set of cut sets is given by $\rho(U, S, \Psi_{TLE})$.

The set of MCSs can be computed as the set of minimal such valuations, i.e. the set of valuations $\gamma \in \rho(U)$ such that for each $\gamma' \in \rho(U)$, $\gamma' \subseteq \gamma$ implies $\gamma' = \gamma$ (where we define $\gamma' \subseteq \gamma$ iff $\gamma'(u)$ implies $\gamma(u)$ for each $u \in U$). This can be computed with standard BDD-based operations.

5 Formal Problem and Solution

5.1 Formalization of Modes and Mode Transitions

An operational mode can be considered from the formal point of view as a macro state, i.e. a set of concrete states. For example, in the EPS case study described above, the *master-slave* mode, where the primary channel is in master mode and the backup channel is in slave mode, includes various states where the power may or may not be supplied to the channels, the data has been provided or not, the cores are processing the data, the comparator state represents the consistency of the cores' output, etc.

On this line, a mode transition is achieved with a sequence of state transitions. For example, in order to switch from *master-slave* to *master-passive*, the system performs different state transitions, where for example a core of the backup channel fails, the comparator silences the output torque, and the channel goes to passive mode.

Formally, we define a mode of a system $S = \langle V, E, I, T \rangle$ as a set of states of S. A mode can be therefore represented by a propositional formula over the state variables V. With abuse of notation, given a formula m over V, the mode m refers to the set of states satisfying m.

Given two modes m_1 and m_2, a mode transition from m_1 to m_2 is a sequence of $s_0, \ldots, s_n$ such that $n > 0$ and there exists a trace σ of S and $i \geq 0$ such that

- for k, $0 \leq k \leq n$, $\sigma_{i+k} = s_k$ (the sequence is part of the trace σ of S);
- for k, $0 \leq k < n$, $s_k \models m_1$ and $s_n \models m_2$ (the sequence leads from m_1 to m_2);
- $i = 0$ or $\sigma_{i-1} \models \neg m_1$ (the sequence is maximal as it is either the first mode transition of σ or is preceded by another mode transition leading to m_1).

5.2 Model Checking Mode Transitions

It is easy to prove that S has a mode transition from m_1 to m_2 (denoted by $S \models_\exists m_1 \Rightarrow m_2$) iff $S \models_\exists \mathbf{F}(m_1 \wedge \mathbf{X} m_2)$. In fact, one can see that the definition is one-to-one with the LTL formula $\mathbf{F}(\mathbf{Z} \neg m_1 \wedge m_1 \wedge \mathbf{X}(m_1 \mathbf{U} m_2))$. We proved also with a model checker that this formula is equivalent to $\mathbf{F}(\mathbf{Z} \neg m_1 \wedge m_1 \mathbf{U}(m_1 \wedge \mathbf{X} m_2))$ and to $\mathbf{F}(m_1 \wedge \mathbf{X} m_2)$.

We can also generate with parameter synthesis the set of events that occur in mode transitions between m_1 and m_2. Let us introduce a parameter p_e for every event $e \in E$ and define the formula ψ_E as $\psi_E := \bigwedge_{e \in E} e \rightarrow p_e$. Then, we build the LTL formula: $\mathbf{F}((\mathbf{Z} \neg m_1) \wedge ((m_1 \wedge \psi_E) \mathbf{U}(m_1 \wedge \psi_E \wedge \mathbf{X} m_2)))$.

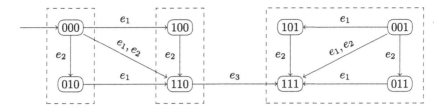

Fig. 2. States and transitions for the system in Example 1.

5.3   Discussion

The analysis discussed in the previous section is quite related to the problem of understanding which events cause a mode transition. A deeper look at the problem shows that it is not what we need.

Example 1. Consider for example the transition system shown in Fig. 2 formalized by $\langle \{b_1, b_2, b_3\}, \{e_1, e_2, e_3\}, \neg b_1 \wedge \neg b_2 \wedge \neg b_3, T_1 \rangle$, where T_1 is a disjunction of conjuctions representing the set of transitions (for example, the transition from state 000 to state 100 is represented by $\neg b_0 \wedge \neg b_1 \wedge \neg b_2 \wedge e_1 \wedge \neg e_2 \wedge \neg e_3 \wedge b_0' \wedge \neg b_1' \wedge \neg b_2'$). In the figure, the states are labeled by the value of the variables b_1, b_2, b_3. Thus for example, the state 001 assigns b_1 and b_2 to false and b_3 to true.

Suppose we are interested in the transitions from mode $m_1 = b_1 \wedge \neg b_3$ and $m_2 = b_3$, which correspond to the central and right dashed boxes respectively. The mode transitions are two: 110, 111 and 100, 110, 111. The events that occur in these transitions are e_3 and e_2, e_3. Thus, it seems that the cause of the mode transition is e_3 (since it labels the only incoming transition into m_2). However, also e_2 is necessary to reach m_2, but not necessarily to reach m_1: in some traces e_2 occurs before entering mode m_1. Hence this interpretation is not captured by the definition in Sect. 5.2.

5.4   Problem Definition

Intuitively, given a transition system $\langle V, E, I, T \rangle$ and two modes m_1 and m_2, we are interested in the sets of events in E that are necessary to go from m_1 to m_2. We call such set of events *Minimal Transition Cut Set* (MTCS) for $m_1 \Rightarrow m_2$ and we denote by $MTCS(m_1, m_2)$ the set of all MTCSs for $m_1 \Rightarrow m_2$. For simplicity, we assume that an event can occur only once. The framework can be extended to consider multiple occurrences of the same event. Note that: 1) a MTCS for $m_1 \Rightarrow m_2$ should not contain the events needed to reach m_1; 2) the event in a MTCS for $m_1 \Rightarrow m_2$ may occur even before m_1.

We formalize the definition of Transition Cut Sets (TCSs) and MTCSs as follows:

Definition 1. $F \in TCS(m_1, m_2)$ iff $F \subseteq E$ and there exist a trace σ and $i, j \in \mathbb{N}$ s.t.

1. $i < j$, $\sigma(j) \models m_2$, and $\sigma(k) \models m_1$ for all k, $i \leq k < j$ (i.e., it contains a mode transition from m_1 to m_2);
2. there exists $C \in MCS(m_1)$ such that $C \cap F = \emptyset$ and for each $e \in C$ there exists k, $0 \leq k < i$, such that $\sigma(k) \models e$ (i.e., F does not contain a MCS necessary to reach m_1);
3. for each $e \in E \setminus C$, if there exists k, $0 \leq k < j$, such that $\sigma(k) \models e$, then $e \in F$ (i.e., F contains all other events occurring until m_2).

The set $MTCS(m_1, m_2)$ is the set of cut sets in $TCS(m_1, m_2)$ that are minimal: $MTCS(m_1, m_2) := \{F \in TCS(m_1, m_2) \mid \forall F' \in TCS(m_1, m_2) \; (F' \subseteq F \rightarrow F' = F)\}$

5.5   Solution Based on Parameter Synthesis

In this section, we reduce the problem of finding $MTCS(m_1, m_2)$ to a parameter synthesis problem. We first compute $MCS(m_1)$. We introduce a parameter p_e for every event $e \in E$. Finally, we build the LTL formula:

$$\Psi(m_1, m_2) := \bigvee_{C \in MCS(m_1)} \mathbf{F}(m_1 \wedge \mathbf{Y} \bigwedge_{f \in C} \mathbf{O}f \wedge \mathbf{X}(m_1 \mathbf{U}(m_2 \wedge \mathbf{YH} \bigwedge_{e \notin C} e \rightarrow p_e)))$$

Theorem 1. Given a TS $S = \langle V, E, I, T \rangle$ and two modes m_1 and m_2,

$$TCS(m_1, m_2) = \{F \subseteq E \mid S \models_\exists \gamma_F(\Psi(m_1, m_2))\}$$

where γ_F is an assignment to parameters defined as follows: $\gamma_F(p_e) = \top$ iff $e \in F$.

Proof. Given $F \subseteq E$, we prove that $F \in TCS(m_1, m_2)$ iff $S \models_\exists \gamma_F(\Psi(m_1, m_2))$.

Note that, for any trace σ of S, $\sigma \models \gamma_F(\Psi(m_1, m_2))$ iff there exists $C \in MCS(m_1)$ and $\sigma \models \mathbf{F}(m_1 \wedge \mathbf{Y} \bigwedge_{f \in C} \mathbf{O}f \wedge \mathbf{X}(m_1 \mathbf{U}(m_2 \wedge \mathbf{YH} \bigwedge_{e \notin C} e \rightarrow \gamma_F(p_e))))$.

Thus, $\sigma \models \gamma_F(\Psi(m_1, m_2))$ iff there exists $C \in MCS(m_1)$, $i \geq 0$ such that $\sigma, i \models m_1$ and $\sigma, i \models \mathbf{Y} \bigwedge_{f \in C} \mathbf{O}f$, $\sigma, i+1 \models m_1 \mathbf{U}(m_2 \wedge \mathbf{YH} \bigwedge_{e \notin C} e \rightarrow \gamma_F(p_e))$.

Thus, $\sigma \models \gamma_F(\Psi(m_1, m_2))$ iff there exists $C \in MCS(m_1)$, $i, j \geq 0$ such that 1) $i < j$ and $\sigma, j \models m_1$ and for all k, $i \leq k < j$, $\sigma, i \models m_1$; 2) $\sigma, i \models \mathbf{Y} \bigwedge_{f \in C} \mathbf{O}f$, 3) $\sigma, j \mathbf{YH} \bigwedge_{e \notin C} e \rightarrow \gamma_F(p_e))$. These are the three conditions of Definition 1. In fact, 3) holds iff $\sigma, k \models e$ for some k, $0 \leq k < j$ implies $\gamma_F(p_e))$.

Once we obtain the set *tcs* of Transition Cut Sets, we can compute the minimal ones (*MTCS*) as described in Sect. 4.5.

6   Experimental Evaluation

6.1   Implementation

We have implemented the solution for computing $MTCS$ described in Sect. 5.5 as a command in the xSAP tool [2]. A model in xSAP is written in the SMV language; it can be manually specified or it can be the result of fault injection (the functionality to automatically extend a nominal model with the fault specification – see [2] for more details). Modes can be specified as Boolean expressions, or implicitly as a set of discrete domain state variables (in the latter case, modes correspond to all the possible evaluations of the given variables). The user can either choose to compute $MTCS$ for one pair of given modes m_1 and m_2 or for all pairs of distinct modes taken from a given set of modes.

For each event to be considered in the analysis, a corresponding parameter is created. For each mode m_1, $MCS(m_1)$ is computed using parameter synthesis and stored for the computation of $MTCS(m_1, m_2)$, for all target modes m_2. For each pair of modes $\langle m_1, m_2 \rangle$, the LTL formula $\Psi(m_1, m_2)$ described in Sect. 5.5 is constructed and used for the parameter synthesis. The output of the parameter synthesis problem is a region, i.e. a Boolean formula over the set of parameters. Each parameter is replaced by the corresponding event and the corresponding minimal models are computed and printed. The command provides an option to print all modes and transitions in dot format.

6.2   Application to the EPS Case Study

We modeled the EPS system informally described in Sect. 3 in SMV language[1]. We separately defined the nominal model and the xSAP fault extension instructions. Then, using fault injection, we created the extended (faulty) model, on which we ran the $MTCS$ computation routine. We created two variants of the EPS (nominal) models, a simple and a complex one. The simple model does not contain internal components of the channels. The behavior of the model is also simplified by ignoring the possibility of a channel reset. The complex model, on the other hand, also models cores, a comparator, a watchdog and the reset action of the channels. We first focus on the simple model to demonstrate the functionality of our approach. Then, we analyze its scalability using the complex model.

The simple model is composed of two channels pd and sd, the energy supply and vehicle bus for each channel $pdEnergy$, $sdEnergy$, $pdBus$, $sdBus$, and a redundant communication com. The modules representing these components interact as described in Sect. 3. In our analysis, we are interested in all events that can cause the system mode to change, namely the fault events described in Sect. 3 and the take-over of a channel in *slave* mode (i.e., when it fails to receive a torque request from the other channel and assumes that the other channel has failed). The list of all events for the simple model is shown in the middle column of Table 1.

---

[1] Available at https://es-static.fbk.eu/people/vvozarova/TransitionAnalysis/.

Table 1. The events of the EPS system.

	Simple model	Complex model
Energy supply faults	*pdEnergy.fault*	*pdEnergy.fault*
	sdEnergy.fault	*sdEnergy.fault*
Vehicle bus faults	*pdBus.fault*	*pdBus.fault*
	sdBus.fault	*sdBus.fault*
Communication faults	*com.request_ to_ pd_ fault*	*com.can.request_ to_ pd_ fault*
	com.request_ to_ sd_ fault	*com.can.request_ to_ sd_ fault*
		com.uart.request_ to_ pd_ fault
		com.uart.request_ to_ sd_ fault
Channel faults	*pd.fault*	*pd.core1.fault*
	sd.fault	*pd.core2.fault*
		pd.comparator.compare_ fault
		pd.comparator.forward_ fault
		sd.core1.fault
		sd.core2.fault
		sd.comparator.compare_ fault
		sd.comparator.forward_ fault
Channel take-over recovery	*pd.takes_ over*	*pd.takes_ over*
	sd.takes_ over	*sd.takes_ over*
Channel reset recovery		*pd.reset*
		sd.reset

We carried out the *MTCS* analysis on all system modes of the simple model. The modes, along with their criticality, are shown in Fig. 3. We ran the parameter synthesis routine for all pairs of distinct modes and obtained a set of minimal cut sets over the events. For illustration purposes, Fig. 4a shows a few selected transitions between modes *master-slave, slave-master, master-master* and *slave-slave*. The edge labels correspond to the sets of events found by our analysis for the respective transitions. The graph shows that *pdBus.fault* is necessary to reach *slave-master* mode. In case no other fault occurs, the *sd* channel takes over in the following cycle. If the communication link to the *sd* channel fails at the same time as *pdBus*, the system reaches *slave-master* mode in one cycle. If the communication fails, the *sd* channel wrongly assumes that *pd* has failed and goes to the critical *master-master* mode.

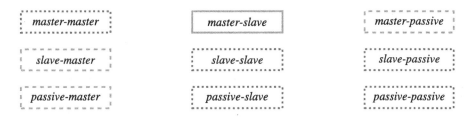

Fig. 3. Possible combinations of channel modes. The green mode (solid border) is a nominal functional mode. The orange modes (dashed) are modes with degraded nominal function, but acceptable for a specific duration. The red modes (dotted) are critical and can lead to erroneous behaviour. (Color figure online)

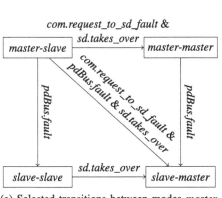

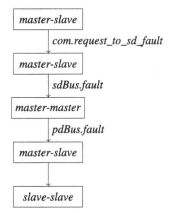

(a) Selected transitions between modes *master-slave*, *slave-master*, *master-master* and *slave-slave* with *MTCS* found by our procedure.

(b) Sequence of mode transitions, where in the last transition no fault occurs.

Fig. 4. Found *MTCS* (left) and occured events (right) in selected mode transitions.

Notice that if we used the formula presented in Sect. 5.2, that monitors only events that occur in m_1, different cut sets would be found. This is possible because some faults take one cycle to propagate. For example, there is a sequence of mode transitions containing transition from *master-slave* to *slave-slave* on which no fault occurs. The sequence is visualized in Fig. 4. The effect of each fault is visible in the next cycle. The communication fault causes *sd* to go to *master*. The *sd* vehicle bus fault causes *sd* to go back to slave, analogously *pd* vehicle bus fault causes *pd* to go to slave. As a result, only one minimal cut set for *master-slave* to *slave-slave* transition is found, and that is an empty set.

To test the scalability of our procedure, we created a more complex model with more detailed communication and channel. Specifically, we modeled the redundancy of the communication by introducing two submodules *com.can* and *com.uart* with the same functionality as the original module. The communication fails only if both submodules fail. The channel is extended by adding two core modules *core1* and *core2*, *comparator* and *watchdog*. The comparator ensures that if a core fails, the channel goes to *passive* mode. However, if the comparator is faulty, the channel can either wrongly stay in the nominal mode or go to *passive* even when both cores are working correctly. If the watchdog recognizes that either a core or the comparator is faulty, it resets the channel to its initial mode. The list of all events is given in the last column of Table 1. The communication faults are replaced by faults in *com.can* and *com.uart*, the channel faults are replaced by core and comparator faults, and we additionally monitor the reset event of the channel.

6.3   Scalability Results

We tested the implemented procedure for both simple and complex model. The simple model contains 10 events and 7 nominal modules (more modules are introduced after the fault extension). The complex model contains 20 events and 17 nominal modules. We ran the experiments on a machine with Intel(R) Core(TM) i5 CPU and 16 GB RAM. The results are in Table 2. The results show that the procedure is applicable for models with many events and complex behaviour. Table 3 shows numbers of found minimal cut sets and their cardinality for all mode transitions.

Table 2. Outcome of the *MTCS* analysis for both the simple and complex models. We report used memory and time, and the number of generated *MTCS* for all transitions between distinct modes (72 in total).

Simple model			Complex model		
Time (s)	Mem (MB)	MTCSs	Time (s)	Mem (MB)	MTCSs
56.56	392.1	63	621.84	1047.0	354

Table 3. Number of *MTCS* found for each transition from one mode (left) to another (top) for the EPS system. Cells with dash '–' are self loops on which the analysis was skipped. Cells with 'x' are transitions with no cut sets found (the transition is not feasible). The number of cut sets is followed by the cardinality of the sets in parentheses.

Simple model

	MM	MS	MP	SM	SS	SP	PM	PS	PP
MM	–	1(1)	2(1)	1(2)	2(2)	2(2)	2(1)	2(2)	4(2)
MS	1(2)	–	2(1)	1(3)	1(1)	2(2)	2(3)	2(1)	4(2)
MP	x	x	–	x	x	1(1)	x	x	2(1)
SM	x	x	x	–	1(1)	2(1)	2(1)	2(2)	4(2)
SS	x	x	x	1(1)	–	2(1)	2(2)	2(1)	4(2)
SP	x	x	x	x	x	–	x	x	2(1)
PM	x	x	x	x	x	x	–	1(1)	2(1)
PS	x	x	x	x	x	x	1(1)	–	2(1)
PP	x	x	x	x	x	x	x	x	–

Complex model

	MM	MS	MP	SM	SS	SP	PM	PS	PP
MM	–	1(1), 1(2), 2(3)	4(1)	1(0)	1(1), 1(2), 2(3)	4(1)	1(0)	1(1), 1(2), 2(3)	4(1)
MS	1(3), 4(4)	–	4(1)	2(4), 2(5)	1(1)	4(2)	5(4), 2(5)	4(1)	16(2)
MP	x	4(2)	–	x	4(3)	1(1)	x	16(3)	4(1)
SM	1(2), 2(3)	1(3), 3(4), 4(5), 4(6)	4(3), 8(4)	–	1(1), 1(2), 2(3)	4(1)	4(1)	4(2), 4(3), 8(4)	16(2)
SS	1(3), 2(4)	1(2), 2(3)	4(3), 8(4)	1(1)	–	4(1)	4(2)	4(1)	16(2)
SP	x	4(4), 8(5)	1(2), 2(3)	x	4(2)	–	x	16(3)	4(1)
PM	4(1)	4(2), 4(3), 8(4)	16(2)	x	x	x	–	1(1), 1(2), 2(3)	4(1)
PS	4(3)	4(2)	16(3)	x	x	x	1(1)	–	4(1)
PP	x	16(4)	4(2)	x	x	x	x	4(2)	–

7 Conclusions

In this paper, we extended model-based safety analysis techniques to consider the transition between operational modes in complex systems. We propose new techniques based on parameter synthesis and symbolic model checking. We evaluated the approach in an industrial automotive case study describing the architecture of an ECU implementing multiple safety mechanisms for functional safety.

The directions for future development are manifold: 1. to investigate optimization techniques to increase the scalability; 2. to extend the method to consider the negation of events (when an event must not occur in the mode transition, thus going beyond the monotonic case and MCS); 3. to extend the method to consider multiple occurences of an event; 4. to extend the method to consider more general notions of causality; 5. to investigate how ordering of events influences mode transitions; 6. to embed the techniques in system and safety engineering processes involving the design of fault detection and recovery components and the specification of safety contracts on components.

References

1. Abele, A.: Transformation of a state description into a qualitative fault tree. In: Praxisforum Fehlerbaumanalyse & Co. (2019)
2. Bittner, B., et al.: The xSAP safety analysis platform. In: Chechik, M., Raskin, J.-F. (eds.) TACAS 2016. LNCS, vol. 9636, pp. 533–539. Springer, Heidelberg (2016). https://doi.org/10.1007/978-3-662-49674-9_31
3. Bozzano, M., Cimatti, A., Griggio, A., Mattarei, C.: Efficient anytime techniques for model-based safety analysis. In: Kroening, D., Păsăreanu, C.S. (eds.) CAV 2015. LNCS, vol. 9206, pp. 603–621. Springer, Cham (2015). https://doi.org/10.1007/978-3-319-21690-4_41
4. Bozzano, M., Cimatti, A., Tapparo, F.: Symbolic fault tree analysis for reactive systems. In: Namjoshi, K.S., Yoneda, T., Higashino, T., Okamura, Y. (eds.) ATVA 2007. LNCS, vol. 4762, pp. 162–176. Springer, Heidelberg (2007). https://doi.org/10.1007/978-3-540-75596-8_13
5. Caltais, G., Leue, S., Mousavi, M.R.: (De-)Composing causality in labeled transition systems. In: Proceedings of the CREST Workshop (2016)
6. Cimatti, A., Griggio, A., Mover, S., Tonetta, S.: Parameter synthesis with IC3. In: Proceedings of FMCAD, pp. 165–168. IEEE (2013)
7. Coudert, O., Madre, J.C.: Implicit and incremental computation of primes and essential primes of boolean functions. In: Proceedings of the Design Automation Conference (DAC 1992), pp. 36–39. IEEE Computer Society Press (1992)
8. ECSEL-JU: Multi-Annual Strategic Plan (MASP), Private Members Board of the ECSEL Joint Undertaking - ECSEL GB 2019.134 (2020)
9. Halpern, J.: A modification of the Halpern-Pearl definition of causality. In: Proceedings of the IJCAI, pp. 3022–3033 (2015)
10. Kabir, S., et al.: A model-based extension to HiP-HOPS for dynamic fault propagation studies. In: Bozzano, M., Papadopoulos, Y. (eds.) IMBSA 2017. LNCS, vol. 10437, pp. 163–178. Springer, Cham (2017). https://doi.org/10.1007/978-3-319-64119-5_11
11. Manna, Z., Pnueli, A.: The Temporal Logic of Reactive and Concurrent Systems: Specification. Springer-Verlag, New York (1992). https://doi.org/10.1007/978-1-4612-0931-7
12. McMillan, K.L.: Symbolic Model Checking. Kluwer Academic, Dordrecht (1993)
13. Ortmeier, F., Reif, W., Schellhorn, G.: Deductive cause-consequence analysis (dcca). IFAC Proc. Vol. **38**(1), 62–67 (2005)
14. Pnueli, A.: The temporal logic of programs. In: Proceedings of the SFCS, pp. 46–57 (1977)

Efficient Translation of Safety LTL to DFA Using Symbolic Automata Learning and Inductive Inference

Georgios Giantamidis[1,2(✉)], Stylianos Basagiannis[1], and Stavros Tripakis[3]

[1] United Technologies Research Centre Ireland, Cork, Ireland
GiantaGE@utrc.utc.com
[2] Aalto University, Otaniemi, Finland
[3] Northeastern University, Boston, MA, USA

Abstract. Safety LTL properties are ubiquitous in the verification of safety critical systems. There is already evidence that translating safety properties into DFA rather than Büchi automata results in faster verification times. Conventional translation strategies can in some cases use unnecessarily large amounts of resources. We develop a symbolic adaptation of the L^* active learning algorithm tailored to efficiently translate safety LTL properties into symbolic DFA. We demonstrate how an inductive inference procedure can be used to provide additional input to the algorithm that greatly improves performance for certain important families of properties. For completeness, we also provide an outline and examples of how such a procedure can be implemented. Finally, we compare with state of the art LTL translators and provide experimental evidence where our approach significantly outperforms conventional translation strategies.

Keywords: Linear Temporal Logic · Safety properties · Automata learning · Symbolic automata · Inductive inference

1 Introduction and Motivation

Safety properties are pervasive in model based design. Informally, they capture the notion that 'nothing bad should ever happen', which, in turn, can be used to express a great variety of requirements of safety critical systems. A widespread formalism that can be used to describe safety properties is *Safety LTL* (Linear Temporal Logic) [28]. Safety LTL specifications can be used in a variety of ways in the model based design process: They can be used for formal verification of the system, for runtime monitoring during testing, for generating test-cases and, even before any system model is created, satisfiability tests can be performed on them to reveal potential inconsistencies in the original requirements.

This work was partially supported by the Irish Development Agency (IDA) for UTRC Ireland related to Network of Excellence in Aerospace Cyber Physical Systems.

© Springer Nature Switzerland AG 2020
A. Casimiro et al. (Eds.): SAFECOMP 2020, LNCS 12234, pp. 115–129, 2020.
https://doi.org/10.1007/978-3-030-54549-9_8

An important step in the procedures mentioned above is translation of LTL formulas into automata. In particular, it is possible to translate safety LTL formulas to Deterministic Finite Automata (DFA), which is generally desirable, as it has been shown to reduce verification times [26]. In an agile, continuous integration workflow where during prototyping every small change in the requirements triggers a cascade of testing and verification actions that must be performed as fast as possible to keep iteration times low, efficient translation of safety LTL properties into DFA is of paramount importance.

The problems of translating LTL to automata and specifically safety LTL to DFA have received a lot of attention over the years, and while the worst case theoretical complexity w.r.t number of states is exponential on the formula length for non-deterministic automata and doubly exponential on the formula length for deterministic automata, approaches that perform quite well in practice have been developed [3,8,15,19,21]. Such approaches are generally based on syntactic manipulation of the LTL formula and typically construct an automaton the states of which correspond to subformulas of the original formula, which can subsequently be determinized/minimized. One major drawback of these approaches is that this intermediate automaton can be considerably larger than the final result, which can lead to unnecessarily excessive resource consumption during translation. Another limitation is that, to the best of our knowledge, existing implementations of such approaches cannot take into account a priori knowledge about the target automaton that might be available.

In this work, we present a novel approach for safety LTL to symbolic DFA (SDFA) translation that overcomes both these limitations. Specifically:

- We develop a novel algorithm for syntactically safe LTL to SDFA translation.
- Our algorithm returns a minimal (w.r.t. number of states) SDFA and all intermediately constructed SDFA contain strictly fewer states than the result.
- Our algorithm can be extended to take into account a priori information about the target automaton, which results in significant performance boost.
- We provide an outline and examples of how an inductive inference procedure that provides said a priori information can be implemented.
- We provide a prototype implementation and experimental evidence that the proposed approach (i) behaves comparably with state of the art tools on randomly generated formulas and literature benchmarks and (ii) significantly outperforms the state of the art in certain important property families (even without a priori information about the target automaton).

In Sect. 2 we summarize related work on (safety) LTL to DFA translation and (symbolic) automata learning. In Sect. 3 we introduce the necessary preliminary concepts and algorithms. In Sect. 4 we describe the proposed algorithm and its properties. In Sect. 5 we present our experimental evaluation results. Finally, in Sect. 6 we conclude with some ideas for future work.

2   Related Work

The more general problem of translating LTL to Omega (e.g. Büchi, Rabin etc.) automata has been studied extensively before [3,8,15,19]. The state of the art here is Spot [3] and, more recently, Rabinizer [19]. The problem of translating safety LTL to DFA has also received a great amount of attention [16,20,21]. This is justified by the fact that using deterministic automata can improve verification times [26]. To the best of our knowledge [21] is the state of the art on translators specialized to turn safety LTL to DFA, hence we compare against it in our experimental evaluation. Spot and Rabinizer are also able to generate deterministic automata if requested, therefore we compare against them as well.

Automata learning and in general grammatical inference is a field that has received a lot of attention over the years [12]. Algorithms here generally fall into two categories, passive learning (learning from examples) and active learning (learning with queries). Symbolic automata learning is an area that recently received some attention [13,22]. Variations of this problem have been studied earlier as well [17]. Note that, while we do not claim to improve the state of the art in symbolic automata learning, our extension of L^* makes specific assumptions about the system to be learned, which enable a more efficient approach than using a generic learning algorithm.

3   Preliminaries

3.1   Linear Temporal Logic

Linear Temporal Logic (LTL) [24] is a widespread formalism used in model checking based formal verification. The typical automata theoretic model checking approach requires the negation of the LTL expressed property to first be transformed into an automaton on infinite words, for example a Büchi automaton. Then, this automaton is composed with an automaton representing the system, and the resulting product is checked for emptiness.

LTL properties can be classified into two broad categories: *safety* properties and *liveness* properties [4]. Informally, safety properties state that 'something bad never happens', while liveness properties state that 'something good eventually happens'.

Syntactic Safety Subset of LTL. Safety LTL properties can also be characterized syntactically. Any property built out of operators in the *syntactic safety subset* of LTL is guaranteed to be a safety property. Specifically, every propositional formula (i.e. a formula built of atomic propositions, $\neg$, $\wedge$ and $\vee$) is a syntactically safe formula, and if formulas f and g are syntactically safe, so are formulas $f \wedge g$, $f \vee g$, Gf, Xf, fWg, where G, X, and W are, respectively, the *globally*, *next* and *weak until* LTL operators. We omit the formal definition of the semantics of these operators and refer the reader to [28] which we follow in this work. Note that it is possible to express any safety LTL property by only using the syntactic safety subset of LTL.

Bad Prefixes. Every safety LTL formula ϕ can be translated into a DFA which accepts all *bad prefixes* of ϕ. A bad prefix of ϕ is a finite trace σ such that all infinite continuations of σ violate ϕ. Kupferman and Vardi [20] further classify safety LTL formulas as *intentionally safe, accidentally safe* and *pathologically safe* based on the *informativeness* of their bad prefixes. Intuitively, accidentally safe and pathologically safe formulas contain some redundancy; for example, $G(p \vee X(q \wedge \neg q))$ is accidentally safe, $G(p \vee F(q \wedge \neg q))$ is pathologically safe, and both are equivalent to Gp, which is intentionally safe. Since it is possible to write any safety LTL formula as an intentionally safe formula, we will only consider intentionally safe formulas here (however, note that our algorithm handles accidentally safe formulas as well, but not pathologically safe ones, since these do not belong in the syntactic safety subset of LTL).

3.2   Symbolic DFA and Symbolic Traces

In this work, we use the definition of symbolic automata from [11]. Symbolic DFA are able to encode the state machine described by a DFA in a more succinct way, by means of allowing predicates drawn from a boolean algebra to compactly represent transitions between states.

Figure 1 shows two monitors for the safety property $G(p \rightarrow Xq)$ expressed as both an SDFA and a DFA ($\top$ as a transition label stands for 'true'). Notice that while the number of states is the same in the two versions, the number of transitions can generally differ drastically. This is very important for the performance of the learning algorithm we employ, as reducing the number of transitions also reduces the amount of book-keeping needed.

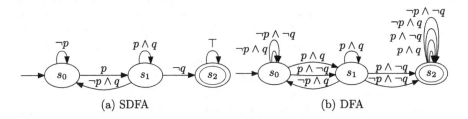

(a) SDFA   (b) DFA

Fig. 1. Monitors for $G(p \rightarrow Xq)$

Given a set of atomic propositions $\{p_1, p_2, \ldots, p_m\}$ we define a *finite symbolic trace* to be a finite sequence $a_1 \cdot a_2, \cdots, a_n$, where each a_i is either $\top$ or a conjunction of literals (a literal being an atomic proposition, p_i, potentially negated).

3.3   Active Automata Learning

Our approach is based on Angluin's L^* algorithm for active automata learning [6]. In this setting, a *learner* tries to identify an automaton by submitting queries to a *teacher*. These can be *membership queries*, where the learner submits a word and gets back an 'accept' or 'reject' answer, or *equivalence queries*, where a hypothesis automaton is submitted and either the process ends with success or a counterexample is generated which drives more queries.

There are four important data structures involved in a run of the L^* algorithm: A *RED* set of words that represent state candidates for the learned automaton, a *BLUE* set of words that correspond to 1-step successors of states in *RED*, a set of suffixes, *SFX* that are used to distinguish states in $RED \cup BLUE$ and the *observation table*, *OBS*, which stores information about words in *RED* and *BLUE* w.r.t. their behavior on the suffixes in *SFX*. The set $RED \cup BLUE$ is prefix closed and the set *SFX* is suffix closed. The rows of *OBS* are labeled by states in $RED \cup BLUE$ and its columns by elements of *SFX*. The entry of *OBS* at row $w \in RED \cup BLUE$ and column $s \in SFX$ represents the result of the membership query for the word $w \cdot s$, where dot denotes concatenation. In other words, if the target automaton accepts the word $w \cdot s$, then $OBS(w, s)$ is set to 1, otherwise it is set to 0. We say that $p, q \in RED \cup BLUE$ are *SFX*-equivalent if $\forall s \in SFX : OBS(p, s) = OBS(q, s)$. Otherwise, we say that p and q are *SFX*-distinct. We say that *OBS* is (i) *complete* if $\forall w \in RED \cup BLUE, \ s \in SFX : OBS(w, s)$ is set to either 1 or 0, (ii) *closed* if $\forall b \in BLUE \ \exists r \in RED : r, b$ are *SFX*-equivalent, and (iii) *consistent* when $\forall p, q \in RED$: if p, q are *SFX*-equivalent then their 1-step successors $p \cdot \alpha, q \cdot \alpha$ are also *SFX*-equivalent, for each letter α in the alphabet.

A brief description of the algorithm follows:

1. Initially, *RED* and *SFX* only contain the empty word, and *BLUE* contains the 1-letter successors of the empty word.
2. Membership queries are used to make *OBS* complete, closed and consistent, promoting states from *BLUE* to *RED* as needed (to enforce closedness), updating *BLUE* to include the 1-step successors of any new *RED* states, as well as potentially adding elements in *SFX* (to enforce consistency).
3. Once *OBS* is complete, closed and consistent, a hypothesis DFA is constructed.
4. An equivalence query is performed to check whether the hypothesis is correct.
5. (a) If the hypothesis is incorrect, we obtain a counterexample in the form of a word on which the hypothesis and the target behave differently. We add the counterexample and all its prefixes in *RED* and go to step 2.
   (b) Otherwise, we have found the target automaton and we are done.

The L^* algorithm is guaranteed to terminate and yield a minimal automaton after at most n equivalence queries and a number of membership queries bounded by a polynomial quadratic on n and linear on m, where n is the number of states of the learned machine and m the maximum length of any counterexample word returned by the teacher.

Several variants of the algorithm have been proposed over the years that improve on the original algorithm and extend it to other formalisms. In our implementation we use a variant where the counterexample and all of its suffixes are added in *SFX* instead of having *RED* updated as mentioned in step 5a above, as done in [27]. We chose to do so because this introduces a new important invariant: throughout the algorithm, all states in *RED* are pairwise *SFX*-distinct. In turn, this makes constructing the hypothesis DFA easier: we can simply collect all states in *RED* without worrying that one of them may be equivalent to another. Another nice property of this variant is that *OBS* is guaranteed to be consistent throughout the algorithm, which allows us to skip consistency checking and enforcement in step 2 above.

4 Proposed Approach

Problem Definition and Approach Overview. The problem we are solving can be formulated as follows: 'Given a syntactically safe LTL formula Φ, construct a minimal (w.r.t number of states) symbolic DFA that accepts all bad prefixes of Φ and nothing else'. Note that the returned DFA must accept the *bad* prefixes of Φ, i.e. all finite traces satisfying $\neg\Phi$. The proposed algorithm is a symbolic extension of Angluin's L^* tailored for LTL to SDFA translation. Membership queries are performed by recursive traversal of the LTL formula itself, as explained in Sect. 4.2 that follows. As for equivalence queries, we employ a symbolic model checker as explained in Sect. 4.3. Our method is *symbolic* in the sense that we use a symbolic alphabet (set of predicates) for the learned DFA and employ a lazy alphabet refinement strategy in which we begin with a single, all-encompassing predicate, $\top$, and gradually refine it as needed.

4.1 Safety LTL on Finite Symbolic Traces

In order to be able to perform membership queries, it is imperative that we define a semantics for syntactically safe LTL on finite symbolic traces that will allow us to identify bad prefixes. We introduce a four-value semantics where evaluating a formula on a symbolic trace can yield a value of *True*, *False*, *Unknown* or *Refine(proposition, index)*, the last one being parametrized by the proposition that needs refinement and the position in the symbolic trace this needs to happen.

Let $\sigma := a_1 \cdot a_2 \cdots a_n$ be a finite symbolic trace of length n and Φ a syntactically safe LTL formula. The function $\texttt{eval}(\Phi, \sigma, i)$, which returns the evaluation of Φ on the suffix of σ that begins with a_i is defined as follows:

```
eval(p,σ,i) :=
    if ¬p is a conjunct in a_i: return False     eval(⊤,σ,i) := return True
    if  p is a conjunct in a_i: return True      eval(⊥,σ,i) := return False
    return Refine(p,i)

eval(φ ∨ ψ,σ,i) :=
    let e_φ = eval(φ,σ,i), e_ψ = eval(ψ,σ,i)
    if either e_φ or e_ψ is True: return True
    if e_φ (resp. e_ψ) is False: return e_ψ (resp. e_φ)
    if e_φ (resp. e_ψ) is Unknown: return e_ψ (resp. e_φ)
    # now, both e_φ and e_ψ are refinement requests
    if e_φ.index > e_ψ.index: return e_φ
    return e_ψ
```

```
eval(φ ∧ ψ, σ, i) :=
  let eφ = eval(φ, σ, i),  eψ = eval(ψ, σ, i)
  if either eφ or eψ is False: return False
  if eφ (resp. eψ) is True: return eψ (resp. eφ)
  if eφ (resp. eψ) is Unknown: return eψ (resp. eφ)
  # now, both eφ and eψ are refinement requests
  if eφ.index > eψ.index: return eφ
  return eψ

eval(¬φ, σ, i) :=                         eval(Xφ, σ, i) :=
  let eφ = eval(φ, σ, i)                    if i ≥ n: return Unknown
  if eφ is True: return False               return eval(φ, σ, i + 1)
  if eφ is False: return True
  return eφ

eval(φWψ, σ, i) :=                        eval(Gφ, σ, i) :=
  return eval(ψ ∨ (φ ∧ X(φWψ)), σ, i)      return eval(φ ∧ XGφ, σ, i)
```

where p is an atomic proposition and ϕ, ψ are syntactically safe LTL formulas.

4.2   Membership Queries and Lazy Alphabet Refinement

Given the semantics defined in 4.1, we are now able to explain how membership queries work. Recall that when the L^* algorithm submits a membership query it receives an 'accept' or 'reject' answer. In our case, we want a membership query mem_q(Φ, σ) to return 'accept' iff the symbolic trace σ is a bad prefix for the formula Φ. Therefore, if the result of eval$(\Phi, \sigma, 1)$ is $False$, mem_q(Φ, σ) returns 1 (accept). If the result of eval$(\Phi, \sigma, 1)$ is $True$ or $Unknown$, mem_q(Φ, σ) returns 0 (reject). In the case eval$(\Phi, \sigma, 1)$ returns a refinement request, the symbolic trace will be duplicated with one copy now containing the positive literal and the other copy the negative literal of the proposition for which refinement was requested, and two separate membership queries will be issued subsequently.

During a run of the L^* algorithm, whenever a word is added to RED, its successors with all letters of the alphabet are added to $BLUE$ (this also happens during initialization). This means that if we have a formula containing 10 atomic propositions, every time a word is added to RED, $2^{10} = 1024$ words will be added to $BLUE$. However, there is a high chance (depending on the formula, of course) that many of these entries actually represent the same state, which implies that a lot of time can potentially be wasted on membership queries that provide essentially the same information. What we do to address this issue is add, instead, a single entry to $BLUE$ that symbolically represents all 1-step successors of the state added to RED. For example, if the word added to red is $p \cdot p \wedge q$, we add to $BLUE$ the word $p \cdot p \wedge q \cdot \top$. Whether the latter actually corresponds to different states will be revealed later, as membership queries are submitted. Suppose, for example, that the algorithm issues the query mem_q$(G(p \rightarrow Xq), p \cdot p \wedge q \cdot \top)$ or, equivalently, mem_q$(G(\neg p \vee Xq), p \cdot p \wedge q \cdot \top)$. Since p holds at step 2, but we do not know what happens to q at step 3, a refinement request for q at position 3 is issued. Then, the word will be split accordingly and the following two membership queries will be performed: mem_q$(G(\neg p \vee Xq), p \cdot p \wedge q \cdot q)$, mem_q$(G(\neg p \vee Xq), p \cdot p \wedge q \cdot \neg q)$, the former of which returns $Unknown$ and the latter *False*. And since we now know that $p \cdot p \wedge q \cdot \neg q$ is a bad prefix for the formula, the corresponding cell in *OBS* will be set to 1. Accordingly, the cell corresponding to $p \cdot p \wedge q \cdot q$ will be set to 0, which would also be the case for a result of value *True*.

The astute reader may wonder here why we need both values *True* and *Unknown* if the purpose of a membership query is to detect whether a word is a bad prefix or not. The answer has to do with the behavior of *True* and *Unknown* w.r.t. refinement requests: *True* and *False* have 'priority' over *Refine*, which in turn has 'priority' over *Unknown*, as can be seen in the definitions of `eval` for $\phi \vee \psi$ and $\phi \wedge \psi$ above. This ensures that on one hand we perform refinement when necessary, but on the other hand do not refine without a real need to do so. For the same reason, we heuristically perform first the refinement request that refers to the latest position in the trace.

4.3   Equivalence Queries

Equivalence queries are implemented by employing NuSMV [9], a symbolic model checker. Whenever an equivalence query needs to be issued, a hypothesis automaton is constructed, encoded in the language of NuSMV and then model checked against the following properties:

LTLSPEC $\Phi \leftrightarrow G$ *state* $\neq$ *accept*   LTLSPEC $\neg\Phi \leftrightarrow F \; G$ *state* $=$ *accept*

where Φ is the LTL formula we want to translate, *state* is a variable holding the current state of the encoded hypothesis automaton and *accept* is a value denoting its (unique) accepting state. Note that in order to perform the above checks, NuSMV does *not* internally translate the LTL formula into an automaton (which would defeat the purpose of the proposed algorithm). Rather, it translates the LTL formula into a CTL one with added fairness constraints and then applies a symbolic model checking algorithm [10,14,25].

Counterexample handling is a bit involved, since what NuSMV returns is a description of an infinite trace. What we do is we lazily enumerate all finite prefixes of this infinite counterexample in order of increasing length and pick the first one that reveals a problem in the hypothesis. We opted for choosing the shortest possible counterexample because small counterexample length means less subsequent membership queries, and while longer counterexamples might reveal more new states, this is not guaranteed.

Another interesting direction to explore here would be, instead of model checking against the formulas mentioned above, to simply obtain the symbolic tableau NuSMV internally builds for Φ and compare this with the hypothesis automaton to examine whether behavior appearing in the former is missing from the latter and vice versa. It is not immediately obvious how this comparison would be performed, as the two representations are quite different in nature; nevertheless, this is something worth exploring, as it could potentially increase the efficiency of equivalence queries.

4.4   Properties and Complexity

Minimality. The proposed algorithm (i) returns a minimal (w.r.t. number of states) SDFA and (ii) guarantees that all intermediate SDFA hypotheses contain strictly fewer states than the returned result. Both (i) and (ii) follow directly from the properties of the L^* algorithm: The initial hypothesis contains a single state, and the number of states of subsequent hypotheses is monotonically increasing until it reaches the value corresponding to the minimal automaton.

Membership Query Complexity. Based on the definitions for `eval` in 4.1, in order to compute `eval` on a node in the formula tree of the form $\phi \wedge \psi$, $\phi \vee \psi$, $\neg\phi$, $X\phi$, each of its children needs to be considered at most once. Similarly, in order to compute `eval` on a node of the form $G\phi$ or $\phi W \psi$, each of its children needs to be considered at most n times, where n is the trace length. It is easy to see that with arbitrary nesting of operators in the safety subset of LTL, each node in the tree of the formula will need to be examined at most n^{m+1} times, where m is the total number of G and W operators in the formula. Therefore, the complexity of a single membership query is polynomial on the trace length and exponential on the formula length.

Equivalence Query Complexity. A bound for performing an equivalence query can be given by a bound on translating the safety LTL formula into CTL with fairness constraints and a bound on symbolic model checking of the hypothesis automaton. As the hypothesis automaton can reach a number of states doubly exponential on the length of the safety LTL formula, and the model checking step is linear on the size of the automaton, the worst-case complexity of equivalence queries is at least doubly exponential on the length of the formula to be translated. This result motivated the search for a modified approach that eliminates equivalence queries altogether, which we present in the following.

4.5   A Priori Information and Inductive Inference

The observation that equivalence queries are needed in order to discover states of the target automaton raises an interesting question: What if we have some sort of state information beforehand? This could be the actual states represented as words or something else like distinguishing suffixes collectively allowing to differentiate all states of the target automaton. The former would not be enough; if we simply put these words in *RED* we would violate an important invariant of the algorithm: Since *SFX* would only contain the empty word, potentially many of the words in *RED* would be *SFX*-equivalent. Therefore, distinguishing suffixes would need to also be put in *SFX*. As it turns out, the latter alone is enough, since, as long as the required distinguishing suffixes are present, all states of the target automaton will be discovered and put in *RED* in the process of filling the observation table, updating *BLUE* and promoting states from *BLUE* to *RED* as needed, without the need for any equivalence queries.

In the rest of this section we discuss how we could obtain such information for two counter property families (parametrized properties that express some sort of counting by means of repetition/nesting of X operators) taken from aerospace domain use-cases, shown in Table 1.

Table 1. Counter family formulas

N	Counter family A	Counter family B
1	$G(\neg p \vee X(\neg p \vee \neg q \vee r \vee Xr))$	$G(\neg p \vee X(\neg q \vee r))$
2	$G(\neg p \vee X(\neg p \vee X(\neg p \vee \neg q \vee r \vee Xr)))$	$G(\neg p \vee X(\neg q \vee (r \wedge Xr)))$
3	$G(\neg p \vee X(\neg p \vee X(\neg p \vee X(\neg p \vee \neg q \vee r \vee Xr))))$	$G(\neg p \vee X(\neg q \vee (r \wedge X(r \wedge Xr))))$

Suppose that we need to translate a formula of one of the families above for $N = 50$. What we could do is first translate formulas corresponding to small values of N, which would be fast since the formula size is small, then obtain the corresponding distinguishing suffixes (this can be easily done with breadth-first search), and finally employ an inductive inference procedure to identify a relation between N and the set of distinguishing suffixes, which, in turn, can be used to derive the required information for $N = 50$. Providing such an inductive inference procedure and formally analyzing its properties is outside the scope of this paper. However, for completeness, we outline a simple approach, generic enough to work on the property families listed above:

1. Identify base cases to be excluded from the following steps.
2. Identify how many suffixes are introduced from SDFA(N − 1) to SDFA(N)
3. For each newly introduced suffix in SDFA(N), identify a function to construct it from suffixes in SDFA(N − 1).

We first show example runs of the procedure outlined above on the two property families and then will explain how each individual step can be implemented in a general way. The relation between N and sets of distinguishing suffixes is shown in Table 2.

Table 2. Counter family formula suffixes

N	Suffixes for counter family A	Suffixes for counter family B
1	$\{a, \ ba\}$	$\{a\}$
2	$\{a, \ ba, \ cba\}$	$\{a, \ b, \ ca\}$
3	$\{a, \ ba, \ cba, \ ccba\}$	$\{a, \ b, \ ca, \ da, \ cca\}$
4	$\{a, \ ba, \ cba, \ ccba, \ cccba\}$	$\{a, \ b, \ ca, \ da, \ cca, \ dca, \ ccca\}$
5	$\{a, \ ba, \ cba, \ ccba, \ cccba, \ ccccba\}$	$\{a, \ b, \ ca, \ da, \ cca, \ dca, \ ccca, \ dcca, \ cccca\}$

where, for family A, we have $a := \neg p \wedge q \wedge \neg r$, $b := p \wedge q \wedge \neg r$ and $c := p \wedge q \wedge r$. We treat N = 1 as the base case, observe that when moving from N − 1 to N one new suffix is added, and notice that this suffix can be constructed by prepending c to the longest suffix from step N − 1. For family B, we have $a := p \wedge q \wedge \neg r$, $b := p \wedge \neg q \wedge \neg r$, $c := \neg p \wedge q \wedge r$ and $d := \neg p \wedge \neg q \wedge r$. In this case, we treat N = 1 and N = 2 as base cases, and observe that two new suffixes are added when moving from N − 1 to N, which can be generated by taking the longest suffix from step N − 1 and (i) replacing the front letter with d for one, and (ii) prepending the letter c for the other.

Generalizing the above approach, step 1 (identifying base cases) can be performed by always treating N = 1 as a base case and then adding those cases the suffixes of which contain less distinct letters than the following cases, while steps 2 and 3 can easily be formulated as *Syntax Guided Synthesis* [5] problems and solved as such.

5 Experimental Evaluation

We implemented a prototype version of the proposed algorithm (we refer to this as 'Proposed' throughout this Section) in the programming language D [1] and compared against scheck v1.2 [21], Spot v2.6.1 [3] and Rabinizer v4 [19][1] on (i) 500 randomly generated syntactically safe LTL formulas, (ii) 54 formulas from the Spot benchmarks [2], as well as (iii) the 2 counter formula families from Sect. 4.5 and their conjunction. The 500 random formulas were generated using the Spot command line tools, and specifically the command:

```
randltl -n -1 4 --tree-size=10..30 -r | \
ltlfilt --lbt --syntactic-safety --size=10..25 -u -n 500
```

In short, the above means that we want 500 unique syntactic safety formulas with up to 4 atomic propositions, of length between 10 and 25. The 54 Spot benchmark formulas were taken from [2] and were the result of filtering the 184 formulas in that page for syntactic safety. The 2 counter formula families come from industrial (United Technologies Research Centre) requirements for aerospace domain digital hardware verification[2]. All experiments were run on an Ubuntu 14.04 laptop with a 1.6 GHz Intel Celeron processor and 4 GB of RAM. The results are summarized in Table 3 and Figs. 2 and 3 (memory consumption generally closely follows running time in all cases).

As can be seen in Table 3, the proposed approach behaves comparably to others on small formulas. We argue that there is potential for improvement here by addressing some implementation details: In our prototype implementation, communication with NuSMV involves a lot of process and file I/O, which can

---

[1] To be fair to Rabinizer, since it is implemented in Java, we deducted 0.4 seconds (the measured JVM startup time) from the elapsed time in all experiments with it.
[2] Note that formulas of this kind with many (typically > 50) nested next operators, expressing timing requirements for FPGAs, appear very frequently in this domain.

Table 3. Execution times (in seconds) for 500 random and 54 Spot formulas

Algorithm	500 random formulas		54 Spot formulas	
	Average	Median	Average	Median
Proposed	0.0693	0.0457	0.1262	0.0545
Spot	0.0397	0.0373	0.0406	0.0401
scheck	0.0082	0.0065	0.0161	0.0072
Rabinizer	1.4821	1.3668	1.8128	1.6885

cause considerable overhead (this is especially true for the latter, since hard disk access is orders of magnitude slower than RAM access). In addition to that, the current implementation of equivalence queries does not take advantage of the fact that parts of past SDFA hypotheses exist in future ones – an incremental model checking approach would be of great benefit here. This last issue, in particular, is responsible for some spikes in running time that drive the average away from the median in our case. Regarding the size of the corresponding minimal automata, the average and median number of states are 5.4 and 5 in the random formulas case, and 4.1 and 4 for the Spot formulas. Note that, in all cases, all tools except Rabinizer return a minimal automaton.

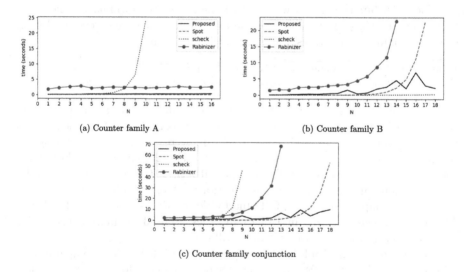

(a) Counter family A

(b) Counter family B

(c) Counter family conjunction

Fig. 2. Results on counter formulas

Where our learning approach shines is in translating the longer counter formulas (Fig. 2). It performs better asymptotically, as the number of next operators increases. Even if the automata grow linearly in size with the number of X operators ($N + 3$ states for counter family A and $2N + 1$ states for counter

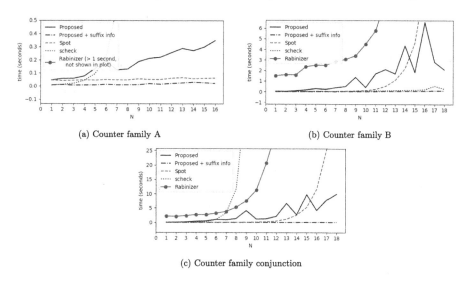

(a) Counter family A   (b) Counter family B

(c) Counter family conjunction

Fig. 3. Effect of suffix information on counter formulas

family B and their conjunction), scheck, Spot and Rabinizer require exponential time in at least one of the property families and in their conjunction, while our approach requires only linear time in all cases. This is a direct manifestation of the main drawback of conventional translation approaches; we remind here that our approach provides theoretical guarantees that this intermediate result explosion does not happen. Also note that for counter family B as well as for the conjunction of counter family formulas Rabinizer does not return minimal automata (it returns automata that grow exponentially in size with N).

Taking into account a priori information about the target automaton gives a significant additional boost to the proposed approach, as shown in Fig. 3. Note that, while not very clear in the figures, the proposed approach using suffix information performs better than all other tools on both counter formulas (and their conjunction) for all values of N. These graphs also provide an idea of the overhead introduced by the current implementation of equivalence queries due to the non-incremental model checking approach in NuSMV as well as communication delays (process and file I/O).

6   Conclusion and Future Work

In this work we presented a learning-based approach for translating safety LTL to DFA. We studied its theoretical properties and demonstrated its performance in practice. The proposed approach is comparable with existing ones in formulas of small size. Moreover, by guaranteeing that intermediate results do not explode in size, it outperforms existing approaches in long instances of important property families, by orders of magnitude. In addition, unlike existing approaches, it can take into account a priori information about the target automaton, which leads to even better performance.

We believe that the proposed approach nicely complements existing LTL translators in the sense that, performance-wise, a hybrid approach where (i) existing translators are used for small formulas and for inductive inference of the suffix information, and (ii) the proposed approach with the previously derived suffix information is used for longer formulas, would behave best.

In the future, we plan to improve our learning-based approach by employing more L^* optimizations (e.g. parallel membership queries, TTT algorithm [18]), and by using an incremental model checking approach for equivalence queries. We also plan to extend this work to translate general (not just safety) LTL properties to Büchi automata as well [7,23].

References

1. D programming language. https://dlang.org/
2. Spot 1.0 benchmarks. https://www.lrde.epita.fr/~adl/ijccbs/
3. Duret-Lutz, A., Lewkowicz, A., Fauchille, A., Michaud, T., Renault, É., Xu, L.: Spot 2.0—a framework for LTL and ω-automata manipulation. In: Artho, C., Legay, A., Peled, D. (eds.) ATVA 2016. LNCS, vol. 9938, pp. 122–129. Springer, Cham (2016). https://doi.org/10.1007/978-3-319-46520-3_8
4. Alpern, B., Schneider, F.B.: Recognizing safety and liveness. Distrib. Comput. **2**(3), 117–126 (1987)
5. Alur, R., et al.: Syntax-guided synthesis. In: 2013 Formal Methods in Computer-Aided Design, pp. 1–8, October 2013
6. Angluin, D.: Learning regular sets from queries and counterexamples. Inf. Comput. **75**(2), 87–106 (1987)
7. Angluin, D., Fisman, D.: Learning regular omega languages. In: Auer, P., Clark, A., Zeugmann, T., Zilles, S. (eds.) ALT 2014. LNCS (LNAI), vol. 8776, pp. 125–139. Springer, Cham (2014). https://doi.org/10.1007/978-3-319-11662-4_10
8. Babiak, T., Kretínský, M., Rehák, V., Strejcek, J.: LTL to Büchi automata translation: fast and more deterministic. CoRR, abs/1201.0682 (2012)
9. Cimatti, A., et al.: NuSMV 2: an opensource tool for symbolic model checking. In: Brinksma, E., Larsen, K.G. (eds.) CAV 2002. LNCS, vol. 2404, pp. 359–364. Springer, Heidelberg (2002). https://doi.org/10.1007/3-540-45657-0_29
10. Clarke, E.M., Grumberg, O., Hamaguchi, K.: Another look at LTL model checking. Formal Methods Syst. Des. **10**(1), 47–71 (1997)
11. D'Antoni, L., Veanes, M.: The power of symbolic automata and transducers. In: CAV (2017)
12. de la Higuera, C.: Grammatical Inference: Learning Automata and Grammars. Cambridge University Press, New York (2010)
13. Drews, S., D'Antoni, L.: Learning symbolic automata. In: TACAS (2017)
14. Emerson, E.A., Lei, C.-L.: Efficient model checking in fragments of the propositional Mu-Calculus (Extended Abstract). In: LICS (1986)
15. Gastin, P., Oddoux, D.: Fast LTL to Büchi automata translation. In: Berry, G., Comon, H., Finkel, A. (eds.) CAV 2001. LNCS, vol. 2102, pp. 53–65. Springer, Heidelberg (2001). https://doi.org/10.1007/3-540-44585-4_6

16. Geilen, M.: On the construction of monitors for temporal logic properties. Electron. Notes Theoret. Comput. Sci. **55**(2), 181–199 (2001). RV 2001, Runtime Verification (in connection with CAV 2001)
17. Howar, F., Steffen, B., Merten, M.: Automata learning with automated alphabet abstraction refinement. In: Jhala, R., Schmidt, D. (eds.) VMCAI 2011. LNCS, vol. 6538, pp. 263–277. Springer, Heidelberg (2011). https://doi.org/10.1007/978-3-642-18275-4_19
18. Isberner, M., Howar, F., Steffen, B.: The TTT algorithm: a redundancy-free approach to active automata learning. In: Bonakdarpour, B., Smolka, S.A. (eds.) RV 2014. LNCS, vol. 8734, pp. 307–322. Springer, Cham (2014). https://doi.org/10.1007/978-3-319-11164-3_26
19. Křetínský, J., Meggendorfer, T., Sickert, S., Ziegler, C.: Rabinizer 4: from LTL to your favourite deterministic automaton. In: Chockler, H., Weissenbacher, G. (eds.) CAV 2018. LNCS, vol. 10981, pp. 567–577. Springer, Cham (2018). https://doi.org/10.1007/978-3-319-96145-3_30
20. Kupferman, O., Vardi, M.Y.: Model checking of safety properties. Formal Methods Syst. Des. **19**(3), 291–314 (2001)
21. Latvala, T.: Efficient model checking of safety properties. In: Ball, T., Rajamani, S.K. (eds.) SPIN 2003. LNCS, vol. 2648, pp. 74–88. Springer, Heidelberg (2003). https://doi.org/10.1007/3-540-44829-2_5
22. Maler, O., Mens, I.-E.: Learning regular languages over large alphabets. In: Ábrahám, E., Havelund, K. (eds.) TACAS 2014. LNCS, vol. 8413, pp. 485–499. Springer, Heidelberg (2014). https://doi.org/10.1007/978-3-642-54862-8_41
23. Maler, O., Pnueli, A.: On the learnability of infinitary regular sets. In: Proceedings of the Fourth Annual Workshop on Computational Learning Theory, COLT 1991, San Francisco, CA, USA, pp. 128–138. Morgan Kaufmann Publishers Inc. (1991)
24. Manna, Z., Pnueli, A.: The Temporal Logic of Reactive and Concurrent Systems: Specification. Springer, New York (1991). https://doi.org/10.1007/978-1-4612-0931-7
25. Rozier, K.Y.: Survey: linear temporal logic symbolic model checking. Comput. Sci. Rev. **5**(2), 163–203 (2011)
26. Sebastiani, R., Tonetta, S.: "More deterministic" vs. "Smaller" Buchi automata for efficient LTL model checking. In: Geist, D., Tronci, E. (eds.) CHARME 2003. LNCS, vol. 2860, pp. 126–140. Springer, Heidelberg (2003). https://doi.org/10.1007/978-3-540-39724-3_12
27. Shahbaz, M., Groz, R.: Inferring mealy machines. In: Cavalcanti, A., Dams, D.R. (eds.) FM 2009. LNCS, vol. 5850, pp. 207–222. Springer, Heidelberg (2009). https://doi.org/10.1007/978-3-642-05089-3_14
28. Sistla, A.P.: Safety, liveness and fairness in temporal logic. Formal Aspects Comput. **6**(5), 495–511 (1994)

Security Modelling and Methods

Automated Attacker Synthesis
for Distributed Protocols

Max von Hippel$^{(\boxtimes)}$, Cole Vick, Stavros Tripakis$^{(\boxtimes)}$,
and Cristina Nita-Rotaru$^{(\boxtimes)}$

Northeastern University, Boston, MA 02118, USA
{vonhippel.m,stavros,c.nitarotaru}@northeastern.edu
vick.c@husky.neu.edu

Abstract. Distributed protocols should be robust to both benign malfunction (e.g. packet loss or delay) and attacks (e.g. message replay). In this paper we take a formal approach to the automated synthesis of attackers, i.e. adversarial processes that can cause the protocol to malfunction. Specifically, given a formal *threat model* capturing the distributed protocol model and network topology, as well as the placement, goals, and interface of potential attackers, we automatically synthesize an attacker. We formalize four attacker synthesis problems - across attackers that always succeed versus those that sometimes fail, and attackers that may attack forever versus those that may not - and we propose algorithmic solutions to two of them. We report on a prototype implementation called KORG and its application to TCP as a case-study. Our experiments show that KORG can automatically generate well-known attacks for TCP within seconds or minutes.

Keywords: Synthesis · Security · Distributed protocols

1 Introduction

Distributed protocols represent the fundamental communication backbone for all services over the Internet. Ensuring the correctness and security of these protocols is critical for the services built on top of them [9]. Prior literature proposed different approaches to correctness assurance, e.g. testing [12,26], or structural reasoning [11]. Many such approaches rely on manual analysis or are ad-hoc in nature.

In this paper, we take a systematic approach to the problem of security of distributed protocols, by using formal methods and synthesis [10]. Our focus is the automated generation of *attacks*. But what exactly is an attack? The notion of an attack is often implicit in the formal verification of security properties: it is a counterexample violating some security specification. We build on this idea. We provide a formal definition of *threat models* capturing the distributed protocol model and network topology, as well as the placement, goals, and capabilities of potential *attackers*. Intuitively, an attacker is a process that, when composed with the system, results a protocol property violation.

A. Casimiro et al. (Eds.): SAFECOMP 2020, LNCS 12234, pp. 133–149, 2020.
https://doi.org/10.1007/978-3-030-54549-9_9

By formally defining attackers as processes, our approach has several benefits: first, we can ensure that these processes are *executable*, meaning attackers are programs that reproduce attacks. This is in contrast to other approaches that generate a *trace* exemplifying an attack, but not a program producing the attack, e.g. [5,39]. Second, an explicit formal attacker definition allows us to distinguish different types of attackers, depending on: what exactly does it mean to violate a property (in some cases? in all cases?); how the attacker can behave, etc. We distinguish between ∃-attackers (that sometimes succeed in violating the security property) and ∀-attackers (that always succeed); and between attackers *with recovery* (that eventually revert to normal system behavior) and attackers without (that may attack forever). We make four primary contributions.

- We propose a novel formalization of threat models and attackers, where the threat models algebraically capture not only the attackers but also the attacker goals, the environmental and victim processes, and the network topology.
- We formalize four attacker synthesis problems – ∃ASP, R-∃ASP, ∀ASP, R-∀ASP – one for each of the four combinations of types of attackers.
- We propose solutions for ∃ASP and R-∃ASP via reduction to model-checking. The key idea of our approach is to replace the vulnerable processes - the victim(s) - by appropriate "gadgets", then ask a model-checker whether the resulting system violates a certain property.
- We implement our solutions in a prototype open-source tool called KORG, and apply KORG to TCP connection establishment and tear-down routines. Our experiments show KORG is able to automatically synthesize realistic, well-known attacks against TCP within seconds or minutes.

The rest of the paper is organized as follows. We present background material in Sect. 2. We define attacker synthesis problems in Sect. 3 and present solutions in Sect. 4. We describe the TCP case study in Sect. 5, present related work in Sect. 6, and conclude in Sect. 7.

2   Formal Model Preliminaries

We model distributed protocols as interacting processes, in the spirit of [1]. We next define formally these processes and their composition. We use 2^X to denote the power-set of X, and ω-exponentiation to denote infinite repetition, e.g., $a^\omega = aaa\cdots$.

2.1   Processes

Definition 1 (Process). *A* process *is a tuple* $P = \langle AP, I, O, S, s_0, T, L \rangle$ *with set of* atomic propositions *AP, set of* inputs *I, set of* outputs *O, set of* states *S, initial state $s_0 \in S$, transition relation $T \subseteq S \times (I \cup O) \times S$, and (total) labeling function $L : S \to 2^{AP}$, such that: $AP, I, O,$ and S are finite; and $I \cap O = \emptyset$.*

Let $P = \langle \mathrm{AP}, I, O, S, s_0, T, L \rangle$ be a process. For each state $s \in S$, $L(s)$ is a subset of AP containing the atomic propositions that are true at state s. Consider a transition (s, x, s') starting at state s and ending at state s' with label x. If the label x is an input, then the transition is called an *input transition* and denoted $s \xrightarrow{x?} s'$. Otherwise, x is an output, and the transition is called an *output transition* and denoted $s \xrightarrow{x!} s'$. A transition (s, x, s') is called *outgoing* from state s and *incoming* to state s'.

A state $s \in S$ is called a *deadlock* iff it has no outgoing transitions. The state s is called *input-enabled* iff, for all inputs $x \in I$, there exists some state $s' \in S$ such that there exists a transition $(s, x, s') \in T$. We call s an *input state* (or *output* sate) if all its outgoing transitions are input transitions (or output transitions, respectively).

A process P is *deterministic* iff all of the following hold: (i) its transition relation T can be expressed as a function $S \times (I \cup O) \to S$; (ii) every non-deadlock state in S is either an input state or an output state, but not both; (iii) input states are input-enabled; and (iv) each output state has only one outgoing transition. Determinism guarantees that: each state is a deadlock, an input state, or an output state; when a process outputs, its output is uniquely determined by its state; and when a process inputs, the input and state uniquely determine where the process transitions.

A *run* of a process P is an infinite sequence $r = \big((s_i, x_i, s_{i+1})\big)_{i=0}^{\infty} \subseteq T^{\omega}$ of consecutive transitions. We use runs(P) to denote all the runs of P. A run over states $s_0, s_1, \ldots$ induces a sequence of labels $L(s_0), L(s_1), \ldots$ called a *computation*.

2.2 Composition

The composition of two processes P_1 and P_2 is another process denoted $P_1 \parallel P_2$, capturing both the individual behaviors of P_1 and P_2 as well as their interactions with one another. We define the asynchronous parallel composition operator $\parallel$ with rendezvous communication as in [1].

Definition 2 (Process Composition). *Let $P_i = \langle AP_i, I_i, O_i, S_i, s_0^i, T_i, L_i \rangle$ be processes, for $i = 1, 2$. For the composition of P_1 and P_2 (denoted $P_1 \parallel P_2$) to be well-defined, the processes must have no common outputs, and no common atomic propositions. Then $P_1 \parallel P_2$ is defined below:*

$$P_1 \parallel P_2 = \langle AP_1 \cup AP_2, (I_1 \cup I_2) \setminus (O_1 \cup O_2), O_1 \cup O_2, S_1 \times S_2, (s_0^1, s_0^2), T, L \rangle \quad (1)$$

where the transition relation T is precisely the set of transitions $(s_1, s_2) \xrightarrow{x} (s_1', s_2')$ such that, for $i = 1, 2$, if the label $x \in I_i \cup O_i$ is a label of P_i, then $s_i \xrightarrow{x} s_i' \in T_i$, else $s_i = s_i'$. $L : S_1 \times S_2 \to 2^{AP_1 \cup AP_2}$ is the function defined as $L(s_1, s_2) = L_1(s_1) \cup L_2(s_2)$.

The labeling function L is total as L_1 and L_2 are total. Since we required the processes P_1, P_2 to have disjoint sets of atomic propositions, L does not change the logic of the two processes under composition. Note that the composition of two processes is a process. Additionally, $\parallel$ is commutative and associative [1].

2.3   LTL

LTL [28] is a linear temporal logic for reasoning about computations. In this work, we use LTL to formulate properties of processes. The syntax of LTL is defined by the following grammar: $\phi ::= p \mid q \mid ... \mid \phi_1 \wedge \phi_2 \mid \neg\phi_1 \mid \mathbf{X}\phi_1 \mid \phi_1\mathbf{U}\phi_2$, where the $p \mid q \mid ...$ are any atomic propositions $\in$ AP, and ϕ_1, ϕ_2 can be any LTL formulae.

Let σ be a computation. If σ satisfies an LTL formula ϕ we write $\sigma \models \phi$. If $\neg(\sigma \models \phi)$, then we write $\sigma \not\models \phi$. The satisfaction relation for LTL is formally defined as follows: $\sigma \models p$ if p is true in $\sigma(0)$; $\sigma \models \mathbf{X}p$ if p is true in $\sigma(1)$; $\sigma \models \mathbf{F}p$ if there exists some $K \geq 0$ such that p is true in $\sigma(K)$; $\sigma \models \mathbf{G}p$ if for all $K \geq 0$, p is true in $\sigma(K)$; $\sigma \models p\mathbf{U}q$ if there exists some $K \geq 0$ such that for all $k_1 < K \leq k_2$, p is true in $\sigma(k_1)$ and q is true in $\sigma(q_2)$; and $\sigma \models \phi_1 \wedge \phi_2$ if $\sigma \models \phi_1$ and $\sigma \models \phi_2$.

An LTL formula ϕ is called a *safety property* iff it can be violated by a finite prefix of a computation, or a *liveness property* iff it can only be violated by an infinite computation [2]. For a process P and LTL formula ϕ, we write $P \models \phi$ iff, for every computation σ of P, $\sigma \models \phi$. For convenience, we naturally elevate our notation for satisfaction on computations to satisfaction on runs.

3   Attacker Synthesis Problems

We want to synthesize attackers automatically. Intuitively, an attacker is a process that, when composed with the system, violates some property. There are different types of attackers, depending on what it means to violate a property (in some cases? in all cases?), as well as on the system topology (threat model). Next, we define the threat model and attacker concepts formally, followed by the problems considered in this paper.

3.1   Threat Models

A *threat model* or *attacker model* prosaically captures the goals and capabilities of an attacker with respect to some victim and environment. Our threat model captures: how many attacker components there are; how they communicate with each other and with the rest of the system; and the attacker goals.

Definition 3 (Input-Output Interface). *An* input-output interface *is a tuple* (I,O) *such that* $I \cap O = \emptyset$ *and* $I \cup O \neq \emptyset$. *The* class *of an input-output interface* (I,O), *denoted* $\mathcal{C}(I,O)$, *is the set of processes with inputs* I *and outputs* O. *Likewise,* $\mathcal{C}(P)$ *denotes the input-output interface the process* P *belongs to (e.g. Fig. 2).*

Definition 4 (Threat Model). *A threat model is a tuple* $(P, (Q_i)_{i=0}^m, \phi)$ *where* $P, Q_0, ..., Q_m$ *are processes, each process* Q_i *has no atomic propositions (i.e., its set of atomic propositions is empty), and* ϕ *is an LTL formula such that* $P \parallel Q_0 \parallel ... \parallel Q_m \models \phi$. *We also require that the system* $P \parallel Q_0 \parallel ... \parallel Q_m$ *satisfies the formula* ϕ *in a non-trivial manner, that is, that* $P \parallel Q_0 \parallel ... \parallel Q_m$ *has at least one infinite run.*

In a threat model, the process P is called the *target process*, and the processes Q_i are called *vulnerable processes*. The goal of the adversary is to modify the vulnerable processes Q_i so that composition with the target process violates ϕ. (We assume that prior to the attack, the protocol behaves correctly, i.e., it satisfies ϕ.) See Fig. 1.

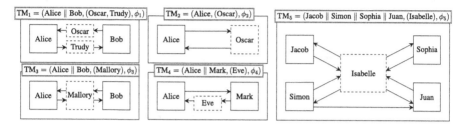

Fig. 1. Example Threat Models. The properties ϕ_i are not shown. Solid and dashed boxes are processes; we only assume the adversary can exploit the processes in the dashed boxes. TM_1 describes a distributed on-path attacker scenario, TM_2 describes an off-path attacker, TM_3 is a classical man-in-the-middle scenario, and TM_4 describes a one-directional man-in-the middle, or, depending on the problem formulation, an eavesdropper. TM_5 is a threat model with a distributed victim where the attacker cannot affect or read messages from Simon to Juan. Note that a directed edge in a network topology from Node 1 to Node 2 is logically equivalent to the statement that a portion of the outputs of Node 1 are also inputs to Node 2. In cases where the same packet might be sent to multiple recipients, the sender and recipient can be encoded in a message subscript. Therefore, the entire network topology is *implicit* in the interfaces of the processes in the threat model according to the composition definition.

3.2   Attackers

Definition 5 (Attacker). *Let* $\mathrm{TM} = (P, (Q_i)_{i=0}^{m}, \phi)$ *be a threat model. Then* $\boldsymbol{A} = (A_i)_{i=0}^{m}$ *is called a* TM-attacker *if* $P \parallel A_0 \parallel ... \parallel A_m \not\models \phi$, *and, for all* $0 \leq i \leq m$: A_i *is a deterministic process;* A_i *has no atomic propositions, and* $A_i \in \mathcal{C}(Q_i)$.

The existence of a $(P, (Q_i)_{i=0}^{m}, \phi)$-attacker means that if an adversary can exploit all the Q_i, then the adversary can attack P with respect to ϕ. Note that an attacker $\boldsymbol{A}$ cannot succeed by blocking the system from having any runs at all. Indeed, $P \parallel A_0 \parallel ... \parallel A_m \not\models \phi$ implies that $P \parallel A_0 \parallel ... \parallel A_m$ has at least one infinite run violating ϕ.

Real-world computer programs implemented in languages like C or JAVA are called *concrete*, while logical models of those programs implemented as algebraic transition systems such as processes are called *abstract*. The motivation for synthesizing abstract attackers is ultimately to recover exploitation strategies that actually work against concrete protocols. So, we should be able to translate an abstract attacker (Fig. 2) into a concrete one (Fig. 8). Determinism guarantees that we can do this. We also require the attacker and the vulnerable processes to have no atomic propositions, so the attacker cannot "cheat" by directly changing the truth-hood of the property it aims to violate.

For a given threat model many attackers may exist. We want to differentiate attacks that are more effective from attacks that are less effective. One straightforward comparison is to partition attackers into those that always violate ϕ, and those that only sometimes violate ϕ. We formalize this notion with $\exists$-attackers and $\forall$-attackers.

Definition 6 ($\exists$-Attacker vs $\forall$-Attacker). *Let A be a $(P, (Q_i)_{i=0}^m, \phi)$-attacker. Then A is a $\forall$-attacker if $P \parallel A_0 \parallel ... \parallel A_m \models \neg\phi$. Otherwise, A is an $\exists$-attacker.*

A $\forall$-attacker A always succeeds, because $P \parallel A \models \neg\phi$ means that *every* behavior of $P \parallel A$ satisfies $\neg\phi$, that is, *every* behavior of $P \parallel A$ violates ϕ. Since $P \parallel A \not\models \phi$, there must exist a computation σ of $P \parallel A$ such that $\sigma \models \neg\phi$, so, a $\forall$-attacker cannot succeed by blocking. An $\exists$-attacker is any attacker that is not a $\forall$-attacker, and every attacker succeeds in at least one computation, so an $\exists$-attacker sometimes succeeds, and sometimes does not. In most real-world systems, infinite attacks are impossible, implausible, or just uninteresting. To avoid such attacks, we define an attacker that produces finite-length sequences of adversarial behavior, and then "recovers", meaning that it behaves like the vulnerable process it replaced (see Fig. 3).

Definition 7 (Attacker with Recovery). *Let A be a $(P, (Q_i)_{i=0}^m, \phi)$-attacker. If, for each $0 \leq i \leq m$, the attacker component A_i consists of a finite directed acyclic graph (DAG) ending in the initial state of the vulnerable process Q_i, followed by all of the vulnerable process Q_i, then we say the attacker A is an attacker with recovery. We refer to the Q_i postfix of each A_i as its recovery.*

Note that researchers sometimes use "recovery" to mean when a system undoes the damage caused by an attack. We use the word differently, to mean when the property ϕ remains violated even under *modus operandi* subsequent to attack termination.

3.3   Attacker Synthesis Problems

Each type of attacker - $\exists$ versus $\forall$, with recovery versus without - naturally induces a synthesis problem.

Problem 1 ($\exists$-Attacker Synthesis Problem ($\exists$ASP)). Given a threat model TM, find a TM-attacker, if one exists; otherwise state that none exists.

Problem 2 (Recovery $\exists$-Attacker Synthesis Problem (R-$\exists$ASP)). Given a threat model TM, find a TM-attacker with recovery, if one exists; otherwise state that none exists.

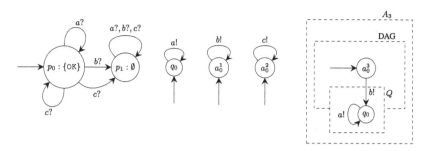

Fig. 2. From left to right: processes P, Q, A_1, A_2, A_3. Let $\phi = \mathbf{G}\,\mathtt{OK}$, and let the interface of Q be $\mathcal{C}(Q) = (\emptyset, \{a, b, c\})$. Then $P \parallel Q \models \phi$. A_1 and A_2 are both deterministic and have no input states. Let $\mathcal{C}(A_1) = \mathcal{C}(A_2) = \mathcal{C}(Q)$. Then, A_1 and A_2 are both $(P, (Q), \phi)$-attackers. A_1 is a $\forall$-attacker, and A_2 is an $\exists$-attacker. A_3 is a $\forall$-attacker with recovery consisting of a DAG starting at a_0^3 and ending at the initial state q_0 of Q, plus all of Q, namely the recovery.

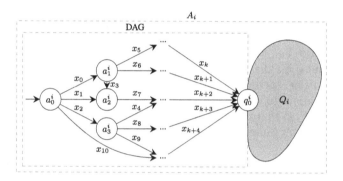

Fig. 3. Suppose $\boldsymbol{A} = (A_i)_{i=0}^m$ is an attacker with recovery for $\mathrm{TM} = (P, (A_i)_{i=0}^m, \phi)$. Further suppose A_i has initial state a_0^i, and Q_i has initial state q_0^i. Then A_i should consist of a DAG starting at a_0^i and ending at q_0^i, plus all of Q_i, called the *recovery*, indicated by the shaded blob. Note that if some Q_i is non-deterministic, then there can be no attacker with recovery, because Q_i is a subprocess of A_i, and all the A_is must be deterministic in order for $\boldsymbol{A}$ to be an attacker.

We defined $\exists$ and $\forall$-attackers to be disjoint, but, if the goal is to find an $\exists$-attacker, then surely a $\forall$-attacker is acceptable too; we therefore did not restrict the $\exists$-problems to only $\exists$-attackers. Next we define the two $\forall$-problems, which remain for future work.

Problem 3 ($\forall$-Attacker Synthesis Problem ($\forall$ASP)). Given a threat model TM, find a TM-$\forall$-attacker, if one exists; otherwise state that none exists.

Problem 4 (Recovery $\forall$-Attacker Synthesis Problem (R-$\forall$ASP)). Given a threat model TM, find a TM-$\forall$-attacker with recovery, if one exists; otherwise state that none exists.

4 Solutions

We present solutions ∃ASP and R-∃ASP for any number of attackers, and for both safety and liveness properties. Our success criteria are soundness and completeness. Both solutions are polynomial in the product of the size of P and the sizes of the interfaces of the Q_is, and exponential in the size of the property ϕ [35]. For real-world performance, see Sect. 5.

We reduce ∃ASP and R-∃ASP to model-checking. The idea is to replace the vulnerable processes Q_i with appropriate "gadgets", then ask a model-checker whether the system violates a certain property. We prove that existence of a violation (a counterexample) is equivalent to existence of an attacker, and we show how to transform the counterexample into an attacker. The gadgets and the LTL formula are different, depending on whether we seek attackers without or with recovery.

4.1 Gadgetry

A computation σ is a *lasso* if it equals a finite word α, then infinite repetition of a finite word β, i.e., $\sigma = \alpha \cdot \beta^\omega$. A prefix α of a computation σ is called a *bad prefix* for P and ϕ if P has ≥ 1 runs inducing computations starting with α, and every computation starting with α violates ϕ. We naturally elevate the terms *lasso* and *bad prefix* to runs and their prefixes. We assume a *model checker*: a procedure $\mathrm{MC}(P, \phi)$ that takes as input a process P and property ϕ, and returns $\emptyset$ if $P \models \phi$, or one or more violating lasso runs or bad prefixes of runs for P and ϕ, otherwise [2].

Attackers cannot have atomic propositions. So, the only way for A to *attack* TM is by sending and receiving messages, hence the space of attacks is within the space of labeled transition sequences. The *Daisy Process* nondeterministically exhausts the space of input and output events of a vulnerable process.

Definition 8 (Daisy Process). *Let $Q = \langle \emptyset, I, O, S, s_0, T, L \rangle$ be a process with no atomic propositions. Then the* daisy *of Q, denoted $\mathrm{DAISY}(Q)$, is the process defined below, where $L' : \{d_0\} \to \{\emptyset\}$ is the map such that $L'(d_0) = \emptyset$.*

$$\mathrm{DAISY}(Q) = \langle \emptyset, I, O, \{d_0\}, d_0, \{(d_0, w, d_0) \mid w \in I \cup O\}, L' \rangle \qquad (2)$$

Next, we define a *Daisy with Recovery*. This gadget is an *abstract process*, i.e., a generalized process with a non-empty set of initial states $S_0 \subseteq S$. Composition and LTL semantics for abstract processes are naturally defined. We implicitly transform processes to abstract processes by wrapping the initial state in a set.

Definition 9 (Daisy with Recovery). *Given a process $Q_i = \langle \emptyset, I, O, S, s_0, T, L \rangle$, the* daisy with recovery *of Q_i, denoted $\mathrm{RDAISY}(Q_i)$, is the abstract process $\mathrm{RDAISY}(Q_i) = \langle AP, I, O, S', S_0, T', L' \rangle$, with atomic propositions $AP = \{recover_i\}$, states $S' = S \cup \{d_0\}$, initial states $S_0 = \{s_0, d_0\}$, transitions $T' = T \cup \{(d_0, x, w_0) \mid x \in I \cup O, w_0 \in S_0\}$, and labeling function $L' : S' \to 2^{AP}$ that takes s_0 to $\{recover_i\}$ and other states to $\emptyset$. (We reserve the symbols* *recover$_0$,...* *for use in daisies with recovery, so they cannot be sub-formulae of the property in any threat model.)*

4.2   Solution to ∃ASP

Let TM $= (P, (Q_i)_{i=0}^m, \phi)$ be a threat model. Our goal is to find an attacker for TM, if one exists, or state that none exists, otherwise. First, we check whether the system $P \parallel \text{DAISY}(Q_0) \parallel ... \parallel \text{DAISY}(Q_m)$ satisfies ϕ. If it does, then no attacker exists, as the daisy processes encompass any possible attacker behavior. Define a set R returned by the model-checker MC:

$$R = \text{MC}(P \parallel \text{DAISY}(Q_0) \parallel ... \parallel \text{DAISY}(Q_m), \phi) \tag{3}$$

If $R = \emptyset$ then no attacker exists. On the other hand, if the system violates ϕ, then we can transform a violating run into a set of attacker processes by projecting it onto the corresponding interfaces. Choose a violating run or bad prefix $r \in R$ arbitrarily. Either $r = \alpha$ is some finite bad prefix, or $r = \alpha \cdot \beta^\omega$ is a violating lasso. For each $0 \le i \le m$, let α_i be the projection of α onto the process $\text{DAISY}(Q_i)$. That is, let $\alpha_i = []$; then for each (s, x, s') in α, if x is an input or an output of Q_i, and q, q' are the states $\text{DAISY}(Q_i)$ embodies in s, s', add (q, x, q') to α_i. For each α_i, create an incomplete process A_i^α with a new state s_{j+1}^α and transition $s_j^\alpha \xrightarrow{z} s_{j+1}^\alpha$ for each $\alpha_i[j] = (d_0^i, z, d_0^i)$ for $0 \le j < |\alpha_i|$. If $r = \alpha \cdot \beta^\omega$ is a lasso, then for each $0 \le i \le m$, define A_i^β from β_i in the same way that we defined A_i^α from α_i; let A_i' be the result of merging the first and last states of A_i^β with the last state of A_i^α. Otherwise, if $r = \alpha$ is a bad prefix, let A_i' be the result of adding an input self-loop to the last state of A_i^α, or an output self-loop if Q_i has no inputs. Either way, A_i' is an incomplete attacker. Finally let A_i be the result of making every input state in A_i' input-enabled via self-loops, and return the attacker $A = (A_i)_{i=0}^m$. An illustration of the method is given in Fig. 4.

Theorem 1 (∃ASP Solution is Sound and Complete). *Let* TM $= (P, (Q_i)_{i=0}^m, \phi)$ *be a threat model, and define R as in Eq. 3. Then the following hold. 1) $R \ne \emptyset$ iff a TM-attacker exists. 2) If $R \ne \emptyset$, then the procedure above eventually returns a TM-attacker.*

4.3   Solution to R-∃ASP

Let TM $= (P, (Q_i)_{i=0}^m, \phi)$ be a threat model as before. Now our goal is to find a TM-attacker *with recovery*, if one exists, or state that none exists, otherwise. The idea to solve this problem is similar to the idea for finding attackers without recovery, with two differences. First, the daisy processes are now more complicated, and include recovery to the original Q_i processes. Second, the formula used in model-checking is not ϕ, but a more complex formula ψ to ensure that the attacker eventually recovers, i.e., all the attacker components eventually

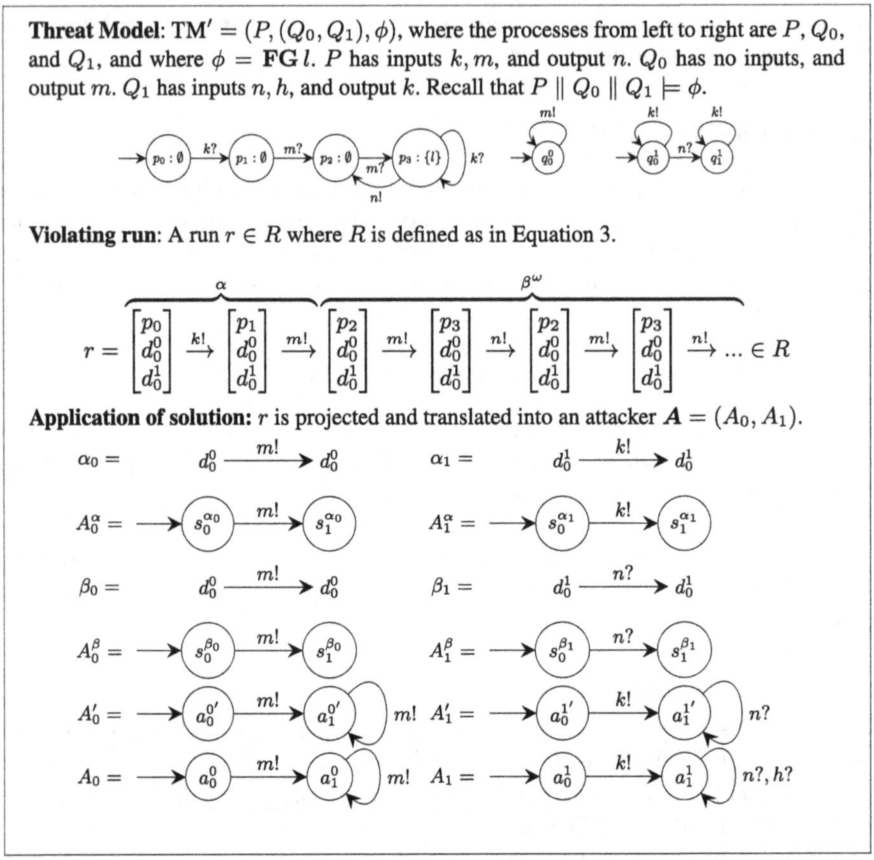

Threat Model: $\text{TM}' = (P, (Q_0, Q_1), \phi)$, where the processes from left to right are P, Q_0, and Q_1, and where $\phi = \mathbf{FG}\, l$. P has inputs k, m, and output n. Q_0 has no inputs, and output m. Q_1 has inputs n, h, and output k. Recall that $P \parallel Q_0 \parallel Q_1 \models \phi$.

Violating run: A run $r \in R$ where R is defined as in Equation 3.

$$r = \overbrace{\begin{bmatrix} p_0 \\ d_0^0 \\ d_0^1 \end{bmatrix} \xrightarrow{k!} \begin{bmatrix} p_1 \\ d_0^0 \\ d_0^1 \end{bmatrix}}^{\alpha} \xrightarrow{m!} \overbrace{\begin{bmatrix} p_2 \\ d_0^0 \\ d_0^1 \end{bmatrix} \xrightarrow{m!} \begin{bmatrix} p_3 \\ d_0^0 \\ d_0^1 \end{bmatrix} \xrightarrow{n!} \begin{bmatrix} p_2 \\ d_0^0 \\ d_0^1 \end{bmatrix} \xrightarrow{m!} \begin{bmatrix} p_3 \\ d_0^0 \\ d_0^1 \end{bmatrix} \xrightarrow{n!} \dots}^{\beta^\omega} \in R$$

Application of solution: r is projected and translated into an attacker $A = (A_0, A_1)$.

Fig. 4. Example threat model TM' on top, followed by a violating run in R, followed by translation of the run into attacker.

recover. We define the property ψ so that in prose it says "if all daisies eventually recover, then ϕ holds". We then define R like before, except we replace daisies with daisies with recovery, and ϕ with ψ, as defined below.

$$\psi = \Big(\bigwedge_{0 \leq i \leq m} \mathbf{F}\, \text{recover}_i \Big) \implies \phi \tag{4}$$

$$R = \text{MC}(P \parallel \text{RDAISY}(Q_0) \parallel \dots \parallel \text{RDAISY}(Q_m), \psi) \tag{5}$$

If $R = \emptyset$ then no attacker with recovery exists. If any Q_i is not deterministic, then likewise no attacker with recovery exists, because our attacker definition requires the attacker to be deterministic, but if Q_i is not and $Q_i \subseteq A_i$ then neither is A_i.

Otherwise, choose a violating run (or bad prefix) $r \in R$ arbitrarily. We proceed as we did for $\exists$ASP but with three key differences. First, we define α_i

by projecting α onto RDAISY(Q_i) as opposed to DAISY(Q_i). Second, for each $0 \leq i \leq m$, instead of using A_i^β if r is a lasso, or adding self-loops to the final state if r is a bad prefix, we simply glue A_i^α to Q_i by setting the last state of A_i^α to be the initial state of Q_i. (The result of gluing is a process; the initial state of A_i^α is its only initial state.) Third, instead of using self-loops to input-enable input states, we use input transitions to the initial state of Q_i. This ensures the pre-recovery portion is a DAG. Then we return $\boldsymbol{A} = (A_i)_{i=0}^m$.

Theorem 2 (R-∃ASP Solution is Sound and Complete). *Let* TM $=$ $(P, (Q_i)_{i=0}^m, \phi)$ *be a threat model, and define R as in Eq. 5. Assume all the $Q_i s$ are deterministic. Then the following hold. 1) $R \neq \emptyset$ iff a TM-attacker with recovery exists. 2) If $R \neq \emptyset$, then the procedure described above eventually returns a TM-attacker with recovery.*

5   Case Study: TCP

Implementation. We implemented our solutions in an open-source tool called KORG. We say an attacker $\boldsymbol{A}$ for a threat model TM $= (P, (Q_i)_{i=0}^m, \phi)$ is a *centralized attacker* if $m = 0$, or a *distributed attacker*, otherwise. In other words, a centralized attacker has only one attacker component $\boldsymbol{A} = (A)$, whereas a distributed attacker has many attacker components $\boldsymbol{A} = (A_i)_{i=0}^m$. KORG handles ∃ASP and R-∃ASP for liveness and safety properties for a centralized attacker. KORG is implemented in PYTHON 3 and uses the model-checker SPIN [15] as its underlying verification engine.

TCP is a fundamental Internet protocol consisting of three stages: connection establishment, data transfer, and connection tear-down. We focus on the first and third stages, which jointly we call the connection routine. Our approach and model (see Fig. 5, 6) are inspired by SNAKE [19]. Run-times and results are listed in Table 1.

Fig. 5. TCP threat model block diagram. Each box is a process. An arrow from process P_1 to process P_2 denotes that a subset of the outputs of P_2 are exclusively inputs of P_1. PEERs 1 and 2 are TCP peers. A *channel* is a directed FIFO queue of size one with the ability to detect fullness. A full channel may be overwritten. 1TON, NTo1, 2TON, and NTo2 are channels. Implicitly, channels relabel: for instance, 1TON relabels outputs from PEER 1 to become inputs of NETWORK; NETWORK transfers messages between peers via channels, and is the vulnerable process.

Threat Models. Rather than communicating directly with the NETWORK, the peers communicate with the channels, and the channels communicate with the NETWORK, allowing us to model the fact that packets are not instantaneously transferred in the wild. We use the shorthand CHAN!MSG to denote the event where MSG is sent over a channel CHAN; it is contextually clear who sent or received the message. We abstract the lower network stack layer TCP relies on with NETWORK, which passes messages between 1TON ‖ 2TON and NTO1 ‖ NTO2. We model the peers symmetrically.

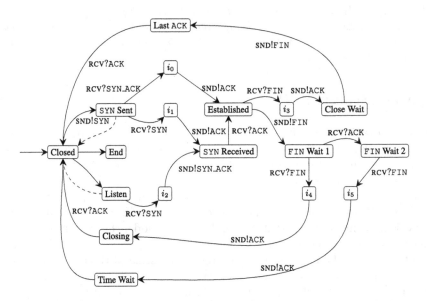

Fig. 6. A TCP peer. For $i = 1, 2$, if this is PEER i, then SND $:= i$TON and RCV $:=$ NTOi. All the states except $i_0, ..., i_5$, and End are from the finite state machine in the TCP RFC [29]. The RFC diagram omits the implicit states $i_0, ..., i_5$, instead combining send and receive events on individual transitions. In the RFC, Closed is called a "fictional state", where no TCP exists. We add a state End to capture the difference between a machine that elects not to instantiate a peer and a machine that is turned off. We label each state s with a single atomic proposition s_i. Dashed transitions are *timeout transitions*, meaning they are taken when the rest of the system deadlocks.

Given a property ϕ about TCP, we can formulate a threat model TM as follows, where we assume the adversary can exploit the lower layers of a network and ask if the adversary can induce TCP to violate ϕ:

$$\text{TM} = (\text{PEER 1} \parallel \text{PEER 2} \parallel \text{1TON} \parallel \text{2TON} \parallel \text{NTO1} \parallel \text{NTO2}, (\text{NETWORK}), \phi)$$
$$(6)$$

We consider the properties ϕ_1, ϕ_2, ϕ_3, giving rise to the threat models $\text{TM}_1, \text{TM}_2, \text{TM}_3$.

TM$_1$: No Half-Closed Connection Establishment. The safety property ϕ_1 says that if PEER 1 is in Closed state, then PEER 2 cannot be in Established state.

$$\phi_1 = \mathbf{G}(\text{Closed}_1 \implies \neg\text{Established}_2) \tag{7}$$

KORG discovers an attacker that spoofs the active participant in an active-passive connection establishment (see message sequence chart in Fig. 7), as described in [13].

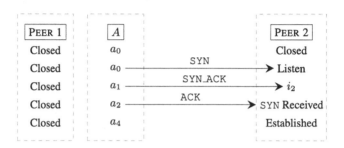

Fig. 7. Time progresses from top to bottom. Labeled arrows denote message exchanges over implicit channels. The property is violated in the final row; after this recovery may begin.

TM$_2$: Passive-Active Connection Establishment Eventually Succeeds. The liveness property ϕ_2 says that if it is infinitely often true that PEER 1 is in Listen state while PEER 2 is in SYN Sent state, then it must eventually be true that PEER 1 is in Established state.

$$\phi_2 = (\mathbf{GF}(\text{Listen}_1 \wedge \text{SYN Sent}_2)) \implies \mathbf{F}\,\text{Established}_1 \tag{8}$$

KORG discovers an attack where a SYN packet from PEER 2 is dropped. The corresponding attacker code is given in the PROMELA language of SPIN in Fig. 8.

```
Nto1 ! ACK; Nto2 ! ACK; 2toN ? SYN; /* ... recovery ... */
```

Fig. 8. Body of PROMELA process for a TM$_2$-attacker with recovery generated by KORG. PEER 2 transitions from Closed state to SYN Sent state and sends SYN to PEER 1. The attacker drops this packet so that it never reaches PEER 1. PEER 1 then transitions back and forth forever between Closed and Listen states, and the property is violated. Because SPIN attempts to find counterexamples as quickly as possible, the counterexamples it produces are not in general minimal.

TM$_3$: Peers Do Not Get Stuck. The safety property ϕ_3 says that the two peers will never simultaneously deadlock outside their End states. Let S_i denote the set of states in Fig. 6 for PEER i, and $S_i' = S_i \setminus \{\text{End}\}$.

$$\phi_3 = \bigwedge_{s_1 \in S_1'} \bigwedge_{s_2 \in S_2'} \neg\mathbf{FG}(s_1 \wedge s_2) \tag{9}$$

For the problem with recovery, KORG discovers an attacker that selectively drops the ACK sent by PEER 1 as it transitions from i_0 to Established state in an active/passive connection establishment routine, leaving PEER 2 stranded in SYN Received state, leading to a violation of ϕ_3. Similar bugs exist in real-world implementations, e.g. [31].

Performance. Performance results for Case Study are given in Table 1. Our success criteria was to produce realistic attackers faster than an expert human could with pen-and-paper. We discovered attackers in seconds or minutes as shown in Table 1.

Table 1. For each property ϕ_i, we asked KORG 10 times to generate 10 attackers with recovery, and 10 without, on a 16 GB 2018 Intel© Core^{tm} i7-8550U CPU running Linux Mint 19.3 Cinnamon. KORG may generate duplicate attackers, so for each property (Column 1), we list the average time to generate a unique attacker without recovery (Column 2) or with (Column 3), and the total number of unique attackers found without recovery (Column 4) or with (Column 5). E.g., for ϕ_3, of 100 attackers with recovery generated over about four hours, five were unique and 95 duplicates, so KORG took about 2.3 min per attacker, or, 45 min per unique attacker. Instructions and code to reproduce these results are given in the GitHub repository.

Property	Avg. Runtime (s) Unique attacker		Unique attackers found	
	∃ASP	R-∃ASP	∃ASP	R-∃ASP
ϕ_1	0.32	0.49	7	5
ϕ_2	0.45	0.48	5	5
ϕ_3	876.74	2757.98	4	5

6   Related Work

Prior works formalized security problems using game theory (e.g., FLIPIT [34], [22]), "weird machines" [7], attack trees [37], Markov models [33], and other methods. Prior notions of attacker quality include $\mathcal{O}$-complexity [6], expected information loss [30], or success probability [25,36], which is similar to our concept of ∀ versus ∃-attackers. The formalism of [36] also captures attack consequence (cost to a stakeholder).

Attacker synthesis work exists in cyber-physical systems [3,18,25,27], most of which define attacker success using bad states (e.g., reactor meltdown, vehicle collision, etc.) or information theory (e.g., information leakage metrics). Problems include the *actuator attacker synthesis problem* [23]; the *hardware-aware attacker synthesis problem* [32]; and the *fault-attacker synthesis problem* [4].

Maybe the most similar work to our own is PROVERIF [5], which verifies properties of, and generates attacks against, cryptographic protocols. We formalize the problem with operational semantics (processes) and reduce it to model checking, whereas PROVERIF uses axiomatic semantics (PROLOG clauses) and reduces it to automated proving. Another similar tool is NETSMC [39], a model-checker that efficiently finds counter-examples to security properties of stateful networks.

Existing techniques for automated attack discovery include model-guided search [16,19] (including using inference [8]), open-source-intelligence [38], bug analysis [17], and genetic programming [21]. The generation of a failing test-case for a protocol property is not unlike attack discovery, so [24] is also related.

This paper focuses on attacker synthesis at the protocol level, and thus differs from the work reported in [20] in two ways: first, the work in [20] synthesizes mappings between high-level protocol models and execution platform models, thereby focusing on linking protocol design and implementation; second, the work in [20] synthesizes correct (secure) mappings, whereas we are interested in synthesizing attackers.

7   Conclusion

We present a novel formal framework for automated attacker synthesis. The framework includes an explicit definition of threat models and four novel, to our knowledge, categories of attackers. We formulate four attacker synthesis problems, and propose solutions to two of them by program transformations and reduction to model-checking. We prove our solutions sound and complete; these proofs are available online [14]. Finally, we implement our solutions for the case of a centralized attacker in an open-source tool called KORG, apply KORG to the study of the TCP connection routine, and discuss the results. KORG and the TCP case study are freely and openly available[1].

Acknowledgments. This material is based upon work supported by the National Science Foundation under NSF SaTC award CNS-1801546. Any opinions, findings, and conclusions or recommendations expressed in this material are those of the author(s) and do not necessarily reflect the views of the National Science Foundation. The authors thank four anonymous reviewers. Additionally, the first author thanks Benjamin Quiring, Dr. Ming Li, and Dr. Frank von Hippel.

References

1. Alur, R., Tripakis, S.: Automatic synthesis of distributed protocols. SIGACT News **48**(1), 55–90 (2017)
2. Baier, C., Katoen, J.P.: Principles of Model Checking. MIT Press, Cambridge (2008)
3. Bang, L., Rosner, N., Bultan, T.: Online synthesis of adaptive side-channel attacks based on noisy observations. In: 2018 IEEE European Symposium on Security and Privacy, pp. 307–322. IEEE (2018)

---

[1] http://github.com/maxvonhippel/AttackerSynthesis.

4. Barthe, G., Dupressoir, F., Fouque, P.A., Grégoire, B., Zapalowicz, J.C.: Synthesis of fault attacks on cryptographic implementations. In: Proceedings of the 2014 ACM SIGSAC Conference on Computer and Communications Security, pp. 1016–1027 (2014)
5. Blanchet, B.: An efficient cryptographic protocol verifier based on prolog rules. In: 14th IEEE Computer Security Foundations Workshop, pp. 82–96. IEEE Computer Society, Cape Breton (2001)
6. Branco, R., Hu, K., Kawakami, H., Sun, K.: A mathematical modeling of exploitations and mitigation techniques using set theory. In: 2018 IEEE Security and Privacy Workshops (SPW), pp. 323–328. IEEE (2018)
7. Bratus, S., Locasto, M.E., Patterson, M.L., Sassaman, L., Shubina, A.: Exploit programming: from buffer overflows to weird machines and theory of computation. USENIX Login **36**(6), 13–21 (2011)
8. Cho, C.Y., Babic, D., Poosankam, P., Chen, K.Z., Wu, E.X., Song, D.: MACE: model-inference-assisted concolic exploration for protocol and vulnerability discovery. In: USENIX Security Symposium, vol. 139 (2011)
9. Chong, S., et al.: Report on the NSF workshop on formal methods for security (2016)
10. Church, A.: Application of recursive arithmetic to the problem of circuit synthesis (1957). https://doi.org/10.2307/2271310
11. Dijkstra, E.W., et al.: Notes on structured programming (1970). http://www.cs.utexas.edu/users/EWD/ewd02xx/EWD249.PDF. Accessed 11 May 2020
12. Duran, J.W., Ntafos, S.: A report on random testing. In: Proceedings of the 5th International Conference on Software Engineering, pp. 179–183. IEEE Press (1981)
13. Friedrichs, O.: A simple TCP spoofing attack (1997). http://citi.umich.edu/u/provos/papers/secnet-spoof.txt. Accessed 3 Jan 2020
14. von Hippel, M., Vick, C., Tripakis, S., Nita-Rotaru, C.: Automated attacker synthesis for distributed protocols (2020). arXiv preprint arXiv:2004.01220
15. Holzmann, G.: The Spin Model Checker. Addison-Wesley, Boston (2003)
16. Hoque, E., Chowdhury, O., Chau, S.Y., Nita-Rotaru, C., Li, N.: Analyzing operational behavior of stateful protocol implementations for detecting semantic bugs. In: 2017 47th Annual IEEE/IFIP International Conference on Dependable Systems and Networks (DSN), pp. 627–638. IEEE (2017)
17. Huang, S.K., Huang, M.H., Huang, P.Y., Lai, C.W., Lu, H.L., Leong, W.M.: Crax: software crash analysis for automatic exploit generation by modeling attacks as symbolic continuations. In: 2012 IEEE Sixth International Conference on Software Security and Reliability, pp. 78–87. IEEE (2012)
18. Huang, Z., Etigowni, S., Garcia, L., Mitra, S., Zonouz, S.: Algorithmic attack synthesis using hybrid dynamics of power grid critical infrastructures. In: 2018 48th Annual IEEE/IFIP International Conference on Dependable Systems and Networks, pp. 151–162. IEEE (2018)
19. Jero, S., Lee, H., Nita-Rotaru, C.: Leveraging state information for automated attack discovery in transport protocol implementations. In: 2015 45th Annual IEEE/IFIP International Conference on Dependable Systems and Networks, pp. 1–12. IEEE (2015)
20. Kang, E., Lafortune, S., Tripakis, S.: Automated synthesis of secure platform mappings. In: Dillig, I., Tasiran, S. (eds.) CAV 2019. LNCS, vol. 11561, pp. 219–237. Springer, Cham (2019). https://doi.org/10.1007/978-3-030-25540-4_12
21. Kayacik, H.G., Zincir-Heywood, A.N., Heywood, M.I., Burschka, S.: Generating mimicry attacks using genetic programming: a benchmarking study. In: 2009 IEEE Symposium on Computational Intelligence in Cyber Security, pp. 136–143. IEEE (2009)

22. Klaška, D., Kučera, A., Lamser, T., Řehák, V.: Automatic synthesis of efficient regular strategies in adversarial patrolling games. In: Proceedings of the 17th International Conference on Autonomous Agents and MultiAgent Systems, pp. 659–666. International Foundation for Autonomous Agents and Multiagent Systems (2018)
23. Lin, L., Zhu, Y., Su, R.: Synthesis of actuator attackers for free (2019). arXiv preprint arXiv:1904.10159
24. McMillan, K.L., Zuck, L.D.: Formal specification and testing of QUIC. In: Proceedings of the ACM Special Interest Group on Data Communication, pp. 227–240. ACM (2019)
25. Meira-Góes, R., Kwong, R., Lafortune, S.: Synthesis of sensor deception attacks for systems modeled as probabilistic automata. In: 2019 American Control Conference, pp. 5620–5626. IEEE (2019)
26. Myers, G.J.: The Art of Software Testing. John Wiley & Sons, Hoboken (1979)
27. Phan, Q.S., Bang, L., Pasareanu, C.S., Malacaria, P., Bultan, T.: Synthesis of adaptive side-channel attacks. In: 2017 IEEE 30th Computer Security Foundations Symposium, pp. 328–342. IEEE (2017)
28. Pnueli, A.: The temporal logic of programs. In: 18th Annual Symposium on Foundations of Computer Science, pp. 46–57. IEEE (1977)
29. Postel, J., et al.: Rfc 793 Transmission Control Protocol (1981)
30. Srivastava, H., Dwivedi, K., Pankaj, P.K., Tewari, V.: A formal attack centric framework highlighting expected losses of an information security breach. Int. J. Comput. Appl. **68**(17), 26–31 (2013)
31. Øhenryouly: [Solved] TCP connection blocked in SYN_SENT status (2007). https://bbs.archlinux.org/viewtopic.php?id=33875. Accessed 3 Jan 2020
32. Trippel, C., Lustig, D., Martonosi, M.: Security verification via automatic hardware-aware exploit synthesis: the CheckMate approach. IEEE Micro **39**(3), 84–93 (2019)
33. Valizadeh, S., van Dijk, M.: Toward a theory of cyber attacks (2019). arXiv preprint arXiv:1901.01598
34. Van Dijk, M., Juels, A., Oprea, A., Rivest, R.L.: FlipIt: The game of "stealthy takeover". J. Cryptol. **26**(4), 655–713 (2013)
35. Vardi, M.Y., Wolper, P.: An automata-theoretic approach to automatic program verification. In: Proceedings of the First Symposium on Logic in Computer Science, pp. 322–331. IEEE Computer Society (1986)
36. Vasilevskaya, M., Nadjm-Tehrani, S.: Quantifying risks to data assets using formal metrics in embedded system design. In: Koornneef, F., van Gulijk, C. (eds.) SAFECOMP 2015. LNCS, vol. 9337, pp. 347–361. Springer, Cham (2015). https://doi.org/10.1007/978-3-319-24255-2_25
37. Wideł, W., Audinot, M., Fila, B., Pinchinat, S.: Beyond 2014: formal methods for attack tree-based security modeling. ACM Comput. Surv. **52**(4), 1–36 (2019)
38. You, W., et al.: Semfuzz: semantics-based automatic generation of proof-of-concept exploits. In: Proceedings of the 2017 ACM SIGSAC Conference on Computer and Communications Security, pp. 2139–2154 (2017)
39. Yuan, Y., Moon, S.J., Uppal, S., Jia, L., Sekar, V.: NetSMC: a custom symbolic model checker for stateful network verification. In: 17th USENIX Symposium on Networked Systems Design and Implementation. USENIX Association, Santa Clara (2020)

An Attacker Modeling Framework for the Assessment of Cyber-Physical Systems Security

Christopher Deloglos$^{(\boxtimes)}$, Carl Elks, and Ashraf Tantawy

Virginia Commonwealth University, Richmond, VA 23220, USA
{delogloscj,crelks,amatantawy}@vcu.edu

Abstract. Characterizing attacker behavior with respect to Cyber-Physical Systems is important to assuring the security posture and resilience of these systems. Classical cyber vulnerability assessment approaches rely on the knowledge and experience of cyber-security experts to conduct security analyses and can be inconsistent where the experts' knowledge and experience are lacking. This paper proposes a flexible attacker modeling framework that aids in the security analysis process by simulating a diverse set of attacker behaviors to predict attack progression and provide consistent system vulnerability analysis. The model proposes an expanded architecture of vulnerability databases to maximize its effectiveness and consistency in detecting CPS vulnerabilities while being compatible with existing vulnerability databases. The model has the power to be implemented and simulated against an actual or virtual CPS. Execution of the attacker model is demonstrated against a simulated industrial control system architecture, resulting in a probabilistic prediction of attacker behavior.

Keywords: CPS · Security · Attacker modeling

1 Introduction

To secure systems from known and emerging threats, systems engineers and security analysts alike need to integrate an attacker's view of potential vulnerabilities into their design, development, and analysis process as early as possible. To date, this attacker perspective activity has been largely a manual process conducted by subject matter experts who examine a system and identify possible vulnerabilities and weaknesses. Understanding the potential threat behaviors and capabilities of a cyber-actor or threat agent with respect to a cyber or cyber-physical system (CPS) is critical for risk assessment and the development of effective security countermeasure solutions [11,17].

A promising way forward is the use of formal attacker models that attempt to characterize and capture the expected behavior of attackers against a CPS. Developing accurate attacker-models, however, is difficult due to the number

© Springer Nature Switzerland AG 2020
A. Casimiro et al. (Eds.): SAFECOMP 2020, LNCS 12234, pp. 150–163, 2020.
https://doi.org/10.1007/978-3-030-54549-9_10

of factors that influence and encompass attacker behavior. To understand the behavior of an attacker many questions may be asked such as "Who is the attacker?", "What resources are at the attacker's disposal?", and "What is the motivation of the attacker?". Quantifying the answers to these questions, however, is challenging in the absence of absolute metrics and incomplete situation awareness. To partially address these challenges, in this paper we present a novel modular attacker modelling framework (AMF) that is: (1) capable of capturing and quantifying complex attacker behavior and, (2) is readily extensible to incorporate new or emerging aspects of attacker behavior.

2 Related Work

In attacker modeling, a common approach is to create a correlation model where the designer selects a series of attacker properties such as skill level, resources, intent, and motivation, and attempts to develop cumulative correlation functions that effectively predict attacker behavior when applied to real-world attackers [10]. Rocchetto et al. performed a literature search and created a six-profile model able to effectively describe attacker profiles from the majority of cited literature [20]. The use of this method, however, requires the user to be aware of the skill level of the attacker. In order to apply Rocchetto's method to a realistic attacker model, a probability mass function is used to simulate the non-determinism in the skillset of an unknown attacker.

Orojloo et al. [18] proposed an attack modeling approach that applied attack trees to model how characteristics of a particular attack (access, knowledge required, skill required, and level of user interaction) influence the behavior of an attacker. While serving as an effective foundation, the attack tree method as proposed by Orojloo requires a comprehensive perspective of the CPS which must be created through a manual process for each CPS under consideration. This design process becomes tedious when considering a large CPS or one with multiple attack vectors to a single target.

A common approach to representing attacker behavior against a CPS is application of the Markov decision process (MDP) [8,12]. The size of the Markov model explodes, however, when considering a large CPS with multiple nodes, each having multiple potential actions. Markov representation also lacks the ability to clearly depict the nature of various paths an attacker may take through a system. An alternate to the full MDP is the Partially Observable Markov Decision Process (POMDP) as in [7]. This model allows the application of the Markov methodology while limiting the state-space of the model to a single attack-path. We propose an alternate scheme using a one-step look-ahead formalism as a solution.

Automation of the attack-analysis process for a complex CPS was explored in [13], where the ADVISE method is proposed. The ADVISE method requires as input a description of the system, a description of the adversary, a list of the desired security metrics, and a description of all vulnerability information pertaining to the system. In application to a real system, researching, compiling, and organizing all vulnerability information related to a CPS is a monumental task. Databases such as the Common Attack Pattern Enumeration and Classification (CAPEC), the Common Weakness Enumeration (CWE), the Common Vulnerabilities and Exposures (CVE), and the Common Platform Enumeration (CPE) have been applied to attack modeling to aid in vulnerability research [9,14]. We propose the application of CAPEC, CWE, CVE, and CPE search engines as an aid for the generation of a hybrid action database.

Due to the diversity of CPSs, attacker models are often defined within the context of a specific system [5,9,14]. In this paper, we propose a modular AMF that is capable of modeling complex attacker behavior against a full CPS and is readily expandable to include additional aspects of attacker behavior. The authors propose two components of the attacker model as novel. First, the authors propose a formalization between an attacker profile and an attacker's behavior that allows the prediction of the behavior of profile-specific attackers against a CPS. This approach allows an attacker-specific security review and aids in prioritizing the relevance of attacks and vulnerabilities in a CPS. Second, the authors propose a modular scheme for describing cyber-physical system architectures as well as the attack progression of an attacker through cyber-physical systems.

The remainder of the paper is organized as follows. Section 3 describes the attacker-modeling framework. A case study is explored in Sect. 4. Section 5 summarizes the work and proposes future research directions.

3   Overview of the Attacker Model

Traditional attacker behavior is captured as a series of observations regarding the attacker motivation and decision process. These observations are captured in the proposed AMF as *rules*. A rule may be formally defined as a facet of an attacker's behavior which observes a cause/effect relationship between an influencing parameter and the attacker's actions. The proposed AMF accepts a series of rules which together define the behavior of the attacker. The attacker model overview in Fig. 1 depicts the relationship between the attacker and the CPS. Sample rules defining attacker behavior are implemented in modules such as the CPS Knowledge and the Target Node Selection modules. This provides a test-bed to explore the role and influence of individual rules on the composite attacker decision process. This also provides a flexible framework that allows validation of the AMF against a particular dataset where the rules the AMF implements may be refined and calibrated to achieve a model that accurately reflects the behavior of a known attacker or set of attackers.

Relationships between modules are characterized by connected arrows, where upstream modules occur earlier in the attacker decision process. The proposed attacker model operates on a cyclical action/feedback scheme where an *action* is some step the attacker performs in the attack process and *feedback* is any information the attacker receives as a result of the action. The progression of the attack through the CPS is described as the *attack state*. The attack state represents a single action and is a tuple of static *properties* and dynamic *variables*. Properties are information that is static throughout the attack process and in Fig. 1 includes the Action Database and the Attacker Profile. Variables include information that changes as the attack progresses such as the attacker CPS Knowledge. The action performed for each state of the attack is a product of all static properties and dynamic variables and is discussed further in Sect. 3.6.

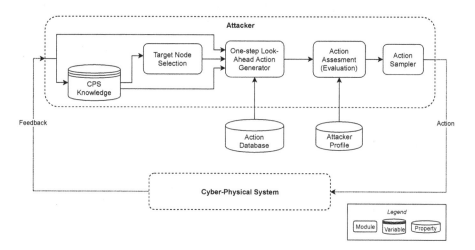

Fig. 1. Attacker model overview

3.1 Cyber-Physical System

In the proposed attacker-modeling framework, the CPS is modeled and described as a composition of *nodes*, *edges*, *attack vectors*, and *entry points*. A node represents a machine or other potentially vulnerable device that has functional purpose within the CPS. An edge represents a communication link between two nodes that may be used to transmit information, while an attack vector is any edge that may be used for an attack. An entry point is an edge directed into the CPS from outside the CPS that may be used by an attacker to gain access to the system. Establishing well-formed boundaries between nodes of the CPS and relationships between them allows a formal description of a Cyber-Physical System. Programming tools such as SysML [1] utilize the node/edge system description scheme and may be readily integrated with the CPS design process for attacker model automation.

3.2 CPS Knowledge

We begin with making the reasonable assumption that as the attack or probing progresses, the attacker will begin to learn information about the target system.

This behavior is captured in the CPS knowledge module. The rules that the CPS knowledge module implements are:

- When starting an attack, the attacker only has knowledge of the system entry points.
- As the attack progresses the attacker will discover new information about the CPS.
- If a node is compromised, all nodes it is connected to are discovered and added to the CPS knowledge.

Information about the CPS is fed into the attacker's CPS knowledge module as feedback. If a node is compromised it is considered owned by the attacker and capable of performing pivoting attacks. The initial attacker CPS knowledge is simplified for demonstration purposes, but in a more complex application could include behaviors involving the attacker's discovery of the target system. More complex rules may be applied to node ownership such as defining levels of ownership (based on privilege escalation).

3.3   Target Node Selection

When the attacker goes to perform an action against a system, the attacker must first select a target node. The rules that the target node selection module implements are:

- The attacker will only target nodes that exist in the attacker's CPS Knowledge.
- The attacker will not target a node if it is already compromised.
- The attacker will not target a node if the attacker has exhausted all qualified actions against it.
- If an attacker targets a node, the attacker will not change targets until exhausting all actions against it.
- If more than one target is valid, the attacker will select a target node at random from amongst the valid nodes.

Several additional rules may be added to capture the tendency of an attacker to target nodes associated with the end-goal (often referred to as the honey-pot).

3.4   Action Database

The purpose of the Action Database module is to capture behaviors influenced by the actions available to the attacker. The action database contains descriptions of all actions known about the CPS. Each action within the database contains several fields of information including the action profile, the action description, the target criteria, and a list of prerequisite actions. The *action profile* contains a quantitative description of the user and use-case of the action, which is used for quantifying a relationship between each action and the attacker profile defined for the attacker model as discussed further in Sect. 3.6. The *action description* is a plain-text description of how the action works in as much detail as is possible. The *target criteria* defines what system(s) the action is valid against. The *prerequisite attacks* describe any actions that must be completed before this action may be attempted.

A critical component to the viability of the attacker model is the database population scheme. CAPEC [16], CWE [2], CVE [15], and CPE [3] are amongst the most popular and provide different approaches to cataloguing attacks, attack descriptions, and attack relationships. Search engines that make use of online attack and vulnerability databases aid in effectively generating an action database for the attacker model. One tool that was applied to populate the action database for the case study in Sect. 4 was the CYBOK tool [6], which is a literal search engine for CAPEC, CWE, and CVE capable of generating vulnerability data for individual queries or entire systems.

3.5   One-Step Look-Ahead Generator

The one-step look-ahead generator applies the attacker's knowledge of the CPS to filter out all attacks that are invalid for the current attack state. Filters are non-probabilistic in nature and may depend on any information regarding the current state of the attack or the description of the node. This attacker model applies three filters.

1. The attacker will only consider actions that meet the target criteria
2. The attacker will not consider an action that has already been performed on the target
3. The attacker will not consider an action if the edge relating the current node to the target node is not a viable propagation path for that action

We define $\mathcal{A}$ as the set of all m known actions in the action database and $\Phi \subseteq \mathcal{A}$ as the set of actions known by the attacker. The three filters are defined as $\Phi_{target} \subseteq \Phi$, $\Phi_{ex} \subseteq \Phi$, and $\Phi_{vect} \subseteq \Phi$ for filters 1, 2, and 3 respectively. The set of actions that are valid for the attacker to perform in the given state of the attack (Φ_{valid}) are then defined by Eq. 1, where the attack space can be visualized in Fig. 2.

$$\Phi_{valid} = \Phi_{ex} \cap \Phi_{vect} \cap \Phi_{target} \qquad (1)$$

3.6   Action Assessment

When an attacker goes to select an action, characteristics about the attacker will influence the selection of the attack. This behavior is captured in the action assessment module. The rules applied here are:

- An attacker's behavior is dependent on one or more primary influencing factors.
- Actions may have properties that allow them to be correlated to attackers.
- An attacker's attack selection decision can be predicted by evaluating the sum of influencing factors between an attacker and an action.

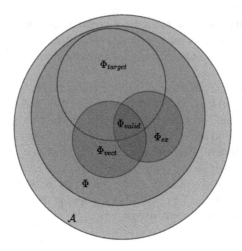

Fig. 2. The intersection of action selection filters applied to the action database.

The action assessment module calculates the probability of the attacker performing each of the actions based on probability functions that take as operands the attacker profile, the attack profile, and the current state of the attack.

Attacker Profiles and Attack Profiles. *Attacker profiles* are a topic well covered in literature with no recognized standards for what characteristics best model an attacker. The purpose of an attacker profile is to capture characteristics about an attacker that influence the attacker's behavior, thereby describing the expected behavior of the attacker. The characteristics that define the attacker profile are termed attacker *properties*. Rocchetto et al. [20] performed a literature review on attacker profiles for CPSs in an attempt to find a unifying attacker profiling model to describe various attackers from multiple different research studies. In conclusion, Rocchetto proposed a set of six attacker profiles composed of twenty-nine attacker properties that effectively described the majority of attacker profiles in the referenced literature.

An *action profile* is often represented as a set of properties describing the characteristics of the action [20]. This, however, implies linearly proportionality to an attacker profile, which is not universally true. For example, an attacker with a high skill set is not necessarily more likely to perform an attack that requires a high skill set when an easier attack may succeed as well. We capture this behavior by defining an attack profile as the profile of the attacker expected to use that attack. Because attacker behavior is constantly changing as technology evolves, this profiling technique may be reinforced by empirical data from records of attack history. Collaborations such as MITRE's ATT&CK framework [4] may aid in assessment of current threat actors. This facilitates an attacker model that can better emulate realistic and relevant threats by allowing the user to base the relationship between attackers and their actions off of current attacker data.

As such, we define an attacker profile (Δ) as an n-dimensional space of attacker properties (δ_i) such that $\Delta = \{\delta_1, \delta_2, \ldots, \delta_n\}$ for an attacker profile having n properties. An example attack space can be seen in Fig. 3 where the attacker profile and several action profiles are plotted in the 3-dimensional space. The probability of an attacker performing an action is a function of the distance between the attacker profile and the action profile in n-dimensional space.

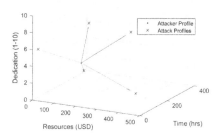

Fig. 3. An example 3-dimensional attack space showing the attacker profile and several action profiles.

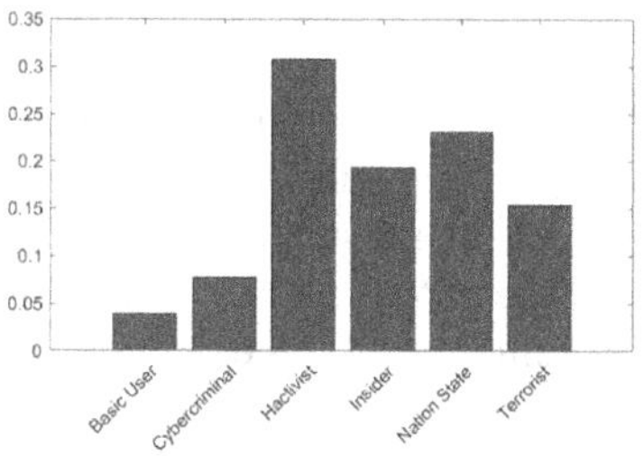

Fig. 4. An example of a probability mass function for a probabilistic attacker profile against a nuclear power plant.

Probabilistic Attacker Profiles. In applying Rocchetto's attacker profiles to an attacker model it is important to note that in a real-world application one cannot assume which attacker will be attacking a system. In order to simulate this non-deterministic behavior, two types of attacker profiles are adopted which are the *static attacker profile* and the *probabilistic attacker profile*. A static attacker profile represents one of the six attacker profiles defined by Rocchetto et al. [20]. A probabilistic attacker profile may be represented as a probability mass function (PMF) of the six profiles. The PMF is generated by assigning each of the six attacker profiles ($\Delta_1, \ldots, \Delta_6$) a likelihood of attacking (l_i) such that $0 \le l_i \le 1$. The Probability of attack of a specific attacker profile is calculated using:

$$P(\Delta_i) = \frac{l_i}{\sum_{j=1}^n l_j} \tag{2}$$

where $\sum_{j=1}^n P(\Delta_j) = 1$. The PMF in Fig. 4 is an example probabilistic attacker profile designed to mimic the probability of attackers against a nuclear power plant. At the beginning of the attack analysis process, the probabilistic attacker profile is sampled to obtain a discrete attacker profile which is recognized as the attacker for the remainder of the attack process.

Attack Probability Functions. The probability that the attacker will perform an attack at any given time is calculated using the attack probability function.

Attacker properties may be one of three types which are sets, bounded ranges, and unbounded ranges. Non-ordered sets are considered to have a scaled property value $\gamma = 1$ if the attacker profile property and the attack profile property match and $\gamma = 0$ otherwise. Ordered set values may be mapped to the scaled property range $(0 \leq \gamma \leq 1)$ using Fuzzy set theory as demonstrated by Patil et al. in [19].

Bounded ranges are numerical ranges where the value of a property (ε) may only fall between a lower bound (ε_L) and an upper bound (ε_H). Bounded ranges are linearly mapped to the scaled property value $(\gamma : 0 \leq \gamma \leq 1)$ using:

$$\gamma = \frac{\varepsilon - \varepsilon_L}{\varepsilon_H - \varepsilon_L} \tag{3}$$

Several scaling functions exist for unbounded ranges such as the percent-difference function, the logistic function, and the hyperbolic tangent. The value weighting in these functions, however, is non-linear, which does not properly scale different property values where a score considered median is represented by a numerically large or numerically small value (>100 or <1 respectively). Therefore, we propose converting the unbounded property values to a bounded range by first evaluating the maximum (γ_{max}) and minimum (γ_{min}) values for all actions within the database, then using the local maximum and minimum to scale the unbounded range.

We designate the set of m available actions in the action database as $\mathcal{A} = \{A_1, A_2, \ldots, A_m\}$. Each action A_i $(i = 1, 2, \ldots, m)$ has an associated set of scaled property values $\Gamma_i = \{\gamma_i^1, \gamma_i^2, \ldots, \gamma_i^n\}$. For a given attacker profile (Δ) with n scaled property values $\Theta = \{\theta_1, \theta_2, \ldots, \theta_n\}$, the distance (d_i) between the attacker and each action is calculated by the distance between the two profiles in n-dimensional space using:

$$d_i = f(\Theta; \Gamma_i) = \sqrt{\sum_{j=1}^{n} \frac{1}{\beta_j^2} \left(\theta_j - \gamma_i^j\right)^2} \tag{4}$$

where β_j is a criticality factor such that $\{\beta \in \mathbb{R} | 0 \leq \beta \leq 1\}$ which increases the distance for properties with a $\beta < 1$ criticality. The score of each action (s_i) is inversely proportional to d_i and calculated using the function:

$$s_i = 1 - \frac{d_i}{\sum_{j=1}^{m} d_j} \qquad i = 1, \ldots, m \tag{5}$$

This equation is unique in that it calculates the inverse of the distance without applying a nonlinear value-weighting as is observed in the inverse function or exponential functions such as the Softmax function. According to the score for each action, the probability that the attacker will take action A_i is calculated using the function:

$$P[A_i] = \frac{s_i}{\sum_{j=1}^{m} s_j} \tag{6}$$

Equation (6) has the intuitive interpretation that the higher the score the attacker gets for an action, the higher the probability that this action will be chosen by the attacker.

3.7   Action Sampler

The last module in the attacker model is the action sampler module. The action sampler module implements the following rule: After evaluating the attacks, the attacker is more likely to choose an attack with a high probability than an attack with a low probability.

The action sampler receives as inputs all attacks for the target system with their attack probability values and selects one of the actions by sampling a weighted randomizing function ($rand_w()$) mapped to the probabilities of the set of probabilistic actions $\Delta = \{A_i, P[A_i]\}$. This action is then performed by the attacker against the CPS.

4   Case Study

For application of the proposed AMF, we observe the Industrial Control System (ICS) in Fig. 5 composed of nodes and communication channels. This example ICS is used to control a simulated exothermic continuous stirred tank reactor (CSTR) using an NI cRIO controller. The target for the attack is the Basic Process Control System (BPCS, N4). Control or disruption of the BPCS by the attacker indicates a successful attack.

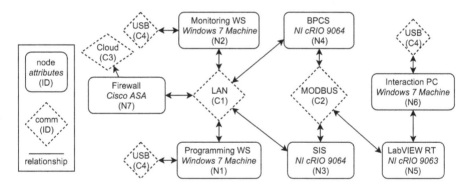

Fig. 5. Case study ICS relational diagram

4.1   ICS Formal Description

The ICS consists of 7 nodes, each composed of key attributes included in Fig. 5. The system is described as having 4 entry points which include N1, N2, and N6 via infected USB and N7 via remote access. Six properties are selected as a subset of those described by Rocchetto et al. [20] to describe the attacker and action profiles which include Access, Finances, Knowledge, Manpower, Motivation, and Tools. Access, Motivation, and Tools are defined as set properties with values of {Direct, Wireless, Offsite} for Access and {Low, Medium, High} for Motivation and for Tools. Knowledge is defined as a bounded property with a

$0 \leq$ Knowledge ≤ 10 range. Finances and Manpower are defined as unbounded properties. These properties are not intended to be a holistic description of the attacker behavior, but rather to demonstrate the principles and dynamics of the different types of profile properties. The criticality factor is kept at unity (1) for all profile properties. The attacker profile PMF in Fig. 4 was defined as a set of 6 attacker profiles with property values in Table 1. CAPEC, CWE, CVE, and CPE databases were used to search for vulnerability information. The CAPEC and CWE databases were used to identify potential attack patterns and weaknesses respectively, aiding in the discovery of associated CVEs. Table 2 contains a sample profile set for the vulnerabilities found for the ICS nodes.

Table 1. Attacker profiles and property values

Profile	Access	Finances	Knowledge	Manpower	Motivation	Tools
Basic user	Offsite	100	2	40	Low	Low
Cybercriminal	Offsite	1000	5	160	Medium	High
Hactivist	Wireless	500	6	1500	High	Medium
Insider	Onsite	100	7	10	Medium	Medium
Nation state	Offsite	1000000	9	100000	High	High
Terrorist	Onsite	10000	4	1000	High	Medium

Table 2. Case study action profiles

ID	Name	Targets	A	F	K	Mp	Mo	T
V1	Remote-Access trojan	Windows 7 machine	Offsite	0	3	20	Low	Low
V2	CVE-2017-2779	Windows 7 machine	Onsite	10000	9	5000	High	Mid
V3	CVE-2017-2775	Windows 7 machine	Offsite	6000	10	8000	High	Mid
V4	MODBUS MITM	NI cRIO 9064/9063	Onsite	50000	9	500	High	Mid
V5	MODBUS DOS	NI cRIO 9064/9063	Offsite	40000	6	200	High	Mid
V6	Code injection	NI cRIO 9064	Onsite	100	4	300	Mid	Low
V7	Watering-Hole	Windows 7 machine	Offsite	2000	6	300	Mid	Mid
V8	CVE-2014-4115	Windows 7 machine	Onsite	1200	7	800	High	High
V9	CVE-2010-2568	Windows 7 machine	Onsite	10000	8	2000	High	High
V10	CVE-2019-1713	Cisco ASA	Offsite	5000	9	100	High	Mid

A = Access, F = Finances, K = Knowledge, MP = Manpower, M = Motivation, T = Tools

4.2 Attacker Model Execution

Sampling the PMF results in the selection of the Nation State attacker. The attacker profile is then evaluated against the CPS. Initial attacker knowledge assumed includes the entry vectors E1, E2, E3, and E4, along with the corresponding existence of nodes N1, N2, N6, and N7. The modeling cycle in Fig. 1

begins and is repeated until either the target is reached or there are no actions remaining for the attacker to perform. Figure 6 shows the progression of the attack as a POMDP, including each decision the attacker made in the attacker process and the probability of each decision.

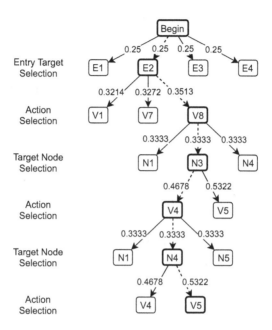

Fig. 6. Diagram of attacker CPS Knowledge upon completion of the attack, including attack progression.

4.3 Attack Review

The steps taken to complete the attack in Fig. 6 represent one of many possible attacks that may have been performed by the attacker. The attacker was able to compromise the CPS by exploiting three vulnerabilities. Step 1 used an infected USB thumb-drive to gain access to the monitoring workstation. Step 2 used a MODBUS man-in-the-middle attack to take over the SIS cRIO. Step 3 used a MODBUS DOS attack to disrupt the operation of the BPCS.

5 Conclusion and Future Work

The Attacker Modeling Framework we present significantly builds upon existing research and injects a more theoretical foundation for system behavior and attacker causality models. The flexibility of the framework readily integrates a variety of complex attacker behaviors. The proposed attack probability functions quantify the influence of attacker characteristics on the attacker's decision process and provide probabilistic predictions for the attacker behavior.

Preliminary findings indicate that the proposed method scales well; specifically with respect to the decision space of a traditional MDP or attack-tree analysis methods which would grow exponentially. The POMDP analysis framework provides manageable attack scenarios describing system vulnerabilities and putting the attack process in the context of the CPS. The case study shows the benefit of the attacker decision-by-decision analysis, allowing the cyber analyst and system engineers to have deeper insights into potential vulnerability pathways into and through the CPS.

Proposed future work includes,

1. The implementation of additional rules defined in related literature
2. The development of a tool to aid in attack scenario design and automation of the attack analysis process
3. Exploration of different techniques to train and calibrate the AMF
4. The application of the AMF to recorded attacker data-sets from behavioral analysis studies
5. The integration of a penetration-testing framework such as Metasploit into the attacker-model for analysis against a SCADA test-bed

Acknowledgement. This research was made possible by NPRP 9-005-1-002 grant from the Qatar National Research Fund (a member of The Qatar Foundation). The statements made herein are solely the responsibility of the authors.

References

1. SysML Open Source Project. https://sysml.org/
2. CWE - Common Weakness Enumeration (2018). https://cwe.mitre.org/index.html
3. CPE - Common Platform Enumeration (2019). https://nvd.nist.gov/products/cpe
4. ATT&CK for Industrial Control Systems. In: MITRE (2020). https://doi.org/10.1109/isie.2010.5636886, https://collaborate.mitre.org/attackics/index.php/
5. Adepu, S., Mathur, A.: Generalized attacker and attack models for cyber physical systems. In: Proceedings - International Computer Software and Applications Conference, vol. 1, pp. 283–292. IEEE Computer Society (8 2016). https://doi.org/10.1109/COMPSAC.2016.122
6. Bakirtzis, G., Simon, B.J., Collins, A.G., Fleming, C.H., Elks, C.R.: Data-driven vulnerability exploration for design phase system analysis. IEEE Syst. J. https://doi.org/10.1109/JSYST.2019.2940145
7. Carin, L., Cybenko, G., Hughes, J.: Quantitative Evaluation of Risk for Investment Efficient Strategies in Cybersecurity: The QuERIES Methodology. Duke University, Technical Report (2008)
8. Chen, Y., Hong, J., Liu, C.C.: Modeling of intrusion and defense for assessment of cyber security at power substations. IEEE Trans. Smart Grid **9**(4), 2541–2552 (2018). https://doi.org/10.1109/TSG.2016.2614603
9. Ekelhart, A., Kiesling, E., Grill, B., Strauss, C., Stummer, C.: Integrating attacker behavior in IT security analysis: a discrete-event simulation approach. Inf. Technol. Manag. **16**(3), 221–233 (2015). https://doi.org/10.1007/s10799-015-0232-6
10. Heckman, R.: Attacker Classification to Aid Targeting Critical Systems for Threat Modelling and Security Review. Technical Report, ROCKYH (2005)

11. Knowles, W., Prince, D., Hutchison, D., Disso, J.F.P., Jones, K.: A survey of cyber security management in industrial control systems. Int. J. Crit. Infrastruct. Prot. **9**, 52–80 (2015). https://doi.org/10.1016/j.ijcip.2015.02.002, https://www.sciencedirect.com/science/article/pii/S1874548215000207

12. Kriaa, S., Bouissou, M., Piètre-Cambacédès, L.: Modeling the stuxnet attack with BDMP: towards more formal risk assessments. In: 7th International Conference on Risks and Security of Internet and Systems, CRiSIS 2012 (2012). https://doi.org/10.1109/CRISIS.2012.6378942

13. LeMay, E., Ford, M.D., Keefe, K., Sanders, W.H., Muehrcke, C.: Model-based security metrics using ADversary VIew security evaluation (ADVISE). In: Proceedings of the 2011 8th International Conference on Quantitative Evaluation of Systems, QEST 2011, pp. 191–200 (2011). https://doi.org/10.1109/QEST.2011.34

14. Mili, S., Nguyen, N., Chelouah, R.: Transformation-based approach to security verification for cyber-physical systems. IEEE Syst. J. **13**(4), 1–12 (2019). https://doi.org/10.1109/jsyst.2019.2923818

15. MITRE: CVE - Common Vulnerabilities and Exposures. Common Vulnerabilities and Exposures (2016). https://doi.org/10.1016/0272-7757(91)90035-N, https://cve.mitre.org/

16. MITRE Corporation: CAPEC - Common Attack Pattern Enumeration and Classification (CAPEC) (2011). http://www.https.com//capec.mitre.org/index.htmlcapec.mitre.org/index.html

17. Mo, Y., et al.: Cyber-physical security of a smart grid infrastructure. Proc. IEEE **100**(1), 195–209 (2012). https://doi.org/10.1109/JPROC.2011.2161428

18. Orojloo, H., Abdollahi Azgomi, M.: Predicting the behavior of attackers and the consequences of attacks against cyber-physical systems. Secur. Commun. Netw. **9**(18), 6111–6136 (2016). https://doi.org/10.1002/sec.1761

19. Patil, S.K., Kant, R.: A fuzzy AHP-TOPSIS framework for ranking the solutions of knowledge management adoption in supply chain to overcome its barriers. Exp. Syst. Appl. **41**(2), 679–693 (2014). https://doi.org/10.1016/j.eswa.2013.07.093

20. Rocchetto, M., Tippenhauer, N.O.: On attacker models and profiles for cyber-physical systems. In: Askoxylakis, I., Ioannidis, S., Katsikas, S., Meadows, C. (eds.) ESORICS 2016. LNCS, vol. 9879, pp. 427–449. Springer, Cham (2016). https://doi.org/10.1007/978-3-319-45741-3_22

Predicting Railway Signalling Commands Using Neural Networks for Anomaly Detection

Markus Heinrich[1]([✉])[iD], Dominik Renkel[1], Tolga Arul[1][iD],
and Stefan Katzenbeisser[2]

[1] Department of Computer Science, Technische Universität Darmstadt,
Darmstadt, Germany
{heinrich,arul}@seceng.informatik.tu-darmstadt.de
[2] Faculty of Computer Science and Mathematics, University of Passau,
Passau, Germany
stefan.katzenbeisser@uni-passau.de

Abstract. We propose a new anomaly detection system to defend against semantic attacks on the command and control communication in safety-critical railway signalling networks. To this end, we train artificial neural network on the communication of signal boxes connected to their signals, points, and train detection system. We show that it is possible to predict the next command with knowledge of only few previously transmitted datagrams. We optimize the parameters of the artificial neural network, determine the optimal number of previous datagrams, and show that our approach is viable in railway stations of various size. Using the artificial neural network, we construct an anomaly detection system to classify each observed datagram to raise an alert in case of deviant behaviour. We further optimize the anomaly detection's threshold and show that our classifier is able to operate with a false positive rate of 0.03 and a false negative rate of 0.04.

Keywords: Anomaly detection · Artificial neural network · Artificial intelligence · Critical infrastructure protection · Cybersecurity · Railway signalling · Safety and security co-engineering · Semantic attack

1 Introduction

Railway signalling systems, like many industrial control systems (ICSs), increasingly leverage commercial off-the-shelf (COTS) hardware, shared communication networks and open protocols in order to exploit the benefits of standardized products. At the same time, this transformation exposes railway signalling to a range of new security threats [1,9–12] because standard products lower the threshold for attacks, as readily available attack tools can be applied to railway networks and known vulnerabilities can be exploited. Physical protection of the

© Springer Nature Switzerland AG 2020
A. Casimiro et al. (Eds.): SAFECOMP 2020, LNCS 12234, pp. 164–178, 2020.
https://doi.org/10.1007/978-3-030-54549-9_11

railway signalling infrastructure is virtually impossible due to its spatial extension along the railway tracks. This provides a large attack surface for adversaries
with little chance of being caught and sufficient time to perform attacks on signalling devices and networks with serious consequences such as train collisions
and derailments.

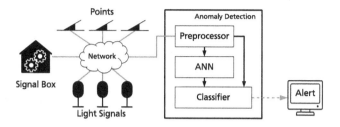

Fig. 1. Overview of a railway signalling network and the anomaly detection system

Securing safety-critical signalling infrastructure is a difficult task because
security measures must not interfere with the safety functionality mandatory in
railway transportation. Interference could, for example, result from a security
application introducing delay in safety-related communication, such that safety
components are unable to meet response time requirements and subsequently
violate the system's fail-safe property. Another cause of friction between railway
safety and security is the difference in the duration of the system lifecycle. For
safety, a system is subject to a long lasting certification process and is assumed
safe forever. In contrast, for security, new vulnerabilities and attacks become
public permanently such that systems are required to be updated and patched
frequently.

We propose an anomaly detection system that does not interfere with safety
communication because it is sufficient to monitor the safety datagram transmission to be able to classify it. Our system can be integrated in existing railway signalling networks and be trained on traces of their command and control
communication. Anomaly detection systems for semantic attacks have been proposed for other critical infrastructures (CIs) as well [3,5,7]. However, they are
not immediately applicable to railway transportation because semantic attacks
rely on domain knowledge that cannot be transferred easily. We investigate the
capabilities of artificial neural networks (ANNs) for the use as an anomaly detection system in railway signalling. Our hypothesis is that the commands in a
modern, computer-based railway signalling system can be predicted with the
help of an ANN that is presented with a short trace of recently observed commands. We run experiments for the parameters of an ANN on three datasets
of datagrams containing the command and control network traffic of three railway stations. In particular, we test the effect of the number of recently observed
commands presented to the ANN on the accuracy of the prediction. Also, we
experiment with different layer arrangements. After optimizing the parameters

and training models, we construct an anomaly detection system for railway signalling networks. The anomaly detection system can be embedded in a variety of countermeasures of a defence in depth concept that defends safety-critical railway signalling against cyberattacks. Such a security architecture is proposed by Heinrich et al. [6].

Figure 1 shows an overview of a railway signalling network where our proposed anomaly detection system is employed. A signal box uses an Ethernet-based communication network to send command and control datagrams to its associated field elements (FEs) depicted as light signals and points in the figure. The anomaly detection is an additional network component that is able to observe all network communication, e.g., using a monitoring port of the network's central router. It comprises a preprocessor to prepare the observed commands for the ANN. As we use the ANN to predict the next observed command and control datagram, a classifier is appended to the ANN's output that compares the prediction to the observed datagram and raises an alert in case of a deviation. The alert can be forwarded for further actions to a monitoring system such as a security information and event management (SIEM) system that is located e.g., in a security operations center (SOC) responsible to supervise railway signalling.

We aim to defend against an attacker performing semantic attacks on the command and control layer of railway signalling with the goal to provoke a train derailment or collision. This could be an attacker who gained access to the signal box and issues malicious commands to the infrastructure on its behalf. Instead of overcoming the physical protection of the building where the signal box is located, the attacker can as well compromise the insufficiently protected signalling network to inject malicious commands to the FEs. The commands on their own issued by the attacker appear to be licit, but issued at the wrong time they can be harmful. A countermeasure against semantic attacks is required to take the context of previous commands into account. However, we assume that our attacker can not compromise an FE itself. Protection against attacks on the FEs requires physical barriers, hardware tamper resistance, and secure storage [6], which are not in the scope of this paper. Due to the utilization of COTS hard- and software and the increasingly interconnected fashion of ICSs, the physical presence of the attacker is no longer required to execute semantic attacks. Tampering with railway operation is possible from remote locations and is not limited to a single railway station as it can be scaled to a multitude of stations via the communication network. Similarly, it is possible that a malware specifically crafted for railway signalling infects the communication networks to manipulate the FEs in the described way. Stuxnet is the infamous proof that such attacks have already been carried out in the past. A well targeted attack of this magnitude could have a serious impact on railway transportation and thus the society.

2   Related Work

To the best of our knowledge, there is no work investigating anomaly detection in railway signalling networks. There are a few works that utilize the semantics of the monitored network to construct and intrusion or anomaly detection system for other CIs. ANNs have been employed for network anomaly detection several times, but our application to railway signalling and the preprocessor and classifier to facilitate the integration of an ANN are novel in the literature.

Caselli et al. [3] describe an intrusion detection system (IDS) that defends against sequence attacks on the command and control communication of a CI. Sequence attacks are a specific type of semantic attack that concern the misplacement of system operation events that are licit if considered individually. We investigate sequence attacks on the CI of railway signalling in this paper.

Jin et al. [7] employ the semantics of the controlled process to infer anomaly detection rules similar to the idea behind our work that the inherent logic (semantics) of railway operation can be learned by an ANN and further utilized for anomaly detection. The work of Jin et al. is based on electricity networks, where they developed invariants to verify across defined locations of the network. The Linear Invariant Checker and Bus-zero-sum Checker are derived from physical laws that are always valid in an electrical grid.

Carcano et al. [2] study intrusion detection in supervisory control and data acquisition (SCADA) systems that have been subject to a safety analysis process such that possible critical states of the system are known. They model the critical states and define a metric for the IDS to calculate the distance of the currently observed state to any critical state and subsequently raise an alert if the system assumes a critical state. Our ANN learns a model of the system's normal states and determines with the classifier whether the observed action transforms the system into a state outside the model and thus a critical state.

Debar et al. [4] use a trace of Unix commands to model the user's behaviour and predict the next command with the help of an ANN. In combination with an expert system, they construct an IDS to detect break-ins into the supervised computer system.

Heinrich et al. [6] propose an architecture to embed a variety of security measures into safety-critical railway signalling to build defence in depth and describe the environment in which our anomaly detection system is supposed to work in more detail.

The insufficient cybersecurity protection of railway transportation is also discussed by Valdivia et al. [12] as well as the coexistence of safety and security in the domain. They demand a network IDS that does not interfere with any safety functionality. We present an anomaly detection system that fulfils this requirement.

Kwon et al. [8] provide a survey of deep learning-based network anomaly detection. They provide a taxonomy of anomaly-based IDS that includes many techniques but focuses on ANNs and discusses types of ANN that have been studied for network anomaly detection.

3 Building and Training the ANN

We explain how we build and configure an ANN to predict the next issued command based on the recently observed commands. We use three realistic datasets of network communication that we preprocess to be able to feed the commands into an ANN. Equivalent preprocessing of the supervised network is required for a real-world application of our anomaly detection. Then, we test different ANN models and optimize their parameters on the datasets.

Table 1. Overview of datasets

	Station 1	Station 2	Station 3
Number of datagrams	178 346	605 966	810 191
Number of FEs ($|i|$)	21	70	184
$|s|$ (FE state)	11	11	11
$|d| = |i| + |s|$ (datagram)	$21 + 11 = 32$	$70 + 11 = 81$	$184 + 11 = 195$

3.1 Dataset

To train and evaluate our ANNs, we use three datasets gathered over a period of three years in TU Darmstadt's signalling lab[1]. The lab simulates real-world railway operation with tracks, signals, points, and trains in scale 1:87 and is used among other things to qualify traffic controllers of a German railway operator. We summarize signals, points and train detection systems (TDSs) under the term field element (FE). Signal boxes, FEs, and their operation are accurately simulated in the signalling lab, including the network traffic and datagrams. Hence, our datasets contain realistic traffic between the signal boxes and their FEs. Each dataset contains datagrams from one railway station comprised of one signal box that are pairwise independent with respect to railway signalling. Table 1 shows the size of the datasets (number of datagrams) and the size of the stations (number of FEs), which corresponds to the complexity of its track topology.

Our dataset contains three types of FEs: light signals, points and TDSs all of which are identified by their names. The latter monitor the vacancy of track sections. Each datagram consists of an FE identifier (its name) and the successive state the FE is set to. A datagram is sent via the signalling network only if a state of an FE changes. To ensure safe train movement through the infrastructure, the signal box receives reports on the vacancy of track sections from the TDSs and sends commands to the points and light signals according to the desired route of the train. We use the first 80 % of our dataset as training set and the remaining 20 % as test set. The order of the datagrams in the datasets matters because it inherently represents the state of the station's FEs at that time. Therefore, randomly sampling datagrams from the dataset for training and test set is not possible as it would not maintain the inherent order.

---

[1] http://www.eisenbahnbetriebsfeld.de/.

3.2   Preprocessing Datagrams

We model each datagram d as a pair of vectors $d = (i, s)$ containing the FE's identifier and state. We use the notation $|v|$ to denote the length of vector v. To feed the vectors to the ANN, we use one-hot encoding. For Station 1, vector i encoding the identifier is a 21 bit vector as Station 1 has 21 FEs. The vector is filled with 0s and exactly one value is set to 1 to encode the datagram's FE identifier. For Station 2, the vector has length 70 and for Station 3, it has length 184. To one-hot encode the state of the considered FE, 11 bit are sufficient. Points and TDSs assume two states each: left or right and clear or occupied respectively. For the various clear and stop states of the signals, we need 9 more bits in the state vector, resulting in a total of 11. Hence, we use vectors of length 32, 81 and 195 and thus the same number of neurons on the input and output layer to encode each datagram. The lengths $|i|$, $|s|$, and $|d|$ corresponding to the dataset are summarized in Table 1.

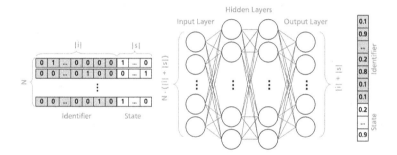

Fig. 2. ANN architecture

3.3   ANN Architecture

As architecture for our ANN, we use four fully connected (dense) layers: one input layer, two hidden layers and an output layer, as sketched in Fig. 2. The amount of neurons in the input layer is determined by the size of the encoded datagram $|d|$ and the number of past datagrams N presented to the ANN. Figure 2 depicts the input vector on the left, split in one-hot encoded identifier and state with N datagram vectors. The encoded identifier is shown with a grey background, the state with a white. The vectors of the N datagrams are flattened in the preprocessing to form a large vector with length $N * (|i| + |s|)$ containing all values concatenated. We perform experiments with different types and sizes of layers. A summary is given in Table 2. Model A utilizes a constant size of hidden layers, independent from the input or output layers, and thus independent from the station's size that we train the model on. In Model B, the size of the first hidden layer depends on the size of the input layer, while the size of the second hidden layer depends on the size of the output layer. We have performed experiments with long short-term memory (LSTM) cells as well. We use $|\boldsymbol{d}|$ LSTM units and N time steps in Model C and choose to not use a second hidden layer.

3.4   Determining Hyper-Parameters

With a few pilot experiments, we determine suitable values for the batch size and number of epochs in the training phase. For the batch size, that determines how many samples are presented to the ANN before the weights are adjusted, we decide that a value of 512 suits our purpose as a trade-off between training duration and accuracy. The number of epochs determines how many times the entire dataset is presented to the ANN for training. For our further tests we use 10 training epochs as we can not observe any significant improvement beyond 10 rounds. For the input and dense hidden layers we use the ReLU function as activation. Due to the one-hot encoding, we pass the output layer's activation through a sigmoid function that translates the activation to the interval $[0, 1]$.

Table 2. ANN layer types and sizes

Layer	Model A		Model B		Model C	
	Type	Size	Type	Size	Type	Size
Input layer	Dense	$N \cdot |\boldsymbol{d}|$	Dense	$N \cdot |\boldsymbol{d}|$	Dense	$|\boldsymbol{d}|$
Hidden layer	Dense	128	Dense	$2N \cdot |\boldsymbol{d}|$	LSTM	$(N, |\boldsymbol{d}|)$
Hidden layer	Dense	128	Dense	$2|\boldsymbol{d}|$	–	
Output layer	Dense	$|\boldsymbol{d}|$	Dense	$|\boldsymbol{d}|$	Dense	$|\boldsymbol{d}|$

Table 3. Optimal length of history (N) and accuracy for each model and dataset

	Model A	Model B	Model C
Station 1	18 (98.78 %)	14 (98.84 %)	3 (97.57 %)
Station 2	14 (99.13 %)	9 (99.18 %)	8 (98.90 %)
Station 3	12 (99.59 %)	7 (99.61 %)	9 (99.53 %)

3.5   Optimizing Specific Parameters

The hypothesis of this paper is that a small number of previously observed datagrams (N) in the signalling network is sufficient to predict the next command. To validate the hypothesis, we train our models on the datasets starting from $N = 1$ and increase N by 1 until we find a maximum in the accuracy on the test set. Table 3 shows for each dataset and each model which value of N achieved the best accuracy on the test set.

Figure 3 depicts accuracy and loss on the training and test sets. We present Station 2 with Model B as an example, while finding the optimal parameter N. The learning curve for the other datasets and models look similar and their results are shown in Table 3. The measured accuracy is presented as the mean of 8 trainings with the same parameters to cope with the indeterminism of training an ANN. Thus, we print the standard deviation in Fig. 3 as well. However, in most cases it is so small that it collapses with the graph. The maximum accuracy appears at $N = 9$ and the minimum loss at $N = 7$. Both points are marked in the figure.

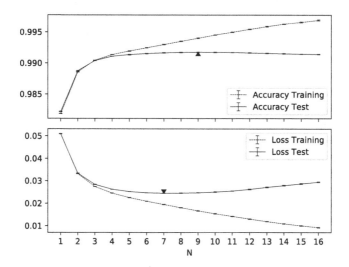

Fig. 3. Accuracy and loss while optimizing N for Station 2 with Model B

Table 4. Mean training duration for $N = 10$ and the optimal N shown in Table 3

	Model A		Model B		Model C	
	$N = 10$	$N = opt$	$N = 10$	$N = opt$	$N = 10$	$N = opt$
Station 1	22.4 s	29.9 s	36.0 s	51.5 s	67.4 s	30.6 s
Station 2	125.9 s	145.2 s	387.0 s	355.4 s	465.1 s	387.1 s
Station 3	284.6 s	321.9 s	2845.5 s	1437.5 s	1366.1 s	1221.0 s

Table 4 shows the mean training time including the preprocessing and evaluation on the test set for our datasets and models. The duration increases in proportion to N and dataset size. We use TensorFlow[2] to perform the experiments on eight Intel(R) Xeon(R) CPU E5-2620 v2 @ 2.10GHz processors running

---

[2] https://www.tensorflow.org/.

Debian 9. 30 GB of memory are sufficient to train the largest model. We now
have determined the parameters to operate our ANN with and we have shown
that our hypothesis is valid that a small number of datagrams are sufficient to
predict the next with adequate accuracy.

4   Constructing an Anomaly Detection Classifier

Due to the lack of anomaly examples (attacks) and a labelled dataset we can
not directly train a classifier to distinguish anomalies. This would require a
dataset with approximately the same amount of normal and anomalous traces,
otherwise the classifier would be strongly biased towards the larger group of
examples (normal traces in our case). Thus, we construct a classifier for anomaly
detection out of the ANN's prediction of the next datagram. We predict the next
transmitted datagram based on the trace of N previously observed datagrams
and compare it to the actually observed datagram. The prediction is a $|d|$-
dimensional vector $\hat{y} = (\hat{i}, \hat{s})$ of values in $[0, 1]$ describing the ANN's estimation
of the next datagram's identifier and state. The closer one value in $\hat{y}$ is to 1, the
more likely the ANN estimates the respective entry in the observed datagram
y to be 1. Once we observe the next datagram $y = (i, s)$ in the signalling
network, we split it into FE identifier i and state s parts. We compare the
observed datagram (y) to our prediction $(\hat{y})$ by applying one of the two following
comparators:

Activation: We check whether the observed identifier was predicted with an
output value (neuron activation) greater than a defined threshold. As the
observed identifier is one-hot encoded, the desired activation value is the dot
product of the prediction vector and observed vector: $i \cdot \hat{i}$.
Rank: We sort the predictions in $\hat{i}$ by their value and apply the same order
to i. Then we check whether the observed identifier has a rank less than or
equal to a threshold (e.g., whether it is in the top 3).

To merge identifier and state into a combined classifier, we follow the decision
tree depicted in Fig. 4. First, we compare the observed datagram's identifier i
with the prediction $\hat{i}$ as explained above $(cmp(i, \hat{i}))$. If the prediction is below
the identifier threshold t_i, we classify the observed datagram as an anomaly. If
the prediction is above or equal to t_i, we proceed to compare the state s of the
observed datagram with the prediction $\hat{s}$ $(cmp(s, \hat{s}))$. If the prediction is below

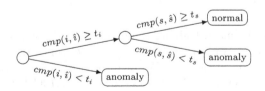

Fig. 4. Decision tree visualizing the combined classifier

the state threshold t_s, we classify the observed datagram as an anomaly. Only if the datagram passes both thresholds, we accept it as normal. The thresholds for the rank comparator work analogously with the rank less than or equal to the threshold classifying as normal and otherwise as anomaly. We introduce the rank as a comparator as it offers the advantage of being independent from the absolute output of the ANN. It is possible that for some benign predictions, all activations are below the absolute activation threshold while the rank threshold accepts the highest (most likely) predictions even if their absolute value is low.

5 Evaluation

To evaluate our model and classifier, we determine the false positive rate (FPR) and false negative rate (FNR) dependent on a threshold for the prediction's activation and rank. We first explain this for identifier and state independently. Subsequently, we use the combined classifier and evaluate the combined FPR and FNR as well. In our terminology, a true positive is an anomalous, malicious datagram and a true negative correspondingly a normal, benign datagram. Accordingly, a false positive is a benign datagram that is falsely considered to be an anomaly. Vice versa, a false negative is a malicious datagram that is not detected as anomaly. Also, we need to demonstrate that our classifier is indeed capable of distinguishing benign from malicious datagrams by showing that normal datagrams are above the thresholds and anomalies are below. The FPR can easily be determined from the test data of our dataset by plotting the activation of the correct output neuron ($i \cdot \hat{i}$ and $s \cdot \hat{s}$) as well as its rank among all neurons respectively. The FNR however, we cannot determine from our dataset because it does not contain anomalies to test against. Hence, we manually create attack vectors by randomly selecting a trace of $l > N$ consecutive datagrams from our test set. With expert knowledge, we craft a malicious datagram $l + 1$ that would set the railway infrastructure to a hazardous state if issued after the selected sequence and therefore must be classified as anomaly. The concrete malicious datagram depends on the current infrastructure configuration represented by the trace of l datagrams. Generally, attack vectors split into three categories: First, the attacker tries to switch a point a train is about to run over or is already running over it to cause a derailment or collision. Second, the attacker swaps the state of a TDS to make trains appear or disappear on the infrastructure, which increases the chance that another train is routed into an already occupied section causing a collision. Third, the attacker sets a signal to clear that protects an occupied track section such that an approaching train collides with the train occupying the section behind the signal. The experts verify that executing the malicious datagram after the set of l datagrams would lead to a train derailing or a collision. We ensure that each attack category receives the same fraction ($1/3$) of malicious datagrams in our attack vector set which contains 99 attack vectors for each station. Subsequently, we calculate the FNR by presenting the last N datagrams of each attack vector to the ANN and the classifier. The fraction of undetected attack vectors yields the FNR. Ideally, we would expect the malicious datagrams to receive an activation close to 0 because they should be very unlikely to appear next from what the ANN learned in the training phase.

Figure 5 shows the FPR and FNR for FE identifier and FE state independently. In fact, the state is dependent on the identifier, which we evaluate in Sect. 5.1. As an example for comparing the identifiers $(i, \hat{i})$ by activation, we chose a threshold of 0.2, such that every datagram whose identifier is predicted with an activation greater than 0.2 is classified as normal and classified as anomaly if below 0.2. In Fig. 5a, we see that this threshold would perform with a FPR of 0.167 (thick black line) and a FNR of 0.010 (thick dashed grey line). The thin lines depict the rates for comparing the state $(s, \hat{s})$ of the FE.

Figure 5b shows the rates for the rank comparator of the output neuron. As an example for comparing the identifiers $(i, \hat{i})$ by rank, we chose to accept all commands whose prediction are at least in the top 10. In Fig. 5b, we see that this threshold would perform with a FPR of 0.030 (thick black line) and a FNR of 0.152 (thick dashed grey line). The rates of the FE's state (thin lines) reach 0 and 1 respectively for smaller ranks than the rates for the identifier because there are fewer states to rank than identifiers ($|\hat{s}| < |\hat{i}|$). For both figures, we use the results of Station 2 and Model B with $N = 9$.

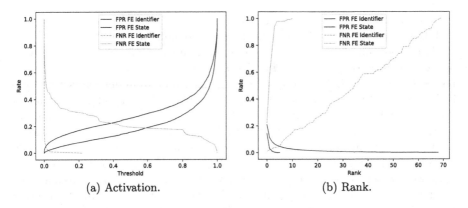

(a) Activation.   (b) Rank.

Fig. 5. FPR and FNR based on the correct output neuron's activation and rank

5.1   Evaluating the Combined Classifier

To receive meaningful evaluation data, we need to calculate FNRs and FPRs on the combined classifier for the identifier and state. It is important to note that the two thresholds are not necessarily set to the same value. This becomes apparent in the case of ranks as the identifier threshold can be in a range from 1 to $|i|$ (70 in this evaluation of Station 2) while the state threshold can only range from 1 to $|s|$ (11). Hence, the FPR and FNR are functions dependent on two dimensions t_i and t_s. We sample the function for a predefined set of thresholds on our datasets to find a suitable pair $t = (t_i, t_s)$ to operate the classifier on. The

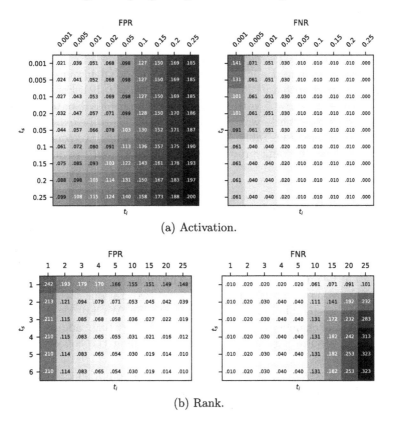

(a) Activation.

(b) Rank.

Fig. 6. Combined FPR and FNR for (a) activation and (b) rank

resulting heatmap for the neuron's activation is depicted in Fig. 6a. The values in the squares depict the achieved FPR or FNR respectively for t_i on the x-axis and t_s on the y-axis. The darker the square, the higher the rate. For example, an activation threshold of $t = (0.005, 0.001)$ yields a FPR of 0.039 costing a FNR of 0.071. If the prediction's rank is used for the classifier, a FPR of 0.01 at $t = (25, 6)$ corresponds to a high FNR of 0.323 as shown in Fig. 6b.

Especially Fig. 6b shows that most of the classification depends on the FE's identifier as there is more improvement of the rates in the x-axis than in the y-axis. We observe that fewer false positives appear with smaller thresholds and fewer false negatives appear with higher thresholds independent from whether the activation or the rank is used as comparator. The optimal choice of t_i and t_s, however, depends on the trade-off between FNR and FPR hence the importance of a low FNR versus a low FPR. In general, a lower FPR should be preferred over a lower FNR as false positives raise an alert where there is actually no attack on the system. Too many false positives reduce the confidence of the anomaly detection's users in the system and occupies the resources to process such an alert. On the contrary, missing a few actual attacks (false negatives) can be compensated because it is very likely that an attacker issues multiple malicious commands of which a single one classified as anomaly is sufficient to draw attention to the attacked system.

A reasonably balanced point between FPR and FNR in our opinion is $t_i = 0.001$ and $t_s = 0.01$ with a FPR of 0.027 and a FNR of 0.101. For the rank, such point is $t_i = 10$ and $t_s = 5$ with a FPR of 0.03 and a FNR of 0.04. Models A and C operate with slightly worse performance as it is to be expected from the proportion of accuracy in Table 3. From our experience, we conclude that the classifier based on the rank produces better results than the activation-based classifier.

6   Discussion

From the preprocessing we apply, it is already apparent that an ANN needs to be trained and optimized individually for each railway station. This includes in particular the length of history (N) and the thresholds. Not only is the ANN dependent on the number of FEs. But also the inter-dependencies of FEs learned by the ANN are significantly different between two stations such that a trained model is not transferable to another railway station. We indeed presume that a certain amount of changes to a station's track topology (e.g., adding or removing points) would require a re-training as well, including the collection of a new dataset to train on.

To train and test our ANN, we utilize datasets comprising several hundred thousand datagrams (confer Table 1) gathered over the course of three years. Fortunately, our preliminary experiments have shown that already a fraction of about 10 % of our datasets' size produces good results at the cost of one or two basis points of accuracy. Consequently, it is possible to reduce the dataset accumulation time. On top of that, real-world railway stations operate almost 24 h a day on 7 days per week, which is not the case in TU Darmstadt's signalling lab. Hence, sufficient training data for a real-world railway station can be collected significantly faster.

While data collection and model training can consume a lot of time and resources (see Table 4), the actual prediction can be performed quickly and in advance before the next datagram is observed. The anomaly detection holds the ANN model and a queue of N last datagrams. Before the next datagram appears, the prediction can be performed on the queue such that only the comparison needs to take place after a datagram arrives. This ensures that the anomaly detection can react in time to each incoming datagram. After the classification, the new datagram is pushed into the queue and the next prediction can already be performed such that the anomaly detection is prepared for the arrival of another datagram. In terms of computational resources, the CPU and memory intensive training (see Sect. 3.5) can be performed offline and is anyway required only once until the railway infrastructure changes. Our largest model (Model B for Station 3) requires as few as 18 MB of storage. Once the model is loaded into memory, a commercially available machine can perform the classification in a fraction of a second.

The anomaly detection mitigates application level denial-of-service (DoS) attacks that try to simulate occupied track segments, because random track sections becoming occupied are not contained in the training set and thus are outside the anomaly detection's perception of normality. Accordingly, the attacker cannot occupy some or all sections of her choice at once. The attacker's strategy to remain undetected by the anomaly detection is to follow correct train operation, by setting the points correctly, setting a signal to clear and then occupying one track section after the other as a real train would do. This would not raise an alert as it corresponds to the expected behaviour but would as well not be invisible to traffic controllers.

Our anomaly detection system can be attached to the communication network of a railway station as a dedicated machine as indicated by Fig. 1. It requires network monitoring capabilities to observe the transmitted commands. With this layout and alerts being processed by staff in a SOC, the system itself does not interfere with railway's safety functionality as the actual decision for intervention is transferred to a human. It is possible to allow the anomaly detection system to directly suppress commands that it classifies as anomaly. However, this kind of intervention requires a detailed study of safety interference.

7   Conclusion

We have demonstrated a neural network-based anomaly detection system that can be installed without interference in railway signal boxes. By performing our experiments on railway stations of different sizes, we have shown that our method is scalable to large networks. With only 14, 9, or 7 datagrams of history, we have shown that it is possible to predict the next action in a railway signalling network with an accuracy of 98.84 %, 99.18 %, and 99.61 %. We demonstrated a classifier that takes the prediction and the actual observed datagram and determines whether it is an anomaly or not. We have shown that the classifier based on the rank of the ANN's prediction can operate with a FPR of 0.03 and a FNR of 0.04 and produces better results than the classifier solely based on the activation. The concrete trade-off between false positives and false negatives however should be adjusted by domain experts for each station individually.

Acknowledgement. The work presented in this paper has been partly funded by the German Federal Ministry of Education and Research (BMBF) under the project "HASELNUSS: Hardwarebasierte Sicherheitsplattform für Eisenbahn-Leit- und Sicherungstechnik" (ID 16KIS0597K).

References

1. Bloomfield, R., Bloomfield, R., Gashi, I., Stroud, R.: How secure is ERTMS? In: Ortmeier, F., Daniel, P. (eds.) SAFECOMP 2012. LNCS, vol. 7613, pp. 247–258. Springer, Heidelberg (2012). https://doi.org/10.1007/978-3-642-33675-1_22

2. Carcano, A., Coletta, A., Guglielmi, M., Masera, M., Fovino, I.N., Trombetta, A.: A multidimensional critical state analysis for detecting intrusions in SCADA systems. IEEE Trans. Ind. Inform. **7**(2), 179–186 (2011). https://doi.org/10.1109/TII.2010.2099234

3. Caselli, M., Zambon, E., Kargl, F.: Sequence-aware intrusion detection in industrial control systems. In: Proceedings of the 1st ACM Workshop on Cyber-Physical System Security, pp. 13–24. ACM (2015). https://doi.org/10.1145/2732198.2732200

4. Debar, H., Becker, M., Siboni, D.: A neural network component for an intrusion detection system. In: IEEE Computer Society Symposium on Research in Security and Privacy, pp. 240–250. IEEE (1992). https://doi.org/10.1109/risp.1992.213257

5. Fovino, I.N., Coletta, A., Carcano, A., Masera, M.: Critical state-based filtering system for securing SCADA network protocols. IEEE Trans. Ind. Electron. **59**(10), 3943–3950 (2011). https://doi.org/10.1109/tie.2011.2181132

6. Heinrich, M., et al.: Security requirements engineering in safety-critical railway signalling networks. Secur. Commun. Netw. (2019). https://doi.org/10.1155/2019/8348925

7. Jin, X., Bigham, J., Rodaway, J., Gamez, D., Phillips, C.: Anomaly detection in electricity cyber infrastructures. In: Proceedings of CNIP (2006)

8. Kwon, D., Kim, H., Kim, J., Suh, S.C., Kim, I., Kim, K.J.: A survey of deep learning-based network anomaly detection. Cluster Comput. **22**(1), 949–961 (2017). https://doi.org/10.1007/s10586-017-1117-8

9. Schlehuber, C., Heinrich, M., Vateva-Gurova, T., Katzenbeisser, S., Suri, N.: Challenges and approaches in securing safety-relevant railway signalling. In: 2017 IEEE European Symposium on Security and Privacy Workshops (EuroS&PW), pp. 139–145. IEEE (2017). https://doi.org/10.1109/eurospw.2017.63

10. Schlehuber, C., Heinrich, M., Vateva-Gurova, T., Katzenbeisser, S., Suri, N.: A security architecture for railway signalling. In: Tonetta, S., Schoitsch, E., Bitsch, F. (eds.) SAFECOMP 2017. LNCS, vol. 10488, pp. 320–328. Springer, Cham (2017). https://doi.org/10.1007/978-3-319-66266-4_21

11. Temple, W.G., Tran, B.A.N., Chen, B., Kalbarczyk, Z., Sanders, W.H.: On train automatic stop control using balises: attacks and a software-only countermeasure. In: 2017 IEEE 22nd Pacific Rim International Symposium on Dependable Computing (PRDC), pp. 274–283. IEEE (2017). https://doi.org/10.1109/prdc.2017.52

12. Valdivia, L.J., Adin, I., Arrizabalaga, S., Anorga, J., Mendizabal, J.: Cybersecurity-the forgotten issue in railways: security can be woven into safety designs. IEEE Veh. Technol. Mag. **13**(1), 48–55 (2018). https://doi.org/10.1109/mvt.2017.2736098

Automated Anomaly Detection in CPS Log Files
A Time Series Clustering Approach

Tabea Schmidt[(✉)], Florian Hauer, and Alexander Pretschner

Department of Informatics, Technical University of Munich, Munich, Germany
{tabea.schmidt,florian.hauer,alexander.pretschner}@tum.de

Abstract. When *Cyber-Physical Systems* (CPS) work incorrectly we would like to know the reason for this behavior. Experts inspect log files of CPS to get an idea about what went wrong. The large amount of information, which is stored in those log files, and the complexity of CPS pose a challenge to experts that try to manually detect anomalies in the system's behavior. We propose to automate anomaly detection in CPS log files by applying a clustering approach to find time spans, in which the regarded system behaves abnormal. With our approach, we aim to significantly reduce the time and effort that is needed by experts to discover anomalies in the log files without having to build a model of the system first. The results from our evaluation show that our generic approach can effectively find anomalies for different types of CPS.

Keywords: Anomaly detection · CPS · Time series data · Clustering · Unsupervised machine learning · Log analysis

1 Introduction

In *Cyber-Physical Systems* (CPS), the physical components of the systems are connected, controlled and monitored by software components. The sensors of the systems are permanently collecting data. On the one hand, this data is stored in log files and, on the other hand, it is processed by software components. We can find CPS in a broad range of application domains. Examples from different fields are unmanned aerial vehicles (UAVs), autonomous cars or smart grids [12].

In the following, we will take a look at a single UAV as an example for CPS. The UAV has the mission to fly to a specified waypoint to deliver a package. When the UAV reaches the waypoint, the package is damaged. As the company that wanted to deliver an intact package, we are interested in the reason for the damage of the package. A UAV normally logs at each time stamp more than 100 parameters including sensor data, messages and status of components. A flight of ten minutes yields a log file with 6,000 time stamps if the data is logged every 100 ms. If each of the 100 parameters is logged at each time stamp, the resulting log file contains 600,000 parameter values. An expert that tries to find the reason for the damage of the package will take a look at the behavior of

© Springer Nature Switzerland AG 2020
A. Casimiro et al. (Eds.): SAFECOMP 2020, LNCS 12234, pp. 179–194, 2020.
https://doi.org/10.1007/978-3-030-54549-9_12

the UAV during its flight by inspecting the log file. Throughout this process, the expert will look for anomalies in the behavior of the UAV. These anomalies in the system's behavior depict undesired behavior of the system, which can result, for example, from failures of the system or attacks on the system. When searching the log file for an anomaly, the expert might have to take a look at all 600,000 parameter values in the worst case. In the best case for anomaly detection, the UAV crashes during its flight, hinting that the underlying fault is probably located at the end of the log file. However, this is not necessarily the case. A short anomaly might occur that needs some time to manifest and to result in a crash. Then, taking a look at only the last parameter values will not reveal the anomaly and the expert still needs to inspect up to 600,000 parameter values. Even if the anomaly is located at the end of the log file, there are additional challenges that the expert has to handle. These are described in the following: The system's behavior might look normal when the expert only regards a single parameter each time. This means that the expert additionally needs to take the interaction of different parameters into account to detect abnormal behavior of the system. Also, the particular set of interactions that the expert needs to review to detect an anomaly is not known beforehand.

Therefore, we propose to automate the anomaly detection in CPS log files by using a clustering approach. With our approach, we reduce the log files of a CPS to the time spans, in which the system behaves abnormal. In this way, the expert does not need to review the complete log files. This saves him or her a large amount of time and effort when trying to discover an anomaly.

Previous approaches of anomaly detection in CPS log files [5,16] work with a model that describes the normal behavior of the system. This means that a complete and fine-tuned model of the system is needed to effectively detect anomalies in the log files of this system. If we want to apply these approaches to detect anomalies for different systems, we need to create a model for each of those systems. Our proposed approach for detecting anomalies is not dependent on a model of the system. When inspecting CPS log files, we aim to find time spans, in which the system does not behave as in the other parts of the log files. In this way, we create a generic approach, which can be applied to log files of any type of CPS without having to train or learn a model of the system beforehand.

The **contribution of this paper** is the following: We provide a generic approach to detect time spans, in which a CPS behaves abnormal. For this purpose, we apply clustering on the multidimensional time series data from the log files of the system. We evaluate our proposed anomaly detection approach with two CPS data sets, which include failures and attacks as abnormal behavior. One of these data sets includes log files from a UAV, whereas the other one contains data from an industrial water plant.

An overview of our proposed process for detecting anomalies in CPS log files is presented in Sect. 2. We then describe our clustering approach in detail in Sect. 3. Subsequently, Sect. 4 demonstrates the results of our experiments on two data sets. In Sect. 5 we discuss related work in the area of automated anomaly detection for CPS. Finally, we conclude our work in Sect. 6.

2   Anomaly Detection

When a CPS works incorrectly, we would like to find the reason for this behavior. Abnormal behavior can, for example, be caused by a failure within the system or by an attack launched on the system. When investigating the reason for the incorrect behavior, experts take a look at the log files of the system. In those log files, the parameter values of the system such as sensor data, messages or status of components are logged over the execution time of the system.

As mentioned earlier, there exist two main challenges for manually detecting anomalies in CPS log files: (i) the large amount of information included in the log files and (ii) the general complexity of CPS. Due to these challenges, we propose an automated approach to reduce the amount of information that needs to be inspected by the expert and enable easier detection of anomalies in CPS log files. Figure 1 depicts an overview of our proposed approach.

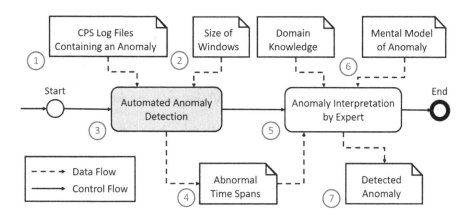

Fig. 1. Automated anomaly detection in CPS log files.

CPS log files (1) are the input to our approach. These log files include the logged parameter values over the execution time of the CPS. Additionally, they contain the anomaly that we are interested in discovering.

In this paper, we focus on the automated anomaly detection approach (3), which takes the CPS log files as input. We divide the log files into a number of time spans and compare the behavior of the parameters in these time spans. Therefore, we need as a second input the size of these time spans (2), which we call "windows". We will discuss different options for estimating this variable in this paper. Additionally, we would like to inspect methods for estimating a good window size in future work. With our clustering approach, we aim to detect time spans in the log files, in which the regarded system behaves abnormal (4).

In the next step, an expert can use the discovered abnormal time spans of the log files to interpret the abnormal behavior of the system (5). To detect anomalies in the provided time spans of the log files, additional expert knowledge (6) is necessary. To find an anomaly in the provided time spans, the expert will need to have domain knowledge and a mental model of the anomaly to discover. This means that the expert has to know how the parameter values of the regarded system normally behave to detect anomalies.

As a result of this process, the expert might be able to detect the anomaly (7) in a reduced amount of time and effort. Our clustering approach provides time spans, in which the system does not behave normally. Thus, it is possible that also rare behaviors are represented in these time spans. The expert will not be able to detect an anomaly if only rare behavior is included in the provided time spans. If this is the case, we propose to change the window size and run the automated anomaly detection again.

3   Detecting Anomalies with Time Series Clustering

In this chapter, we explain the technical details of our method. In Fig. 2, we provide an overview of the methodology of our proposed approach for automated anomaly detection in CPS log files. With our approach, we try to find those time spans in which the system behaves abnormal. We expect these abnormal behaviors to be different from the normal behavior of the system. Additionally, we anticipate the abnormal behavior to only appear rarely. The idea is, therefore, to cluster the data and then look at the small clusters to detect anomalies in the system's behavior.

CPS have a list of parameters $P = p_1, p_2, ..., p_n, ..., p_N$ that are logged over time. A CPS log file $L = p_1(ts_0), p_2(ts_0), ..., p_1(ts_1), ..., p_N(ts_T)$ consists of parameter values $p_n(ts_t)$ for each recorded time stamp ts_t with $t \in [0, T]$. The parameter value $p_n(ts_t)$ is logged at time stamp t and represents the parameter with index n in the list of parameters P. When trying to find anomalies in the log file of CPS, we might encounter the problem of log-heterogeneity [4]. Different components of CPS might generate differently formatted log files. In this case, we need to pre-process these log files to bring them into one format L. [4] presents various techniques that can be used for this pre-processing step. We will divide the log files into smaller windows w_j for clustering with $j \in [1, J]$. Each window has the same size $windowSize$, which has to be specified beforehand by the expert. More details about this step can be found in the next subsection. The result of our proposed approach will be a list of windows, in which the system behaves abnormal. We use the variable $AW = aw_1, ..., aw_F$ to represent this list of abnormal windows.

3.1   Window Slicing

When we use a clustering approach to detect anomalies in CPS log files, we need to first divide the log files into subsequent time spans. Then, we can compare the behavior of the parameters P in these time spans. We cut the time series data of the log files $L_1, ..., L_L$ into consecutive windows w_j. Each window has a size of $windowSize$ and the first window of each log file starts at ts_0. The

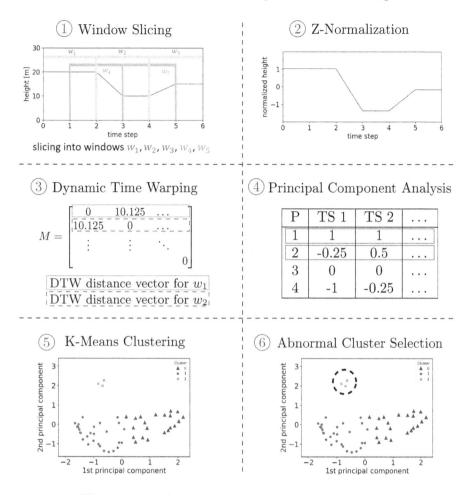

Fig. 2. Methodological overview of our proposed approach.

variable *windowSize* has to be specified by the expert beforehand. One way of estimating this variable is to take the knowledge about the system's behavior and its previously occurred anomalies into account. After detecting several anomalies in the system, we expect the expert to be able to estimate a good *windowSize* for each of these anomalies. Another approach is to execute the automated anomaly detection several times with different window sizes to find a good estimate. In our experiments, we discovered that a clustering with a low inertia value leads to good results for detecting anomalies, but not necessarily to the best results. Receiving good results for low inertia values seems intuitive since the inertia value represents the internal cohesion of the clusters. A low inertia value stands for a high internal cohesion within the clusters. An optimization technique can be used to find a window size, with which the lowest inertia values can be achieved. We believe that optimizing for a low inertia value will not be sufficient to find

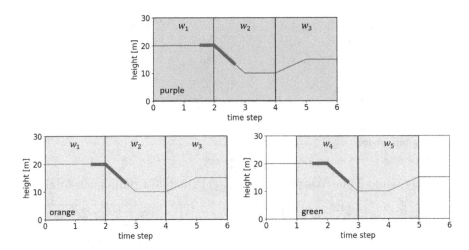

Fig. 3. If the log file L is only cut into the three purple windows w_1, w_2 and w_3 the abnormal behavior marked in bold might be missed. Therefore, we propose to instead use the five orange and green windows w_1, w_2, w_3, w_4 and w_5 to represent the log file. (Color figure online)

the best results for detecting anomalies though. In the future, we would like to assess several methods and optimization criteria for estimating a good value for the size of the windows. In this work, we will assume that the expert knows a good estimate of $windowSize$.

When slicing our data into windows w_j, we might run into the problem that the anomaly is lying directly on the border of two windows. Figure 3 illustrates this problem. In this figure, the abnormal behavior is located at the border of the windows w_1 and w_2. If the abnormal behavior wraps around the border of two windows w_j and w_{j+1}, it might not be detected since its effect on the complete behavior of w_j or w_{j+1} might be too small. Thus, we decided to consider additional windows that start with an offset at time stamp $ts_0 + (windowSize/2)$. These windows have the same size as the previously regarded windows. In this way, we can find the complete abnormal behavior in at least one window as long as we choose $windowSize$ large enough for the behavior to fit in.

3.2 Z-Normalization

Since we want to detect anomalies in the behavior of a system, we are not interested in the absolute values of the parameters p_n. Instead, we would like to compare how the parameter values change throughout the log files. Essential for us is, for example, that the UAV reduces its height by 5 m in 1 s. Whether the UAV decreased its height starting from 20 m or 15 m is instead not relevant for the anomaly detection. To concentrate on the structure of the time series we apply *Z-Normalization* on the data from the log files as proposed in [6]. In this way, we equalize the amplitudes and spatial differences between the time series. This enables the clustering algorithm to focus on the structure of the time series. To compute the normalized data points we need to look at each parameter p_n separately. For each parameter p_n we have to compute the mean and standard deviation over all time steps t_n in the log files. Then, we can calculate the normalized data point $p'_n(ts_t)$ for each data point $p_n(ts_t)$ by using the computed mean and standard deviation values.

3.3   Dynamic Time Warping

To compute the distance and therefore the similarity between two or more time series, *Dynamic Time Warping* (DTW) is commonly used [3,13]. With this method, we can find equal time series even if they are distorted along the temporal axis. Since we want to find equal behaviors in the log files that might be slightly distorted, this method seems to be suited very well for our approach.

To compute the DTW distance between two windows $w_1 = w_{1_1}, ..., w_{1_a}$ and $w_2 = w_{2_1}, ..., w_{2_b}$, we need to calculate the cumulative distances $D(w_{1_a}, w_{2_b})$ between the points of the time series.

$$D(w_{1_a}, w_{2_b}) = \delta(w_{1_a}, w_{2_b}) + min \begin{Bmatrix} D(w_{1_{a-1}}, w_{2_{b-1}}) \\ D(w_{1_a}, w_{2_{b-1}}) \\ D(w_{1_{a-1}}, w_{2_b}) \end{Bmatrix}$$

In this function, δ represents the Euclidean distance between the single data points w_{1_a} and w_{2_b} [3,19].

In the third step of our methodology, we compute the DTW distance of all parameter values p_n of one window to the parameter values p_n of all other windows. Our goal is to gain a single DTW distance value $D(w_i, w_j)$ between two windows w_i and w_j. To achieve this, we first need to calculate the DTW distance of these two windows for each parameter: $D_{p_n}(w_i, w_j)$ for $p_n \in P$. In a next step, we have to aggregate these single distance values of all parameters $D_{p_n}(w_i, w_j)$ to obtain a single DTW distance $D(w_i, w_j)$ for the two windows w_i and w_j. We use the sum of squares to aggregate these values. If two windows depict an identical behavior, the resulting DTW distance between these windows $D(w_i, w_j)$ will be 0. The matrix representing the DTW distances between all windows will be the input for the clustering algorithm in a subsequent step. Using DTW to calculate the distances between several time series enables us to work with data from different types of CPS. Since DTW can work on time series of different length and independent of the underlying parameters, we create a generic approach that is not tailored to one specific system.

3.4   Principal Component Analysis

Before clustering the derived DTW distances, the dimensionality of the data first needs to be reduced to gain decent clustering results. A *Principal Component Analysis* (PCA) [1] can be used for this purpose. It generates principle components by combining redundant or similarly behaving features of the data. This results in a decreased dimensionality of the data. We apply the PCA with a retained variance of 0.95 as suggested by the literature. This means that we only reduce the dimensionality of the data until the specified variance is met. In this way, we can cluster data that includes a high number of parameters p_n and, thus, do not need to limit our analysis on only a few selected parameters.

3.5   K-Means Clustering

After applying the PCA, we can cluster the data and gain decent clustering results. We decided to use the clustering algorithm *K-Means*, which is suitable and often used for clustering time series data [13]. Additionally, the results from the algorithm are easier to interpret than results from other techniques. We compute the *K-Means* clustering for all possible number of clusters. Subsequently, we apply the elbow method on the inertia values of the resulting clusterings to determine the optimal number of clusters k. Instead of manually guessing the location of the elbow, we let the *Kneedle* algorithm, presented in [20], find the point of maximum curvature in the inertia values. The resulting clusters $C = c_1, ..., c_k$ represent similar behaviors of the system parameters P throughout the log files. In the next step, we have to select those clusters from C, which represent the abnormal behavior of the system.

3.6   Abnormal Cluster Selection

For detecting anomalies we are interested in the abnormal behavior of the system. In this paper, we assume that our system behaves normally most of its execution time. This means that the number of time stamps in which abnormal behavior occurs will be small. Therefore, we expect the abnormal behavior to differ from the normal behavior of the system and to appear only rarely. In our clustering, this is represented by separate clusters that include only a small amount of instances.

To determine the number of small clusters that we should regard as abnormal, we suggest using the occurrence rate of the anomaly to detect. This rate can, for example, be the failure rate of the system or the attack rate on the system. Depending on how often the system fails or gets attacked, we should consider a different amount of clusters as abnormal. We assume that an expert can provide such an occurrence rate from his or her knowledge about the system. This knowledge can include the expert's experience with the system, a mental model of the anomaly to detect or reports on the system's processing.

In a first step, the list of clusters C needs to be rearranged to enable the selection of the abnormal clusters. The list of clusters C is sorted by the number of instances that the clusters contain. This yields a sorted list of clusters $CS = cs_1, cs_2, ..., cs_k$ with $size(cs_1) \leq size(cs_2) \leq ... \leq size(cs_k)$. Additionally, we need to specify the maximum number of abnormal windows that should be collected. This number can be computed based on the occurrence rate r of the anomaly to detect. The maximal number of abnormal windows is the product of the occurrence rate r and the number of all windows. In the next step, the selection of clusters starts from the beginning of CS to gain the smallest clusters first. When a cluster is selected, all windows w_i from this cluster are added to the list of abnormal windows AW. Clusters are selected from the beginning of CS until the maximum number of abnormal windows is reached. The result of this step is the list of abnormal windows AW for the regarded log files.

4   Evaluation

In our experiments, we aim to evaluate how effectively the proposed approach can detect abnormal time spans in CPS log files. The intended result is a reduced amount of time and effort that needs to be invested by an expert to find an anomaly in CPS log files. Therefore, a high recall value is important for us. The resulting list of abnormal windows AW should include all anomalies. Otherwise, the expert will not be able to find the anomalies in the reduced amount of windows that we provide. If the precision values are too low, the amount of windows that the expert needs to inspect is too large to save time and effort. However, we believe that as long as we can save the expert time and effort during the anomaly detection, the precision values do not need to be as high as the recall values. This means that the list of abnormal windows AW is allowed to contain some windows with normal behavior as long as their quantity remains small. We use two data sets from different CPS in our experiments to emphasize the generic applicability of our approach. Both data sets contain labels about the included failures and attacks. In the experiments, we only use these labels to compute precision and recall values for our proposed method. These labels are not used by our clustering algorithm at any time.

4.1   Implementation and Experimental Setup

In our implementation, we use methods from the scikit-learn machine learning library [18] for computing PCA and K-Means. Additionally, we use the *Kneedle* algorithm from [20].

The experiments are run on a machine with an *Intel Xenon E5-2687W* processor with 15 cores and 128 GB of RAM. The K-Means algorithm is run 10 times with different beginning seeds. The run with the smallest inertia value is chosen. Our experiments take 6 s to 16 min, depending on the length of the log files and the size of the windows.

4.2   Data Sets

ALFA Data Set. [10,11] the first data set in our experiments is the ALFA data set, which includes log files of a fixed-wing Unmanned Aerial Vehicle (UAV). This data set encompasses 36 log files, which describe the behavior of the UAV while various failures occur. The log files include four different types of failures: aileron, elevator, engine and rudder failures. For each log file L, the specific failure and its occurrence time are given. Our list of parameters P for this data set consists of the main eight features of the UAV:

$$P = pitch, roll, yaw, velocity, position, orientation, air speed, wind estimation$$

This data set includes failures of different categories that vary widely in their behavior. To yield more detailed results, we conduct our experiments separately for each of those failure types. This allows us to explore whether or not there are specific types for which our approach performs considerably better or worse compared to the other types. In this way, we can understand how well the clustering separates the abnormal behavior of each of those failure types from the normal behavior of the system. To perform this category-specific analysis, we combine all log files that contain failures of one category into one log file L. Then, our approach is applied to this single log file L to find abnormal behaviors that represent the failures of this specific category.

SWaT Data Set. [7] as a second data set, we use the SWaT data set collected by the *Centre for Research in Cyber Security, Singapore University of Technology and Design* (iTrust). The institute collected data from an industrial water treatment plant and launched 36 attacks on it during execution. In our experiments, we use the data that was recorded over six days in 2015 and work with a resolution of one data point per minute. This means that we regard all parameter values once per minute. The list of parameters P for this data includes the most dominant features of the water plant. These can be found in [7], where the authors provide an overview of the process of their test bed.

$$P = lit101, lit301, lit401, p101, p201, p203, p205, p301, p401, p501, p602,$$
$$fit201, fit401, ait201, ait202, aitT203, ait402, ait503, ait504, dpit301$$

Since we do not have further knowledge about this water plant, we do not know what the parameters in P stand for or which effects they have on the system. But, we are still able to apply our clustering approach to find abnormal time spans without this further knowledge.

The data set does not provide a subdivision of the attacks into attack categories that are based on the behavior of the attack types. Therefore, we will consider all data from this data set at the same time in our experiments. We thus apply our clustering approach to a log file L, which includes all data from the data set.

4.3   Experimental Results

When applying our proposed clustering approach to the log files $L_1, ..., L_L$ in the experiments, we will get a list of abnormal windows AW as a result. To evaluate

Table 1. The characteristics of the ALFA and the SWaT data set as well as the window size, which achieves the best values in the experiments for each category.

Data set	Failure/attack category	Failure/attack rate	Best window size
ALFA	Aileron failure	0.3365	100
ALFA	Elevator failure	0.1114	109
ALFA	Engine failure	0.1350	138
ALFA	Rudder failure	0.1921	33
SWaT	All attacks	0.1205	34

our approach, we compare the resulting abnormal windows $aw_i \in AW$ with the time spans that were labeled to include a failure or an attack in the data sets.

For computing precision, recall and F_1 values for the evaluation of our approach, we need a clear definition of true positives (TP), false positives (FP), true negatives (TN) and false negatives (FN). A block in the following definitions is a set of parameter values of subsequent time stamps from the log files. Each block has a size of $windowSize/2$ and the first block starts at time stamp ts_0.

- TP are blocks that include an anomaly and are correctly marked as 'abnormal' by our proposed approach.
- FP are blocks that contain no anomaly and are wrongly marked as 'abnormal' by our clustering approach.
- TN are blocks that include no anomaly and are correctly marked as 'normal' by our proposed approach.
- FN are blocks that contain an anomaly and are wrongly marked as 'normal' by our clustering approach.

As mentioned earlier, the abnormal clusters are selected depending on the occurrence rate of the anomaly. In our experiments, this is the failure rate of the system or attack rate on the system. Normally, an expert would provide this occurrence rate. Since we do not know the specific systems of the used data sets, we will instead estimate the occurrence rate of the anomalies from the included labels. For this purpose, we divide the total number of time stamps with the number of time stamps in which a failure or attack occurs concerning the labels. Table 1 displays the calculated failure or attack rates for the two data sets in our experiments.

Additionally, this table shows the window size per category which achieves the best results in the experiments. We mentioned several methods for estimating a good window size in Sect. 3.1. Since we are not familiar with the particular systems of the data sets, we have to find the best window sizes differently than experts would normally do. We decided to run our proposed clustering approach on the log files $L_1, ..., L_L$ for each category and data set with the size of the window $windowSize \in [10, 200]$. The best window size can be determined by looking at the resulting F_1 scores. Note that this process is only possible if we can compute the F_1 scores. The window size with the highest F_1 score is the optimal window size for finding anomalies in the regarded log files.

Table 2 presents the precision values, recall values and F_1 scores computed in our experiments. These values were calculated using the following formulas and the aforementioned definitions of TP, FP and FN:

$$precision = \frac{TP}{TP + FP} \qquad recall = \frac{TP}{TP + FN} \qquad F_1 = 2 * \frac{1}{\frac{1}{precision} + \frac{1}{recall}}$$

Table 2. The results of the experiments displaying the calculated precision and recall values as well as the F_1 score for the ALFA and the SWaT data set.

Data set	Failure/attack category	Precision	Recall	F_1 score
ALFA	Aileron failure	0.6848	0.8889	0.7736
ALFA	Elevator failure	0.8571	1.0000	0.9231
ALFA	Engine failure	0.6545	0.7500	0.6990
ALFA	Rudder failure	0.8209	0.9167	0.8661
SWaT	All attacks	0.8669	0.7357	0.7959

We can detect aileron failures from the ALFA data set with a precision of 0.6848, a recall of 0.8889 and a resulting F_1 score of 0.7736. For elevator failures, we can achieve even better results. The precision value raises to 0.8571 and we can identify all failures, which is presented by a recall value of 1.0. A precision of 0.6545 and a recall of 0.75 can be obtained for engine failures of the ALFA data set. When clustering the rudder failures from the same data set, we accomplish high precision and recall values of 0.8209 and 0.9167. The results of the SWaT data set show that we can detect attacks with a precision value of 0.8669 and a recall value of 0.7357. We can achieve high recall values for the SWaT data set and all categories in the ALFA data set. This shows that our proposed approach can detect a large amount of the included failures and attacks as abnormal behaviors of the system. From a practical perspective, the precision values for aileron and engine failures are high enough to save the expert time when trying to find an anomaly even though they are not as high as in the other categories. For elevator failures, rudder failures and all attacks in the SWaT data set, we achieve high precision values above 80%. This shows that we can efficiently reduce the amount of information that the expert needs to review.

In the following, we will compare the results of our experiments on the SWaT data set with results from experiments on the same data set in the literature. The authors of [9] present two model-based anomaly detection methods in their paper. They compare the performance of (1) *Deep Neural Networks* (DNN) and (2) *one-class Support Vector Machines* (SVM) on the SWaT data set. The parameters of these two unsupervised machine learning algorithms need to be fine-tuned to achieve good results. To train the DNN, a high amount of time and data is necessary. For the SVM approach the classification boundary between normal and abnormal behavior needs to be learned beforehand. A third method for anomaly detection on the SWaT data set is evaluated in [14] and called (3) *TABOR*. The authors propose to first train a *Bayesian Network* (BN) to recognize the normal behavior of the sensors and actuators of the system. Then, this BN is used to distinguish between normal and abnormal behavior of this specific system. We will focus the comparison on the number of anomalies that were detected by each of these approaches. We were not able to compare other values from these papers since the authors use different methods to compute TP, FP and FN. The SWaT data set includes 36 attacks. From [9], we can obtain that the (1) DNN-based approach detects 13 and the (2) SVM-based solution finds 20 attacks. These numbers are derived from Table 3 in [9] and not computed by ourselves. The method (3) *TABOR* can discover 24 attacks in the data set, which is displayed in Table 4 in [14]. We compare these numbers that were directly derived from the two papers, with the performance of our approach. With our proposed approach, we can detect 23 of the 36 attacks. This shows that we can discover more attacks in the SWaT data set than the (1) DNN-based and (2) SVM-based methods. Also, we detect only one attack less than the third method called (3) *TABOR*. This indicates that we can effectively detect anomalies in the SWaT data set compared to current literature. Most importantly, we can apply our approach to log files of different CPS without the need to fine-tune a large number of parameters or learn a model beforehand. Our evaluations, therefore, show the generic applicability of our proposed approach and its efficiency in comparison with other approaches from the literature.

5   Related Work

Automating anomaly detection in Cyber-Physical Systems is a broad research field. Anomalies are either identified by working on log files of the system [5, 8, 9, 15] or by monitoring parameters of the system in real-time [2, 17]. We decided to develop an approach that a posteriori detects anomalies in CPS log files.

For anomaly detection in log files [8] proposes the *Local Outlier Factor* algorithm, which statistically computes the reachability distance to the neighboring points. In contrary to this approach, we plan to develop a method which is per se suited to work on time series data by using *Dynamic Time Warping* as our distance metric. In [15], a hierarchical clustering approach is applied to log files to detect reoccurring failures. A representative sequence is chosen for each cluster. The authors of [5] build a *Finite State Automaton* for each component of the system from its log files to represents the normal work process of each component. In the next step, both approaches compare new log files with the representative sequences or *Finite State Automata* to detect anomalies. In these two papers, the normal behavior and representative sequences are derived from previously collected log files of the system. In this way, they are only able to detect reoccurring failures and anomalies and need to build a new model for each new system. Our approach, on the contrary, can be applied to log files of any CPS without having to train or learn a model beforehand. The authors of [9] suggest to use unsupervised machine learning approaches to find anomalies in log files from a water purification plant. In this approach, the authors do not need to build a fine-tuned model of the system. They still need to tune different parameters before they can start the learning phase of their machine learning approaches though. In contrary to this, the expert only needs to set a single variable in our approach. For real-time anomaly detection, [17] monitors one specific parameter (motor temperature) and [2] defines process invariants, which have to hold as long as the system is in a specified state. The invariants are derived from a model of the system. We aim for detecting anomalies of different origins, instead of focusing on only one parameter of the system as [17] suggests. Our goal is to a-posteriori find abnormal behaviors in CPS log files. In this way, we want to create an approach that is independent of the system itself and where we do not need to create a fine-tuned model of our system as needed in [2].

6   Conclusion

We first outlined the challenges of manually detecting anomalies in CPS log files. A large amount of logged parameter values, as well as the high complexity of these systems, complicate the manual discovery of anomalies. Therefore, we propose to automate this process by applying a clustering approach to the multidimensional time series data. The abnormal behavior is expected to occur only rarely and to differ from the normal behavior of the system. Thus, we anticipate the abnormal behaviors from the log files in separate and small clusters. For the selection of the abnormal clusters, the occurrence rate of the anomaly is utilized. We assume that an expert can provide this occurrence rate from previously collected data and his or her knowledge of the domain and system. In our experiments with two data sets from different types of CPS, we could show that our generic approach can effectively detect anomalies in the log files. Naturally, there exists a trade-off between the analytical run-time of our proposed approach and the size of the log files. If we encounter the problem of not possessing enough computational power, we have to reduce the size of the log files. This can, for example, be achieved by reducing the number of data points per time unit or by having an expert predict which parts of the log files should be considered in the analysis.

There is no need to create a fine-tuned model of the regarded system in our approach. The only variable that needs to be set is the size of the windows, in which the data is cut. We expect that the expert will be able to set this variable properly after discovering several anomalies in a system. Another option is the use of optimization techniques to find a good estimate of the window size. In this paper, we assume that the expert knows a good estimate of this variable. We would like to investigate various methods and optimization criteria for assessing a good window size in the future. Additionally, we would like to expand our experiments to several other types of CPS to strengthen the generic applicability of our proposed solution.

References

1. Abdi, H., Williams, L.J.: Principal component analysis. Wiley Interdisc. Rev. Comput. Stat. **2**(4), 433–459 (2010)
2. Adepu, S., Mathur, A.: Using process invariants to detect cyber attacks on a water treatment system. In: Hoepman, J.-H., Katzenbeisser, S. (eds.) SEC 2016. IAICT, vol. 471, pp. 91–104. Springer, Cham (2016). https://doi.org/10.1007/978-3-319-33630-5_7
3. Berndt, D.J., Clifford, J.: Using dynamic time warping to find patterns in time series. In: KDD Workshop, Seattle, WA, vol. 10, pp. 359–370 (1994)
4. Caporuscio, M., Flammini, F., Khakpour, N., Singh, P., Thornadtsson, J.: Smart-troubleshooting connected devices: Concept, challenges and opportunities. Future Gener. Comput. Syst. **111**, 681–697 (2019)
5. Fu, Q., Lou, J.G., Wang, Y., Li, J.: Execution anomaly detection in distributed systems through unstructured log analysis. In: 2009 Ninth IEEE International Conference On Data Mining, pp. 149–158. IEEE (2009)
6. Gillian, N., Knapp, B., O'modhrain, S.: Recognition of multivariate temporal musical gestures using N-dimensional dynamic time warping. In: Nime, pp. 337–342 (2011)
7. Goh, J., Adepu, S., Junejo, K.N., Mathur, A.: A dataset to support research in the design of secure water treatment systems. In: Havarneanu, G., Setola, R., Nassopoulos, H., Wolthusen, S. (eds.) CRITIS 2016. LNCS, vol. 10242, pp. 88–99. Springer, Cham (2017). https://doi.org/10.1007/978-3-319-71368-7_8
8. Harada, Y., Yamagata, Y., Mizuno, O., Choi, E.H.: Log-based anomaly detection of CPS using a statistical method. In: 2017 8th International Workshop on Empirical Software Engineering in Practice (IWESEP), pp. 1–6. IEEE (2017)
9. Inoue, J., Yamagata, Y., Chen, Y., Poskitt, C.M., Sun, J.: Anomaly detection for a water treatment system using unsupervised machine learning. In: 2017 IEEE International Conference on Data Mining Workshops (ICDMW), pp. 1058–1065. IEEE (2017)
10. Keipour, A., Mousaei, M., Scherer, S.: Alfa: a dataset for UAV fault and anomaly detection. arXiv, arXiv–1907 (2019)
11. Keipour, A., Mousaei, M., Scherer, S.: Automatic real-time anomaly detection for autonomous aerial vehicles. In: 2019 International Conference on Robotics and Automation (ICRA), pp. 5679–5685. IEEE (2019)
12. Lee, E.A.: Cyber physical systems: Design challenges. In: 2008 11th IEEE International Symposium on Object and Component-Oriented Real-Time Distributed Computing (ISORC), pp. 363–369. IEEE (2008)
13. Liao, T.W.: Clustering of time series data-a survey. Pattern Recogn. **38**(11), 1857–1874 (2005)
14. Lin, Q., Adepu, S., Verwer, S., Mathur, A.: Tabor: a graphical model-based approach for anomaly detection in industrial control systems. In: Proceedings of the 2018 on Asia Conference on Computer and Communications Security, pp. 525–536 (2018)
15. Lin, Q., Zhang, H., Lou, J.G., Zhang, Y., Chen, X.: Log clustering based problem identification for online service systems. In: Proceedings of the 38th International Conference on Software Engineering Companion, pp. 102–111. ACM (2016)
16. Lou, J.G., Fu, Q., Yang, S., Xu, Y., Li, J.: Mining invariants from console logs for system problem detection, In: USENIX Annual Technical Conference, pp. 23–25 (2010)

17. Lu, H., et al.: Motor anomaly detection for unmanned aerial vehicles using reinforcement learning. IEEE Internet Things J. **5**(4), 2315–2322 (2017)
18. Pedregosa, F., et al.: Scikit-learn: machine learning in Python. J. Mach. Learn. Res. **12**, 2825–2830 (2011)
19. Petitjean, F., Gançarski, P.: Summarizing a set of time series by averaging: from steiner sequence to compact multiple alignment. Theoret. Comput. Sci. **414**(1), 76–91 (2012)
20. Satopaa, V., Albrecht, J., Irwin, D., Raghavan, B.: Finding a "kneedle" in a haystack: detecting knee points in system behavior. In: 2011 31st International Conference On Distributed Computing Systems Workshops, pp. 166–171. IEEE (2011)

Assurance of Learning-Enabled Systems

Assuring the Safety of Machine Learning for Pedestrian Detection at Crossings

Lydia Gauerhof[1,2]([✉]), Richard Hawkins[2]([✉]), Chiara Picardi[2], Colin Paterson[2], Yuki Hagiwara[1], and Ibrahim Habli[2]

[1] Corporate Research Robert Bosch GmbH, Renningen, Germany
lydia.gauerhof@de.bosch.com
[2] University of York, York, UK
richard.hawkins@york.ac.uk

Abstract. Machine Learnt Models (MLMs) are now commonly used in self-driving cars, particularly for tasks such as object detection and classification within the perception pipeline. The failure of such models to perform as intended could lead to hazardous events such as failing to stop for a pedestrian at a crossing. It is therefore crucial that the safety of the MLM can be proactively assured and should be driven by explicit and concrete safety requirements. In our previous work, we defined a process that integrates the development and assurance activities for MLMs within safety-related systems. This is used to incrementally generate the safety argument and evidence. In this paper, we apply the approach to pedestrian detection at crossings and provide an evaluation using the publicly available JAAD data set. In particular, we focus on the elicitation and analysis of ML safety requirements and how such requirements should drive the assurance activities within the data management and model learning phases. We explain the benefits of the approach and identify outstanding challenges in the context of self-driving cars.

Keywords: Machine Learning · Safety argument · Self-driving car · Safety assurance process

1 Introduction

The assurance of safety-related systems which utilise Machine Learnt Models (MLMs) can only be achieved when arguments concerning the safety of the MLM are provided in the context of the overall system into which the model is deployed. For safety-related applications, the performance of the model is just one aspect that may be of interest; we must also take a much broader view of which aspects are important to assure the safety of the MLM. These aspects should be defined in the form of explicit Machine Learning (ML) safety requirements and should drive the way in which the MLM is trained and verified, with a particular focus on the quality and suitability of the training and verification data sources.

© Springer Nature Switzerland AG 2020
A. Casimiro et al. (Eds.): SAFECOMP 2020, LNCS 12234, pp. 197–212, 2020.
https://doi.org/10.1007/978-3-030-54549-9_13

In [15] we introduced a process for generating assurance arguments for MLMs. This process integrates development and assurance activities and can be used to incrementally generate the safety assurance argument and evidence that can be used to form a safety case for the MLM within the safety related context. We also described the structure of such arguments in the form of safety argument patterns [15]. Although some simple illustrative examples were provided, the details of how to implement the process activities, and the nature of the evidence that is generated were not provided. This paper seeks to address this by considering the safety-related automated driving scenario of a self-driving car approaching a pedestrian crossing. For this scenario we use a MLM for detection of pedestrians at the crossing that is trained on a publicly available dataset [17]. In particular, by considering this credible scenario and its associated safety implications, the primary contribution of the paper is that it shows how safety requirements can be systematically and traceably generated and refined across the different lifecycle phases of the MLM, particularly focussing on the data management and model learning requirements.

The rest of this paper is structured as follows. Section 2 provides an overview of our MLM safety assurance process. In Sect. 3 we describe the autonomous driving scenario that we used for our experiment and introduce the safety requirements for the system. Section 4 details the ML requirements that we derived for the scenario. Section 5 assesses the degree to which these requirements are satisfied for the data management and model learning stages of the lifecycle respectively. Section 6 discusses related work, draws conclusions from the paper and discusses our future work.

2   Model Learning Safety Assurance Process

The process we developed for assuring the safety of MLMs was presented in [15]. We split the ML lifecycle into five stages: requirements elicitation, data management, model learning, model verification and model deployment. Traditionally ML development has focused on data collection and model performance. For safety-related systems, a much broader view of ML development is required. In particular, the requirements elicitation stage must ensure that the ML requirements reflect the intent of the broader system-level safety requirements [9]. The model verification stage must provide an independent check that the requirements are satisfied and this must be particularly focused on the verification of explicit safety requirements. The model deployment stage must ensure that the learnt model will be acceptably safe when integrated into the larger system. To ensure that each lifecycle stage provides what is required to support a safety case, we can define a set of desired properties (desiderata) for each stage. It is important to have a clear and sufficient set of desiderata. For the work reported in this paper, we have used the assurance desiderata proposed by Ashmore et al. in [1].

To ensure the desiderata are satisfied, specific ML safety requirements must be specified for each lifecycle stage. This is the focus of this paper. These ML requirements must relate to the specific safety requirements determined for the system into which the MLM will be deployed. The relationship between safety requirements at a system level and detailed ML requirements is not always obvious. For example, a safety requirement may define the need to identify all stop signs in an urban environment in sufficient time for the vehicle to stop comfortably. Turning this into specific and meaningful ML requirements relating to desiderata such as data coverage, model robustness or model accuracy is challenging and rarely discussed in a way that is justifiably traceable to system safety requirements. This paper describes how this may be done for a credible automotive scenario, focussing on ML safety requirements for data management and model learning. As part of a safety case, it must be demonstrated that the defined ML safety requirements are met. We discuss the activities that may be performed during the ML lifecycle to generate evidence to support this.

3 Pedestrian Detection at Crossings Scenario: Vehicle-Level Safety Requirements

We consider a MLM that is being used to identify pedestrians at pedestrian crossings so that an autonomous vehicle is able to stop safely. We consider that a car (the Ego vehicle) is driving autonomously in an urban environment and is approaching a crossing. We can specify a safety requirement on the Ego vehicle as follows:

Ego Shall Stop at the Crossing If a Pedestrian is Crossing
At this level the safety requirement is defined for the vehicle as a whole. It is important to note that this safety requirement would apply to the vehicle irrespective of the use of ML as part of the implementation. Based on system level safety analysis, other safety requirements could be identified (such as that the Ego vehicle should not stop unnecessarily at a crossing) but we do not consider those within this paper.

In order to elicit safety requirements for the MLM it is first necessary to identify the safety requirements that apply to the relevant system component, in this case the object detection component. The safety process decomposes the system level safety requirement to the different components of the Ego vehicle. This takes account of the proposed system architecture for the vehicle as well as the relevant operating scenarios and operating environment as discussed below.

Ego is able to sense the environment using a Bosch stereo video camera [12] that is fitted above the rear view mirror. The camera has an image size of 1280×960 pixels and a frame rate of 30 images per second. The images are sent to the object detection component that identifies pedestrians in the images and creates bounding boxes around each pedestrian. Figure 1 shows an example of an image in which all pedestrians in the scene were successfully identified. These are indicated by the green bounding boxes in the image. In this case, the image has also been annotated with white bounding boxes which show the ground truth. This indicates that even though all objects were successfully detected errors in the bounding boxes still remain. By contrast, Fig. 2 shows an image from the same crossing in which there are several identification errors in the object detection, with pedestrians who were not spotted by the object detection indicated by blue boxes in the scene.

Fig. 1. An ideal pedestrian detection at crossings. (Color figure online)

Fig. 2. An example of missed detections at crossings. (Color figure online)

It is crucial that the context within which the vehicle is expected to function is clearly and explicitly specified. For road vehicles this is normally done through the specification of the Operational Design Domain (ODD) [7]. J3016 defines an ODD as "operating conditions under which a given driving automation system or feature thereof is specifically designed to function, including, but not limited to, environmental, geographical, and time-of-day restrictions, and/or the requisite presence or absence of certain traffic or roadway characteristics" [19].

One of the reasons for specifying the ODD is to reduce the complexity of the input space. For instance, particular geographical areas and country-specific circumstances, such as traffic signs, can be excluded. Also weather conditions such as snow, and time of day such as night, may be excluded, meaning that Ego would not operate autonomously under such conditions. Measures are put in place to ensure operation does not occur under the excluded conditions [5]. There are a number of approaches to structuring the ODD, such as equivalence classes [18]. There are also a number of ODD ontologies that have been suggested [7,11].

In the driving scenario in this paper, the ODD specifies that Ego operates on roads in the UK and in daylight, and that the weather conditions may be variable. In order to make our scenario concrete, we assume that pedestrians will only cross the road at the crossing, so we do not here consider pedestrians stepping off the pavement into the road.

Based on this we are able to specify safety requirements on the object detection component. This component is implemented in our example system using an MLM, in this case classification using a Convolutional Neural Network (CNN) based on SqueezeNet and localisation based on a Region Proposal Network (RPN). It is important to note however that at this point, the safety requirements could apply equally to the component whether it was a MLM or a more traditional software component.

To elicit the safety requirements we first consider the performance required of the object detection in order to satisfy the high-level safety requirement. Table 1 defines three performance related requirements. The justification for these requirements is provided below.

Table 1. Performance and robustness requirements for object detection.

Performance	
RQ1:	When Ego is 50 m from the crossing, the object detection component shall identify pedestrians that are on or close to the crossing in their correct position
RQ1.1:	In a sequence of images from a video feed any object to be detected should not be missed more then 1 in 5 frames
RQ1.2:	Position of pedestrians shall be determined within 50 cm of actual position
Robustness	
RQ2:	The object detection component shall perform as required in all situations Ego may encounter within the defined ODD
RQ3:	The object detection component shall perform as required in the face of defined component failures arising within the system

For RQ1, 50 m is specified as this is the minimum distance at which a decision to stop must be made if Ego is to stop comfortably at the maximum assumed speed. Stopping safely at a crossing requires consideration of this comfortable braking distance for the Ego vehicle; it would not be acceptable to brake excessively for pedestrians. The maximum comfortable braking distance will depend upon the speed of Ego and the road surface conditions. We assume for this scenario that comfortable braking loses roughly 20 kph per second on a damp road, so if Ego is travelling at 60 kph in the urban area it will take around 50 m to stop comfortably. This requires that Ego has sufficient confidence in the identification of pedestrians at 50 m, prior to this point Ego will be detecting the possible presence of pedestrians, however the uncertainty in those identifications may be relatively high.

RQ1 assumes that any pedestrian close to the crossing is intending to cross. This is certainly a conservative assumption that may result in some unrequired stopping, but is made here to simplify the scenario. In practice this could be mitigated through trajectory prediction for pedestrians (so for example pedestrians close to, but moving away from, the crossing would be rejected). It is taken that any pedestrian within one metre of the crossing is considered to be close to the crossing for the purposes of this scenario. Any pedestrians further away than this are assumed to be not intending to cross prior to Ego arriving at the crossing.

RQ1.1 and RQ1.2 further refine RQ1 by considering how good the performance of pedestrian identification and positioning needs to be in the context of the high-level system safety requirement and the system architecture. RQ1.1 is based upon the frame rate of the video feed as described above, and considers the fact that the ML model is deployed to a pipeline in which computational power is limited. As such the model may be unable to identify all objects in the scene for every frame at run-time. However the frame rate is such that the subsequent component into which the output of object detection is fed will ignore single frame changes in detections. RQ1.2 is based upon an assessment that 50 cm discrepancy in position provides a sufficient safety margin for pedestrians.

In addition to requirements on performance, it is also necessary for the performance of the object detection to be robust to the different situations that Ego may encounter. Table 1 defines two requirements relating to robustness. RQ2 is justified on the basis that if a situation that Ego encounters is outside of the defined ODD then the system will revert to a fail-safe or a manual drive mode (it is not required for object detection to cope with such situations). The safety of such transitions would be handled at the vehicle level. RQ3 acknowledges that the system components cannot be assumed to always perform perfectly. Object detection must therefore be able to cope with some defined failures or degradation. It should be noted that any failures in other system components that are not specified or are unanticipated must still be dealt with, but this would be done as part of the vehicle level safety case.

As the object detection is implemented using a MLM, these safety requirements on object detection must be interpreted to be meaningful for ML to enable assurance of the MLM to be demonstrated. In the next section we describe how ML safety requirements are derived.

4   ML Safety Requirements Elicitation

In order to create a safety argument for the MLM, it is necessary to specify concrete and meaningful ML safety requirements, i.e. traceable to the vehicle and component-level safety requirements as discussed in Sect. 3. That is, the ML requirements must be sufficient to ensure that the safety requirements identified in Sect. 3 are satisfied. The ML safety requirements are defined with a consideration of each phase of the ML lifecycle and the identified desiderata for each phase. In this paper we focus on the requirements for the data management and model learning phases.

Tables 2, 3 and 4 show the ML requirements that we have derived for these phases of the lifecycle. The tables enumerate requirements for each of the identified desiderata. For the data management phase, the desiderata we use are that the data should be relevant (Table 2), complete (Table 3), accurate (Table 4), and balanced (Table 4). These desiderata are consistent with the work of Ashmore et al. in [1] where the desiderata are discussed in more detail. The ML requirements reflect these ML desiderata within the context of the safety requirement we have identified for object detection in our scenario. A justification for these requirements is provided below.

Table 2. ML requirement elicitation for the **Relevant** desiderata of the **Data Management** lifecyle phase.

RQ4:	All data samples shall represent images of a road from the perspective of a vehicle
RQ5:	Crossings included in data samples shall be of a type found on UK roads
RQ6:	Pedestrians included in data samples shall be of a type that may use crossings on UK roads
RQ7:	The format of each data sample shall be representative of that which is captured using sensors deployed on the ego vehicle
RQ8:	Each data sample shall assume sensor positioning which is representative of that be used on the ego vehicle

If we first consider the requirements relating to the 'Relevant' desiderata, we must specify requirements that define which data is relevant to the safety requirements. Any data that is not relevant should be excluded from the data set. In order to have relevance in this context, the data sample must be an image that features a road as it may appear to Ego vehicle, and where this includes features of interest these should be relevant to the operational domain. In this case the features of interest are crossings and pedestrians. Relevant images would be expected to include some or all of these features. RQ4 to RQ6 capture this requirement for relevant data samples.

In addition the format of each image must be relevant. Since we understand the way in which images will be captured on the Ego vehicle, we can identify

Table 3. ML requirement elicitation for the **Complete** desiderata of the **Data Management** lifecyle phase.

RQ9:	The data samples shall include sufficient range of environmental factors within the scope of the ODD
RQ10:	The data samples shall include sufficient range of pedestrians within the scope of the ODD
RQ11:	The data samples shall include images representing a sufficient range of distances from the crossing up to that required by the decision making aspect of the perception pipeline
RQ12:	The data samples shall include examples with a sufficient range of levels of occlusion giving partial view of pedestrians at crossings
RQ13:	The data samples shall include a sufficient range of examples reflecting the effects of identified system failure modes

Table 4. ML requirement elicitation for the **Accurate** and **Balanced** desiderata of the **Data Management** lifecyle phase.

	Accurate
RQ14:	All bounding boxes produced shall be sufficiently large to include the entirety of the pedestrian
RQ15:	All bounding boxes produced shall be no more than 10% larger in any dimension than the minimum sized box capable of including the entirety of the pedestrian
RQ16:	All pedestrians present in the data samples must be correctly labelled
	Balanced
RQ17:	The data shall have a comparable representation of samples for each relevant class and feature (any class must not be under-represented with respect to the other classes or features)

factors that are important to ensure the images are of a relevant format. In this case the relevant factors are the type of image created by the sensors and the position of the sensors in the vehicle. Physical properties of sensors can have a profound impact on the data gathered and it is often easier to collect data from publicly available sets or test harnesses which differ from the final deployed system. For example, the lenses on two different cameras will have different levels of distortion, vignetting and chromatic aberration. In order to ensure that issues of distributional shift, due to sensor variation, are avoided we can specify a requirement to ensure that the sensors used in training and deployment are not materially different (RQ7). The images, even if not generated from the Ego vehicle itself, must reflect the position of Ego's sensors. RQ8 defines this requirement.

We next consider the desiderata 'Complete'. From the robustness requirement RQ2 we know the data must include sufficient examples to reflect different situations Ego may encounter. Through consideration of the defined ODD we know these must include, for example, variations in the environment (a defined range of lighting and weather conditions), and in pedestrians (a defined range of ages, sizes, numbers of people and variations in gait and pose). It should be noted that an explicit enumeration of the scope of such variables is particularly critical when using MLMs in order to ensure robustness can be achieved. Experience has shown us that complex ML models can become over reliant on features in the image (over-fitting) if insufficient variation in those features is present in the data. By ensuring that a range of pedestrian features are present in the data sets we are less likely to produce models which fail to perform appropriately in the real world. RQ9 and RQ10 capture these requirements with referenced to the ODD, it is crucial therefore that the ODD is clearly documented and validated as part of the vehicle safety process. As well as exploring the scope of the ODD to consider different situations, we must also consider the impact on the images of the distance of Ego from the crossing (affecting the size of image features), and the possibility of occlusions in the image (we have discussed these effects in more detail in [2]. RQ11 and RQ12 address this issue.

From the robustness requirement RQ3 it has already been identified that the object detector must perform acceptably in the face of system failures. We acknowledge that the performance of a sensor will degrade over time, for example a camera lens will become scratched. Since this is generally unavoidable we must be confident that the performance of the object detection is not impacted by normal wear and tear. This means that the data used in the ML lifecycle must include sufficient examples that reflect the effects of these system failures on the images that are obtained. The relevant failures must be identified through failure analysis of the system (for example this could be linked to the outputs of an FMEA). RQ13 is specified to address this issue.

Another desiderata that must be considered is 'Accurate'. The performance of MLMs is highly dependent on the quality of the data from which they learn and as such all labelling should be accurate. The performance requirement RQ1.2 specifies a performance requirement on the prediction of the pedestrian's position. In order to assess this performance it is necessary to compare model predictions with the ground truth labels encoded in the training and testing data sets. RQ14 is therefore specified to ensure that the bounding box added to the dataset contains the whole of the pedestrian. If any part of the pedestrian, for example an arm or a leg, were not included inside the bounding box then when the model performance were assessed with reference to the bounding box a model could be deemed to meet the performance requirements when it actually breached the 50 cm required by RQ1.2. Whilst this requirement specifies a minimum size for the bounding box, it does not consider a maximum size. It would be possible to meet RQ14 by creating very large boxes around every pedestrian, however this is likely to make the system unusable as free space is essentially identified as containing a pedestrian. RQ15 addresses this issue by specifying a limit on the size of the bounding box.

The performance requirement RQ1.1 may be interpreted as an ML requirement to avoid false negatives. This leads to a requirement on the accuracy of the training data. The training data is labelled (by a human) to identify the pedestrians in each image. Manual labelling of data is error prone and drawing bounding boxes in particular is difficult. If the images are labelled incorrectly such that the pedestrians are not identified in the image then this can lead to false negatives in the output of the MLM as well. RQ16 is specified to address this.

Finally RQ17 addresses the desiderata 'Balanced'. The requirements have already specified the need for relevance and coverage in the data, it is also important that certain features are not over or under represented in the data set. Again the relevant classes and features can be identified through consideration of the ODD.

Having defined explicit ML safety requirements it is then necessary to demonstrate that the ML requirements are satisfied. In Sect. 5 we discuss whether the data we used in this experiment meet the ML safety requirements and whether additional activities are required to support a safety case. Section 5.2 then discusses this for the model that is learnt.

5   Satisfying ML Safety Requirements

In order to investigate the sufficiency of the requirements defined in this paper we considered an experimental object detection MLM consisting of a CNN trained using the JAAD dataset [17]. In this section the data management and model learning for this MLM is assessed against the defined requirements to determine whether the requirements are satisfied. This highlighted areas where the MLM is insufficient from a safety assurance perspective, and identified additional assurance activities that would be required. This highlights the key role of an explicit elicitation of ML safety requirements in assuring MLMs.

5.1   Assessing the Data Management Safety Requirements

In this section, we discuss each data requirement presented in Tables 2, 3 and 4 with reference to the JAAD dataset used in our experiment.

RQ4–5: In the dataset there are 25 videos relative to pedestrian crossing at designated and signalised crossings. For each of these videos approximately 82,000 image samples can be extracted. The recordings were done during 240 h of driving across several locations in North America and Eastern Europe. Even if some of the crossings could be considered similar between Eastern Europe and UK (e.g. zebra and pegasus crossings), the data does not meet this requirements because UK locations are not included in the recording and therefore not all UK pedestrians crossings types are considered. In particular it can be easily noted that Pelican crossings are not included in the data. Augmenting the data by synthesising missing images can partially solve the problem, but the data samples generated must be very close to real world images. A better solution could be to undertake additional data collection in different UK crossing locations.

RQ6: When considering the JAAD dataset, we see that many classes of pedestrian are included, e.g. examples of children are included as is a man pushing a buggy. There are however some relevant omissions from this including people with disabilities, and people with different colour skin or ethnicity. When considering if there are any particular characteristics of UK pedestrians it seems important given the UK climate to ensure there are images of people carrying umbrellas or wearing waterproof jackets. These are not found in the data. Therefore the dataset could not be said to meet this requirement as more data would need to be collected that included the missing categories.

RQ7: The cameras used for the recording of the dataset are describe in [16]. The resolution of the three cameras are compatible with the one deployed in the ego vehicle (see Sect. 3). Consequently, this requirement can be considered satisfied.

RQ8: The camera recording the data used is positioned inside the car below the rear view mirror as described in [16]. In the ego vehicle the camera is mounted inside the car above the rear view mirror. Although the position is not exactly the same of the ones used for the data recording the distance is not significant and as such the requirement is satisfied.

RQ9–10: The data represents some different weather conditions (e.g. snow and rain). They do not consider different positions of the sun or different daytime lighting (e.g. sunset). Limited visibility weather conditions like fog are also not included, even though this is part of the ODD. The data includes pedestrians of different ages and height, as well as different walking speeds. No running pedestrians are included however. Although there are a sufficient range of examples for some features, for others the data is found to be lacking. Augmentation techniques can be applied to address this, for example by varying the colour of pixel or the orientation of pedestrians to the camera as done in previous work (e.g. [6]). In particular, Zhang and colleagues [20] described a method, through the use of a Generative Adversial Network (GAN), to synthesize scenes for autonomous driving simulating different weather conditions and then different lighting conditions. Further, possible evidence for supporting the argument in order to satisfy the requirements can be represented by performance graphs showing the difference between original and augmented data and how the different features included influence the performance. The data include some busy crossings that have groups of up to a maximum of 11 people. The performance of the MLM in identifying pedestrians when in groups compared to individuals could be used as evidence of this requirement. If performance is seen to be worse for groups, then more data samples for groups of people should be included.

RQ11: In most of the images included in the dataset, the pedestrians are very close to the car so do not respect the distance necessary for the pipeline decision making (in excess of 50 m). The dataset would therefore be inappropriate against this requirement.

RQ12: There is partial occlusion of pedestrians in some of the data samples. For example, some pedestrians are occluded by gates or by the car in front of the Ego vehicle. Again, the number of occluded data samples could be increased through synthesis. For example artificial masking of pedestrians could be used to help meet the requirement.

RQ13: Data samples derived from identified failures in the system are not present in the dataset. Also the classifier is not tested with adversarial attacks. For these reasons the requirements are not satisfied. In order to satisfy these requirements failures need to be identified and recorded in a report that can be used as evidence to support the argument. After failures are identified, corresponding data samples need to be added to the data set.

Req.14–16: While the process used to generate the dataset is described in [16], there is limited information regarding the generation of bounding boxes. Piotr's annotation toolbox [8] is used to define the bounding boxes and annotate the images. However, there is no information regarding the process to ensure that these are correct with respect to ground truth. The accuracy of the labelling is a function of the skills of the individuals undertaking the task and the validation processes used during labelling.

RQ17: Using a public dataset results in a lack of information and control in the number of data samples recorded for each feature of interest. Features that are under-represented have to be identified and possibly over-sampled in order to improve the performance of the classifier in presence of these features. Augmentation approaches can be used here, as well as other techniques for detecting and mitigating rare classes, such as [14].

In short, a public dataset such as JAAD is not sufficient to satisfy the ML safety requirements for our scenario. This result is not unexpected, but it highlights the role of explicit ML safety requirements in both highlighting deficiencies, and identifying necessary actions. Public datasets can however be useful for an exploratory analysis in order to refine the requirements as suggested by Gelman and colleagues [10].

5.2 Assessing the Model Learning Safety Requirements

In this section we discuss the ML safety requirements that relate to the learned model itself as presented in Table 1, with reference to the model used in our experiment.

RQ1: In order to evaluate classifiers in the automotive domain it is common practice to use the log average miss rate (LAMR) [13]. Having constructed a convolution neural network as an MLM, we calculated the LAMR for images in the dataset. When considering all pedestrians larger than 50 pixels in the image, we obtain an LAMR of 29.03%. We note that for those pedestrians between 50 and 75 pixels this increases to 46.78%. These results are shown in Fig. 3a and Fig. 3b with more detail provided in Table 5.

RQ1.1: The JAAD dataset does provide a labelling which allows for each object to be tracked through frames. However, at present we do not have access to a

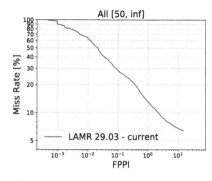 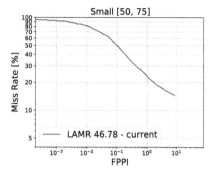

a) MR vs. FPPI for pedestrians larger than 50*px* in height.

b) MR vs. FPPI for pedestrians detection of the size 50*px* to 75*px*.

Fig. 3. Miss rate (MR) vs. false positive per image (FPPI) for pedestrian detection with different heights.

pipeline which allows us to generate evidence to evaluate whether the MLM meets this requirement. This remains as future work.

RQ2: The images in the data set only cover 5 locations with the vast majority of videos captured in one location. Some of the images included weather features, for example LAMR results are shown in Table 6 for LAMR under snow conditions. Even these cases are restricted since snow is lying on the ground, so variations such as falling snow are missing. The generation of the JAAD database used for training required considerable effort, especially in the labelling of objects within the scene. In order to assess the ability of the MLM to operate at locations other than those in the JAAD dataset would require additional data collection and significant labelling effort. Without this, it is impossible to assess if the requirement could be met using this MLM.

Table 5. Log average miss rate (LAMR) of pedestrian detection with different heights of bounding boxes and occlusion severity (the smaller, the better).

Heights	in Pixels	LAMR in %	LAMR in %	LAMR in %
		No occlusion	Occlusion 25%–75%	Occlusion >75%
Small	50–75	46.78	54.12	62.18
Medium	75–100	20.22	28.91	36.49
Large	100–200	7.96	16.14	25.72
Huge	200–400	7.47	13.18	19.05
Giant	400–600	10.76	21.18	31.03

RQ3: The JAAD videos were not captured using sensors traditionally used for autonomous vehicles. Instead, consumer video cameras were employed. In order

to evaluate the effects of sensor wear, we would need to either simulate wear on the images, which would require a wear model to be validated, or we would need to collect data using sensors which had been subjected to appropriate wear, e.g. lens scratches etc. This new set could then be used as a test set on the candidate MLM. At present no such wear model or testing set exists and we can not therefore assess if the requirement is met.

Table 6. Log average miss rate (LAMR) of pedestrian detection with different heights and occlusion severity under the **snow conditions**

Heights	in Pixels	LAMR in %	LAMR in %	LAMR in %
		No occlusion	Occlusion 25%–75%	Occlusion >75%
Small	50–75	39.30	47.01	55.89
Medium	75–100	13.78	19.08	27.65
Large	100–200	9.08	19.92	32.21
Huge	200–400	4.44	7.92	12.39
Giant	400–600	–	15.77	34.00

6   Discussion and Conclusions

There is no established approach to the assurance of MLMs for use in safety-related applications. Within the automotive domain, established safety standards such as ISO26262 do not consider MLMs. Traditional testing methods and test coverage metrics used for safety-related software, such as Modified Condition Decision Coverage, are not applicable to Neural Networks [3]. To try to close this gap, Cheng et al. introduced metrics for measuring NN dependability attributes including robustness, interpretability, completeness and correctness. Building upon this and other works, in [4] they introduce an "NN-dependability-kit" that could be used to support the development of a safety argument. Their work is not however driven by specific requirements that are explicitly and traceably linked to system-level safety analysis. Being able to demonstrate and justify this link is crucial to creating a compelling safety case.

This traceable link between system safety requirements and ML safety requirements is the focus of our work reported in this paper. This is important for two reasons: to maintain the link with vehicle-level hazardous events (and their mitigation) and to ensure that safety considerations are addressed in the detailed ML lifecycle phases. In particular, as we have shown in this paper, the ML safety requirements can be used to drive and scope the safety assurance activities. In this paper we have focused on the ML safety requirements for the data management and model learning phases. In our ongoing work, we intend to extend this to consider ML verification and deployment, which are two crucial aspects for a compelling safety case. Furthermore, formalizing these requirements in contract-based design allows machine support for refinement checks within a component-based system [2]. We hope that this work is of benefit to both researchers and engineers and helps inform the current debate concerning the safety assurance and regulation of autonomous driving.

Acknowledgements. This work is funded by the Assuring Autonomy International Programme https://www.york.ac.uk/assuring-autonomy.

References

1. Ashmore, R., Calinescu, R., Paterson, C.: Assuring the machine learning lifecycle: desiderata, methods, and challenges (2019). http://arxiv.org/abs/1905.04223
2. Burton, S., Gauerhof, L., Sethy, B.B., Habli, I., Hawkins, R.: Confidence arguments for evidence of performance in machine learning for highly automated driving functions. In: Romanovsky, A., Troubitsyna, E., Gashi, I., Schoitsch, E., Bitsch, F. (eds.) SAFECOMP 2019. LNCS, vol. 11699, pp. 365–377. Springer, Cham (2019). https://doi.org/10.1007/978-3-030-26250-1_30
3. Cheng, C., Nührenberg, G., Huang, C., Ruess, H., Yasuoka, H.: Towards dependability metrics for neural networks. In: 2018 16th ACM/IEEE International Conference on Formal Methods and Models for System Design (2018)
4. Cheng, C.H., Huang, C.H., Nührenberg, G.: nn-dependability-kit: engineering neural networks for safety-critical autonomous driving systems. arXiv:1811.06746 (2018)
5. Colwell, I., Phan, B., Saleem, S., Salay, R., Czarnecki, K.: An automated vehicle safety concept based on runtime restriction of the operational design domain. In: 2018 IEEE Intelligent Vehicles Symposium (IV) (2018)
6. Crispell, D., Biris, O., Crosswhite, N., Byrne, J., Mundy, J.L.: Dataset augmentation for pose and lighting invariant face recognition. arXiv:1704.04326 (2017)
7. Czarnecki, K.: Operational world model ontology for automated driving systems–part 1: road structure. Waterloo Intelligent Systems Engineering Lab (WISE) Report (2018)
8. Dollár, P.: Piotr's computer vision matlab toolbox (PMT). https://github.com/pdollar/toolbox
9. Gauerhof, L., Munk, P., Burton, S.: Structuring validation targets of a machine learning function applied to automated driving. In: Gallina, B., Skavhaug, A., Bitsch, F. (eds.) SAFECOMP 2018. LNCS, vol. 11093, pp. 45–58. Springer, Cham (2018). https://doi.org/10.1007/978-3-319-99130-6_4
10. Gelman, A., Loken, E.: The garden of forking paths: Why multiple comparisons can be a problem, even when there is no "fishing expedition" or "p-hacking" and the research hypothesis was posited ahead of time. Columbia University, Department of Statistics (2013)
11. Geyer, S., et al.: Concept and development of a unified ontology for generating test and use-case catalogues for assisted and automated vehicle guidance. IET Intell. Transp. Syst. **8**, 183–189 (2013)
12. GmbH, R.B.: Stereo video camera product data sheet. https://www.bosch-mobility-solutions.com/media/global/products-and-services/passenger-cars-and-light-commercial-vehicles/driver-assistance-systems/lane-departure-warning/stereo-video-camera/product-data-sheet-stereo-video-camera.pdf. Accessed 28 Feb 2020

13. Liu, S., Huang, D., Wang, Y.: Adaptive NMS: refining pedestrian detection in a crowd. CoRR abs/1904.03629 (2019). http://arxiv.org/abs/1904.03629
14. Paterson, C., Calinescu, R.: Detection and mitigation of rare subclasses in neural network classifiers. arXiv preprint arXiv:1911.12780 (2019)
15. Picardi, C., Paterson, C., Hawkins, R., Calinescu, R., Habli, I.: Assurance argument patterns and processes for machine learning in safety-related systems. In: Proceedings of the Workshop on Artificial Intelligence Safety (SafeAI 2020), pp. 23–30. CEUR Workshop Proceedings (2020)
16. Rasouli, A., Kotseruba, I., Tsotsos, J.K.: Are they going to cross? A benchmark dataset and baseline for pedestrian crosswalk behavior. In: Proceedings of the IEEE Conference on Computer Vision and Pattern Recognition (2017)
17. Rasouli, A., Kotseruba, I., Tsotsos, J.K.: It's not all about size: on the role of data properties in pedestrian detection. In: Leal-Taixé, L., Roth, S. (eds.) ECCV 2018. LNCS, vol. 11129, pp. 210–225. Springer, Cham (2019). https://doi.org/10.1007/978-3-030-11009-3_12
18. Rosenwald, G.W., Liu, C.-C.: Rule-based system validation through automatic identification of equivalence classes. IEEE Trans. Knowl. Data Eng. **9**, 24–31 (1997)
19. SAE: J3016, taxonomy and definitions for terms related to on-road motor vehicle automated driving systems (2013). https://saemobilus.sae.org/content/j3016_201401
20. Zhang, M., Zhang, Y., Zhang, L., Liu, C., Khurshid, S.: DeepRoad: GAN-based metamorphic testing and input validation framework for autonomous driving systems. In: Proceedings of the 33rd ACM/IEEE International Conference on Automated Software Engineering (2018)

Safety-Aware Hardening of 3D Object Detection Neural Network Systems

Chih-Hong Cheng[✉]

DENSO AUTOMOTIVE Deutschland GmbH,
Freisinger Str. 21, 85386 Eching, Germany
c.cheng@denso-auto.de

Abstract. We study how state-of-the-art neural networks for 3D object detection using a single-stage pipeline can be made safety aware. We start with the safety specification (reflecting the capability of other components) that partitions the 3D input space by criticality, where the *critical area* employs a separate criterion on robustness under perturbation, quality of bounding boxes, and the tolerance over false negatives demonstrated on the training set. In the architecture design, we consider symbolic error propagation to allow feature-level perturbation. Subsequently, we introduce a specialized loss function reflecting (1) the safety specification, (2) the use of single-stage detection architecture, and finally, (3) the characterization of robustness under perturbation. We also replace the commonly seen non-max-suppression post-processing algorithm by a safety-aware *non-max-inclusion* algorithm, in order to maintain the safety claim created by the neural network. The concept is detailed by extending the state-of-the-art PIXOR detector which creates object bounding boxes in bird's eye view with inputs from point clouds.

1 Introduction

For perceiving the environment in automated driving, techniques for detecting object presence in 3D have been predominantly implemented using deep neural networks. While state-the-the-art implementations for 3D object detection achieve superior performance, for building trust over the created artifact, the underlying engineering process should be *safety-aware*. Concretely, for certification authorities, it is essential to demonstrate that the safety specification is reflected in the design of the neural network and is aligned with the design of the post-processing algorithm.

In this paper, we study how safety concepts can be integrated into engineering 3D object detection networks with single-stage detection. Our process starts by defining the *critical area* and the associated quality attributes. Intuitively, the critical area is the area nearby the ego vehicle where failed detection of an object may lead to immediate safety risks. How one defines the critical area can be dependent on the capability of the ego vehicle, such as maximum braking forces. Apart from detecting the presence of objects, the quality of detection should also be dependent on the safety characteristics of other components in the system

© Springer Nature Switzerland AG 2020
A. Casimiro et al. (Eds.): SAFECOMP 2020, LNCS 12234, pp. 213–227, 2020.
https://doi.org/10.1007/978-3-030-54549-9_14

such as motion planners. For instance, some collision avoidance algorithms may assign a fixed buffer around the bounding boxes (provided by the perception module as input) to perform planning. If the size of the real object exceeds the predicted bounding box by the buffer size, physical collisions, although unaware by motion planners, may appear. The separation of the critical area and the non-critical area leads to the separation of the corresponding architectural design and the definition of the loss function, where the subsequent design is *guided by safety* for the critical area and but is *driven by performance* for the non-critical area. We then restrict ourselves to the training and the post-processing pipeline, and exemplify how a single-stage detection network such as PIXOR [19] and its post-processing algorithm should be altered. For prediction in the critical area, we adapt training techniques that incorporate feature-level perturbation, and define a loss function over perturbed worst case, the label, and the allowed tolerance. We also provide a mathematically proven bound to associate (i) the tolerance in prediction-label difference and (ii) the required buffer to ensure that a prediction contains the labeled bounding box. For post-processing, we use an alternative *non-max-inclusion* algorithm, which intuitively enlarges the predicted bounding box by considering other predictions on the same object with a slightly lower probability. The use of non-max-inclusion is conservative, but it ensures that the safety claims made in the neural network remain valid after post-processing.

By including this concept to the development process, one immediate benefit is for certification authorities to obtain profound transparency regarding how safety concepts can be demonstrated in the concrete design of neural networks and the following post-processing algorithm. Our proposal does not prohibit the use of standard training with commonly seen loss functions (e.g., mean square error). Instead, one may use parameters trained with standard approaches as initializing parameters; subsequently, perform parameter fine-tuning under special loss functions that consider area-criticality and robustness. Our proposal also does not prohibit the use of other further post-processing algorithms such as utilizing time-series data, as in single-stage detection networks, non-max-suppression is executed immediately on the output of the neural network, and our proposal merely replaces non-max-suppression by a customized algorithm.

In summary, our primary contributions are (i) an exemplification of the safety concept reflected into the architecture design and the corresponding post-processing; (ii) a formally stated constraint associating the quality of the prediction and the its effect on the interacting components such as planners; and (iii) the extension of provable robustness into single-stage object detection networks.[1]

2   Related Work

There exist many novel neural network architectures that can perform object detection from point clouds, including PIXOR [19], VeloFCN [9], PointRCNN [13], Vote3Deep [4], among others. Our work starts with the idea of refining the PIXOR

---

[1] Due to space limits, we refer readers to https://arxiv.org/abs/2003.11242 for proofs of the lemmas and our preliminary evaluation.

system to make (i) the design of neurons, (ii) the design of the loss function, and (iii) the immediate post-processing algorithm linked to requirements imposed from the safety argumentation and capabilities from other components. This makes the overall system design driven by safety rather than by performance, in contrast to existing design methodologies. For example, standard PIXOR only sets the loss to zero when the prediction perfectly matches the label. Our extension sets the loss to be zero, so long as the prediction is close to the label by a fixed tolerance. This allows the loss to be overloaded on cases with perturbation, where the perturbed input also leads to zero loss, so long if the produced output falls into the tolerated bound. Another example is to use the non-max-inclusion post-processing algorithm that enables to maintain provable guarantees in contrast to the standard non-max-suppression algorithm.

For engineering robust neural networks, the concept in this paper is highly related to the work of provably robust training [11,12,14–18]. While current research results target simple classification or regression tasks, our focus is to extend these results such that the technique scalably applies to single-stage object detection neural networks that produce a vector of outputs on each grid.

Lastly, we are also aware of fruitful research results in safety certification of machine learning components, with some focusing on safety argumentation [1, 5,8,10] while others on testing and formal verification (see [7] for a survey on results in formal verification, testing, and adversarial perturbation). While these works contribute to the overall vision of rigorous safety engineering of neural networks, these results do not touch the construction of the neural networks. In this way, our research well complements these results as we focus on constructing the neural network (architecture and the loss function) and the immediate post-processing algorithm such that they can reflect the safety argument.

3   Neural Networks and the PIXOR Architecture

A deep neural network is comprised of N layers where operationally, the n-th layer for $n \in \{1, \ldots, N\}$ of the network is a function $g^{(n)} : \mathbb{R}^{d_{n-1}} \to \mathbb{R}^{d_n}$, with d_n being the dimension of layer n. Given an input in $\in \mathbb{R}^{d_0}$, the output of the n-th layer of the neural network $f^{(n)}$ is given by the functional composition of the n-th layer and the previous layers $f^{(n)}(\text{in}) := \circ_{i=1}^{n} g^{(i)}(\text{in}) = g^{(n)}(g^{(n-1)} \ldots g^{(2)}(g^{(1)}(\text{in})))$. Given input in, the prediction of the neural network is thus $f^{(N)}(\text{in})$. We use $g_j^{(n)}$ to denote the j-th neuron in layer n, and for fully connected layers, computing $g_j^{(n)}$ is done by a weighted sum (characterized by the weight matrix W_j^n and bias b_j) followed by applying a nonlinear activation function ρ_j^n, i.e., $g_j^{(n)} := \rho_j^n((\sum_{k=1}^{d_{(n-1)}} W_{jk}^n g_k^{(n-1)}(\text{in})) + b_j)$. Note that such a definition allows to represent commonly seen architecture variations such as residual blocks or top-down branches that are used in PIXOR. Given a tensor v, we use subscript $v_{\langle i,j \rangle}$ to extract the tensor by taking the i-th element in the first dimension and j-th element in the second dimension. Lastly, define the *training set* for the neural network to be $\mathcal{T} := \{(\text{in}, \text{lb})\}$ where for every input in $\in \mathbb{R}^{d_0}$, $\text{lb} \in \mathbb{R}^{d_N}$ is the corresponding label.

PIXOR [19] is a *single-stage detector* neural network that, based on the input as point clouds, directly predicts the final position and orientation of an object. By single-stage, we refer to neural networks where there exists no intermediate step of proposing possible areas (region proposal) in 3D for suggesting the potential existence of an object in the area. In this paper, we follow the original formulation in [19] to only detect the presence of a "car" as in the KITTI dataset [6]. One can easily extend the network architecture to include other object types.

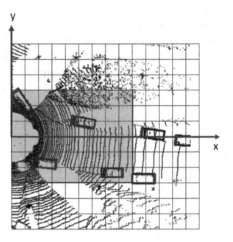

The input dimension d_0 of the PIXOR network is (L, W, H). Provided that the positive direction of the x coordinate facing in the front windshield of the car, the positive direction of the y coordinate facing to the left of driver, and the positive direction of the z coordinate facing up, each $\text{in}_{\langle i,j,k \rangle}$ contains the density of the lidar point cloud centered at the point $(i\alpha + \frac{\alpha}{2}, (j - \frac{W}{2})\alpha + \frac{\alpha}{2}, k\alpha + \frac{\alpha}{2})$ with α being the size of the grid. Figure 1 illustrates how grids are mapped to the physical 2D dimension.

Fig. 1. Visualizing the relation between grids and x-y coordinates. The bottom-left grid has an index $\langle 0, 0 \rangle$, and its center point is translated to the x-y coordinate equaling $(\frac{\alpha}{2}, -\frac{11\alpha}{2})$.

The output dimension for the network is $d_L = (\frac{L}{\beta}, \frac{W}{\beta}, 7)$ with β being the down-scaling factor. The output $f^{(N)}(\text{in})_{\langle i,j \rangle}$, i.e., the output at grid $\langle i, j \rangle$, is a 7 tuple $(pr, \cos(\theta), \sin(\theta), dx, dy, \log(w), \log(l))$, where $\langle i, j \rangle$ is matched to the physical area in 2D centered by point $(i\alpha\beta + \frac{\alpha\beta}{2}, (j - \frac{W}{2\beta})\alpha\beta + \frac{\alpha\beta}{2})$ with $\alpha\beta$ being the size of the output grid. The output of the network essentially predicts, for each grid in $\langle i, j \rangle$ in the 2D plane, if there is a vehicle nearby. In the original PIXOR paper [19], the grid size α is set to $0.1\,\text{m}$ and β is set to 4, meaning that the output grid has a physical quantity of $0.4 \times 0.4\,\text{m}^2$. Figure 2 shows the visualization of the output relative to the center of the grid. One direct consequence is that it is possible for multiple grids to create prediction over the same vehicle (as the grid size is very small), by having a different displacement value dx and dy to the center of the vehicle. Therefore, a post-processing algorithm called *non-max-suppression* is introduced. The idea is to first pick the output grid whose prediction probability is the largest while being larger than the *class threshold* α. Subsequently, create the prediction as a bounding box, and remove every prediction whose bounding box overlaps with the previously created bounding box (for the same type) by a certain threshold, where the degree of overlapping is computed using the intersection-over-union (IoU) ratio. For the example in Fig. 2, the vehicle prediction on the right will be neglected as the probability ($pr = 0.8$) is less than the prediction probability from the left grid ($pr = 0.9$). Note that *such a post-processing algorithm, its computation is not integrated the training and the inference of neural networks.*

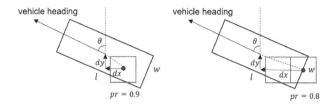

Fig. 2. The output of the PIXOR network for a single grid; the red dot represents the centering position of the grid. Both two grids have positive prediction on the existence of the same vehicle. (Color figure online)

4 Safety Goals and the Proposed Safety Arguments

We define the safety goal by first considering the *critical area*. Intuitively, a critical area is an area where object detection should be processed with care, as detection miss or an object prediction of the wrong size may lead to unsafe consequences. The precise definition of the critical area and the associated quality attribute can be driven by multiple factors such as the specification of labeling quality, the capability of motion planners, and the capability of maximum breaking. In the following, we create the following sample specification and describe the underlying rationale.

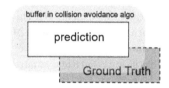

Fig. 3. Understanding the quality of prediction. The area of ground truth that is outside the buffer of the collision avoidance algorithm imposes risk of collision.

(**S1: Critical area**) The critical area are output grids $\langle i, j \rangle$ where $i \in [0, \gamma_L]$ and $j \in [\frac{W}{2\beta} - \gamma_W, \frac{W}{2\beta} + \gamma_W]$. Figure 1 shows an example where critical area (in light yellow) is in grid $\langle i, j \rangle$ with $i \in [0, 9]$ and $j \in [3, 8]$.

(**S2: Demonstrate no false negative in critical area**) *If there exists an object in the critical area, it should be "detected". The system may fail to detect an object outside the critical area but there is no immediate danger (such as hitting an object). The meaning of "detected" is detailed as follows: the predicted bounding box (of the vehicle) should deviate from the ground truth with a fixed tolerance.* In later sections, we provide the mathematical formulation to quantify the meaning of tolerance in prediction.

- The rationale is that we assume that the collision avoidance algorithm takes a fixed buffer in its planning, and it fully trusts the output of the object detection. Therefore, any prediction that deviates from the ground truth with an amount more than the tolerance can create the risk for collision (see Fig. 3 for an illustration).
- The "if" condition in the specification implies that safety constraint is only on false negatives (undetected objects) and is not on false positives (ghost objects). In other words, reducing false positives is a performance specification and (within the scope of this paper) is not considered as a safety specification.[2]

(S3: High performance outside the critical area) For objects outside the critical area, the prediction should achieve reasonable performance, but *no hard constraints are imposed.*

Therefore, we employ two philosophies in designing the quality attributes for object detection. Within the critical area, the quality attribute is *safety-driven* - performance shall never sacrifice safety. This implies that a neural network that creates tighter bounding boxes but may fail to detect an object in the critical area is not allowed. Based on the specification, the training of neural networks may reduce false positives that appeared inside the critical area, but it is only a performance improvement. Outside the critical area, the quality attribute is *performance-driven* - positives and false negatives are allowed for object detection outside the critical area. However, the training of neural networks may try to reduce them. Lastly, in this example, we do not enforce perfection between the prediction given input and the associated ground truth label. As demonstrated in later sections, this is reflected by having a zero loss so long as the prediction deviates from the ground truth by the tolerance.

Following the safety specification listed above, we are considering the following safety arguments in the architecture design and post-processing to support the key safety specification **(S2)**. Note that the listed items are partial and can be further expanded to create a stronger supporting argument.

(A1: Safety-aware loss function) The first argument is a careful definition of a loss function that reflects the requirement listed above. In particular, for critical and non-critical areas, different loss functions are applied.
(A2: Robust training for critical area) For generating predictions inside the critical area, the second argument is to deploy specialized training mechanisms such that one has a theoretical guarantee on robust prediction over data used in training, provided that the robust loss has dropped to zero.[3]

---

[2] This paper targets automated driving systems (SAE J3016 level 3 and up); for ADAS systems (SAE J3016 level 2) such as automatic emergency braking, false negatives are less critical due to the driver taking ultimate control, but avoiding false positives are considered to be safety-critical due to potential rear collision.

[3] It is almost impossible to use standard loss functions while demonstrating zero loss, as zero loss implies perfection between prediction and labels. Our robust training and our defined robust loss can, as demonstrated in later sections, enable zero loss (subject to parameters used) in practical applications.

(**A3: Conservative post-processing**) For post-processing algorithms that are independent of the neural network but crucial to the generated prediction, they should act more conservatively in the critical area.

5   Architecture Design, Loss, and Post-processing

In this section, we detail how we extend the architecture of PIXOR to incorporate a safety-aware loss function, to integrate a new post-processing algorithm, and finally, to apply robust training techniques. Recall that PIXOR has a *backbone network* $g_{backbone}$ and a *header network* g_{header}. Intuitively, the backbone network creates high-level features from high dimensional inputs, and the header network produces predictions from high-level features.

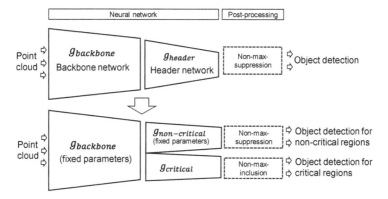

Fig. 4. Hardening a standard object detection network system (top) to a safety-aware one that differentiates between critical and non-critical areas (down)

We illustrate the proposed network architecture and the associated post-processing pipeline in Fig. 4. We start by training a standard PIXOR network as a baseline model. It is tailored for optimal performance but is not safety-aware. In the hardened neural network, we create two header networks $g_{critical}$ and $g_{non.critical}$, with both connected to the backbone network $g_{backbone}$. Parameters in $g_{backbone}$ are fixed, i.e., they are not subject to further change. $g_{non.critical}$ is used to perform object detection for the non-critical area, and $g_{critical}$ is used to perform object detection for the critical area. In this paper, we present two variations to engineer $g_{critical}$ together with their associated theoretical guarantees. Lastly, for the critical area, a non-standard post-processing algorithm (*non-max-inclusion*) is used rather than the standard non-max-suppression algorithm which is used for non-critical areas.

(*Engineering $g_{non.critical}$*). For $g_{non.critical}$ to perform object detection in non-critical areas, it is created by taking g_{header} and subsequently, remove all neurons in the final layer that generate predictions for critical areas. Naturally, such a header network can be used for making predictions that are outside the critical area. We do not perform further training to change any learned parameters.

5.1 Post-processing Algorithm for the Critical Area (Addressing A3)

For the post-processing in the critical area, we alternatively propose the *non-max-inclusion* algorithm. The underlying idea is illustrated using Fig. 5, where a PIXOR network generates the prediction of the same object on two adjacent grids. Standard non-max-suppression (Fig. 5-b) picks the grid that produces the largest prediction probability and suppresses other predictions with high intersection-over-union (IoU); in Fig. 5-b the bounding box with probability equaling 0.89 is suppressed. Nevertheless, as there is no ground truth in operation, it is uncertain which bounding box is correct. Therefore, a conservative post-processing algorithm should include both bounding boxes, as demonstrated in Fig. 5-c. Overall, the non-max-inclusion algorithm proceeds as follows.

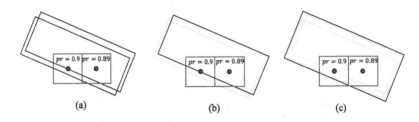

Fig. 5. Explaining non-max-inclusion

1. Sort all bounding boxes with their prediction probabilities (from high to low), and store them to a list L_{all}. Remove all boxes whose probability is lower than the class threshold α.
2. Remove from L_{all} the first bounding box B (i.e., the box with the highest probability), and create a sub-list $L_B = \{B\}$ containing only B.
3. For each bounding box prediction $B' \in L_{all}$, if the prediction B' has high IoU with the original bounding box B, remove B' from L_{all} and add B' to L_B and do not consider it afterwards.
4. Finally, build the final bounding box $\hat{B}$ which contains all bounding boxes of L_B and use it as the final prediction for B.
5. Proceed to step 2 until L_{all} is empty.

5.2 Engineering $g_{critical}$ - Variation 1 (Addressing A1)

In the following, we introduce the first variation for engineering $g_{critical}$ addressing (**A2**), where we create $g_{critical}$ by first taking g_{header}, followed by removing all connections to final layer neurons that generate predictions for non-critical areas. In contrast to $g_{non.critical}$, the parameters for weights and bias (from g_{header}) will be further adjusted due to the newly introduced loss function.

(Loss Function Inside the Critical Area). For a labeled data $(\text{in}, \text{lb}) \in \mathcal{T}$, we need to define the loss for every output grid $\langle i, j \rangle$ that is inside the critical area, and the overall loss is the sum of loss from each grid. In particular, the loss function shall reflect the safety specification:

– If in the ground truth, there exists a vehicle centered at output grid $\langle i, j \rangle$, then the loss for output grid $\langle i, j \rangle$ is 0 so long as

  • for the 1st output prediction, i.e., the predicted probability, it is greater than *class threshold* α, as the post-processing algorithm uses α as the threshold, and
  • for the k-th output prediction where $k > 1$, the distance between the output and the label is bounded by δ_k.

– If in the ground truth, there does not exist a vehicle centered at output grid $\langle i, j \rangle$, then loss for output grid $\langle i, j \rangle$ is 0 so long as
  • the prediction probability is less than *class threshold* α, as for the post-processing algorithm, it uses α as the threshold.

Definition 1. *Let function* $\text{dist}(v, \text{low}, \text{up})$ *return the minimum distance between value* v *to the interval* $[\text{low}, \text{up}]$. *That is,* $\text{dist}(v, \text{low}, \text{up}) := \min(|v - \text{low}|, |v - \text{up}|)$.

The following definition of loss captures the above mentioned concept.

Definition 2. *Given* $(\text{in}, \text{lb}) \in \mathcal{T}$, *define the loss between the prediction* $\text{out} := f^{(n)}(\text{in})$ *and the ground truth* lb *at output grid* $\langle i, j \rangle$ *to be*

$$\text{loss}_{\langle i,j \rangle}(\text{out}, \text{lb}) := \begin{cases} \text{dist}(\text{out}_{\langle i,j,1 \rangle}, \alpha, \infty) + \eta & \text{if } \text{lb}_{\langle i,j,1 \rangle} = 1 \\ \text{dist}(\text{out}_{\langle i,j,1 \rangle}, -\infty, \alpha) + \eta & \text{otherwise } (\text{lb}_{\langle i,j,1 \rangle} = 0) \end{cases}$$

where $\eta := \sum_{k=2}^{7} \text{dist}(\text{out}_{\langle i,j,k \rangle}, \text{lb}_{\langle i,j,k \rangle} - \delta_k, \text{lb}_{\langle i,j,k \rangle} + \delta_k)$

At the end of this section, we provide technical details on how to implement the loss function using state-of-the-art machine learning framework PyTorch.

(Connecting Zero Loss with Buffer Size). To avoid scenarios shown in Fig. 3, the following lemma provides a conservative method to enlarge the predicted bounding box, such that the enlarged bounding box guarantees to contain the ground truth bounding box so long as the computed loss value $\text{loss}_{\langle i,j \rangle}(\text{out}, \text{lb})$ equals 0.

Lemma 1. *For the labelled data* $(\text{in}, \text{lb}) \in \mathcal{T}$, *given* $\text{out} := f^{(n)}(\text{in})$, *let* θ *be the angle produced by* $\text{out}_{\langle i,j,2 \rangle}$ *and* $\text{out}_{\langle i,j,3 \rangle}$. *If* $\text{loss}_{\langle i,j \rangle}(\text{out}, \text{lb}) = 0$ *and if* $\text{lb}_{\langle i,j,1 \rangle} = 1$, *then enlarging the prediction bounding box by*

– *enlarging the predicted width with* $d + d_w$
– *enlarging the predicted length with* $d + d_l$

guarantees to contain the vehicle bounding box from label lb at grid $\langle i, j \rangle$, *where* d, d_l *and* d_w *need to satisfy the following:*

- $d > \sqrt{(\delta_4)^2 + (\delta_5)^2}$,
- $d_l > max_{\alpha \in [-\kappa, \kappa]} \frac{1}{2}(10^{out\langle i,j,6\rangle + \delta_6} \sin \alpha + 10^{out\langle i,j,7\rangle + \delta_7} \cos \alpha - 10^{out\langle i,j,7\rangle})$,
- $d_w > max_{\alpha \in [-\kappa, \kappa]} \frac{1}{2}(10^{out\langle i,j,6\rangle + \delta_6} \cos \alpha + 10^{out\langle i,j,7\rangle + \delta_7} \sin \alpha - 10^{out\langle i,j,6\rangle})$,

and the interval $[-\kappa, \kappa]$ *used in* d_l *and* d_w *satisfies the following constraints:*

$$\forall \alpha \in [\frac{-\pi}{2}, \frac{\pi}{2}] : (|\cos(\theta) - \cos(\theta + \alpha)| \leq \delta_2 \wedge |\sin(\theta) - \sin(\theta + \alpha)| \leq \delta_3)$$
$$\rightarrow \alpha \in [-\kappa, \kappa] \quad (1)$$

A conservative computation of d_l and d_w independent of the generated prediction can be done by further assuming the maximum length and width of a vehicle for the observed output, e.g., a vehicle can have at most 6 m in length ($10^{out\langle i,j,7\rangle} \leq 6$) and 2.5 m in width ($10^{out\langle i,j,6\rangle} \leq 2.5$); the assumptions shall be monitored in run-time to check if one encounters prediction that generates larger vehicle bounding boxes. As $\delta_2, \ldots, \delta_7$ are constants, and by setting $[-\kappa, \kappa]$ to be a constant interval (which is related to the value of δ_2 and δ_3)[4], the minimum value for d_l and d_w can be computed using numerical approximation solvers such as Mathematica or Sage.

(Connecting the Prediction and the Post-processing Algorithm). As a consequence, given $(\text{in}, \text{lb}) \in \mathcal{T}$, provided that $\text{loss}_{\langle i,j \rangle}(\text{out}, \text{lb}) = 0$ and $\text{lb}_{\langle i,j,1\rangle} = 1$, one ensures the following:

1. By enlarging the bounding box created from the prediction using Lemma 1, the enlarged bounding box is guaranteed to contain the bounding box created by the label.
2. The non-max-inclusion algorithm never removes any bounding box with prediction probability smaller than α,

Therefore, the resulting list of bounding boxes after post-processing is *guaranteed to have one bounding box that completely contains the ground truth.* This implies that situation in Fig. 3 does not occur in (in, lb).

---

[4] The interval $[-\kappa, \kappa]$ is essentially a *conservative upper bound* on the deviated angle between prediction and the ground truth, where their associated sine and cosine value differences are bounded by δ_2 and δ_3. As an example, if between the predicted angle and the ground truth, we only allow the sine and cosine value to only differ by at most 0.1 (i.e., $\delta_2 = \delta_3 = 0.1$), it is easy to derive that κ can be conservatively set to $\frac{\pi}{18}$, i.e., (10°), rather than the trivial value $\frac{\pi}{2}$. This is because an angle difference of 10° can already make sine and cosine value differ by 0.15, thereby creating non-zero loss. Therefore, conservatively setting $[-\kappa, \kappa]$ to be $[-\frac{\pi}{18}, \frac{\pi}{18}]$ in computing d_l and d_w surely covers all possible angle deviation constrained by zero loss.

(Problems in Using Standard Post-processing Algorithm). Notice that the above mentioned guarantee *does not hold when replacing non-max-inclusion with non-max-suppression*, as the enlarged bounding box from the prediction at $\langle i, j \rangle$ (which has the guarantee of containing the ground truth) can be removed, so long as there exists another bounding box from a nearby output grid $\langle i', j' \rangle$ that (i) has higher predicted probability value (i.e., $\mathsf{out}_{\langle i',j',1 \rangle} \geq \mathsf{out}_{\langle i,j,1 \rangle}$) and (ii) has a huge area overlap with the one from grid $\langle i, j \rangle$.

5.3   Engineering $g_{critical}$ - Variation 2 (Addressing A1 and A2)

We propose an improvement for engineering $g_{critical}$ which considers feature-level robustness, thereby also addressing **A2**. The underlying idea is illustrated in Fig. 6, where parameters to be learned are the same between the first variation and the second variation. The difference lies in how values are propagated in training (value propagation in variation 1 versus bound propagation in variation 2) and in how the loss is computed (loss accounting tolerance in variation 1 versus symbolic loss accounting tolerance in variation 2).

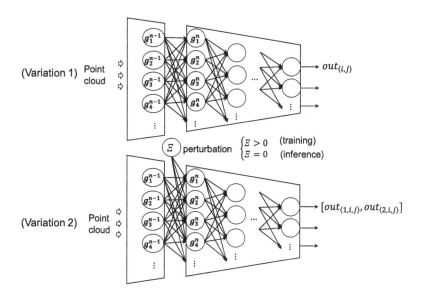

Fig. 6. Introducing feature-level perturbation in engineering $g_{critical}$

- (First layer in $g_{critical}$) For every neuron in $g_{critical}$ receiving values produced from the backbone network, we require that it takes an additional input parameter $\Xi \geq 0$ that characterizes the maximum amount of *perturbation*, and subsequently computes a conservative bound accounting all possible perturbation. Let n be the starting layer index of $g_{critical}$. During training, we require neuron g_j^n to compute, subject to the condition $-\Xi \leq \xi_1, \ldots, \xi_{d_{(n-1)}} \leq \Xi$, values lowerb_j^n and upperb_j^n where

- lowerb$_j^n$ $\leq$ min $\rho_j^n (\sum_{i=1}^{d_{(n-1)}} W_{ji}^n (g_i^{(n-1)}(\text{in}) + \xi_i) + b_j^n)$ and
- upperb$_j^n$ $\geq$ max $\rho_j^n (\sum_{i=1}^{d_{(n-1)}} W_{ji}^n (g_i^{(n-1)}(\text{in}) + \xi_i) + b_j^n)$.

In other words, the interval [lowerb$_j^n$, upperb$_j^n$] acts as a *sound over-approximation* over all possible computed values by taking input $g_i^{(n-1)}(\text{in})$ and by having it boundedly perturbed.

- (Other layers in $g_{critical}$) For other layers, during training, a neuron takes the bound computed by the previous layer and computes again a sound over-approximation over possible outputs. In other words, during training, the j-th neuron at layer n' ($n' > n$) computes lowerb$_j^{n'}$ and upperb$_j^{n'}$ such that

- lowerb$_j^{n'}$ $\leq$ min $\rho_j^{n'} (\sum_{i=1}^{d_{(n'-1)}} W_{ji}^n v_i^{(n'-1)} + b_j^{n'})$ and
- upperb$_j^{n'}$ $\geq$ max $\rho_j^{n'} (\sum_{i=1}^{d_{(n'-1)}} W_{ji}^n v_i^{(n'-1)} + b_j^{n'})$,

where for $i \in 1, \ldots, d_{(n'-1)}$, lowerb$_i^{n'-1}$ $\leq$ v$_i^{(n'-1)}$ $\leq$ upperb$_i^{n'-1}$.

Here we omit technical details, but one can implement above mentioned bound computation in state-of-the-art ML training framework using abstract interpretation techniques such as dataflow analysis [3]. Using dataflow analysis, under $\Xi = 0$ the computation turns exact, meaning that the lower-bound and the upper-bound should collide, i.e., lowerb$_j^{n'}$ = upperb$_j^{n'}$. In the rest of the paper, we always assume that Assumption 1 holds. This implies that during inference, one may set Ξ to 0 and can use the computed lower-bound as the prediction.

Assumption 1. *Assume that when $\Xi = 0$, the computation of lowerb$_j^n$, upperb$_j^n$, lowerb$_j^{n'}$, upperb$_j^{n'}$ for every input in $\in \mathbb{R}^{d_o}$ is exact, i.e., lowerb$_j^n$ = upperb$_j^n$ and lowerb$_j^{n'}$ = upperb$_j^{n'}$.*

(Characterizing Robust Loss). During training, as each output is no longer a single value but a bound incorporating the effect of perturbation, the loss function should be adjusted accordingly. For simplifying the notation, for each output at grid indexed $\langle i, j \rangle$, we add another dimension in the front to indicate the lower and the upper bound. That is, use out$_{\langle 1,i,j \rangle}$ and out$_{\langle 2,i,j \rangle}$ for indicating the computed lower- and upper-bound at grid $\langle i, j \rangle$.

Definition 3. *At output grid $\langle i, j \rangle$, define the robust loss between the range of possible values out (computed using perturbation bound Ξ and the input in) and the ground truth lb to be*

$$
\text{robust\_loss}_{\langle i,j \rangle}(\text{out}, \text{lb}) := \begin{cases} \text{dist}(\text{out}_{\langle 1,i,j,1 \rangle}, \alpha, \infty) + \frac{\eta_l + \eta_u}{2} & \text{if } \text{lb}_{\langle i,j,1 \rangle} = 1 \\ \text{dist}(\text{out}_{\langle 2,i,j,1 \rangle}, -\infty, \alpha) + \frac{\eta_l + \eta_u}{2} & \text{otherwise } (\text{lb}_{\langle i,j,1 \rangle} = 0) \end{cases}
$$

where

- $\eta_l := \sum_{k=2}^7 \text{dist}(\text{out}_{\langle 1,i,j,k \rangle}, \text{lb}_{\langle i,j,k \rangle} - \delta_k, \text{lb}_{\langle i,j,k \rangle} + \delta_k)$ *and*
- $\eta_u := \sum_{k=2}^7 \text{dist}(\text{out}_{\langle 2,i,j,k \rangle}, \text{lb}_{\langle i,j,k \rangle} - \delta_k, \text{lb}_{\langle i,j,k \rangle} + \delta_k)$

The rationale for the design of robust loss is as follows: If the ground truth indicates that there exists an object at grid $\langle i,j \rangle$, then we hope that any input under perturbation should still reports the existence of that object. This is characterized by the probability lower-bound $\mathsf{out}_{\langle 1,i,j,1 \rangle}$ being larger than the class threshold α. On the other hand, if the ground truth states that no object exists at grid $\langle i,j \rangle$, then all possible input perturbation can report absence, so long when the probability upper-bound $\mathsf{out}_{\langle 2,i,j,1 \rangle}$ is less than the class threshold α. Finally, when η_l and η_u are both 0, both the lower-bound and the upper-bound due to perturbation are within tolerance. In other words, the perturbation never leads to a prediction that exceeds the label by tolerance.

Under Assumption 1, $\mathsf{robust\_loss}_{\langle i,j \rangle}(\mathsf{out}, \mathsf{lb})$ can be viewed as a generalization of $\mathsf{loss}_{\langle i,j \rangle}(\mathsf{out}, \mathsf{lb})$: When $\varXi = 0$, computing $\mathsf{robust\_loss}_{\langle i,j \rangle}(\mathsf{out}, \mathsf{lb})$ essentially computes the same value of $\mathsf{loss}_{\langle i,j \rangle}(\mathsf{out}, \mathsf{lb})$ due to the colliding lower- and upper-bounds $(\mathsf{out}_{\langle 1,i,j,k \rangle} = \mathsf{out}_{\langle 2,i,j,k \rangle})$ making $\eta_l = \eta_u$.

Finally, given $(\mathsf{in}, \mathsf{lb}) \in \mathcal{T}$, Lemma 2 (implicitly yet mathematically) characterizes the allowed perturbation on in to maintain the prediction under tolerance. If the symbolic loss at grid $\langle i,j \rangle$ equals zero and the label indicates the existence of an object at grid $\langle i,j \rangle$, then any input in' that are close to in (subject to Eq. 2) should also positively predict the existence of an object (i.e., the first output should be larger than α). The result can also be combined with Lemma 1 to avoid the situation illustrated in Fig. 3.

Table 1. Implementing the loss function

Function on single input	Batched implementation in PyTorch
$\mathsf{dist}(\mathsf{v}, \mathsf{low}, \mathsf{up})$	`torch.max(torch.clamp(low - v, min=0),` `torch.clamp(v - up, min=0))`
If lb=1 then x; else (i.e., lb=0) y	`torch.mul(lb, x) + torch.mul(1 - lb, y)`

Lemma 2.   *Given* $(\mathsf{in}, \mathsf{lb}) \in \mathcal{T}$, *under the condition* $\mathsf{robust\_loss}_{\langle i,j \rangle}(\mathsf{out}, \mathsf{lb}) = 0$ *where* out *is computed using* in *with perturbation bound* $\varXi := \xi$ *($\xi > 0$) at layer n, then for any* in' *where the following condition holds,*

$$\forall m \in \{1, \ldots, d_{(n-1)}\} : |g_m^{(n-1)}(in') - g_m^{(n-1)}(in)| \leq \xi \tag{2}$$

the prediction out′ *that is computed using* in′ *without perturbation (i.e., using inference with* $\varXi = 0$*), is guaranteed to have the following properties.*

(a) If $\mathsf{lb}_{\langle i,j,1 \rangle} = 1$ *then* $\mathsf{out}'_{\langle 1,i,j,1 \rangle} \geq \alpha$.
(b) If $\mathsf{lb}_{\langle i,j,1 \rangle} = 0$ *then* $\mathsf{out}'_{\langle 1,i,j,1 \rangle} \leq \alpha$.
(c) For $k \in \{2, \ldots, 7\}$, $|\mathsf{out}'_{\langle 1,i,j,k \rangle} - \mathsf{lb}_{\langle i,j,k \rangle}| \leq \delta_k$.

(Implementing the Loss Function). As state-of-the-art neural network training frameworks such as TensorFlow or Pytorch always operate on batches of data, it is important that the previously mentioned loss functions can be implemented with batch support. Overall, the loss function defined in Definition 2 and 3 is a composition from two elements, namely (i) to apply Definition 1 and (ii) to perform case split depending on the value of the label, which can only be 1 or 0. Table 1 details how to implement these two elements in PyTorch.

6   Concluding Remarks

In this paper, we exemplified how to extend a state-of-the-art single-stage 3D detector neural network (PIXOR) in a safety-aware fashion. By safety-aware, our goal is to reflect the safety specification into the architectural design, the engineering of the loss function, and the post-processing algorithm. Our proposed hardening is compatible with standard training methods while being complementary to other critical activities in the safety engineering of machine learning systems such as rigorous data collection, testing (for understanding the generalizability) or interpretation (for understanding the decision of networks). In our example, the tolerance concept integrated inside the loss function avoids unrealistic-and-unreachable perfection in training, allows integrating the idea of provable robustness, and finally, enables connecting the specification to capabilities or limitations from other components such as motion planners.

For future work, we are interested in migrating the concept and the research prototype into real systems, as well as reflecting other safety specifications into the design of the architecture and the loss function. Yet another direction is to consider how other architectures used in multi-view 3D reconstruction (e.g., MV3D network [2]) can also be made safety-aware.

References

1. Burton, S., Gauerhof, L., Sethy, B.B., Habli, I., Hawkins, R.: Confidence arguments for evidence of performance in machine learning for highly automated driving functions. In: Romanovsky, A., Troubitsyna, E., Gashi, I., Schoitsch, E., Bitsch, F. (eds.) SAFECOMP 2019. LNCS, vol. 11699, pp. 365–377. Springer, Cham (2019). https://doi.org/10.1007/978-3-030-26250-1_30
2. Chen, X., Ma, H., Wan, J., Li, B., Xia, T.: Multi-view 3D object detection network for autonomous driving. In: CPVR, pp. 1907–1915 (2017)
3. Cousot, P., Cousot, R.: Abstract interpretation: a unified lattice model for static analysis of programs by construction or approximation of fixpoints. In: POPL, pp. 238–252. ACM (1977)
4. Engelcke, M., Rao, D., Wang, D.Z., Tong, C.H., Posner, I.: Vote3Deep: fast object detection in 3D point clouds using efficient convolutional neural networks. In: ICRA, pp. 1355–1361. IEEE (2017)
5. Gauerhof, L., Munk, P., Burton, S.: Structuring validation targets of a machine learning function applied to automated driving. In: Gallina, B., Skavhaug, A., Bitsch, F. (eds.) SAFECOMP 2018. LNCS, vol. 11093, pp. 45–58. Springer, Cham (2018). https://doi.org/10.1007/978-3-319-99130-6_4

6. Geiger, A., Lenz, P., Stiller, C., Urtasun, R.: Vision meets robotics: the KITTI dataset. Int. J. Robot. Res. **32**(11), 1231–1237 (2013)
7. Huang, X., et al.: A survey of safety and trustworthiness of deep neural networks. arXiv preprint arXiv:1812.08342 (2018)
8. Koopman, P., Kane, A., Black, J.: Credible autonomy safety argumentation. In: SSS (2019)
9. Li, B., Zhang, T., Xia, T.: Vehicle detection from 3D lidar using fully convolutional network. arXiv preprint arXiv:1608.07916 (2016)
10. Matsuno, Y., Ishikawa, F., Tokumoto, S.: Tackling uncertainty in safety assurance for machine learning: continuous argument engineering with attributed tests. In: Romanovsky, A., Troubitsyna, E., Gashi, I., Schoitsch, E., Bitsch, F. (eds.) SAFE-COMP 2019. LNCS, vol. 11699, pp. 398–404. Springer, Cham (2019). https://doi.org/10.1007/978-3-030-26250-1_33
11. Raghunathan, A., Steinhardt, J., Liang, P.: Certified defenses against adversarial examples. In: ICLR (2018)
12. Salman, H., et al.: Provably robust deep learning via adversarially trained smoothed classifiers. arXiv preprint arXiv:1906.04584 (2019)
13. Shi, S., Wang, X., Li, H.: PointrRCNN: 3D object proposal generation and detection from point cloud. In: CPVR, pp. 770–779 (2019)
14. Sinha, A., Namkoong, H., Duchi, J.C.: Certifying some distributional robustness with principled adversarial training. In: ICLR (2018)
15. Tsuzuku, Y., Sato, I., Sugiyama, M.: Lipschitz-margin training: scalable certification of perturbation invariance for deep neural networks. In: NeuIPS, pp. 6541–6550 (2018)
16. Wang, S., Chen, Y., Abdou, A., Jana, S.: MixTrain: scalable training of formally robust neural networks. arXiv preprint arXiv:1811.02625 (2018)
17. Wong, E., Kolter, Z.: Provable defenses against adversarial examples via the convex outer adversarial polytope. In: ICML, pp. 5283–5292 (2018)
18. Wong, E., Schmidt, F., Metzen, J.H., Kolter, J.Z.: Scaling provable adversarial defenses. In: NeuIPS, pp. 8400–8409 (2018)
19. Yang, B., Luo, W., Urtasun, R.: PIXOR: real-time 3D object detection from point clouds. In: CPVR, pp. 7652–7660 (2018)

Model-Centered Assurance
for Autonomous Systems

Susmit Jha, John Rushby[✉], and Natarajan Shankar

Computer Science Laboratory, SRI International, Menlo Park, CA 94025, USA
Susmit.Jha@sri.com, {Rushby,Shankar}@csl.sri.com

Abstract. The functions of an autonomous system can generally be partitioned into those concerned with perception and those concerned with action. Perception builds and maintains an internal model of the world (i.e., the system's environment) that is used to plan and execute actions to accomplish a goal established by human supervisors.

Accordingly, assurance decomposes into two parts: a) ensuring that the model is an accurate representation of the world as it changes through time and b) ensuring that the actions are safe (and effective), given the model. Both perception and action may employ AI, including machine learning (ML), and these present challenges to assurance. However, it is usually feasible to guard the actions with traditionally engineered and assured monitors, and thereby ensure safety, given the model. Thus, the model becomes the central focus for assurance.

We propose an architecture and methods to ensure the accuracy of models derived from sensors whose interpretation uses AI and ML. Rather than derive the model from sensors bottom-up, we reverse the process and use the model to predict sensor interpretation. Small prediction errors indicate the world is evolving as expected and the model is updated accordingly. Large prediction errors indicate surprise, which may be due to errors in sensing or interpretation, or unexpected changes in the world (e.g., a pedestrian steps into the road). The former initiate error masking or recovery, while the latter requires revision to the model. Higher-level AI functions assist in diagnosis and execution of these tasks.

Although this two-level architecture where the lower level does "predictive processing" and the upper performs more reflective tasks, both focused on maintenance of a world model, is derived by engineering considerations, it also matches a widely accepted theory of human cognition.

1 Introduction

Autonomous systems—those, such as self-driving cars, that are capable of independent decision making—typically use software that employs methods of Artificial Intelligence (AI) such as Machine Learning (ML) and time-constrained best-efforts deduction. It is generally impossible to predict the behavior of such software in all cases, as it can differ from case to case with little generalization. Consequently, it is difficult to provide assurance to justify confidence that an autonomous system is fit for use in critical contexts.

© Springer Nature Switzerland AG 2020
A. Casimiro et al. (Eds.): SAFECOMP 2020, LNCS 12234, pp. 228–243, 2020.
https://doi.org/10.1007/978-3-030-54549-9_15

One primitive way to seek assurance is through a large number of realistic tests. For self-driving cars, this is known as "collecting miles" and involves real and simulated driving through many scenarios and over large distances [1]. However, studies including one by the RAND Corporation [2], show that the quantity of testing required to substantiate acceptable safety is infeasibly vast, ranging from hundreds of millions to tens of billions of test miles.

An alternative that is endorsed for unmanned aircraft [3], for example, is to use conventional software as a monitor[1] for autonomous functions. The monitor is assured by conventional methods and overrides the autonomous software when it detects a potential safety violation and substitutes safe alternative behavior. Monitors have their own difficulties, however, but to examine them we first need to review the architecture of autonomous systems.

The functions of an autonomous system generally can be partitioned into those concerned with perception and those concerned with action. The purpose of perception is to build a model of the system's "world" (i.e., its environment) that is used for planning and executing actions to accomplish a goal established by human supervisors (e.g., the destination of a self-driving car) while maintaining required invariants, such as safety. This is an instance of model-based control, where the novelty is that the model is built with the aid of perception functions that employ AI and ML.

The overall case for safety depends on both perception (how good is the model of the world?) and action (how safe are the selected actions, given the model of the world?). Although AI and ML may be needed to construct an action plan, conventional software can check its safety, given a model of the world. Because it operates in uncertain environments (e.g., a self-driving car does not know what other road users may do) the checking software needs to consider all possibilities. Mobileye promote a safety model of this kind: "Responsibility-Sensitive Safety" (RSS) requires that the action software, and hence its monitor, should not be the cause of an accident no matter what other vehicles do [4]. With these interpretations, the action functions of an autonomous system can be checked or monitored by conventional software that can be assured by conventional means. However, the monitors also need a model of the environment and this complicates the argument for their assurance.

One possibility is that a monitor builds its own model, which might be very crude. For example, the monitor for a self-driving car might comprise a set of functions similar to those of an "Advanced Driver Assistance System" (ADAS) for human drivers, including "Forward Collision Warning," "Automatic Emergency Braking," "Blind Spot Warning," and "Rear Cross Traffic Warning and Rear Automatic Emergency Braking." Here, the "models" are derived very directly from radar and other sensors. These "last second" protections work well for human drivers but might be less effective for the unpredictable failures of autonomous systems. Furthermore, because they are unconnected to the larger plan constructed by action software, these protections may sometimes prove counterproductive. For example, the primary system might choose to give a

---

[1] The terms "guard," or "shield," or "safety bag" are also used.

cyclist or pedestrian a wide berth, but a "lane keeping assist" ADAS-like function operating as a monitor could override and steer back toward the cyclist or walker.

We can distinguish "independent" vs. "integrated" monitors at this point. An independent monitor uses its own sensing and decides whether or not to intervene without much reference to the primary action system. In addition to "last second" protections, a second function of an independent monitor could be to check whether the primary system is operating within specified "Operational Design Domains" (ODDs) [5]; these are circumstances, such as "on a freeway, in daylight," for which the system was designed and is considered safe. In both cases, since it is performing different functions than the primary, it is plausible that such a monitor could provide strong protection using only assured conventional software in its sensing and interpretation (i.e., model-building) functions. We endorse such monitors for "within ODD" and "last second" protection, but prefer integrated monitors for overall assurance.

An integrated monitor evaluates the plan produced by action software, looking several time units ahead. To do this, it needs a model of the world and this model needs to resemble that of the primary system more than do the models of independent monitors. If an integrated monitor builds its own model using assured conventional software, then it seems this is likely to generate false alarms as it will be less accurate than the ML-enabled model of the primary system, or else it invites the question why the primary could not also use conventional software. On the other hand, if the monitor itself uses AI and ML software then we face the original problem of how this can be assured. And if the monitor does use AI and ML software, then a case can be made that it should use some or all of the same sensors and software as the primary system, because a redundant system will be expensive yet surely the recipient of less development and validation resources than the primary system, and therefore less capable and less trustworthy.

In the following, we will assume an integrated monitor that either uses the same model as the primary system or uses much the same sensors and software to build an alternative "shadow" model optimized for its different function. We will refer to the model used by the monitor, whether it be the primary model or its own specialized one, as the *assured model* because it is the focus for safety and therefore the architecture of the system should be directed to ensuring its accuracy. We call this "model-centered assurance" and it is the approach that we advocate. If the assured and primary models are separate, they both will be constructed and maintained in the way we describe below, but the details will be adjusted for their different functions.

The next section develops the idea of model-centered assurance and its key components: predictive processing and the dual-process architecture. Section 4 outlines the case for assurance, and Sect. 5 provides brief conclusions. The paper provides neither mathematics nor a case study. We are grateful to the organizers and reviewers for allowing us to present a purely conceptual paper. The underlying mathematics is well known in other fields and we provide references later; we are working on a case study and hope to report soon.

2   Model-Centered Assurance

If a world model is to be the focus for assurance, we need to consider the properties needed for safety, and the hazards to these. The intuitive property required of the model is fidelity to the real world, at least insofar as required to plan safe actions. In particular, if M is a model of world W, then any actions planned and shown to be safe using M should be safe when executed in W. The inverse need not be true; that is, there can be safe actions in the real world that do not appear so in the model. Thus, the model does not need to be a strictly accurate representation of the world: it can be conservative or, as we say, *safely approximate*.

In the absence of monitors, the model could be expressed in the variables of some latent space discovered by ML. But requirements for assurance monitors will surely be expressed in naturalistic terms ("don't hit a pedestrian") and the model must therefore represent these fairly directly. Hence, in model-centered assurance, the model must be a *naturalistic* one. Beyond that, the content of the model and submodels constructed by perception functions will be determined by the system and its purpose and goals. For a self-driving car, the overall model will represent something like an annotated map of its surroundings: it will include the layout of the local roads and junctions, information about nearby vehicles and pedestrians, locations of fixed objects (e.g., mailboxes), road signs and their interpretation, traffic signals, and so on. It is a design choice whether there is one model or a coordinated collection of submodels. A typical submodel is a list of detected objects in the vicinity of the *ego* vehicle, giving the location, size, velocity, type, and inferred intent of each; another might be an occupancy grid (a discretized probabilistic 2D map, describing the occupancy of each "square"); and another might be a representation of traffic lanes. Inputs from many different sensors (e.g., GPS location and map data, odometry, lidar, radar, proximity sensors, cameras etc.) will be interpreted and fused to create the world model and its submodels. All of these data sources present challenges in interpretation but we will focus on image data from cameras since this is the most widely studied and discussed, and among the most challenging.

Lin and colleagues [6] outline a representative vision processing pipeline for a self-driving car: image data from the cameras are fed in parallel to an object detector and a localizer; the object detector discovers the objects of interest around the vehicle, such as other vehicles, pedestrians, and traffic signals; the detected objects are then passed to an object tracker that associates objects with their past movements and predicts the future trajectories of moving objects [7]; in parallel, the localizer determines the location of the *ego* vehicle. Subsequently, the object movement information from the object tracker and vehicle location information from the localizer are combined and projected onto the same 2 or 3 dimensional coordinate space by a sensor fusion engine to create the model used by the action functions.

The object detector is usually based on (semi) supervised learning using a convolutional neural network. This is a deep learning neural network architecture that typically comprises some layers of artificial neurons arranged to perform convolution, some to do pooling, and some fully connected. The number and arrangement of layers of each type are determined by experiment and constitute the developer's "secret sauce." During subsequent training, a vast number of images are fed to the network together with correct (human generated) data on the objects they contain. During the training process, the weights in the neural network are adjusted until it detects objects with high accuracy and reliability.

Now although deep neural networks such as those employed in object detectors are astonishingly effective at their tasks, we must heed Judea Pearl's observation that at bottom all they are doing is extremely sophisticated curve fitting [8]. We tune the network architecture and its weights so that training data is detected and classified with high accuracy and reliability (but without "overfitting") and we hope that live data is detected equally well. This hope has to rest on the assumption that real world data is smooth in a way that matches the implicit curve of the neural network. But the lesson from safety-critical systems is that their failures are often associated with unanticipated cases that are discontinuous from their neighbors.

This concern is exemplified by so-called "adversarial examples" [9]. These are typically minor modifications to an input image that are indiscernible to a human observer but cause an image classifier to change its output, often drastically and inappropriately. Masks have been developed that will cause misclassification when overlayed on any image input to a given classifier, and there are universal examples that will disrupt any classifier [10]. Furthermore, there are patterns that can be applied to real world artifacts (e.g., small images that can be stuck to traffic signs) that will cause them to be misread by an object classifier [11]. There is much work on detection and defense against such attacks but their effectiveness is limited: for example, Carlini and Wagner [12] demonstrate that ten different methods for detecting adversarial examples are easily bypassed.

In our opinion these concerns and defenses miss the true significance of adversarial examples. Their significance is not that a classifier can be mislead by carefully manipulated inputs, but that they demonstrate that classifications are fragile: that is, for every correctly classified image, there may be several incorrectly classified ones just a few pixel changes away. And why wouldn't this be, when all that the learning-enabled components are doing is curve fitting? Shamir and colleagues present an analysis that confirms and quantifies this interpretation [13], while Kilburtus and colleagues argue that this kind of "anti-causal" learning via curve-fitting has inherent challenges in achieving generalization [14].

The inevitable conclusion is that although many learning-enabled systems driven by neural networks exhibit amazing performance, it is reckless to assume this performance is robust. These systems will always exhibit more failures than can be tolerated in safety-critical systems and this cannot be fixed by adjustments to the interpretation function because it derives from the fact that the learning-enabled software is not interpreting the world in any meaningful sense, but merely applying statistical correlation to patterns of pixels. The question then is: can we locate these learning-enabled components in an architecture or context where their failures can be detected and masked or tolerated?

Some such methods attempt to assess "confidence" in the quality of the current learning-enabled judgment. One way to do this is to estimate whether the current input is similar to those encountered during training. Pimentel *et al* review methods for doing this [15]. A popular modern method uses a variational autoencoder [16] to learn the training data distribution and to compress it to a smaller "latent" space, from which a decoder can reconstruct the original input. In live operation, encoding and decoding the current input will usually result in an image close to the original if it is similar to the training data, and distant if not. Measures such as "Mahalanobis distance" can be used to assess the distance between an image and its reconstruction. Another approach attempts to locate the portions of the input that most directly contribute to the current judgment and checks that these are related to the feature concerned [17]. We consider it prudent to employ methods such as these but, as with defenses against adversarial examples, we note that they can often be defeated by changes to a few pixels and do not contribute greatly to assurance.

A different class of methods employs diversity and fault tolerance. All fault tolerance is based on redundancy, but it requires more than mere replication. For example, some of the best performing learning-enabled systems for image and speech recognition employ "ensembles" in which several different systems cooperate or compete to generate results [18]. However, while this approach can improve already impressive behavior, it does not deliver assurance—because we have no reason to suppose that failures of the component systems are independent, and no reason to trust any individual system.

However, although diverse interpretations of the same sensors may not fail independently, it is plausible that different sensors, particularly different kinds of sensors, may do so. Hence, sensor fusion over different kinds of sensor may be able to detect or mask some failures, although this may not be straightforward to achieve, as illustrated by the fatal accident between an Uber self-driving car and a pedestrian in Arizona on 18th March 2018 [19]. The Uber car used three sensor systems to build a simple object tracker model (recall Lin's vision processing pipeline [6]): cameras, radars, and lidar. In each of these sensor systems, its own object detector indicates the position of each detected object and attempts to classify it as, for example, a vehicle, a pedestrian, a bicycle, or other. The object tracker fuses these inputs using a "prioritization schema that promotes certain tracking methods over others, and is also dependent on the recency of the observation" [19, page 8]. In the case of the Arizona crash, this resulted in a "flickering" identification of the victim as the sensor systems' own classifiers changed their identifications, and as fusion performed by the object tracker preferred first one sensor system, then another, as listed below [19, Table 1].

- 5.6 s before impact, victim classified as *vehicle*, by radar
- 5.2 s before impact, victim classified as *other*, by lidar
- 4.2 s before impact, victim classified as *vehicle*, by lidar
- Between 3.8 and 2.7 s before impact,
  classification alternated between *vehicle* and *other*, by lidar
- 2.6 s before impact, victim classified as *bicycle*, by lidar

- 1.5 s before impact, victim classified as *unknown*, by lidar
- 1.2 s before impact, victim classified as *bicycle*, by lidar

The deeper harm of this "flickering" identification is that "if the perception system changes the classification of a detected object, the tracking history of that object is no longer considered when generating new trajectories" [19, page 8]. Consequently, the object tracker never established a trajectory for the victim and the vehicle collided with her even though she had been detected in some form or other for several seconds.

There are two related problems here: one is that the object tracker maintains a rather impoverished model of the world, the other is that its method of sensor fusion and model update pays no attention to the prior state of the model. The purpose of perception in autonomous systems is to build a model that accurately reflects the world; the model therefore encodes a lot more information than does an individual sensor sample and we should be cautious about making large updates to the model on the basis of such an individual sample.

The tenet of Model-Centered Assurance is that the model is the focus of attention, and the goal of perception is to ensure that it is an accurate (or "safely approximate") representation of the world. When a sensor samples the world, its interpretation software delivers some representation and we need to decide how to incorporate this into the world model. On the one hand, the information from the sensor is new but, on the other, its interpretation is possibly erroneous. Furthermore, the model is the repository of much accumulated information, so the method of model update must maintain its overall accuracy and coherence.

These considerations suggest a radical alternative to the traditional relationship between sensors and model: instead of operating "bottom up," we invert this to derive a framework for perception known as *predictive processing* (PP).

2.1 Predictive Processing

The world causes the sense impressions that our sensors report, but standard bottom-up methods of sensor interpretation attempt to reason backwards or "anti-causally" from sense impressions to their causes. This is inherently fraught with difficulty because many different configurations in the world can cause the same sense impressions. The idea of predictive processing is to reason causally: if we have an accurate model of the world, we can use it to predict the impressions that the world will cause our sensors to perceive. This is valuable for several reasons. The first is that it assists the lower levels of sensor interpretation (which may still operate anti-causally) by telling them what to look for.

Consider the component of a car's vision system concerned with detecting traffic lanes. This can be accomplished by a computer vision algorithm (e.g., based on the Hough Transform [20]) that looks for more-or-less straight lines painted on the road. A bottom-up approach will perform this algorithm afresh as each camera frame is processed. But this is inefficient—the traffic lanes in the current image frame are likely to be similar to those in the previous few frames and we should surely use this to seed the search—and it is fragile, as missing or scuffed lane markers might cause lanes to go undetected where they could be detected if we knew where to look, or could even be extrapolated from previous images. A better approach builds a model of the road and its traffic lanes and projects this forward in time to guide the algorithm in its search for lanes in the current image by predicting their location. The lanes found by the algorithm will generally be very close to those predicted by the model, so the information returned by the vision system to the system that maintains the model could be just the *difference* between them: that is, the *prediction error*.

In general, there will be uncertainty in the world model. This might be represented as a collection of candidate models: for example, one model might suppose that a detected object is a bicycle, another that it is a pedestrian, and we will favor the one that has the least prediction error (bicycles generally go in the same direction as the traffic, while pedestrians tend to go across it, so the two models will predict different locations for the object in the next frame).

This is an example of "analysis by synthesis," meaning that we formulate hypotheses (i.e., candidate world models) and favor those whose (synthesized) predictions match the sensed data. Enabling this approach is the second reason why PP is so valuable. In practical applications, we need to consider the level of the predictions concerned: do we use the world model to synthesize the raw data (e.g., pixels) that we predict the sensor will detect (which can be done using autoencoders), or do we target some higher level of its local interpretation (e.g., detected objects)? The best choice is a topic for experimental research, but we would expect a level of representation comparable to that produced by an object detector to be suitable.

Rather than (or in addition to) multiple candidate models, we could use probability distributions to represent uncertainty about model parameters. Implementations of this approach often employ Bayesian methods, although there are many variations [21]. The component that maintains the model will then send its predictions to the vision (or other sensor) component as a *prior* distribution and the vision system will return a *posterior* one. This kind of Bayesian inference typically generates intractable integrals, so implementations employ methods known as *Variational Bayes* that turn the problem into iterative optimization of the posterior models to minimize prediction error [16].

There is strong similarity between this approach and a Kalman Filter. As here, a Kalman filter maintains a model of the system state, which is the estimated value of each of its state variables together with their estimated accuracies, and predicts their values at the next timestep. Sensors sample these values, and the state variables are updated in a way that favors their predicted values when these are believed to have high accuracy, and the sensor values otherwise.

In a further, and perhaps surprising similarity, the top-down approach is widely believed to be the way perception works in human (and other) brains, as first proposed by Helmholtz in the 1860s [22]. *Predictive Processing* [23], also known as predictive *coding* [24] and predictive *error minimization* [25], posits that the brain builds models of its environment and uses these to predict its sensory input, and that much of its activity can be seen as (an approximation to) iterative Bayesian optimization of its models to minimize prediction error. PP has prior "predictions" flowing from models down to sense organs and Bayesian "corrections" flowing back up that cause the posterior models to track reality. ("Free Energy" [26] is a more all-encompassing theory that includes actions: the brain "predicts" that the hand, say, is in a certain place and to minimize prediction error the hand actually moves there.) This is consistent with the fact that the brain has more neural pathways going from upper to lower levels than vice versa: models and predictions flow down, and only corrections flow up.

As we noted, PP can be seen as extending the idea of Kalman filtering from classical representations of state (i.e., a set of continuous variables, as in control theory) to more complex models, where we also have representations of object "type" and "intent" and so on. Thus, fields as varied as neuroscience, control theory, signal processing, and sensor fusion all employ methods similar to PP, but under different names and derived by different histories.

The model-centered architecture is portrayed in Fig. 1 (ignore the dark pink box on the right labeled "Level 2 model refinement" for the time being). The black arrows from "Level 1 model construction" to sensors and their low-level

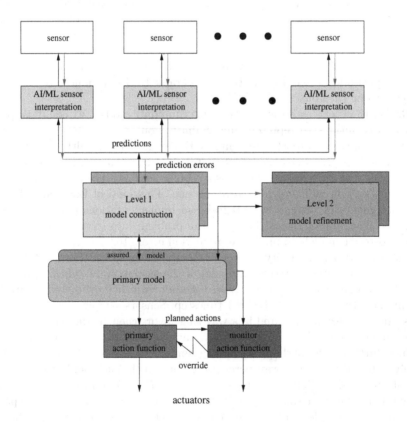

Fig. 1. Primary/monitor two-level architecture with predictive processing. (Color figure online)

interpretation indicate the top-down predictions of PP (inverted in the picture), while red arrows indicate prediction errors returned to model construction. If the assured model is separate from the primary model, then it and its mechanisms are indicated by the "shadows" behind the corresponding primaries.

The third and perhaps most crucial benefit of PP in a model-centered approach to assured autonomy is that prediction error provides a continuous assessment of the accuracy of the model and a systematic purchase on situations that warrant further investigation. Small prediction errors indicate that all is proceeding satisfactorily (we will see later that this may not be so and we need to separately verify the absence of systemic misinterpretations, but the basic inference is correct). Large prediction errors constitute *surprise* and indicate a failure of some kind, a flaw in the model, or an unexpected development in the world. Prediction error thus provides a single, uniform method for runtime verification and failure detection, so that assurance for the autonomous system is itself autonomous. For example, disappearance of previously detected objects because they are occluded by an overturned truck will trigger surprise even if our object detector fails to recognize the truck (cf. Tesla crash, Taiwan 1 Jun 20).

There are just three possible responses to surprise: we can adjust the sensor(s), adjust the model, or adjust the world. Selection and coordination among these is best performed by a separate function that has access to knowledge and more comprehensive methods for reasoning about the world, as we now describe.

2.2   Dual-Process Architecture

Suppose we are driving on a freeway when the object detector of a camera indicates a bicycle in front of us. In fact, what has been seen is a picture of a bicycle painted on the rear of a van. The object detector has seen the van in earlier frames and correctly labeled it but, now that we are closer, it is able to resolve the picture and labels the object as a bicycle, or perhaps as a van with confidence x and bicycle with confidence y. PP will have predicted it is definitely a van, so we have a large prediction error and need to decide how to proceed.

Now, we are on a freeway and the local "Laws and Rules of the Road" specify that bicycles are not allowed on freeways (this is not always so, but we will ignore special cases for the purpose of illustration). If our object detector had access to this information it could make the inference that the detected object cannot be a bicycle and must be a van. Such knowledge and methods of inference seem a useful augmentation to model-centered assurance—the more the system knows, the less it needs to sense—but pose the question how they should be incorporated into the architecture. The capabilities seem too general and universal to be added to the interpretation functions of individual sensors, so it seems they could be added to the model construction function. However, we now think of model construction as a predictive processing loop that sends predictions to sensors and updates the model according to prediction errors. The higher level knowledge and inferences that we now contemplate seem asynchronous to this loop and more focused on analysis and augmentation of the world model

and the response to surprise. Accordingly, we propose that these capabilities—
essentially, the deductive AI functions of the system—are located in a separate
"model refinement" function that is shown as dark pink in Fig. 1. Furthermore,
we suggest that it is useful to think of the two methods of model update as
occurring on two levels: basic (PP) model construction at Level 1, and more
inferential refinement at the higher Level 2.

Just as predictive processing has independent engineering justification, but
also happens to coincide with a current theory of human cognition, so the two-
level architecture coincides with a related "dual-process" theory [27,28], recently
popularized by Kahneman as separate "fast and slow" systems of human thought
[29]. In human cognition, *System 1* is unconscious, fast, and specialized for routine tasks; *System 2* is conscious, slow, easily fatigued, and capable of deliber-
ation and reasoning—it is what we mean by "thinking." These correspond to
Levels 1 and 2 in the architecture of Fig. 1.

We have implicitly suggested that Level 1 Model Construction maintains a
single assured world model (that may have several components) and that Level 2
Model Refinement embellishes this. However, it is believed that humans maintain
a hierarchy of models [24, 26] and this seems a good approach for autonomous
systems as well. The idea is that a PP loop operates between each adjacent pair
(in the hierarchy) of models, so that the lower level is like a sensor for the upper
level, with priority and update frequency determined by the size of prediction
errors. We will not pursue this more elaborate architecture here, but it seems an
interesting prospect for future consideration.

In general, the purpose of Level 2 Model Refinement is to respond to and
minimize "surprise" and one way to approach the latter is to augment the world
model with additional information that encodes "situation awareness." This can
be the result of hypothetical and counterfactual reasoning, so that things not
seen but "that might be there" are explicitly added to the model as "ghosts"
(objects with low probability). For example, by reasoning about lines of sight and
occluded vision, we could deduce that "we will be unable to see any vehicle that
might be behind that truck." We could then add a ghost vehicle to the occupancy
grid location behind the truck and this will influence the action functions. When
the truck no longer occludes our vision, sensors will confirm or deny presence of
the ghost, but neither outcome will constitute a surprise or a hazard because the
action functions will not have committed to a choice that would be dangerous
for either outcome. Dually, we might determine that a detected vehicle may be
unable to see us because a truck is in the way, and this can be incorporated in the
model as increased uncertainty on the likely motions of the vehicle concerned.

In another example, detection of many brake lights up ahead can be used to
infer some kind of problem and this will be represented as increased uncertainty
in the world model. In this way, what might otherwise be the surprising manifestation of an unanticipated situation will instead develop as gradual changes
in uncertainty or the resolution of ghosts into real objects. Observe that these
refinements to the world model make it more conservative: that is, they reduce

the options available to action functions, so that faults in this type of Level 2 reasoning cannot make the world model less safe.

Level 2 aims to minimize surprise but, when surprise happens, it must deal with it. We noted earlier that there are three possible responses: we can adjust the sensors, the model, or the world (or a combination of these). When surprise takes the form of a large prediction error from one sensor, or group of similar sensors, it is reasonable to assume it is a temporary glitch in sensing (e.g., reflections confusing radar) or interpretation (e.g., adversarial-type inputs) and to ignore the afflicted sensor(s) for a while and trust to local continuity in the world, or diversity and redundancy among other sensors, to maintain an accurate model.

Alternatively, analysis may suggest that prediction errors are due to a persistent cause in the external world, such as cameras dazzled by the sun. A suitable response might then be to change lanes to get in the shade of a nearby truck—in other words, to make a change in the world (specifically, our location in it).

If prediction errors persist, or afflict an entire class of sensor, then it may be a hardware or system problem—in which case Level 2 may coordinate with the fault tolerance functions of the underlying platform—or it may be some environmental challenge, such as fog. In this situation, lane-detection by cameras may fail, but Level 2 may be able to substitute some alternative method of "sensing" for model update, such as inferring location of the traffic lanes from the motions of neighboring cars as revealed by radar and proximity sensors.

When many sensors register large prediction errors, then the cause of the surprise is likely to be that the world did not evolve as the model predicted, and the appropriate response is to make changes in the model so that it conforms to information from the sensors. In extreme cases, this may require rebuilding the model from scratch, using some frames of bottom-up anti-causal interpretation.

We have motivated and introduced the two key aspects of our model-centered approach for autonomous systems: predictive processing and dual-process architecture. We now develop an outline assurance argument.

3   Toward an Assurance Argument

In routine operation, an autonomous system employing our model-centered approach will maintain a comprehensive naturalistic model of the world, possibly comprised of several components including (e.g., for cars) a detected objects list and an occupancy grid. The model is updated in an automated and regular manner using predictive processing, which provides continuous feedback on the quality of the model and available sensor data. For each sensor, the system will generate a prediction for the interpretation of its next frame. This can allow the sensor to focus its resources and interpretation in the most productive manner. Each sensor will report its prediction error; a small error indicates the model is aligned with the world and will cause a modest update to the model; a large error indicates a "surprise" that could be due to either a fault in the sensor or its interpretation, a flaw in the model, or an unexpected development in the world.

The most basic branch in an assurance case for this architecture is to be sure that small prediction errors really do guarantee that the model is a safely approximate representation of the world. The primary hazard to this claim is that the system's perception of the world could be systematically distorted—a hallucination. For example it could be blind to red cars: sensors will report no red cars, leading to construction of a world model without red cars; this will generate predictions lacking red cars that are confirmed by the sensors. So all seems well—until we collide with a red car, or are otherwise surprised by their existence. We refer to these perception faults as *systemic* and their characteristic is that they occur in some significant region of the input space and for significant periods of time, leading to misperception of the world. Other systemic faults might concern measurement rather than existence: for example, a sensor might displace objects 10 ft to the left or miscalculate bounding boxes by 10%; and others might concern identification, such as misreading stop signs as something else.

Systemic faults must be excluded or eliminated during development. A reasonable way to detect residual systemic faults—and to provide evidence for their absence—is by testing, and a plausible way to perform this is in simulation. We generate a simulated model of the world and a rendering of it is presented to the sensor interpretation and model construction functions under test; the model they construct is then compared to the original. A few million miles of simulated travel through representative scenarios [1] with some injection of degradation (e.g., rain and fog) into the rendering, could provide reasonable assurance for the absence of systemic faults. Note that this is not the same as "collecting miles" as we are looking only for systemic faults, whereas those who collect miles are also seeking exceptionally rare "corner case" and "fat tail" failures.

Assuming adequate evidence that small prediction errors guarantee the model is safely approximate, the next major branch in the assurance case is to show that the responses to large prediction errors (i.e., surprise) maintain the property. This divides into case analysis over the causes of surprise. First is a hardware fault of some kind, and we assume that this is safely handled by the underlying fault-tolerant platform (possibly in coordination with Level 2 model refinement).

Next is some fault in sensor interpretation or model construction that is localized in space and time (i.e., not systemic); we call these *local* perception faults and rely on assumed local continuity of the world to justify freezing or extrapolating afflicted values for a few frames; alternatively, if redundant sensors are available, we assume failure independence and favor these. Failure independence seems a plausible assumption, especially for sensors using different phenomena.

When prediction errors persist for more than a few frames, or are shared by multiple sensors, then we have a genuine surprise (the model is inaccurate, or the world has not evolved as expected) and Level 2 functions will orchestrate repair or regeneration of the model, or take action in the world, as described in the previous section. We will not drive this sketch of an assurance case into these details as they will be specific to each system. However, we note that the primary purpose of the AI functions at Level 2 is to resolve uncertainties in sensor interpretation (e.g., the bicycle/van example mentioned earlier), and to reduce future surprise through augmentations to the model that anticipate its evolution and promote situation awareness. These activities all increase the conservatism of the model and can only enhance the safety of its approximation to the real world.

This safety argument is quite different than could be constructed for traditional bottom-up sensor interpretation and fusion: predictive processing provides an intrinsic structure to the case analysis that suggests the argument can be made deductive [30]. Of course, much remains to be investigated, including a search for defeaters and quantifiable assessment of confidence and risks. A critical next step will be to assess confidence that surprises are always generated when they should be, which might be done by fault injection (e.g., perturbing interpretation of sensors, or the modeled world presented to them) in simulation.

4 Conclusion

We have described an architecture for autonomous systems that promotes their safety and assurance. The focus of the architecture is the "safely approximate" accuracy of an assured world model maintained by the perception functions. Given this model, the action functions can be guarded by monitors driven by traditional software and assured in traditional ways.

In the proposed architecture, sensor interpretation is driven top-down from the model—the reverse of the usual direction—using predictive processing. Small prediction errors confirm accuracy of the model and sensor interpretation, given that testing confirms absence of systemic faults. Large prediction errors indicate either a fault in sensor interpretation, or a departure between the model and the world (a surprise). The uniformity of prediction error as the single basis for runtime assurance and fault detection means that assurance is itself autonomous. AI functions located at a second level provide situation awareness and other measures to reduce future surprise and to deal with it when it occurs.

Although this dual-process architecture with predictive processing is derived by engineering considerations, it corresponds with current theories of human cognition and suggests fruitful comparisons. Mathematical formulations of predictive processing are well-developed in cognitive science [26] and in machine learning, where it is associated with "generative" and "variational" methods [16].

In current work, we are performing experimental evaluations of the approach and plan to report our experience and propose key challenges.

Acknowledgments. We thank the reviewers for their constructive comments, and Bev Littlewood of City, University of London, and Wilfried Steiner of TTTech Vienna for their challenges and discussion. The work was funded by DARPA contract FA8750-19-C-0089. We would also like to acknowledge support from the US Army Research Laboratory Cooperative Research Agreement W911NF-17-2-0196, and National Science Foundation (NSF) grant 1740079. The views, opinions and/or findings expressed are those of the authors and should not be interpreted as representing the official views or policies of the Department of Defense or the U.S. Government.

References

1. Thorn, E., Kimmel, S., Chaka, M.: A framework for automated driving system testable cases and scenarios. DOT HS 812 623, NHTSA, Washington DC (2018)
2. Kalra, N., Paddock, S.M.: Driving to safety: How many miles of driving would it take to demonstrate autonomous vehicle reliability? Transp. Res. Part A Policy Pract. **94**, 182–193 (2016)
3. ASTM: Standard Practice for Methods to Safely Bound Flight Behavior of Unmanned Aircraft Systems Containing Complex Functions (2017). ASTM F3269-17
4. Shalev-Shwartz, S., Shammah, S., Shashua, A.: On a formal model of safe and scalable self-driving cars. arXiv preprint arXiv:1708.06374 (2017)
5. NHTSA: Automated driving systems 2.0: A vision for safety. DOT HS 812 442, Washington DC (2018)
6. Lin, S.C., et al.: The architectural implications of autonomous driving: constraints and acceleration. ACM SIGPLAN Notices **53**, 751–766 (2018)
7. Koller, D., Daniilidis, K., Thórhallson, T., Nagel, H.-H.: Model-based object tracking in traffic scenes. In: Sandini, G. (ed.) ECCV 1992. LNCS, vol. 588, pp. 437–452. Springer, Heidelberg (1992). https://doi.org/10.1007/3-540-55426-2_49
8. Pearl, J., Mackenzie, D.: The Book of Why: The New Science of Cause and Effect. Basic Books, New York (2018)
9. Szegedy, C., et al.: Intriguing properties of neural networks. arXiv:1312.6199 (2013)
10. Moosavi-Dezfooli, S.M., Fawzi, A., Fawzi, O., Frossard, P.: Universal adversarial perturbations. In: Proceedings of the IEEE Conference on Computer Vision and Pattern Recognition, pp. 1765–1773 (2017)
11. Brown, T.B., et al.: Adversarial patch. arXiv preprint arXiv:1712.09665 (2017)
12. Carlini, N., Wagner, D.: Adversarial examples are not easily detected: bypassing ten detection methods. In: Proceedings of the 10th ACM W'shop on AI & Security, pp. 3–14 (2017)
13. Shamir, A., Safran, I., Ronen, E., Dunkelman, O.: A simple explanation for the existence of adversarial examples with small Hamming distance. arXiv preprint arXiv:1901.10861 (2019)
14. Kilbertus, N., Parascandolo, G., Schölkopf, B.: Generalization in anti-causal learning. arXiv preprint arXiv:1812.00524 (2018)
15. Pimentel, M.A.F., Clifton, D.A., Clifton, L., Tarassenko, L.: A review of novelty detection. Sig. Process. **99**, 215–249 (2014)
16. Kingma, D.P., Welling, M.: Auto-encoding variational Bayes. arXiv preprint arXiv:1312.6114 (2013)
17. Jha, S., Jang, U., Jha, S., Jalaian, B.: Detecting adversarial examples using data manifolds. In: MILCOM 2018, pp. 547–552. IEEE (2018)
18. Ju, C., Bibaut, A., van der Laan, M.: The relative performance of ensemble methods with deep convolutional neural networks for image classification. J. Appl. Stat. **45**, 2800–2818 (2018)
19. National Transportation Safety Board: Vehicle Automation Report; Tempe, AZ (2019). HWY18MH010
20. Duda, R.O., Hart, P.E.: Use of the Hough transformation to detect lines and curves in pictures. Commun. ACM **15**, 11–15 (1972)
21. Spratling, M.W.: A review of predictive coding algorithms. Brain Cogn. **112**, 92–97 (2017)

22. von Helmholtz, H.: Handbuch der Physiologischen Optik III, vol. 9. Verlag von Leopold Voss, Leipzig, Germany (1867)
23. Wiese, W., Metzinger, T.K.: Vanilla PP for philosophers: a primer on Predictive Processing. MIND Group, Frankfurt am Main (2017). Many papers: https:// predictive-mind.net/papers
24. Clark, A.: Whatever next? Predictive brains, situated agents, and the future of cognitive science. Behav. Brain Sci. **36**, 181–204 (2013)
25. Hohwy, J.: The Predictive Mind. Oxford University Press, Oxford (2013)
26. Friston, K.: The free-energy principle: A unified brain theory? Nat. Rev. Neurosci. **11**, 127 (2010)
27. Frankish, K.: Dual-process and dual-system theories of reasoning. Philos. Compass **5**, 914–926 (2010)
28. Evans, J.S.B.T., Stanovich, K.E.: Dual-process theories of higher cognition: Advancing the debate. Perspect. Psychol. Sci. **8**, 223–241 (2013)
29. Kahneman, D.: Thinking. Fast and Slow. Farrar, Straus and Giroux (2011)
30. Bloomfield, R., Rushby, J.: Assurance 2.0: A Manifesto. arXiv:2004.10474 (2020)

A Safety Framework for Critical Systems Utilising Deep Neural Networks

Xingyu Zhao[1], Alec Banks[2], James Sharp[2], Valentin Robu[1], David Flynn[1], Michael Fisher[3], and Xiaowei Huang[3(✉)]

[1] Heriot-Watt University, Edinburgh EH14 4AS, UK
{xingyu.zhao,v.robu,d.flynn}@hw.ac.uk
[2] Defence Science and Technology Laboratory, Salisbury SP4 0JQ, UK
{abanks,jsharp1}@dstl.gov.uk
[3] University of Liverpool, Liverpool L69 3BX, UK
{mfisher,xiaowei.huang}@liverpool.ac.uk

Abstract. Increasingly sophisticated mathematical modelling processes from Machine Learning are being used to analyse complex data. However, the performance and explainability of these models within practical critical systems requires a rigorous and continuous verification of their safe utilisation. Working towards addressing this challenge, this paper presents a principled novel safety argument framework for critical systems that utilise deep neural networks. The approach allows various forms of predictions, e.g., future reliability of passing some demands, or confidence on a required reliability level. It is supported by a Bayesian analysis using operational data and the recent verification and validation techniques for deep learning. The prediction is conservative – it starts with partial prior knowledge obtained from lifecycle activities and then determines the worst-case prediction. Open challenges are also identified.

Keywords: Safety cases · Quantitative claims · Reliability claims · Deep learning verification · Assurance arguments · Safe AI · Bayesian inference

1 Introduction

Deep learning (DL) has been applied broadly in industrial sectors including automotive, healthcare, aviation and finance. To fully exploit the potential offered by DL, there is an urgent need to develop approaches to their certification in safety critical applications. For traditional systems, safety analysis has aided engineers in *arguing* that the system is sufficiently safe. However, the deployment of DL in critical systems requires a thorough revisit of that analysis to reflect the novel characteristics of Machine Learning (ML) in general [2,10,27].

Compared with traditional systems, the behaviour of learning-enabled systems is much harder to predict, due to, *inter alia*, their "black-box" nature and the lack of traceable functional requirements of their DL components. The

© Springer Nature Switzerland AG 2020
A. Casimiro et al. (Eds.): SAFECOMP 2020, LNCS 12234, pp. 244–259, 2020.
https://doi.org/10.1007/978-3-030-54549-9_16

"black-box" nature hinders the human operators in understanding the DL and makes it hard to predict the system behaviour when faced with new data. The lack of explicit requirement traceability through to code implementation is only partially offset by learning from a dataset, which at best provides an incomplete description of the problem. These characteristics of DL increase apparent non-determinism [25], which on the one hand emphasises the role of *probabilistic measures* in capturing uncertainty, but on the other hand makes it notoriously hard to estimate the probabilities (and also the consequences) of critical failures.

Recent progress has been made to support the Verification and Validation (V&V) of DL, e.g., [23,47]. Although these methods may provide evidence to support low-level claims, e.g., the local robustness of a deep neural network (DNN) on a given input, they are insufficient by themselves to justify overall system safety claims. Here, we present a safety case framework for DL models which may in turn support higher-level system safety arguments. We focus on DNNs that have been widely deployed as, e.g., perception/control units of autonomous systems. Due to the page limit, we also confine the framework to DNNs that are fixed in the operation; this can be extended for online learning DNNs in future.

We consider safety-related properties including reliability, robustness, interpretability, fairness [6], and privacy [1]. In particular, we emphasise the assessment of DNN *generalisation error* (in terms of inaccuracy), as a major reliability measure, throughout our safety case. We build arguments in two steps. The first is to provide initial confidence that the DNN's generalisation error is bounded, through the assurance activities conducted at each stage of its lifecycle, e.g., formal verification on the DNN robustness. The second step is to adopt *proven-in-use/field-testing* arguments to boost the confidence and check whether the DNN is indeed sufficiently safe for the risk associated with its use in the system.

The second step above is done in a statistically principled way via Conservative Bayesian Inference (CBI) [8,46,49]. CBI requires only *limited and partial* prior knowledge of reliability, which differs from normal Bayesian analysis that usually assumes a *complete* prior distribution on the failure rate. This has a unique advantage: partial prior knowledge is more convincing (i.e. constitutes a more realistic claim) and easier to obtain, while complete prior distributions usually require extra assumptions and introduces optimistic bias. CBI allows many forms of prediction, e.g., posterior expected failure rate [8], future reliability of passing some demands [46] or a posterior confidence on a required reliability bound [49]. Importantly, CBI guarantees conservative outcomes: it finds the worst-case prior distribution yielding, say, a maximised posterior expected failure rate, and satisfying the partial knowledge. We are aware that there are other extant dangerous pitfalls in safety arguments [25,27], thus we also identify *open challenges* in our proposed framework and map them onto on-going research.

The key contributions of this work are:

a) A very first safety case framework for DNNs that mainly concerns *quantitative* claims based on structured heterogeneous safety arguments.

b) An initial idea of mapping DNN lifecycle activities to the reduction of decomposed DNN generalisation error that used as a primary reliability measure.

c) Identification of open challenges in building safety arguments for quantitative claims, and mapping them onto on-going research of potential solutions.

Next, we present preliminaries. Sect. 3 provides top-level argument, and Sect. 4 presents how CBI approach assures reliability. Other safety related properties are discussed in Sect. 5. We discuss related work in Sect. 6 and conclude in Sect. 7.

2   Preliminaries

2.1   Safety Cases

A safety case is a comprehensive, defensible, and valid justification of the safety of a system for a given application in a defined operating environment, thus it is a means to provide the grounds for confidence and to assist decision making in certification [12]. Early research in safety cases mainly focus on their formulation in terms of claims, arguments and evidence elements. The two most popular notations are CAE [12] and GSN [26]. In this paper, we choose the latter to present our safety case framework.

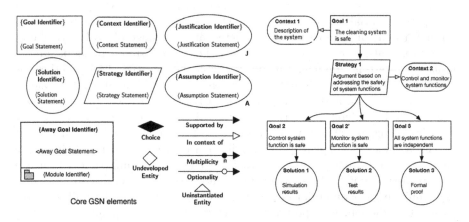

Fig. 1. The GSN core elements and an example of using GSN

Figure 1 shows the core GSN elements and a quick GSN example. Essentially, the GSN safety case starts with a top *goal* (claim) which then is decomposed through an argument *strategy* into sub-goals (sub-claims), and sub-goals can be further decomposed until being supported by *solutions* (evidence). A claim may be subject to some *context* or *assumption*. An *away goal* repeats a claim presented in another argument module. A description on all GSN elements used in this paper can be found in [26].

2.2 Deep Neural Networks and Lifecycle Models

Let (X, Y) be the training data, where X is a vector of inputs and Y is a vector of outputs such that $|X| = |Y|$. Let X be the input domain and Y be the set of labels. Hence, $X \subset$ X. We may use x and y to range over X and Y, respectively. Let $\mathcal{N}$ be a DNN of a given architecture. A network $\mathcal{N} :$ X $\rightarrow \mathcal{D}(Y)$ can be seen as a function mapping from X to probabilistic distributions over Y. That is, $\mathcal{N}(x)$ is a probabilistic distribution, which assigns for each possible label $y \in$ Y a probability value $(\mathcal{N}(x))_y$. We let $f_{\mathcal{N}} :$ X $\rightarrow$ Y be a function such that for any $x \in$ X, $f_{\mathcal{N}}(x) = \arg\max_{y \in Y}\{(\mathcal{N}(x))_y\}$, i.e. $f_{\mathcal{N}}(x)$ returns the classification label. The network is trained with a parameterised learning algorithm, in which there are (implicit) parameters representing e.g., the number of epochs, the loss function, the learning rate, the optimisation algorithm, etc.

A comprehensive ML *Lifecycle Model* can be found in [4], which identifies assurance desiderata for each stage, and reviews existing methods that contribute to achieving these desiderata. In this paper, we refer to a simpler lifecycle model that includes several phases: initiation, data collection, model construction, model training, analysis of the trained model, and run-time enforcement.

2.3 Generalisation Error

Generalisability requires that a neural network works well on all possible inputs in X, although it is only trained on the training dataset (X, Y).

Definition 1. *Assume that there is a ground truth function* $f :$ X $\rightarrow$ Y *and a probability function* $O_p :$ X $\rightarrow [0, 1]$ *representing the operational profile. A network* $\mathcal{N}$ *trained on* (X, Y) *has a generalisation error:*

$$G_{\mathcal{N}}^{0-1} = \sum_{x \in X} 1_{\{f_{\mathcal{N}}(x) \neq f(x)\}} \times O_p(x) \tag{1}$$

where 1_S *is an indicator function – it is equal to 1 when* S *is true and 0 otherwise.*

We use the notation $O_p(x)$ to represent the probability of an input x being selected, which aligns with the *operational profile* notion [35] in software engineering. Moreover, we use 0-1 loss function (i.e., assigns value 0 to loss for a correct classification and 1 for an incorrect classification) so that, for a given O_p, $G_{\mathcal{N}}^{0-1}$ is equivalent to the reliability measure *pfd* (the expected probability of the system failing on a random demand) defined in the safety standard IEC-61508. A "frequentist" interpretation of *pfd* is that it is the limiting relative frequency of demands for which the DNN fails in an infinite sequence of independently selected demands [48]. The primary safety measure we study here is *pfd*, which is equivalent to the generalisation error $G_{\mathcal{N}}^{0-1}$ in (1). Thus, we may use the two terms interchangeably in our safety case, depending on the context.

3   The Top-Level Argument

Figure 2 gives a top-level safety argument for the top claim **G1** – the DNN is sufficiently safe. We first argue **S1**: that all safety related properties are satisfied. The list of all properties of interest for the given application can be obtained by utilising the Property Based Requirements (PBR) [34] approach. The PBR method is a way to specify requirements as a set of properties of system objects in either structured language or formal notations. PBR is recommended in [2] as a method for the safety argument of autonomous systems. Without the loss of generality, in this paper, we focus on the major quantitative property: reliability (**G2**). Due to space constraints, other properties: interpretability, robustness, etc. are discussed in Sect. 5 but remain an undeveloped goal (**G3**) here.

More properties that have a safety impact can be incorporated in the framework as new requirements emerge from, e.g., ethical aspects of the DNN.

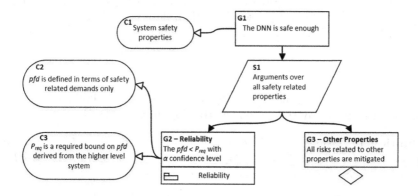

Fig. 2. The top-level safety argument

Despite the controversy over the use of probabilistic measures (e.g., *pfd*) for the safety of conventional software systems [29], we believe probabilistic measures are useful when dealing with ML systems since arguments involving their inherent uncertainty are naturally stated in probabilistic terms.

Setting a reliability goal (**G2**) for a DNN varies from one application to another. Questions we need to ask include: (i) What is the appropriate reliability measure? (ii) What is the quantitative requirement stated in that reliability measure? (iii) How can confidence be gained in that reliability claim?

Reliability of safety critical systems, as a probabilistic claim, will be about the probabilities/rates of occurrence of failures that have safety impacts, e.g., a dangerous misclassification in a DNN. Generally, systems can be classified as either: continuous-time systems that are being continuously operated in the active control of some process; or on-demand systems, which are only called upon to act on receipt of discrete demands. Normally we study the failure rate (number of failures in one time unit) of the former (e.g., flight control software) and the probability of failure per demand (*pfd*) of the latter (e.g., the emergency shutdown system of a nuclear plant). In this paper, we focus on *pfd* which aligns with DNN classifiers for perception, where demands are e.g., images from cameras.

Given the fact that most safety critical systems adopt a *defence in depth design* with safety backup channels [28], the required reliability (p_{req} in **G2**) should be derived from the higher level system, e.g., a 1-out-of-2 (1oo2) system in which the other channel could be either hardware-only, conventional software-based, or another ML software. The required reliability of the whole 1oo2 system may be obtained from regulators or compared to human level performance (e.g., a target of 100 times safer than average human drivers, as studied in [49]). We remark that deriving a required reliability for individual channels to meet the whole 1oo2 reliability requirement is still an open challenge due to the dependencies among channels [30] (e.g., a "hard" demand is likely to cause both channels to fail). That said, there is ongoing research towards rigorous methods to decompose the reliability of 1oo2 systems into those of individual channels which may apply and provide insights for future work, e.g., [7] for 1oo2 systems with one hardware-only and one software-based channels, [28,48] for a 1oo2 system with one possibly-perfect channel, and [15] utilising fault-injection technique. In particular, for systems with duplicated DL channels, we note that there are similar techniques, e.g., (i) ensemble method [39], where a set of DL models run in parallel and the result is obtained by applying a voting protocol; (ii) simplex architecture [45], where there is a main classifier and a safer classifier, with the latter being simple enough so that its safety can be formally verified. Whenever confidence of the main classifier is low, the decision making is taken over by the safer classifier; the safer classifier can be implemented with e.g., a smaller DNN.

As discussed in [8], the reliability measure, *pfd*, concerns system behaviour subject to *aleatory* uncertainty ("uncertainty in the world"). On the other hand, *epistemic* uncertainty concerns the uncertainty in the "beliefs about the world". In our context, it is about the human assessor's *epistemic* uncertainty of the reliability claim obtained through assurance activities. For example, we may not be *certain* whether a claim – the *pfd* is smaller than 10^{-4} – is true due to our imperfect understanding about the assurance activities. All assurance activities in the lifecycle with supportive evidence would increase our *confidence* in the reliability claim, whose formal quantitative treatment has been proposed in [11,32]. Similarly to the idea proposed in [46], we argue that all "process" evidence generated from the DNN lifecycle activities provides initial confidence of a desired *pfd* bound. Then the confidence in a *pfd* claim is acquired incrementally through operational data of the trained DNN via CBI – which we describe next.

4 Reliability with Lifecycle Assurance

4.1 CBI Utilising Operational Data

In Bayesian reliability analysis, assessors normally have a prior distribution of *pfd* (capturing the *epistemic* uncertainties), and update their beliefs (the prior distribution) by operational data. Given the safety-critical nature, the systems under study will typically see *failure-free* operation or very *rare failures*. Bayesian inference based on such non or rare failures may introduce dangerously optimistic bias if using a *Uniform* or *Jeffreys prior* which describes not only one's prior knowledge, but adds extra, unjustified assumptions [49]. Alternatively, CBI is a technique, first described in [8], which applied Bayesian analysis with only *partial* prior knowledge; by partial prior knowledge, we mean the following typical forms:

- $\mathbb{E}[pfd] \leq m$: the prior mean *pfd* cannot be worse than a stated value;
- $Pr(pfd \leq \epsilon) = \theta$: a prior confidence bound on *pfd*;
- $\mathbb{E}[(1 - pfd)^n] \geq \gamma$: prior confidence in the reliability of passing n tests.

These can be used by CBI either solely or in combination (e.g., several confidence bounds). The partial prior knowledge is far from a complete prior distribution, thus it is easier to obtain from DNN lifecycle activities (**C4**). For instance, there are studies on the generalisation error bounds, based on how the DNN was constructed, trained and verified [5,21]. We present examples on how to obtain such partial prior knowledge (**G6**) using evidence, e.g. from formal verification on DNN robustness, in the next section. CBI has also been investigated for various objective functions with a "posterior" flavour:

- $\mathbb{E}[pfd \mid$ pass n tests]: the posterior expected *pfd* [8];
- $Pr(pfd \leq p_{req} \mid k$ failures in n tests): the posterior confidence bound on *pfd* [48,49]; the p_{req} is normally a small *pfd*, stipulated at higher level;
- $\mathbb{E}[(1 - pfd)^t \mid$ pass n tests]: the future reliability of passing t demands in [46].

Example 1. In Fig. 3, we plot a set of numerical examples based on the CBI model in [46]. It describes the following scenario: the assessor has θ confidence that the software *pfd* cannot be worse than ϵ (e.g., 10^{-4} according to SIL-4), then after n failure-free runs (the x-axis), the future reliability of passing t demands is shown on the y-axis. We may observe that stronger prior beliefs (smaller ϵ with larger θ) and/or larger n/t ratio allows higher future reliability claims.

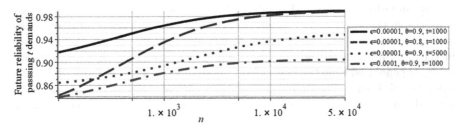

Fig. 3. Numerical examples based on the CBI model in [46]

Depending on the objective function of interest (**G2** is an example of a posterior confidence bound) and the set of partial prior knowledge obtained (**G6**), we choose a corresponding CBI model[1] for **S2**. Note, we also need to explicitly assess the impact of CBI model assumptions (**G5**). Published CBI theorems abstract the stochastic failure process as a sequence of independent and identically distributed (i.i.d.) Bernoulli trials given the unknown *pfd*, and assume the operational profile is constant [8,46,49]. Although we identify how to justify/relax those assumptions as open challenges, we note some promising ongoing research:

a) The i.i.d. assumption means a constant *pfd*, which may not hold for a system update or deployment in a new environment. In [31], CBI is extended to a *multivariate* prior distribution case coping with scenarios of a *changing pfd*, which may provide the basis of arguments for online learning DNNs in future.

b) The effect of assuming independence between successive demands has been studied, e.g., [20]. It is believed that the effect is negligible given non or rare failures; note this requires further (preferably conservative) studies.

c) The changes to the operational profile is a major challenge for all proven-in-use/field-testing safety arguments [27]. Recent research [9] provides a novel conservative treatment for the problem, which can be retrofitted for CBI.

The safety argument via CBI is presented in Fig. 4. In summary, we collect a set of partial prior knowledge from various lifecycle activities, then boost our posterior confidence in a reliability claim of interest through operational data, in a conservative Bayesian manner. We believe this aligns with the practice of applying management systems in reality – a system is built with claims of sufficient confidence that it may be deployed; these claims are then independently assessed to confirm said confidence is justified. Once deployed, the system safety performance is then monitored for continuing validation of the claims. Where there is insufficient evidence systems can be fielded with the risk held by the operator, but that risk must be minimised through operational restrictions. As confidence then grows these restrictions may be relaxed.

4.2 Partial Prior Knowledge on the Generalisation Error

Our novel CBI safety argument for the reliability of DNNs is essentially inspired by the idea proposed in [46] for conventional software, in which the authors seek prior confidence in the (quasi-)perfection of the software from "process" evidence like formal proofs, and effective development activities. In our case, to make clear the connection between lifecycle activities and their contributions to the generalisation error, we decompose the generalisation error into three:

$$G_{\mathcal{N}}^{0-1} = \underbrace{G_{\mathcal{N}}^{0-1} - \inf_{\mathcal{N} \in \mathbb{N}} G_{\mathcal{N}}^{0-1}}_{\text{Estimation error of } \mathcal{N}} + \underbrace{\inf_{\mathcal{N} \in \mathbb{N}} G_{\mathcal{N}}^{0-1} - G_{f,(X,Y)}^{0-1,*}}_{\text{Approximation error of } \mathbb{N}} + \underbrace{G_{f,(X,Y)}^{0-1,*}}_{\text{Bayes error}} \qquad (2)$$

---

[1] There are CBI combinations of objective functions and partial prior knowledge haven't been investigated, which remains as open challenges.

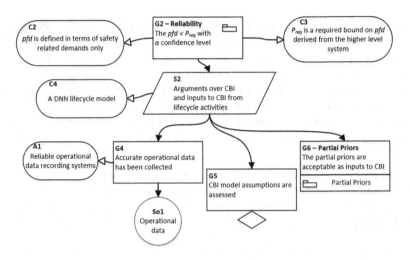

Fig. 4. The CBI safety argument

a) The *Bayes error* is the lowest and irreducible error rate over all possible classifiers for the given classification problem [19]. It is non-zero if the true labels are not deterministic (e.g., an image being labelled as y_1 by one person but as y_2 by others), thus intuitively it captures the uncertainties in the dataset (X, Y) and true distribution f when aiming to solve a real-world problem with DL. We estimate this error (implicitly) at the **initiation** and **data collection** stages in activities like: necessity consideration and dataset preparation etc.

b) The *Approximation error of* N measures how far the best classifier in N is from the overall optimal classifier, after isolating the Bayes error. The set N is determined by the architecture of DNNs (e.g., numbers of layers), thus lifecycle activities at the **model construction** stage are used to minimise this error.

c) The *Estimation error of* $\mathcal{N}$ measures how far the learned classifier $\mathcal{N}$ is from the best classifier in N. Lifecycle activities at the **model training** stage essentially aim to reduce this error, i.e., performing optimisations of the set N.

Both the Approximation and Estimation errors are reducible. We believe, the *ultimate goal* of all lifecycle activities is to reduce the two errors to 0, especially for safety-critical DNNs. This is analogous to the "possible perfection" notion of traditional software as pointed to by Rushby and Littlewood [28,42]. That is, assurance activities, e.g., performed in support of DO-178C, can be best understood as developing evidence of possible perfection – a confidence in *pfd* = 0. Similarly, for safety critical DNNs, we believe ML lifecycle activities should be considered as aiming to train a "possible perfect" DNN in terms of the two *reducible* errors. Thus, we may have some confidence that the two errors are both 0 (equivalently, a prior confidence in the *irreducible* Bayes error since the other two are 0), which indeed is supported by on-going research into finding globally optimised DNNs [17]. Meanwhile, on the **trained model**, V&V also provides prior knowledge as shown in Example 2 below, and **online monitoring** continuously validates the assumptions for the prior knowledge being obtained.

Example 2. We present an illustrative example on how to obtain a prior confidence bound on the generalisation error from formal verification of DNN robustness [23,40]. *Robustness* requires that the decision making of a neural network cannot be drastically changed due to a small perturbation on the input. Formally, given a real number $d > 0$ and a distance measure $|| \cdot ||_p$, for any input $x \in X$, we have that, $f_{\mathcal{N}}(x) = f_{\mathcal{N}}(x')$ whenever $||x' - x||_p \leq d$.

Figure 5 shows an example of the robustness verification in a one-dimensional space. Each blue triangle represents an input x, and the green region around each input x represents all the neighbours, x' of x, which satisfy $||x' - x||_p \leq d$ and $f_{\mathcal{N}}(x) = f_{\mathcal{N}}(x')$. Now if we assume $Op(x)$ is uniformly distributed (an assumption for illustrative purposes which can be relaxed for other given $Op(x)$ distributions), the generalisation error has a lower bound – the chance that the next randomly selected input does not fall into the green regions. That is, if ϵ denotes the ratio of the length not being covered by the green regions to the total length of the black line, then $G_{\mathcal{N}}^{0-1} \leq \epsilon$. This said, we cannot be certain about the bound $G_{\mathcal{N}}^{0-1} \leq \epsilon$ due to assumptions like: (i) The formal verification tool itself is perfect, which may not hold; (ii) Any neighbour x' of x has the same ground truth label of x. For a more comprehensive list, cf. [14]. Assessors need to capture the doubt (say $1 - \theta$) in those assumptions, which leads to:

$$Pr(G_{\mathcal{N}}^{0-1} \leq \epsilon) = \theta. \tag{3}$$

We now have presented an instance of the safety argument template in Fig. 6. The solution **So2** is the formal verification showing $G_{\mathcal{N}}^{0-1} \leq \epsilon$, and **G8** quantifies the confidence θ in that result. It is indeed an open challenge to rigorously develop **G8** further, which may involve scientific ways of eliciting expert judgement [36] and systematically collecting process data (e.g., statistics on the reliability of verification tools). However, we believe this challenge – evaluating confidence in claims, either quantitatively or qualitatively (e.g., ranking with low, medium, high), explicitly or implicitly – is a fundamental problem for all safety case based decision-makings [11,16], rather than a specific problem of our framework.

The sub-goal **G9** represents the mechanism of online monitoring on the validity of offline actives, e.g., validating the environmental assumptions used by offline formal verifications against the real environment at runtime [18].

Fig. 5. Formal verification on DNN robustness in an one-dimensional space

5   Other Safety Related Properties

So far we have seen a reliability-centric safety case for DNNs. Recall that, in this paper, reliability is the probability of misclassification (i.e. the generalisation error in (1)) that has safety impacts. However, there are other DNN safety related properties concerning risks not directly caused by a misclassification, like interpretability, fairness, and privacy; discussed as follows.

Interpretability is about an explanation procedure to present an interpretation of a single decision within the overall model in a way that is easy for humans to understand. There are different explanation techniques aiming to work with different objects, see [22] for a survey. Here we take the instance explanation as an example – the goal is to find another representation $\mathtt{expl}(f_\mathcal{N}, x)$ of an input x, with the expectation that $\mathtt{expl}(f_\mathcal{N}, x)$ carries simple, yet essential, information that can help the user understand the decision $f_\mathcal{N}(x)$. We use $f(x) \Leftrightarrow \mathtt{expl}(f_\mathcal{N}, x)$ to denote that the explanation is consistent with a human's explanation in $f(x)$. Thus, similarly to (1), we can define a probabilistic measure for the instance-wise interpretability:

$$I_\mathcal{N} = \sum_{x \in X} (f(x) \not\Leftrightarrow \mathtt{expl}(f_\mathcal{N}, x)) \times O_p(x) \qquad (4)$$

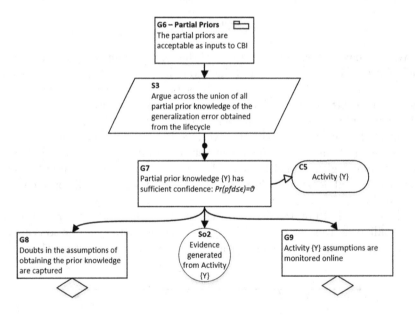

Fig. 6. A template of safety arguments for obtaining partial prior knowledge

Then similarly as the argument for reliability, we can do statistical inference with the probabilistic measure $I_\mathcal{N}$. For instance, as in Example 2, we (i) firstly define the robustness of explanations in norm balls, measuring the percentage of space that has been verified as a bound on I_N, (ii) then estimate the confidence of the robust explanation assumption and obtain a prior confidence in interpretability, (iii) finally Bayesian inference is applied with runtime data.

Fairness requires that, when using DL to predict an output, the prediction remains unbiased with respect to some protected features. For example, a financial service company may use DL to decide whether or not to provide loans to an applicant, and it is expected that such decision should not rely on sensitive features such as race and gender. *Privacy* is used to prevent an observer from determining whether or not a sample was in the model's training dataset, when it is not allowed to observe the dataset directly. Training methods such as [1] have been applied to pursue differential privacy.

The lack of fairness or privacy may cause not only a significant monetary loss but also ethical issues. Ethics has been regarded as a long-term challenge for AI safety. For these properties, we believe the general methodology suggested here still works – we first introduce bespoke probabilistic measures according to their definitions, obtain prior knowledge on the measures from lifecycle activities, then conduct statistical inference during the continuous monitoring of the operation.

6   Related Work

Alves *et al.* [2] present a comprehensive discussion on the aspects that need to be considered when developing a safety case for increasingly autonomous systems that contain ML components. In [10], a safety case framework with specific challenges for ML is proposed. [44] reviews available certification techniques from the aspects of lifecycle phases, maturity and applicability to different types of ML systems. In [27], safety arguments that are being widely used for conventional systems – including conformance to standards, proven in use, field testing, simulation and formal proofs – are recapped for autonomous systems with discussions on the potential pitfalls. Similar to our CBI arguments that exploit operational data, [24,33] propose utilising continuously updated arguments to monitor the weak points and the effectiveness of their countermeasures. The work [3] identifies applicable quantitative measures of assurance for learning-enabled components.

Regarding the safety of automated driving, [41,43] discuss the extension and adaptation of ISO-26262, and [13] considers functional insufficiencies in the perception functions based on DL. Additionally, [37,38] explores safety case patterns that are reusable for DL in the context of medical applications.

7   Discussions, Conclusions and Future Work

In this paper, we present a novel safety argument framework for DNNs using probabilistic risk assessment, mainly considering quantitative reliability claims, generalising this idea to other safety related properties. We emphasise the use of probabilistic measures to describe the inherent uncertainties of DNNs in safety arguments, and conduct Bayesian inference to strengthen the top-level claims from safe operational data through to continuous monitoring after deployment.

Bayesian inference requires prior knowledge, so we propose a novel view by (i) decomposing the DNN generalisation error into a composition of distinct errors and (ii) try to map each lifecycle activity to the reduction of these errors. Although we have shown an example of obtaining priors from robustness verification of DNNs, it is non-trivial (and identified as an open challenge) to establish a quantitative link between other lifecycle activities to the generalisation error. Expert judgement and past experience (e.g., a repository on DNNs developed by similar lifecycle activities) seem to be inevitable in overcoming such difficulties.

Thanks to the CBI approach – Bayesian inference with limited and partial prior knowledge – even with sparse prior information (e.g., a single confidence bound on the generalisation error obtained from robustness verification), we can still apply probabilistic inference given the operational data. Whenever there are sound arguments to obtain additional partial prior knowledge, CBI can incorporate them as well, and reduce the conservatism in the reasoning [8]. On the other hand, CBI as a type of proven-in-use/field-testing argument has some of the fundamental limitations as highlighted in [25, 27], for which we have identified on-going research towards potential solutions.

We concur with [27] that, despite the dangerous pitfalls for various existing safety arguments, credible safety cases require a heterogeneous approach. Our new quantitative safety case framework provides a novel supplementary approach to existing frameworks rather than replace them. We plan to conduct concrete case studies and continue to work on the open challenges identified.

Acknowledgements and Disclaimer. This work is supported by the UK EPSRC (through the Offshore Robotics for Certification of Assets [EP/R026173/1] and its PRF project COVE, and End-to-End Conceptual Guarding of Neural Architectures [EP/T026995/1]) and the UK Dstl (through projects on Test Coverage Metrics for Artificial Intelligence). Xingyu Zhao and Alec Banks' contribution to the work is partially supported through Fellowships at the Assuring Autonomy International Programme.

This document is an overview of UK MOD (part) sponsored research and is released for informational purposes only. The contents of this document should not be interpreted as representing the views of the UK MOD, nor should it be assumed that they reflect any current or future UK MOD policy. The information contained in this document cannot supersede any statutory or contractual requirements or liabilities and is offered without prejudice or commitment. Content includes material subject to © Crown copyright (2018), Dstl. This material is licensed under the terms of the Open Government Licence except where otherwise stated. To view this licence, visit http://www.nationalarchives.gov.uk/doc/open-government-licence/version/3 or write to the Information Policy Team, The National Archives, Kew, London TW9 4DU, or email: psi@nationalarchives.gsi.gov.uk.

References

1. Abadi, M., et al.: Deep learning with differential privacy. In: ACM SIGSAC CCS'16 (2016)

2. Alves, E., Bhatt, D., Hall, B., Driscoll, K., Murugesan, A., Rushby, J.: Considerations in assuring safety of increasingly autonomous systems. Technical report NASA/CR-2018-220080, NASA, July 2018
3. Asaadi, E., Denney, E., Pai, G.: Towards quantification of assurance for learning-enabled components. In: EDCC 2019, pp. 55–62. IEEE, Naples, Italy (2019)
4. Ashmore, R., Calinescu, R., Paterson, C.: Assuring the machine learning lifecycle: Desiderata, methods, and challenges. arXiv preprint arXiv:1905.04223 (2019)
5. Bagnall, A., Stewart, G.: Certifying the true error: Machine learning in Coq with verified generalization guarantees. In: AAAI 2019, vol. 33, pp. 2662–2669 (2019)
6. Barocas, S., Hardt, M., Narayanan, A.: Fairness and Machine Learning. fairmlbook.org (2019). http://www.fairmlbook.org
7. Bishop, P., Bloomfield, R., Littlewood, B., Popov, P., Povyakalo, A., Strigini, L.: A conservative bound for the probability of failure of a 1-out-of-2 protection system with one hardware-only and one software-based protection train. Reliab. Eng. Syst. Saf. **130**, 61–68 (2014)
8. Bishop, P., Bloomfield, R., Littlewood, B., Povyakalo, A., Wright, D.: Toward a formalism for conservative claims about the dependability of software-based systems. IEEE Trans. Softw. Eng. **37**(5), 708–717 (2011)
9. Bishop, P., Povyakalo, A.: Deriving a frequentist conservative confidence bound for probability of failure per demand for systems with different operational and test profiles. Reliab. Eng. Syst. Saf. **158**, 246–253 (2017)
10. Bloomfield, R., Khlaaf, H., Ryan Conmy, P., Fletcher, G.: Disruptive innovations and disruptive assurance: assuring machine learning and autonomy. Computer **52**(9), 82–89 (2019)
11. Bloomfield, R.E., Littlewood, B., Wright, D.: Confidence: its role in dependability cases for risk assessment. In: DSN 2007, pp. 338–346. IEEE, Edinburgh (2007)
12. Bloomfield, R., Bishop, P.: Safety and assurance cases: past, present and possible future - an adelard perspective. In: Dale, C., Anderson, T. (eds.) Making Systems Safer, pp. 51–67. Springer, London (2010)
13. Burton, S., Gauerhof, L., Heinzemann, C.: Making the case for safety of machine learning in highly automated driving. In: Tonetta, S., Schoitsch, E., Bitsch, F. (eds.) SAFECOMP 2017. LNCS, vol. 10489, pp. 5–16. Springer, Cham (2017). https://doi.org/10.1007/978-3-319-66284-8_1
14. Burton, S., Gauerhof, L., Sethy, B.B., Habli, I., Hawkins, R.: Confidence arguments for evidence of performance in machine learning for highly automated driving functions. In: Romanovsky, A., Troubitsyna, E., Gashi, I., Schoitsch, E., Bitsch, F. (eds.) SAFECOMP 2019. LNCS, vol. 11699, pp. 365–377. Springer, Cham (2019). https://doi.org/10.1007/978-3-030-26250-1_30
15. Chen, L., May, J.H.R.: A diversity model based on failure distribution and its application in safety cases. IEEE Trans. Reliab. **65**(3), 1149–1162 (2016)
16. Denney, E., Pai, G., Habli, I.: Towards measurement of confidence in safety cases. In: International Symposium on Empirical Software Engineering and Measurement, pp. 380–383 (2011)
17. Du, S.S., Lee, J.D., Li, H., Wang, L., Zhai, X.: Gradient descent finds global minima of deep neural networks. arXiv e-prints p. arXiv:1811.03804 (Nov 2018)
18. Ferrando, A., Dennis, L.A., Ancona, D., Fisher, M., Mascardi, V.: Verifying and validating autonomous systems: towards an integrated approach. In: Colombo, C., Leucker, M. (eds.) RV 2018. LNCS, vol. 11237, pp. 263–281. Springer, Cham (2018). https://doi.org/10.1007/978-3-030-03769-7_15
19. Fukunaga, K.: Introduction to Statistical Pattern Recognition. Elsevier, New York (2013)

20. Galves, A., Gaudel, M.: Rare events in stochastic dynamical systems and failures in ultra-reliable reactive programs. In: FTCS 1998, pp. 324–333. Munich, DE (1998)

21. He, F., Liu, T., Tao, D.: Control batch size and learning rate to generalize well: theoretical and empirical evidence. In: NIPS 2019, pp. 1141–1150 (2019)

22. Huang, X., et al.: A survey of safety and trustworthiness of deep neural networks. arXiv preprint arXiv:1812.08342 (2018)

23. Huang, X., Kwiatkowska, M., Wang, S., Wu, M.: Safety verification of deep neural networks. In: Majumdar, R., Kunčak, V. (eds.) CAV 2017. LNCS, vol. 10426, pp. 3–29. Springer, Cham (2017). https://doi.org/10.1007/978-3-319-63387-9_1

24. Ishikawa, F., Matsuno, Y.: Continuous argument engineering: tackling uncertainty in machine learning based systems. In: Gallina, B., Skavhaug, A., Schoitsch, E., Bitsch, F. (eds.) SAFECOMP 2018. LNCS, vol. 11094, pp. 14–21. Springer, Cham (2018). https://doi.org/10.1007/978-3-319-99229-7_2

25. Johnson, C. W.: The increasing risks of risk assessment: on the rise of artificial intelligence and non-determinism in safety-critical systems. In: The 26th Safety-Critical Systems Symposium, p. 15. Safety-Critical Systems Club, York, UK (2018)

26. Kelly, T.P.: Arguing safety: a systematic approach to managing safety cases. Ph.D. thesis, University of York (1999)

27. Koopman, P., Kane, A., Black, J.: Credible autonomy safety argumentation. In: 27th Safety-Critical System Symposium Safety-Critical Systems Club, Bristol, UK (2019)

28. Littlewood, B., Rushby, J.: Reasoning about the reliability of diverse two-channel systems in which one channel is "possibly perfect". TSE **38**(5), 1178–1194 (2012)

29. Littlewood, B., Strigini, L.: 'Validation of ultra-high dependability...' - 20 years on. Safety Systems, Newsletter of the Safety-Critical Systems Club 20(3) (2011)

30. Littlewood, B., Povyakalo, A.: Conservative bounds for the pfd of a 1-out-of-2 software-based system based on an assessor's subjective probability of "not worse than independence". IEEE Trans. Soft. Eng. **39**(12), 1641–1653 (2013)

31. Littlewood, B., Salako, K., Strigini, L., Zhao, X.: On reliability assessment when a software-based system is replaced by a thought-to-be-better one. Reliab. Eng. Syst. Saf. **197**, 106752 (2020)

32. Littlewood, B., Wright, D.: The use of multilegged arguments to increase confidence in safety claims for software-based systems: a study based on a BBN analysis of an idealized example. IEEE Trans. Softw. Eng. **33**(5), 347–365 (2007)

33. Matsuno, Y., Ishikawa, F., Tokumoto, S.: Tackling uncertainty in safety assurance for machine learning: continuous argument engineering with attributed tests. In: Romanovsky, A., Troubitsyna, E., Gashi, I., Schoitsch, E., Bitsch, F. (eds.) SAFE-COMP 2019. LNCS, vol. 11699, pp. 398–404. Springer, Cham (2019). https://doi.org/10.1007/978-3-030-26250-1_33

34. Micouin, P.: Toward a property based requirements theory: system requirements structured as a semilattice. Syst. Eng. **11**(3), 235–245 (2008)

35. Musa, J.D.: Operational profiles in software-reliability engineering. IEEE Softw. **10**(2), 14–32 (1993)

36. O'Hagan, A., et al.: Uncertain Judgements: Eliciting Experts' Probabilities. Wiley, Chichester (2006)

37. Picardi, C., Habli, I.: Perspectives on assurance case development for retinal disease diagnosis using deep learning. In: Riaño, D., Wilk, S., ten Teije, A. (eds.) AIME 2019. LNCS (LNAI), vol. 11526, pp. 365–370. Springer, Cham (2019). https://doi.org/10.1007/978-3-030-21642-9_46

38. Picardi, C., Hawkins, R., Paterson, C., Habli, I.: A pattern for arguing the assurance of machine learning in medical diagnosis systems. In: Romanovsky, A., Troubitsyna, E., Bitsch, F. (eds.) SAFECOMP 2019. LNCS, vol. 11698, pp. 165–179. Springer, Cham (2019). https://doi.org/10.1007/978-3-030-26601-1_12
39. Ponti Jr., M.P.: Combining classifiers: from the creation of ensembles to the decision fusion. In: SIBGRAPI 2011, pp. 1–10. IEEE, Alagoas, Brazil (2011)
40. Ruan, W., Wu, M., Sun, Y., Huang, X., Kroening, D., Kwiatkowska, M.: Global robustness evaluation of deep neural networks with provable guarantees for the hamming distance. In: IJCAI 2019, pp. 5944–5952 (2019)
41. Rudolph, A., Voget, S., Mottok, J.: A consistent safety case argumentation for artificial intelligence in safety related automotive systems. In: ERTS 2018 (2018)
42. Rushby, J.: Software verification and system assurance. In: 7th International Conference on Software Engineering and Formal Methods, pp. 3–10. IEEE, Hanoi, Vietnam (2009)
43. Schwalbe, G., Schels, M.: Concept enforcement and modularization as methods for the ISO 26262 safety argumentation of neural networks. In: ERTS 2020 (2020)
44. Schwalbe, G., Schels, M.: A survey on methods for the safety assurance of machine learning based systems. In: ERTS 2020 (2020)
45. Sha, L.: Using simplicity to control complexity. IEEE Softw. 18(4), 20–28 (2001)
46. Strigini, L., Povyakalo, A.: Software fault-freeness and reliability predictions. In: Bitsch, F., Guiochet, J., Kaâniche, M. (eds.) SAFECOMP 2013. LNCS, vol. 8153, pp. 106–117. Springer, Heidelberg (2013). https://doi.org/10.1007/978-3-642-40793-2_10
47. Sun, Y., Wu, M., Ruan, W., Huang, X., Kwiatkowska, M., Kroening, D.: Concolic testing for deep neural networks. In: ASE2018, pp. 109–119. ACM (2018)
48. Zhao, X., Littlewood, B., Povyakalo, A., Strigini, L., Wright, D.: Modeling the probability of failure on demand (pfd) of a 1-out-of-2 system in which one channel is "quasi-perfect". Reliab. Eng. Syst. Saf. 158, 230–245 (2017)
49. Zhao, X., Robu, V., Flynn, D., Salako, K., Strigini, L.: Assessing the safety and reliability of autonomous vehicles from road testing. In: The 30th International Symposium on Software Reliability Engineering, pp. 13–23. IEEE, Berlin, Germany (2019)

Assurance Argument Elements for Off-the-Shelf, Complex Computational Hardware

Rob Ashmore[(⊠)] and James Sharp

Defence Science and Technology Laboratory, Fareham, Hants PO17 6AD, UK
{rdashmore,jsharp1}@dstl.gov.uk

Abstract. There are many aspects to the safe use of artificial intelligence. To date, comparatively little attention has been given to the specialist computational hardware that is used, especially within embedded systems. Consequently, there is a need to identify evidence that would support a compelling assurance argument for the safe use of off-the-shelf, large scale, complex system-on-chip designs. To that end, we summarise issues related to the use of multi-core processors in aviation, which contextualises our problem. We also discuss a collection of considerations that provide evidence to support a compelling assurance argument.

Keywords: Artificial intelligence · Computational hardware · Machine learning · Safety · Security

1 Introduction

Artificial Intelligence (AI), especially that enabled by Machine Learning (ML), is being used in an increasing number of applications, some with potential safety impacts. This has motivated a large body of work aimed at specific aspects of AI, including: susceptibility to adversarial examples [21]; explainability [19]; formal specification [16]; through-lifecycle assurance [4]; and ML safety engineering [24]. Less attention has been paid to the assurance of the computational hardware that supports AI. Correct functioning of this hardware is necessary for the correct functioning of AI. This hardware is also significantly more complex than anything that is currently being used in other safety-critical domains (e.g. aviation).

We briefly discuss (in Sect. 2) the introduction of Multi-Core Processors (MCPs) into the aviation domain, which provides helpful context. We then (in Sect. 3) present a structured set of evidence-generating activities that support the hardware-related portion of an assurance argument. Since it represents the most common case, we focus on the use of large-scale, complex, off-the-shelf hardware, in the form of System-on-Chips (SoCs). For brevity, we refer to this as AI-enabling hardware. A sumary is provided (in Sect. 4).

© Crown 2020
A. Casimiro et al. (Eds.): SAFECOMP 2020, LNCS 12234, pp. 260–269, 2020.
https://doi.org/10.1007/978-3-030-54549-9_17

2 Multi-core Processors in Aviation

Before discussing modern AI-enabling hardware it is informative to review the introduction of MCPs in the aviation domain.

Use of MCPs is beneficial because they provide increased computational power. It is necessary because many single-core processors are becoming obsolete. However, the introduction of MCPs has faced challenges and proceeded at a controlled, relatively slow pace. A review of relevant guidance material suggests that the two main challenges were interference and non-determinism [9]. Interference happens when one application unintentionally (and, typically, adversely) affects the behaviour of another. Use of shared resources, for example, interconnects and lower-level caches is a typical cause. Unless it is understood and mitigated, interference will make behaviour non-deterministic.

There are four main aspects to assuring the use of MCPs in aviation:

- Control the configuration of the MCP;
- Understand and mitigate potential interference paths;
- Verify behaviour of software applications running on the MCP;
- Implement architectural protections (beyond the level of the MCP).

3 AI-Enabling System-on-Chip

Approaches that support use of MCPs are insufficient to support the assurance of AI-enabling hardware. There are two main reasons for this. Firstly, SoCs are significantly more complex than MCPs. Secondly, aviation-related MCP guidance takes a traditional approach to safety, protecting against random chance events. We adopt a wider view that incorporates both safety and security.

We follow the aviation domain guidance in asserting that a SoC should be assured in the context of the software associated with a particular deployment. Providing generally-applicable assurance that a SoC can be used for all possible software applications is practically impossible.

The following subsections discuss topics that would be expected to contribute to an assurance argument for AI-enabling hardware. The subsections follow the four main aspects of MCP use in the aviation domain, as shown in Table 1; italics show cases where the subsection is of indirect relevance to the aspect.

Due to space limitations, the subsections do not cover all aspects of hardware assurance. Our focus on off-the-shelf, physical items means that considerations applied during design and manufacturing considerations are outside our scope.

3.1 Configuration

Configuration settings can significantly change hardware behaviour, for example, by controlling cache allocations and changing power management strategies. Consequently, it is important that configuration settings are documented, justified, controlled and monitored (including at run time).

Table 1. Considerations and relationships to main aspects of MCP use in the aviation domain (*italic* text shows an indirect relationship).

Aspect of MCP use	Consideration (Subsection)
Control configuration	Configuration (3.1)
	Host and Target (3.3)
Manage interference paths	Interference paths (3.2)
	Worst-Case Execution Time (3.5)
Verify behaviour	Host and Target (3.3)
	Test Coverage (3.4)
	Worst-Case Execution Time (3.5)
	Logging (3.6)
	Safety Islands (3.7)
	Hardware-Based Trojans (3.8)
Architectural protections	System-Level Architecture (3.9)

Microcode updates, can significantly change detailed behavioural aspects, for example, speculative execution [22]. Consequently, management of configuration settings needs to include management of microcode updates.

Particular attention also needs to be paid to debug features. These features are not intended to be used in operational settings, so they may be developed with less rigour. Debug features also provide access to low-level information, which should not generally be exposed during operational use.

3.2 Interference Paths

Initially, potential interference paths should be identified from a theoretical perspective. Buses, caches and interconnects are obvious candidates; interrupt handling routines may also be relevant. This theoretical investigation should inform an empirical investigation, which relies on software. Applications intended to be run on the system should be considered, as well as "enemy processes", which are deliberately designed to try and cause interference [13].

Much of the literature related to interference paths considers multiple software applications interfering with each other, with effects on timing. AI-enabling hardware may introduce the possibility of "self-interference", with an effect on computation results. For example, the order in which floating point numbers are summed can change the result of the summation. Unless care is taken, this effect could occur in parallelised calculations [23].

3.3 Host and Target

AI is often developed on "host" hardware, before deployment on to "target" hardware, embedded within the operational system. Differences between host and target hardware can lead to unexpected effects.

We note that some AI-enabling hardware may be suitable for developing neural networks. This may allow the same hardware to be used for development and operation. Provided the same configuration settings were used in both settings, this would largely mitigate the concerns discussed in this subsection.

Numerical precision may differ between host and target (e.g. to allow deployment on constrained hardware [12]). Exhaustively running all samples (from the Training, Test and Verification (TTV) data sets) through operational software on the target hardware protects against consequences of this difference. Whilst conceptually simple, this may be impractical. If so, a sampling-based approach may be used, provided samples are chosen with care. Useful inspiration may be drawn from approaches used to design computer-based experiments [18].

The approaches discussed above are focused on the performance of the final ML-trained model on the target hardware. From an engineering perspective, this can lead to increased risk late in a project, with host-target differences only becoming apparent towards the end of the activity. To reduce this risk there may be benefit in using simple models, that are quick to develop and analyse, to identify key differences between host and target hardware.

Large-scale, on-chip integration can increase the importance of Process Variation (PV), which occurs as a result of manufacturing imperfections. These imperfections can lead to significant variations in power consumption and timing violations [17]. Consequently, there is value in supplementing the generally-applicable testing outlined above with some level of test on each and every SoC.

3.4 Test Coverage

A complete discussion of software assurance issues is outside the scope of this paper, but a brief discussion of test coverage is relevant. Here, we follow [4], which also provides an overview of general ML assurance issues. When considering test coverage, it is helpful to consider four different domains, or sets of inputs:

1. The *input domain* space, $\mathcal{I}$, which is the set of inputs that the model can accept.
2. The *operational domain* space, $\mathcal{O} \subset \mathcal{I}$, which is the set of inputs that the model may be expected to receive when used operationally.
3. The *failure domain* space, $\mathcal{F} \subset \mathcal{I}$, which is the set of inputs the model may receive if there are failures elsewhere in the system.
4. The *adversarial domain* space, $\mathcal{A} \subset \mathcal{I}$, which is the set of inputs the model may receive if it is being attacked by an adversary.

Separate coverage arguments should be provided for all of these domains. The argument relating to $\mathcal{I}$ should consider the number of inputs tested and their distribution across the input space (potentially informed by designs for computer experiments [18]); situation coverage [2] may be useful when thinking about $\mathcal{O}$; coverage of $\mathcal{F}$ should be informed by analysis of system architecture, focusing on subsystems that acquire data that is subsequently used as an input to an ML model; and coverage of $\mathcal{A}$ should be based on an understanding of possible attacks [10].

3.5   Worst-Case Execution Time

One reason MCPs are of concern in aviation is their potential effect on Worst-Case Execution Time (WCET). This could be important if an AI-enabling SoC is being used as part of a vehicle control loop, for example. Activities discussed above, notably understanding interference paths and test coverage, should provide helpful information to support assurances related to WCET.

In addition, particular inputs may affect execution time. For example, it is well-known that poorly-implemented cryptographic routines can show significant timing differences depending on inputs [15]. This may not be apparent for typical neural networks, where each input follows the same path through the program code. However, input-dependent timing may be apparent in some algorithms (e.g. bypassing later layers of a neural network [11]).

Specific bit patterns may also affect timing. For example, in traditional (i.e. non-AI) computing, subnormal numbers can have a significant effect on execution time [3]. If the operational software is based on floating point numbers then bit patterns provide another aspect of measuring coverage across $\mathcal{I}$.

3.6   Logging

Learning from incidents is an important part of a good safety culture. Sufficient AI-related information needs to be logged to support this learning. From our perspective, logging raises two key questions.

Firstly, whether logging relies on features of the SoC or whether it uses other system features (e.g. recording inputs and outputs at the SoC boundary). If SoC features are used then logging may create a new interference path, or emphasise a previously-identified one.

Secondly, (assuming SoC features are used), whether logging-related demands are constant, or whether they vary depending on the prevailing situation. Varying logging demands are another factor that can affect WCET.

3.7   Safety Islands

A large-scale, complex SoC intended for embedded use within a safety-related context may include a "safety island". This is a specific set of isolated hardware that is dedicated to fault handling [7].

In the case of off-the-shelf hardware, full details of any safety island are unlikely to be available. Nevertheless, areas of potential interference between the safety island and the rest of the SoC should be identified. This is a special case of interference path analysis.

The safety island would be expected to detect and respond to failures elsewhere on the SoC. This functionality should be examined as part of test activities (e.g. by inducing failures in different parts of the SoC).

3.8   Hardware-Based Trojans

Hardware-based Trojans are an acknowledged potential vulnerability in software systems [1]. Consequently, they present a notable threat to the use of AI in safety-related systems.

Theoretically, full control of the entire supply chain is sufficient to protect against hardware-based Trojans. In reality, the size and dynamic nature of the supply chain mean this level of control is impossible. Supply chain monitoring is important, but a multi-layered argument is needed.

Thinking about the standard cyber security Confidentiality, Integrity and Availability (CIA) triad, availability should be detectable and manageable by traditional safety measures. From a system perspective, this is the same situation as a hardware failure of the SoC. Handling this situation will require system-level architectural features. If there is a means of checking the AI output then traditional safety measures should also be able to detect loss of integrity. If the output cannot easily be checked then, as before, system-level architectural features should protect against the hazard that "AI provides an undetectable incorrect result". Confidentiality is very difficult to protect. System-level architectural designs, which, from a confidentiality perspective, treat the SoC as an untrusted "black box" may be the most appropriate way of mitigating this risk.

3.9   System-Level Architecture

Activities to support the use of computational hardware in safety-related domains can be split between fault prevention and fault tolerance, with the latter subdividing into fault detection and fault recovery. (This represents a significantly simplified view of the concepts and taxonomy of dependable and secure computing [6].) Much of the previous discussion has focused on prevention. Tolerance is typically achieved through system-level architectural design.

Tolerance can be achieved by using some form of diversity. Historically, one option involved using multiple, independent software teams. Experience has shown there are difficulties with this approach: it is costly; and it is difficult to quantify its benefits, which might not be as much as first appears [14]. ML development approaches change the cost-profile of software development [5]. They replace some expensive human effort for potentially less-expensive compute power. This may make diversity cheaper to achieve. Furthermore, the large number of samples in the TTV data sets may make it easier to measure diversity.

Diversity could also be achieved by using different ML development tools [20] or using different AI-enabling hardware. Another form of diversity could be achieved by combining an AI channel with a monitor channel implemented using traditional software techniques [8]. This would reduce the assurance burden borne by the AI channel (and the AI-enabling hardware). However, defining a suitable monitor is a non-trivial task.

4 Summary

Some form of assurance argument will be needed to support the use of AI in safety-related applications. Considerations related to AI-enabling hardware, typically large-scale, complex, off-the-shelf SoCs, will be an important part of that argument. This argument needs to investigate the hardware in the context of the hosted software applications. In loose terms we require confidence that:

- It will work, in general;
- It will work, in unlikely situations;
- Errors (i.e. failures to work) will be detected;
- Information will be protected (i.e. security).

Information to support those assertions should be generated from a variety of activities. Examples (mapped to subsections of this paper) are indicated in Table 2: ★ marks activities that directly support an assertion; ☆ marks activities where support is indirect.

Table 2. Support provided by activities to assertions (★ indicates direct support, ☆ indicates indirect support).

Activity (Subsection)	Work, in general	Work, in unlikely	Detect errors	Protect information
History of previous use (3-Intro)	☆			
Document and justify config. (3.1)	★	★	☆	☆
Run-time checks on config. (3.1)	★	☆		☆
Microcode updates (3.1)	★	★		☆
Control debug features (3.1)	☆	☆		★
Theoretical interference (3.2)	☆	☆		★
Empirical interference: apps (3.2)	★	☆		
Empirical interference: enemy procs (3.2)	★	★		
Self-interference (3.2)	☆	★		
Effects of numerical precision (3.3)	☆	★		
Exhaustive coverage of TTV data sets (3.3)	★	★		
Sampled coverage of TTV data sets (3.3)	★	☆		
Simple host-target comparisons (3.3)	★	☆		
Test coverage of $\mathcal{I}$ (3.4)	★	☆	★	
Test coverage of $\mathcal{O}$ (3.4)	☆	★	★	
Test coverage of $\mathcal{F}$ (3.4)	★	★	☆	
Test coverage of $\mathcal{A}$ (3.4)		☆		★
Testing on each and every SoC (3.4)	★	☆		
Effect of specific inputs on WCET (3.5)	★	☆		
Effect of specific bit patterns on WCET (3.5)	★	★		
Potential effect of logging (3.6)	☆	☆		
Safety island independence (3.7)		☆	★	
Safety island functionality (3.7)		☆	★	
Partial control of supply chain (3.8)		☆		☆
Monitoring SoC manufacturer errata (3.8)		☆		★
Wrapping Intellectual Property (IP) cores (3.8)				★
Multiple AI channels (3.9)	☆	☆	★	
AI and non-AI channels (3.9)			★	

Collectively, these activities cover the assertions we wish to make. This provides some confidence that a compelling assurance argument can be made to support the use of AI-enabling hardware in a safety-related system. However, there is a danger that Table 2 can be interpreted too favourably. There is much work to be done before all of the activities are well understood and routinely implemented as part of general engineering practice. Whilst this paper provides a signpost towards a compelling argument, we still have some way to go before we reach that destination.

References

1. Adee, S.: The hunt for the kill switch. IEEE Spectr. **45**(5), 34–39 (2008)
2. Alexander, R., Hawkins, H.R., Rae, A.J.: Situation coverage-a coverage criterion for testing autonomous robots. University of York (2015)
3. Andrysco, M., Kohlbrenner, D., Mowery, K., Jhala, R., Lerner, S., Shacham, H.: On subnormal floating point and abnormal timing. In: 2015 IEEE Symposium on Security and Privacy, pp. 623–639. IEEE (2015)
4. Ashmore, R., Calinescu, R., Paterson, C.: Assuring the machine learning lifecycle: desiderata, methods, and challenges. arXiv arXiv:1905.04223 (2019)
5. Ashmore, R., Madahar, B.: Rethinking diversity in the context of autonomous systems. In: Engineering Safe Autonomy, 27th Safety-Critical Systems Symposium, pp. 175–192 (2019)
6. Avizienis, A., Laprie, J.C., Randell, B., Landwehr, C.: Basic concepts and taxonomy of dependable and secure computing. IEEE Trans. Dependable Secure Comput. **1**(1), 11–33 (2004)
7. Bello, L.L., Mariani, R., Mubeen, S., Saponara, S.: Recent advances and trends in on-board embedded and networked automotive systems. IEEE Trans. Industr. Inf. **15**(2), 1038–1051 (2018)
8. Caseley, P.: Claims and architectures to rationate on automatic and autonomous functions. In: 11th International Conference on System Safety and Cyber-Security (SSCS 2016), pp. 1–6. IET (2016)
9. Certification Authorities Software Team (CAST): Multi-core processors. Tech. rep. CAST-32A. Federal Aviation Administration, November 2016
10. Chakraborty, A., Alam, M., Dey, V., Chattopadhyay, A., Mukhopadhyay, D.: Adversarial attacks and defences: a survey. arXiv arXiv:1810.00069 (2018)

11. Gopinath, D., Converse, H., Pasareanu, C.S., Taly, A.: Property inference for deep neural networks. arXiv arxiv:1904.13215v2 (2019)
12. Gysel, P., Pimentel, J., Motamedi, M., Ghiasi, S.: Ristretto: a framework for empirical study of resource-efficient inference in convolutional neural networks. IEEE Trans. Neural Netw. Learn. Syst. **29**(11), 5784–5789 (2018)
13. Iorga, D., Sorensen, T., Donaldson, A.F.: Do your cores play nicely? a portable framework for multi-core interference tuning and analysis. arXiv arXiv:1809.05197 (2018)
14. Knight, J.C., Leveson, N.G.: An experimental evaluation of the assumption of independence in multiversion programming. IEEE Trans. Softw. Eng. **1**, 96–109 (1986)
15. Kocher, P.C.: Timing attacks on implementations of Diffie-Hellman, RSA, DSS, and other systems. In: Koblitz, N. (ed.) CRYPTO 1996. LNCS, vol. 1109, pp. 104–113. Springer, Heidelberg (1996). https://doi.org/10.1007/3-540-68697-5_9
16. Luckcuck, M., Farrell, M., Dennis, L., Dixon, C., Fisher, M.: Formal specification and verification of autonomous robotic systems: a survey. arXiv arXiv:1807.00048 (2018)
17. Nicopoulos, C., et al.: On the effects of process variation in network-on-chip architectures. IEEE Trans. Dependable Secure Comput. **7**(3), 240–254 (2008)
18. Pronzato, L., Müller, W.G.: Design of computer experiments: space filling and beyond. Stat. Comput. **22**(3), 681–701 (2012)
19. Ribeiro, M.T., Singh, S., Guestrin, C.: Why should I trust you?: explaining the predictions of any classifier. In: Proceedings of the 22nd ACM SIGKDD International Conference on Knowledge Discovery and Data Mining, pp. 1135–1144 (2016)
20. Srisakaokul, S., Wu, Z., Astorga, A., Alebiosu, O., Xie, T.: Multiple-implementation testing of supervised learning software. In: Proceedings of the AAAI-18 Workshop on Engineering Dependable and Secure Machine Learning Systems, pp. 384–391 (2018)
21. Szegedy, C., et al.: Intriguing properties of neural networks. In: Proceedings of the 2nd International Conference on Learning Representations, pp. 1–10 (2014)
22. Taram, M., Venkat, A., Tullsen, D.: Context-sensitive fencing: securing speculative execution via microcode customization. In: Proceedings of the Twenty-Fourth International Conference on Architectural Support for Programming Languages and Operating Systems, pp. 395–410 (2019)
23. Teh, J.S., Samsudin, A., Al-Mazrooie, M., Akhavan, A.: GPUs and chaos: a new true random number generator. Nonlinear Dyn. **82**(4), 1913–1922 (2015)
24. Varshney, K.R.: Engineering safety in machine learning. In: Proceedings of the 11th IEEE Information Theory and Applications Workshop, pp. 447–451 (2016)

Quantifying Assurance in Learning-Enabled Systems

Erfan Asaadi, Ewen Denney, and Ganesh Pai[✉]

KBR, Inc., NASA Research Park, Moffett Field, CA 94035, USA
{easaadi,edenney,gpai}@sgt-inc.com

Abstract. Dependability assurance of systems embedding machine learning (ML) components—so called *learning-enabled systems* (LESs)—is a key step for their use in safety-critical applications. In emerging standardization and guidance efforts, there is a growing consensus in the value of using assurance cases for that purpose. This paper develops a quantitative notion of assurance that an LES is dependable, as a core component of its assurance case, also extending our prior work that applied to ML *components*. Specifically, we characterize LES assurance in the form of *assurance measures*: a probabilistic quantification of confidence that an LES possesses system-level properties associated with functional capabilities and dependability attributes. We illustrate the utility of assurance measures by application to a real world autonomous aviation system, also describing their role both in *i)* guiding high-level, runtime risk mitigation decisions and *ii)* as a core component of the associated *dynamic assurance case.*

Keywords: Assurance · Autonomy · Confidence · Learning-enabled systems · Machine learning · Quantification

1 Introduction

The pursuit of developing systems with increasingly autonomous capabilities is amongst the main reasons for the emergence of *learning-enabled systems* (LESs), i.e., systems embedding machine learning (ML) based software components. There is a growing consensus in autonomy standardization efforts [1] on the value of using *assurance cases* (ACs) as the mechanism by which to convince various stakeholders that an LES can be relied upon. ACs have been successfully used for safety assurance of novel aviation applications where—like LESs—regulations

---

This work was supported by the Defense Advanced Research Projects Agency (DARPA) and the Air Force Research Laboratory (AFRL) under contract FA8750-18-C-0094 of the Assured Autonomy Program. The opinions, findings, recommendations or conclusions expressed are those of the authors and should not be interpreted as representing the official views or policies of DARPA, AFRL, the Department of Defense, or the United States Government.

A. Casimiro et al. (Eds.): SAFECOMP 2020, LNCS 12234, pp. 270–286, 2020.
https://doi.org/10.1007/978-3-030-54549-9_18

and standards continue to be under development [2]. However, LESs pose particular assurance challenges [3] and existing AC technologies may not be sufficient, requiring a framework where the system and its AC evolve in tandem [4]. Here too, there are specific additional challenges: first, structured arguments[1] in many ACs are effectively *static*, i.e., they are usually developed prior to system deployment under assumptions about the environment and intended system behavior. Evolution of the system or its ML components (e.g., via online learning, or by adaptation in operation) can render invalid a previously accepted AC. In principle, although it is possible to dynamically evolve structured arguments [4], since their role is primarily to convince human stakeholders, it makes more sense for such updates to happen between missions at well-defined points.

Second, an operational evaluation of the extent of assurance in an LES (or its ML components, where appropriate) is a valuable system-level indicator of continued fitness for purpose. That, in turn, can facilitate potential intervention and counter-measures when assurance drops below an acceptable level during a mission. Indeed, *online assurance updates* that are aimed at machine consumption must necessarily be in a computable form, e.g., using a formal language, such as a logic, or as a quantification. So far as we are aware, prevailing notions of ACs do not yet admit such evaluation. Prior efforts at AC confidence assessment [5,6] have focused on the argument structure rather than the system itself, and face challenges in repeatable, objective validation due to their reliance on subjective data. They have also not been applied to LESs. Thus, there is a general need to capture a computable form of assurance to bolster an otherwise qualitative AC. Note that although a qualitative AC may well refer to quantitative evidence items, here we are identifying the necessity to have quantified assurance as a core facet of LES ACs.

This paper focuses on the problem of assurance quantification, deferring its use in dynamic updates to future work. The main contribution is an approach to characterize assurance in an LES through uncertainty quantification (UQ) of system-level dependability attributes, demonstrated by application to an aviation domain LES.

2   Methodology

Previously [7], we have described how assurance of ML *components* in an LES can be characterized through UQ of component-level properties associated with the corresponding (component-level) dependability attributes. Here, we extend our methodology to the system-level, relying on the following concepts: *assurance* is the provision of (justified) confidence that an *item*—i.e., a (learning-enabled) component, system, or service—possesses the relevant assurance properties. An *assurance property* is a logical, possibly probabilistic characteristic associated

---

[1] The systematic reasoning that captures the rationale why specific conclusions, e.g., of system safety, can be drawn from the evidence supplied.

with *dependability attributes* [8] and functional capabilities. One or more assurance properties applied to a particular item give an *assurance claim*[2]. An *assurance measure* characterizes the extent of confidence that an assurance property holds for an item through a probabilistic quantification of uncertainty. It can be seen as implementing a UQ model on which to query the confidence in an assurance property.[3]

In general, we can define multiple assurance properties (and assurance measures), based on the LES functionality and dependability attributes for which assurance is sought. For example, the proposition *"the aircraft location does not exceed a specified lateral offset from the runway centerline during taxiing"* is a system-level assurance claim associated with the attribute of *reliability*. Similarly, the assurance property *"the aircraft does not veer off the sides of the runway during taxiing"* is associated with the attribute of *system safety*. Such assurance properties directly map to the claims made in the structured arguments of an LES assurance case. Thus, we can leverage the methodology for creating structured arguments [9] to also specify assurance properties.

For quantification, we mainly consider assurance measures for those system-level properties that can be reasonably and feasibly quantified. For example, assurance measures for the preceding example quantify the uncertainty that the aircraft location does not exceed, respectively, the specified lateral offset from the runway centerline (reliability), and half the width of the runway pavement (safety), over the duration of taxiing.

LESs used in safety-critical applications, especially aviation, are effectively stochastic dynamical systems. The insights from this observation are that we can: *i)* capture LES behavior through model-based representations of the underlying stochastic process; *ii)* view system-level assurance properties as specific realizations of particular random variables (RVs) of that process; and *iii)* express confidence in the assurance properties—i.e., the assurance measures—by propagating uncertainty through the model to determine the distributions over the corresponding RVs.

One challenge is selecting an appropriate model and representation of the stochastic process to be used to model LESs. Although there is not a generic answer for this, such a model could be built, for example, by eliciting the expected system behavior from domain experts, by transforming a formal system description, using model fitting and statistical optimization techniques applied to (pre-deployment) system simulation and execution traces, or through a combination of the three. For LESs, a formal system description may be often unavailable. As such, we rely on elicitation and statistical techniques, using Bayesian models where possible, making allowance to admit and use other well-known, related stochastic process models—such as Markov chains—and leveraging data from analytical representations of system dynamics, simulations, and execution. The Bayesian concepts of *credible* intervals and regions—determined on the

---

[2] Henceforth, we do not distinguish assurance properties from assurance claims.

[3] When the assurance property is itself probabilistic, the corresponding assurance measure is deterministic, i.e., either 0 or 1.

posterior distribution of the RVs for assurance properties—give a formal footing to the intuitive, subjective notion of confidence that usually accompanies claims in assurance arguments, and ACs in general [10].

3   Illustrative Example – Runway Centerline Tracking

System Description. To show our methodology is feasible, we now apply it to quantify assurance in an aviation domain LES supplied by our industrial collaborators: a unmanned aircraft system (UAS) embedding an ML component, trained offline using supervised learning, to support an autonomous taxiing capability. The broader goal is to enable safe aircraft movement on a runway without human pilot input. Figure 1 shows a simplified *pipeline architecture* used to realize this capability. A deep convolutional neural network (CNN) implements a perception function that ingests video images from a wing-mounted camera pointed to the nose of the aircraft. The input layer is (360×200) pixels $\times 3$ channels wide; the network size and complexity is of the order of 100 layers with greater than two million tunable parameters. Effectively, this ML component performs regression under supervised learning producing estimates of *cross track error* (CTE)[4] and *heading error* (HE)[5] as output. These estimates are input to a classical proportional-integral-derivative (PID) controller that generates the appropriate steering and actuation signals.

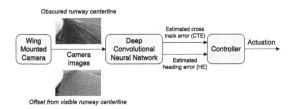

Fig. 1. Pipeline architecture to implement an autonomous taxiing capability in a UAS.

3.1   Assurance Properties

The main objective during taxiing (autonomously, or under pilot control) is to safely follow the runway (or taxiway) centerline. Safety during taxiing entails avoiding *lateral runway overrun*, i.e., not veering off the sides of the runway pavement. Although avoiding obstacles on the runway is also a safety concern,

---

[4] The horizontal distance between the aircraft nose wheel and the runway centerline.

[5] *Heading* refers to the compass direction in which an object is pointed; heading error (HE) here, is thus the angular distance between the aircraft heading and the runway heading.

it is a separate assurance property that we do not consider in this paper. Thus, safety can be achieved here, in part, by meeting a performance objective of maintaining an acceptable lateral offset (ideally zero) on either side of the runway centerline during a taxi *mission* from starting taxi to stopping (or taking off).[6] In other words, the closer the aircraft is to the runway centerline during taxiing, the less likely it is to veer off the sides of the runway.

This performance objective relates to the attribute of reliability, where *taxi failure* is considered to be the violation of the specified lateral offset. Here, we focus on the corresponding assurance property, `AssuredTaxi` : $|\text{CTE}_a|$ < `offset`, where `offset` $= 2\,\text{m}$ is the maximum acceptable lateral offset on either side of the runway centerline for this application and aircraft type. CTE_a, which is the true (or actual) CTE for the UAS, is a signed, real valued scalar; the absolute value gives the magnitude of the offset, and the sign indicates where the UAS is located relative to the centerline, i.e., to its left or its right.

3.2 Assurance Quantification

Model Choice. The assurance measure corresponding to `AssuredTaxi`, establishes $\Pr\left(|\text{CTE}_a| < 2\,\text{m}\right)$, which characterizes the uncertainty (or conversely, confidence) in the true (or actual) CTE (CTE_a) relative to the specified offset. CTE_a evolves in time as the PID controller responds to *estimates* of CTE and HE, themselves the responses of the deep CNN component, to runway images captured by the wing mounted camera (see Fig. 1). CTE_a is thus uncertain and depends on other variables, of which those that can be observed are the estimated CTE (CTE_e), estimated HE (HE_e), and a sequence of images. We can also model the controller behavior in terms of a time series evolution of CTE_a since, during taxiing, the true CTE at a given time is affected by the controller actuation signals at prior times.

An abstracted model of LES behavior is reflected in the joint distribution of the relevant observed and uncertain variables. In fact, a *dynamic Bayesian network* (DBN) [11] is a convenient and compact representation of this joint distribution, as we will see subsequently in this section. It takes into account the temporal evolution of the variables and their (known or assumed) conditional independence relations. Thus, to determine the assurance measure, we effectively seek to quantify the (posterior) distribution over CTE_a, given a sequence of runway images, the estimates of CTE and HE produced by the ML component, and the controller behavior, as a query over the corresponding DBN model.

Model Variables. Model variables can be discrete or continuous, and there are tradeoffs between information loss and computational cost involved in the choice. Table 1 lists the discrete variables we have chosen, giving the interval boundaries for their states. The choice of the intervals that constitute the states of the variables has been based, in part, on: *i)* domain knowledge, *ii)* an assessment

---

[6] Our industry collaborators elicited the exact performance objectives from current and proficient professional pilots.

Table 1. DBN model variables.

Description	Variable	Interval Boundaries for States
True CTE *Uncertain discrete variable with 9 states*	CTE_a	[-½w, -2, -1.43, -0.85, -0.28, 0.28, 0.85, 1.43, 2, ½w]
Outlier detection outcome *Observed Boolean variable*	D	[0, 1]
CNN estimate of CTE *Observed discrete variable with 6 states*	CTE_e	[-½w, -2, -1, 0, 1, 2, ½w]
CNN estimate of HE *Observed discrete variable with 3 states*	HE_e	[-20, -3, 3, 20]

of the data sampled from the environments used for training and testing the CNN, and *iii)* the need to develop an executable model that was modest in its computational needs.

Here, w is the width of the runway in meters, and negative values represent CTE measured on the left of the runway centerline. The HE is given in degrees, while D is dimensionless. An additional variable (I, not shown in Table 1) models the runway image captured from the camera video feed as a vector of values in the range [0 . . . 1] representing normalized pixel values. The Boolean variable D represents the detection of outliers in camera image data. Such outliers may manifest due to various causes, including camera errors and *covariate shift*, i.e., when the data input to the CNN has a distribution different from that of its training data. Note that the LES shown in Fig. 1 does not indicate whether or not it includes a mechanism to detect outliers or covariate shift. However, we include this variable here, motivated by our earlier work on component-level assurance quantification of the CNN [7], which revealed its susceptibility to outlier images. In fact, D models a runtime monitor for detecting out of distribution (OOD) inputs to the CNN.

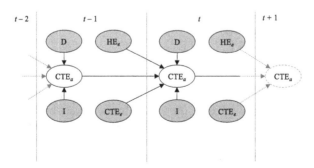

Fig. 2. DBN structure for assurance quantification, showing two adjacent slices at times $t - 1$, and t; shaded nodes represent observed variables, clear nodes are the uncertain, latent variables.

Model Structure. Each variable in Table 1 is indexed over time: we will denote a variable X at time t as $X^{(t)}$. The causal ordering of the model variables (Fig. 2) informs the structure of the DBN: the estimated CTE and HE at time t are inputs to the controller which, in turn, impacts the future location of the aircraft at time $t + \varepsilon$. The directed links between the corresponding variables in adjacent time slices capture this dependency. For example, in Fig. 2, these are the directed links $\mathrm{CTE}_e^{(t-1)} \to \mathrm{CTE}_a^{(t)}$, and $\mathrm{HE}_e^{(t-1)} \to \mathrm{CTE}_a^{(t)}$ (and likewise for the preceding and subsequent time slices). The directed links $\mathrm{CTE}_a^{(t-1)} \to \mathrm{CTE}_a^{(t)}$ model the correlation between actual vehicle position over time, also capturing vehicle inertia.

At time t, the runway image $I^{(t)}$ influences the belief about the true aircraft location, i.e., the states of $\mathrm{CTE}_a^{(t)}$, with the node D modeling the associated structural uncertainty. This reflects the intuition that upon detecting an outlier image (more generally an OOD input), we are no longer confident that the image seen is an indicator of the actual aircraft location. Figure 2 reflects these dependencies by the directed edges $\mathrm{CTE}_a^{(t)} \leftarrow I^{(t)}$, and $\mathrm{CTE}_a^{(t)} \leftarrow D^{(t)}$, respectively.

Figure 2 shows two adjacent time slices of the DBN structure, although the actual structure is unrolled for T time steps, the duration of taxiing, to compute the assurance measure over the taxi phase. At time t, this is, in fact, the sum of the probability mass over the seven states of $\mathrm{CTE}_a^{(t)}$ that lie within the interval $[-2, 2]$ (see Table 1). By unrolling the DBN for an additional ε time steps and propagating the uncertainty through the model from the time of the last observations, the model can provide an assurance forecast.

Probability Distributions. To complete the DBN model specification, we need to specify the conditional probability distributions (CPDs) over the model variables, as encoded by its structure. One way to identify the CPDs is through uncertainty quantification of the physical system model [12]. Practically, the latter may not be available, especially for LESs.

Another alternative—the approach we take here—is to assume a functional form for the CPDs that is then tuned based on execution and simulation data. Specifically, to construct the CPD represented by the transition edge between the time slices, i.e., $\Pr(\mathrm{CTE}_a^{(t)} \mid \mathrm{CTE}_a^{(t-1)}, \mathrm{CTE}_e^{(t-1)}, \mathrm{HE}_e^{(t-1)})$, we chose a multinomial distribution with a uniform prior, tuned using the maximum a posteriori probability (MAP) estimate on simulation data. This choice was advantageous in the sense that the DBN produces a uniform posterior distribution over CTE_a when the observed variables take on values from a distribution different from that of the data used to build the CPDs. For this example, the simulation data comprised sequences of runway images, estimated CTE and HE as produced by the CNN, and true CTE. Section 4 gives more details on the simulation platform and data gathered.

To determine the emission probability $\Pr(\mathrm{CTE}_a^{(t)} \mid I^{(t)})$, first we used the Gaussian process (GP) model underpinning our prior work on component-level assurance quantification [7]. In brief, the idea is to use a GP to model the error performance of the CNN (i.e., its accuracy) on its input (i.e., runway images).

Then, adding the error distribution to the estimate of CTE gives the distribution over the true CTE. However, for high dimensional data (such as images), this is computationally expensive. Instead, in this paper we used an ensemble of decision trees [13] as a classifier that ascribes a probability distribution over the states of CTE_a, given a runway image, I. This approach builds uncorrelated decision trees such that their combined estimate is more accurate than that of any single decision tree. To identify the decision rules, we used supervised learning over the collection of runway images and corresponding true CTE, sampled from the same environments used to train and test the CNN (see Sect. 4). For this example, we built 280 decision trees with terminal node size of at least 10, by randomly sampling 100 data points using the *Gini index* as a performance metric, selecting the model parameters to balance classification accuracy and computational resources.

4 Experimental Results

We now present some results of our experiments in quantifying LES assurance in terms of the assurance measure, $\Pr\left(|CTE_a| < 2\,\mathrm{m}\right)$, based upon simulations of constant speed taxiing missions.

Simulation Setup. We use a commercial-off-the-shelf flight simulator instrumented to reflect the pipeline architecture of Fig. 1. The simulation environment includes various airports and runways with centerlines of varying quality, e.g., portions of the centerline may be obscured at various locations (see Fig. 1). We can create different training and test environments by changing various simulation settings, among which two that we have selected are: *i)* weather induced visibility (*clear* and *overcast*), and *ii)* the time of day (*07:30 am* to *2:00 pm*). Two such environments are, for example, "*Clear at 07:30 am*", and "*Overcast at 12:15 pm*". More generally, we can construct environments such as "*Clear Morning*", "*Overcast Afternoon*", and so on. The former refers to the collection of data sampled from the environment having clear weather, and the time of day incremented in steps of 15 and 30 min from *07:30 am* until *noon*. A similar interpretation applies to other such environments.

From these environments, we gathered images via automated screen capture (simulating the camera output) whilst taxiing the aircraft on the airport runway, using different software controllers, as well as different CNNs for perception: i.e., the same CNN architecture described in Sect. 3, but trained by our industrial collaborators with data drawn from the various environments identified earlier. In tandem, for each image, we collected true CTE (from internal simulation variables), along with estimates of CTE and HE. We used several such data sets, one for each of the different environments identified above, from which data samples were drawn to build the CPDs of the DBN model. Here, note that these data samples were *not* identical to those used to train and test the CNN, even though the samples were drawn from the collection of environments common to both the LES and the DBN.

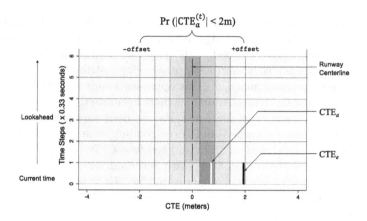

Fig. 3. Visualization of predicted uncertainty in true cross track error, $\mathrm{CTE}_a^{(t)}$, to quantify assurance in runway centerline tracking as the assurance measure, $\mathrm{Pr}(\mathtt{AssuredTaxi})$.

Uncertainty Quantification. Figure 3 shows the results of assurance quantification for one test scenario, visualized as a probability surface overlaid on a stretch of the runway, itself shown as a grid. The horizontal axis—discretized using the interval boundaries for the states of CTE_a (see Table 1)—gives the true aircraft location, which is uncertain during taxiing. Thus, moving from left to right (or vice versa) constitutes lateral aircraft movement. The vertical axis (discretized into 6 steps, each of duration 0.33 s) represents the number of time slices for which the DBN model is unrolled. We selected this based on the time taken for the UAS to laterally depart the runway after violating the 2 m bound, given: runway dimensions, maximum allowed taxiing speed, and other constraints on the UAS dynamics, e.g., non-accelerating taxiing.

At $t = 0$, the horizontal axis gives the aircraft location at the current time. The time steps $t = 1, \ldots, 6$ are *lookahead times* for which the horizontal axis gives the *predicted* location of the aircraft relative to the centerline, given the CNN estimates of CTE and HE at $t = 0$. Thus, moving from the bottom to the top of Fig. 3 represents forward taxiing, i.e., the temporal evolution of aircraft position over the runway. Each cell of the grid formed by discretizing the two axes is, therefore, a state of CTE_a at a given time, shaded such that darker shades

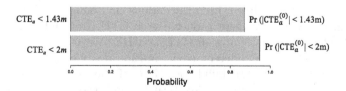

Fig. 4. $\mathrm{Pr}(\mathtt{AssuredTaxi})$ for $\mathtt{offset} = 2\,\mathrm{m}$ and $\mathtt{offset} = 1.43\,\mathrm{m}$.

indicate lower uncertainty (or higher confidence) and lighter shades indicate higher uncertainty (or lower confidence). Thus, the row at $t = 0$ shows the DBN estimate of uncertainty over CTE_a at the current time. Similarly, each row for $t = 1,\ldots,5$ shows the *predicted* uncertainty over CTE_a for those lookahead times, given that the last known values for the observed variables are at $t = 0$. The solid white line in Fig. 3 at $t = 0$ is *ground truth*, i.e., the true CTE at the current time based on internal simulation variables. Although this may not be otherwise available during taxiing, we show it here primarily for model validation, i.e., to show that the interval (state of CTE_a) estimated by the DBN to be the least uncertain is also the one that includes the ground truth. The solid black line is CTE as estimated by the CNN (i.e., CTE_e) at the current time.

Recall that assured taxiing involves maintaining CTE_a between a 2 m lateral offset on either side of the centerline. To quantify assurance in this property, we sum up the probability mass in each cell between the two offsets. Figure 4 shows the assurance measure, $\Pr(|CTE_a^{(t=0)}| < \texttt{offset})$ computed for two different offset values: 2 m and 1.43 m.[7] The interval $[-2, 2]$ is a Bayesian *credible interval* within which the true CTE lies with probability $\approx 95\%$, based on Fig. 4. In other words, *the DBN model is $\approx$95% confident that the aircraft is truly located within 2 m of the runway centerline.* In general, the expected (and desired) DBN behavior is to be more uncertain over longer term assurance forecasts, when there are no additional observations with which to update the posterior distributions on the assurance measures.

Sufficient Assurance. We must select a threshold on the assurance measure to establish what sufficient assurance constitutes, based on which we can assert whether or not the assurance claim holds. The criterion we have selected here is: when the DBN is $\geq$30% confident that the true UAS location exceeds the allowed lateral offset, the assurance claim does not hold, i.e., $\Pr(|CTE_a^{(t)}| \geq 2\,\mathrm{m}) \geq 0.3 \Rightarrow \neg(\texttt{AssuredTaxi})$. We determined this threshold under conservative assumptions about vehicle behavior, leveraging the engineering judgment of our industry collaborators, to balance the tradeoff between safety (avoiding runway overrun) and mission effectiveness (not stopping too often).

5   Discussion

We now evaluate how the DBN performs relative to the LES, in the context of ground truth. The intent is to show that it is a reasonable (i.e., valid) *reference model* of the system suitable for runtime use (i.e., simple and abstract), based on which to make certain decisions, e.g., whether or not to stop taxiing. Moreover, we must also show that the software implementation of the DBN can be relied upon. In this paper, we primarily address the former, leaving the latter for future work.

---

[7] The introduction of a second offset was motivated by our industry collaborators to integrate the assurance measure on the LES platform.

Validity. We compare how well the DBN and the LES can discriminate between *true positive* and *true negative* situations when their respective outputs are transformed into a classification on a plurality of image data drawn from multiple simulated taxiing scenarios for different test environments unseen by both the DBN and the LES.

A true positive (negative) situation for the DBN is one where it indicates that the assurance property is satisfied (not satisfied) based on the criterion for sufficient assurance (see Sect. 4), and ground truth data also indicates that it is truly the case that the UAS location is within (exceeds) the allowed lateral offset from the runway centerline. Likewise for the LES, a true negative (positive) situation is one where the CNN estimate of CTE indicates (does not indicate) an offset violation i.e., $CTE_e \geq 2\,m$ (equivalently, $CTE_e < 2\,m$), and so does ground truth data.

Table 2. DBN Performance evaluation for runway centerline tracking.

Perception Component	Test Environment	LES Performance		DBN Model Performance	
		Sensitivity	Specificity	Sensitivity	Specificity
CNN trained on *Clear Afternoon* and *Overcast Afternoon* environments	*Clear at 07:30am*	0.85	0.95	1	1
	Clear at 10:15am	0.83	0.87	1	1
	Overcast at 07:30am	0.87	0.85	1	1
CNN trained on *Clear Morning* and *Clear Afternoon* environments	*Overcast at 12:15pm*	1	0.01	0.8	0.99
	Clear at 11:45am	1	0.2	0.98	0.8
	Clear at 07:30am	1	NA	1	NA

Table 2 shows our evaluation results in terms of *sensitivity* (true positive rate) and the *specificity* (true negative rate) of both the DBN model and the LES, varying the embedded CNN used for perception. The variability arises from using CNNs trained under two different training environments. We also used these training environments to build the DBN for both LES variants using ≈37000 image samples. These samples were not the same as those that were used to train the CNN variants: indeed, we did not have access to the actual training data for the different CNNs. Also, the test environments listed in the table (and, therefore, the resulting test data), are unseen during the development of both LES variants, and the DBN models of the same.

Based on Table 2, in the context of the sensitivity and specificity metrics shown, as well as the criterion for sufficient assurance, we are cautiously optimistic in claiming that the DBN models the LES reasonably well. For the test environments "*Clear at 11:45 am*", and "*Overcast at 12:15 pm*", the DBN has a lower sensitivity than the LES, however its specificity is substantially better. This suggests that the LES may be biased in its estimates of CTE for those operating conditions.

Suitability. The DBN model structure—in particular, the conditional independence relations encoded by the structure—is informed by (our knowledge of) the causal impacts of the identified variables and the system dynamics, and the resulting assumptions. We note that it is always possible to relax these assumptions and learn the DBN structure as well as its parameters. However, in most cases, especially when there is limited data available, structure learning can be an unidentifiable problem, or can produce a non-unique solution. In our case, the conditional independence assumptions used have turned out to be neither too strong to affect model performance nor too conservative to impose a problem in identifying the CPDs given limited data.

Our assessment in Table 2 does *not* compare the DBN and the CNN that estimates CTE. Indeed, the latter is a learned, static regression function for a *component*, that associates a vector of real values with a real-valued scalar, whereas here we are assessing a stochastic process model of a (learning-enabled) *system* (i.e., the DBN) against the system itself. When we use the DBN for runtime assurance, we implement it as a software component integrated into the LES. This can be viewed as an item to which we can apply our own assurance methodology, i.e., as in Sect. 2, and [7]. Thus, although we have not formulated assurance properties for the DBN, sensitivity and specificity are probabilistic performance metrics (albeit in a frequentist sense) that we can view as assurance measures in their own right, that we have now applied to our model.

The validation above is admittedly not exhaustive although the following observations are worth noting: the DBN is a relatively simple and abstract model of the time-series evolution of the *system*, whose estimates can be updated through Bayesian inference given observed data. Thus, it is amenable to applying other verification techniques including inspection, and formal verification.

Moreover, the DBN *does not* produce point estimates of CTE; rather, in quantifying confidence in a system-level assurance property, a by-product is the uncertainty in true CTE given as a probability distribution over the range of admissible values of CTE_a. Thus, in unseen situations where the CNN can produce an inaccurate estimate of CTE (see Fig. 3), the DBN gives a distribution over possible values of true CTE. As such, it is more conservative in potentially unsafe scenarios. Based on this assessment, we submit that the DBN is a reasonable and suitable runtime reference model of the LES for the autonomous taxiing application, when used for centerline tracking.

Utility. A key advantage of an abstract assurance quantification model is a small implementation footprint for runtime integration into the LES. As indicated in Sect. 1, one of the primary motivations for quantified assurance measures is to provide feedback signals (in a computable form) to the LES, that can be acted on, e.g., by a *Contingency Management System* (CMS), in operation. In this work, the assurance measure values were translated into commands to either *stop*, *slow down*, or *continue* based on *i)* the chosen decision thresholds (Sect. 4), and *ii)* a simple model of the system-level effect (i.e., likelihood of lateral runway overrun) given the assurance measure and current system state.[8] In general, deciding between a series of options in the presence of conflicting and uncertain outcomes is a special case of *decision making under uncertainty* [14]. We plan to investigate such techniques as future work to develop a principled approach to contingency management using assurance measures.

The aim of *run-time assurance*, also known as *run-time verification*, is to provide updates as to whether a system satisfies specified properties as it executes [15]. This is done using a run-time *monitor*, which evaluates the property using values extracted from the state of the system and its environment. In a sense, therefore, the notion of assurance measure we have described here is a kind of monitor. However, it is worth making several distinctions. A monitor relates directly to properties of the system, whereas an assurance measure characterizes *confidence* in our knowledge of such properties. Second, an assurance measure seeks to aggregate a range of sources of information, including monitors. Thus it can be seen as a form of *data fusion*. Third, monitors typically provide values that relate to the current state of the system, whereas the assurance measures we have defined are predictive, intended to give a probabilistic quantification on dependability attributes.

In general, our approach to assurance quantification admits other models including runtime monitors: recall that the node $D^{(t)}$ in Fig. 2 is a runtime monitor detecting data distribution shift in the input image at time t. Indeed, our framework is not intended to replace runtime verification, and the assurance measures generated show the assurance contribution of the runtime monitors, additionally providing an assurance/uncertainty forecast. We are not aware of existing runtime verification techniques that do this.

6   Related Work

The work in this paper is closely related to our earlier research on assurance case confidence quantification [5]. There, although confidence estimation in an assurance claim also uses Bayesian techniques, it relies primarily on the argument structure to build the model. Similarly, based on the structure of an argument, the use of an evidential theory basis has been explored for confidence quantification in assurance claims [6]. However, neither work has been applied to LES assurance quantification. Moreover, in this paper the focus is on those properties where quantification is possible, relying upon models of the system that can be assessed against objective, measured data.

This paper is a natural extension of our prior work on quantifying assurance in ML components [7]: the assurance property we consider there is CTE_e *accuracy*. Assurance quantification then entails using Gaussian processs (GPs) to determine the uncertainty in the error of CTE_e, which is inversely proportional to accuracy. However, the data used are not (and need not be) time dependent

---

[8] Although the content of integrating assurance measures with a CMS is very closely related to the work here, it is not in scope for this paper, and will be the topic of a forthcoming article.

and the model used applies regardless of whether or not the aircraft position has violated `AssuredTaxi`. Indeed, despite a high assurance CNN that accurately estimates CTE, it is nevertheless possible to violate `AssuredTaxi`. However, in this paper we model the LES as a stochastic process, including any runtime mitigations, e.g., a monitor for detection OOD images. As such, the models used for UQ are a generalization of that in [7] to time-series behavior.

As previously indicated (Sect. 1), one of the motivations is to support dynamic assurance cases (ACs). Our prior work [4] first explored this concept, which has subsequently been tailored for so-called *self-adaptive software* [16]. Again, neither work has considered LESs, although self-adaptation is one of the properties that LESs can exhibit. In [4], confidence quantification has been situated as a core principle of dynamic assurance which has also motivated this paper to an appreciable degree. However, that work relies on the quantification methodology in [5]. In [16], assurance quantification employs probabilistic model checking, which can be leveraged for LESs if they can be represented using state-space models, e.g., as in [17] which uses hybrid model checking instead. Neither technique is incompatible with the stochastic processes-based modeling approach that we have adopted. As such, they may be a candidate means to check properties of the stochastic models that we build as a means of (meta-)assurance.

Dynamic safety management as an assurance concept has also been proposed as a run-time assurance method [18], but it is largely speculative about applicability for LESs. The idea of *requirements-aware* runtime models [19] is very closely related to our notion of building a reference model. Quantified and probabilistic guarantees in reinforcement learning have been explored in developing assured ML components in [20]. That work is also closely related to what we have presented here, though its focus is mainly on assurance of correctness properties that have a safety impact. Additionally, the assurance approach there is *intrusive* in the sense that the ML component being built is modified. In our case, assurance quantification does not modify the ML components. *Benchmarking* of uncertainty estimation techniques [21] has also been investigated, although mainly in the context of image classification. It is unclear if the reported results translate to assurance quantification as applied in this paper. However, the benchmarking principles and metrics used could be candidates for evaluating various system models built using our approach.

Kalman filters have long been used to address uncertainty during state estimation, and have some similarities to our approach. A Kalman filters is a special case of a DBN where amongst the main assumptions are that sensor errors are distributed as zero mean Gaussians, and that the uncertainty does not vary between sensing outputs. In contrast, our model uses discrete distributions, admitting varying sensor uncertainty for each image input, in a more general graphical model that has a different structure, whilst including detections of OOD inputs.

7   Conclusion and Future Work

We have described our approach to quantifiable assurance using assurance measures, run-time computations of uncertainty (conversely, confidence) in specified assurance properties, and their application to learning-enabled systems (LESs). Assurance measures complement design-time assurance activities, each of which forms part of an overall dynamic assurance case (DAC). In collaboration with system integrators from industry, we have applied our framework to an aviation platform that employed supervised learning using a deep CNN. Collaboration was crucial to develop the contingency management capability, which relied on engineering judgment to tradeoff safety risk reduction and achieving performance objectives. Feedback from the end-users (i.e., our industry collaborators) was also essential in refining the final visualizations of the assurance measure that we ultimately deployed in the system (based on Fig. 4). Those are intended to provide insight into the system assurance state for safety observer crew.

We have shown that our methodology can feasibly quantify assurance in system-level properties of an aviation domain LES, though we have used classical UQ techniques. Our work in quantifying assurance in LESs is ongoing, and we will be developing assurance measures for other autonomous platforms in the context of more complex mission objectives that require additional ML components and learning schemes.

The work in this paper is one strand of our overall approach to assurance through DACs. The diverse components of an assurance case, including structured arguments, safety architecture [22], as well as the assurance measures described here, each represent one facet of an integrated DAC. There are close connections between the probabilistic models underlying assurance measures and the safety architecture, as well as between assurance properties and claims in an assurance arguments. Our future work will place these connections on a rigorous basis. In part, this can be achieved through use of a high-level *domain-specific language* (DSL) that will let us i) abstract from the details of the individual probabilistic models, and ii) conversely, allow compilation into a range of different models, whilst making more explicit the connections to domain concepts used elsewhere in the assurance case.

A related avenue of future work is providing comprehensive assurance for our approach itself, and in turn, the assurance measures produced. From a verification standpoint, we can consider *correctness* properties entailing i) consistency between the quantification model and the other DAC components, e.g., the risk scenarios captured by a safety architecture, and ii) correctness of the low-level implementation against the higher level specification embodied by the quantification model.

Additionally, assurance measure validity is related, in part, to the limits of the statistical techniques used to infer the underpinning stochastic models, and the data used to build them.

Indeed, one of the challenges we faced in this work was obtaining sufficient useful data. Moreover, the quality of the data gathered also plays a key role in corroborating that the assurance quantification models sufficiently represent the system behavior across its intended operational profile. We believe that a more principled approach to specifying a variety of training data should be possible (e.g., to include various types of perturbed and adversarial inputs), and that such specifications could be derived from the DSL used to specify the assurance measures themselves. The dynamic nature of assurance cases (ACs) will also bear further investigation, to see how real-time updates provided by assurance measures during a mission can inform updates between missions, to the qualitative arguments of ACs.

References

1. Underwriter Laboratories Inc.: Standard for Safety for the Evaluation of Autonomous Products UL 4600, April 2020
2. Clothier, R., Denney, E., Pai, G.: Making a risk informed safety case for small unmanned aircraft system operations. In: 17th AIAA Aviation Technology, Integration, and Operations Conference (ATIO 2017), AIAA Aviation Forum, June 2017
3. McDermid, J., Jia, Y., Habli, I.: Towards a framework for safety assurance of autonomous systems. In: Espinoza, H., et al. (eds.) 2019 AAAI Workshop on Artificial Intelligence Safety (SafeAI 2019), CEUR Workshop Proceedings, January 2019
4. Denney, E., Habli, I., Pai, G.: Dynamic safety cases for through-life safety assurance. In: IEEE/ACM 37th IEEE International Conference on Software Engineering (ICSE 2015), vol. 2, pp. 587–590, May 2015
5. Denney, E., Pai, G., Habli, I.: Towards measurement of confidence in safety cases. In: 5th International Symposium on Empirical Software Engineering and Measurement (ESEM 2011), pp. 380–383, September 2011
6. Wang, R., Guiochet, J., Motet, G., Schön, W.: Safety case confidence propagation based on Dempster-Shafer theory. Int. J. Approximate Reasoning **107**, 46–64 (2019)
7. Asaadi, E., Denney, E., Pai, G.: Towards quantification of assurance for learning-enabled components. In: 15th European Dependable Computing Conference (EDCC 2019), pp. 55–62. IEEE, September 2019
8. Avižienis, A., Laprie, J.C., Randell, B., Landwehr, C.: Basic concepts and taxonomy of dependable and secure computing. IEEE Trans. Dependable Secure Comput. **1**(1), 11–33 (2004)
9. Denney, E., Pai, G.: Tool support for assurance case development. J. Autom. Softw. Eng. **25**(3), 435–499 (2018)
10. Hawkins, R., Kelly, T., Knight, J., Graydon, P.: A new approach to creating clear safety arguments. In Dale, C., Anderson, T. (eds.) Advances in Systems Safety, pp. 3–23 (2011)
11. Murphy, K.P.: Machine Learning: A Probabilistic Perspective. MIT Press, Cambridge (2012)
12. Najm, H.N.: Uncertainty quantification and polynomial chaos techniques in computational fluid dynamics. Annu. Rev. Fluid Mech. **41**(1), 35–52 (2009)
13. Criminisi, A., Shotton, J., Konukoglu, E.: Decision forests: a unified framework for classification, regression, density estimation, manifold learning and semi-supervised learning. Found. Trends Comput. Graphics Vision **7**(2–3), 81–227 (2012)

14. Kochenderfer, M.J.: Decision Making Under Uncertainty: Theory and Application. MIT Press, Boston (2015)

15. Moosbrugger, P., Rozier, K.Y., Schumann, J.: R2U2: monitoring and diagnosis of security threats for unmanned aerial systems, pp. 1–31, April 2017

16. Calinescu, R., Weyns, D., Gerasimou, S., Iftikhar, M.U., Habli, I., Kelly, T.: Engineering trustworthy self-adaptive software with dynamic assurance cases. IEEE Trans. Software Eng. **44**(11), 1039–1069 (2018)

17. Ivanov, R., Weimer, J., Alur, R., Pappas, G.J., Lee, I.: Verisig: verifying safety properties of hybrid systems with neural network controllers. In: 22nd ACM International Conference on Hybrid Systems: Computation and Control, HSCC 2019, pp. 169–178 (2019)

18. Trapp, M., Schneider, D., Weiss, G.: Towards safety-awareness and dynamic safety management. In: 14th European Dependable Computing Conference, EDCC 2018, pp. 107–111, September 2018

19. Bencomo, N., Garcia-Paucar, L.H.: RaM: causally-connected and requirements-aware runtime models using Bayesian learning. In: 22nd IEEE/ACM International Conference on Model Driven Engineering Languages and Systems, MODELS 2019, September 2019

20. Bouton, M., Karlsson, J., Nakhaei, A., Fujimura, K., Kochenderfer, M.J., Tumova, J.: Reinforcement learning with probabilistic guarantees for autonomous driving. Computing Research Repository (CoRR) arXiv:1904.07189v2 [cs.RO], May 2019

21. Henne, M., Schwaiger, A., Roscher, K., Weiss, G.: Benchmarking uncertainty estimation methods for deep learning with safety-related metrics. In: Espinoza, H., et al. (eds.) 2020 AAAI Workshop on Artificial Intelligence Safety (SafeAI 2020), CEUR Workshop Proceedings, vol. 2560, pp. 83–90, February 2020

22. Denney, E., Pai, G., Whiteside, I.: The role of safety architectures in aviation safety cases. Reliab. Eng. Syst. Saf. **191**, 106502 (2019)

Practical Experience and Tools

Cyber-Security of Neural Networks in Medical Devices

Uwe Becker$^{(\boxtimes)}$ ⓘ

Draegerwerk AG, Moislinger Allee 53-55, 23558 Luebeck, Germany
uwe.becker@draeger.com

Abstract. European and national initiatives, as well as changes in the standards, have led to a dramatic increase in the demand for interconnected medical devices during the last few years. In addition to the increased connectivity of devices in a larger network, economic reasons demand for AI (artificial intelligence) enhanced support functions even in the medical devices domain. Both connectivity and the usage of AI in safety-relevant devices are the basis for new and additional challenges for the manufacturers. The more devices become networked, the more they become targets of cyber-attacks. This means that safety of medical devices can no longer be guaranteed without adequate cyber-security measures. These cyber-security measures must cover the whole design of the devices including their internal neural networks to ensure that the inferences are free from influences from attackers. Modern, advanced attack vectors demand for very advanced countermeasures to ensure or even increase cyber-security of medical devices in this environment. This industrial experience paper will show the required concert of measures that is accompanied by a security informed safety analysis from the earliest steps of development to increase general safety and security in the design of a modern intensive care ventilator.

Keywords: Medical devices · Neural networks · AI · CNN · DNN · Cyber-security · Systems engineering · Safety-informed security · STPA-SafeSec

1 Introduction

The number of attacks on IT systems continuously increases with a steeper or even dramatic increase in the recent years [1]. In parallel do European and national initiatives push towards connectivity of medical devices. Some markets and the new standard for intensive care ventilators require connectivity. Cyber-security threats and the demand for interconnection of devices requires intensive consideration during the development of devices. Open standards should be used for data interfaces.

As cyber-security vulnerabilities in devices can severely affect safety, good cyber-security practice is required for certification of medical devices. Motivation, skills, required knowledge, and access of an attacker are not questioned. Existing vulnerabilities will be exploited in a health-care environment. The exploit may be a starting point for an attack on the device or on other devices in the network. (See the attack

© Springer Nature Switzerland AG 2020
A. Casimiro et al. (Eds.): SAFECOMP 2020, LNCS 12234, pp. 289–297, 2020.
https://doi.org/10.1007/978-3-030-54549-9_19

on the braking system of a car via the entertainment system [2]). Traffic from a device inside a network is often viewed as trustworthy and fewer checks are performed on it.

Risk management must shift from a safety centered focus towards a more cyber-security oriented one [3, 4] to adequately consider vulnerabilities and sophisticated attacks. Security engineering, as part of systems engineering, ensures that security principles, concepts, methods, and practices are applied during design and life cycle. Systems security engineering aims to protect the assets of a system by a) hardening the system, b) making the system survivable, and c) limiting damage to the system.

This industrial experience report will describe which measures were taken to increase cyber-security during the design of a new intensive care ventilator system. The paper is organized as follows: The next chapter identifies the cyber-security threats found during the design of the medical ventilator system. Section 3 describes the measures taken in hardware to mitigate the threats. Section 4 highlights the software measures used for threat mitigation. The report concludes with a summary.

2   Cyber-Security Threats

As modern devices often are permanently connected to a network, they have to cope with the resultant threats. Designs shall at least avoid default passwords, weak encryption, and easy to crack authentication. It is of utmost importance to never compromise the essential function of a medical device. An essential function is the function or capability that is required to maintain basic safety, essential performance, a minimum of clinical functionality (specified by the manufacturer), and operational availability for the medical device [22, 23]. The devices have to continue their operation and deliver their performance according to the current settings i.e. continue the current therapy. Values and curves have to be in accordance with the actual measurements. Therapy decisions based on wrong values may lead to harm to the patient.

STPA-SafeSec is used for combined safety and security analysis and to include both safety and cyber-security into risk management. This holistic analysis approach helps to identify potential hazards in every step of the design [4], ensures better (optimal) design decisions [3–5], helps to optimize the design, and guarantees best possible output [5]. Safety is no longer given without security. Both have to be considered and built-in by design. A risk analysis resolves the conflict if safety and security considerations result in conflicting requirements. In the resulting trade-off between the two, there is a tendency towards safety in order to maximize patient safety.

A security analysis considers all external connections and consequences of attacks. A ventilator has interfaces for software update, remote alarm systems, legacy interfaces, connections to other devices, connections to hospital information systems, and sensor connections. Interfaces are the destination of an attack or are the entry point for an attack on other parts of a system e.g. a device's neural network or its control part.

The demand for support from neural networks increases with the increase of budget pressure, lack of time for intensive care, and lack of personnel. It is estimated that billions of Euros can be saved because of better analysis of risk factors and earlier reaction on pre-indicators or alarm signals that identify beginning diseases, development of complications, or slow increase of severity of an already existing disease. Diagnosis may be exacter and faster with the support of artificial intelligence enhanced devices in general. Specialized hardware has reduced the time required for training from weeks to a few hours, enabling more sophisticated networks and new applications. Since 2019 neural networks are marketed not only to provide proposals for treatment but also for clinical decisions. Widespread use for other decisions and closed-loop controls is expected. Risk management can no longer rely on the judgement of a human in the loop as the output of neural networks is directly used for the next steps. This may require a safety system if the output may cause harm to a patient. The importance of cyber-security increases. The neural networks must never be the weakest link in the security chain.

We consider the whole signal processing chain except sensors and actuators that can only be tampered after opening the device. We protect the respective control loop instead. Sensors connected via plugs or provided by other systems are considered thoroughly as sensor data may be tampered to let the control loop become unstable. Even interfaces intended for read-only access may introduce vulnerabilities as they may allow random code execution or access to all parts of a system. Software update requires at least two-factor authentication and only allows update but no downgrade. Updates may only be performed if no patient is connected and only verified and certified code is allowed for execution. Data should be encrypted to guarantee authenticity and integrity. There is no interface backward compatibility. Successful attacks already exploited vulnerabilities re-introduced by a software downgrade or backward compatibility.

3   Hardware Measures for Threat Mitigation

A concerted approach of hardware and software measures is used to fulfill the requirements from the STPA-SafeSec analysis and to increase both safety and security. Hardware measures cover as much as possible of the interfaces and the complete signal processing chain. All unused interfaces are disabled. Security starts with system boot, as a root of trust is required to ensure running un-compromised software only. During a high assurance boot, the boot-loader checks its own integrity and integrity and signature of the operating system and applications. The processor only executes code that is signed with a valid certificate stored in its secure memory. Execution prevention of random code is ensured. Data written or read from external devices is encrypted and its validity and integrity is checked. Hardware measures protect the inputs of the system. The connection of internal sensors cannot be changed without changing/damaging the device. Sensors users can connect, identify themselves and protect the sequence of data to ensure authenticity and correct order. Measures prohibit tampering of their data. Remote sensors identify themselves by device and sensor ID. Signals are encoded to defend against attacks that involve faking sensor signals and replay attacks. The new generation of sensors even supports pre-processing of data within the sensor to off-load the device (more computing power available for security features). Some sensors are realized redundantly to detect faulty sensors and wrong control actions. The validity of other (e.g. pressure) sensor outputs is checked by combining the outputs of second and additional (e.g. second pressure + flow) sensors.

Hardening the control system to provide breathing gas, one of the main parts of a ventilator, covers the complete signal processing chain including sensors, pre-processing of data, the inference of the neural network, and actuators. An attack resulting in the control system assuming wrong or delayed actuator behavior can render the system unstable [9, 10]. If it is not possible to avoid tampering, measures have to be taken to detect it. Actuators either provide direct status feedback (e.g. a valve position) or feedback is provided via the current the actuator draws. Actuators are checked to judge whether the signals received from the sensors are plausible and whether they behave as expected. The response of the sensors indicates the expected change of the controlled parameter and can therefore be verified against an expected response.

A secure FPGA is used to realize the neural network since to harden the complete control loop requires to protect the computation of the controller. It uses an encrypted and protected input stream to avoid malicious configuration with wrong/tampered input. The configuration bit-stream is stored in special chips. These chips have individual identification registers that are also used to encrypt and protect the configuration data. To an attacker, every bit-stream looks different because of the chips' unique identification bits. This prevents simple copying of the content. During configuration, the FPGA performs an "Identification Friend or Foe" process. Only if this process is successful, the FPGA is configured and performs as expected. The internal memory of the FPGA, especially the part used for purposes of the neural network, is configured to be an error-correcting memory (ECC memory) and is write-protected during normal use. Weights, activation functions and code are stored in ECC memory to protect them against random bit flips caused by attacks (and other external influences).

Safety-relevant inputs are read-in via two different channels. Safety-relevant outputs are checked against the outputs of a second system. The second system will detect wrong and unexpected outputs and will keep the system in the safe operation area by issuing the appropriate commands. The second system may be realized as identical system or as hardware and/or software diverse system. A second system sometimes is required to reach a defined safety level and may help to defend against cyber-attacks. A neural network, even with different architecture, acting as second system for another neural network is not preferred as both of them would be susceptible to the same adversarial attack patterns. Adversarial patches constructed for one type of neural network [8, 16] are also able to attack other types of neural networks. They perform a kind of black-box attack. To avoid attacks affecting both channels, the second channel has to use a different technology e.g. a very different classifier. The usage of a random forest classifier for online detection of certain main features has turned out to be a good choice for the ventilator design. Random forest is a tree-based algorithm suitable for multi-value classification and regression. It can classify objects with high accuracy and detection rate, is relatively robust, and not affected by the same adversarial patterns. Our hardware and software diverse solution uses heuristics to check inputs and outputs of the main neural network in parallel to the random forest classifier.

The probability for a mismatch between the random forest classifier and the neural network increases with the size of the detection classes. One may have to narrow down the detection space to only detect the most important and most critical pattern. Additional classifiers may be implemented to detect more patterns and reduce the probability of false negatives. Where possible, the outputs of the neural network and of a small rule-based system are compared. A set of few, very simple rules such as pressure at a certain level and tidal volume below a threshold or resistance above a threshold are used to verify the output and to check for plausibility of the inference. In addition, out-of-bounds detection to detect signals at or above defined boundaries or physiological values is used. The confidence indicator is modified on a detected mismatch between the output of the neural network and the results of the second channel.

Neural networks explore a rather large high-dimensional search space. Training data typically is only concentrated in a relatively small area of this search space. Small perturbations can easily nudge the input to a point the network has never seen before. Carefully crafted noise added to input signals can make the network recognize it as something different or something defined by an attacker. Such attacks work in every domain [8, 13, 16]. The easiest way to defend against them is to filter the inputs or to make the neural network process otherwise pre-processed data. We use high-pass filters, band-pass filters, and fast Fourier transforms (FFT) on some inputs to let the network process data in the frequency domain. This effectively eliminates the (adversarial) noise and is easy to implement in FPGA hardware. Although neural networks are non-linear, the activation function ReLU (**re**ctifier **l**inear **u**nit) is linear from 0 on. ReLU eases training but may be pushed to relatively high values. It increases the attack surface as it allows prediction of the (linear) results. The non-linear sigmoid or hyperbolic tangent (tanh) activation functions are preferable. It is much harder to predict the inference results for non-linear activation functions. The downside of the chosen tanh activation function is that the learning phase takes longer. But Shanuel's conjecture [7] is still fulfilled and mathematical proofs are still possible.

Defending against small perturbations alone is insufficient because larger local perturbations can also break classifiers [8]. The larger perturbations exploit the way classification tasks are constructed. While the data to be analyzed may contain several items, only one target label is considered true, and the network must learn to detect the most "salient" item. The attack exploits this feature by producing inputs much more salient than items in the real world. We use a technique known as defensive distillation [15] to protect against this. Distillation increases the resilience to adversarial perturbations with only marginal influence on detection capabilities. A distillation procedure transfers knowledge form larger deep neural network (DNN) to smaller ones. It requires a trained larger DNN with a softmax output layer. A softmax layer normalizes the output of the last hidden layer into a probability vector F(X), assigning a probability to each class for input X. Its parameter called temperature plays a central role. A high temperature forces probability vectors with relatively large (similar) values for each class. For a DNN with N outputs, the probability vector will converge to 1/N for $T \rightarrow \infty$. The smaller the temperature, the more discrete the probability distribution will be. The probability vectors are used to label training data. The label been called soft labels as opposed to hard class labels. The smaller DNN is then trained at high softmax temperature using a combination of soft and hard class labels. This allows it to benefit from both types of labels and to converge towards an optimal solution. The soft labels encode additional knowledge, namely the relative difference between classes. This allows better generalization around training points thus increasing robustness. The best temperature for the distillation process is selected in an iterative approach. Different temperatures are tried, and the results are compared. The optimal temperature is the best compromise between reduction in detection rate and resilience to adversarial perturbations. During normal operation the temperature is set back to allow discrete probability vectors during classification. Distillation has the advantage to reduce the size of DNN architectures or ensembles of DNN architectures and their computing resource needs without loss of accuracy. In addition, it reduces gradients used in adversarial sample creation by about a factor of 10^{30}. The minimum number of items to be modified to create adversarial samples is increased by nearly a factor of eight. The detection problem for the medical ventilator is comparable to the detection problem of the MNIST data set. Therefore, we achieve comparable results with detection rates above 99%.

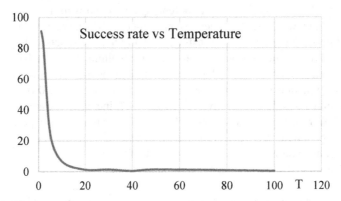

Fig. 1. Success rate of adversarial attacks vs. distillation temperature T.

4   Software Measures for Threat Mitigation

To enhance cyber-security defense, a combination of redundancy, diversity, and hardening [21] reduces the attack surface as far as possible. Different threats call for different measures and weaknesses of measures should be as "complimentary" as possible [20]. Of course, the standard measures such as stack randomization and running tasks at different privilege levels are implemented. Closed-loop controls using data from other medical devices fall back to a local operating mode if the connection is lost or an attack is detected. Unfortunately, it was found that the only possible defense against some attacks such as "arp flooding" is to shut-down the respective interface. This effectively is a denial of service of this interface (at least for a certain amount of time) but prevents a denial of service of the complete system.

To decrease the attack surface, code that is not used during normal operation is compiled-out of the firmware. This is code used for testing, for simulating inputs, for debugging, or to train a neural network. Simulation or demo modes only work in a special mode of the device, which does not permit patient connection. To minimize the attack surface, partial reconfiguration of FPGAs should not be used whenever possible to avoid denial of service (DoS) attacks by applying the wrong configuration for a certain mode of operation. Secure, encrypted storage of configuration data is mandatory to detect and prevent any change in the configuration. Data confidentiality is increased by avoiding storage of data as far as possible. Non-frequently used data is requested from the hospital information system instead of storing it on the machine.

Check tasks are one of the hardening measures. The task run in standby mode applies several test-patterns and checks the responses of the important system components, including the neural network, against known answers [6]. Another check task is run during normal operation and closely works together with the device's so-called safety-system. Heuristics, plausibility checks, and values from redundant or diverse systems are used to check the correct function of the (sub-) system under test. Safety-relevant subsystems use canaries around their data to indicate a possible change. Weights, activation functions, and code of the neural network are in write-protected memory. Their syndrome and the canaries are checked on a regular basis to detect any change. Heuristics, checking for out-of-bounds values, and checking against a small number of training patterns are used to double-check the inference outputs [6].

Recent advances in neural network architecture have reduced the sparsity of the detection space by reducing the number of parameters up to a factor of 35 [11, 12]. Nevertheless, the reduction of the attack surface did not prohibit adversarial attacks. It is mandatory to employ additional measures to avoid or at least detect an attack. The neural network is in application mode only. It does not learn or improve during the application. This will avoid many problems e.g. negative side effects by reward hacking. The rewards required for unsupervised learning can cause a change of the intended strategy towards a strategy that maximizes rewards but has negative long-term side effects. For example, the ventilator system could change the ventilation strategy to maximize short-term oxygenation at the expense of long-term lung damage [17, 18].

The neural network was crafted using a multi-stage approach with several iterations to minimize its attack surface. An initial architecture underwent distillation and optimization steps. In our experiments, we found that a suitable published DNN proven to provide high accuracy for a similar task is a very good starting point. The initial architecture used 2 convolutional layers with 32 filters and a max pooling layer, 2 convolutional layers with 64 filters and a max pooling layer, 2 fully connected layers with 200 tanh functions and a softmax layer for 16 output classes. One reason for subsequent iteration steps is to make the DNN fit into the target FPGA and to fulfill the performance requirements when deployed. The initial DNN is distilled to fit into the FPGA's 300 neurons network. Another reason is to minimize the attack surface and to increase the robustness of the DNN [19]. Training of the initial DNN is done with great care and carefully selected training patterns. The training set was augmented by noise added to the pattern to be detected. The next steps only start after the accuracy of the initial DNN is sufficiently high. Distillation steps reduce both the size of the network and the gradient values. Weights below a certain value are electable for pruning. We found that structured pruning might have larger effects on the accuracy of a network obtained by distillation as it has on the initial DNN. Structured pruning of the initial DNN may not result in a structured neural network or in a reduced number of neurons after distillation. Results largely depend on the architecture and sometimes also on the application. Distillation uses an iterative process to find the optimal temperature. Different pruning and optimization steps are done during additional iterations. They require additional time for completion but result in smaller and better implementations. The last step of the network design is a pruning step. It is advantageous not to prune all eligible neurons to avoid unused neurons. This will hinder an attack by activating unused neurons.

Madry et al. [14] showed that doubling the number of neurons could yield a considerable effect (a plus in the range of 5% of accuracy). Smaller changes in their number had only an insignificant effect in our experiments and in the experiments of others. Increasing the training data or the number of layers will only slightly improve accuracy. The largest effect on accuracy is obtained by specialization. I.e. training the network on small parts of a task has the largest effect (e.g. for autonomous driving, use one network to control straight cruising and use another to drive through curves).

The internal gradients and thus the attack surface were further reduced by applying additional MinMax training patterns suggested by Madry et al. [14]. This second training step is applied to the network after the distillation, pruning, and optimization steps. The training patterns include adversarial pattern and are kind of maximum noise pattern added to the pattern of interest. The fast gradient sign method and the forward derivative method can be used to create the adversarial patterns [13, 16]. Both methods are based on the sensitivity of the differentiating functions over the architecture and the parameters. Together with the distillation process, a significant reduction of the gradients and thus the possibility for adversarial attacks was obtained. The countermeasures increased resilience to adversarial perturbations from about 96% to a value below 0.7‰. This reduced possibility for successful attacks is considered acceptable for the use case. It renders attacks to the real-time system to be infeasible.

5 Summary

The development of a medical ventilator system has been described. It has been shown that it is a necessity to use good cyber-security development practices also throughout the complete development of medical devices. The use of neural networks in modern devices creates special challenges to ensure cyber-security. Nevertheless, the combined use of advanced methods and techniques can reduce the risk for the patients to an acceptable level. Especially the combination of MinMax training patterns and defensive distillation resulted in high robustness against adversarial attacks.

A combination of measures was used to increase the robustness of sensors against tampering attacks. Future evaluation and feedback from the field will show whether the sensors may require some additional kind of tamper detection to avoid processing of tampered or faked signals. Another future improvement could be the inclusion of a BBN (Bayesian Belief Network) into the analysis. This type of network helps to take into account unforeseen future threats. This, of course, would come with the extra effort to generate the required graph. Depending on the system, the extra effort can be quite high. It is currently under investigation whether the extra effort is justified.

References

1. Symantec Corp.: ISTR: Internet Security Threat Report, vol. 24 (2019)
2. https://www.theregister.co.uk/2015/07/24/car_hacking_using_dab/

3. https://www.wired.com/2015/07/hackers-remotely-kill-jeep-highway/

4. Schmittner, C., Ma, Z., Puschner, P.: Limitation and improvement of STPA-Sec for safety and security co-analysis. In: Skavhaug, A., Guiochet, J., Schoitsch, E., Bitsch, F. (eds.) SAFE-COMP 2017. LNCS, vol. 9923, pp. 195–209. Springer, Cham (2017). https://doi.org/10.1007/978-3-319-45480-1_16

5. Friedberg, I., McLaughlin, K., Smith, P., Laverty, D., Sezer, S.: STPA-SafeSec: safety and security analysis for cyber-physical systems. J. Inf. Secur. Appl. **34**, 183–196 (2017)

6. Becker, U.: STPA guided systems engineering. In: Gallina, B., Skavhaug, A., Schoitsch, E., Bitsch, F. (eds.) SAFECOMP 2018. LNCS, vol. 11094, pp. 164–176. Springer, Cham (2018). https://doi.org/10.1007/978-3-319-99229-7_15

7. Becker, U.: Increasing safety of neural networks in medical devices. In: Romanovsky, A., Troubitsyna, E., Gashi, I., Schoitsch, E., Bitsch, F. (eds.) SAFECOMP 2019. LNCS, vol. 11699, pp. 127–136. Springer, Cham (2019). https://doi.org/10.1007/978-3-030-26250-1_10

8. Wilkie, A.J.: Schanuel's conjecture and the decidability of the real exponential field. In: Hart, B.T., Lachlan, A.H., Valeriote, M.A. (eds.) Algebraic Model Theory, pp. 223–230. Springer, Dordrecht (1997). https://doi.org/10.1007/978-94-015-8923-9_11

9. Brown, T.B., Mané, D., Roy, A., Abadi, M., Gilmer, J.: Adversarial Patch (2018). arXiv:1712.09665v2

10. Lobo, J.P., Charchalakis, P., Stipidis, E.: Safety and security aware framework for the development of feedback control systems, University of Brighton (2012)

11. Cárdenas, A.A., Amin, S., Sastry, S.: Secure Control: Towards Survivable Cyber-Physical Systems. University of California, Berkley (2008)

12. Wu, B., et al.: Shift: A Zero FLOP, Zero Parameter Alternative to Spatial Convolutions, December 2017. arXiv:1711.08141v2

13. Zhang, X., Zhou, X., Lin, M., Sun, J.: ShuffleNet: An Extremely Efficient Convolutional Neural Network for Mobile Devices, December 2017. arXiv:201707.01083v2

14. Eykholt, K., et al.: Robust Physical-World Attacks on Deep Learning Visual Classification, April 2018. arXiv:1707.08945v5

15. Madry, A., Makelov, A., Tsipras, D., Schmidt, L., Vladu, A.: Towards Deep Learning Models Resistant to Adversarial Attacks, September 2019. arXiv:1706.06083v4

16. Papernot, N., McDaniel, P., Wu, X., Jha, S., Swami, A.: Distillation as a Defense to Adversarial Perturbations against Deep Neural Networks, March 2016. arXiv:1511.04508v2

17. Papernot, N., McDaniel, P., Swami, A., Harang, R.: Crafting Adversarial Input Sequences for Recurrent Neural Networks, April 2016. arXiv:1604.08275v1

18. Challen, R., Denny, J., Pitt, M., Gompels, L., Edwards, T., Tsaneva-Atanasova, K.: Artificial intelligence, bias and clinical safety. BMJ Qual. Saf. (2019). https://doi.org/10.1136/bmjqs-2018-008370

19. Prasad, N., Cheng, I.-F., Chivers C.: A reinforcement learning approach to weaning of mechanical ventilation in intensive care units, April 2017. arXiv:1704.06300v2

20. Yu, F., Qin, Z., Liu, C., Zhao, L., Wang, Y., Chen, X.: Interpreting and evaluating neural network robustness. In: Proceedings of the Twenty-Eighth International Joint Conference on Artificial Intelligence (IJCAI-19), pp 4199–4205 (2019)

21. Littlewood, B., Strigini, L.: Redundancy and diversity in security. In: Samarati, P., Ryan, P., Gollmann, D., Molva, R. (eds.) ESORICS 2004. LNCS, vol. 3193, pp. 423–438. Springer, Heidelberg (2004). https://doi.org/10.1007/978-3-540-30108-0_26

22. Laszka, A., Abbas, W., Vorobeychik, Y., Koutsoukos, X.: Synergistic security for the Industrial Internet of Things: Integrating Redundancy, Diversity, and Hardening (2018). arXiv:1808.09090v1

23. IEC CD TR 60601-4-5: Medical electrical equipment – Part 4-5 Guidance and interpretation – Safety related technical security specifications for medical devices (2019)

FASTEN.Safe: A Model-Driven Engineering Tool to Experiment with Checkable Assurance Cases

Carmen Cârlan[1](✉) and Daniel Ratiu[2]

[1] fortiss GmbH, Munich, Germany
carlan@fortiss.org
[2] Siemens Corporate Technology, Munich, Germany
daniel.ratiu@siemens.com

Abstract. The Goal Structuring Notation (GSN) is popular among safety engineers for modeling assurance cases. GSN elements are specified using plain natural language text, this giving safety engineers great flexibility to express their arguments. However, pure textual arguments introduce ambiguities and prevent automation. Currently, assurance cases are verified by manual reviews, which are error prone, time consuming, and not adequate for today's systems complexity and agile development methodologies. In this paper we present our research tool *FASTEN.Safe*, which extends GSN with a set of higher-level modeling language constructs capturing recurring argumentation patterns and integrating formal system models. This allows automatically checking 1) the intrinsic consistency of assurance models, 2) the consistency of arguments with system models and 3) the verification of safety claims themselves by using external verification tools. *FASTEN.Safe* is open source and allows experimenting with language abstractions to bridge the world of GSN-based arguments that are common among safety engineers and the world of formal methods that enable automation. Last but not least, we report on the preliminary experience gained with *FASTEN.Safe*.

Keywords: Assurance cases · GSN · NuSMV · Language engineering

1 Introduction

Explicit modeling of assurance cases supports engineers in reasoning about the system safety and communicating with third-parties. Assurance cases are central artifacts of the safety assurance engineering process, an explicit model of an assurance case entailing the core of the argument that the system is safe.

The Goal Structuring Notation (GSN) is a compact graphical representation for argumentations and one of the most prominent notations used for modeling assurance cases, containing a small number of constructs that are intuitive to understand and easy to use by practitioners [1]. Using models for assurance arguments brings structure and enables the application of well-formedness rules

© Springer Nature Switzerland AG 2020
A. Casimiro et al. (Eds.): SAFECOMP 2020, LNCS 12234, pp. 298–306, 2020.
https://doi.org/10.1007/978-3-030-54549-9_20

– e.g., no circular reasoning is allowed. Claims within GSN elements are specified using plain natural language text, safety engineers having great flexibility to express their arguments. However, pure text-based claims introduce ambiguities and prevent automation. The only validation method of text-based claims within assurance cases are manual reviews, this causing two challenges. First, such reviews prove to be tedious when complex systems are built. Second, manual reviews are not suitable for a more agile development mindset, where change requests of safety critical components are frequent and their impact on the assurance argument should be immediately evaluated.

In our work, we explore the way in which assurance cases can be made checkable, yet easy to understand by practitioners. To this end, we extend GSN language constructs with specialized constructs (DSLs) that reference formally specified system models. This enables automated consistency checks both within assurance cases and with the models linked therein. Further, given the integrated automated verification engines, the verification of the satisfaction of safety claims by the referenced system models can be triggered from the assurance case model and the verification results lifted at the level of the assurance cases. Our long-term vision is to make assurance case models central artefacts for starting verification activities in the context of agile development of safety-critical systems.

Contributions and Structure. The main contribution of this paper is *FASTEN.Safe*[1], a new tooling approach to build extensible and semantically rich assurance cases that are linked with formally defined system models in order to increase the rigour of the assurance cases specification and to enable automated verification of assurance cases. *FASTEN.Safe* is an extension of FASTEN, a *FormAl SpecificaTion ENvironment* described in [9], released under EPL 1.0 license and available on github[2]. The rest of the paper is organized as follows: Sect. 2 presents a set of GSN extensions that make automated checks possible, Sect. 3 describes our preliminary experience with using these extensions, in Sect. 4 we present the related work and Sect. 5 concludes the paper.

2   Checkable Assurance Cases

To facilitate automation for safety assurance, our approach is to check the assurance case directly by 1) ensuring its intrinsic consistency, 2) enabling automatic consistency checks with system models, and 3) firing up checks of various system aspects that are modeled outside of the assurance case itself. These checks make the assurance case a central engineering artifact that is to be checked and facilitates automation for safety assurance.

Running Example: Airbag of a Car. To facilitate the understanding, we introduce in the following *FASTEN.Safe* features "by example". We use system

---

[1] https://sites.google.com/site/fastenroot/home.
[2] https://github.com/mbeddr/mbeddr.formal.

models of an airbag and integrate them with assurance case elements. The airbag
system's main functionality is specified by the following functional requirement:
FR_01: *The purpose of an airbag is to slow a vehicle occupant's motion as
evenly as possible using a bag designed to inflate extremely quickly, then quickly
deflate during a crash scenario.* Based on this requirement, a list of hazards is
derived. Hazard **H1** is mitigated by implementing, among others, the following
derived safety requirement: **SR_01**: *The airbag shall inflate only after a collision.* This requirement is then refined in the system's architecture, as described
by Arts et al. [2]. The architecture comprises a top-level component, named
`airbag_system`, containing the following subcomponents: 1) the `Sensor`, which
detects collisions and sends messages encoded by an End-2-End (E2E) protection
mechanism (specific to the AUTOSAR standard) to the airbag controller, 2) the
`Link` that connects the components, and 3) the `Device`, entailing the airbag's
controller. All components are specified in a black-box manner, the requirements
being specified via formal contracts expressed in LTL. While functional requirement **FR_01** is formalized as *post(1) collision_post* postcondition, postcondition
post(2) no_collision formalizes safety requirement **SR_01**. The bus guarantees
that the airbag system functions correctly even when failures such as message
corruption and deletion occur. To express this failure model, we specify precondition `pre(1) collision pre`.

Tool Architecture. In Fig. 1, we present an overview over our tooling platform
built using the Jetbrains' MPS language workbench[3]. *FASTEN.Safe* is a platform that allows experimentation with different modeling abstractions for the
development of safety critical systems. The tool addresses four concerns – 1) hazard and risk analysis (HARA), 2) requirements specification, 3) formal modeling
of system architecture [9] and 4) safety argumentation. To enable verification of
architecture models, *FASTEN.Safe* integrates the NuSMV verification engine.
At its core, *FASTEN.Safe* features an implementation of the Goal Structuring

DSLs Extensions	Extensions of GSN which Integrate Formal Models			
	SMV-based Requirements Specification		Contract-based Design	Patterns
Core	HARA	Requirements	SMV	Architecture	GSN
Platform	JetBrains MPS			
Verification Engines	NuSMV	...		...

Fig. 1. Overview over the FASTEN DSL-stack developed using JetBrains' MPS. FAS-
TEN integrates verification engines as external tools and provides support for their
input languages. In blue we highlight the parts that belong to *FASTEN.Safe* – they
comprise an implementation of GSN language and a set of patterns. Specialized GSN
entities (blue-hashed) reference formally specified elements of system models (hashed).
(Color figure online)

---

[3] https://www.jetbrains.com/mps/.

Notation (GSN) language. Additionally, to support automatic checks, we implemented extensions of the GSN language with specific types of goals, strategies or solutions, integrating other safety and system models.

Checkable Assurance Cases are modeled via the instantiation of a special type of GSN-based patterns, based on state-of-the-art patterns, for which we provide special language constructs integrated with system models, and which come with automated checks. In the following we introduce three categories of such checks.

2.1   Type I Checks: Intrinsic Consistency of the Safety Case

GSN has rules for how to connect GSN elements among each other to obtain a syntactically correct argumentation. However, it does not regard the semantic validity of an argumentation. GSN patterns go a step further and enable a higher intrinsic consistency since they re-use several entities together. To ensure the validity of the arguments created via instantiation, the patterns come with instructions on how to instantiate them. However, unless the instantiation is done automatically, there is no guarantee that the instantiation will generate a valid argumentation. To ensure valid instantiation of patterns, *FASTEN.Safe* provides special types of GSN entities via language extensions, which may only be connected via special types of connections, which extend the GSN *supported by* and *in context of* connections. For example, the *Argument over Hazards Strategy* can only be supported by sub-goals of type *Hazards Mitigation Goal*.

2.2   Type II Checks: Consistency with System Models

The second category of checks ensures the consistency between the assurance case and system models. To this end, we propose specialized entities extending GSN elements, which are integrated with different types of models, specifying the system at different levels of abstraction (e.g., hazards, requirements, architecture). As the system models are created in the same tool as the safety case model, deeper integration can be achieved.

Examples of patterns that may undergo such checks are arguments that all hazards, or all safety requirements have been addressed, as proposed by Hawkins and Kelly [7]. These patterns entail specialized GSN strategies integrated with hazards and, respectively, requirements models. Consistency checks are then executed on these strategies, ensuring that for each element in the list, an argumentation leg exists. In Fig. 2, on the left hand side, we depict the hazards mitigation checkable pattern; on the right hand side, we depict the patterns' instantiation with hazards from the airbag example. The automated checks are enabled by having specialized goals for claiming hazard mitigation – each goal referencing a specific hazard – and specialized relationships between the strategy and the goals. An error from our checks is triggered as the GSN model does not contain argumentation legs regarding the mitigation of H3 and H4 hazards.

Another example for type II checks is a pattern for arguing about the satisfaction of a requirement in a contract-based design setting, entailing specialized GSN entities integrated with the components architecture (see Fig. 3). The structure of this pattern reassembles the structure of the argument on component level pattern proposed by Warg et al. [10]. Automated checks will trigger errors given any inconsistencies between the components specified in the system architecture and the GSN model (e.g., ensure that there is a correctness implementation claim for each direct sub-component of the top-system).

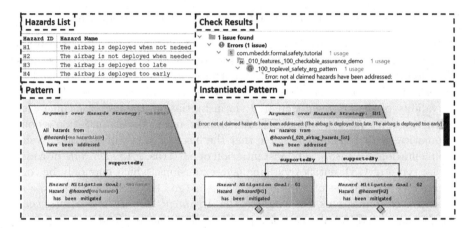

Fig. 2. On top-left a list of hazards of an airbag is presented. On bottom-left the checkable pattern containing specialized GSN strategy and goal is depicted, whereas on bottom-right the instantiation of the pattern for the airbag system is presented. On top-right the consistency checking results are displayed – in this example a check fails since not all hazards have a corresponding *Hazard Mitigation Goal*.

2.3   Type III Checks: Verification of Safety Claims

The third type of checks that can be executed on an assurance case model are verifications of the satisfaction of claims within the safety case by the referenced system model via external verification tools. GSN elements expressing a system property may be specialized as verifiable entities, by integrating them with the formal specification of the respective system property. Such specialized entities are integrated with external tools capable to verify the respective property type. Verification goals are always supported by specialized solutions, which automatically integrate the verification results whenever the verification is executed.

For example, the satisfaction of a safety requirement formalized as an assume-guarantee contract can be reflected by a specialized strategy supported by three main strands of argument, each comprising a specialized, checkable goal (see Fig. 3). First, an argument about the correct refinement of the contract of the upper-level component by the contracts of the subcomponents should exist. Contract refinement checks ensure that the guarantees of an upper-level component is not weakened by the contracts of its subcomponents and the assumptions of the upper-level component is strong enough to satisfy the assumptions of sub-components (*Refinement Check* goal).

Second, A/G compatibility checks ensure that the composition of subcomponents is consistent (*Compatibility Check* goal). Third, the correct implementation of each corresponding subcomponent shall be argued (*Implementation Check* goal). In the case when subcomponents are hierarchical, the implementation check is again potentially performed via a CBD strategy. In the case when subcomponents are atomic, a model checker (in our case NuSMV) is used to verify if the implementation (an SMV module) of an atomic subcomponent satisfies its contract (i.e., $A \rightarrow G$). These goals are checkable, meaning that their claim is checked with NuSMV and, if the verification is not successful, an error is triggered in the assurance case editor. Each of the verification goals has a special solution that is automatically updated with the corresponding model checking results as evidence. Specialized solutions enable the automatic integration of NuSMV results as evidence in assurance cases, whenever the verification is (re)executed. The verification results are interpreted and the solution's

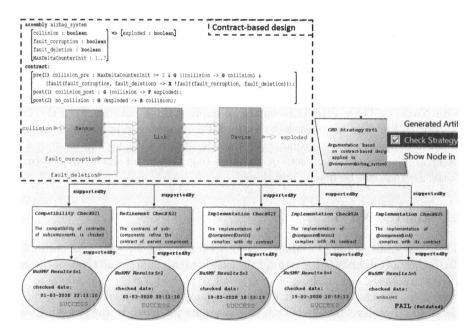

Fig. 3. The top-left side presents the interface definition of the `airbag_system` in terms of ports and contracts (pre-/postconditions) and the architectural decomposition. The bottom side displays the GSN argument about the correct implementation of a requirement based on contract-based design. The argument contains specialized entities (e.g., *CBD Strategy* is a specialization of *Strategy*) that are linked to corresponding system models. NuSMV can be started directly on the *CBD Strategy* node (right) and the results are lifted in and reflected in the corresponding solutions.

editor displays whether the verification is successful or not. Thereby, the safety engineer can see at a glance which goals have been invalidated after a change was implemented. Furthermore, a solution is annotated as *outdated* when either the referenced formal models or the claims within the safety case change, thus making the verification results stale.

3   Experience

Using the Extensions. We are currently evaluating the benefits of using checkable assurance cases by collecting feedback from safety engineering practitioners who used *FASTEN.Safe* in different projects from automotive domain and piloting the functionality in realistic projects. The most important benefits so far seem to be 1) the immediate feedback in the editor signalizing when assurance cases and system models get desynchronized, and 2) the possibility to start verification activities of claims from the assurance case itself, thereby making the trace between system model changes and assurance cases more transparent. Further, the feedback of practitioners is that, on longer term, based on the management of changes on system models and the assessment of their impact on the assurance case, our approach could support continuous verification of assurance cases, thus enabling the integration of assurance cases in a continuous delivery pipeline.

Developing the Extensions. As presented in Sect. 2, we have created a set of extensions of GSN constructs covering strategies and claims about hazards, requirements, specification of safety properties via LTL and their verification with NuSMV. These extensions suffice to express three patterns from the literature [7,10]. The language workbench MPS allows easy implementation of extensions in a modular fashion. On the conceptual side, we are looking for other argumentation fragments or patterns (e.g., based on safety architecture patterns) that can be made checkable.

4   Related Work

There is a vast amount of tooling approaches for developing assurance cases [8]. To the best of our knowledge, none of the existing tools support all types of checks (I-III). Another distinguishing characteristic of *FASTEN.Safe*, that allows us to implement the checks, is that it features language extensions of GSN that raise the abstraction level at which assurance cases are modeled. In the following, we compare *FASTEN.Safe* with existing assurance case modeling tools.

The most comprehensive automation support is provided by AdvoCATE [6] and AMASS tool platform [5], both tools supporting references from assurance case models to other system models (e.g., hazards, requirements or system architecture). AdvoCATE supports the automated creation and assembly of assurance arguments based on patterns instantiation, hierarchical abstraction for arguments, integration of formal methods in assurance arguments and verification of safety claims. The AMASS platform scopes at supporting assurance activities.

For example, similarly to AdvoCATE, AMASS supports automated generation of model-based verification evidence, based on which, via pattern instantiation, assurance case fragments are automatically generated. While AdvoCATE and AMASS use patterns described directly in GSN to increase automation, we lift recurring patterns at language level via DSL abstractions. This allows us to define a richer set of consistency checks both for ensuring the intrinsic consistency of arguments and their consistency with existing system and safety models (checks of Type I and II). Furthermore, similar to our approach, in AdvoCATE analyses performed by external verification tools (e.g. model checkers) can be triggered directly based on the higher level entities.

Another category of approaches aims at automated construction of assurance cases based on system models and existing verification results. The Evidential Tool Bus (ETB) supports the construction and maintenance of assurance cases by automatic generation of claims and evidence from the outputs of verification tools [4]. ENTRUST supports automatic instantiation of assurance case patterns with information from design-time and runtime system models and verification tools [3]. In contrast to these tools, the automation enabled in *FASTEN.Safe* checks the argumentation constructed by the engineer and does not re-generate entire argumentation fragments. In *FASTEN.Safe* changes in system models are immediately reflected in the assurance case via failed constraints.

5 Conclusions

In this paper we presented *FASTEN.Safe*, which is a platform for modeling assurance cases based on GSN and experimenting with semantically rich extensions for expressing safety arguments. Our work formalizes a subset of published GSN patterns using domain specific constructs and links them to system models that are amenable to automated checks. Our long term goal is to make GSN-based arguments automatically checkable. This would enable incremental safety assurance via (semi-)automated maintenance of safety cases, thereby facilitating the development of safety-critical systems in more agile settings. Next, we plan to identify more semantically rich extensions capturing assurance case patterns and to integrate other verification engines (e.g. for performing quantitative analyses). Furthermore, we intend to use the tool within real-world projects.

References

1. GSN community standard version 1, November 2011
2. Arts, T., Dorigatti, M., Tonetta, S.: Making implicit safety requirements explicit. In: Bondavalli, A., Di Giandomenico, F. (eds.) SAFECOMP 2014. LNCS, vol. 8666, pp. 81–92. Springer, Cham (2014). https://doi.org/10.1007/978-3-319-10506-2_6
3. Calinescu, R., Weyns, D., Gerasimou, S., Iftikhar, M.U., Habli, I., Kelly, T.: Engineering trustworthy self-adaptive software with dynamic assurance cases. IEEE Trans. Softw. Eng. 44(11), 1039–1069 (2018)

4. Cruanes, S., Hamon, G., Owre, S., Shankar, N.: Tool integration with the evidential tool bus. In: Giacobazzi, R., Berdine, J., Mastroeni, I. (eds.) VMCAI 2013. LNCS, vol. 7737, pp. 275–294. Springer, Heidelberg (2013). https://doi.org/10.1007/978-3-642-35873-9_18

5. de la Vara, J.L., Parra, E., Ruiz, A., Gallina, B.: The amass tool platform: an innovative solution for assurance and certification of cyber-physical systems. In: Proceedings of the 26th International Conference on Requirements Engineering: Foundation for Software Quality, vol. 2584. CEUR-WS (2020)

6. Denney, E., Pai, G.: Tool support for assurance case development. Autom. Softw. Eng. **25**(3), 435–499 (2017). https://doi.org/10.1007/s10515-017-0230-5

7. Hawkins, R., Kelly, T.: A software safety argument pattern catalogue, vol. 30. The University of York, York (2013)

8. Maksimov, M., Fung, N.L.S., Kokaly, S., Chechik, M.: Two decades of assurance case tools: a survey. In: Gallina, B., Skavhaug, A., Schoitsch, E., Bitsch, F. (eds.) SAFECOMP 2018. LNCS, vol. 11094, pp. 49–59. Springer, Cham (2018). https://doi.org/10.1007/978-3-319-99229-7_6

9. Ratiu, D., Gario, M., Schoenhaar, H.: FASTEN: an open extensible framework to experiment with formal specification approaches. In: FormaliSE (2019)

10. Warg, F., Blom, H., Borg, J., Johansson, R.: Continuous deployment for dependable systems with continuous assurance cases. In: ISSRE Workshops (2019)

Threat Analysis and Risk Mitigation

On Validating Attack Trees with Attack Effects

Hideaki Nishihara[1(✉)] , Yasuyuki Kawanishi[1,2] , Daisuke Souma[1,2] ,
and Hirotaka Yoshida[1]

[1] SEI-AIST Cyber Security Cooperative Research Laboratory, Cyber Physical
Security Research Center, National Institute of Advanced Industrial Science and
Technology (AIST), Osaka, Japan
{h.nishihara,hirotaka.yoshida}@aist.go.jp
[2] Cyber-Security R&D Office, Sumitomo Electric Industries, Ltd., Osaka, Japan
{kawanishi-yasuyuki,souma-daisuke}@sei.co.jp

Abstract. Threats or attacks can be decomposed into more primitive
attacks/events by attack trees. These trees can show possible scenarios of threats. In addition, the quantitative properties of attacks, called
attributes, can be integrated along with the tree structures. This paper
introduces a formal system for attack trees focusing on refinement scenarios, and enriches attack trees with effects of attacks, which allows the
evaluation of the validity of attack decomposition systematically. The
property that sub-attacks refine an attack is described by the relationship among their effects, that is defined as consistency of a branch. Consistent attack trees support a systematic approach for the entire attack
tree process. Furthermore the effects of attacks in consistent attack trees
are well-behaved as an attribute. These ideas are applied to the case
study of a vehicular network system. As an application, possible degrees
of mitigation for attacks in attack trees are discussed.

1 Introduction

Progress in information technology has contributed to the evolution of various
systems worldwide. In particular, cyber-physical systems now have more flexible
and finer functionalities, and cooperate with other systems via networks. However, security threats on these systems have also increased. Protecting a system
from security threats has become an important issue recently.

Attack trees are major tools in analyzing the security of a system. These
trees represent the decomposition of threats in the form of **AND/OR**-trees
(Examples are presented graphically in Fig. 1, 4), as well as fault trees represent
structures of faults in a system in safety domain. We can analyze every scenario
for a threat in a sub-tree of the attack tree [20]. Moreover we can evaluate the
quantitative properties of the threat along with the corresponding attack tree.

Simple and intuitive descriptions of attack trees allow various extensions
of the concepts. Examples include adding other types of nodes, connecting
trees expressing defenses, and specifying the maximum number of children of

© Springer Nature Switzerland AG 2020
A. Casimiro et al. (Eds.): SAFECOMP 2020, LNCS 12234, pp. 309–324, 2020.
https://doi.org/10.1007/978-3-030-54549-9_21

a node [23]. Specifically, to distinguish causal relationships among sub-attacks, attack trees are extended to ones with *sequential conjunctions* [1,8,13].

Fortunately attack trees are well formulated in some research [1,8,13,15]; formal syntax and semantics are provided, the quantitative attributes are related to attacks formally, or attacks are linked to state transitions of the target system. However, all the aspects of attack trees are not supported by formal approach.

In particular, relations among attacks around a branch have not been discussed thoroughly. In an attack tree, a branch represents a concretization of the parent, another branch shows preceding events for the parent, or those are mingled together at the other branch. Resulting attack trees tend to be diverse, and it is a problem from the practical viewpoint. Although there are several studies [1,2,7] dedicated to this issue, the frameworks proposed in these research works are deemed rather indirect. Methodologies for considering the consistency of attack trees simply are required.

This paper tackles this problem by introducing the effects of attacks. An effect, considered as the post-condition of an event, is tightly related to an attack, and therefore we can discuss the abstract-refinement relation around a branch with the help of effects rather than attacks alone. Furthermore, when an attack depends on another one, they are related with effects, that is, the effect of the preceding attack works as the pre-condition of the subsequent attack. We define the consistency of a branch by logical conditions in terms of effects. This approach allows checking the validity of each branch in an attack tree with sequential conjunctions. As a result, attack trees and analyses for them can be described in more rigorous way.

In order to discuss intermediate nodes in attack trees with effects, we define a novel semantics of attack trees. Horne et al. [8] provided a semantics of attack tree with sequential conjunctions, which took values in the set of directed graphs whose nodes were labeled with primitive attacks. Here, a primitive attack corresponds to a leaf node in an attack tree. It meant that attack trees were interpreted as combinations of only primitive attacks. However, the focus on this paper is to investigate relationships among an attack and its sub-attacks, especially at intermediate nodes. Here we consider that an attack tree expresses a collection of inseparable refinement scenarios. The semantics proposed in this paper takes value in the powerset of sub-trees without **OR** branches. These subtrees can derive directed graphs labeled by the leaf nodes in the attack tree, and therefore, the semantics can be related to the semantics proposed by Horne et al.

As an application of attack trees with effects, we evaluate countermeasures and possible mitigation for attacks. A countermeasure or mitigation eliminate some part of the consequences (i.e. effects) of attacks. Hence, the mitigated effects and the residuals can be described as fragments of effects. It enables to link the mitigation to the consistency of attack decomposition. To date, obtained results are rather rough; the cancellations of effects of the sub-attacks tend to be stronger than that of the parent. With a vehicular network system and its threats, this paper analyzes possible countermeasures in detail from this viewpoint.

Generally, an attack tree process for a threat consists of the following three steps: identification of the target, tree construction, and analysis. The first step is commonly conducted in system engineering, such as system development or risk management. To conduct the step in a systematic way, it is possible to follow the established methodologies like with SysML [6]. Moreover, formal analyses with attack trees have been developed for the third step. With the use of attributes, logical or quantitative properties of a threat are integrated according to the tree structure, and in this way we can evaluate the threat rigorously. However, systematic approach to the tree construction, the second step of the process, seems to be overlooked, as we pointed ambiguous relationships among attacks. Our results support tree constructions by observing consistency in a more direct, simpler and formal way. As a result, all steps in the attack tree process can be approached systematically, contributing into an improvement of attack tree analysis.

Organization. Section 2 deals with theoretical aspects of attack trees. Attack trees with sequential conjunctions and attributes are defined formally, after reviewing related works. Next, we introduce the concept of effects of attacks in Sect. 3. Consistent attack decompositions are also discussed with the use of effects. Based on this discussion, Sect. 4 illustrates a case study on threats on a vehicular network system. Moreover we attempt to estimate which grades are required for mitigation against attacks in attack trees. Finally, conclusions and future research directions are outlined in Sect. 5.

2   Attack Trees with Sequential Conjunctions

2.1   Overview of Attack Trees

Here, we review attack trees, particularly, about formal descriptions related to this paper and practical applications of them. Comparison with fault trees used in the safety domain are discussed in the last part of this section.

The concept of attack trees was firstly introduced by Schneier [20]. He expressed the decomposition of an attack as an **AND/OR** tree, and demonstrated several examples of evaluating of attacks using the tree. That is, an attack was evaluated by integrating the evaluations of sub-attacks along with the tree structure. Subsequently, this idea was formalized by Mauw and Oostdijk [15]. They specified a formal syntax of attack trees and defined the corresponding semantics as a set of multisets consisting of primitive attacks. Moreover they discussed the equivalence and transformations of attack trees compatible with the semantics. They also introduced evaluations of attack trees as *attributes*. An attribute was defined as a function from the nodes of an attack tree to a set, where the function values did not conflict with **AND** and **OR** decomposition. Indeed, the attribute of an attack in an attack tree was calculated with attribute values of the attack's children.

Attack trees have been applied in various domains for the purpose of attack modelling, although in many cases, the concept was not defined formally.

Security analyses together with attack trees were conducted for cyber-physical systems recently. The paper [21] showed an attack tree for an implantable medical device, and checked whether communication protocols for the device had vulnerabilities or not. The paper [3] analyzed security about a railway system. Attack tree was applied to identify detailed attack scenarios, while effect identification and risk evaluation was done with failure modes, vulnerabilities, effects analysis (FMVEA). In EVITA [18] for the automotive domain, attack trees were considered as major tools to identify attack scenarios and to estimate attack potentials. However approaches to build trees were not discussed there, other than considering abstract structures of trees. JASO TP 15002 [12] for automobiles suggested tree decompositions of selected threats to analyze how these threats could be realized. In DO-356 [17] for the aviation domain, tree diagrams were introduced to analyze security aspects. These diagrams were referred to as threat trees, as they were focused on the threat condition events and vulnerability events as well as attacks.

The idea of attack trees is rather simple, which allows various extensions. Wang et al. [23] classified many variants of attack trees. Fovino and Masera [4] enriched nodes of attack trees with related information such as assertions, vulnerabilities, and operations. With the enrichment, attacks or threats can be analyzed from several viewpoints in the research. The simplicity of attack trees also allows wider interpretations, and it means engineers may experience difficulties in building attack trees. To the best of our knowledge, most related studies have neither explicitly discussed the guidance for attack decompositions nor the validity of decompositions in detail. Although [1, 2, 7] discussed this issue, their frameworks dealt with attacks indirectly.

One of the major extensions of attack trees was to add a new type of branches, that is, sequential conjunction. In several cases, sub-attacks of an attack have causal dependency, and therefore it is natural to consider an attack tree together with the order of attack executions. Attack trees with sequential conjunction were discussed by Jhawar et al. [13] and by Horne et al. [8]. Their studies incorporated Mauw and Oostdijk's formalization [15], and the multiset semantics was extended to sets of graphs representing possible sequences of primitive attacks. Audinot et al. [1] also focused on attack trees with sequential conjunctions. They used pre-conditions and post-conditions of attacks for labels of nodes instead of attacks themselves. The semantics was given as the sets of the target's behaviors that satisfied the corresponding pre-conditions and post-conditions. Their framework shows the relationship among the parent node and its children of a branch clearly, but actual events by attacks are not presented explicitly. Furthermore, a transition model expressing possible behaviors in the target system should be prepared in advance. They discussed the consistency[1] of decomposition by comparing the semantics of nodes around a branch.

In safety domain, fault trees have been used for reliability analysis of systems since the 1960s. Fault trees were presented as **AND/OR**-trees as same as attack trees, but showed causal decompositions [9, 19]. In the literature, attack trees and

---

[1] It is called *correctness* properties in their paper.

fault trees were often dealt with similarly. For example interpretations were given as sets of labels on the leaf nodes in the tree, or properties of the uppermost event of the tree were quantitatively calculated with the properties of leaf nodes [15,19]. Moreover, with recent observation that security threats caused harms in safety-critical systems, the integration of attack trees and fault trees were proposed [5] to connect security analysis and safety analysis.

2.2 Formulation

We provide a formal definition of attack trees. Its syntax is defined inductively, and the semantics represents possible scenarios of attack refinements. In the sequel, we denote attack trees, including sequential conjunctions.

Definition 1. *An attack tree is a labeled tree with three types of branches:*

$$t ::= Lf(n) \mid Nd(n, op, \langle t, t, \dots, t \rangle),$$
$$op ::= \textbf{AND} \mid \textbf{OR} \mid \textbf{SAND},$$

where $\langle - \rangle$ *means a non-empty finite sequence of its arguments, and where the symbol* n *is a label for the node, which expresses an action or an event.*

Intuitively, $Lf(n)$ corresponds to a primitive attack n, which is no longer decomposed (a *leaf* node in a tree), and $Nd(n', op, \langle t_1, \dots, t_k \rangle)$ corresponds to an attack n', which has sub-attacks $t_1, \dots, t_k$ with type op as its decomposition (an intermediate node in a tree). Attack trees can be diagrammatically represented, as illustrated in Fig. 1. The type of a branch is expressed by a gate symbol under nodes. Around a **SAND** branch ("S"-marked **AND** gate), actions in the child nodes are executed from left to right. The uppermost node of an attack tree is called the root node.

We do not consider the order of children for **AND** or **OR** branches, as well as the type of a branch having only one child. Hence the following equations are assumed for arbitrary subtrees $\{t_j\}_{1 \leq j \leq k}$ and a subtree t:

$$Nd(n, op, \langle t_1, \dots, t_i, t_{i+1}, \dots, t_k \rangle)$$
$$= Nd(n, op, \langle t_1, \dots, t_{i+1}, t_i, \dots, t_k \rangle) \quad (op \in \{\textbf{AND}, \textbf{OR}\})$$
$$Nd(n, op, \langle t \rangle) = Nd(n, op', \langle t \rangle) \quad (op, op' \in \{\textbf{AND}, \textbf{SAND}, \textbf{OR}\}).$$

We denote an attack tree without **OR** branches as an *R-tree*. Intuitively, an R-tree expresses an individual refinement scenario regarding the attack of the root node.

A semantics $[\![\cdot]\!]$ of attack trees is the function which maps an attack tree to a multiset of R-trees.

Definition 2. *The function $[\![\cdot]\!]$ on the set of attack trees is defined by the following rules, where $\bar{t} = \langle t_1, \ldots, t_m \rangle$ and $[\![\bar{t}]\!] = ([\![t_1]\!], \ldots, [\![t_m]\!])$:*

$$[\![Lf(n)]\!] = \{Lf(n)\},$$
$$[\![Nd(n, \mathbf{AND}, \bar{t})]\!] = \{Nd(n, \mathbf{AND}, \langle \tau_1, \ldots, \tau_m \rangle) \mid (\tau_1, \ldots, \tau_m) \in [\![\bar{t}]\!]\},$$
$$[\![Nd(n, \mathbf{SAND}, \bar{t})]\!] = \{Nd(n, \mathbf{SAND}, \langle \tau_1, \ldots, \tau_m \rangle) \mid (\tau_1, \ldots, \tau_m) \in [\![\bar{t}]\!]\},$$
$$[\![Nd(n, \mathbf{OR}, \bar{t})]\!] = \bigsqcup_{1 \leq i \leq n} \{Nd(n, \mathbf{AND}, \langle \tau \rangle) \mid \tau \in [\![t_i]\!]\}.$$

The semantics is based on the idea that decompositions appearing in attack trees are logical refinement. An **OR** branch is interpreted as a multiset union, indicating this branch corresponds to a case division. An aspect of the attack is refined, and possible detailed attacks are listed as sub-attacks. On the other hand an **AND/SAND** branch is interpreted as a factorization of an attack to sub-attacks. The collection of sub-attacks around the branch is inseparable, as a single sub-attack in it does not invoke the original attack. The causal dependency of attacks exists only between children of each **SAND** branch, and does not exist elsewhere, especially between an attack and its sub-attacks.

Comparing our formulation (Definition 1, 2) with those in [8], syntaxes are very similar - the difference is whether a branch is limited to binary or not. However, our semantics keeps intermediate nodes and analyses of them are available, whereas the semantics in [8] only considers leaf nodes.

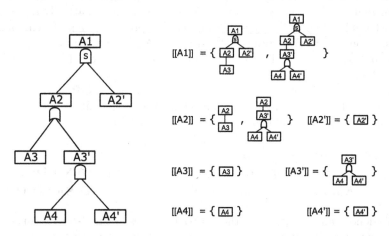

The gates under the node A1, A2, and A3' present **SAND**, **OR**, and **AND** branches respectively. As examples, nodes labeled A4 and A3' are expressed as $Lf(A4)$ and $Nd(A3', \mathbf{AND}, \langle Lf(A4), Lf(A4') \rangle)$.

Fig. 1. Attack trees and their interpretation.

2.3 Attributes

An attribute of an attack tree is defined as a function f from the set of nodes. The codomain D of f is a set with the three operations μ_O, μ_A, and μ_S, corresponding to **OR**, **AND**, and **SAND**, respectively. Around a branch in an attack tree, attribute values of the child nodes are summarized with these operations. Therefore the following equalities are required to hold ($\varphi \in \{\mu_O, \mu_A\}$):

$$\varphi(\langle f(x_1), \ldots, f(x_i), f(x_{i+1}), \ldots, f(x_k)\rangle)$$
$$= \varphi(\langle f(x_1), \ldots, f(x_{i+1}), f(x_i), \ldots, f(x_k)\rangle),$$
$$\mu_A(\langle f(x)\rangle) = \mu_S(\langle f(x)\rangle) = \mu_O(\langle f(x)\rangle).$$

One example of attributes is the minimum number of experts required to perform an attack, discussed in [8]. When we denote the defining function of the attribute by ν, its codomain is defined as the set of natural numbers $\mathbb{N}$ and $(\mu_O, \mu_A, \mu_S) = (\min, \text{Sum}, \max)$. Remark that this attribute is assumed to be determined by the values of lower nodes rigorously. Namely, $\nu(Nd(n, \mathbf{OR}, \bar{t})) = \min\{\nu(t_1), \ldots, \nu(t_k)\}$ where $\bar{t} = \langle t_1, \ldots, t_k\rangle$, and similar equations hold for **AND/SAND** branches. When there is another attribute for which we cannot have the assumption, the equalities may not be expected and we must consider contributions for the attribute by intermediate nodes themselves. Such an attribute will be compatible with the semantics in Definition 2, but not with that in [8] using only leaf nodes.

3   Validating Decompositions with Effects

3.1 Effects of Attacks

An effect is one of the major properties of an attack. It is a situation or a property of a specific entity related to the target system, and is caused by a specific action. Let us consider the attack "Message receive function is interfered" as an example. After the attack, messages may be lost, the function may be unavailable, or some irregular behaviors occur. These situations have not occurred before the attack, and therefore it can be considered that the attack causes these situations. As a result, we can identify the summarized situation "messages are not processed correctly" as the effect of the attack.

Effects are also significant concepts in the areas adjacent to security. In the safety standard ISO/IEC Guide51 [11], negative effects[2] on people, property or the environment, caused by some event are the primary issues to be avoided. In the standard ISO 31000 [10] focused on risk management, a risk is defined as an effect of uncertainty on objectives.

Owing to the above observation for effects, it seems reasonable that *an effect of an attack* meets the following conditions:

---

[2] Those effects are referred to as harms.

- The effect must be directly caused by the corresponding attack; it shows a change of the entity that the attack affects.
- Properties that hold before the attack must not be selected as effects.
- The effect occurs immediately after the corresponding attack; no other properties invoked by the attack occur before the effect occurs.

The effect of an attack can be described by propositional formulas. Logical expressions serve as standard tools to consider relationships and operations on properties. In particular, they allow considering refinement of properties easily. When a property P is refined as P', the inference $P' \Rightarrow P$ holds.

For an attack tree, we assign a formula expressing an effect to a node. In an attack tree diagram, we put the round node labeled by the effect and connect it to the corresponding attack with a blue edge (see Fig. 2).

The effect is considered as an attribute of attack trees. Let us denote the mapping from nodes to effects by ε. The codomain of ε is the set of propositional formulas $\mathcal{P}$, and the three operations are $\mu_O = \vee$ (disjunction), $\mu_A = \wedge$ (conjunction), and $\mu_S = \mu_\rho = \lambda\langle e_1, \ldots, e_r \rangle.e_r$ (the projection to the last element). However the attribute value of the upper node is not always determined by the attribute values of the lower nodes. Their relationship are discussed in the next section.

As effects are strongly connected to attacks, there can be analyses of attack trees with use of effects. One possibility is the treatment of threats. The treatment cancels some part of the effects of an attack, and hence the effectiveness of treatment can be evaluated. In Sect. 4.3, some properties about treatments are observed and applied in the case study.

3.2   Consistent Branches

As a branch in an adequately constructed attack tree represents a decomposition of the attack corresponding to the parent node, a similar structure can be expected with regard to effects around the branch. For instance, the effect of the parent node will include the conjunction of all effects of the child nodes for an **AND** branch, as all of the attacks corresponding to the child nodes are conducted. By contrast, when there are several conflicts among the effects around a branch, the decomposition of the attack will have inconsistencies, such as misunderstanding of the situation, or inadequate refinement. To analyze whether an attack decomposition is valid or not, we introduce the consistency of a branch with the assigned effects as follows.

Definition 3. *A branch in an attack tree is defined as consistent, if the condition below holds regarding its type, where e_P is the effect assigned to the parent node and $e_1, e_2, \ldots, e_r$ are the effects assigned to the children:*

- **OR** *branch: the effect of the parent is inferred from the effect of each child node, i.e. $e_i \Rightarrow e_P$ for each i.*
- **AND** *branch: the effect of the parent is inferred from the conjunction of the effects of all children, i.e., $\bigwedge_i e_i \Rightarrow e_P$.*

– **SAND** *branch: the effect* e_k *is obtained by the k-th attack from the left with assumption* $e_1, \ldots, e_{k-1}$, *and* e_P *is inferred from the rightmost effect* e_r.

These conditions are depicted in Fig. 2.

If all branches in an attack tree are consistent, then the entire attack tree is consistent.

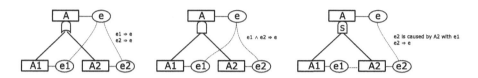

Fig. 2. Consistency of attacks with effects.

Actual examples of attack trees with effects are provided in Sect. 4.2.

As an attribute, effects behave appropriately for a consistent attack tree. The following property is induced straightforwardly.

Proposition 1. *Consider the attribute* ε *as defined above, and take a branch in a consistent attack tree where* e_P, *[resp.* $e_1, e_2, \ldots, e_r$*] is the value of* ε *for the parent [resp. children]. Then the inference* $\nu(\langle e_1, \ldots, e_r \rangle) \Rightarrow e_P$ *holds for* $\nu = \vee$ *[resp.* $\wedge$, μ_ρ*] if the branch is an* **OR** *[resp.* **AND**, **SAND**].

Remark that it is evident that the effect of the root node can be inferred with the effects of the leaf nodes.

4   Case Study

4.1   Process Overview

The security analysis process specified in JASO TP15002 [12] consists of the following five phases: ToE (Target of Evaluation) Definition, Threat analysis, Risk assessment, Define security objectives, and Security requirement selection. In [14], the authors studied concepts and their relationship appearing in the process in detail. It allows refactoring activities and the data dealt with in the security analysis process.

A deliverable of the Risk assessment phase is a list of identified threats on ToE. Threats in this list are prioritized, and significant ones are analyzed in depth using tree diagrams. Countermeasure goals for the threats are discussed in the Define security objective phase.

4.2 Verifying Decompositions

Based on the model in [16], a vehicular network system can be specified as ToE (see Fig. 3). Each module inside the vehicle has its own assets. For example, the assets of the Powertrain module are Control function, Authentication function, Authentication information, and Sensor information.

Here, we consider the identified threat *"Authentication function in Powertrain is interfered via TPMS[3]."* It is estimated significant because the target (Powertrain) is closer to the entry point (TPMS), and the potential damage to the vehicle system is more severe.

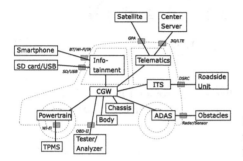

Red boxes indicate entry points. Modules inside the vehicle may be accessed through them.

Fig. 3. The network architecture of ToE.

Figure 4(a) shows an early version of the attack tree (only the upper part is outlined). It should be noted that attacks on node labels include the events that contribute to invoking the parent but are not performed by the attacker. Policies and methods used to construct the tree are rather abstract. Therefore sub-attacks of an attack are intuitively selected; some of sub-attacks do not refine the parent but are expected to occur preceding to the parent. Here, decomposition is interpreted as causal ones implicitly. Moreover only **OR** and **AND** branches are considered. As a result, the following two inconsistencies are found:

1. A temporal-gap among attacks around a branch. The attack A1 has to occur before its parent A0, but the attacks A2 and its parent A0 occur simultaneously.
2. A violated refinement order. The Msg. identification function in A1 refines the Authentication function in A0, whereas Powertrain Software mentioned in A1.1 is a wider entity than Msg. identification function in A1.

These un-structural situations are made explicit by considering the effects of attacks. As mentioned in Sect. 3.1, effects are changes in ToE and its environment caused by specific actions. Here, we identify the entities affected by attacks, and decide effects on them derived from the attacks. The result is illustrated in

---

[3] Tire Pressure Monitoring System.

Node labels:
A0: Authentication function in Powertrain is interfered with via TPMS.
A1: TPMS msg identification function in Powertrain is tampered with.
A1.1: Powertrain Software is tampered with.
A2: TPMS msg identification function in Powertrain is interfered with by DoS.

Effects(Underlined parts are the targets of attacks):
E0: Unintended behaviors in <u>Authentication function</u>.
E1: Installed <u>TPMS msg identification function</u> is invalid.
E1.1: Installed <u>Powertrain Software</u> is invalid.
E2: <u>TPMS msg identification function</u> is not available.

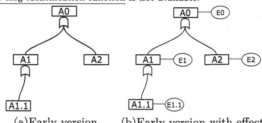

(a)Early version   (b)Early version with effects

Revised node labels:
A1: Unauthorized TPMS msg identification function in Powertrain is invoked.
A1.1: TPMS msg identification function in Powertrain is tampered with by replacing Powertrain software.
A1.2: (Unauthorized) TPMS msg identification function in Powertrain is invoked.

Revised effects:
E1: Unintended behaviors in <u>TPMS msg identification function</u>.
E1.1: Installed <u>TPMS msg identification function</u> is invalid.
E1.2: Unintended behaviors in <u>TPMS msg identification function</u>.

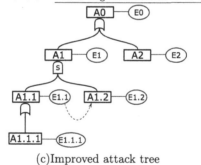

(c)Improved attack tree

Fig. 4. Improvement of an attack tree.

Fig. 4(b). As the non-availability of a sub-function (the effect of A2) is an instance of unintended behaviors (the effect of A0), their occurrences are not separate, i.e. E2 ⇒ E0 holds. On one hand, the existence of adverse software (the effect of A1) does not mean the appearance of unintended behaviors immediately, i.e. E1 ⇒ E0 does not hold. It shows that A1 breaks the consistency of the **OR** branch under A0. Moreover, the branch under A1 is inconsistent, as the fact Powertrain Software is invalid does not imply that Msg. identification function is invalid.

The revised version of the attack tree is outlined in Fig. 4(c). The second inconsistency mentioned above is simply resolved by emphasizing the target(A1.1.1). We modify the node A1 and add a **SAND** branch under it to ensure consistency. At last all branches are consistent in this tree, and the entire attack tree is consistent, as well.

4.3   The Degrees of Possible Mitigation

Attacks can be treated by countermeasures. A countermeasures prevents an attack or modifies its results, and therefore it mitigates the effect of the attack. When the original effect e is weakened to e', e can be expressed as $e' \wedge e''$. Here e'' corresponds to the partial effect the countermeasure cancels, and e' and e'' are independent. In risk management, the four types of treatments are introduced (according to Chapter 6 in [22]): avoidance, limitation/reduction, transference, and acceptance. If we consider them for the purpose of our discussion, then avoidance corresponds to the case when e'' is e itself, and acceptance corresponds to the case when e' coincides e in terms of the same symbols mentioned above. This paper does not consider transference, since it may replace e by another effect and make difficult to estimate the effectiveness of the countermeasure.

Inferences of the properties and corresponding treatments can be related. However the relation is rather rough, that is, two reductions for the effect of an attack cannot be compared by the relations.

Lemma 1. *Let e_p and e_c be properties satisfying $e_c \Rightarrow e_p$. If the mitigated e_p is still inferred from the mitigated e_c, then the mitigation of e_p is weaker than that of e_c. Rigorously, if e_p is weakened by avoidance, then so must be e_c, and if e_p is weakened by reduction, then e_c must be weakened by avoidance or reduction as well.*

The lemma can be proven by a simple observation. Let us split e_p and e_c to $e'_p \wedge e''_p$ and $e'_c \wedge e''_c$ respectively, where e''_p and e''_c are removed by mitigation. Remember that the inference $e_c \Rightarrow e_p$ implies $e'_c \wedge e''_c \Rightarrow e'_p$ and $e'_c \wedge e''_c \Rightarrow e''_p$. If e_p is mitigated by avoidance, that is, $e_p = e''_p$ and e'_p does not actually exist, then the inference $e'_c \Rightarrow e'_p$ is contradictory, unless e'_c does not exist. Similarly, if e_p is mitigated by reduction but e_c is mitigated by acceptance, then e''_p still holds even after mitigation by $e_c \Rightarrow e''_p$.

On the basis of the above lemma, we can restrict mitigation of children in attack trees. However, before stating that, several conditions are assumed for simplicity:

- Children's effects around an **AND** branch are independent. None of them is inferred by other effects, and the countermeasure for an effect is not overridden by countermeasures for other effects.
- Each child's effect around a **SAND** branch is not modified by subsequent attacks. Hence the entire effect by the children around a **SAND** branch is the conjunction of effects by every child.

Proposition 2. *Consider the effect e_p of the parent and $e_1, \ldots, e_k$ of the children around a branch of an attack tree. Then, the mitigation for e_p must be weaker than or equal to that of all children, if the branch is* **OR** *and is still consistent after the mitigation. In the case of the* **AND/SAND** *branch, the mitigation for e_p must be weaker than or equal to the mitigation of at least one child's.*

Let us first consider that the type of the branch is **OR**. According to the semantics, it is sufficient to check the relationship between each child and the parent. The above lemma is applied to an individual child directly, and it is observed that the mitigation of the parent is weaker than that of each child.

Remember that the consistency means $(\wedge_i e_i) \Rightarrow e_p$ when the type of the branch is **AND/SAND**. We can apply the lemma corresponding to e_c as $\wedge_i e_i$, that is, the mitigation for e_p must be weaker than or equal to that of $(\wedge_i e_i)$. It indicates that the mitigation for every e_i must be avoidance if e_p is mitigated by avoidance. Moreover it indicates that the mitigation for all children must not be acceptance if e_p is mitigated by reduction, that is, at least one e_i must be mitigated by reduction or avoidance. Finally, the proposition is obtained.

Remark that we can observe stronger results for **SAND** branches. A weakened effect for a child by avoidance or reduction may become an insufficient precondition of the subsequent attacks. Consequently, the attack is not invoked, and its effect does not occur as well. Therefore, mitigating the leftmost sub-attack by avoidance/reduction is sufficient to mitigate the entire $\wedge_i e_i$ by avoidance.

Considering the case study regarding the vehicular network system. After analyzing significant threats using attack trees, countermeasures are considered for primitive attacks of the threats that serve as labels on leaf nodes. The selected countermeasures are those that will negate the corresponding primitive attacks, but some of them may be overreactions. Proposition 2 supports the determination of whether or not the selections are adequate.

Considering the identified threat "*Authentication information in Infotainment is stolen via BT/WiFi/IR*" (B0) and the attack tree for it (Fig. 5), we note that the threat is less critical, as its effect, *the disclosure of the information*, does not affect the drive control of vehicles immediately. The treatment for the threat can be reduction; for example updating the information after a fixed period of time. By referring to Proposition 2, each sub-attack of B0 can be treated by reduction or avoidance. Similarly, all sub-attacks of B3 must not be mitigated by acceptance. Therefore we have several options: to accept obtaining device (B3.1) and eavesdropping (B3.2) but make it difficult to extract authentication information (B3.3), or to restrict obtaining device (B3.1) and simultaneously restrict opportunities to eavesdrop (B3.2) and to extract the information (B3.3).

5   Conclusion

We define a new formal system of attack trees with sequential conjunction, and the consistency around a branch in terms of effects of attacks. They match the

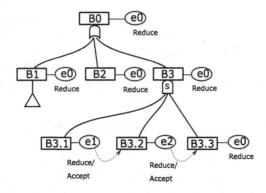

B0: Auth. info. in Infotainment is stolen via BT/Wifi/IR.
B1: Auth. info. in Infotainment is obtained by accessing Infotainment.
B2: Auth. info. in Infotainment is obtained by fake communication request.
B3: Auth. info. in Infotainment is obtained by eavesdropping BT/Wifi/IR.
B3.1: Device to eavesdrop is prepared.
B3.2: Msg.s for authentication are collected.
B3.3: Auth. info. is extracted from eavesdropped Msg.s
e0: Auth. info. is disclosed.
e1: Ready for eavesdropping.
e2: Analyzing Msg.s are available.

Fig. 5. Attack tree with effects and treatment types. The triangle connected to B1 indicates the node is not decomposed here.

interpretation of attack trees as representations of refinement scenarios, and therefore we can discuss the validity of attack trees formally. These ideas lead to and accountable attack models. Consequently, the construction of attack trees is improved, and it becomes possible to analyze attack trees rigorously.

As an application, degrees of mitigation for attacks are measured. Although it is a slightly rough, we show examples and observation for that, with use of a vehicular network system.

There are several issues left to be considered in the future research:

- Our formulation of attack trees does not cover complicated phenomena including the evolution of effects by subsequent attacks, or non-linear relations among effects and attacks. Developing more expressive attack trees will give finer models of attacks appearing in the real world. In addition, semantics should be rigorously related to ones in existing formalizations.
- Research on the derivation of the effects from attacks are required. Additional information, for example a structure of ToE, may allow determining effects in systematic way that reduces informal discussion in attack tree processes, and that validates attack trees entirely at a higher level.
- The evaluation of mitigation can be enhanced. From the practical point of view, it is beneficial if we can evaluate how effective a mitigation is for a specific attack. Further research may refine Proposition 2 and we can choose the most appropriate mitigations for attacks.

References

1. Audinot, M., Pinchinat, S., Kordy, B.: Is my attack tree correct? (Extended version). arXiv:1706.08507 (2017)
2. Audinot, M., Pinchinat, S., Kordy, B.: Guided design of attack trees: a system-based approach. In: Computer Security Foundations Symposium, CSF 2018, pp. 61–75 (2018)
3. Chen, B., et al.: Security analysis of urban railway systems: the need for a cyber-physical perspective. In: Koornneef, F., van Gulijk, C. (eds.) SAFECOMP 2015. LNCS, vol. 9338, pp. 277–290. Springer, Cham (2015). https://doi.org/10.1007/978-3-319-24249-1_24
4. Fovino, I.N., Masera, M.: Through the description of attacks: a multidimensional view. In: Górski, J. (ed.) SAFECOMP 2006. LNCS, vol. 4166, pp. 15–28. Springer, Heidelberg (2006). https://doi.org/10.1007/11875567_2
5. Fovino, I.N., Masera, M., Cian, A.D.: Integrating cyber attacks within fault trees. Reliab. Eng. Syst. Saf. **94**(9), 1394–1402 (2009)
6. Friedenthal, S., Moore, A., Steiner, R.: A Practical Guide to SysML: The Systems Modeling Language, 3rd edn. Morgan Kaufmann Publishers Inc., Burlington (2014)
7. Gadyatskaya, O., Trujillo-Rasua, R.: New directions in attack tree research: catching up with industrial needs. In: Liu, P., Mauw, S., Stølen, K. (eds.) GraMSec 2017. LNCS, vol. 10744, pp. 115–126. Springer, Cham (2018). https://doi.org/10.1007/978-3-319-74860-3_9
8. Horne, R., Mauw, S., Tiu, A.: Semantics for specialising attack trees based on linear logic. Fundam. Inform. **153**(1–2), 57–86 (2017)
9. IEC 61025: Fault tree analysis (FTA) (2006)
10. ISO 31000: Risk management - Guidelines (2018)
11. ISO/IEC Guide 51: Safety aspects - Guidelines for their inclusion in standards (2014)
12. JASO TP15002: Guideline for Automotive Information Security Analysis (2015)
13. Jhawar, R., Kordy, B., Mauw, S., Radomirović, S., Trujillo-Rasua, R.: Attack trees with sequential conjunction. In: Federrath, H., Gollmann, D. (eds.) SEC 2015. IAICT, vol. 455, pp. 339–353. Springer, Cham (2015). https://doi.org/10.1007/978-3-319-18467-8_23
14. Kawanishi, Y., Nishihara, H., Souma, D., Yoshida, H., Hata, Y.: A comparative study of JASO TP15002-based security risk assessment methods for connected vehicle system design. Secur. Commun. Netw. (2019). https://doi.org/10.1155/2019/4614721
15. Mauw, S., Oostdijk, M.: Foundations of attack trees. In: Won, D.H., Kim, S. (eds.) ICISC 2005. LNCS, vol. 3935, pp. 186–198. Springer, Heidelberg (2006). https://doi.org/10.1007/11734727_17
16. Miyashita, Y., et al.: On-vehicle compact and lightweight multi-channel central gateway unit. SEI Tech. Rev. **83**, 5–9 (2016)
17. RTCA DO-356: Airworthiness Security Methods and Considerations (2014)
18. Ruddle, A., et al.: Security requirements for automotive on-board networks based on dark-side scenarios. EVITA Deliverable D2.3 (2009)
19. Ruijters, E., Stoelinga, M.: Fault tree analysis: a survey of the state-of-the-art in modeling, analysis and tools. Comput. Sci. Rev. **15–16**, 29–62 (2015)
20. Schneier, B.: Attack trees. Dr. Dobb's J. **24**(12), 21–29 (1999)

21. Siddiqi, M.A., Seepers, R.M., Hamad, M., Prevelakis, V., Strydis, C.: Attack-tree-based threat modeling of medical implants. In: PROOFS 2018, 7th International Workshop on Security Proofs for Embedded Systems, vol. 7, pp. 32–49 (2018)
22. Susan Snedaker, C.R.: Business Continuity and Disaster Recovery Planning for IT Professionals, 2nd edn. Elsevier, Amsterdam (2014)
23. Wang, J., Whitley, J.N., Phan, R.C.W., Parish, D.J.: Unified parametrizable attack tree. IJISR 1(1/2), 20–26 (2011)

Safety Meets Security: Using IEC 62443 for a Highly Automated Road Vehicle

Dominik Püllen$^{(\boxtimes)}$, Nikolaos Anagnostopoulos, Tolga Arul,
and Stefan Katzenbeisser

University of Passau, Passau, Germany
`dominik.puellen@uni-passau.de`

Abstract. In this work, we conduct and discuss a consensus-based risk analysis for a novel architecture of a driverless and electric prototype vehicle. While well-established safety standards like ISO 26262 provide frameworks to systematically assess risks of hazardous operational situations, the automotive security field has emerged only in the last years. Today, SAE J3061 provides recommendations and high-level guiding principles of how to incorporate security into vehicle systems. ISO/SAE 21434 is a novel automotive security standard, which, however, is still under development. Therefore, we treat the aforementioned architecture as a single Industrial Automation and Control System (IACS) and provide an implementation of the IEC 62443 series. We collaboratively identify threats in a three-round process and define a scoring scheme for automotive risks. As a result, we obtain a tailored bundle of compensating security mechanisms. Based on our work, we suggest improvements for future automotive security standards when it comes to the co-engineering of safety and security.

Keywords: IEC 62443 · Security · Safety · Risk mitigation

1 Introduction

The increasing connectivity and the growing computational power of road vehicles come along with great potential, but likewise lead to security concerns as demonstrated by prior works [6,15,25]. Beside new security challenges, the field of safety is also affected by vehicle automation, because a human being cannot be assumed anymore as a fallback layer. As modern road vehicles are typically complex cyber-physical systems and need to meet legal requirements, a standardized process for risk identification and mitigation is typically applied. Currently, the ISO/SAE 21434 [5] is the most promising candidate for an automotive security standard. It provides risk assessment methods for Intelligent Transportation Systems (ITS). After identifying and decomposing threat scenarios into attack paths, Cybersecurity Assurance Levels (CAL) indicate the estimated security requirements for given items. Moreover, SAE J3061 [3], published in 2016, provides general guidelines for the development of secure automotive components.

© Springer Nature Switzerland AG 2020
A. Casimiro et al. (Eds.): SAFECOMP 2020, LNCS 12234, pp. 325–340, 2020.
https://doi.org/10.1007/978-3-030-54549-9_22

It is inspired by the ISO 26262 [1] safety standard and reuses techniques from existing security models such as EVITA [10] and HEAVENS [2]. Schmittner et al. [20] demonstrate the security analysis of an automotive communication gateway by applying the concept phase of SAE J3061. They derive high-level security requirements, using the Confidentiality, Integrity, and Availability (CIA) triad. While their work focuses on a single component, our objective is to analyze an automated vehicle as a whole. For that purpose, we apply the IEC 62443 standards [4] to a recently announced novel vehicular architecture [24]. We argue, that IEC 62443 overlaps with the main idea of the unpublished ISO/SAE 21434. That is, it provides a risk-based security analysis process, takes into account interfaces to external components (e.g., V2X), identifies and assesses threats, and eventually uses Security Levels (SL) to describe security requirements. When it comes to threats, Petit and Shladover [17] identified 12 sources of potential attacks on automated vehicles and evaluated each one regarding its feasibility, occurrence probability, consequences and mitigation techniques. Beside the goal of a systematic security requirement analysis, our research question concerns the possibility of co-engineering security and safety demands in a vehicular system. In the following, we aim at sharing our lessons learned and suggest improvements for future automotive security standards.

2   Overview of a Novel Vehicular Architecture

In 2018, seven German universities and industry partners announced the development of four fully automated and driverless vehicles [24]. These vehicles are supposed to serve as an evaluation platform for new concepts in various fields, such as automation, modularization, verification, validation, safety, and security. Unlike contemporary vehicles, that typically consist of dozens of Electronic Control Units (ECUs), the novel E/E architecture follows a centralized approach, which is inspired by the human nervous system. That is, four *sensor modules* collect and preprocess radar, Lidar, and camera data. They hand them over to the *cerebrum*, which is responsible for the trajectory and for behavioral planning based on the sensor data. The *brainstem*, in turn, implements and tracks the trajectory and instructs the *spinal cord* to eventually move the vehicles. The latter provides all necessary steering angles and both braking and acceleration torques to four *dynamic modules*, which drive the wheels. In case of failures, the brainstem reflexively enforces an emergency trajectory, by which a safe halt is usually triggered. All aforementioned modules are connected over BroadR-Reach in a ring topology, allowing communication even if a switch breakes down. The dynamic modules are additionally wired over FlexRay, which serves as a supplementary fallback layer. In total, 26 ultrasonic and 2 radar sensors, denoted as *platform sensors*, allow for near-field sensing and are directly connected to the brainstem over CAN. For in-vehicle communication, the Automotive Service-Oriented software Architecture (ASOA) [11] is deployed, a new modular framework, that enables flexible communication, fast and secure updates of ECUs, and easy replacement of hardware components.

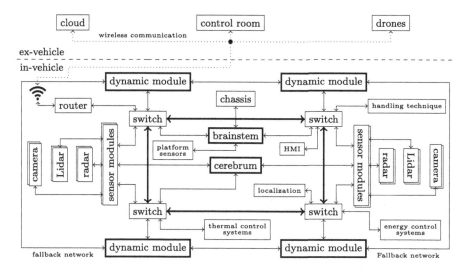

Fig. 1. Overview of the proposed vehicular architecture [12]

Beside the prototype vehicles, a new infrastructural concept provides environmental information such as traffic updates via V2I communication. A *cloud* serves as a collective memory, such that vehicles can incorporate predictive driving behavior by learning from each other. *Drones* collect and share additional traffic information which helps the vehicles to create a realistic environmental model. This information is fed into trajectory planning algorithms on the cerebrum. A *control room* enables the remote control by a human in case automatic maneuvering is not possible anymore. It is only called into action in exceptional situations, in order to meet European legal requirements.

In the following, the term *vehicular architecture* refers to the novel E/E architecture in combination with its external components as illustrated in Fig. 1.

3   Introduction to IEC 62443

The IEC 62443[4] is a series of standards and technical reports that provide a structured risk assessment and mitigation process for Industrial and Automation Control Systems (IACS), alongside with management guidances, policies, and terminology. An IACS typically describes a complex system consisting of various computing units, sensors, actuators, temporarily connected devices, and a human interface, that all collaboratively work on the outcome of a specific product. The overall objective is to identify threats, assess resulting risks, and come up with protection techniques.

As shown in Fig. 2, the actual risk assessment process is described in IEC 62443-3-2 in consecutive steps, denoted as Zone and Conduit Requirements (ZCR). In the first step, all relevant assets of the System Under Consideration

(SUC) are identified (ZCR 1). A high-level security analysis (ZCR 2) gives indication about the worst-case unmitigated risk on each asset and whether further investigation is necessary. Based on the results of this high-level analysis, the SUC is partitioned into zones and conduits (ZCR 3), whereas a zone contains assets with the same or similar security requirements. A conduit is a special zone type, that connects two other zones and therefore, usually describes a network. In ZCR 4, the tolerable risk $r^{\mathrm{tol,max}}$ of each zone is compared with the unmitigated risk r^{u}. If $r^{\mathrm{tol,max}}$ is below r^{u}, no further action is required. Otherwise, a detailed security risk assessment follows in ZCR 5.

The main objective of ZCR 5 is to iteratively reduce the unmitigated security risk of identified *threats* ($\mathcal{T}$) by applying compensating countermeasures. Threats are associated with seven Foundational Requirements ($\mathcal{FR}$). That is, *Identification and Authentication Control* (IAC), *Use Control* (UC), *System Integrity* (SI), *Data Confidentiality* (DC), *Restricted Data Flow* (RDF), *Timely Response to Events* (TRE), and *Resource Availability* (RA). Since the security of a system refers to the mitigation of threats, an exhaustive list of threats and exploitable vulnerabilities is crucial (ZCR 5.1–5.2). Both the impact and the likelihood of each threat (ZCR 5.3–5.4) is determined, in order to compute the unmitigated security risk r^{u} of each threat (ZCR 5.5). Based on these results, a target security level SL-T for each zone is computed. IEC 62443 differentiates between four levels, SL-1, SL-2, SL-3, and SL-4. While SL-0 is implicitly defined as no requirements, SL-1 demands for protection against coincidental violations. SL-2 - SL-4 cover intentional violation with an increasing level of skills, resources, and motivation. Both impact and likelihood are reevaluated (ZCR 5.9) after applying changes to the SUC, e.g., after introducing a new countermeasure. Ideally, this leads to a reduction of the residual risk (ZCR 5.10). A reassessment of the

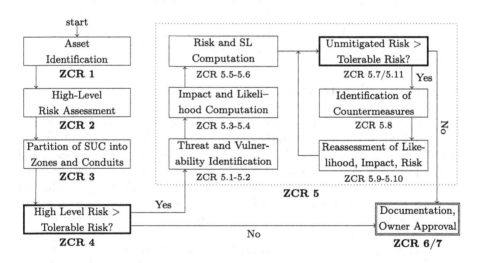

Fig. 2. Simplified workflow of IEC 62443-3-2

high level risk, however, is not caused. Once the unmitigated risk of all threats is below the tolerable risk, the SUC is considered secure.

4   Application of IEC 62443

We consider the presented vehicular architecture as our System Under Consideration (SUC). Since it shares most IACS properties like sensors, actuators, and computing units, we use the IEC 62443 standards for a full security risk analysis. We demonstrate how to implement the generic guidelines ZCR 1–5 of IEC 62443-3-2 with the ultimate goal to create a tailored bundle of security means for a secure and safe operation of the automated vehicles. Our findings may inspire future automotive security standards. As discussed in Sect. 5, all assessments are the results of an expert committee.

4.1   High-Level Risk Analysis (ZCR 1 - ZCR 4)

In **ZCR 1**, our expert team identified a total number of 19 assets in the SUC, i.e., functional components with a potential impact on security and safety. These include both in-vehicle assets (e.g., brainstem, radar) and external ones (e.g., drones, control room).

In **ZCR 2**, a high-level security risk analysis was performed for each asset a_i. For this, IEC 62443-3-2 requires to assess the high-level likelihood $L_{a_i}^{\mathrm{HL}}$ and the high-level impact $I_{a_i}^{\mathrm{HL}}$ of a potential attack on a_i. Since it does not state how this is supposed to happen, we apply a multi-criteria decision making process. More precisely, we implement a Simple Additive Weighting (SAW) approach [19], where predefined evaluation criteria are scored and then ranked according to their importance. As demonstrated in the subsequent paragraphs, evaluation criteria for both likelihood and impact are represented as vectors $\boldsymbol{L}_{a_i}^{\mathrm{HL}} = (L_1\ L_2\ ...\ L_n)^{\intercal}$ and $\boldsymbol{I}_{a_i}^{\mathrm{HL}} = (I_1\ I_2\ ...\ I_m)^{\intercal}$, respectively. The ranking of each criterion is done with the normalized weight matrices $\boldsymbol{W}_{\mathrm{L}}$ and $\boldsymbol{W}_{\mathrm{I}}$, respectively. We compute the scores $L_{a_i}^{\mathrm{HL}}$ and $I_{a_i}^{\mathrm{HL}}$ by summing up the products of each score and its weight, i.e., $L_{a_i}^{\mathrm{HL}} = \boldsymbol{L}_{a_i}^{\mathrm{HL}} \cdot \boldsymbol{W}_{\mathrm{L}}$, respectively $I_{a_i}^{\mathrm{HL}} = \boldsymbol{I}_{a_i}^{\mathrm{HL}} \cdot \boldsymbol{W}_{\mathrm{I}}$, where $\cdot$ is the dot product. Due to normalization, a score of $L_{a_i}^{\mathrm{HL}} = 1$ indicates the highest possible likelihood, while $I_{a_i}^{\mathrm{HL}} = 1$ stands for the worst-case impact. The high-level risk $r_{a_i}^{\mathrm{HL}} = (I_{a_i}^{\mathrm{HL}}, L_{a_i}^{\mathrm{HL}},)$ is mapped to a risk class, using the weighted normalized decision matrix in Table 3. We argue that such a scoring scheme is compliant with current automotive guidelines, as SAE J3061 recommends additive scoring for the assessment of impact factors.

Impact: We describe $\boldsymbol{L}_{a_i}^{\mathrm{HL}} = (\mathrm{PS\ FL\ OL})^{\intercal}$ as a vector of three impact criteria, where PS represents *Passenger Safety*, FL *Financial Loss*, and OL *Operational Limitations* [10]. Each criterion is independently scored by the experts, who use a set of exclusive parameters ($\mathcal{P}$) for this task. Based on its severity, each parameter is mapped on a distinct integer value according to the rules of SAW.

That is, the least severe parameter is associated with 1, which is then incremented by 1 for subsequent parameters. For instance, we differentiate between $\mathcal{P}_{PS} = \{fatal, seriously\ injured, slightly\ injured, no\ injuries\}$ for passenger safety. The parameter $p_0 = no\ injuries$ is associated with 1, $p_1 = slightly\ injured$ with 2, $p_2 = seriously\ injured$ with 3, and $p_3 = fatal$ with 4. Following SAW, we normalize these integer scores with $\widetilde{p}_i = \frac{\min p_j \forall p_j \in \mathcal{P}}{p_i}$ and then rank them with predefined weights. In our case, we use probabilistic weights, yielding 0.3 for both operational limitations and financial loss. As we consider passenger safety the most valuable criterion for an automotive system, we prioritize it with a weight of 0.4. We define $\mathcal{P}_{OL} = \{massive, high, medium, low, none\}$ to assess operational limitations of a potential attack. A *massive* limitation occurs if all traffic comes to an halt. This, for instance, may happen if the control room is taken over by an adversary. *High* limitations lead to traffic jams in a designated area, e.g., when sending fake traffic information. *Medium* constraints occur in case a vehicle can only operate at reduced speed, e.g., when hijacking or deceiving sensors. Finally, *low* limitations are the result of hijacking non-critical assets such as the chassis. Regarding the financial loss, we distinguish between four monetary classes as shown in Table 1. The so-called *Value of a Statistical Life* (VSL) [22] served as a reference value to determine these classes. The VSL indicates the mortality risk reduction benefit for the U.S. government. In 2016, the U.S. Department of Transportation indicated a VSL of \$9.6 million. Since the VSL is not a universal constant, we assume VSL = \$10M for simplicity. Table 1 shows the normalized and weighted scores for each impact parameter.

Table 1. Impact criteria with their normalized and weighted scores

Passenger Safety (PS)	Fatal	Seriously injured	Slightly injured	None	
	0.4	**0.2**	**0.134**	**0.1**	
Operational Limitation (OL)	massive	high	medium	low	none
	0.3	**0.15**	**0.1**	**0.085**	**0.075**
Financial Loss (FL)	]\$10M, ∞]	]\$10K, \$10M[	]\$0, \$10K]	\$0	
	0.3	**0.15**	**0.1**	**0.075**	

During our impact assessments, we encountered the problem of *transitive attack relations*. Theoretically, every asset a_i may be accountable for a worst-case attack if an adversary manipulates a safety-critical asset a_j through a_i, $i \neq j$. As a consequence, all assets would receive the highest impact score, which eventually could result in over-engineering. Therefore, for the assessment of a_i, we focus solely on its functional description, without considering propagating side effects. This, however, does not mean that transitive attacks are left out from the risk analysis, since they are covered by conduits in later steps.

Likelihood: We describe the high-level likelihood $L_{a_i}^{HL} = (IC\ WC\ P\ EI\ B\ TP)^{\mathsf{T}}$ as a six dimensional Boolean vector. That is, we decide for each asset a_i, whether an *Internet Connection* (IC) can be established, a *Wireless Communication*

Table 2. High-level assessments (ZCR 2) and SUC partitioning (ZCR 3)

Asset	Weighted Impact			Weighted Likelihood						HL Risk Class	Zone
	PC	OL	FL	IC	WC	P	EI	B	TP		
Control room	.4	.3	.3	.286	.238	.19	.143	0	0	ex.high	Z_F
Brainstem	.4	.15	.4	.286	0	.19	0	.095	0	ex.high	Z_A
Dynamic module	.4	.15	.15	.286	0	.19	0	.095	0	ex.high	Z_E
Radar	.2	.1	.15	0	0	0	0	.095	.048	Medium	Z_B
Sensor module	.134	.1	.15	.286	0	.19	.143	.095	0	High	Z_A
Chassis	.1	.075	.15	0	0	0	0	.095	0	Low	Z_C
⋮	⋮			⋮						⋮	⋮
HMI	.1	.1	.1	.286	.238	.19	0	.095	.048	High	Z_D

(WC) is possible, a_i is *re-Programmable* (P), a_i has *External Interfaces* (EI) such as ODB2, USB, a_i is directly connected to the in-vehicle *Bus* (B), and whether a_i is produced by a *Third Party* (TP). For instance, $L_{a_i}^{HL} = (1\ 0\ 1\ 0\ 1\ 0)^\intercal$ describes a re-programmable asset, which is connected to the in-vehicle bus and has the ability to establish an Internet connection. The order of the above criteria implicitly shows their ranking, i.e., to what extent they facilitate an attack. Similar to the high-level impact, we assign each criterion a distinct integer. As an Internet connection enables a potential attack the most, it receives the largest value of 6. For each subsequent criterion, we subtract 1 from the value, such that *Third Party* is eventually associated with 1. After normalization, we obtain $W_L = (0.286\ 0.238\ 0.19\ 0.143\ 0.095\ 0.048)^\intercal$. Table 2 gives an overview of the weighted evaluation criteria for both impact and likelihood of a selected number of assets.

In **ZCR 3**, we partition the SUC into zones and conduits, using the results of the high-level security analysis. We obtain nine zones and conduits $ZC = \{Z_A, Z_B, ..., Z_F, C_A, C_B, C_C\}$. Instead of putting all assets with the same high-level risk into one zone, we additionally differentiate between safety-critical and remote assets. For instance, Z_A consists of highly safety-critical in-vehicle assets (brainstem, cerebrum, sensors, router), while the (remote and safety-critical) control room resides in Z_F. In that way, we are able to better address specific safety and security demands. Although the dynamic modules are highly safety-critical,

Table 3. Weighted normalized risk matrix with acceptance ranges

Grey cells: tolerable risk for ZCR 4			Impact ($I_{a_i}^{HL}$)				
			negligible [.235,.26]	minor [.27,.384[	major [.384,.584[	critical [.584,.7[	catastrophic [.7,1]
Likelihood ($L_{a_i}^{HL}$)	trivial	[0,.048]	ex. low	low	medium	high	high
	unlikely	[.048,.191]	ex. low	low	medium	high	high
	possible	[.191,.428]	low	medium	high	high	ex. high
	likely	].428,.714]	medium	medium	high	ex. high	ex. high
	certain	].714,1]	medium	high	ex. high	ex. high	ex. high

they are put into the dedicated zone Z_E, because they are additionally connected between each other over a fallback bus (cf., Fig. 1) and thus, have a significantly different attack surface. The fallback bus is treated in a dedicated conduit (C_C) as well. C_A describes the in-vehicle Ethernet-based communication and C_B is the wireless network that connects external components such as the cloud and the control room. Table 2 shows the zones to which an asset belongs.

In **ZCR 4**, a detailed security analysis follows for a zone $Z_i \in \mathcal{ZC}$, if there is an asset a_i with a high-level risk $r_{a_i}^{\mathrm{HL}} > r_{Z_i}^{\mathrm{tol,max}}$, where $r^{\mathrm{tol,max}}$ denotes the maximum tolerable risk. Since IEC 62443-3-2 does not prescribe how to determine $r^{\mathrm{tol,max}}$, we define both a maximum tolerable impact $I^{\mathrm{tol,max}}$ and likelihood $L^{\mathrm{tol,max}}$. We exclude passenger harm and financial loss, but find low operational limitations tolerable, resulting in $I^{\mathrm{tol,max}} = \boldsymbol{I}_{a_i}^{\mathrm{HL}} \cdot \boldsymbol{W}_{\mathrm{I}} = 0.1 + 0.085 + 0.075 = 0.26$. Similarly, we define the tolerable likelihood. That is, we only consider it non-critical if an asset is manufactured by a third party and/or is connected to the vehicle bus, while *all* other criteria are excluded. These considerations lead to $L_{a_i}^{\mathrm{tol,max}} = \boldsymbol{L}_{a_i}^{\mathrm{HL}} \cdot \boldsymbol{W}_{\mathrm{L}} = (0\ 0\ 0\ 0\ 1\ 1)^{\mathsf{T}} \cdot (0\ 0\ 0\ 0\ 0.095\ 0.048)^{\mathsf{T}} = \boldsymbol{0.143}$. The grayed fields of the risk matrix in Table 3 correspond to the tolerable risk. Since no asset has a tolerable high-level risk, a detailed security analysis is required for all zones and conduits.

4.2 Detailed Risk Analysis (ZCR 5.1 - ZCR 5.10)

The objective of **ZCR 5** is to move the unmitigated risk $r_{Z_i}^{\mathrm{u}}$ of potential threats in a zone $Z_i \in \mathcal{ZC}$ below the maximum tolerable zone risk $r_{Z_i}^{\mathrm{tol,max}}$. This is achieved by applying compensating security countermeasures, which lower $r_{Z_i}^{\mathrm{u}}$ and thus, move the achieved security level SL-A$_{Z_i}$ closer to the target security level SL-T$_{Z_i}$. A security level measures security demands arising from risks, whereas a risk results from a threat on a given asset in combination with at least one vulnerability. Thus, a crucial step for a reasonable risk analysis is the thorough determination of a threat and adversary model, taking into account known vulnerabilities and both the impact and likelihood of the identified threats.

Threat Modeling: A core prerequisite of a risk analysis is an exhaustive list of threats $\mathcal{T}$, since compensating security techniques may not protect the SUC from unidentified threats. During threat identification, we face two core problems: First, it remains impossible to prove completeness for $\mathcal{T}$, even though numerous identification techniques, such as *CIA*, *STRIDE*, and *Threat Trees* have been proposed [21]. Since threats are identified by the expert committee, we claim to have diverse views on the SUC and to obtain a reasonable number of threats. Additionally, we acknowledge the work by Petit and Shladover [17], who identified potential attack surfaces on road vehicles, that inspired our threat identification. Second, a collaborative threat identification process requires a common notion of a threat, when it comes to the *granularity* level. For instance, $t_1 = $ *"The attacker triggers the vehicle brakes."* and $t_2 = $ *"A network man-in-the-middle attacker injects forged braking commands."* are both candidates for threats with the same outcome. However, t_1 is phrased on a purely functional level, while t_2 already addresses *one* potential attack scenario. While the author of t_1 may view the SUC at a coarser granularity level, he potentially misses attack vectors, as more than one vector can lead to the same outcome. In order to obtain threats with a comparable granularity level, we apply a three-round iterative threat identification process, as illustrated in Fig. 3. In a first round, we identify *top-level* threats on a purely functional level, having in mind *what* consequences are possible. After that, each top-level threat is split up into intermediate threats, taking into account *how* they can be realized, i.e., a precise attack vector. Since an attack vector can be used to realize more than one attack, an intermediate threat may appear multiple times. For instance, threats $t_{0\text{-}2}$ and $t_{2\text{-}2}$ in Table 4 are identical and are thus treated equally in succeeding steps.

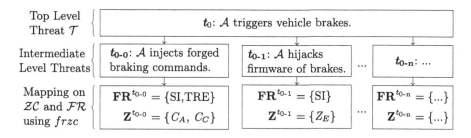

Fig. 3. Three-round iterative threat identification process

In the last round, each intermediate threat is associated with at least one zone or conduit $Z_i \in \mathcal{ZC}$ and at least one foundational requirement $fr \in \mathcal{FR}$, resulting in $\mathcal{T}_{Z_i}^{fr} \subseteq \mathcal{T}$. We formally model $\mathcal{T}_{Z_i}^{fr} = \{t \in \mathcal{T} : \pi_1(frzc(t)) = fr \wedge \pi_2(frzc(t)) = z\}$ with $frzc : \mathcal{T} \to (\mathcal{FR}^{\leq 7} \times \mathcal{ZC}^{\leq 9})$ and π the projection operation. In that way, we identified 63 intermediate threats.

Computation of Zone-Based Security Levels: Based on the identified threats, we derive a target security level SL-T_{Z_i} for each zone $Z_i \in \mathcal{ZC}$ (**ZCR 5.6**). The security model HEAVENS [2] combines a threat level with the impact level to derive a security level. In contrast, IEC 62443-3-2 has no prescribed method to compute a security level. It only recommends to either represent SL-T_{Z_i} as a scalar or as a vector. A scalar value minimizes the effort during verification, because the total number of possible states is kept low. In turn, a scalar may lead to over-engineering, since it does not allow a fine-grained requirement analysis. For instance, a zone requiring a confidentiality level of SL-4 would obtain SL-T_{Z_i} as an overall security level, although precautions regarding other security goals may not be necessary. We express the security level of a zone $Z_i \in \mathcal{ZC}$ as a seven dimensional vector, where each dimension takes into account the unmitigated risks $r_{t_i}^u \in \mathcal{T}_{Z_i}^{fr}$ for a given $fr \in \mathcal{FR}$. In other words, we assign a security level to each foundational requirement and thereby, express to what extent it is affected in Z_i. Precisely, we determine $\mathrm{SL}_{Z_i} = (\mathrm{SL}_{Z_i}^{\mathrm{IAC}}\, \mathrm{SL}_{Z_i}^{\mathrm{UC}}\, ...\, \mathrm{SL}_{Z_i}^{\mathrm{RA}})^{\mathsf{T}}$ where $\mathrm{SL}_{Z_i}^{\mathrm{fr}} = \max(< r_{t_0}^{\mathrm{u}}, r_{t_1}^{\mathrm{u}}, ..., r_{t_n}^{\mathrm{u}} >)$, $r_{t_i}^{\mathrm{u}} \in \mathcal{T}_{Z_i}^{fr}$, $fr \in \mathcal{FR}$. As an example, for the achieved security level of zone Z_A, we obtain $\mathrm{SL\text{-}A}_{ZA} = (\mathrm{SL\text{-}2}\,\mathrm{SL\text{-}3}\,\mathrm{SL\text{-}4}\,\mathrm{SL\text{-}3}\,\mathrm{SL\text{-}2}\,\mathrm{SL\text{-}4}\,\mathrm{SL\text{-}3})^{\mathsf{T}}$.

Similar to the high-level analysis, we express the unmitigated risk $r_{t_i}^{\mathrm{u}}$ of a threat t_i as a combination of likelihood (ZCR 5.4) and impact (ZCR 5.3). We suggest a *cascading parameter approach*, that evaluates likelihood and impact depending on further sizes like *vulnerabilities* and *attacker's capabilities*. This means, any change in one of those parameters immediately propagates to $r_{t_i}^{\mathrm{u}}$. Precisely, the likelihood for a successful threat t_i is determined by the required capabilities for its implementation and by exploitable vulnerabilities (ZCR 5.2). We acknowledge, that the idea of incorporating the attacker's capabilities into the threat likelihood has been already proposed in [16]. Similar to the HEAVENS project[2], we model the attacker's capabilities $\mathcal{AC}$ as three factors, *experience*

Table 4. Mapping of intermediate threats on zones and foundational requirements

Top Layer Threat	No.	Intermediate threat	Z_A	Z_B	...	C_C	IAC	SI	...	RA	Risk class
			Zones& conduits				Functional requirements				
Adversary prevents braking	$t_{0\text{-}0}$	Injection of fake braking commands		x		x		x	x		ex.high
	$t_{0\text{-}1}$	Illegal firmware on dynamic modules		x				x			Low
	$t_{0\text{-}2}$	Manipulation of brainstem firmware	x				x	x			high
	$t_{0\text{-}3}$	Malicious device to vehicle bus		x		x		x		x	ex.high
	$t_{0\text{-}4}$	Impersonation of control room		x			x				High
Manipulation of position	$t_{1\text{-}0}$	Injection of forged position data	x	x		x	x				ex.high
	$t_{1\text{-}1}$	GPS jamming		x						x	High
	$t_{1\text{-}2}$	Illegal firmware on localization ECU	x	x			x				Medium
Passenger Imprisonment	$t_{2\text{-}0}$	Malicious firmware to door control		x			x				Low
	$t_{2\text{-}1}$	DoS on door control				x	x	x		x	ex.high
	$t_{2\text{-}2}$	Manipulation of brainstem firmware	x				x	x			High
Manipulation of traffic data	$t_{3\text{-}0}$	Sending fake traffic data to cloud		x		x	x	x			ex.high
	$t_{3\text{-}1}$	Map poisoning on cerebrum	x				x				Medium
	$t_{3\text{-}2}$	Forging traffic data from drone		x			x	x			High
...	...	...	...	...	...	...	...	...	...	...	...

$\mathcal{E}$, *knowledge* $\mathcal{K}$, and *resources* $\mathcal{R}$, i.e., $\mathcal{AC} = \mathcal{E} \times \mathcal{K} \times \mathcal{R}$. We score each of them independently for all threats t_i. Afterwards, we assign each identified vulnerability a value from $\mathcal{V} = \{severe, medium, negligible\}$. A severe vulnerability, for instance, may be a broken cryptographic protocol or a zero-day exploit, while a medium one requires user privileges. A negligible vulnerability is mostly theoretical, such as quantum attacks. Regarding the impact of t_i, we use the same criteria as we did for the high-level analysis, i.e., by ranking a threat according *Personal Safety*, *Operational Limitations*, and *Financial Loss*. Eventually, we receive a tuple for unmitigated risk $r_{t_i}^{\mathrm{u}}$ of every threat $t_i \in \mathcal{T}$ as illustrated in Table 4, allowing us to compute a target security level for all zones.

4.3   Threat Mitigation and Results

After having computed a security level SL-A$_{Zi}$ for each zone $Z_i \in \mathcal{ZC}$, we iteratively identify and apply compensating countermeasures, such that the unmitigated risk $r_{t_i}^{\mathrm{u}}$ of threat $t_i \in \mathcal{T}_{Z_i}^{fr}, \forall fr \in \mathcal{FR}$ shrinks below the tolerable risk $r_{Z_i}^{\mathrm{tol,max}}$. For this purpose, we constantly compare $r_{t_i}^{\mathrm{u}} \le r_{Z_i}^{\mathrm{tol,max}}$ by reassessing all parameters, that impact likelihood and impact (ZCR 5.7-5.10). For instance, a compensating countermeasure for the foundational requirement *System Integrity* in zone Z_A is data authentication. Assuming the verifiable authenticity of in-vehicle traffic, the required capabilities to inject fake braking commands without being recognized (c.f. threat $t_{0\text{-}0}$ in Table 4) rise significantly, since an attacker would need to circumvent cryptographic protection. This, in turn, makes $t_{0\text{-}0}$ less likely and consequently, $r_{t_{0\text{-}0}}^{\mathrm{u}}$ decreases. Beforehand, the expert committee defines a tolerable risk $r_{Z_i,fr}^{\mathrm{tol,max}}$ for each zone $Z_i \in \mathcal{ZC}$ and foundational requirement $fr \in \mathcal{FR}$. Precisely, they determine the tuple $r_{Z_i,fr}^{\mathrm{tol,max}} = (I_{Z_i,fr}^{\mathrm{tol,max}}, L_{Z_i,fr}^{\mathrm{tol,max}})$ and compare it with all $r_{t_i}^{\mathrm{u}}$, $t_i \in \mathcal{T}_{Z_i}^{fr}$. For instance, the maximum tolerable likelihood of the foundational requirement *Use Control* for zone Z_F (control room) is set to *extremely low*, because only individuals with assigned privileges are allowed to remotely control a vehicle. According to Table 3, this leads to $L_{C_F,\mathrm{UC}}^{\mathrm{tol,max}} = 0.191$. As the high-level analysis in Sect. 4.1 has revealed, the malicious operation of the control room can lead to life-threatening situations. Therefore, we set the maximum tolerable impact $I_{Z_F,\mathrm{UC}}^{\mathrm{tol,max}}$ to *extremely low*, i.e., $I_{Z_F,\mathrm{UC}}^{\mathrm{tol,max}} = 0.26$. As a result, we obtain $r_{Z_F,\mathrm{UC}}^{\mathrm{tol,max}} = (I_{Z_F,\mathrm{UC}}^{\mathrm{tol,max}}, L_{Z_F,\mathrm{UC}}^{\mathrm{tol,max}}) = (0.26, 0.191)$.

Depending on the security level, IEC 62443-3-3 provides countermeasures for each foundational requirement. However, we argue, that most of them are not directly applicable to our SUC, since they have not been designed for automotive challenges. That is, *real-time behavior*, *resource-constrained* control units, and a high *reliability*. For example, a security level SL-2 of the foundational requirement *Identification and Authentification Control* demands for public key infrastructure certificates. This, however, is hardly applicable to in-vehicle communication, because public key certificates lead to unacceptable overhead, as they come along with long certification chains and demanding cryptographic operations. As a consequence, we looked for alternative, more lightweight, and resource-saving solutions. In particular, the work of El-Rewini et al. [9] inspired us, as they provide an extensive survey on automotive security frameworks. As a result, we obtain a detailed list of security mitigation techniques for each zone, that protect against the 63 identified threats. They can be summarized as follows:

Authenticated In-Vehicle Communication: A core prerequisite of safety-critical in-vehicle conduits and zones (Z_A, Z_E, C_A, C_B) is the ability to verify the authenticity of data streams. In this way, the injection of fake commands becomes difficult. A promising alternative technique are implicit certificates in combination with distinct physical memory characteristics [18], avoiding potentially long and resource-consuming certification chains. Related work [9] illustrates additional solutions for the wide variety of in-vehicle communication protocols.

Integrity of In-Vehicle Control Units: Since both the SUC and contemporary road vehicles possess an increasingly large number of external interfaces, and the ability to remotely update control units, adversaries, residing inside the ECUs, must be prevented. In our case, we propose to treat the brainstem as a trust anchor, that verifies the integrity of all control units before the vehicle start. For this purpose, we suggest *Remote Attestation* (RA), a technique, allowing to prove the integrity of a device to a third party. Kohnhäuser et al. [13] show how to use RA in the automotive domain.

Malicious Behavior Detection: During the security analysis, high-risk threats on safety-critical assets were associated with the foundational requirement *Timely Response to Events* (TRE). Specifically, adversaries connecting to the in-vehicle bus may be able to flood the in-vehicle network (DoS attack) and thus to cause failures. We find an anomaly-based intrusion detection system [8] for safety-critical in-vehicle traffic (i.e., conduits C_A, C_B) a suitable compensating countermeasure. Also, inter-vehicle communication (i.e., zone C_C) is prone to DoS attacks, for which, however, many mitigation frameworks have been presented [23].

Data Separation: The initial design of the SUC provides a single in-vehicle bus for all data flows. Consequently, user input and potentially safety-critical data streams are mixed, which may lead to the delayed transmission of safety-critical demands. As our risk analysis revealed threats affecting the foundational requirement *Restricted Data Flow* for in-vehicle traffic, the presented vehicular architecture requires means to separate data flows. Both physical and virtual data separation achieve this goal. For our SUC, we configure VLAN priority levels for the Ethernet-based in-vehicle network and use the arbitration logic of the CAN bus. The FlexRay network inherently realizes a TDMA-based schedule, allowing to reserve dedicated time slots for critical data.

Access Control: An integral part of the SUC is the control room, that enables human remote control in case of emergency situations. In order to distinguish between legitimate and illegitimate remote control, an access control system is necessary at the vehicle's edge. This is highlighted by the risk analysis, that exposes the importance of user authentication, in particular when it comes to the communication between the vehicle and its exterior. Since the router is the only gateway to the external world, access control mechanisms have to be implemented in the corresponding zone (Z_A). This includes a strict deny-by-default policy and mutual identity checks.

5 Discussion

Our analysis particularly highlights the demand for system integrity and timely responses, since a significant number of threats are mapped on the corresponding foundational requirements. Both software and communication integrity are key factors for a safe driving state. This evidence coincides with related work [17], that considers the injection of fake messages as one of the severest attacks on modern vehicles.

Although our analysis yields effective means to protect against the identified threats, we lack techniques to handle actual security incidents during vehicle operation. We need means to assess them in real-time and to adopt appropriate (safety) measures. We plan to address this problem in future work. Regarding our security requirement analysis, we want to stress the following points:

Quality of Assessments: For our consensus-based risk analysis, we presented a scoring scheme, using Simple Additive Weighting (SAW) as a decision support system. In order to obtain reasonable and consistent assessments, and to ensure a broad insight into the SUC, we engaged an expert committee, consisting of eight computer scientists and mathematicians from the *Securing Engineering Lab*[1] of the *Technische Univeristät Darmstadt*. As a first step, the experts have been thoroughly introduced to the novel vehicular architecture in a Q&A session. Afterwards, we established the presented set of evaluation criteria based on related work and empirical values. As both the threat identification process and all assessments have been jointly accomplished by the expert committee, we argue to properly address subjectivity and vagueness. However, we admit, that a higher committee heterogeneity in terms of educational background may yield even better results. Regarding the proposed scoring scheme, we currently assign a fixed probabilistic weight to each evaluation criterion. We consider the Fuzzy Analytic Hierarchy Process (FAHP) [7] an effective alternative to determine preference weight, but leave this for future work.

Safety and Security Co-Engineering: We pursued the question of what changes are necessary for a safety-aware security risk analysis in the automotive domain. As safety and security demands may contradict, the possibility of prioritization is crucial. We find the mapping of risks onto zones and foundational requirements a promising technique, because it allows fine-grained solutions for large-scale systems. The partition of the SUC into zones and conduits should take safety criteria into consideration. In addition, we suggest the following adaptions:

---

[1] http://www.seceng.de.

- So far, the seven foundational requirements are purely security-related. We suggest extending them with safety requirements such as *reliability*, *redundancy*, and *real-time behavior*. By doing so, the unmitigated risk of a threat or of a hazardous situation would take both safety and security dimensions into account. The presented vector-driven approach allows prioritization, by pointing out which foundational requirement is affected most by a set of threats. Appropriate countermeasures can be deduced in that way.
- The countermeasures listed in IEC 62443-3-3 need to be adjusted for the automotive domain. Instead of user-oriented, potentially computationally heavy systems (e.g., PKI, multi-factor authentication, ...), lightweight and resource-saving techniques (e.g., implicit certification, hardware-based security, ...) are worthwhile. There has been extensive work on automotive security with numerous frameworks, covering many automotive challenges [8,9,14,23], that should be included in a future standard.
- A common set of evaluation criteria and a consistent scoring scheme for automotive systems is desirable, in order to make analysis results comparable. We presented a scheme, that incorporates both security and safety criteria for risk assessment.

5.1 Comparison to ISO/SAE DIS 21434

The high-level risk analysis and the subsequent partition into zones and conduits allow for efficient identification of relevant assets. Besides, the analysis process becomes more scalable, since uncritical assets are excluded from further steps. The use of foundational requirements as a reference point enables the clear establishment of mitigation techniques.

While the detailed risk analysis of IEC 62443-3-2 begins with the identification of threats, the novel ISO/SAE DIS 21434 starts from potential damage scenarios and traces them back to attack paths. More precisely, the risk assessment methods are comprised of seven steps (I-VII). Initially, damage scenarios are identified, which may occur through compromised assets (I). A damage scenario is triggered by a set of adverse actions, a so-called threat scenario, which are enumerated in (II). The impact of each damage scenario is assessed according to four core categories of consequences, *Safety*, *Financial*, *Operational*, and *Privacy* (III). Subsequently, each threat scenario is decomposed into attack paths in a top-down or bottom-up approach (IV). The feasibility of each path is assessed according to a pre-defined scale (V), resulting in a risk value (VI) for each threat scenario, which also incorporates the impact of the damage scenario. Finally, risk reduction methods shall be realized (VII). In case the risk for a threat scenario has to be reduced, a Cybersecurity Assurance Level (CAL) reveals requirements for the affected item.

At first glance, the risk analysis process of ISO/SAE DIS 21434 and IEC 62443 have little in common. On closer inspection, however, both standards do share similar concepts. The CAL is similar to the SL-T value, which is only determined if the risk is too large. Instead of our iterative threat identification process and conduits, attack paths cover propagating effects of adverse actions. While the idea of decomposing threat scenarios into attack paths is the most promising feature of ISO/SAE 21434, our work reveals requirements that are not yet met by ISO/SAE 21434. Unlike IEC 62443, the novel automotive standard prescribes assessment criteria and parameters. However, it insists on neither underlying cybersecurity requirements nor mitigation techniques, contrary to IEC 62443. For the sake of a common minimum security perception, suggestions of countermeasures for specific CALs would be helpful, in particular, because road vehicles are generally subjected to the same safety and legal requirements. Also, consistent scoring schemes and a dedicated process to identify relevant critical assets of a potentially complex architecture would be desirable.

6 Conclusion

In this work, we presented a consensus-based implementation of the generic IEC 62443 cybersecurity standard for a novel vehicular architecture. In particular, we identified risk evaluation criteria and developed an additive scoring scheme to assess automotive risks. Furthermore, we introduced a hierarchical threat model for a collaborative threat identification process. We used a cascading parameter approach to express risks as zone-based vectors, yielding fine-grained security levels, that express security requirements. We conclude that especially data and software integrity, the separation of safety-critical commands, and the ability to detect anomalies are crucial for automated vehicles. Based on our lessons learned, we find as essential for a future standard the systematic partition of a potentially complex vehicular architecture into relevant assets, the computation of security levels with regard to cybersecurity reference goals, the treatment of transitive adverse actions, and the suggestion of mitigation techniques. We also make suggestions on how to incorporate safety requirements into a future standard. In particular, a safety-aware automotive security standard should use a redefined set of foundational requirements, including safety objectives such as reliability, redundancy, and real-time behavior. Although IEC 62443 has been originally designed for IACS, we promote its applicability to the automotive domain in combination with the adaptions suggested in this work.

Acknowledgement. This work has been accomplished within the project "UNICARagil" (FKZ 16EMO0392). We acknowledge the financial support for the project by the Federal Ministry of Education and Research of Germany (BMBF). We also thank the *Security Engineering Group* for their support in assessing, scoring, and ranking security parameters.

References

1. ISO 26262 Road vehicles - Functional Safety. Standard, International Organization for Standardization (2011)
2. Healing vulnerabilities to enhance software security and safety (HEAVENS) project (2016). https://research.chalmers.se/en/project/5809. Accessed 25 Feb 2020

3. SAE J3061 - Cybersecurity Guidebook for Cyber-Physical Vehicle Systems. Standard, Society of Automotive Engineers (2016)
4. ISA-62443 Security for Industrial Automation and Control Systems. Standard, International Society of Automaton (2017)
5. ISO/SAE DIS 21434:2020(E): Road vehicles - cybersecurity engineering (2020)
6. Checkoway, S., et al.: Comprehensive experimental analyses of automotive attack surfaces. In: USENIX Security Symposium, vol. 4, pp. 447–462 (2011)
7. Chen, V.Y., et al.: Fuzzy mcdm approach for selecting the best environment-watershed plan. Appl. Soft Comput. **11**(1), 265–275 (2011)
8. Cho, K.T., Shin, K.G.: Fingerprinting electronic control units for vehicle intrusion detection. In: 25th USENIX Security Symposium, pp. 911–927 (2016)
9. El-Rewini, Z., et al.: Cybersecurity challenges in vehicular communications. Veh. Commun., 100214 (2019)
10. Henniger, O., et al.: Securing vehicular on-board IT systems: the Evita project. In: VDI/VW Automotive Security Conference, p. 41 (2009)
11. Kampmann, A., et al.: A dynamic service-oriented software architecture for highly automated vehicles. In: 2019 ITSC, pp. 2101–2108. IEEE (2019)
12. Keilhoff, D., et al.: UNICARagil – new architectures for disruptive vehicle concepts. 19. Internationales Stuttgarter Symposium. P, pp. 830–842. Springer, Wiesbaden (2019). https://doi.org/10.1007/978-3-658-25939-6_65
13. Kohnhäuser, F., et al.: Ensuring the safe and secure operation of electronic control units in road vehicles. In: 2019 IEEE Security and Privacy Workshops (SPW)
14. Mejri, M., et al.: Survey on VANET security challenges and possible cryptographic solutions. Veh. Commun. **1**(2), 53–66 (2014)
15. Nie, S., Liu, L., Du, Y.: Free-fall: Hacking tesla from wireless to CAN bus, pp. 1–16. Briefing, Black Hat USA (2017)
16. Ben Othmane, L., et al.: Incorporating attacker capabilities in risk estimation and mitigation. Comput. Secur. **51**, 41–61 (2015)
17. Petit, J., Shladover, S.E.: Potential cyberattacks on automated vehicles. IEEE Trans. Intell. Transp. Syst. **16**(2), 546–556 (2014)
18. Püllen, D., et al.: Using implicit certification to efficiently establish authenticated group keys for in-vehicle networks. In: 2019 IEEE VNC, pp. 1–8 (2019)
19. Putra, D.W.T., Punggara, A.A.: Comparison analysis of Simple Additive Weighting (SAW) and weigthed product (WP) in decision support systems, p. 01003 (2018)
20. Schmittner, C., Ma, Z., Reyes, C., Dillinger, O., Puschner, P.: Using SAE J3061 for automotive security requirement engineering. In: Skavhaug, A., Guiochet, J., Schoitsch, E., Bitsch, F. (eds.) SAFECOMP 2016. LNCS, vol. 9923, pp. 157–170. Springer, Cham (2016). https://doi.org/10.1007/978-3-319-45480-1_13
21. Shevchenko, N., Chick, T.A., O'Riordan, P., Scanlon, T.P., Woody, C.: Threat modeling: a summary of available methods, July 2018
22. U.S. DoT: Revised departmental guidance 2016: Treatment of the value of preventing fatalities and injuries in preparing economic analyses (2016)
23. Verma, K., et al.: Prevention of DoS attacks in VANET. Wireless Pers. Commun. **73**(1), 95–126 (2013)
24. Woopen, T., et al.: UNICARagil-disruptive modular architectures for agile, automated vehicle concepts. Aachener Kolloquium GbR (2018)
25. Yan, C., Xu, W., Liu, J.: Can you trust autonomous vehicles: Contactless attacks against sensors of self-driving vehicle. DEF CON **24** (2016)

Threat Analysis Framework for Safety Architectures in SCDL

Kenji Taguchi[1]([✉])(iD), Ryo Kurachi[2](iD), Kiyoshi Sasaki[3], Nobuhiko Nakamura[4],
Kazuki Tomonaga[5], and Shuhei Yamashita[6]

[1] CAV Technologies, Kyoto, Japan
`kenji.taguchi@cav-tech.co.jp`
[2] Nagoya University, Nagoya, Japan
`kurachi@nces.i.nagoya-u.ac.jp`
[3] Marelli Corporation, Saitama, Japan
`kiyoshi.sasaki@marelli.com`
[4] Vector Japan Co., Ltd., Tokyo, Japan
`nobuhiko.nakamura@vector.com`
[5] Mitsubishi Electric, Himeji, Japan
`Tomonaga.Kazuki@ea.MitsubishiElectric.co.jp`
[6] DVN GL, Yokohama, Japan
`shuhei.yamashita@dnv.co.jp`

Abstract. Cybersecurity threats have become a reality for safety critical systems such as automobiles, railways and avionics witnessing cybersecurity incidents and research reports from white hackers. Threat analysis plays an important role to identify potential threats in early stages of the system development and it is a common understanding that the threat analysis for safety critical systems need to assess an effect caused by threats against safety. In this paper, we propose a threat analysis framework on safety concepts required by ISO 26262 in an architecture description language SCDL (Safety Concept Description Language) specifically designed for safety concepts modeling in ISO 26262 and demonstrate the effectiveness of our framework on a case study. Our research result shows the potential usage of SCDL for threat analysis and effect analysis between functional safety and cybersecurity.

Keywords: SCDL · Safety architecture · ISO 26262 · Security · Threat analysis

1 Introduction

Cybersecurity threats have become a reality for safety critical systems such as automobiles, railways and avionics, witnessing cybersecurity incidents and research reports from white hackers. Although threat analysis has already been practiced in various industrial domains in the past, it is now a common understanding that the threat analysis for safety critical systems needs to assess an effect caused by threats against safety. This makes us doubt whether the threat

© Springer Nature Switzerland AG 2020
A. Casimiro et al. (Eds.): SAFECOMP 2020, LNCS 12234, pp. 341–354, 2020.
https://doi.org/10.1007/978-3-030-54549-9_23

analysis methods used in the IT (Information Technology) are readily applicable for safety critical systems. An engineering discipline that considers the interaction between safety and security is called safety and security co-engineering [1], and a part of it is an attempt to combine safety analysis and threat analysis [2]. However, we have not found any practical and effective threat analysis methods which fully utilize the work-products produced from functional safety activities in ISO 26262 [3] yet. Particularly we are deeply concerned with how to carry out threat analysis with the safety concept in ISO 26262, since it is the first work product to be produced at the concept phase, an earliest phase in ISO 26262. The safety concept is a *specification of the functional safety requirements, with associated information, their allocation to elements within the architecture, and their interaction necessary to achieve the safety goals.* Unfortunately how to produce a safety concept in a certain formalism/modeling language is not explicitly stated in ISO 26262. In order to address this issue, one of the authors of this paper designed an architecture description language (ADL) called "Safety Concept Description Language (SCDL)" [4], which has been widely used for developing safety architectures in automotive industry in Japan. In this paper we propose a threat analysis framework for SCDL which fully utilizes a safety concept modelled in SCDL. This framework enables to show the followings:

+ Safety goal violations due to security attacks
+ Protection by safety mechanisms against security attacks

We show how safety goal violation can be caused by cybersecurity threats and how safety architecture alone can prevent safety goals against them. These are of great concerns for safety engineers and an effective analysis on these at early stages help develop safe and secure automotive architecture. It might not be certain why the latter is crucial at the first sight, so we quote a famous hacking case study on Jeep by C. Miller and C. Valasek in [5]. In their case study, in order to take over control of the car, they place an Electronic Control Unit (ECU) under the diagnostic mode and inject control messages instead of that ECU. However the safety mechanism prevents putting an ECU under the diagnostic mode while the car is at high speed. In fact, the same phenomenon happened when Tencent attacked Tesla Model S in [6]. The safety aspect of these case studies are largely ignored from the security experts, but this is the very issue of which safety engineers have a great concern.

The paper is organized as follows: The next section explains the SCDL language and threat analysis. The case study is explained in the Sect. 3 and related work is presented in the Sect. 4. Finally we conclude the paper in the Sect. 5.

2   Background

In this section, all necessary background knowledge for this paper is explained.

2.1   SCDL

The main purpose of the SCDL (Safety Concept Description Language) is to provide a full support for analysis and design of safety architectures that include safety mechanisms in vehicle development in order to develop the safety concept more easily than required by ISO 26262. The language specification of SCDL has been developed by SCN-SG (Safety Concept Notation Study Group) [7] led by Yamashita, one of the authors of this paper and the language specification is open to the public and currently three tools are available. In this section we will explain the syntax of SCDL for readers to understand the case study modelled in SCDL.

Table 1. Definition of symbol for SCDL.

Symbol	Description
<<FSR>> D(D) FSR-2-1 Command Checking / <<NFSR>> D NFSR-1 Independence Requirement 1	A requirement is expressed in a rectangle and with its assigned "ASIL" presented in a small rectangle located at the upper right corner of the rectangle. In this rectangle, the type of requirement is expressed at the top (FSR for Functional Safety Requirements, NSFR for Non-Functional Safety Requirements and FR for Functional Requirements), the Requirement ID of the requirement at the middle left, and the name of the requirement at the bottom
ITEM-1 Item D	An Item and element is expressed in a rectangle and assigned "ASIL" is presented in a small rectangle located at the upper right corner of the rectangle
ReqG-1	Balloon type notation can be used for the requirement group using an ellipsoid and connecting lines. Requirements group includes "SM (Safety Mechanism)" and "MF (Main Functionality)". The latter is now called "IF (Intended Functionality)"
EL-6 Locator ECU QM / <<FR>> QM FR-5 Location Data Acquision	Requirement rectangle can be located within an element rectangle
I-1	"Interaction" between two requirements is expressed with a one direction arrow
SI-2	"System boundary interaction" is expressed with a block type arrow which stands for some interaction outside of the system
Pair-1	Pairing between requirement groups is illustrated with a bidirectional arrow
EL-2 ElementB / I-1 FR-2 - ReqB	"Interface" can be used to define interfaces which appears on the crossing point of inter-requirement interaction line and element boundary line, and is expressed with a square

The SCDL provides symbols for requirements, requirement group, item and elements, and relations between them such as interactions, system boundary interactions and requirements group pairing. The SCDL allows an allocation of a requirement to an element, which is a faithful interpretation of functional safety standards in general. For instance, ISO 26262 states that *The functional safety requirements shall be allocated to the elements of the system architectural design.* An item and an element are specific terms in ISO 26262 which roughly mean system and system component respectively. The graphical representation of the symbols and their definitions are shown in Table 1.

2.2 Safety Activities in ISO 26262

According to a Functional Safety Concept (FSC) in ISO 26262, which specifies safety requirements and elements to achieve safety goals, and safety architecture is the substantial work product derived from safety activities in the concept phase. Figure 1 depicts safety activities related to produce a FSC. The deliverable of "3-7.4.2 Derivation of functional safety requirements" is in fact the safety architecture, which will be specified in SCDL. For more detailed explanation, please refer to ISO 26262-3:2018 [3].

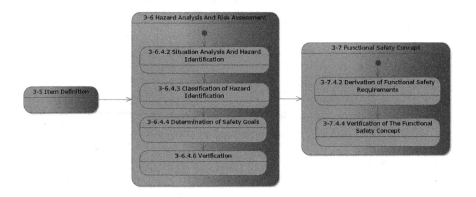

Fig. 1. Activities for deriving FSC.

2.3 Criteria on Threat Analysis

There are several threat analysis methods proposed by several authors. We consider the following as substantial criteria for threat analysis. That is, a threat analysis method should provide means to analyze or model at least some of these criteria.

1. Where does an attack come from
2. What should be protected from an attack
3. What boundary should be protected from an attack
4. How does an attack reach the target
5. What kind of attacks are possible
6. How may attacks are necessary

The first criterion "Where does an attack come from" is to analyze the "Attack Surface", which is a potential entry point for an attack where an unauthorized user (i.e., attacker) can intrude. The second criterion "What should be protected from an attack" is to analyze the "Asset" which is a part of the system to be targeted by an attacker. We classify assets into two kinds, one is "Information Asset" for information/data and "Functional Assets" for functionality of the system. The third criterion "What boundary should be protected from an attack" is to analyze the "Trust Boundary", which specifies the area of protection from attacks in the entire system architecture. The fourth criterion "How does an attack reach the target" is to analyze the "Attack Path" which begins with an attack surface up until reaching the assets to be protected. This is sometimes called "multi-stage attack". The fifth criterion "What types of attack are possible" is an identification method to analyze potential attacks on attack surfaces and assets. The final criterion "How many attacks are necessary" is a security version of multiple faults. Sometimes just a single attack on an attack surface or an asset is not be enough to achieve an attacker's goal and multiple attacks on multiple attack surfaces and/or assets are necessary in some cases. This is different from the attack path already explained, since an attack path is a continuation of a single attack, which can be divided into stages (e.g., some system component).

Our interpretation of those criteria in SCDL is as follows:

1. Attack surface
   - Interactions and system boundary interactions
2. Assets
   - Requirements for functional assets and Interactions and system boundary interactions for information assets
3. Trust boundary
   - Elements
4. Attack path
   - Any paths consisting of requirements and interactions.
5. Attack identification
   - Any attack identification methods such as STRIDE.
6. Multiple attacks
   - A combination of attacks on attack surfaces and/or assets which causes a safety goal violation.

SCDL does not provide any model elements for representation of any data or information or any holder for them. So the reasonable interpretation of information asset is interaction which represents passing data/information between elements or sending them from outside of the system.

2.4   Threat Analysis Process

The threat analysis process we use in this paper is shown in Fig. 2.

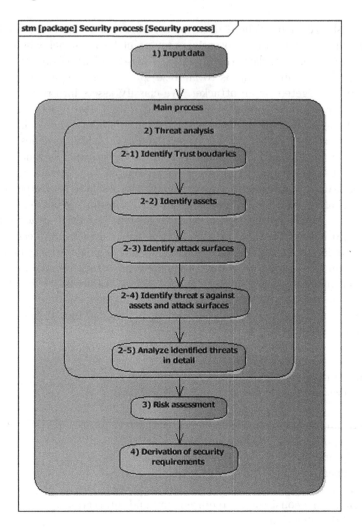

Fig. 2. The process of threat analysis to safety architecture.

It starts with 1) Input data, which includes a FSC specified in SCDL and relevant system information. We adopt the process that threat analysis process follows safety activities in ISO 26262. It then goes on to 2) Threat analysis.

2–1) Identify the trust boundary in a FSC in the given SCDL model.
2–2) Identify functional assets (requirements) and information assets (interaction and system boundary interactions between elements).
2–3) Identify attack surfaces (interactions between elements or boundary interactions)
2–4) Identify threats against assets and attack surfaces using some guide-word such as STRIDE.

2–5) Analyze identified threats in detail using methods, e.g., attack trees [8].

The process depicts further activities such as risk assessment of identified attacks and derivation of security requirements. But this paper only deals with 1) up to 2–4). After completing 2–4), we will assess whether identified attack(s) would violate safety goals.

3   Case Study and Analysis Results

In this section, we will explain our case study and show our results on threat analysis based on our proposed framework explained in the previous section.

3.1   Case Study

Figure 3 shows our case study on the Parking Assist System, in which the safety architecture in FSC modelled in SCDL is depicted. An intended safety goal for this case study is "Does not generate unintended control values against user intention" and ASIL level "D" is allocated to that safety goal, which is not depicted in the model. This system automatically parks a vehicle based on "Map data", "Positioning Information", and "Sensor Input" following "User Operation" which let the "Smartphone" (EL-1) generate "GO/NOGO" command. As safety measures, two safety mechanisms are implemented on the vehicle. One is "Command Checking" (FSR-2-1), which covers malfunctions of the "Command Generation" (FR-1) and "Command Reception" (FSR-2). The other is "Arbitration" (FSR-3-1) and "Monitor" (FSR-3-2), which cover malfunction of "Control Value Generation" (FSR-3). The safety goal is a requirement that the vehicle (EL-2) must achieve, therefore there is no safety mechanism on the smartphone.

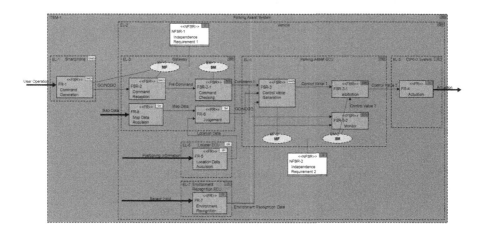

Fig. 3. Parking assist system.

3.2   Threat Analysis Framework

The first step for threat analysis is to identify the trust boundary. In this case
study, the whole vehicle (EL-2) is identified as the trust boundary, which secures
the safety measures to achieve the safety goal. This is depicted as a dashed yellow
line in Fig. 4.

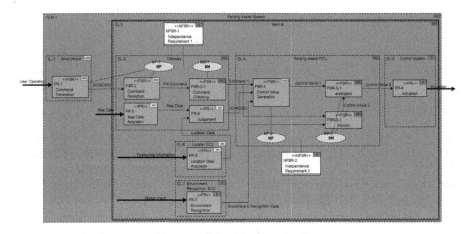

Fig. 4. Trust boundary. (Color figure online)

We then identify assets, which are classified as functional assets (Table 2)
and as information assets (Table 3) respectively.

Table 2. Functional assets.

ID	Requirement	Classification
FR-1	Command Generation	FSR
FSR-2	Command Reception	FSR
FSR-2-1	Command Checking	FSR
FSR-3	Control Value Generation	FSR
FSR-3-1	Arbitration	FSR
FSR-3-2	Monitor	FSR
FR-4	Actuation	FR
FR-5	Location Data Acquisition	FR
FR-6	Judgement	FR
FR-7	Environment Recognition	FR
FR-8	Map Data Acquisition	FR

Table 3. Information asset.

Information asset	Position
User Operation	External
GO/NOGO	External
Map Data	External
Map Data, from FR-8	–
Pre Command	–
Command 1	–
Control Value 1, 2, 3	–
Location Data	–
Positioning Information	External
Sensor Input	External
GO/NOGO, from FR-6	–
Environment Recognition Data	–
Actuation	External

Potential attack surfaces will be identified taking all interactions into account summarized in Table 4. An effective threat analysis for interactions in principle would require technical information such as communication protocol/media (e.g., Bluetooth, CAN) on them, but this kind of detailed technical information is basically not available at the concept level. We regard system boundary interactions and interactions in Fig. 4 as attack surfaces and carry out threat analysis on them.

Table 4. Identified attack surfaces.

Name	Kind
GO/NOGO	Interaction
Map Data	System boundary interaction
Positioning Information	System boundary interaction
Sensor input	System boundary interaction

STRIDE is a collection of capital letters extracted from typical threats, i.e., Spoofing, Tampering, Repudiation, Information Disclosure, Denial of Service and Elevation of Privilege and adopted in SDL (Secure Development Lifecycle) which is used to identify potential threats on trust boundary [19]. We will adopt STRIDE for identifying threats on system boundary interactions and assets.

The following Table 5 shows the analysis result for interactions:

Table 5. Application of STRIDE.

Interaction	Type of Interaction	S	T	R	I	D	E
User operation	System boundary interaction	✓	✓		✓	✓	
GO/NOGO	Interaction	✓	✓		✓	✓	
Map data	System boundary interaction	✓	✓		✓	✓	
Positioning Information	System boundary interaction	✓	✓		✓	✓	
Sensor Input	System boundary interaction	✓	✓		✓	✓	

This table reads like "Spoof the map data", "Tamper the map data", "Eavesdrop the map data", "Disrupt the transmission of the map data" The Table 6 shows analysis results applying STRIDE against assets:

For instance, **T**ampering "Command checking" is to change its functionality to something else. **D**enial of service to "Command checking" is to disrupt its function, e.g., to delay its function. **E** for "Command checking" is to override this function.

The aim of attack is to damage the vehicle by "Parking a vehicle at an inappropriate place". For the sake of brevity, we only take one example analysis and explain it step by step. Let's take a case of "Spoofing User Operation". The result of this attack is an unintended issue of the "GO" command which will be accepted by the Command Reception" (FSR-2). However, whether the place is not appropriate for parking can be judged by location information obtained by "Map Data" and "Location Data" which will be used by the "Judgement" (FR-6) requirement. This would prevent this attack.

Now we will consider multiple attacks which include the above attack and "Tampering Map Data". We assume here that the map data is tampered with to include some obstacles, which would damages the car. In this case, self location information is not helpful to prevent this attack and "GO" command is eventually issued from "Judgement" (FR-6), which will be received by "Control Value Generation" (FSR-3). FSR-3 also receives "Environment Recognition Data" from "Environment Recognition" (FR-7) which is originally from "Sensor Input". This "Environment Recognition" detects the surrounding environment of the vehicle and might find some obstacles. This would prevent this multiple attacks.

Table 6. Application of STRIDE against assets.

(Functional) Asset	S	T	R	I	D	E
Command Checking		✓			✓	✓
Control value generation		✓			✓	✓
Arbitration		✓			✓	✓
Monitor		✓			✓	✓

Finally we will consider multiple attacks which include the above attack plus "Spoofing Sensor Input". The typical example of spoofing sensor input is adversarial attacks, which is widely studied nowadays in relation to machine learning techniques for image recognition. In this case, unintended "Control Value 1" is generated by "Control Value Generation" (FSR-3) and this violates the safety goal "Does not generate unintended control values against user intention". Unfortunately the safety mechanism "FSR-3-1" and "FSR-3-2" would not help for FSR-3, since the same spoofed data are processed in both requirements.

This analysis shows how we can find potential combination of attacks and how those attacks would violate safety goals. In order to do this, we assess possible effects on requirements by tracing through interactions from attack surfaces until we could reach any possible safety goal violation.

3.3   Discussion

As was demonstrated by the case study in the previous section, we have shown that the threat analysis framework we propose for the safety architecture required by ISO 26262 is effective to identify potential threats to the safety architecture and to check the safety goal violation.

We successfully mapped six attack analysis criteria to our framework and how multiple attacks on multiple attack surfaces would result in the safety goal violation. We could also show that some attacks would be prevented by safety architecture to some extent.

Please notice that this analysis framework is limited to safety architecture modeled in SCDL so that non safety threats will be overlooked by this framework.

4   Related Work

We will compare our work with security extensions of Architecture Description Language (ADL) and some other graphical modeling notations similar to SCDL. There exist a number of ADLs, but we only focus on ADL related to automotive systems, that is, EAST-ADL [9], AADL (Architecture Analysis and Design Language) [10] and a security extension of SysML [16].

EAST-ADL was developed under the project ITEA EAST-EEA and further extended to integrate AUTOSAR [18]. The biggest difference between SCDL and EAST-ADL is that in SCDL we can allocate requirements to the element, ASIL is allocated to requirements and items/elements, and requirements can be grouped under some particular groups such as safety mechanism.

The security extension of EAST-ADL called SAM (Security Abstraction Model) [15] proposes a new meta-model for security properties for EAST-ADL. SAM does not provide specific threat analysis technique for safety architecture model in EAST-ADL and the work does not state any relation between safety and security interactions such as safety goal violation by potential attacks. We believe that our framework could be applied to EAST-ADL and could do similar analysis on FSC in EAST-ADL.

AADL is developed by SAE and CMU/SEI and has been extended to include error models as the Error Mode Annex [11] and security models as the Security Annex [12]. Security architectures modeled in AADL is based on MILS [13] and was applied to avionics. Later AADL is enhanced to target IoT (Internet of Things). AADL Security Annex is entirely based on a different idea of security and there is no work on AADL, which focuses on safety and security interactions.

SysML stems from UML (Unified Modeling Language) to support the systems engineering development and its profile is defined by UML metamodel. Security extensions of UML were proposed by several researchers such as misuse cases and UMLsec [14]. One notable security extension of SysML is cp/TARA (common platform for Threat Analysis and Risk Assessment) [17] by one of the authors of this paper. The cp/TARA extends block definition diagrams and requirements diagrams to include security features (e.g., assets and attack surfaces, various kinds of security requirements compliant to J3061 [20]) to support threat analysis on architectural elements and refinement of security requirements. The cp/TARA is in fact the most similar approach to our framework, but it only provides threat analysis to system architecture and does not deal with any safety and security interactions.

The above comparison shows that our threat analysis framework helps analyze not only potential threats against the safety architecture but also safety goal violation to assess any effects of security against safety, which are not dealt with in related work.

5   Conclusion

In this paper, we presented a threat analysis framework which fully utilizes the safety concept modelled in SCDL, an architecture description language specifically designed for modeling safety concepts specified in ISO 26262. We demonstrated the security analysis method provided by the framework on a case study and showed that it is effective in threat analysis as well as assessment of violation of safety by security threats. This result also showed that SCDL can be used for threat analysis at the concept phase in ISO 26262.

This paper is our preliminary results on our efforts of investigating interactions between functional safety and cybersecurity for automotive systems and we think the followings are our future work:

Feedback loop to safety: We have adopted a process in which the safety activities in the concept phase in ISO 26262 come first, then moves on to threat analysis. We need to establish how a feedback cycle could be achieved going backward to safety activities and a method to assess impact on them.

Process Integration: There would be several ways to integrate functional safety process with cybersecurity process (e.g., [21]). We would like to investigate whether other types of integration could be possible and see how our framework can be applied.

Level of abstraction in ISO 26262: SCDL is primarily designed for the concept phase, but currently it is extended to deal with other phases such as the system level. The concept phase which is the most abstract in terms of model specification does not deal with physical interfaces/communication media. However the next phase is the system level, which in fact deals with physical interfaces/communication media (e.g., CAN, Bluetooth). We are planning to extend our framework for the system level and see how the abstract threat model obtained in the concept phase could be enhances to accommodate the level of abstraction at the system level.

Acknowledgements. We would like to thank all the members of the SCDL Security SWG, particularly Mr. Toshio Muramastu and Fumiaki Kohno for the discussions on the issues addressed in this paper, and Gaio Technology for organizing the SWG and assisting the model construction.

References

1. Schmittner, C., Ma, Z., Gruber, T., Schoitsch, E.: Safety and security co-engineering of connected, intelligent, and automated vehicles. ERCIM News **109** (2017)
2. Schmittner, C., Ma, Z., Smith, P.: FMVEA for safety and security analysis of intelligent and cooperative vehicles. In: SAFECOMP Workshops, pp. 282–288 (2014)
3. International Organization for Standardization: ISO 26262:2018 Road Vehicles - Functional Safety (2018)
4. Safety Concept Notation Study Group: SCDL Specification Version 1.4 (2018)
5. Miller, C., Valasek, C.: Remote Exploitation of an Unaltered Passenger Vehicle (2015)
6. Nie, S., Liu, L., Du, Y.: Free-fall: hacking tesla from wireless to CAN bus. In: Black Hat (2016)
7. SCN-SG: https://ssl.scn-sg.com/main/
8. Schneier, B.: Attack trees. Dr. Dobb's J. **24**(12), 21–29 (1999)
9. EAST-ADL Domain Model Specification, Version V2.1.12 (2013)
10. Feiler, P.H., Gluch, D.P.: Model-Based Engineering with AADL: An Introduction to the SAE Architecture Analysis & Design Language. Addison-Wesley, Boston (2013)
11. Delange, J., Feiler, P., Gluch, D.P., Hudak, J.: AADL Fault Modeling and Analysis Within an ARP4761 Safety Assessment, CMU/SEI-2014-TR-020 (2014)
12. Ellison, R., Householder, A., Hudak, J., Kazman, R., Woody, C.: Extending AADL for Security Design Assurance of Cyber-Physical Systems, CMU/SEI-2015-TR-014 (2015)
13. Boettcher, C., DeLong, R., Rushby, J., Sifre, W.: The MILS component integration approach to secure information sharing. In: Proceedings of Digital Avionics Systems Conference (DACS) (2008)
14. Jürjens, J.: Secure Systems Development with UML. Springer, Heidelberg (2005). https://doi.org/10.1007/b137706
15. Zoppelt, M., Tavakoli Kolagari, R.: SAM: a security abstraction model for automotive software systems. In: Hamid, B., Gallina, B., Shabtai, A., Elovici, Y., Garcia-Alfaro, J. (eds.) CSITS/ISSA -2018. LNCS, vol. 11552, pp. 59–74. Springer, Cham (2019). https://doi.org/10.1007/978-3-030-16874-2_5

16. Friendenthal, S., Moore, A., Steiner, R.: A Practical Guide to SysML, 3rd edn. Elsevier, Amsterdam (2015)
17. Taguchi, K.: Mission Possible - Advanced Threat Analysis Tool for All, Autosec China (2019)
18. AUTOSAR: https://www.autosar.org/standards/
19. Shostack, A.: Threat Modeling: Designing for Security. Wiley, Hoboken (2014)
20. SAE International: Cybersecurity Guidebook for Cyber-Physical Vehicle Systems (2016)
21. Taguchi, K., Souma, D., Nishihara, H.: Safe & sec case patterns. In: Koornneef, F., van Gulijk, C. (eds.) SAFECOMP 2015. LNCS, vol. 9338, pp. 27–37. Springer, Cham (2015). https://doi.org/10.1007/978-3-319-24249-1_3

Cyber-Physical Systems Security

Efficient Load-Time Diversity for an Embedded Real-Time Operating System

Joachim Fellmuth[✉], Julian Hartmer, Hanno Skowronek, and Sabine Glesner

Software and Embedded Systems Engineering, Technische Universität Berlin,
Berlin, Germany
{joachim.fellmuth,sabine.glesner}@tu-berlin.de
{hartmer,h.skowronek}@campus.tu-berlin.de

Abstract. Cyber-physical systems (CPS) are threatened by cyber attacks just as any computing system. Even worse, due to them being embedded into the physical world, consequences can be catastrophic. The widespread use of unsafe languages and limited operating system protections makes code-reuse attacks particularly dangerous to smaller CPS. Existing effective countermeasures are either not applicable because resources are limited, or they introduce an unacceptable overhead. In this work, we propose a fine-grained load-time software diversity approach that is enabled by compile-time preparations. Its linear-time loading algorithm makes it feasible for resource-constrained CPS. We demonstrate our approach by fully diversifying an application including the real-time operating system FreeRTOS on an ARM real-time microcontroller. Our performance evaluation using the TACLe benchmark suite shows that the worst-case execution time overhead is acceptable.

Keywords: Security · Real-time · FreeRTOS · CPS · WCET

1 Introduction

Code-reuse attacks can be mounted on real-time cyber-physical systems just as on general-purpose computing systems. However, these systems are mostly not as well protected as larger systems. The problem is that existing countermeasures are not applicable to resource-constrained real-time systems or do not offer comprehensive protection. We solve this problem by proposing a load-time artificial software diversity approach that does not require sophisticated hardware such as a memory mapping unit (MMU), special instructions or hardware virtualization. At the same time, requirements of real-time systems are met: Only safe diversifying transformations are used to keep safety guarantees intact, and the timing overhead for loading and executing the program is predictable and boundable. The level of security against code-reuse is very high, because almost the entire instruction memory is covered and the possible number of variants is very large.

© Springer Nature Switzerland AG 2020
A. Casimiro et al. (Eds.): SAFECOMP 2020, LNCS 12234, pp. 357–371, 2020.
https://doi.org/10.1007/978-3-030-54549-9_24

The rise of code-reuse attacks started when *data execution prevention* was introduced as a very effective measure against code-injection attacks [19] as the primary way to exploit memory errors. Since code-reuse was first proposed [17], various countermeasures and in turn more sophisticated attacks were introduced [3,5,12], even for embedded systems [4,22]. The common idea of code-reuse attacks is to inject addresses of existing functions or code chunks (so-called gadgets) into the data locations used for the control flow (i.e. return addresses on the stack) rather than injecting the code itself.

In general-purpose systems, user processes work under the protection of the operating system. A major difficulty of an attack is the interaction with the operating system via system calls in order to make an effect onto the system state. This is less complex in systems with reduced or no operating system, where the interaction with the environment is more direct. Hence, once the control flow is diverted, the malicious code may reach its goal faster. An example is the diversion of the control flow to an `inflate` function of an airbag, which is not complex, but may have horrific consequences.

Artificial software diversity is a general term for approaches that have been proposed as countermeasures against code-reuse attacks. Their common idea is that hiding information from the attacker makes the success of attacks unlikely. The attacker has to guess information that the attack relies on - such as instruction addresses. Diversity is agnostic to the kind of attack - in contrast to many approaches using control flow integrity (CFI), which protect specifically against certain types of attacks. This makes diversity a universal countermeasure against any code-reuse, even against yet unknown attack types. At compile-time, all information is available and creating variants with equivalent behavior is straight-forward. However, a complex deployment and updating infrastructure is necessary. Load-time diversity is easier to distribute and the most secure: Executing a different variant each time a program is started prevents the attacker to learn from failed attempts.

Larger operating systems, such as Windows and Linux, use address space layout randomization (ASLR), where start addresses of certain code sections are randomized at load-time. This works in a large virtual 64-bit address space, but is not secure enough for smaller systems [18]. We use more fine-grained diversity, while protecting the whole binary. However, existing load-time approaches [7,21] for fine-grained diversity use disassemblers to perform transformations in the code, which has a large overhead in the loading process and introduces potential software errors, as disassembly is not sound [23]. Also, it is not feasible to ship the infrastructure that is required to disassemble and recompile the program with every device. We address these issues with the following contributions:

– We propose an efficient loading algorithm for **safe, fine-grained diversification**. Necessary information is collected in a compile-time phase, allowing for a **fast linear-time loading** of the code.
– We show how diversification works when using the **ARM instruction set and its limited address lengths** without having to recompile at load-time.

– We demonstrate the applicability of the approach on a real-time system using **FreeRTOS**[1], making it **the first fully diversified operating system** with fine-grained diversity, suitable for small embedded devices.

In addition to the FreeRTOS case study we evaluate the load time, the impact of diversity on the worst-case execution time (WCET) and the program size. Our evaluation uses TACLe benchmark [9], a benchmark suite commonly used in literature on WCET analysis. Me measured WCET over all variants of a benchmark to be only 0.87% higher the average than that of the initial variant.

The rest of this work is organized as follows: Sect. 2 briefly introduces the concept of artificial diversity. Section 3 introduces our approach in general, which is continued in Sect. 4 with its application onto the real-time operating system FreeRTOS on an ARM microcontroller. Section 5 offers experimental results. In Sect. 6 we discuss related work, and a conclusion is drawn in Sect. 7.

2   Background

Artificial software diversity is best described as an automatic altering of code in order to hide implementation details. The variations that are possible to perform automatically correspond to the choices a compiler makes between semantically equivalent options. Examples are the selection of equivalent instructions or the order of instructions with independent data flow. We use *reordering and relocation of independent code fragments* as the only diversifying transformations at load-time. A *fragment* is defined as a set of instructions located continuously in adjacent memory locations. *Independent* means that there is no indirect control flow between two adjacent fragments. The transformations allow to choose freely which instruction marks a fragment end, as long as there is no implicit control flow to the subsequent instruction. We define *function level diversity* a fragmentation granularity where all return instructions define a fragment end. This kind of diversity is also known as function reordering. In *block level diversity*, unconditional jumps *and* return instructions are fragment ends.

By not using insertions of instructions at random locations, the timing impact and memory requirements can be made boundable and predictable, which is crucial for real-time systems. It also means that the set of fragments F and their sizes are fixed at compile time and equal in all variants, and therefore each instruction i is mapped to a single fragment.

3   Compiler-Guided Load-Time Diversification

3.1   Threat Model

We assume a powerful threat model: The devices are assumed to employ data execution prevention, e.g. by using a memory protection unit (MPU). A memory mapping unit (MMU), and therefore memory paging, virtualization and process isolation, is not required. Attackers have unlimited resources to develop exploits prior to an attack. They have access to a reference hardware that enables them to gain full access to the program code, including fragment boundaries and sizes. However, they cannot access the entire code of the system under attack. Using these assumptions, we can expect an exploit for an existing vulnerability to be found eventually.

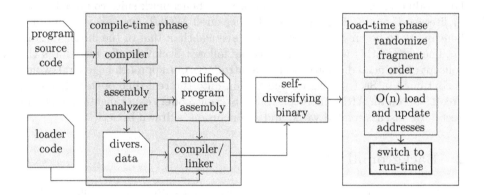

Fig. 1. Approach overview.

3.2 Approach Overview

Our approach is based on the idea that the binary can be equipped with enough information about the diversification so that the loader can operate efficiently and safely without disassembling the program. The required information is similar to the more coarse-grained relocation information that is used for the variable positioning of objects by linkers. Figure 1 illustrates the approach. It is split in two phases: In the compile-time phase, the program is converted to an assembler file suitable for diversification, where addresses are still symbolic. Fragment positions and references to code segments such as branch targets are extracted here, which could otherwise only be gathered by a disassembling process at load-time. Together with this information, the program is packed as a payload into the loader application, making it a self-diversifying binary. The loader itself operates in phase two: It first determines a random fragment order and then loads the program fragments to the designated positions while updating all relevant addresses. After the program is loaded, the loader deletes all information that would reveal the order and launches the diversified program.

3.3 Diversification Data

As described in Sect. 2, we are limiting the diversifying transformations to relocation and reordering of code fragments. Fragments are split at unconditional jumps for *block-level diversity* or only return instructions for *function-level diversity*. Any granularity can be used in this phase. We collect the set of fragment starting addresses fAdr:$\{A\}$ and sizes fSiz:$\{N\}$, where A is the set of the addresses in the instruction memory, as part of the *diversification data*.

To keep the code's functionality equal to the initial fragment order, the control flow and data accesses have to adjusted to the new fragment order. This re-writing of addresses requires knowledge of the locations of all instructions whose behavior might change (i.e. instructions that target code addresses that might change).

Figure 2 illustrates, which addresses are invalidated by fragment reordering: Each data reference or branch that points to a location outside its own fragment with a relative address, and all absolute references pointing to sections that may be shuffled. These references are depicted using red arrows (dashed for data accesses, solid for branches). Invalidated addresses have to be updated in the loading process. Irrelevant for diversification are relative branches within the fragment (green, dotted arrow).

The respective instruction addresses are collected in two tables rel:$\{A \rightarrow F\}$ and abs:$\{A \rightarrow F\}$, each table mapping instruction addresses to target fragments.

It is also possible that multiple code sections with different access

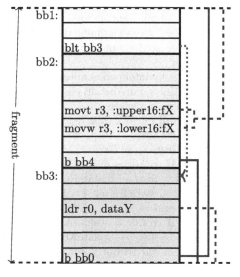

Fig. 2. Invalid branch addresses.

rights are shuffled (or not) separately. In this case, also section information with *s.address* : A and *s.shuffle* : *boolean* are collected.

Using the symbolic address information available at assembler level, this approach can support all branches and data accesses that may be used in the original program, with one exception: The intentional use of non-symbolic absolute addresses in code sections.

3.4   Compile-Time Phase

The compile-time phase consists of the following fully automated steps:

1. Compile the program to a low-level representation, where instructions are fixed, but addresses are symbolic. We use the LLVM compiler to create a single assembly file without directives of variable size.
2. Re-write parts of the program not compatible with relocation, such as short addresses. In ARM, it applies to PC-relative load instructions (Sect. 4.1).
3. Analyze the program to extract diversification data (see Sect. 3.3).
4. Compile the program and extract the section binaries.
5. Compile the loader program and pack the diversification data and program binary as payload into the loader.

Algorithm 1. Diversified Program Loading.

Require: fAdr, fSiz   // fragment locations and sizes
Require: rel, abs   // relative and absolute address tables
Require: sInfo   // section infos
Ensure: Program diversified and loaded
 1: order, order' ← $[1..|F|]$
 2: seed ← obtainRandomSeed()
 3: **for all** s ∈ sInfo | s.shuffle **do**
 4:      order',seed ←randomFragmentOrder(seed, order', s.address)
 5: **end for**
 6: fAdr' ← updateFragLocations(fAdr, order, order')
 7: curRelEntry, curAbsEntry ← 0
 8: **for all** f ∈ order **do**
 9:      **for all** i ∈ [0 .. (fSiz[f]-1)] **do**
10:          srcAdr ← fAdr[f]+i
11:          instr ← src[srcAdr]
12:          **if** srcAdr = rel[curRelEntry].adr **then**
13:              instr ← updateRelAddress(instr, srcAdr, rel.dst, fAdr, fAdr')
14:              curRelEntry += 1
15:          **end if**
16:          **if** srcAdr = abs[curAbsEntry].adr **then**
17:              instr ← updateAbsAddress(instr, abs.dst, fAdr, fAdr')
18:              curAbsEntry += 1
19:          **end if**
20:          dst[fAdr'[f]+i] = instr
21:      **end for**
22: **end for**

3.5 Load-Time Phase

The loader code starts up after each reset. Algorithm 1 describes the loading process in detail: First, a random seed is taken from variable sources such as analogous inputs. With this, the order of fragments to be shuffled is randomized using a linear shuffling algorithm [8]. The new order is then used to determine the new fragment locations in the target program. The loading algorithm then iterates linearly though all instructions and copies them to the predetermined locations. If an instruction is encountered that needs updating, its address is in the current position (`curRelEntry` and `curAbsEntry`, respectively) of the address tables `rel` and `abs`. They are sorted, so they can be processed linearly as well. Absolute addresses can be replaced directly with the new address. A relative address a of an instruction in fragment f_x targeting a position in fragment f_y can be updated as follows:

$$a' ← a + (fAdr(f_x) - fAdr'(f_x)) - (fAdr(f_y) - fAdr'(f_y))$$

After copying the code to the target position, `order'` and `fAdr'` are deleted, so that potential attackers do not get access to all memory layout information using a single information leak. After that, the execution can be switched to the actual program to be executed. The user program then has to set the access rights to the parts of the memory so that the entire loader area is not executable, the diversified program is not writable and its RAM sections are not executable.

3.6 Complexity and Security

The algorithms in the loader are all linear: The complexity of the randomization is $O(|F|)$, and that of the loading is $O(n)$, with n as the number of instructions.

Due to space reasons, and because we are using a well-studied type of diversity, we refrain from quantifying the security increase of the diversification approach in this work in detail, and refer to the discussion in [7]. Fine-grained diversification results in a specific address possibly being located in any address of the target address space. Therefore the randomness is limited to the size of that target space. The probability of a successful attack performed with simple guesses depends largely on the vulnerability, the attack and the contents of the rest of the code. If multiple addresses need to be guessed correctly by the attacker in a fairly large target address space, the probability of success becomes prohibitively low. Hence [7] argue for general-purpose systems that a small number of fragments provides a security level high enough. If it suffices to guess few addresses for simpler attacks in a small address space, brute-force might still be feasible for an attacker, or attacks on a large number of devices become worthwhile. Therefore, the systems we target require a much higher fragmentation.

With our approach, we are able to diversify (fine-grained) almost all executable code, with the exception of starting points such as interrupt tables. In the example we discuss in Sect. 4, this is a small code section of eight instructions. These are vulnerable to direct memory leaks (read access to instruction memory) and of course control-flow attacks, if they are useful gadgets themselves. Note that the loader code itself is not loaded, and can therefore be protected from being leveraged in attacks using appropriate memory protection settings.

A reasonable part of the defense should be a fail-safe mode that prohibits multiple attempts. Another aspect to this is the fact that a simple program crash and restart as a reaction to a successful defense against an attack is not feasible in an embedded real-time system anyway - the program should respond to aborts with proper protections for critical functionality.

4 FreeRTOS Diversification on ARM

To demonstrate the applicability of our approach to real-time systems, we implemented it using the real-time operating system FreeRTOS [1]. This is freely available with ports to many microcontrollers. Our reference implementation uses a LAUNCHPAD-XL2 TMS57012 microcontroller (MCU). That features an ARM Cortex-R4f core, specifically designed for safety-critical real-time systems. The ARM Cortex-R4f allows to protect twelve memory regions of variable sizes using an *MPU* (memory protection unit), so that data execution prevention can be applied effectively.

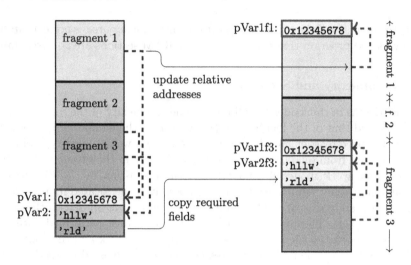

Fig. 3. Converting literal pools to fragment pools.

4.1 Diversity with the ARM Instruction Set

The first step of diversifying a program is addressing the specifics of the instruction set. The ARM Cortex-R4f uses the 32-bit ARM instuction set, which can be diversified with only minor changes. It features the following uses of addresses in the instruction memory (at assembler level):

- Conditional branches and jump instructions always use relative addressing, with an address distance of ± 32MB. This suffices for many smaller real-time systems. If there exists a risk of creating higher address distances during shuffling, long jumps have to be used. We use the rel table to collect all branches with possibly varying distance, i.e. targeting other fragments.
- Absolute addresses can be saved as 32 bit words, e.g., the instruction .word LABEL1 saves the address LABEL1. If LABEL1 is targeting a code section to be shuffled, it is stored in the abs table.
- Move instructions with addresses as half-word immediates are stored to the abs table as pairs, to be updated together (e.g. movw :upper16:LABEL).
- Load instructions with pc-relative addressing (LDR, ADR, VLDR) are the most complex. The largest possible relative distance is 1024 bytes, which is too short for diversification when located in another fragment. ARM compilers create *literal pools*, were constant data is stored to be used by close-by instructions, possibly being used multiple times (The pseudo instruction LTORG helps creating these pools in hand-written assembler). These pools have to be repeated so that they are located at most 1024 bytes from the instruction. With our diversification, however, the pool might be part of another fragment and therefore be relocated much further. To solve that, we rewrite the program, so that there are no literal pools based on absolute distance from the instruction, but as part of the fragment the data is accessed in. Figure 3 illustrates the idea: Each constant data entry of literal pool is copied to the

fragments using it, creating *fragment pools* that serve the same purpose. Fragment sizes have to be limited accordingly.

Programs limited to the use of addresses using labels can be diversified safely using these addressing modes. Using hard-coded immediate operands pointing to a section to be shuffled, however, is not supported.

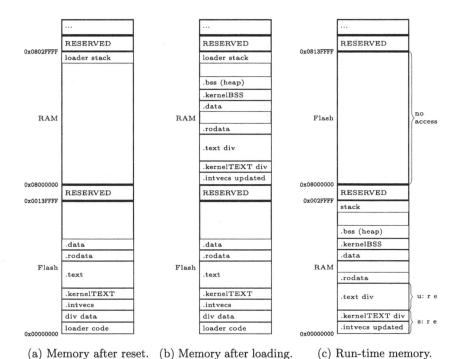

(a) Memory after reset.   (b) Memory after loading.   (c) Run-time memory.

Fig. 4. Memory layout of FreeRTOS on TMS57012.

4.2   FreeRTOS on ARM Cortex-R4

After establishing how to diversify and update each instruction, we can move to illustrating *what* to diversify *where*, using the algorithms presented in Sect. 3.5. Figure 4 shows the memory layout. FreeRTOS uses a kernel as well as a user part of the operating system. The kernel part contains the OS parts during operation, such as the scheduler and heap management. The user part contains the OS initialization code (before real user tasks are executed) and the user tasks. Kernel instructions can only be accessed in ARM access modes other than the user mode, which is secured by the MPU. This difference in access modes has to be preserved, but we also want to shuffle the kernel section as well in case the attacker manages to attack kernel parts or switch to a privileged mode. So the sections to be shuffled separately are `.text` and `.kernelTEXT`. There is a third code section (`.intvecs`), which contains the interrupt table, located at address 0x0. In that section, the instructions are fixed and can not be shuffled. However, they have to be updated during loading. All remaining sections have fixed target addresses and contain no instructions to be updated.

The Cortex R4 allows switching the execution from the initial flash memory to RAM, which we use for the loading process. The loader is located in the flash, starting from address zero (see Fig. 4a). It is packed with the diversification data and program sections as payload, which is why they are located successively in the flash. The loader then copies the code sections to their target locations in RAM (starting at 0x08000000), while shuffling and updating addresses, if necessary. The other sections are copied as well. See Fig. 4a for the result. After loading, the execution is switched to RAM, which also switches the start addresses of both memories. All sections are linked towards their target locations after the switch, to avoid unnecessary data address updates in the code. Also, all sections are located such that there are no conflicts in their target RAM location. The loader in the flash, including its interrupt table, are now out of the way and only the target program is executable. During its initialization it has to configure the MPU to set the appropriate access permissions (Fig. 4c).

Note that the flash can still be used as a read-only memory in this experimental setup. The memory sacrifice for diversification is large nevertheless. However, the controller also allows flashing from RAM execution, which would allow a second loader stage to diversify code in the flash.

5 Evaluation

We evaluated our approach using the TACLe benchmarks [9] *kernel* suite, a benchmark commonly used to evaluate tools and analyses for WCET estimation. These 25 programs contain many aspects of program execution. They are single-path benchmarks, which allows us to generate WCET estimates without having to handle the parameter space. For real-time systems, the WCET is the relevant performance measure (in contrast to general-purpose systems, where the average performance is more important). The benchmarks were extended by standard library operations such as `div` and `memcpy` to be compiled for the controller. The benchmark size ranges from 2.8kB to 40.82kB, and in *basic block level*, the number of fragments ranges from 95 to 447 (21–75 in *function level*). To fully evaluate the capability of our approach to diversify an entire real-time system - including an operating system and its access levels as described in Sect. 4 - we added our program **pacemaker**. It is an actual real-time system scale case study using five FreeRTOS tasks. This is our largest benchmark (78692kB, 2464 fragments in *basic block level*, 958 in the .kernelTEXT section of the code).

We performed our measurements on a *TMS57012*, as described in Sect. 4.

5.1   Load Time

Figure 5 depicts the load times for all benchmarks over their respective code size. It demonstrates that the loading process has linear complexity, but also depends on data size, fragmentation and the number of addresses to be updated. The upper straight line in the chart shows the average load time of approx. 0.2 ms/kB in *function-level diversity* and 3.1 ms/kB in *block-level diversity*. Our pacemaker benchmark requires 26.6 ms to load.

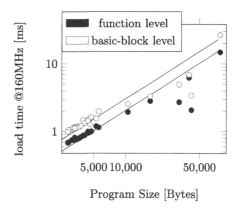

Fig. 5. Load times.

5.2   Run Time (WCET)

We performed run-time measurements with at least 100 executions (different program variants) of the TACLe benchmark programs to evaluate the runtime impact of the diversity on the WCET. Although the system does not have a cache and its branch prediction is address-independent, the execution time depends on the location of the code. Our measurements are summarized in Fig. 6. Each mark represents the average of WCET measurements for all executions of a benchmark relative to the non-diversified program, and the error bars show the distribution of these measurements. It shows that the average performance only worsens slightly (0.01% for function-level, 0.03% for block-level). Relevant to us, however, is an overall WCET for all executions of a benchmark. The average overall WCET is 0.86% higher than the original runtime for *function-level diversity*, and 0.87% for *block-level diversity*. The highest increase was observed for `bitcount` at block level, with 3.2%.

Note that, due to the single-path property of the TACLe benchmarks, the execution path does not depend on external inputs, therefore the measured WCET is actually an upper bound for the specific variant it was measured with. We refrained from using static WCET analysis in this work, because a detailed enough timing model of the controller is not publicly available. Our diversification approach does not change the CFG or instructions of the code, therefore the timing variations that can be observed are caused by address-dependent speculative hardware elements, likely small-scale bulk loading of instructions in the prefetch unit of the processor. In earlier work, we have proposed static WCET cache analyses [11] and branch prediction analyses [10]. These are able to obtain a WCET estimate as an upper bound for all variants of the code, and they are applicable when using the diversifying transformations proposed in this work. They support a range of cache and branch prediction architectures, and demonstrate that the timing impact is boundable and can be estimated in the magnitude of state-of-the-art static analyses.

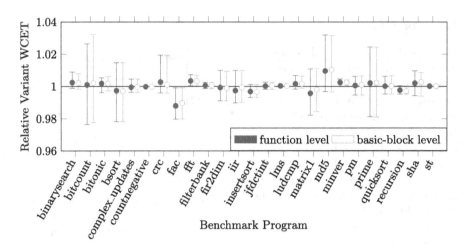

Fig. 6. Distribution of WCET measurements in TACLEBench variants.

5.3 Memory Overhead

The flash memory overhead (binary size) for the diversification of the programs is depicted in Fig. 7. The sizes for instructions and data as well as the additional diversification data are shown, compared to the total size of the original program. The impact of the literal pool transformation is the amount by which the program sections exceed the 100% line (negligible). The diversification data size in average is 7.4% of the initial binary size in average for *function-level diversity*, and 32% for *block-level diversity*. The loader itself takes up 6.4 kB of flash memory.

5.4 Applicability and Security

At last, there is to mention that all the mentioned programs could be diversified without modifications to the existing instructions. There was not a single use of absolute non-symbolic addressing that is not supported by our approach. We did not use any functions from pre-compiled libraries, hence avoiding program parts whose source code was not available.

We created three different exploits for typical vulnerabilities as part of the pacemaker case study, which could be fend off by our diversity countermeasure. The attacks are using buffer overflows, and demonstrate the execution of unwanted functionality, privilege escalation and keeping the controller in spinlock after attack. The question remains how likely it is for the attacker to *guess* the gadget locations correctly and reach their goal before the system crashes and restarts in a safe mode. Our exploits required four to six gadgets to reach their goal, which is less than is usually required to prepare for a system call in a general-purpose system. Our approach can support any granularity of fragments, at the performance trade-off presented in our measurement results.

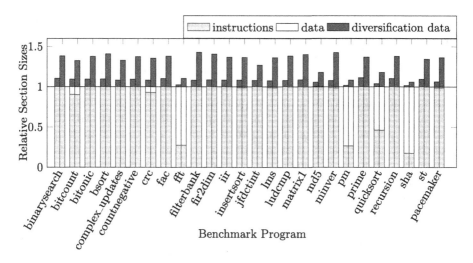

Fig. 7. Sizes relative to original program size for function-level (l)/block-level (r).

6 Related Work

A large number of countermeasures against code-reuse attacks have been proposed. We concentrate on approaches relevant to real-time systems that can cover the entire instruction memory. Many are randomization-based (Larsen et al. [14] presents an excellent overview). Among these, we concentrate on load-time approaches.

Control-flow integrity (CFI) [2,20] is the idea of protecting the control-flow using instrumentation code to check if it is diverted. Full CFI protection suffers from large performance overhead, and partial instrumentation possibly discloses vulnerabilities. Specialized protections such as canaries or shadow stacks only protect certain vulnerabilities and cannot cope with unknown attacks.

Address space layout randomization (ASLR) [16] is section level diversity, which is widely deployed in larger systems. It has been demonstrated that ASLR can be easily brute-forced in systems with 32-bit address space (or lower). A system without an MMU has a much smaller address space, even at 32-bit address width. Also, a single information leak reveals all addresses of the code.

Binary Stirring [21] and Xifer [7] are load-time block-level diversification approaches designed for general-purpose computers with regular operating systems. They use a disassembler before diversification, which is not feasible to be deployed to smaller real-time systems, and may violate safety guarantees as disassembling is generally unsound [23]. Disassembling also causes long load times and requires a disassembler and compiler to be shipped. Splitting blocks at random locations creates timing behavior that cannot be statically bounded. Moreover, Xifer is used with the ARM instruction set, but handles its specialties (e.g. address lengths) by recompiling. This will result in different instructions and their timings over variants, impairing the execution time predictability.

AVRAND [15] uses page-level diversity for an AVR-based microcontroller. The solution relies on rewriting the whole code so that it only uses absolute addressing, which would not be possible on ARM. Also it is not clear if the solution could diversify a whole operating system including privilege modes.

EPOXY [6] is a lightweight operating system that aims to protect real-time systems by adding instrumentation to vulnerable instructions in privileged mode, also features a simplified safe stack and compiler-based diversity. MINION [13] uses memory view switching, aiming to reduce the code parts of the process accessible by the attacker. Both approaches are limited by the granularity of access rules and the precision of the included CFG and data flow analyses, leaving parts of the program unprotected. The randomization of EPOXY is compiler based, while we propose a more secure load-time approach.

7 Conclusion

We propose a safe and efficient load-time diversification algorithm that uses detailed addressing information obtained at compile-time. To demonstrate its potential, we used it to create the first fully diversified embedded operating system, featuring interrupts, task scheduling, privileged modes and memory access restrictions. Our experimental results show that the performance overhead is low and the load times are very small while scaling well. The system is fully automated, and, once integrated into the tool chain, does not require any input from the developer. The price to pay for the considerable security gain, however, is increased memory usage. As the number of fragments can be reduced variably, our approach allows finding a suitable security trade-off.

In future work we are planning to extend the diversity algorithm to larger memory sections, spreading the code sections into unused areas and diversify data sections.

References

1. FreeRTOS. https://www.freertos.org/. Accessed 11 Nov 2019
2. Abadi, M., Budiu, M., Erlingsson, U., Ligatti, J.: Control-flow Integrity Principles, Implementations, and Applications. ACM Trans. Inf. Syst, Secur. (2009)
3. Bletsch, T., Jiang, X., Freeh, V.W., Liang, Z.: Jump-oriented programming: a new class of code-reuse attack. In: ACM Symposium on Information, Computer and Communications Security (2011)
4. Buchanan, E., Roemer, R., Shacham, H., Savage, S.: When good instructions go bad: generalizing return-oriented programming to RISC. In: Computer and Communications Security (2008)
5. Checkoway, S., Davi, L., Dmitrienko, A., Sadeghi, A.R., Shacham, H., Winandy, M.: Return-oriented programming without returns. In: ACM Conference on Computer and Communications Security (2010)
6. Clements, A.A., et al.: Protecting bare-metal embedded systems with privilege overlays. In: 2017 IEEE Symposium on Security and Privacy (SP), May 2017

7. Davi, L.V., Dmitrienko, A., Nürnberger, S., Sadeghi, A.R.: Gadge me if you can: secure and efficient ad-hoc instruction-level randomization for x86 and ARM. In: ACM SIGSAC Information, Computer and Communications Security (2013)
8. Donald, E.K.: The art of computer programming. Sorting and searching (1999)
9. Falk, H., et al.: TACLeBench: a benchmark collection to support worst-case execution time research. In: Proceedings of the 16th International Workshop on WCET Analysis (WCET 2016), July 2016
10. Fellmuth, J., Zell, J., Glesner, S.: Evaluating software diversity in branch prediction analyses for static wcet estimation. In: 2019 IEEE 25th International Conference on Embedded and Real-Time Computing Systems and Applications (RTCSA), pp. 1–6, August 2019. https://doi.org/10.1109/RTCSA.2019.8864568
11. Fellmuth, J., Göthel, T., Glesner, S.: Instruction caches in static WCET analysis of artificially diversified software. In: Altmeyer, S. (ed.) 30th Euromicro Conference on Real-Time Systems (ECRTS 2018). Leibniz International Proceedings in Informatics (LIPIcs), vol. 106, pp. 21:1–21:23. Schloss Dagstuhl-Leibniz-Zentrum fuer Informatik, Dagstuhl, Germany (2018). https://doi.org/10.4230/LIPIcs.ECRTS.2018.21, http://drops.dagstuhl.de/opus/volltexte/2018/8982
12. Goktas, E., Athanasopoulos, E., Bos, H., Portokalidis, G.: Out of control: Overcoming control-flow integrity. In: IEEE Symposium on Security and Privacy (2014)
13. Kim, C.H., et al.: Securing real-time microcontroller systems through customized memory view switching. In: Network and Distributed Systems Security Symposium (NDSS) (2018)
14. Larsen, P., Homescu, A., Brunthaler, S., Franz, M.: SoK: Automated Software Diversity. In: IEEE Symposium on Security and Privacy (2014)
15. Pastrana, S., Tapiador, J., Suarez-Tangil, G., Peris-López, P.: AVRAND: a software-based defense against code reuse attacks for AVR embedded devices. In: Caballero, J., Zurutuza, U., Rodríguez, R.J. (eds.) DIMVA 2016. LNCS, vol. 9721, pp. 58–77. Springer, Cham (2016). https://doi.org/10.1007/978-3-319-40667-1_4
16. PaX Team: PaX address space layout randomization (ASLR) (2003)
17. Shacham, H.: The geometry of innocent flesh on the bone: Return-into-libc without function calls (on the x86). In: Computer and Communications Security (2007)
18. Shacham, H., Page, M., Pfaff, B., Goh, E.J., Modadugu, N., Boneh, D.: On the effectiveness of address-space randomization. In: ACM Conference on Computer and Communications Security (2004)
19. Szekeres, L., Payer, M., Wei, T., Song, D.: SoK: Eternal War in Memory. In: IEEE Symposium on Security and Privacy (SP) (2013). https://doi.org/10.1109/SP.2013.13
20. Walls, R.J., Brown, N.F., Le Baron, T., Shue, C.A., Okhravi, H., Ward, B.: Control-Flow Integrity for Real-Time Embedded Systems. In: ECRTS 2019
21. Wartell, R., Mohan, V., Hamlen, K.W., Lin, Z.: Binary stirring: Self-randomizing instruction addresses of legacy x86 binary code. In: Computer and communications security (2012)
22. Weidler, N.R., et al.: Return-oriented programming on a resource constrained device. Sustainable Computing: Informatics & Systems (2018)
23. Wenzl, M., Merzdovnik, G., Ullrich, J., Weippl, E.: From hack to elaborate technique - a survey on binary rewriting. In: ACM Computing Surveys (CSUR) (2019)

Towards an Automated Exploration of Secure IoT/CPS Design-Variants

Lukas Gressl[1]($\boxtimes$), Michael Krisper[1], Christian Steger[1], and Ulrich Neffe[2]

[1] Graz University of Technology (TU Graz), Graz, Austria
{gressl,michael.kripser,steger}@tugraz.at
[2] NXP Semiconductors Austria GmbH, Gratkorn, Austria
ulrich.neffe@nxp.com

Abstract. The advent of the Internet of Things (IoT) and Cyber-Physical Systems (CPS) enabled a new class of connected, smart, and interactive devices. With their continuous connectivity and their access to valuable information in both the digital and physical world, they are highly attractive targets for security attackers. Integrating them into the industry and our daily used devices adds new attack surfaces. These potential threats call for special care of security vulnerabilities during the design of IoT devices and CPS. Due to their resource-constrained nature, designing secure IoT devices and CPS poses a complex task, considering the selectable hardware components and task implementation alternatives. Researchers proposed a range of automatic design tools to support system designers in their task of finding the optimal hardware selection and task implementations. Said tools offer a limited way of modeling attack scenarios for a system under design. The framework proposed in this paper aims at closing this gap, offering system designers a way to consider security attacks and security risks during the early phase of system design. It offers designers the possibility to model security constraints from the view of potential attackers, assessing the probability of successful security attacks and the resulting security risk, alike. We demonstrate the framework's feasibility and performance by revisiting an industry partner's potential system design of a future IoT device.

Keywords: Cyber security · Embedded system design · Secure IoT systems · Secure CPS · Secure embedded consumer devices

1 Introduction

The increasing utilization of the Internet of Things (IoT) in the commercial market and cyber-physical systems (CPS) in the industry, opened a new attack surface. In the last decades, numerous cybersecurity exploits have been documented [1,11]. The ongoing integration of such systems demands the consideration of cybersecurity exploits throughout the whole system design process. Introducing security measures causes additional performance delay and power consumption, contradicting the systems' requirements for fast response

© Springer Nature Switzerland AG 2020
A. Casimiro et al. (Eds.): SAFECOMP 2020, LNCS 12234, pp. 372–386, 2020.
https://doi.org/10.1007/978-3-030-54549-9_25

times and high energy efficiency [19]. Considering the hardware and task implementation alternatives, finding the optimal solution satisfying performance and security poses a multi-objective optimization problem. Designers rely on automatic design space exploration (DSE) tools are used. There exist both classical DSE tools focusing on performance and power consumption [8,13], and DSE frameworks offering the consideration of security constraints in a limited way [6,7,10,16,18,20].

The framework presented in this paper introduces a new approach to introducing security constraints in early IoT/CPS design, based on both attack graphs and risk trees. Among a set of possible hardware components and task implementation alternatives, the framework finds the optimal selection of hardware components and task placements considering the system's power consumption, performance, security attack mitigation capability, and security risk exposure. In this paper, we make the following contributions: (i) To the best of our knowledge, the framework presented here is the first to allow the consideration of security constraints modeled as Bayesian attack graphs (BAGs) and risk trees during early IoT/CPS design. (ii) We integrate both approaches and show their advantages and disadvantages. (iii) We show the framework's feasibility based on a secure consumer device use case and the scalability of our approach.

The paper is structured as follows: Sect. 2 discusses related projects in DSE, security attack and risk modeling; Sect. 3 describes the security modeling approach, the framework's design and implementation; Sect. 4 shows the impact of both security modeling approaches on the secure consumer device use-case; Sect. 5 gives a conclusion and discusses future work.

2   Related Work

Network administrators commonly use attack graphs when modeling attack scenarios on networks. They model attacks as consecutive steps, represented as nodes within the graph. Modeling them as BAGs adds information about the dependency of the distinct steps and the probability of their successful execution [3,12]. Attack tree analysis (ATA) and fault tree analysis (FTA), generally used in safety analysis, use a similar modeling approach. Both scientists and engineers commonly use ATA and FTA [2]. RISKEE describes risk propagation within a system, and assesses said risk based on a tree representation [9].

A range of DSE tools considering functional safety or security constraints, in addition to the classical optimization goals, e.g., performance, power consumption, and others, have been presented in recent years [6,7,14,16–18,20]. A range of these tools focus on the abstract representation of security constraints in the design space, such as restricting the mapping of security vulnerable tasks to processor types with security extensions [16], integration of security functions into system design [20], or securing control loops [10]. In [5], security constraints and mitigation capabilities are introduced based on distinct security levels. Other works consider distinct security problems, e.g., integration of intrusion detection tasks [6], consideration of network security [7], or optimization of communication protocols regarding message authentication [18]. These works cannot directly integrate the attacker's perspective on the system into the DSE. Hence, they do not reflect the effect of security mechanism integration on distinct attack scenarios.

Contrasting, the framework presented in this paper allows the direct representation of security constraints in the form of BAGs and risk trees, allowing the representation of the overall system's attack vulnerability and monetary security risk. Depending on the used modeling approach, the designer directly sees the effect of the system partitioning and task allocation on both security risk and security attack vulnerability. The framework allows the seamless interchange between the risk tree and the BAG representation for describing the security constraints posed on the IoT device/CPS under design. Considering the security performance and power overhead of the distinct solutions allows a detailed assessment of the costs and benefits of particular system designs, including their security attack mitigation capabilities.

3   Proposed Methodology

The framework allows the designer to model the system's functionality, available architecture components, and security attack scenarios using four perspectives, as shown in Fig. 1. The work presented in [4] describes a preliminary approach to introducing security attack vulnerability into DSE. In this paper, we present a more elaborate approach, allowing the designers to describe the dependencies of the distinct security assets using rule sets. Furthermore, this paper introduces the usage of risk trees in addition to the BAG based approach. This usage of risk trees allows the framework to perform more detailed modeling of the impacts caused by successfully performed security attacks, shown in Sect. 4. However, the usage of risk trees induces additional computation time, also described in Sect. 4. The following paragraphs shortly describe the models behind the distinct perspectives serving as an input to the framework.

System Architecture and Task Representation
A task graph describes the system's functionality with its nodes representing the tasks and the edges modeling the task's dependencies (logical channels). Each task performs operations (OP) on a set of data entities coming with a set of security requirements (SR). High-level hardware components represent the system architecture, including communication buses that connect these components. Each hardware component has security mechanisms (SM) and mitigation capabilities. Each SM comes with a distinct performance overhead and power consumption. For each possible implementation of a task on a hardware component, the designers estimate the implementation's worst-case execution time (WCET).

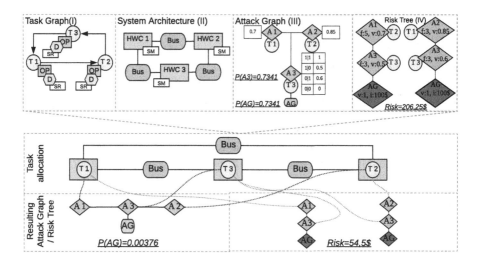

Fig. 1. Framework overview. Inputs consist of: tasks (T) operating (OP) on data entities (D) with security requirements (SR); Hardware components (HWC) connected via communication buses; Attacks modeled as BAGs or risk trees. Outputs consist of: HWC selection and T allocation; security vulnerability ($P(AG)$) and security risk.

Security Constraint Representation

The sets for OP, SR, SM, security operations ($SecOp$), and attack types (AT) are defined by the designer. The designer also defines a set of rules stating the relations between: OP, SR and $SecOp$; SR and AT; $SecOp$ and SM. The rules are described by input sets (in), connected with boolean operators, and a resulting output set (out), e.g. $(in_a \vee in_b) \wedge in_c \mapsto out_x$. Given the tasks and their $SecOp$, the framework calculates the set of secure communications ($secCom$). A $secCom$ is spanned between two tasks (a source (t_{src}) and a destination task (t_{dst})) performing the same communication securing operations ($secOpComm \in SecOp$) on a particular data entity.

Security Attack View: The framework allows the designer to model cybersecurity threats as BAGs or risk trees. In both methods, each attack (excluding goals) aims at a certain task and comes with a distinct attack type taken from AT. Based on the defined ruleset, each attack type aims at a specific security requirement (defined in SR) of the data handled by the attacked task. Within the BAG, each node represents a distinct attack step, with its leafs describing attack goals. The edges define paths an attacker must traverse to reach an attack goal. Each attack has a distinct success probability provided using a conditional probability table. The attack goals' success probabilities are defined by their marginals in the joint distribution table, calculated by the Bayesian chain rule. Each goal has a maximum allowed success probability defined by the designer.

Risk based Attack Trees: The risk-based method uses RISKEE [9], which is a methodology for risk assessment based on attack trees with the enhancement of also modeling the consequences (impacts) of an attack, and accounting for multiple attacks over time (in the form of attack frequencies) instead of just simulating single events. The key feature of RISKEE is the usage of probability distributions for the estimation of uncertain values (which are inherent in risk assessment), providing a benefit compared to classical single-point estimates, which neglect uncertainties. The mean risk value, which is one of the results returned by RISKEE, is used as a metric for each defined attack goal. Attack goals come with a maximum allowed mean risks defined by the designer. By integrating RISKEE into the framework, we are the first to allow the consideration of risk-based security constraints during the automatic DSE for IoT/CPS.

Security Attack Mitigation: Additionally to the SM, each hardware component defines to what extend said mechanisms are capable of mitigating attacks. This attack mitigation ($m \in \mathbb{R} : m \in [0,1]$) states the component's defensive capabilities. Assessing the attack mitigation is based on the judgment of the attacker's expertise and available time for breaking said defensive capabilities. Designers can deduce this mitigation capability from security assessments such as Common Criteria $(CC)^1$, from historical data recording known security incidents, or by expert judgments if no other information is available. The estimated mitigation factor reduces the attack probabilities (BAG) or vulnerabilities (RISKEE) $\lambda, \lambda_m \in \mathbb{R}$ of all attacks on tasks allocated on this particular hardware component, giving the mitigated probability λ_m ($\lambda_m = \lambda * (1 - m)$).

Secure Task Allocation and Partitioning: Based on the system's architecture, functionality, and the given attack scenarios, the framework finds a system partitioning and task allocations which meet the defined security constraints and optimizes either for performance or power consumption. Figure 1 depicts the BAG and RISKEE based approach and the influence of the partitioning and task allocation on the attack success probability and risk value. Hence, the task allocation must comply with a set of restrictions. (I) All tasks directly communicating with each other must be allocated on the same component or different components connected via a communication bus. (II) Each task must map to a hardware component capable of executing its $SecOp$, according to the rules defining the mapping of $SecOp$ to SM. (III) Any task allocation and platform partitioning must fulfill the security attack constraints (in both the BAG- or RISKEE-based security attack modeling approach), meaning that for all attack goals, the defined thresholds on attack success probability or mean risk value must lie within the defined bounds.

Performance and Power Consumption Calculation: The execution times of the individual tasks depend on their component allocations, as each possible implementation of a task on a given component comes with a distinct WCET. Hence, the overall system performance depends on the selected components and the task allocations. The system power consumption consists of the component's

---

[1] https://www.commoncriteriaportal.org/.

static power dissipation and their dynamic power consumption, induced by the task implemented on them. Additionally, each component comes with a distinct security performance and power overhead for each SM. For each $secComm$, the framework adds the performance and power overhead of the SM used by the $secOpComm$ of t_{src} and t_{dst} to the tasks' overall execution times and the component's power consumption, alike. For all tasks performing $SecOp$ not included in any $secComm$, the framework considers the performance and power consumption overheads as well. The $secComm$ must be considered separately, as a task can be both t_{src} and t_{dst} in different $secComm$. Without this consideration, the number of SM executions would not be integrated into the security overhead calculation correctly.

Optimization of Security Calculation: The implementation of the framework is based on the open-source $DeSyDe$ framework[2]. The framework spends its main computational effort calculating the attack probabilities (ap)/risks for each partitioning and task allocation, as for every new allocation or component selection, the BAG/RISKEE must be recalculated based on the altering attack mitigation. The framework orders the components in descending order according to their mitigation capabilities. In each calculation of the ap/risks, the framework checks if any of the said ap/risks do not fulfill the predefined limits. Upon reaching this break condition, the framework renders all further allocations on components with lesser mitigation capabilities to be insecure. Both the RISKEE and BAG based methods use the same graph structure. Hence, it is feasible to make a comparison between both methods. Opposed to BAGs, in which attack nodes can have multiple parents, the current design of RISKEE only considers single path attack scenarios. Hence, to guarantee a similar structure of the attack scenarios, the framework implements a graph-unwrapping method, turning a BAG into a set of RISKEE trees representing said BAG.

4   Experiments and Results

Using the framework, an use case based on a secure ranging system targeted for the consumer market was revisited. Table 1 describes the security rules defined by the designer to model the security aspects of the use case. The set of OP defines reading (r), writing (w) and storing (s) of data. The set of $SecOp$ defines

Table 1. Security rules defined to model security aspects of the use case.

$SecOp$ derived from OP and SR	AT attacking SR	$SecOp$ using SM
$OP, SR \mapsto SecOp$	$AT \mapsto SR$	$SecOp \mapsto SM$
$(r \vee w) \wedge conf \mapsto so_{enc}$	$at_{inf} \mapsto conf$	$so_{enc} \vee so_{auth} \mapsto sm_{crypt}$
$(r \vee w) \wedge auth \mapsto so_{auth}$	$at_{spoof} \mapsto auth$	$(so_{enc} \vee so_{auth}) \wedge internal \mapsto sm_{te}$
$s \wedge (auth \vee conf \vee int) \mapsto so_{sst}$	$at_{tamp} \mapsto int$	$so_{sst} \mapsto sm_{tss}$

---

[2] https://github.com/forsyde/DeSyDe.

Table 2. Hardware components with security options. Mitigation factor (MF), performance (Perf) given in μs, and power consumption (PWC) in mW.

HWC	Security feature description	MF	Perf			PWC		
			sm_{crypt}	sm_{tss}	sm_{te}	sm_{crypt}	sm_{tss}	sm_{te}
AP	HW crypto; TEE	0.8	50	/	5	60	/	5
	SW crypto-lib sc sec., TEE	0.7	60	/	5	50	/	5
	SW crypto-lib sc sec.	0.5	40	/	/	50	/	/
	SW crypto functional	0.3	30	/	/	30	/	/
SE	HW crypto, sec store, (EAL 6+)	0.99	500	50	15	60	20	10
	HW crypto, sec store, (EAL 5+)	0.95	500	50	15	60	20	10
	HW crypto, sec store, (EAL 4+)	0.9	500	50	15	60	20	10
UR	HW crypto, TZ, HW firewall	0.8	80	/	15	50	/	10
	HW crypto, TZ	0.7	80	/	5	45	/	5
	HW crypto, 2 separate MCUs	0.85	80	/	20	50	/	10
	SW crypto-lib sc sec., TZ	0.5	160	/	5	90	/	5
	SW crypto functional	0.3	60	/	/	30	/	/

encryption (so_{enc}), authentication (so_{auth}) and secure storage (so_{sst}). The set of SR defines confidentiality ($conf$), authenticity ($auth$) and integrity (int). The set of security mechanisms (SM) defines cryptographic functionalities (sm_{crypt}), task encapsulation (sm_{te}) and tamper safe storage (sm_{tss}). The restriction of *internal* holds if both t_{src} and t_{dst} of $secComm$ are placed on the same hardware component.

The system consists of a ranging node and a ranging anchor. The node authenticates to the anchor using a shared secret (master key) and setting up a secure session (session key). Within this session, node and anchor perform a two way ranging secured by a continually updated ranging key. The node determines its distance to the anchor in a secure way, without comprising its distance to potentially spying devices, or receiving faked ranging messages from attackers. The functionality consists of two phases, the authentication and the ranging phase, which is described by a task graph comprising 46 nodes. The authentication phase uses an external radio (e.g., Bluetooth Low Energy), the ranging phase uses ultra-wideband. Table 2 lists the security-relevant options for the hardware components available for both the anchor and the node device, giving their estimated performance (Perf) and power consumption (PWC) for their distinct SM. The devices consist of an application processor (AP), a secure element (SE), and a UWB Radio (UR). The security options comprise hardware supported cryptography (HW crypto), side-channel (sc) secured software cryptography library (SW crypto-lib sc sec.), software-based but not tested cryptography (SW crypto functional), Trusted Execution Environment (TEE) and Trust Zone (TZ), secure storage (sec. store), and hardware firewall (HW firewall). Only the SE offers secure storage.

Table 3. WCETs of security relevant tasks given in μs.

Device	Task name	SR	AP	SE	UR
Key	Create challenge	c,a	100	150	–
Lock	Check challenge	c,a	100	170	120
Key & Lock	Derive session key	c,a,i	100	110	
Key & Lock	Derive ranging key	c,a	–	190	140
Lock	Start session	c,a	80	170	120
Key & Lock	Create secure nonce	c,a	–	120	200
Key & Lock	Create ranging message	c,a	120	–	–
Lock	Calculate distance	c,a	–	350	230

The attacks on the overall system comprise the disclosure of the key material, faking the secure authentication, which builds on a challenge request-response exchange, hijacking the ranging session, and compromising the exchanged ranging frames. Security analysts modeled these attacks using 56 nodes, both for the BAG and the RISK tree. Table 3 lists all security-relevant tasks as identified by modeling the attack scenarios, including their SR and WCETs on the hardware components on which system designers considered their implementations. Confidentiality (c), authenticity (a) and integrity (i) were considered as SR. The assessment of the attack success probabilities of the distinct attack steps for the BAG and the vulnerabilities for the RISKEE based approach were estimated using the Common Vulnerability Scoring System [15], using its *Base Metrics*.

We used the described use case as input to the framework and configured it to find the fastest, the most secure, the fastest secure, and most power-efficient and secure solution, both using the BAG and RISKEE based method. The overall system power consumption and performance was normalized. We assume that the described system performs distance-based access control. Hence, an attacker breaking the session key temporarily gains access to the secured location and might acquire the authorization to perform further criminal actions. Depending on the secured location, a successful attack might enable the disclosure of secret information, the theft of valuable items, or other critical actions. An attacker who can also disclose the keyless entry system's master key could perform such an attack on multiple locations, depending on the key distribution policy.

Table 4. Most secure and fastest solution.

HWC	Options (most secure)	Options (fastest)
AP (node & anchor)	HW crypto; TEE	SW crypto functional
SE (node & anchor)	EAL 6+	EAL 4+
UR (node & anchor)	HW crypto; 2 separate MCUs	SW crypto functional
avg ap/avg rv	0.0005/114.4$	0.016/4911$
norm perf.	~2.57	1.0

Based on these considerations and a documented real-life incident[3], risk experts set the impact of disclosing the system's session key to 100.000$, the impact of disclosing the master key to 10.000.000$. This estimation bases on the assumption that with the session key, the attacker can only access one car temporarily. However, with the master key, the attacker might gain access to multiple cars. In this latter case, also the experts considered the reputational damage. They set the frequency for disclosing the session key to 10, and the frequency for the master key disclosure to 5 per year. We modeled these estimated impacts and frequencies in the RISKEE based approach. One must note that the attacks' vulnerabilities and the attack success probabilities are equal for the RISKEE and BAG based approach. We set the maximum allowed risk value of 1.000$ for all attack goals. For the BAG based method, we configured the framework to regard all solutions, in which at least one attack goal's attack success probability exceeds the threshold of 0.002, as insecure. Table 4 describes the fastest, and the most secure system architecture found by the framework. The table shows that the framework can correctly identify optimal solutions based on distinct optimization criteria.

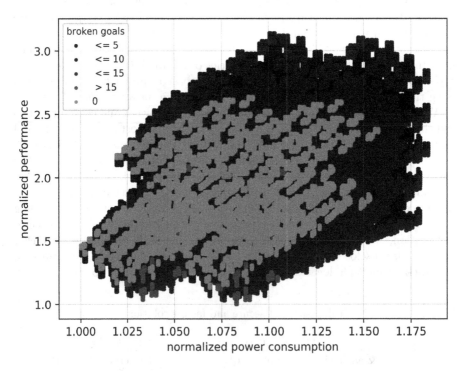

Fig. 2. Solution space identified by the framework using the BAG based method.

---

[3] https://www.wired.com/story/hackers-steal-tesla-model-s-seconds-key-fob/.

Figures 2 and 3 show all solutions found by the framework based on their normalized system performance, power consumption and the number of exceeded security goals for BAG and RISKEE based security constraint calculation, respectively. Both the BAG and the RISKEE based method only consider a small number of solutions to meet their respective security constraints. Both approaches found the same solution space. Out of 5.898.240, the RISKEE based method only considered 320, the BAG 1.643 solutions to be secure. In comparison, the RISKEE method reduced the solution space of a secure solution by another 80.52%. Considering the solutions found using the BAG and the RISKEE based method, one must notice the difference in the selection of options for the distinct hardware components. This difference only comes from the frequency and the impact with which the risk experts considered the attacks on the key material in the RISKEE based approach. The BAG based method does not reflect these two attributes.

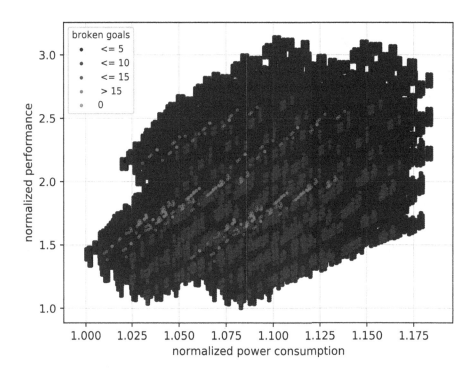

Fig. 3. Solution space identified by the framework using the RISKEE based method.

Figures 5 and 4 show the numbers of found solutions ordered by their average attack success probability and average mean risk, respectively. One can see that for the BAG based calculation, the majority of the found solutions (41.67%) has an average attack success probability of less than a fourth (~ 0.0005) of the solution with the highest attack success probability. Considering the RISKEE

Table 5. Fastest secure solutions found based on average attack probability (avg ap), average risk value (avg rv) and performance.

HWC	Fastest secure (BAG)	Fastest secure (RISKEE)
AP (node & anchor)	HW crypto; TEE	HW crypto; TEE
SE (node)	EAL 4+	EAL 6+
SE (anchor)	EAL 4+	EAL 5+
UR	HW crypto, TZ, HW firewall	HW crypto, TZ, HW firewall
avg ap/avg rv	0.00069	199.5$
norm. perf.	~1.13	~1.35

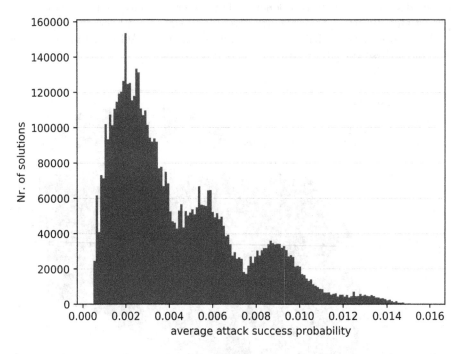

Fig. 4. BAG based solutions found by the framework categorized according to their average attack success probability. Stepsize of $9.95 * 10^{-5}$.

based calculation, the majority of solutions (64%) identified by the framework lies between 1406$ and 2700$ of the average mean risk value. For both calculation approaches, the framework found the least number of solutions (1.58% and 0.4% respectively for BAG and RISKEE based approach) in the most insecure fourth considering their average attack success probability/average mean risk. Table 5 describes the fastest secure solution found by the BAG and RISKEE method. Table 6 the most power-efficient secure solutions, given their average attack probability and average mean risk. One must notice that for both the secure solutions with optimal performance and power consumption, the RISKEE based solution

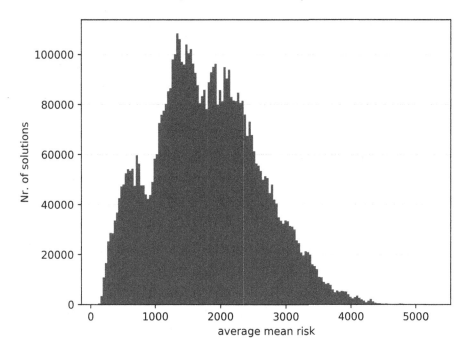

Fig. 5. RISKEE based solutions found by the framework categorized according to their average mean risk. Stepsize of 31.

chooses options with higher security attack mitigation capabilities than the BAG based approach, for both the SE and the AP of the anchor and node device. The increased level of security chosen for the SE is due to the high impact, with which the disclosure of the session key and the master key comes.

Said impact increases the influence of a successful key disclosure on the average mean risk of the overall system dramatically. A similar result can be seen when considering the most power-efficient and secure solutions, regarding their average attack success probability and mean risk value, respectively. Also, for this optimization criteria, the BAG based method chose less secure options for the SE, but also for the node's AP, compared to the RISKEE based method.

Based on these results, we observed that a risk-based analysis, such as provided by RISKEE, improves the level of detail with which one can model attack scenarios. This higher granularity in the security constraints comes with additional computational overhead. The use case scenarios were executed on a system comprising 16 GB of RAM and a Intel® Core™ i7-4600U CPU with 2.10 GHz.

Table 7 shows the results of assessing the framework's scalability and the computational overhead of calculating the security constraints using the BAG and RISKEE based methods. We executed both methods with attack graphs comprising 18, 37, and 56 attack nodes (AN), both with and without using the break criteria for the calculation of secure solutions, as described in Sect. 3. It includes the ratio between the execution times of the full security constraint

Table 6. Most power efficient and secure solutions found based on average attack probability (avg ap), average risk value (avg rv) and power consumption (power cons).

HWC	Most power eff. secure (BAG)	Most power eff. secure (RISKEE)
AP (node)	SW crypto-lib sc sec.; TEE	HW crypto; TEE
AP (anchor)	SW crypto-lib sc sec.; TEE	SW crypto-lib sc sec. TEE
SE (node)	EAL 4+	EAL 6+
SE (anchor)	EAL 4+	EAL 4+
UR (node)	HW crypto, TZ, HW firewall	HW crypto, TZ, HW firewall
UR (anchor)	HW crypto, TZ, HW firewall	HW crypto, TZ, HW firewall
avg ap/rv	0.00074	198.67$
power cons	~1.014	~1.025

Table 7. Computational overhead for BAG and RISKEE based security constraint calculation for attack graphs with different number of attack nodes (AN).

# of AN	BAG (break)	BAG	RISKEE (break)	RISKEE
18	502s	551s/1.09	2021s	3509s/1.74
37	1943s	2052s/1.05	3315s	5597s/1.69
56	8556s	9337s/1.09	15826s	23670s/1.5

calculation and the optimized approach, both for the BAG and RISKEE based calculation. For the BAG based method, one must notice that the break criteria can speed up the calculation by ~5% to ~9%. For the RISKEE based method, the calculation time is reduced by ~50% to ~70%. In general, one can see that the RISKEE based method can capture more details for calculating security constraints. However, its calculation takes ~2.5 to ~6.3 times longer, when compared to the BAG based method. The higher reduction of the computational overhead for the RISKEE based method comes from the relatively higher risk calculation delay induced by this method. Hence, the more risk calculation the framework can skip, the higher the speedup of the overall calculation becomes. This speedup also shows that the attack probability calculation using the BAGs is much more efficient.

The consumer device based use case shows the difference in the BAG and RISKEE based calculation of secure system solutions. We show that the additional information regarding an attack's impact and frequency, used in the RISKEE based approach, can lead to vastly different results regarding the security constraints. This additional information leads to more time-consuming computation. Considering the maximal calculation time of the RISKEE based method (~6 h 30 min), a more efficient approach must be found. For future work, we will develop a combination of BAG and RISKEE based attack graphs.

5   Conclusion and Future Work

In this paper, we presented a DSE framework, which offers the designers to model cybersecurity threats as BAGs or risk trees. Thereby, the DSE framework automatically calculates a set of security constraints from these modeled security attack scenarios and finds an optimal and secure system partitioning and task allocation, with additional consideration of performance, power consumption, and other constraints. Based on a commercial consumer device use case, we showed the framework's feasibility and the distinct methods' scalabilities.

The approach's main limitation is the source from which to draw the information about the attack success probabilities and the attack frequencies for both BAG and RISKEE based calculation. At the moment, only security expert knowledge serves as input. One must also consider the same limitation for the assessment of the mitigation capabilities of hardware components. No method has yet been published on how to rate a system's ability to withstand security attacks. Hence our assumptions for the component's mitigation capabilities are based on CC certifications. In future work, we will focus on proposing such a method and on a combined calculation utilizing both the BAG and the RISKEE approach within the DSE framework.

Acknowledgment. Project partners are NXP Semiconductors Austria GmbH and the Technical University of Graz. This work was supported by the Austrian Research Promotion Agency (FFG) within the project UBSmart (project number: 859475).

References

1. Al-Mhiqani, M.N., et al.: Cyber-security incidents: a review cases in cyber-physical systems. Int. J. Adv. Comput. Sci. Appl. **9**(1), 499–508 (2018)
2. Ammann, P., et al.: Scalable, graph-based network vulnerability analysis. In: Proceedings of the 9th ACM Conference on Computer and Communications Security (2002)
3. Feng, N., et al.: A security risk analysis model for information systems: causal relationships of risk factors and vulnerability propagation analysis. Inf. Sci. **256**, 57–73 (2014)
4. Gressl, L., et al.: Consideration of security attacks in the design space exploration of embedded systems. In: 2019 22nd Euromicro Conference on Digital System Design (DSD) (2019)
5. Gressl, L., et al.: A security aware design space exploration framework. In: Proceedings of the 14th International Conference on Systems ICONS 2019. ThinkMind (TM) Digital Library (2019)
6. Hasan, M., et al.: A design-space exploration for allocating security tasks in multi-core real-time systems. In: Proceedings of the 2018 Design, Automation and Test in Europe Conference and Exhibition, DATE 2018 (2018)
7. Kang, E.: Design space exploration for security. In: IEEE Cybersecurity Development Design (2016)
8. Knerr, B.: Heuristic optimisation methods for system partitioning in HW/SW co-design. Ph.D. thesis, Vienna University of Technology (2008)

9. Krisper, M., Dobaj, J., Macher, G., Schmittner, C.: RISKEE: a risk-tree based method for assessing risk in cyber security. In: Walker, A., O'Connor, R.V., Messnarz, R. (eds.) EuroSPI 2019. CCIS, vol. 1060, pp. 45–56. Springer, Cham (2019). https://doi.org/10.1007/978-3-030-28005-5_4

10. Li, L.W., et al.: Security-aware modeling and analysis for HW/SW partitioning. In: Proceedings of the 5th International Conference on Model-Driven Engineering and Software Development (2017)

11. Nasser, M., et al.: Cyber-security incidents: a review cases in cyber-physical systems. Int. J. Adv. Comput. Sci. Appl. **9**(1), 499–508 (2018)

12. Poolsappasit, N., et al.: Dynamic security risk management using Bayesian attack graphs. IEEE Trans. Depend. Secure Comput. (2012)

13. Rosvall, K., et al.: Exploring power and throughput for dataflow applications on predictable NoC multiprocessors. In: Proceedings - 21st Euromicro Conference on Digital System Design, DSD 2018 (2018). https://doi.org/10.1109/DSD.2018.00011

14. Roudier, Y., Apvrille, L.: SysML-Sec - a model driven approach for designing safe and secure systems. In: Proceedings of the 3rd International Conference on Model-Driven Engineering and Software Development (2015)

15. Schiffman, M.: Common Vulnerability Scoring System (CVSS) (2019). https://www.first.org/cvss/v3.1/specification-document

16. Stierand, I., et al.: Integrating the security aspect into design space exploration of embedded systems. In: Proceedings of IEEE 25th International Symposium on Software Reliability Engineering Workshops, ISSREW 2014 (2014)

17. Tamas-Selicean, D., Pop, P.: Design optimization of mixed-criticality real-time embedded systems. ACM Trans. Embed. Comput. Syst. **14**(3), 1–29 (2015)

18. Xie, Y., et al.: Security/timing-aware design space exploration of CAN FD for automotive cyber-physical systems. IEEE Trans. Industr. Inf. **15**(2), 1094–1104 (2018)

19. Yu, R., et al.: Deploying robust security in Internet of Things. In: 2018 IEEE Conference on Communications and Network Security, CNS 2018 (2018)

20. Zheng, B., et al.: Cross-layer codesign for secure cyber-physical systems. IEEE Trans. Comput. Aided Des. Integr. Circuits Syst. **35**(5), 699–711 (2016)

Securing Electric Vehicle Charging Systems Through Component Binding

Andreas Fuchs, Dustin Kern, Christoph Krauß$^{(\boxtimes)}$, and Maria Zhdanova

Fraunhofer SIT, Darmstadt, Germany
`christoph.krauss@sit.fraunhofer.de`

Abstract. In Vehicle-to-Grid (V2G) scenarios, Electric Vehicle (EV) batteries serve as distributed energy resources that help stabilize power supply through managed (dis)charging. The effective and safe grid integration is only possible when an Electric Vehicle Charging System (EVCS) responsible for the battery management and V2G communication is counterfeit-free and protected against malicious attacks. By manipulating the EVCS, adversaries can cause financial and physical damage and increase the risk of hazardous situations such as fire and traffic accidents. In this paper, we introduce **secEVCS**, a security architecture for EVCSs, which ensures that only a vehicle with a manufacturer-approved charging system can connect to the grid by securely binding all components of the EVCS. Our solution is based on the enhanced authorization functionality of the Trusted Platform Module (TPM) and protects against the installation of counterfeit products and re-use of secret data stored in scrapped EVCSs. We implemented **secEVCS** using a TPM 2.0 chip and the V2G protocol specified in the ISO 15118 standard to show the feasibility and to evaluate the performance of our solution.

Keywords: Electric vehicle charging · Security · TPM 2.0 · ISO 15118

1 Introduction

The worldwide adoption of EVs, i.e., fully battery-powered and plug-in hybrid vehicles, is growing, with the 5 million mark reached in 2018 [8]. The need to charge EV batteries causes an extra load on electric grids, but their storage capacity can be used by V2G services to handle power fluctuations [3]. The V2G technology allows EVs to communicate with the grid to optimize charging profiles, e.g., to limit the charging rate or to feed energy from batteries back to the grid during high demand. For this purpose, V2G communication protocols such as ISO 15118 [10] were developed. Using these protocols, an EV can inform the grid of its preferences (energy amount, departure time, etc.) and negotiate a grid-friendly (dis)charging schedule. The support for bidirectional power transfer services is provided by the vehicle's EVCS with two connected components: an Electric Vehicle Communication Controller (EVCC) and a Battery Management System (BMS) responsible for the V2G session handling and

© Springer Nature Switzerland AG 2020
A. Casimiro et al. (Eds.): SAFECOMP 2020, LNCS 12234, pp. 387–401, 2020.
https://doi.org/10.1007/978-3-030-54549-9_26

battery management, respectively. As the degradation rate of EV batteries is affected by the charging strategy, ensuring their correct operation during V2G sessions is equally important to servicing the grid [18]. Besides, Li-ion batteries are prone to overheating and can self-ignite due to improper (dis)charging control [1,21].

The possibility to cause safety hazards and the V2G connectivity can provide a strong incentive for malicious attacks aiming to subvert the functioning of the EVCS. For example, if an adversary manipulates the BMS part of the EVCS or replaces it with a tampered one, s/he can damage the battery by deliberately operating it outside of the safe range, which can eventually lead to its failure and the danger of fire or explosion [14,15]. In case several EVCSs connected to the grid are under adversarial control, they can be turned into a botnet of high-wattage devices for a coordinated attack aiming for local power outages or large-scale blackouts [20]. Another critical aspect is the usage of counterfeit components in EVCSs. The growing market and high price of EV batteries attract criminals selling expired or low-quality counterfeit spare parts, which do not meet regulatory standards and are potentially unsafe [17].

In this paper, we propose a new security architecture for EVCSs, further referred to as secEVCS, which guarantees that a vehicle participating in V2G services has a manufacturer-approved configuration of EVCC and BMS by securely binding these components. secEVCS uses a TPM in the EVCC and the Device Identifier Composition Engine (DICE) [25] in the BMS as security anchors. The general idea is to only allow access to a V2G authentication key, which is required for connecting to the grid, if the binding is successfully verified using the TPM's enhanced authorization functionality. secEVCS protects against the installation of counterfeit spare parts and re-use of secrets from scrapped EVCSs. We implemented secEVCS using a hardware TPM and ISO 15118 [10] for V2G communication[1] to evaluate secEVCS under realistic constraints. To our knowledge, TPMs have not been deployed in this scenario yet and the analysis of the trade-offs is missing. Our work aims to close this gap.

The rest of the paper is structured as follows: First, we introduce the necessary background on TPMs to be able to understand the paper in Sect. 2. Next, we discuss related work in Sect. 3. In Sect. 4, we define our system model and in Sect. 5 analyze safety-related security threats. Security and functional requirements are defined in Sect. 6. In Sect. 7, we introduce secEVCS before we describe and evaluate our prototype in Sect. 8. We discuss the applicability of our solution in Sect. 9 and conclude the paper in Sect. 10.

2   Background on Trusted Platform Modules (TPMs)

The TPM 2.0 Library Specification [23] defines a catalog of functionalities that can be used to build the second iteration of the TPM for different platforms.

---

[1] The ISO 15118 standard series is actively adopted by the industry, e.g., the CharIn network (www.charinev.org). While we focus on the current protocol specification, ISO 15118-2, we consider the 2nd edition draft, ISO 15118-20 [11], whenever relevant.

Accompanying the TPM specification, a TPM Software Stack (TSS) 2.0 specification [26] defines multiple Application Programming Interfaces (APIs) for different application scenarios. A TPM is a microchip designed to provide security-related functionalities, e.g., secure storage and usage of cryptographic keys. A central functionality in our solution is the enhanced authorization functionality. All objects of a TPM, e.g., cryptographic keys, can be authorized with a policy that must be satisfied in order to authorize an action on that object. Policy assertions are sent to the TPM before the command being authorized. Our solution also uses the internal Non-Volatile (NV) memory of a TPM, which retains content even if the power is off. This memory can be used to make keys of the TPM persistent but can also be allocated by applications to create indexed strongly monotonic NV counters. In the following, we list the TPM 2.0 commands and policy assertions relevant for our proposed solution.

- **TPM2_Create.** This command is used to create all kinds of objects for the TPM. This includes cryptographic keys usable for authenticating to external entities. During creation, an (enhanced authorization) policy can be provided that restricts usage of the created object.
- **TPM2_Sign.** This command calculates a signature using a private key created via *TPM2_Create*. These signatures can be used for authenticating a device or for asserting data integrity and origin.
- **TPM2_VerifySignature.** The TPM can verify a signature using a provided public key. This operation by itself is much faster when implemented in software and does not require the secure execution environment of a TPM. This operation is to be used in conjunction with *TPM2_PolicySigned*.
- **TPM2_NV_DefineSpace.** This command is used to define an NV index. Depending on the assigned index number, the NV index is either part of the user-owned (storage hierarchy) or of the platform-/OEM-owned (platform hierarchy) areas of the TPM. For the sake of this paper, only OEM-owned indices are used.
- **TPM2_NV_Increment.** This command is used to increment a TPM NV counter value.
- **TPM2_StartAuthSession.** In order to fulfill any authorization policy, the application needs to start a policy session using the *TPM2_StartAuthSession* command. Then the actual policy statements are subsequently satisfied by invoking the corresponding TPM commands.
- **TPM2_PolicyAuthorize.** This command allows the activation of policies *after* the definition of an object. In order to achieve this, a public key is registered with a policy. This policy element then acts as a placeholder for any other policy branch that is signed with the corresponding private key.
- **TPM2_PolicyNV.** The PolicyNV element provides the possibility to include NV-indices in the evaluation of a policy. Amongst other operations, it can be used to test whether an NV counter index has a certain value or whether it is smaller or greater.
- **TPM2_PolicySigned.** This policy element can be used to validate a signature before granting object usage. A public key is registered with the policy. In order to satisfy a *TPM2_PolicySigned*, a TPM generated nonce (from

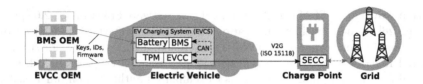

Fig. 1. System overview

TPM2_StartAuthSession) must be signed by the holder of the private key corresponding to the registered public key.

- **TPM2_PolicyTicket.** In order to speed up operations, a *TPM2_Policy Signed* can return a ticket that is valid for a certain amount of time. Instead of having to execute the same sequence of *TPM2_VerifySignature* and *TPM2_PolicySigned*, the ticket can be replayed into a *TPM2_PolicyTicket* command instead. This saves the round trips with the owner of the private key for a predefined amount of time. The expiration time is already denoted in the policy during its creation.

3   Related Work

The use of trusted computing in vehicle communication scenarios is commonly discussed. In [30,31], solutions for privacy-preserving EV charging and billing based on Direct Anonymous Attestation techniques using a TPM are introduced. In [29], the authors use TPM-based remote attestation for identity and integrity verification in the V2X scenario. The authors of [28] propose to use a Mobile Trusted Module for remote attestation in V2G networks. In their system, an EV directly sends its integrity metric to the grid server to verify its trustworthiness. The work in [7] presents a privacy-aware architecture for V2G networks. As part of this solution, a TPM in EV batteries is used for encrypted communication of charging status, accumulation of information in sealed storage and remote attestation. In [19], another security architecture for V2G networks is discussed using a TPM in EV batteries for remote attestation. In [5], the authors propose to include a TPM in a head unit (also called infotainment system) to realize protocols for secure update, remote attestation, and sensitive data protection.

In our previous work [4], we introduce TrustEV, a security architecture for secure provisioning, storage and usage of ISO 15118 credentials in an EV based on TPM 2.0. Similarly, the TPM is used to store and control access to authentication keys of the EVCC. The main feature of TrustEV is the direct import of the ISO 15118 keys created by a third party into the EVCC's TPM. TrustEV can be combined with secEVCS to additionally support secure components binding.

4   System Overview

Figure 1 gives an overview of our assumed system. An Electric Vehicle Charging System (EVCS) comprises a Battery Management System (BMS) with an integrated rechargeable battery and an Electric Vehicle Communication Controller (EVCC) with a TPM providing it with security services (cf. Sect. 2). As TPMs are common in modern cars [9], this assumption is not limiting.

The BMS's major function is to maintain the vehicle's battery within its safe operating range, to monitor its state (i.e., state-of-charge, state-of-health, and state-of-function) and to assess the available energy amount [2]. The BMS also controls battery cooling/heating, operates power switches, and exchanges charging-related data via a Controller Area Network (CAN) bus with the EVCC.

The EVCC is responsible for communication with a Supply Equipment Communication Controller (SECC) of a charge point during V2G service sessions and supports automated authentication of EVs (i.e., Plug&Charge). We assume an EV has to identify and authenticate itself against an SECC by means of a so-called *authentication key* stored in its EVCC before it can connect to the grid for charging. In ISO 15118, this key is part of the vehicle's OEM provisioning or contract certificate. When negotiating a charging schedule for a V2G session with the SECC, the EVCC queries the BMS on such parameters as battery state, allowed current and voltage. Together with the expected departure time and other user-defined charging preferences, this information is crucial for demand-side management aimed to improve efficiency and stability of the grid. Grid-friendly charging behavior can be awarded with reduced tariff rates. While charging, the EVCC periodically receives metering receipts from the SECC for signing that may later be used to bill the EV's driver for the charged energy.

The life-cycle of an EVCS and its components includes several stages. The BMS and the EVCC are produced by respective Original Equipment Manufacturers (OEMs) that provide firmware and cryptographic keys. An automotive OEM creates for an EV a unique Vehicle Identification Number (VIN)[2] and authentication key, while a battery OEM provides a BMS with a unique *identity key*. The cryptographic keys are assumed to be created by OEMs in a secure way and not leaked during manufacturing. When deploying a new EVCS in a vehicle, the EV's manufacturer defines a safety-approved configuration, by binding a BMS to an EVCC. Replacing or updating any of the EVCS's components can be carried out in an authorized repair shop, where a new approved configuration will be created. A drained EV's battery can also be replaced with a fully-charged one in a battery swap station operated by a battery swapping company [22]. We assume backend systems of the OEMs and service providers exchange information securely using a common Public Key Infrastructure (PKI).

5   Safety-Related Security Threats

The EVCS of a vehicle is a safety-critical system. The growing number of reports on self-ignition of EV batteries while charging or in driving [21], shows the potential for adversaries not only to damage EVs and their components but to harm their passengers or people in the vicinity with targeted attacks. In [15,16], the

---

[2] VINs mainly conform to two international standards ISO 3779 and US Standard FMVSS 115; a VIN is always 17 characters long.

authors propose a Security-Aware Hazard and Risk Analysis Method (SAHARA) and use it to identify threats for a BMS and estimate the risk. Threats for BMS and potential effects are also analyzed in [14]. Based on these analyses, we consider the following threat scenarios with their possible safety impact:

Configuration Tampering. An adversary replaces the BMS in the EVCS with one that is not approved by the OEM and/or under full control of the adversary. This could also be done by the EV's driver who aims to extend the range of the vehicle by upgrading the battery [6]. Such action would violate the OEM's warranty. **Impact:** The attack affects the EVCS's integrity and has multiple safety implications. The adversary can modify battery information, e.g., to indicate a larger capacity than given, and control battery functions to, e.g., ignore dangerous operating conditions like overheating in order to damage the battery or cause a fire [18]. Moreover, incompatible EVCS components can incorrectly interpret exchanged data, which can shorten the battery lifetime and lead to hazardous situations. Disrupting demand-side management would also affect the grid.

Charging Contract Hijacking. An adversary uses a scrapped EVCC storing the authentication key of a valid V2G user to charge her/his own vehicle on the uncovered account or to use the access profile to connect to the V2G service. **Impact:** The attack affects the confidentiality of the EV's key and the privacy of the previous user of the scrapped EVCC; the integrity and authenticity of V2G sessions is also breached. The latter can affect grid stability due to unexpected charging behavior or even cause blackouts if the attack is launched in a coordinated manner [20].

Counterfeit BMS. An adversary uses old BMSs with expired or malfunctioning batteries to produce and sell counterfeit products, which can still carry the label of the original manufacturer but are not certified for safe use. **Impact:** The attack affects system integrity and authenticity. Counterfeit batteries often lack required safety protections and can easily catch fire.

6 Security and Functional Requirements

To prevent the threats defined in Sect. 5 with secEVCS, we propose to enable access to an EV's authentication key needed to use V2G services, only if its EVCS is original, i.e., only if a verifiable binding between EVCC and BMS exists. This leads to the following security requirements, which must be fulfilled:

SR_1 *Secure private key storage and usage.* Private keys (e.g., authentication keys, identity keys) shall be protected against leakage during their storage and usage.

SR_2 *Restriction of key usage to trustworthy systems (Key usage authorization).* Access to private keys shall only be possible if the EVCS is trustworthy, i.e., the components configurations are approved by the manufacturer and are not manipulated.

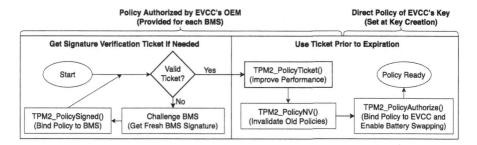

Fig. 2. secEVCS policy verification steps

SR_3 *Revocation support.* It shall be possible to revoke BMS of an EVCS in case it
   is removed from an EV, so that it cannot be used in another manufacturer-
   approved EVCS configuration later on.

   A security solution for EVCSs should bring clear benefits to the automotive and EV battery industry and consumers without unnecessary restricting
legitimate usage scenarios. This results in the following functional requirements:

FR_1 *Minimal performance overhead.* A solution shall not cause undesirable
   delays in EV charging and shall meet timing constraints of standard V2G
   protocols. In ISO 15118, e.g., charging may be delayed by two uses of the
   EVCC's key and key use is bound by strict timing requirements (detailed
   in Sect. 8.2).
FR_2 *Support of legitimate component exchange.* Only legitimate entities shall be
   able to replace or swap the battery (including BMS) and/or EVCC while
   maintaining the manufacturer-approved EVCS configuration.

7   Solution

The general idea of secEVCS is to bind EVCC and BMS of an EV and to allow
access to an authentication key only if this binding can be verified. The authentication key is securely stored and used in the EVCC's TPM and access is only
possible if a TPM enhanced authorization policy is fulfilled. This policy includes
the result of challenge-response protocol between EVCC and BMS.

secEVCS consists of an initial EVCS preparation phase for initializing and
binding EVCC and BMS (cf. Sect. 7.1), the EVCS usage phase (during the lifetime of the EV) supporting the authorization of charging sessions and the swapping of batteries (cf. Sect. 7.2), and performance optimizations (cf. Sect. 7.3).
Figure 2 shows the enhanced authorization policy verification steps as the central part of secEVCS, which are described in more detail below.

7.1   EVCS Preparation

EVCC Preparation. During manufacturing, the OEM generates an authentication key on the EVCC's TPM. This authentication key comes with an authorization policy (*TPM2_PolicyAuthorize()*) that refers to an OEM public key

(cf. Fig. 2 on the right) for policy statements. To use the authentication key, the EVCC software needs to present a policy to the TPM that was authorized (signed) by the OEM. Thus, the newly created key cannot be accessed directly after its generation. The OEM needs to explicitly issue (and sign) a policy statement that describes, under which conditions the authentication key can be used. We use the EV's VIN as policy reference value of the authentication key's policy. This way, this key can only be accessed if a policy is fulfilled that was authorized by the OEM with the corresponding VIN denoted during key generation, i.e., a signed policy addresses the intended EVCC only and cannot be copied to other EVCCs. The EVCC preparation process is represented by InitTPM() in Fig. 3a. If key generation on the TPM is not possible, keys can be also generated outside and imported into the EVCC's TPM (e.g., in ISO 15118 using TrustEV [4]).

BMS Preparation. The BMS is equipped with a DICE [25] (cf. InitDICE() in Fig. 3a), as a cheap alternative to a TPM suitable for highly constrained embedded systems [12]. DICE generates a unique device Identifier (ID) based on a globally unique secret and a measurement of the device's first mutable code using a cryptographically secure one-way function. Hence, any persistent attack to the BMS results in the generation of a different device ID. As the DICE is trusted and has exclusive access to the unique secret, it is impossible for an attacker to recover the secret or generate a valid device ID after a persistent attack. The BMS can use the DICE-generated ID to secure its identity key (e.g., by using the ID as seed to a Key Derivation Function (KDF) and using the resulting key to encrypt the identity key before it is stored). This way, the BMS's identity key is also protected from persistent attacks. With this key, the BMS can authenticate itself using a public key signature. As the BMS' public identity key is required for the binding between EVCC and BMS (see next paragraph), the key is read out by the BMS' OEM and passed to the EVCC's OEM (cf. OEM in Fig. 3a).

BMS and EVCC Binding. At this step, the EVCC's OEM needs to issue (sign) a respective policy (cf. BindingPolicy and PolicySig in Fig. 3a). The policy consists of a *TPM2_PolicySigned()* containing the public key of the BMS. To fulfill this condition, a nonce generated by the TPM must be signed with the BMS' private key and the signature validated by the TPM. Additionally, the policy contains a *TPM2_PolicyNV()* statement that links this policy to a monotonic counter inside the TPM. If a BMS binding needs to be revoked in the future, the OEM can increment the TPM's counter. The signature over this policy by the OEM also includes the VIN as policy reference value as mentioned above. This binding can happen in conjunction with the initial key generation or at a later stage.

7.2   EVCS Usage

Charging Authorization. Access to the authentication key is only possible if the BMS and EVCC binding is successfully verified. This process is shown in Fig. 3b (PolicyCheck() aggregates all policy-related validations). The EVCC first loads the authorized policy (i.e., the BMS binding policy) and policy reference

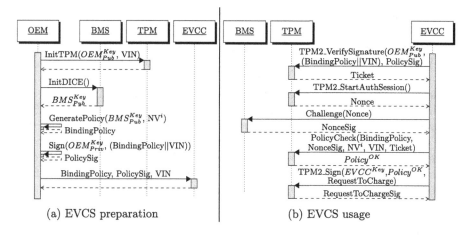

Fig. 3. EVCS sequence diagrams

value, i.e., VIN, and verifies the signature using the OEM's public key. The result is a so-called signature validation ticket. Then, the EVCC starts a policy session (*TPM2_StartAuthSession()*) and sends the session's nonce as a challenge to the BMS. The BMS signs the nonce with its private key and returns the signature and its public key. The EVCC extends its session with a validation of the BMS' signature (*TPM2_PolicySigned()*) and the comparison of the NV-counter (*TPM2_PolicyNV()*). The BMS binding is authorized using the signature validation ticket (*TPM2_PolicyAuthorize()*). After this, the policy session is in a state that grants access to the EVCC's key operations and the EVCC can issue a *TPM2_Sign()* operation to authenticate itself against the charge point.

Battery Swapping. A battery swapping company needs to maintain a backend connection to the OEMs and perform the above BMS binding process. To invalidate the binding to the old BMS, the OEM increments the TPM's counter and then issues (signs) a new policy for the new BMS and the new counter value.

7.3   EVCS Enhancements for Better Performance

The process for key usage described in Sect. 7.2 requires the EVCC to challenge the BMS and perform the policy session assertions for each access to the authentication key. This can lead to undesirable delays when trying to charge an EV (e.g., in our tests it took on average 2.4 s; cf. Sect. 8.2). This can be easily avoided by sending challenges to the BMS independent of the charging sessions and pre-calculating the entire policy session. For example, the EVCC can send a challenge whenever the charging port lid is opened. This way, a correct policy session is always available before the authentication key is to be used.

Another issue is that the EVCC has to send a new challenge to the BMS each time it needs to use the authentication key. This can delay communication protocols between EVCC and SECC using this key not only for charge authorization, but also, e.g., to sign metering receipts. A low performance of the BMS Electronic Control Unit (ECU)[3] and a low throughput of a CAN bus[4], this process (estimated to about 5.8 s) may exceed timing constraints of the protocol.

We address this issue by using a shortcut in the *TPM2_PolicySigned()* command. The command can output a ticket upon validation, which can be used in future policy sessions (within the expiration time) using the *TPM2_PolicyTicket()* command as a replacement (cf. Fig. 2 on the left). This expiration time should not be too short (to gain a speedup) and neither too long (to restrain attacks). An expiration time of 5 min is a good starting point to give a user enough time to initiate charging, while still preventing potential attacks. These 5 min provide enough time to start a second policy session from the beginning.

8   Implementation and Evaluation

In this section, we evaluate our proposed solution. We use ISO 15118-2 [10] as communication protocol between EVCC and SECC. We describe the implemented prototype and evaluate the added overhead. A minimal overhead is important for the usability of secEVCS in terms of compliance to the timing constraints of ISO 15118 on EVCC signature creation as well as for user convenience. Additionally, ISO 15118-20 [11], the upcoming successor of [10], allows for even tighter timing constraints, which are also considered in the evaluation.

8.1   secEVCS Implementation

Our prototype was implemented using three Raspberry Pi 3 Model B running Linux kernel 4.14 to simulate the EVCC, BMS, and SECC. The EVCC-Pi is equipped with an Infineon Iridium 9670 TPM 2.0. EVCC and BMS communicate over regular Ethernet, while SECC and EVCC communicate over power-line communication (PLC) Stamp micro 2 EVBs (similar to PLC over a charging cable). Our test-bed is shown in Fig. 4.

To execute TPM commands, we use the TPM2-TSS[5] and as ISO 15118 implementation we use RISE-V2G[6], integrated with the TrustEV implementation from [4] for *EVCC Preparation* (cf. Sect. 7.1). The challenge-response communication between EVCC and BMS is implemented using the Secure Shell (SSH) protocol [13] to simulate any added security means on the automotive bus.

The expiration time of BMS signatures is set to 5 min. Challenges are sent to the BMS 5 s before start of ISO 15118 communication (to simulate the

---

[3] It can take an ARM Cortex-M0+ without performance optimizations up to 3649 ms to create a signature using the algorithm and parameters defined by ISO 15118 [27].

[4] Transmitting 16 byte nonce, 64 byte EC public key, and 64 byte ECDSA signature in 18 extended CAN frames (16 bytes each with 8 bytes data and 7 bits inter-frame spacing) with 125 kbps Low-Speed CAN takes about 20 ms under optimal conditions.

[5] TPM2-TSS: https://github.com/tpm2-software/tpm2-tss.

[6] RISE-V2G: https://github.com/V2GClarity/RISE-V2G.

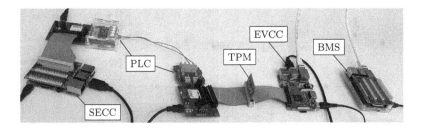

Fig. 4. Test-bed setup

time from opening the charging port lid to plugging in the charging cable) and a minute before the current signature expires. After receiving a signature, *TPM2_PolicySigned()* is called to retrieve the verification ticket. The ticket is used by two processes to pre-calculate multiple policy sessions concurrently. When the authentication key is used in ISO 15118, one of these pre-calculated policies is consumed. We only use two pre-calculation processes along with the ticket generation process, to not exceed three concurrent authorization sessions. While a TPM must be able to support 64 active sessions, it must only be able to hold 3 of those in RAM at a time [24]; hence, exceeding this limit would decrease performance on TPMs that only support the minimums from [24].

8.2   Performance Evaluation

During performance evaluation, we measured the computational overhead created by our prototype from Sect. 8.1 compared to the default RISE-V2G implementation. All measurements were repeated 100 times each using Java's *System.nanoTime()*. During a charging loop, the EVCC alternates between sending charging status and signed metering receipt messages. It tries to send them as fast as possible, reaching 121.9 ms between consecutive receipts. For our measurements, the EVCC sent 10 metering receipts for each of the 100 charging loops.

The time for signing ISO 15118 messages with default RISE-V2G was 15.7 ms and with **secEVCS** 469.8 ms. For comparison, without the parallel pre-calculated policies, the average signature time was 1119.8 ms, and without any of the performance optimizations for **secEVCS**, i.e., with an on-demand challenge to the BMS for each key usage and no policy pre-calculation, the time for signing ISO 15118 messages was 2437.8 ms. Our measurements for **secEVCS** are shown in Fig. 5 (signature #0 is for charge authorization and #1–10 for metering receipts).

With our setup, the time from sending a challenge to the BMS until receiving a signature was 277.6 ms. In Sect. 7.3, we discussed a more realistic device configuration. Extrapolating our measurements to low power ECUs and CAN bus, the measurements for BMS signatures would increase to 3669 ms, leading to ISO 15118 message signing time of 5829.28 ms for **secEVCS** without optimizations. This correlates to the head time used for pre-calculation of sessions and the use of the improvements proposed in Sect. 7.3.

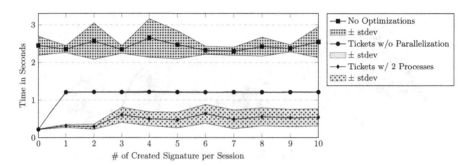

Fig. 5. Mean times of signature creation in a charging session

It is worth noting that with secEVCS there was a significant difference in the times for signing charge authorization requests compared to metering receipts. The former was on average 228.8 ms, whereas the latter – 493.9 ms. Also, the mean time for signing the first 2 receipts of each charging loop was 304.3 ms and the mean time for the 3rd to 10th was 541.3 ms. This is because we have only two processes to pre-calculate policy sessions. Hence, when starting a charging session, there are two policies ready to use and if more than two signatures need to be created, new policy sessions need to be calculated at run-time.

In our setup with 2 parallel policy sessions (n_p), 121.9 ms between metering receipts (t_m), and the signature time of 228.8 ms (t_s) there are only 472.6 ms ($= n_p \times t_m + (n_p - 1) \times t_s$) for policy pre-calculation. Anything above that will increase the signature time. With an average time for policy calculation of 737.4 ms, i.e., an overrun of 264.8 ms, this gives about 500 ms for signatures without full policy pre-calculation. While this should lead to alternating signature times (after a signature with $t_s = 500$, the available time for pre-calculation is 743.8 ms which should allow for a fast signature), we did not experience this effect. Instead, as a result of the parallelization, the times for the 3rd metering receipt signature onward were much less predictable with a standard deviation of 231 ms compared to the times for the first 2 with a standard deviation of 56.4 ms and the time for the authorization signature with a standard deviation of 4.8 ms.

Since in ISO 15118 at most the first two signatures are time-critical, i.e., signing a request for a new authentication key and signing the charge authorization request afterwards can delay the charging start, we argue that the achieved results are acceptable for the use-case. Regarding ISO 15118 compatibility, the only requirements affected by the increased EVCC signature time are the *V2G_EVCC_Sequence_Performance_Time* of 40 s (time for the EVCC to send its next request after a response from the SECC) and the *V2G_SECC_Sequence_Timeout* of 60 s (timeout of the SECC for waiting on the next EVCC request). Even without the performance optimizations, secEVCS stays well within the relevant limits. However, in the 2nd edition ISO 15118-20 [11], the timeout mechanism for metering receipts was changed. The SECC may define its own arbitrary timeout in seconds. Hence, a minimal timeout of 1 s is possible and only the optimized secEVCS would be able to meet this minimum (cf. Fig. 5).

9 Requirements Coverage Discussion

To prevent safety-related threats from Sect. 5, secEVCS verifies the binding between the EVCS components prior to charging. In Sect. 6, we defined the requirements that need to be satisfied by a secure and usable solution. Below we informally discuss how these requirements are covered by secEVCS.

In secEVCS, the EVCC's authentication key is generated and stored in the controller's TPM and can only be accessed by this TPM and used only in its shielded location. Thus, this private key is protected from any attacks that read keys from the memory. As the binding between EVCC and BMS is validated based on a signature by the BMS's identity key, secure storage of this private key is essential for the overall security, too. To protect this key, secEVCS uses DICE. As our solution does not require the BMS to use the TPM's advanced security functions, a smaller security architecture with less hardware requirements was chosen as more appropriate. Due to the relatively high cost of a TPM, it is also desirable to limit their number to externally facing ECUs. Thus, secEVCS meets the security requirement *Secure private key storage and usage (SR_1)*.

The TPM always verifies, whether the EVCC is in a trustworthy state and whether the BMS defined in the configuration provided by its OEM is present, before allowing access to the authentication key. Thus, if an attacker has manipulated or replaced the BMS, or uses a scrapped controller, the EVCC will not be able to authenticate itself for using V2G services. This corresponds to the security requirement *Restriction of key usage to trustworthy systems (SR_2)*.

The security requirement *Revocation support (SR_3)* is fulfilled by the validation of the value of a monotonic counter inside the EVCC's TPM, which can be incremented each time an expired or malfunctioning BMS is exchanged in a repair shop. This way, it will not be possible to use this BMS together with the EVCC for charging because it is not part of the approved configuration anymore.

The functional requirement *Minimal performance overhead (FR_1)* is met as explained in detail in Section 8.2. Requirement *Support of legitimate component exchange (FR_2)* is also fulfilled since only an authorized OEM can register a new BMS with an EVCC's TPM by sending an updated policy.

10 Conclusion

Recent studies indicate fire and traffic incidents caused by manipulated EVCSs as a major safety concern for EVs. In this paper, we proposed secEVCS, a new security architecture aiming to prevent harmful situations by allowing only vehicles with manufacturer-approved charging systems to (dis)charge electric energy at charge points. This guarantee is achieved through securely binding the components EVCC and BMS responsible for charging authentication and management using the enhanced authorization feature of the EVCC's TPM. This binding is verified each time the EV wants to use its authentication credential, which turned out to be challenging with regard to user convenience and communication timeouts. In order to evaluate our solution within realistic constraints, we implemented secEVCS using a TPM 2.0 chip and ISO 15118-2 [10] as a V2G protocol. Also, the upcoming ISO 15118-20 [11] with harder timeouts was considered in our evaluation. While the performance overhead is acceptable for the use case and within the timing constraints of ISO 15118-2, a straightforward approach of TPM-based component binding cannot meet the new requirements. With the new edition, conformance to the standard can only be guaranteed if all proposed secEVCS performance optimizations are in place.

Our results provide a useful reference for future work that can address the shown limitations (e.g., timing conditions or runtime attacks on EVCS) or adopt secEVCS as a security anchor in broadened scenarios, e.g., secure load management. We also plan a collaboration with industry as part of technology transfer.

Acknowledgments. The work was partly funded by the Federal Ministry for Economic Affairs and Energy (BMWi) under the project "LamA-connect" (01MZ19005A) and the TALENTA program of the Fraunhofer-Gesellschaft.

References

1. Blum, A.F., Long, R.T.J.: Hazard assessment of lithium ion battery energy storage systems. Final report, February 2016
2. Brandl, M., et al.: Batteries and battery management systems for electric vehicles. In: Design, Automation Test in Europe Conference Exhibition (DATE) (2012)
3. Clement-Nyns, K., Haesen, E., Driesen, J.: The impact of vehicle-to-grid on the distribution grid. Electr. Power Syst. Res. **81**(1), 185–192 (2011)
4. Fuchs, A., Kern, D., Krauß, C., Zhdanova, M.: TrustEV: trustworthy electric vehicle charging and billing. In: Proceedings of the 35th ACM/SIGAPP Symposium on Applied Computing (2020)
5. Fuchs, A., Krauß, C., Repp, J.: Advanced remote firmware upgrades using TPM 2.0. In: Hoepman, J.-H., Katzenbeisser, S. (eds.) SEC 2016. IAICT, vol. 471, pp. 276–289. Springer, Cham (2016). https://doi.org/10.1007/978-3-319-33630-5_19
6. Gaton, B.: NZ company offers solution to Nissan Leaf owners wanting a bigger battery. The Driven (2019). thedriven.io/2019/08/13/nz-company-offers-solution-to-nissan-leaf-owners-wanting-a-bigger-battery/
7. Ghosh, D.P., Thomas, R.J., Wicker, S.B.: A privacy-aware design for the vehicle-to-grid framework. In: 2013 46th Hawaii International Conference on System Sciences, pp. 2283–2291. IEEE (2013)
8. IEA: Global EV outlook 2019 (2019). www.iea.org/reports/global-ev-outlook-2019
9. Infineon: Volkswagen relies on TPM from Infineon (2019). www.infineon.com/cms/en/about-infineon/press/market-news/2019/INFATV201901-030.html
10. ISO/IEC: Road vehicles - Vehicle-to-Grid Communication Interface - Part 2: Network and application protocol requirements. ISO Standard 15118–2:2014 (2014)
11. ISO/IEC: Road vehicles - Vehicle-to-Grid Communication Interface - Part 2: Network and application protocol requirements. ISO/DIS 15118–2:2018 (2018)
12. Jäger, L., Petri, R., Fuchs, A.: Rolling DICE: lightweight remote attestation for COTS IoT hardware. In: Proceedings of the 12th International Conference on Availability, Reliability and Security. ARES (2017)

13. Lonvick, C.M., Ylonen, T.: The Secure Shell (SSH) Transport Layer Protocol. RFC 4253, January 2006. https://rfc-editor.org/rfc/rfc4253.txt
14. Lopez, A.B., Vatanparvar, K., Deb Nath, A.P., Yang, S., Bhunia, S., Al Faruque, M.A.: A security perspective on battery systems of the internet of things. J. Hardware Syst. Secur. (2017)
15. Macher, G., Sporer, H., Berlach, R., Armengaud, E., Kreiner, C.: SAHARA: a security-aware hazard and risk analysis method. In: 2015 Design, Automation Test in Europe Conference Exhibition (DATE), pp. 621–624, March 2015
16. Macher, G., Höller, A., Sporer, H., Armengaud, E., Kreiner, C.: A combined safety-hazards and security-threat analysis method for automotive systems. In: Koornneef, F., van Gulijk, C. (eds.) SAFECOMP 2015. LNCS, vol. 9338, pp. 237–250. Springer, Cham (2015). https://doi.org/10.1007/978-3-319-24249-1_21
17. Peresson, S.: Counterfeit automotive parts increasingly putting consumer safety at risk. WTR (2019). www.worldtrademarkreview.com/anti-counterfeiting/counterfeit-automotive-parts-increasingly-putting-consumer-safety-risk
18. Sagstetter, F., et al.: Security challenges in automotive hardware/software architecture design. In: 2013 Design, Automation Test in Europe Conference Exhibition (DATE), pp. 458–463, March 2013
19. Saxena, N., Grijalva, S., Chukwuka, V., Vasilakos, A.V.: Network security and privacy challenges in smart vehicle-to-grid. IEEE Wirel. Commun. 24(4), 88–98 (2017)
20. Soltan, S., Mittal, P., Poor, H.V.: BlackIoT: IoT botnet of high wattage devices can disrupt the power grid. In: 27th USENIX Security Symposium (USENIX Security 18), pp. 15–32. USENIX Association, Baltimore, August 2018
21. Sun, P., Bisschop, R., Niu, H., Huang, X.: A review of battery fires in electric vehicles. Fire Technology (2020)
22. Tillemann, L., McCormick, C.: The faster, cheaper, better way to charge electric vehicles. WIRED (2018). www.wired.com/story/the-faster-cheaper-better-way-to-charge-electric-vehicles/
23. Trusted Computing Group: Trusted Platform Module Library Specification, Family 2.0, Level 00, Revision 01.16 edn., October 2014
24. Trusted Computing Group: PC Client Platform TPM Profile (PTP) Specification, Family 2.0, Revision 00.43 edn., January 2015
25. Trusted Computing Group: Hardware Requirements for a Device Identifier Composition Engine. Specification Family 2.0 - Level 00 Revision 78, March 2018
26. Trusted Computing Group: TCG TSS 2.0 Overview and Common Structures Specification, Version 0.90 Revision 03 edn., October 2019
27. Tschofenig, H., Pégourié-Gonnard, M.: Performance investigations. IETF Proceeding 92 (2015)
28. Wang, S., Wang, B., Zhang, S.: A secure solution of V2G communication based on trusted computing. In: 12th IEEE International Conference on Anti-counterfeiting, Security, and Identification (ASID), pp. 98–102. IEEE (2019)
29. Xu, C., Liu, H., Li, P., Wang, P.: A remote attestation security model based on privacy-preserving blockchain for V2X. IEEE Access 6, 67809–67818 (2018)
30. Zelle, D., Springer, M., Zhdanova, M., Krauß, C.: Anonymous charging and billing of electric vehicles. In: Proceedings of the 13th International Conference on Availability, Reliability and Security, ARES, pp. 22:1–22:10. ACM (2018)
31. Zhao, T., Zhang, C., Wei, L., Zhang, Y.: A secure and privacy-preserving payment system for electric vehicles. In: 2015 IEEE International Conference on Communications (ICC), pp. 7280–7285. IEEE (2015)

Fault Injection and Fault Tolerance

Using Hardware-In-Loop-Based Fault Injection to Determine the Effects of Control Flow Errors in Industrial Control Programs

Jens Vankeirsbilck$^{(\boxtimes)}$, Hans Hallez , and Jeroen Boydens

KU Leuven Bruges Campus, Bruges, Belgium
{jens.vankeirsbilck,hans.hallez,jeroen.boydens}@kuleuven.be

Abstract. Embedded systems, which are at the core of many small scale and large scale machines, are affected by external disturbances which can introduce control flow errors. These control flow errors can affect the control program executing on the embedded system, potentially causing sensor signals to be misinterpreted or actuators being miscontrolled. Software-implemented control flow error detection techniques have existed for many years, although there is little literature about these techniques being tested on input/output-driven programs. This paper presents a hardware-in-loop-based fault injection campaign performed on a typical industrial setting, i.e. a small scale factory. Thanks to hardware-in-loop simulation, we can perform the fault injection campaign without the risk of breaking a mechanical or an electrical part. For our fault injection campaign, we considered both the unprotected control program and the version protected with our RACFED error detection technique. The results show that up to 58% of the injected control flow errors can affect the unprotected control program in a dangerous manner. Implementing RACFED clearly lowers this percentage to less than 4%, showing this technique can be used in industrial settings.

Keywords: Hardware-in-the-loop simulation · Fault injection · Control flow error

1 Introduction

Today, industry is becoming more and more data-driven, also known as Industry 4.0 [8]. While the Internet-of-Things makes this shift possible, it also creates a much harsher working environment for embedded systems that are at the core of many small and large scale machines. By interconnecting all these machines, often using wireless communication, electromagnetic interference is now a major form of disturbance for those embedded systems [3,5,12]. Combined with other technology trends such as decreasing transistor feature sizes and lowering supply voltages, embedded systems are inherently more susceptible for external

© Springer Nature Switzerland AG 2020
A. Casimiro et al. (Eds.): SAFECOMP 2020, LNCS 12234, pp. 405–418, 2020.
https://doi.org/10.1007/978-3-030-54549-9_27

disturbances [1,7,11,13,16,24]. These disturbances range from electromagnetic interference and high-energy particles to temperature fluctuations and they may introduce bit-flips in the system's hardware [10,14]. In turn, these bit-flips can cause control flow errors (CFE), unwanted jumps in the system's software. This can lead to misinterpreting sensor readings, erroneously controlling actuators or even crashing programs [9].

To protect embedded systems, many software-implemented CFE detection techniques have been proposed [2,15,18,20,22]. Such techniques add extra control variables and their update instructions to the target programs. At run time, the added instructions are executed and calculate a run-time value for the control variable. At certain points in the target program, the run-time value and the compile-time value of the control variable are compared to one another and a mismatch indicates a CFE has occurred and has been detected. However, these measures are often only validated using data-driven case studies, such as matrix multiplication, fast fourier transform or cyclic redundancy check calculations. To expand the validation of such techniques, we created a small scale factory that enables the validation of CFE detection mechanisms using an input/output-driven case study [23]. In that work, we merely performed a preliminary study on the effects of CFEs on the control programs of the small scale factory. This paper builds upon that work by proposing a hardware-in-loop-based (HIL) fault injection setup. This allows us to execute the control programs of the small scale factory in a simulated environment and enables an extensive fault injection study, without the risk of breaking mechanical or electrical parts.

The remainder of this paper is structured as follows. Section 2 describes the small scale factory and how a CFE detection technique is added to its control programs. Following, Sect. 3 presents the built fault injection setup. Next, the effects of the injected CFEs on those control programs are discussed in Sect. 4. Then, the drawback of this HIL simulation is described in Sect. 5. Finally, future work is presented in Sect. 6 and conclusions are drawn in Sect. 7.

2   Case Study

This section presents our small scale factory and discusses how its control programs are protected against CFEs by implementing our Random Additive Control Flow Error Detection (RACFED) technique.

2.1   Small Scale Factory

Our small scale factory consists of three stations from the Festo-Didactic MPS® series: a distribution station, a testing station and a sorting station [6]. Combined, they represent a closed process, in which workpieces are pushed out of a stacked magazine and transported to the testing area where only the good workpieces are moved to the final station, which in turn sorts them by color. In total, the small scale factory is able to distinct between six types of workpieces.

Regarding the color, it recognizes three types: silver, red and black, and for each color, there are correct workpieces and wrong workpieces.

As the stations' names imply, each station performs a part of that process. The setup is shown in Fig. 1, with the distribution station on the left, the testing station in the middle and the sorting station on the right. To drive each station and thus to execute the control program, we selected an NXP LPC 1768 which is an ARM Cortex-M3 driven microcontroller. We selected the ARM Cortex-M3 because it is an industry leading 32-bit processor. For more information about the functionality of each station and how the control programs are developed, the reader is referred to our previous work [23].

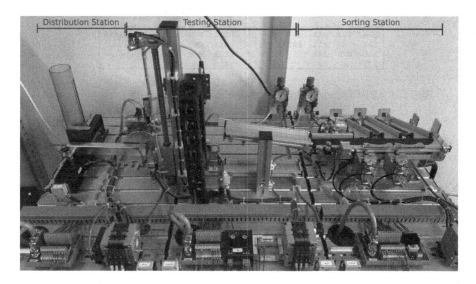

Fig. 1. The small scale factory. On the left the distribution station, in the middle the testing station and on the right the sorting station. The workpiece flow goes from left to right.

2.2   Adding CFE Detection

To make the control programs more fault tolerant, the first step is to apply a CFE detection technique. For this paper, we opted to implement our in-house developed RACFED technique [22]. RACFED detects CFEs by inserting a control variable and its update instructions in the target code. As shown in Fig. 2, RACFED is implemented in the assembly code of a control program, using a basic block as implementation unit. A basic block is a sequence of consecutive instructions with exactly one entry and one exit point. Together, basic blocks and edges which show the intentional paths between basic blocks, a program can be visualized in a control flow graph. In fact, Fig. 2 shows the control flow graph of a sample program, with RACFED implemented. Shown in the normal font are

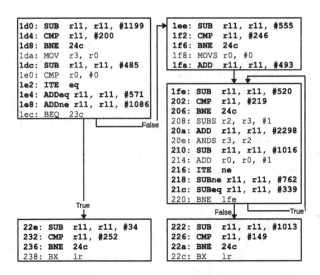

Fig. 2. RACFED implemented for a sample program in the assembly code.

the original program instructions and shown in bold are the instructions inserted by RACFED to detect CFEs, with the control variable held in register r11.

At the beginning of each basic block, a control variable update instruction is inserted. This update instruction is followed by a verification instruction that compares the run-time value of the control variable with its compile-time value. If there is a mismatch between the two values, a CFE is detected and control is transferred to an error handler, here located at address 0x24c. This error handler is defined by the user and is out of scope for this paper. Next, control variable update instructions are inserted after each non-branch instruction. The final control variable update instruction is executed conditionally when the basic block ends in a conditional branch.

Implementing RACFED in the assembly code of the control programs manually would be too time consuming and too error-prone. Therefore, we adjusted the compiler flags of the control programs to use our in-house developed GCC plugin that can automatically add the supported CFE detection techniques to the assembly code [21]. This GCC plugin supports up to ten CFE detection techniques, including RACFED, and currently two instruction set architectures, i.e. ARMv6-M and ARMv7-M. Figure 2 uses ARMv7-M as assembly code, since this is the instruction set of the selected NXP LPC 1768. For more information on RACFED or the GCC plugin[1], the reader is referred to [22] and [21], respectively.

Of course, adding RACFED to the control programs increases the instruction count of those programs, leading to an increase in code size and execution time. Although not important for the small scale factory, since memory is abundant

---

[1] Available as open-source project on https://github.com/MGroupKULeuvenBruges Campus/CFED_Plugin.

and there are no deadlines to be met, we measured both types of overhead. The code size overhead was measured by using the GNU *size* tool on the compiled program, i.e. on the produced *.elf* file. This shows the amount of extra instruction memory needed to store the protected program, relative to the unprotected program. The execution time overhead is measured using an on-board hardware timer of the NXP LPC 1768 and shows the extra time it took for the protected control program to process one workpiece relative to the unprotected control program.

The measurement indicate that using RACFED to detect CFEs has increased the code size of the control programs by a factor of ×1.66 for each station. Nonetheless, this has no impact on the execution time overhead. The time necessary to process one workpiece for the protected control program and the unprotected program is the same. This is because the control program is mainly waiting for the mechanical parts to have moved. During this wait, no instructions are executed, leading to the same execution time for the unprotected and the protected control program. These measurements show that the impact of implementing a software-based CFE detection methods depends from use case to use case.

3   Fault Injection Setup

In order to analyse the effects of CFEs on the control program of each of the stations, we have built a HIL-based fault injection setup. Hardware-in-loop means that the LPC 1768 is removed from its station and is plugged into a hardware simulation of its respective station. This hardware simulation will provide the necessary input signals to the LPC 1768 in order to execute the station control program, and it will analyse the output signals of the LPC 1768. We opted to perform fault injection using a HIL setup to avoid breaking mechanical or electrical parts of the actual stations, as we do not know all potential effects of CFEs on the control programs. This section will first discuss the hardware setup, later the software execution is presented, concluding with the executed experiments.

3.1   Architecture

To inject control flow errors in the control program of each station, we created the architecture illustrated in Fig. 3. As shown, the built setup has four major parts: a computer, a USB-hub, the target LPC 1768 and another LPC 1768 which executes the HIL code to simulate the sensors and actuators of the actual hardware.

Our in-house developed software-implemented fault injection (SWIFI) tool executes on a computer, which is connected to the on-chip debugger of the target LPC 1768 through a USB-hub [19]. Using the on-chip debugger, the SWIFI tool has access to the program counter register of the microcontroller. By injecting bit-flips in this register, CFEs are introduced into the control program. The target LPC 1768 is connected to the computer through the controllable USB-hub to enable hard-resetting the target. From time to time, the communication

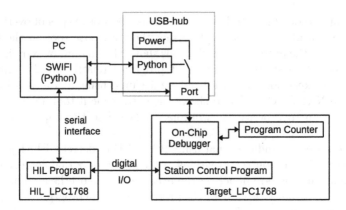

Fig. 3. The hardware setup built for the HIL-based fault injection campaign.

between the computer and the on-chip debugger of the target can get corrupted. To solve this, the SWIFI tool can issue to the USB-hub to power down and re-power the USB-port to which the target is connected. This power-cycling of the USB-port resets the target and enables to establish a new connection between the SWIFI tool and the on-chip debugger of the target.

To make sure that the station control program executes, we developed a HIL program that provides the necessary digital inputs to the target LPC 1768 and that analyses the received digital outputs send by the target. This HIL program also executes on an LPC 1768, indicated as HIL_LPC1768 in Fig. 3. To provide the necessary digital inputs and to analyse the digital outputs of the target, both LPC 1768 are connected through several digital I/O connections. To be able to report the status of the station control program, and to know when to start providing inputs to the target, the HIL LPC 1768 is connected to the computer, and in fact the SWIFI tool, through a serial interface.

3.2 Injecting a CFE

To inject a CFE the following steps are executed:

1. The SWIFI tool determines an origin program counter value for the CFE. Based on that origin value, a destination value is created by flipping a single-bit of the origin value. To make sure the destination value is valid for the current control program, the disassembly file of the control program is provided to the SWIFI tool. The disassembly file holds all valid program counter values for the current program and can thus be used by the tool to select a destination program counter value.
2. Once both the origin and destination of the CFE are selected, a thread is started to inject the defined CFE. This thread waits until the program counter holds the origin value and then corrupts it to the destination value.

3. Once the thread to inject a CFE is started, the SWIFI tool creates a second thread which sends the command to the HIL LPC to start the process of providing the necessary digital inputs to the target LPC to simulate a workpiece that must be processed. Once the HIL LPC has received this command, it will sequentially provide the necessary digital inputs and for each provided digital input, it will check to see if the target LPC provides the correct digital outputs.

Once both threads have executed, the effect of the injected CFE is analyzed. This is done by analyzing the state of the control program and by sending a command to the HIL LPC, which then sends back whether or not all digital outputs from the target LPC were correct. Based on the response of the HIL LPC and the state of the control program, the effect of the CFE is categorized in one of the following four categories:

- **Detected (Det):** The CFE is detected by a software-implemented CFE detection mechanism.
- **Hardware Detected (HD):** The CFE is detected by a hardware measure present in the LPC 1768. Many microcontrollers have error detection mechanisms implemented in their hardware. Such error detection mechanism enable the detection of improper bus usage, stack corruption, etc. This category indicates that the CFE was detected by such a hardware error detection mechanism.
- **Silent Data Corruption (SDC):** The CFE remained undetected and was able to corrupt the execution of the station control program. This means that the HIL LPC responded with an error code, indicating that while processing a simulated workpiece, the target LPC provided incorrect outputs. This is the most dangerous effect a CFE can have and should be avoided as much as possible.
- **No Effect (NE):** The CFE remained undetected but had no effect on the execution of the station control program. This is an indication of the inherent CFE resilience of the control program.

3.3   Executed Experiments

In this paper, we conducted two types of experiments for each station control program. The first type of experiment injected CFEs contained within a control program function. This means that both the origin program counter value and the destination program counter value belong to the same control program function. The results of this type of experiment will be indicated as *IntraFunc* for the remainder of this paper. The second type of experiment injected CFEs that jumped between two control program functions. In these experiments, the origin program counter value belongs to one function, while the destination program counter value belongs to another program function. The results of this type of experiment will be indicated as *InterFunc* in the following sections.

To analyze the effects of CFEs on the unprotected control programs, we injected 1000 IntraFunc and 1000 InterFunc CFEs for each control program function. For the testing station, we executed these experiments twice: once simulating a correct workpiece and once simulating a wrong workpiece. Similarly, we performed these experiments three times for the sorting station: once simulating a silver workpiece, once simulating a red workpiece and finally, once simulating a black workpiece.

To determine the efficiency of RACFED, we repeated this fault injection campaign for the protected version of the control programs. To compensate for the increase in instructions, we injected 2000 IntraFunc and 2000 InterFunc CFEs for each protected control program function.

4   Impact of the Injected CFEs

The results of the fault injection experiments are shown in Fig. 4 and Fig. 5, in which WP stands for workpiece. The two figures show the results of the IntraFunc fault injection campaign and that of the InterFunc fault injection campaign, respectively. In dark-green, the faults detected by RACFED are indicated, in light-green the HD category is represented, the NE category is depicted in orange and because the SDC category represents the worst possible effect of a CFE, it is illustrated in dark-red.

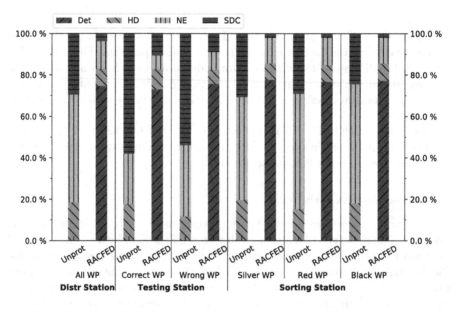

Fig. 4. Results of the IntraFunc fault injection campaign. (Color figure online)

When analyzing the IntraFunc results, it is clear that the unprotected control programs are vulnerable to these types of CFEs. Furthermore, the testing station shows to be even more sensitive to IntraFunc CFEs than the other two stations.

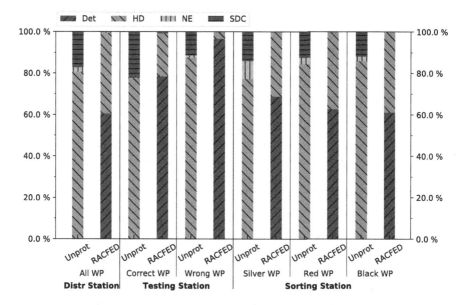

Fig. 5. Results of the InterFunc fault injection campaign. (Color figure online)

As shown in Fig. 4, the IntraFunc CFEs resulted in an SDC ratio of 29.4% for the distribution station and in an average SDC ratio of 28.0% for the sorting station, the testing station reports an average SDC ratio of 56.1%. The data does not show any discrepancies compared to the other two stations. We therefore conclude that the control program for the testing station is just more susceptible to IntraFunc CFEs than its distribution station and sorting station counterparts.

Regarding the global results of the fault injection campaign, the figures indicate that the IntraFunc CFEs resulted in a higher SDC ratio than the InterFunc CFEs for the unprotected control programs. This is due to the hardware error detection mechanisms present in the LPC 1768. A jump between two different control program functions is more likely to corrupt the stack or to be a larger jump, and the hardware error detection mechanisms are implemented to detect such occasions. This is shown in Fig. 5, as the HD category has a minimum value of 77.2%. Therefore, of all injected InterFunc CFEs, only 22.8% or less are not caught by a hardware error detection mechanism and are able to corrupt the workpiece processing. As shown in the figure, most of these InterFunc CFEs do corrupt the processing of a workpiece and are thus categorized as SDC. Intra-Func CFEs on the other hand are smaller jumps and less likely to cause stack corruption, so less likely to trigger the hardware error detection mechanism and thus remain undetected. This is shown in Fig. 4 in which the HD category has a maximum value of 19.7%. This means that 80% of the injected IntraFunc CFEs remain undetected and potentially be registered as SDC.

When looking at the protected control programs, RACFED detects most of the injected CFEs, achieving 60% or higher error detection ratio, and significantly reduces the SDC ratio for all stations, as expected. For the distribution station and the sorting station, the SDC ratio drops below 4% which is within the design limit of the RACFED technique. As explained in the literature, a technique will never reach an SDC ratio of 0% for IntraFunc CFEs, as there are always IntraFunc CFEs that can defeat the technique [22]. To give an example, consider again Fig. 2. A CFE originating at address 0x1d4 and landing at address 0x1dc, skips the program instruction located at 0x1da but does not skip a control variable update and thus remains undetected. While such InterFunc CFEs do exist, they are much more rare and thus a fault injection campaign can report an SDC ratio of 0% for these type of CFEs as is the case for the sorting station.

The IntraFunc results of the testing station differ from those of the other two stations. While RACFED detects 72% of the injected CFEs, the SDC ratio is still 10.5% which is high. Analysis of the data revealed that many of the CFEs causing SDC exploit the weaknesses of RACFED, such as the type of CFE mentioned in the previous paragraph. Another reason for the high SDC ratio is that, due to the memory layout of the program, multiple single-bit bit-flips of the program counter, result in the program jumping to a wait sequence causing an indefinite wait in the program. These wait sequences are used to make sure the mechanical parts are driven for the correct amount of time. When a CFE jumps to such a wait sequence, the waiting time is not initialized or the mechanical part is not actually driven, causing an indefinite wait in the program, which is then categorized as SDC. This shows that, although a CFE detection mechanism is implemented, CFEs can still have devastating effects on the control program.

5   Drawback of the Created Fault Injection Setup

Using the created HIL-based fault injection, we were able to perform an in-depth CFE study on the control programs for our small scale factory. This has revealed that 30% or more of the injected IntraFunc CFEs can corrupt the execution of these control programs, which is much more than our estimate from our preliminary study [23].

The numbers presented in this paper are, however, a *Worst Case* scenario since any deviation from the normal workpiece processing flow is categorized as an SDC. This process does not take the inherent error resilience of the station control programs into account. As described in Sect. 3.2, the created HIL simulation sequentially produces the necessary inputs for the target LPC1768 to correctly process one workpiece, independent from the output of the target. Once all signals to process one workpiece have been produced, no further signals are produced, regardless of the state of the station control program. In the actual small scale factory, however, the sensors might produce signals for the controlling LPC1768 indicating that something went wrong. In turn, the control program can react to those signals and try to correctly process the workpiece.

As an example of this inherent error resilience, consider that the testing station is processing a correct workpiece and that it is in the state **put correct workpiece on airslider**, as shown in Fig. 6. If due to a CFE, the ejection cylinder is not activated, the workpiece will remain on the lift table. Once the remainder of the code is executed, the station will be in the state **wait for workpiece**. Since the workpiece is still on the lift table, the HIL simulation would classify this behavior as an SDC. In the actual small scale factory, however, the workpiece detection sensor detects that the workpiece is still on the lift table and hence sends the signal *new workpiece*, causing the control program to process the workpiece correctly. This means that despite the CFE, the workpiece is processed correctly albeit with a delay. This shows the inherent error resilience of the control program.

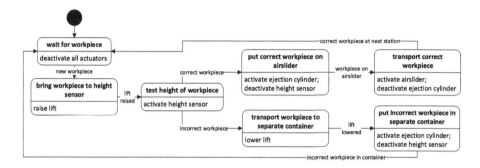

Fig. 6. Flow chart showing the functionality of the testing station.

To have a more realistic simulation of the hardware and to have more realistic fault injection results, another HIL simulator needs to be created. In this new HIL simulator, each major part of each stations should be simulated independently and be reactive to the inputs provided by the target LPC 1768. Where in the current HIL simulation the HIL LPC 1768 is the master and the target LPC 1768 is the slave, these roles should be reversed in the more realistic HIL setup. The current HIL setup has as advantage that detecting whether or not the workpiece was processed correctly is easy. This can now be done by analysing the outputs of the target LPC 1768 for each step in the sequential providing of the inputs. In the more realistic and reactive HIL simulation this would be more difficult, as each simulated part of the station needs to be analysed.

Moreover, such a reactive HIL simulation would allow to test our crude recovery method. As described in our previous work, we implemented a crude recovery method for each of the stations which, simply put, re-executes a certain part of the control program depending on when the CFE is detected. With our current HIL setup, we could not test this recovery mechanism, but with a more reactive HIL simulation this becomes possible. We are currently working on the architecture, hardware selection, etc., for this more reactive HIL simulation.

6 Future Work

As described in Sect. 3.2, non-valid single-bit bit-flip CFE destination values for the program counter are filtered from the pool of possible CFEs to inject. Analysis revealed that 0% to 30% of the single-bit bit-flip values are valid program counter values, i.e. those single-bit bit-flip values are program counter addresses valid for the target program. The other 70% to 100% are non-existing for the target program and CFEs using such values as destination address would be caught by the hardware error detection mechanisms. Although the injected CFEs result in silent data corruption, these values reveal that the program counter is not that sensitive to erroneous bit-flips introduced by external bit-flips.

Therefore, a further study will include bit-flips introduced in the other CPU registers, which are better known as data flow errors. Using the developed HIL setup, bit-flips can be injected in the remaining CPU registers to cause data flow errors risk free. Similarly, the effectiveness of data flow error detection techniques can be evaluated when applied to a more input/output-driven case study [4,17]. Once known, the best performing data flow error detection technique can be combined with RACFED to develop a technique that is able to detect both control flow errors and data flow errors.

7 Conclusions

In this paper, we presented our HIL-based fault injection setup to be able to inject CFEs into the control programs of our small scale factory without the fear of braking anything. For our HIL simulation, we selected the NXP LPC 1768 as hardware platform and developed a HIL control program for each of the three stations in the small scale factory. This HIL control program sequentially provides the inputs to the target LPC 1768 to mimic a workpiece being processed correctly. During this sequential process, the outputs of the target are monitored. At the end, the HIL control program reports back to the fault injection framework whether or not the target LPC 1768 provided the correct outputs or not.

Once set up, we used the HIL-based fault injection setup to inject 1000 Intra-Func and 1000 InterFunc CFEs in each control program function. The results show that, when no CFE detection is present, up to 58% of the injected CFEs can result in the corruption of the processing of a workpiece. This means that due to the CFE, the target LPC 178 produced wrong outputs, which is here classified as a corruption of processing. To analyse the effect of adding a CFE detection technique, we implemented the RACFED technique in each of the control programs and then repeated the fault injection experiments, using 2000 CFEs of each type. Now, a minimum of 60% of the CFEs is detected and the corruption of processing a workpiece is reduced to less than 4% in most cases. This clearly shows the increase in resilience due to the CFE detection technique.

However, due to the sequential and nonreactive nature of the created HIL setup, the numbers shown in this paper represent the *Worst Case* scenario.

Each deviation of the normal procedure to process a workpiece is classified as dangerous. In reality, however, some CFEs are handled by the inherent error resilience of the control program and can result in the correct processing of the workpiece. Unfortunately, the built HIL simulator does not allow for the inherent error resilience to be executed. We are currently looking into new ways to implement a HIL simulator for the small scale factory that is reactive and does allow for this inherent error resilience to take place.

References

1. Abella, J., et al.: Towards improved survivability in safety-critical systems. In: 2011 IEEE 17th International On-Line Testing Symposium. pp. 240–245 (2011). https://doi.org/10.1109/IOLTS.2011.5994536
2. Choi, K., Park, D., Cho, J.: SSCFM: separate signature-based control flow error monitoring for multi-threaded and multi-core environments. Electronics 8(2), 199 (2019). https://doi.org/10.3390/electronics8020166
3. Claeys, T., Catrysse, J., Pissoort, D., Arien, Y.: Stripline set-up for characterizing the effect of corrosion and ageing on the shielding effectiveness of emi gaskets with improved repeatability. In: 2018 International Symposium on Electromagnetic Compatibility (EMC EUROPE), pp. 725–729 (2018). https://doi.org/10.1109/EMCEurope.2018.8485135
4. Didehban, M., Shrivastava, A.: nZDC: a compiler technique for near zero silent data corruption. In: 2016 53nd ACM/EDAC/IEEE Design Automation Conference (DAC), pp. 1–6. IEEE (2016)
5. Estep, N.A., Petrosky, J.C., McClory, J.W., Kim, Y., Terzuoli, A.J.: Electromagnetic interference and ionizing radiation effects on cmos devices. IEEE Trans. Plasma Sci. 40(6), 1495–1501 (2012). https://doi.org/10.1109/TPS.2012.2193600
6. Festo-Didactic: Mps the modular production system. http://www.festo-didactic.com/int-en/learning-systems/mps-the-modular-production-system/stations/
7. Hashimoto, M., Liao, W.: Soft error and its countermeasures in terrestrial environment. In: 2020 25th Asia and South Pacific Design Automation Conference (ASP-DAC), pp. 617–622 (2020)
8. i-SCOOP: Industry 4.0: the fourth industrial revolution - guide to industry 4.0. https://www.i-scoop.eu/industry-4-0/
9. Ibe, E.H., et al.: VLSI design and test for systems dependability. Radiation-Induced Soft Errors (2019). https://doi.org/10.1007/978-4-431-56594-9_3
10. Jagannathan, S., et al.: Temperature dependence of soft error rate in flip-flop designs. In: 2012 IEEE International Reliability Physics Symposium (IRPS), pp. SE.2.1–SE.2.6 (2012). https://doi.org/10.1109/IRPS.2012.6241927
11. Kanekawa, N., Ibe, E.H., Suga, T., Uematsu, Y.: Dependability in Electronic Systems: Mitigation of Hardware Failures, Soft Errors, and Electro-Magnetic Disturbances. Springer, Heidelberg (2011). https://doi.org/10.1007/978-1-4419-6715-2, https://www.springer.com/gp/book/9781441967145
12. Kim, K., Iliadis, A.A.: Critical bit errors in cmos digital inverters due to pulsed electromagnetic interference. In: 2007 International Conference on Electromagnetics in Advanced Applications, pp. 217–220 (2007). https://doi.org/10.1109/ICEAA.2007.4387276

13. Riera, M., Canal, R., Abella, J., Gonzalez, A.: A detailed methodology to compute soft error rates in advanced technologies. In: 2016 Design, Automation Test in Europe Conference Exhibition (DATE), pp. 217–222 (2016)
14. Sierawski, B.D., et al.: Effects of scaling on muon-induced soft errors. In: 2011 International Reliability Physics Symposium. pp. 3C.3.1–3C.3.6 (2011). https://doi.org/10.1109/IRPS.2011.5784484
15. So, H., Didehban, M., Shrivastava, A., Lee, K.: A software-level redundant multi-threading for soft/hard error detection and recovery. In: 2019 Design, Automation Test in Europe Conference Exhibition (DATE), pp. 1559–1562 (2019). https://doi.org/10.23919/DATE.2019.8715089
16. Team, M.M.: International roadmap for devices and systems - 2018 update: More moore. Technical Report, IEEE IRDS (2018). https://irds.ieee.org/images/files/pdf/2018/2018IRDS_MM.pdf
17. Thati, V.B., Vankeirsbilck, J., Penneman, N., Pissoort, D., Boydens, J.: An improved data error detection technique for dependable embedded software. In: IEEE 23rd Pacific Rim International Symposium on Dependable Computing (PRDC), pp. 213–220. IEEE (2018)
18. Tsai, T., Huang, J.: Source code transformation for software-based on-line error detection. In: 2017 IEEE Conference on Dependable and Secure Computing, pp. 305–309 (2017). https://doi.org/10.1109/DESEC.2017.8073852
19. Vankeirsbilck, J., Cauwelier, T., Van Waes, J., Hallez, H., Boydens, J.: Software-implemented fault injection for physical and simulated embedded CPUs. In: IEEE XXVII International Scientific Conference Electronics (ET), pp. 1–4 (2018). https://doi.org/10.1109/ET.2018.8549630
20. Vankeirsbilck, J., Penneman, N., Hallez, H., Boydens, J.: Random additive signature monitoring for control flow error detection. IEEE Trans. Reliab. **66**(4), 1178–1192 (2017). https://doi.org/10.1109/TR.2017.2754548
21. Vankeirsbilck, J., Hallez, H., Boydens, J.: Automatic implementation of control flow error detection techniques. In: Accepted at IASED International Conference on Wireless Networks and Embedded Systems (ICWNES) (2019)
22. Vankeirsbilck, J., Penneman, N., Hallez, H., Boydens, J.: Random additive control flow error detection. In: Gallina, B., Skavhaug, A., Bitsch, F. (eds.) SAFECOMP 2018. LNCS, vol. 11093, pp. 220–234. Springer, Cham (2018). https://doi.org/10.1007/978-3-319-99130-6_15
23. Vankeirsbilck, J., Van Waes, J., Hallez, H., Pissoort, D., Boydens, J.: Control flow errors in an industry 4.0 setup: a preliminary study. In: IEEE International Conference on Systems, Man and Cybernetics (SMC), pp. 2305–2310 (2019). https://doi.org/10.1109/SMC.2019.8914545
24. White, M., Chen, Y.: Scaled cmos technology reliability users guide. Technical Report 20100014217, National Aeronotics and Space Administration (NASA) (2010). https://nepp.nasa.gov/files/16361/08_102_4%20new%20del_White.pdf

On Configuring a Testbed for Dependability Experiments: Guidelines and Fault Injection Case Study

João R. Campos$^{(\boxtimes)}$ (D), Ernesto Costa (D), and Marco Vieira (D)

DEI/CISUC, University of Coimbra, Coimbra, Portugal
{jrcampos,ernesto,mvieira}@dei.uc.pt

Abstract. Several techniques have been developed to experimentally assess the dependability of computer systems, such as fault injection and robustness testing. Given the growing complexity of systems, such approaches often require a large set of experiments to be performed in order to achieve statistical relevance, thus leading to extremely long experimental campaigns. Due to recent developments, there are now various technologies (e.g., multithreading, virtualization) that maximize the use of computer resources. However, taking advantage of such technologies to implement a testbed that accelerates the experimental process is complex and, to the best of our knowledge, no guidelines or examples are easily accessible. This practical experience report overviews the attributes and requirements that should be considered when implementing a testbed to accelerate dependability experiments and presents our experience (in the form of guidelines) on the creation and configuration of a concrete Linux testbed making use of modern technologies. A case study on fault injection is presented to demonstrate the testbed. The ultimate goal is to provide a reflection, guidelines and an example that may facilitate the work of other researchers.

Keywords: Dependability · Testbed · Fault injection

1 Introduction

Various techniques have been proposed to assist in the development of dependable systems, such as robustness testing [16] and fault injection [1]. However, given the growing complexity of computer systems, such techniques often require a large set of experiments to be representative and achieve statistical relevance. This is a time-consuming task and consequently researchers often use heuristics to minimize the test set, possibly compromising the results obtained.

Due to technological developments, there has been a considerable increase in computational power. Moreover, various techniques have been developed at the

Work partially funded by FCT grant SFRH/BD/140221/2018.

A. Casimiro et al. (Eds.): SAFECOMP 2020, LNCS 12234, pp. 419–433, 2020.
https://doi.org/10.1007/978-3-030-54549-9_28

hardware-level, such as running multiple threads on a single core, accelerating the processor for peak loads, and hardware virtualization.

To take advantage of the current computational power and accelerate the experimental process, as well as reducing hardware costs, several works have used multithreading to execute experiments simultaneously on a single machine (e.g., [34,39]). However, besides requiring a completely automated testbed, it also relies on the premise of non-interference, such as software containment and performance isolation. In short, executing experiments simultaneously should not alter the observed behavior/results. In this direction, virtualization techniques have been recurrently used for conducting experiments in the dependability domain (e.g., [14]), as they facilitate the experimental process and its automation, as well as provide software containment (i.e., the misbehavior/failure of a machine does not influence others). However, performance isolation is not so trivial, as, by default, running experiments simultaneously will lead to lower (and inconsistent) individual performance.

As a consequence of all the inherent experimental complexity and current technological solutions, devising and implementing an experimental testbed to assess the dependability of software systems is not straightforward. Furthermore, documentation, guidelines, and examples are not usually available, and thus properly implementing a testbed requires significant effort and expertise to identify all the relevant attributes, requirements, and implementation solutions. This frequently leads researchers to develop simplified testbeds focusing on their specific concerns, often not taking advantage of the computational resources available or neglecting aspects that may negatively influence their results.

This practical experience report attempts to overcome the aforementioned limitations, by overviewing the various concerns and requirements of a testbed for experiment-based dependability research. It focuses on Linux, as it is often the chosen platform for research and it can also be found in the most varied applications. Based on our own experience, it provides guidelines on how to create, configure, and attain the various testbed attributes. These guidelines focus on achieving experiment isolation and complete automation so that multiple experiments can be executed simultaneously without influencing their results. In short, the goal of this paper is to assist and facilitate other researchers in properly setting up their experimental testbeds while leveraging their resources without compromising the results of their experiments. To demonstrate these concepts, a simple case study on fault injection is presented.

2   Background and Related Work

One of the most common dependability assessment techniques is *software testing*, which consists of executing a program with the intent of finding faults [24]. Even after defining adequate test cases it still requires the execution of a considerable number of experiments. While in [18] the authors used parallelization to speed up the testing of a complex system, the fact is that the demand for parallelization is so relevant that there are even studies on parallelizing test suites [4].

A variation of testing, *robustness testing*, attempts to assess to which degree the program functions correctly in the presence of exceptional (e.g., range, invalid) inputs [16]. In [21] a case study is presented on the methods used to achieve automatic regression and robustness testing on the CERN disk storage system, using GitLab-CI, which uses parallelization. Work in large-scale European projects also used parallelization to accelerate robustness testing [41].

Software aging and *rejuvenation* techniques try to mitigate the state and performance degradation over time by restarting an application to a clean internal state [13]. As this degradation happens over time various works use an experiment-based approach to accelerate the process [22]. In [32] the authors use multiprocessing to conduct source-code refactoring, while [8] uses virtual machines to assess, test, and/or isolate the effects of aging. Although most studies do not leverage parallelization, it could be used to expedite the process.

Fault injection has recurrently been used to assess the behavior of a system in the presence of faults [5]. Given the high complexity of modern systems, it requires a significant number of experiments to cover the most relevant faults. In [40] the authors explore the use of simultaneous execution for multiple fault injections while in [39] the impact/validity of running multiple fault injection experiments simultaneously is assessed. Finally, [3] and [34] propose frameworks for fault injection that accelerate the process through simultaneous execution.

Dependability benchmarking intends to characterize the dependability of a system and related measures in the presence of faults in a standardized manner [15]. In [15] various benchmarks are overviewed which could benefit from running experiments simultaneously (e.g., automotive control systems, transactional systems). In [2] the authors evaluate encryption algorithms, that could also take advantage of executing experiments simultaneously.

While some of the previous works actually parallelized experiments others simply made use of multithreading. Such techniques, as well as virtualization, raise some concerns, such as if, and how much, interference exists between experiments [33] and how it affects the results [28].

Existing works often also overlooked the performance independence between experiments, as they were mainly focused on increasing throughput. Although some assess the profile of the experiments between sequential/simultaneous execution (e.g., are the observed failures similar [39]), they do not analyze the actual results/performance. While increasing throughput is indeed relevant, if simultaneous execution compromises the experiments then the results may be invalidated. Although the need for isolation is easy to understand, achieving it is far more complex. So many factors in modern computers non-deterministically influence their performance that even identifying all is not trivial. Besides differences between Operating Systems (OSs) and distributions, the architecture of the system also influences the load distribution (e.g., CPUs shared L# caches).

Concerning software isolation, virtualization has become a go-to solution. If corruption occurs on a given machine, it should not affect the host or other running applications. However, although it allows setting the resources that can be used by each Virtual Machine (VM), this does not guarantee performance isolation (e.g., overprovisioning) [23].

There are two main types of hypervisors (i.e., *Type-I* and *Type-II*), each with various solutions with respective advantages and disadvantages. While *Type-I* hypervisors may offer better isolation [23] they are mostly focused on enterprise solutions and thus usually have a higher cost, alongside limited hardware compatibility, besides limiting the machine to just using virtualization. Moreover, these are specific applications/solutions that may not meet the needs and flexibility required by researchers.

It should be noted that perfect isolation cannot ever be completely guaranteed without using separated physical machines. Still, using adequate techniques it is possible to attain decent levels of isolation, ultimately only requiring to duplicate components that cannot be parallelized (e.g., hard drives). Moreover, this also allows containing (hardware) experimentation costs to run experiments simultaneously (an issue raised in [15]) which is a prominent concern in research.

3   Our Drivers

This work was mainly motivated by the need to conduct large sets (i.e., thousands) of fault injection experiments to generate failure data. Such experiments are time-consuming, but we have access to a dedicated server that has resources to execute multiple experiments simultaneously. Hence, we went into a search for the correct approach to set up an adequate experimental testbed, as no examples or guidelines were yet available. The main drivers for this initiative are:

Containment and Monitoring the main purpose of fault injection is to study the behavior of the system in the presence of faults, which may easily lead to corruption. Hence, each experiment should start with a clean version of the system. Additionally, we also need to monitor the system under test to assess the impact of the injected faults. Due to the risk of abrupt terminations, it must be measured/stored every second.

Automation due to the large number of experiments, the process needs to be as automated as possible to avoid the need for user interaction. It should be possible to automate the entire experimental setup: prepare/configure the host machine, execute the experiments (e.g., launch target machine, run fault injection/workloads, monitor/collect system metrics, detect failures), and terminate the process (e.g., store/process the collected data, restore configurations).

Simultaneous Execution and Isolation as a dedicated server is available we want to leverage it to expedite the experimental process by running multiple experiments simultaneously. However, as it is also intended to assess the impact of injected faults on the performance of the system, identical experiments should produce identical results (i.e., the focus is on consistency and not peak performance). Moreover, this premise should hold even if multiple experiments are running simultaneously, within fair use and share of the resources.

4   Guidelines/Reflections

While the previous drivers are easy to understand, developing a testbed to achieve them is not straightforward. This section overviews the most relevant concepts and provides guidelines and reflections on how to develop a fully automated testbed on Linux. It details how to: i) configure the system to attain performance isolation; ii) leverage virtualization for software containment; iii) monitor the experiments in real-time; and iv) automate the process. A high-level illustration of the approach can be seen in Fig. 1. Briefly, the host contains a controller that is in charge of handling all the workflow (e.g., isolating and controlling the experiments/VMs). Then, each VM sets up the required experiment configurations (e.g., shared folders), injects the faults instructed by the host and executes the workload while monitoring the system.

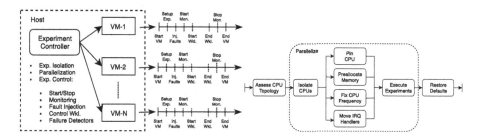

Fig. 1. Experimental process   **Fig. 2.** Performance isolation process

4.1   Simultaneous Execution and Isolation

Running multiple experiments simultaneously allows taking advantage of modern computational power. However, for consistency and repeatability, it should not influence the results of the experiments. Performance isolation is not easy to attain and ultimately it will never be perfect without having dedicated hardware or running the experiments sequentially or in separate machines. Still, some solutions allow achieving decent performance isolation, as discussed next. An overview of the most relevant steps can be seen in Fig. 2.

By default, when executing experiments simultaneously (e.g., through threads/processes), the Linux scheduler will distribute tasks across the cores as it seems best. Hence, to minimize interference/variations each experiment should be allocated to a fixed set of cores. However, one thing is to limit a process to a set of cores and another entirely different is to avoid any other processes from being scheduled to those cores. Two other concepts should also be taken into account. First, Non-Uniform Memory Access (NUMA), a computer memory design where the memory access time depends on its location relative to the processor (i.e., a processor can access its own local memory faster than non-local memory) [17]. Thus, the cores dedicated to an experiment should belong to the same NUMA node. Second, logical cores of a given physical core share resources (e.g. L# caches) and should be used for the same experiment to avoid latency spikes. Hence, each experiment will run in separate physical core(s) (i.e., in parallel).

Isolating CPU Cores. To minimize interference the logical cores required for the experiments should be isolated from the Linux process scheduler. This can either be done using the *isolcpus* kernel parameter (a static approach, which will take effect at boot time) or using *cset-shield/cset-(set)(proc)* functionalities (a runtime approach that creates/defines/isolates sets of cores, known as *cpusets*). While *cset-shield/cset-(set)(proc)* is often the recommended approach, as it provides more control over the isolation, it may not be able to move some processes already running on the intended cores. Still, both approaches may not be able to completely prevent kernel-threads from being scheduled to the isolated cores.

The *cset-shield* program uses a concept of 3 cpusets [36]: *i) root*: contains all cores (unshielded); *ii) system*: contains cores used for system tasks (unshielded); and *iii) user*: contains cores used for dedicated tasks (shielded). All userspace tasks will run in *system*, while *user* has nothing unless specifically set. However, *cset-shield* is only useful if you want to isolate a single experiment (only one *user* cpuset). This way, we need to use *cset-set* (create, adjust, rename, move and destroy cpusets) and *cset-proc* (manage threads and processes) to have finer control of cpusets. The concept is similar to *cset-shield*, but various *user* cpusets will be created (one for each experiment). Keep in mind that the logical cores in each cpuset should take into account physical core affinities and NUMA, otherwise, errors or unwanted variations may occur.

CPU Pinning. After isolating the intended cores, it is necessary to pin specific tasks/processes to them. Although there are various approaches (e.g., taskset) when using *cset-set* it is best to use its counterpart, *cset-proc*, which allows running a program on a given cpuset.

Preallocating Memory. Another technique to minimize interference between experiments is related to memory, which can have a noticeable impact on performance, especially in the case of latency-sensitive applications. Thus, preallocating memory for the experiments and increasing memory page size will help reducing memory access latencies and increase overall performance. Briefly, preallocation dedicates a contiguous area of memory so that it does not require to be dynamically allocated when needed. This provides several advantages, such as guaranteeing that no other process will use that memory, no allocation overhead exists, and no memory fragmentation occurs [9].

Another improvement concerns the size of system pages. In short, the kernel needs to keep a table containing virtual-to-physical address mapping. Small pages (e.g., 2 KB) increases the total amount of entries in the index and therefore increases the time to look up/manage pages. Hugepages (e.g., 1 GB) means that fewer pages will be required, reducing mapping, look-up, and maintenance overhead. Hugepages can be dynamically allocated during runtime. While most modern distributions have some high-level functionality that facilitates this if the system has multiple NUMA nodes some precautions should be taken (e.g., define how many, and how, the experiments will be distributed across the NUMA nodes, and to calculate how many hugepages are required per node).

Limiting CPU Frequencies. Isolating cores, exclusively assigning them to experiments, and isolating memory, may give the (wrong) idea that it is enough. Because energy efficiency is nowadays an important factor in the design of CPUs, cores can be completely turned off temporarily and their running frequency constantly changes depending on several factors (e.g., computational load, temperature). Additionally, specific techniques can also increase the frequency for peak load performance (e.g., Intel®Turbo Boost). This represents a challenge to systematic and repeatable experiments.

The goal is to disable/minimize variations of CPU frequency. While it could be tempting to set it for maximum speed, this may still be overridden (e.g., reaching threshold temperatures). The more reliable way is to set the CPU frequency to its minimum, as it will not go below it. While this will force the CPU to work slower, often the focus is on comparison and repeatability and not on achieving the best performance possible. Thus, a performance penalty is usually acceptable, as far as it is the same for all experiments.

Minor Optimizations. Although often not as significant, we also considered other minor optimizations:

- **Real-time Kernel**: using a real-time kernel may further reduce latency and improve the predictability of thread scheduling. While this typically requires recompiling the kernel, low-latency kernels (often available in repositories) provide good real-time characteristics while keeping reliability [37].
- **Process Scheduler Tuning**: another approach to reduce latency is to set the experiment to use a real-time scheduling policy (e.g., *SCHED_FIFO* [29]).
- **NOHZ Full**: the kernel uses a scheduling-clock that interrupts running applications to run a scheduler. Linux 3.10 introduced a full tickless mode (NOHZ full) that disables the scheduling-clock [20].
- **Interrupt Request (IRQ) Pinning**: IRQs (hardware signals that trigger kernel interrupts) have an affinity property that specifies which cores can process them [10]. This may be altered to avoid using the isolated cores.
- **Offloading Ready-Copy-Update (RCU) Callbacks**: RCU is a lockless mechanism for mutual exclusion [11]. As a consequence, callbacks are often queued to be performed afterward. Seemingly, the *rcu_nocbs* kernel parameter avoids these callbacks on isolated cores [11].

4.2   Using Virtualization

The use of virtualization is becoming a common practice. Besides being able to simulate machines running on different hardware/OS, it also has become the *de facto* approach to contain experiments (i.e., corruption of a VM does neither affect other VMs nor the host). Hence, it is a good solution for an automated testbed for dependability research.

The problem is that although VMs allow defining the guest resources they do not guarantee performance isolation [23]. Although bare-metal (i.e., *Type-I*) hypervisors may offer better isolation [23] they are not ideal for research (e.g., are mostly focused on enterprise solutions, limit the machine to just using virtualization). Additionally, a prerequisite for research is that it must be flexible and easily scripted. While once again there are various alternatives, QEMU [30] (using KVM) is likely the most adequate option. Although QEMU may not be the easiest to get started, it is highly configurable and can be seamlessly scripted.

After creating the necessary cpusets, QEMU can be initialized using the *cset-proc* command, specifying which cpuset to use. When pinning VMs to a cpuset one needs to be sure to leave one logical core for QEMU/system processing.

Concerning the other optimizations previously described, QEMU can be instructed to use hugepages (after properly allocating them) and which NUMA node to use (when applicable). Additionally, to improve latency, the VMs can be run using a real-time process scheduler. Finally, Kernel Same-page Merging (KSM) (used by the KVM) should also be disabled. While this may provide some performance improvements it may also introduce unwanted variations.

4.3   Monitorization

A relevant part of experimental research is monitoring the target system. Although virtualization eases some problems, it also creates new challenges, such as collecting metrics/logs from the VMs. While in some scenarios it may be collected during execution and made available at the end of the experiment, for others (e.g., fault injection, which may abruptly terminate the VM), it should be continuously provided.

One common approach to monitor the state of a system is through its metrics (e.g., CPU/memory). This requires that a set of representative metrics (i.e., that characterize the system) should be chosen and collected. While it is possible to *a priori* select the most relevant metrics, this may require re-running the experiments if they are not adequate. A more generic approach is to monitor as many relevant metrics as possible (without impairing the system) and analyze them post-hoc, enabling possible knowledge discovery (e.g., metrics or synergies that would not have otherwise been inferred).

As a native solution, Linux provides various packages to gather system metrics (e.g., sysstat). Still, most report the data in an unstructured format, and various tools are necessary to monitor the most relevant resources. Concerning free centralized solutions, while there are some well-known options (e.g., Nagio [25]), it is not straightforward to access "real-time" metrics (most are guided towards larger execution times). We adopted Netdata [27], a comprehensive and highly optimized tool that provides real-time monitoring by default. Still, it is possible that with specific configurations other solutions may provide similar results.

4.4   Process Automation

A testbed intended to run large sets of (simultaneous) experiments requires complete automation. This is often achieved through simple scripting (e.g., Bash) or programming languages (e.g., Python). However, more complex applications (e.g., interacting with VMs) may require more specific solutions. *Expect* [19] is a Tool Command Language (TCL) program that "talks" to other programs, characterizing an interaction between user/program. Over the years it has been ported to various programming languages.

Due to its flexibility, ease-of-use, and scientific packages, Python is one of the most adequate languages for research. *Pexpect* (Python's implementation of Expect [35]) allows automatically spawning and controlling applications. Mainly, it is comprised of two methods: *expect* and *sendline*. Briefly, *sendline* can be used to send commands to the application and the *expect* method awaits a successful match with the output given by the command.

5   Case Study

This section presents a case study using a testbed implemented based on the techniques described in Sect. 4. First, we assess the effectiveness of the various techniques in achieving isolation. Afterward, the testbed is used to conduct a fault injection campaign whose goal is to monitor the state (i.e., system metrics) and behavior (i.e., failure/success) of the system in the presence of faults. Note that, the case study is intended only to demonstrate the testbed and not to go into a detailed analysis of the system in the presence of faults.

5.1   Experimental Setup

The experiments were conducted on a PowerEdge R630 with 2 Intel Xeon E5/2650 CPUs (with a NUMA node each, hence the testbed takes this into account). The machine has 64 GB of DDR-4 and 2 Samsung 850 Pro 512 GB SSDs.

For containment/flexibility, the QEMU (with KVM) hypervisor was used. The guest OS (due to fault injector dependencies) is a 32-bits Ubuntu 12.04.3 with kernel 3.7.10. Single-core VMs with 2 GB of memory were used. The host runs 64-bits Ubuntu 18.04.02 with the 5.0.0 low-latency kernel.

We automated the experimental process using Python and Pexpect [35]. System metrics were collected from the VMs using Netdata [27]. Sixteen experiments were run simultaneously (16 was the maximum due to memory constraints).

5.2   Software Implemented Fault Injection (SWIFI)

Software Implemented Fault Injection (SWIFI) is a common technique to assess the dependability of systems. Briefly, fault injection consists of introducing faults that emulate realistic residual faults [1]. Due to the complexity of modern systems, a fault injection campaign may require executing thousands of experiments

[39]. A fault injection environment usually includes various components [12]: a *controller* (which controls the experiment), a *fault injector*, a *fault library/model*, a *monitoring system*, and a *workload* to exercise the system.

We used an updated version [42] of a well-known fault injector [6]. It uses object-code modification to inject bugs into the kernel of a running operating system. For these experiments 10 simultaneous faults, a number commonly used in the literature [6], were injected to increase the chance of triggering a fault. The injected faults range from low-level (e.g., bit-flips, injected in the kernel's address space) to high-level (e.g., memory allocation, injected in the kernel text segment) faults [6]. The latter are the most relevant, which intend to approximate the assembly-level manifestation of real C-level programming errors. They emulate *assignment faults*, *control faults*, *parameter faults*, *omission faults*, and *pointer faults* [7,42]. In total, 17 fault types were considered. Please note that not all injected faults cause faulty behaviors (e.g., bugs inserted on a rarely executed path will rarely produce an error).

Table 1. Experiments isolation

Benchmark	Non-Isolated			Isolated		
	Sequential	Parallel	Par. w/ Host Load	Sequential	Parallel	Par. w/ Host Load
cpu	88860 (173)	81347 (314)	70664 (10456)	38594 (73)	38527 (65)	38370 (96)
io	1620905 (10787)	1375507 (187552)	1373051 (82853)	738995 (2020)	734746 (3362)	730612 (3828)
matrix	1781923 (2976)	1461701 (292359)	1338686 (257073)	775231 (688)	774583 (367)	771314 (1782)
stream	542 (0)	513 (10)	510 (4)	465 (0)	461 (1)	460 (1)
zlib	17372 (228)	15596 (1073)	14414 (1248)	7518 (250)	7630 (20)	7521 (171)
hdd	185388 (28279)	103555 (696)	103191 (789)	169910 (19139)	105453 (7892)	103176 (796)
memthrash	37486 (300)	25686 (3598)	19719 (2135)	30673 (218)	25121 (344)	23562 (1634)
vm	4894297 (213710)	3827312 (665271)	2065351 (593175)	31599440 (530104)	2511423 (207344)	2230932 (78575)

Legend: {operations average} ({standard deviation})

5.3 Workloads

A workload is needed to exercise the system and study the impact of the injected faults. As it may influence the behavior of the system (with and without injected faults) it must be selected considering the technical needs of the system.

In this case study, we used *stress-ng* to generate the workloads. *stress-ng* contains various stressors (e.g., *cpu, hdd, matrix*) designed to exercise several physical subsystems, as well as various kernel interfaces (details can be found at [38]). The workloads executed for 10 min. Besides exercising the system during fault injection it was also used to assess the isolation attained by the various techniques. Sixteen experiments were conducted sequentially to establish a baseline and simultaneously for each stressor (both isolated/non-isolated). To assess the influence of other tasks running on the host, another set of experiments was conducted while a workload was running on a separate session.

5.4 Failure Modes

For these experiments, various types of failure were monitored. More precisely, *Crash* (OS crashes), *Hang* (OS hangs), *Performance* (the performance deviates more than 5%, to tolerate statistical variances, than the lowest baseline value), and *(Filesystem) Corruption* (using Linux *fsck* functionality).

6   Results

This section provides a brief analysis on the simultaneous execution of experiments and on how/which faults led to failures.

6.1 Assessing Isolation

A summary of the results can be seen in Table 1. The first group are those where isolation is noticeable and the second where it is not. The metric used for comparison is *bogo operations* (a throughput measure) [38]. Although it is not an accurate benchmarking metric, it allows comparing the performance across different environments [38].

As can be observed, without isolation all stressors have considerable variation between sequential and parallelized execution, which is further aggravated when the host is executing other tasks (e.g., *cpu* stressor executed 88860, 81347, and 70664 operations respectively). Furthermore, without isolation standard deviations are systematically higher (e.g., the *io* stressor had a standard deviation of 187552 for the non-isolated and only 3362 for the isolated environment). On the other hand, when isolating the experiments it is possible to observe that all the stressors in the first group (i.e., *cpu* to *zlib*) have similar results across the various environments, regardless of having other tasks being performed on the host (e.g., *cpu* stressor executed 38594, 38527, and 38370 operations for the sequential, parallel, and parallel with host load environments).

As expected, benchmarks that stress components that cannot be parallelized were affected by running simultaneous experiments (e.g., *hdd* stressor operations dropped from 169910 to 105453). Also, when comparing the performance of sequential experiments between isolated/non-isolated it is possible to observe that there is a considerable difference (due to limiting the CPU frequency; e.g., when run sequentially the *cpu* stressor executed on average 88860 operations against 38594 on the non-isolated and isolated environment respectively).

Each set of 16 simultaneous experiments took on average approximately 20 min while sequentially it took approximately 3 h and 45 min.

Table 2. SWIFI summary

Fault Type	ALLOC	BCOPY	BRANCH	DSTSRC	FREE	INIT	INTERFACE	INVERSE	LOOP	IRQ	NULL	OFFBYONE	PTR	SIZE	STACK	TEXT	VAR
Non-Fail.	128	49	128	120	127	128	128	128	128	128	127	128	128	127	80	78	128
Invalid	0	79	0	7	1	0	0	0	0	0	0	0	0	0	25	0	0
Hang	0	0	0	0	0	0	0	0	0	0	0	0	0	0	8	0	0
Crash	0	0	0	0	0	0	0	0	0	0	0	0	0	0	15	50	0
Perform.	0	0	0	1	0	0	0	0	0	0	1	0	0	1	0	0	0

(Rows Hang, Crash, Perform. grouped under *Failing*)

6.2 Failures Distribution

2176 fault injection experiments were conducted, 16 (with 10 simultaneous faults eaech) for each of the 17 fault types and 8 stressors in stress-ng [38]. A summary of the outcomes can be seen in Table 2. As shown, different fault types led to different failures. The experiments were divided into *Non-Failing* (no failure occurred), *Invalid* (a failure occurred immediately after injection and thus is not representative of a residual fault, as it would have been detected by traditional validation techniques), and the various types of failures that were observed, *Hang*, *Crash*, and *Performance*.

Overall, 4% of the experiments resulted in "usable" failures, 5% resulted in invalid runs, and 91% did not lead to any (detected) failure. By analyzing the results in detail we could observe that, while some types of faults never lead to any failure (e.g., *inverse, interface*), others (e.g., *stack, text*) quite often do. Additionally, we could also notice that certain types of faults often cause immediate failure (e.g., *bcopy, stack*). Concerning *Crash* failures, they were in fact associated with various errors. The most prevalent (although not present in Table 2 due to space restrictions), was *unable to handle kernel NULL pointer*, which was almost always due to injecting *TEXT* faults. Additionally, all the *tried to execute NX-protected page* errors were due to *STACK* faults. In fact, all recorded *Hang* failures were also due to injecting *STACK* faults. Finally, only 3 experiments presented performance-related failures.

7 Discussion

Using the techniques described in Sect. 4 we created an automated testbed that could take advantage of the system resources through simultaneous executions with minimal interference. In short, the results of experiments run without isolation were considerably different (and with higher variations) between sequential and parallel executions, which worsened when the host was also running other tasks. However, when isolating the experiments (with the exception of workloads that depend on components that cannot be parallelized) the results were similar (and with significantly less variation), regardless of executing the experiments sequentially or in parallel. Additionally, although fixing the cores frequency to its minimum led to lower individual throughput compared to the non-isolated environment, the target frequency could be profiled to reduce the performance gap.

This testbed allowed us to quickly execute a (large) set of experiments (i.e., 2176 experiments took approximately 46 h while executing them sequentially would have taken 22 days). A brief analysis of the results allowed us to observe that only a small set of faults led to "useful" failures. An interesting observation is that simple (emulated) hardware faults (e.g., bitflips in *stack*) led to various failures. Although in recent years software-related faults have been identified as the main cause for outages (hardware faults have become less common), current technology has made hardware components susceptible to particle-induced errors [31]. These results suggest that this may become an issue in the future.

The low failure rate is within expected values according to [26] which defines 5% as an acceptable activation rate for representative faults. Still, some improvements can be made, such as selecting better locations to inject. Due to scope and time restrictions, it was not possible to analyze further why certain faults are more prone to lead to certain failures.

Although the concepts discussed in this paper are not innovative *per se* (most can individually be found online) their combination/integration is not straightforward and not well (if at all) documented. These guidelines should also be considered for a testbed to execute experiments sequentially, as they may also be influenced by other tasks running on the machine.

8 Conclusion

Due to the growing complexity of computer systems, large sets of time-consuming experiments are now required to develop dependable systems. Although various techniques can leverage modern computational power to expedite the experimental process, guidelines and examples on how to do it properly are rare and thus researchers often develop simplified solutions, neglecting relevant aspects.

This paper provided guidelines to assist other researchers in creating and configuring a testbed for conducting experiment-based research for the development of dependable systems on Linux. It highlights the different challenges often faced (e.g., isolation, automation) and gives insights into how to overcome them. Future work includes trying to create/make available a reusable systematic approach/testbed.

References

1. Arlat, J., Crouzet, Y., Laprie, J.C.: Fault injection for dependability validation of fault-tolerant computing systems. In: 1989 The Nineteenth International Symposium on Fault-Tolerant Computing, Digest of Papers, pp. 348–355. IEEE (1989)
2. Awotunde, J., Ameen, A., Oladipo, I., Tomori, A., Abdulraheem, M.: Evaluation of four encryption algorithms for viability, reliability and performance estimation. Niger. J. Technol. Dev. **13**(2), 74–82 (2016)
3. Banabic, R., Candea, G.: Fast black-box testing of system recovery code. In: 7th ACM European Conference On Computer Systems, pp. 281–294. ACM (2012)

4. Candido, J., Melo, L., d'Amorim, M.: Test suite parallelization in open-source projects: a study on its usage and impact. In: 32nd IEEE/ACM International Conference on Automated Software Engineering, pp. 838–848. IEEE Press (2017)

5. Cerveira, F., Barbosa, R., Madeira, H.: Experience report: on the impact of software faults in the privileged virtual machine. In: 28th International Symposium on Software Reliability Engineering (ISSRE), pp. 136–145. IEEE (2017)

6. Chen, P.: The systematic improvement of fault tolerance in the Rio file cache. Digest of Papers. In: Twenty-Ninth Annual International Symposium on Fault-Tolerant Computing (Cat. No.99CB36352), pp. 76–83 (1999). https://doi.org/10.1109/FTCS.1999.781036. http://ieeexplore.ieee.org/lpdocs/epic03/wrapper.htm?arnumber=781036

7. Cotroneo, D., Simone, L.D., Fucci, F., Natella, R.: MoIO : Run-time monitoring for I / O protocol violations in storage device drivers. In: 2015 IEEE 26th International Symposium on Software Reliability Engineering (ISSRE), pp. 472–483 (2015)

8. Cui, L., Li, B., Li, J., Hardy, J., Liu, L.: Software aging in virtualized environments: detection and prediction. In: 2012 IEEE 18th International Conference on Parallel and Distributed Systems, pp. 718–719. IEEE (2012)

9. Grimm, R.: Pros and cons of the various memory allocation strategies. https://www.modernescpp.com/index.php/pros-and-cons-of-the-various-memory-management-strategies. Accessed 15 Nov 2019

10. Hat, R.: Interrupts and irq tuning. https://access.redhat.com/documentation/en-us/red_hat_enterprise_linux/6/html/performance_tuning_guide/s-cpu-irq. Accessed 15 Nov 2019

11. Hat, R.: Offloading RCU callbacks. https://access.redhat.com/documentation/en-us/red_hat_enterprise_linux_for_real_time/7/html/tuning_guide/offloading_rcu_callbacks. Accessed 15 Nov 2019

12. Hsueh, M.C., Tsai, T.K., Iyer, R.K.: Fault injection techniques and tools. Computer **30**(4), 75–82 (1997)

13. Huang, Y., Kintala, C., Kolettis, N., Fulton, N.D.: Software rejuvenation: Analysis, module and applications. In: Twenty-Fifth International Symposium on Fault-Tolerant Computing. Digest of Papers, pp. 381–390. IEEE (1995)

14. Irrera, I., Durães, J., Madeira, H., Vieira, M.: Assessing the impact of virtualization on the generation of failure prediction data. In: Proceedings - 6th Latin-American Symposium on Dependable Computing LADC 2013, pp. 92–97 (2013)

15. Kanoun, K., Spainhower, L.: Dependability Benchmarking For Computer Systems, vol. 72. Wiley, Hoboken (2008)

16. Kropp, N.P., Koopman, P.J., Siewiorek, D.P.: Automated robustness testing of off-the-shelf software components. In: Digest of Papers - 28th Annual International Symposium on Fault-Tolerant Computing FTCS 1998, January 1998, pp. 1–10 (1998)

17. Lameter, C.: Numa (non-uniform memory access): an overview. https://queue.acm.org/detail.cfm?id=2513149. Accessed 15 Nov 2019

18. Lastovetsky, A.: Parallel testing of distributed software. Inf. Softw. Technol. **47**(10), 657–662 (2005)

19. Libes, D.: Exploring Expect: A Tcl-Based Toolkit for Automating Interactive Programs. O'Reilly Media, Inc., Sebastopol (1995)

20. LWN.net: (nearly) full tickless operation in 3.10. https://lwn.net/Articles/549580/. Accessed 15 Nov 2019

21. Makai, J., Peters, A.J., Bitzes, G., Sindrilaru, E.A., Simon, M.K., Manzi, A.: Testing of complex, large-scale distributed storage systems: a CERN disk storage case study. In: EPJ Web of Conferences, vol. 214, p. 05008. EDP Sciences (2019)

22. Matias Jr, R., Trivedi, K.S., Maciel, P.R.: Using accelerated life tests to estimate time to software aging failure. In: 2010 IEEE 21st International Symposium on Software Reliability Engineering, pp. 211–219. IEEE (2010)
23. Matthews, J.N., et al.: Quantifying the performance isolation properties of virtualization systems. In: 2007 workshop on Experimental computer science, p. 6. ACM (2007)
24. Myers, G.J., Sandler, C., Badgett, T.: THe Art of Software Testing. Wiley, Hoboken (2011)
25. Nagios: Nagios. https://www.nagios.com/. Accessed 15 Nov 2019
26. Natella, R., Cotroneo, D., Duraes, J., Madeira, H.: Representativeness analysis of injected software faults in complex software. In: 2010 IEEE/IFIP International Conference on Dependable Systems & Networks (DSN), pp. 437–446. IEEE (2010)
27. Netdata: Netdata. https://www.netdata.cloud/. Accessed 15 Nov 2019
28. Novaković, D., Vasić, N., Novaković, S., Kostić, D., Bianchini, R.: Deepdive: transparently identifying and managing performance interference in virtualized environments. In: Presented as part of the 2013 {USENIX} Annual Technical Conference ({USENIX}{ATC} 13), pp. 219–230 (2013)
29. man Pages, L.: chrt - manipulate the real-time attributes of a process. http://man7.org/linux/man-pages/man1/chrt.1.html. Accessed 15 Nov 2019
30. QEMU: Qemu. https://www.qemu.org/. Accessed 15 Nov 2019
31. Sangchoolie, B., Pattabiraman, K., Karlsson, J.: One bit is (not) enough: an empirical study of the impact of single and multiple bit-flip errors. In: 2017 47th Annual IEEE/IFIP International Conference on Dependable Systems and Networks (DSN), pp. 97–108. IEEE (2017)
32. Santos, H., Pimentel, J.F., Da Silva, V.T., Murta, L.: Software rejuvenation via a multi-agent approach. J. Syst. Softw. **104**, 41–59 (2015)
33. Schwahn, O., Coppik, N., Winter, S., Suri, N.: Assessing the state and improving the art of parallel testing for C. In: 28th ACM SIGSOFT International Symposium on Software Testing and Analysis, pp. 123–133. ACM (2019)
34. Schwahn, O., Coppik, N., Winter, S., Suri, N.: FastFI: accelerating software fault injections. In: Proceedings of IEEE Pacific Rim International Symposium on Dependable Computing PRDC, December 2018, pp. 193–202 (2019)
35. Spurrier, N.: Pexpect. https://pexpect.readthedocs.io/en/stable/. Accessed 15 Nov 2019
36. Ubuntu: cset-shield. http://manpages.ubuntu.com/manpages/trusty/man1/cset-shield.1.html. Accessed 15 Nov 2019
37. Ubuntu: Real-time/low-latency kernel. https://help.ubuntu.com/community/UbuntuStudio/RealTimeKernel. Accessed 15 Nov 2019
38. Ubuntu: stress-ng. https://manpages.ubuntu.com/manpages/artful/man1/stress-ng.1.html. Accessed 15 Nov 2019
39. Winter, S., Schwahn, O., Natella, R., Suri, N., Cotroneo, D.: No PAIN, no gain? the utility of parallel fault injections. In: Proceedings - International Conference on Software Engineering, vol. 1, pp. 494–505 (2015)
40. Winter, S., Tretter, M., Sattler, B., Suri, N.: simFi: from single to simultaneous software fault injections. In: 2013 43rd Annual IEEE/IFIP International Conference on Dependable Systems and Networks (DSN), pp. 1–12. IEEE (2013)
41. Fernández, J.D. (WU), Wouter Dullaert (TF).: D3.3 - scalability and Robustness testing report V1, June 2018
42. Yoshimura, T., Yamada, H., Kono, K.: Is linux kernel oops useful or not? HotDep (2012)

A Classification of Faults Covering
the Human-Computer Interaction Loop

Philippe Palanque[1][✉], Andy Cockburn[2], and Carl Gutwin[3]

[1] ICS-IRIT, Université Paul Sabatier Toulouse 3, Toulouse, France
palanque@irit.fr
[2] Computer Science, University of Canterbury, Christchurch, New Zealand
andy.cockburn@canterbury.ac.nz
[3] Computer Science, University of Saskatchewan, Saskatoon, Canada
gutwin@cs.usask.ca

Abstract. The operator is one of the main sources of vulnerability in command and control systems; for example, 79% of fatal accidents in aviation are attributed to "human error." Following Avizienis et al.'s classification system for faults human error at operation time can be characterized as the operator's failure to deliver services while interacting with the command and control system. However, little previous work attempts to separate out the many different origins of faults that set the operator in an error mode. This paper proposes an extension to the Avizienis et al. taxonomy in order to more fully account for the human operator, making explicit the faults, error states, and failures that cause operators to deviate from correct service delivery. Our new taxonomy improves understanding and identification of faults, and provides systematic insight into ways that human service failures could be avoided or repaired. We present multiple concrete examples, from aviation and other domains, of faults affecting operators and fault-tolerant mechanisms, covering the critical aspects of the operator-side of the Human-Computer Interaction Loop.

Keywords: Human error · Failures · Human-computer interaction loop

1 Introduction

Command and control systems have many potential sources of faults, one of which is the human operator. Operators are a primary source of vulnerability in complex systems: for example, studies have shown that 66% of hull-loss accidents in commercial jet aircrafts [2] and 74% of fatal accidents in general aviation [1] are attributed to human error. However, there is relatively little work on categorizing the different types of operator faults than might contribute to the high frequency of operator errors.

One of the most influential taxonomies of faults was developed by Avizienis and colleagues [6]. It covers some aspects of the human operator and allows for a variety of operator faults, but does not provide a full treatment of the human-computer interaction loop (HCIL). In particular, Avizienis's taxonomy does not address issues such as environmental causes for operator faults (e.g., turbulence that prevents a pilot from pressing

© Springer Nature Switzerland AG 2020
A. Casimiro et al. (Eds.): SAFECOMP 2020, LNCS 12234, pp. 434–448, 2020.
https://doi.org/10.1007/978-3-030-54549-9_29

a button), the different subsystems in a human (perceptual, cognitive, or motor function) that can cause faults, or the difference between failures within the operator (e.g., not having adequate muscular control to guide a vehicle) and failures that are caused by another person (e.g., someone shining a laser pointer into a pilot's eyes).

Because faults stemming from the operator's interaction with a complex system are common and often critical, it is important to better understand the nature and causes of these faults. In identifying this need, Sheikh Bahaei et al. [3–5] extended previous fault taxonomies with a focus on addressing the specific issues arising in augmented reality interaction. More precisely, [3] builds on top of human error taxonomies including Reason [50], Norman [51] or Rasmussen [52] and provides a human error taxonomy using feature diagrams from [53]. In this paper, we pursue a more general approach, expanding on Avizienis's influential fault taxonomy to better characterize and explain operator faults, focusing on internal and external events that induce **error states inside the operator**. This approach contrasts with that of others – in particular, Avizienis's work focused on faults that induce **error states inside the system**. We build on that taxonomy (widely used in dependable computing) and integrate an interactive systems engineering approach with the goal of improving dependable interactive systems.

We add categories in Avizienis's *System boundary* dimension to include causes of operator error that are either internal to the operator or external; we add categories to the *Phenomenological cause* dimension to recognize new sources of faults including environmentally-induced operator faults and faults induced by other people; and we add a new dimension *Human capability* to separate out faults that occur in the operator's perceptual, cognitive, and motor subsystems. These additions provide 24 types of operator faults, many of which have not been considered in previous work. Our expansion provides designers and researchers with new classes of potential faults that cover common and important real-world phenomena, and that improve understanding of how faults occur in the human-computer interaction loop. By showing where operator faults can arise, our work can improve the design of new interactive systems and lead to better evaluation of existing systems and diagnosis of accidents and incidents. We demonstrate that the classification makes it possible to position previous work in the field of HCI addressing fault tolerance, fault prevention, fault removal and fault forecasting.

The paper first provides an introduction to the human-computer interaction loop and the way operators interact with technological systems. Second, we present our expanded taxonomy of operator faults and describe the main structures and categories, with examples from aviation and other task domains. Third, we describe how existing HCI research fits into our framework, and fourth, we discuss amelioration strategies for the new fault categories, using the general approaches of fault removal, fault tolerance, fault prevention, and fault forecasting.

2   The Human-Computer Interaction Loop (HCIL)

The research field of Human-Computer Interaction (HCI) aims to build knowledge about humans interacting with computing systems. The field covers methods, techniques, and tools for designing and developing computing systems adapted to their users. Typical properties that are targeted by HCI research are usability [7], user experience [8], accessibility [9], and acceptance [10]. In order to reach these objectives, HCI promotes iterative user-centered design and development processes [11] that use variable-fidelity prototyping [33] and continuous feedback from real users [12].

These processes do not necessarily lead to robust computing systems: for example, cellphones are less dependable than fixed lines [13], but users may accept reduced dependability if it is accompanied by significant improvements in user experience. In the area of safety-critical systems, however, dependability cannot be compromised for user experience and usability, as people's lives are at stake; in addition, in some domains such as aviation, certification authorities explicitly require a very high level of dependability (e.g., the certification specification requirements in [14]).

These requirements mean that designing interactive systems that are both dependable and usable implies making informed compromises. Making such compromises is not an easy task (as demonstrated in [15]) as it requires blending knowledge from several disciplines like HCI and dependable computing. The following section highlights the principles behind the engineering of interactive systems, providing a holistic view that incorporates the human with the computing system.

2.1 The Human-Computer Interaction Loop

Figure 1 presents an architectural view (from left to right) of the operator, the interactive command and control system, and the underlying system (e.g., an aircraft engine). This architecture is a simplified version of MIODMIT (Multiple Input and Output Devices and Multiple Interaction Techniques), a generic architecture for multimodal interactive systems [26] described in AADL [27]. Following the attribute dimensions of [6] we highlight (top right of Fig. 1) the hardware and software components, and show how the human operator interacts with them (thick dotted lines).

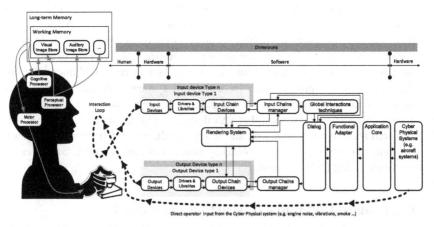

Fig. 1. Architecture of interactive systems with operator, hardware, & software components.

As shown in the figure, interaction mainly takes place though the manipulation of input devices (e.g., keyboard or mouse) and the perception of information from the output devices (e.g., a computer screen or speaker). Another channel usually overlooked is the direct perception by the operator of information produced (usually as a side effect) of the underlying cyber-physical systems (e.g., noise or vibrations from an aircraft engine (represented by the lower dotted line in the figure)).

The top left of the Software section of the diagram corresponds to the interaction technique that uses information from the input devices. Interaction techniques have a tremendous impact on operator performance. Standard interaction techniques encompass complex mechanisms (e.g. modification of the cursor's movement on the screen according to the acceleration of the physical mouse on the desk). This design space is of prime importance and HCI research has explored multiple possibilities for improving performance, such as enlarging the target area for selection on touch screens [29] and providing on-screen widgets to facilitate selection [28].

The right side of the Software section of the architecture corresponds to what is usually called interactive applications. This is where HCI methods such as task analysis are needed for building usable application that fit the operators' work [30].

The left side of Fig. 1 represents the operator's view. The drawing is based on work that models the human as an *information processor* [22], based on previous research in psychology. In that model, the human is presented as a system composed of three interconnected processors. The *perceptive system* senses information from the environment – primarily the visual, auditory, and tactile systems as these are more common when interacting with computers. The *motor system* allows operators to act on the real world. Target selection (a key interaction mechanism) has been deeply studied [32]; for example, Fitts' Law provides a formula for predicting the time needed for an operator to select a target, based on its size and distance [31]. The *cognitive system* is in charge of processing information gathered by the perceptual system, storing that information in memory, analyzing the information and deciding on actions using the motor system. The sequential use of these systems (perceptive, cognitive and motoric) while interacting with computers is called the Human-Computer Interaction Loop (HCIL).

2.2   The Operator as a Service

If we consider the operator as a service provider to the interactive system (by manipulation of input devices for selecting commands and entering data) and a service consumer of information presented by means of the output devices, this service might exhibit failures, i.e., that the delivered service deviates from correct service (as introduced in [6], section 3.3.1, p. 18). While that paper [6] was focusing on faults that might trigger service failure on the software and hardware parts of systems, the taxonomy presented in Sect. 3 will identify faults that might trigger failures in the operator him- or herself by exploiting the human information processor decomposition.

A key abstraction in the HCIL is that of the match between the *variance* in the signal produced by either the user or the system (e.g., the variance in the user's motor movements, or the brightness of the output display) and the *tolerance for variance* in the receiver of the information (e.g., the size of a target in the interface, or the user's visual acuity). If the variance exceeds the tolerance, the operator might enter an error state. For example, the requirements for correct selection of a button on a touchscreen are that the variance in the movement of the finger is less than the extents of the button:

if the button is 2 cm in diameter and the user has a 1 cm variance when aiming for the centre of the button, the button will be selected correctly; if the user has a 3 cm variance in their aiming motion, errors may arise. This variance element is key in the design of user interfaces and interaction techniques. If the button is the size of the entire screen, selection will be faster and the operator will be able to select even in severe turbulence; however, very little information will be presented, thus reducing the effectiveness and efficiency of the application. As described in the next section, various elements of the operator and the external environment can affect both the variance in the signals, and the tolerance for variance, in an operator-system interaction.

3   Taxonomy of Faults for the HCIL

Our taxonomy of operator faults expands on the framework of Avizienis and colleagues [6]. We use Avizienis as a foundation due to its widespread use and influence on the field. Other taxonomies have been introduced (such as Sheikh Bahaei et al.'s taxonomy of fault taxonomies [3]) that cover various aspects of operator error lacking in previous frameworks (such as faults that arise from augmented reality interaction [3]); however, previous work is primarily focused on specific areas rather than general limitations.

   We expand the Avizienis framework in four ways. First, we extend the *System boundary* dimension to recognize that human faults can be **induced in the operator** from external causes. Second, we add new levels to the *Phenomenological cause* dimension to distinguish between faults arising 1) from the operator, 2) from another person, and 3) from the natural world (including the system itself). Third, we introduce the *Human capability* dimension to differentiate faults in the operator's perceptual, cognitive, and motor abilities. Fourth, we add specific fault categories that derive from these dimensions. Figure 2 provides an overview of the taxonomy.

3.1   Changes and Additions to the Fault Dimensions

The Avizienis framework provides several dimensions that characterize faults in terms of when, where, and how they arise: at the highest levels, they distinguish between development and operational faults (*Phase*), faults that are internal or external to the system (*System boundary*), and faults that are natural or human made (*Phenomenological cause*). Although this structure allows for a wide range of fault types (including operator and environmental faults), it does not systematically categorize and describe the ways in which operator faults can occur.

   In particular, the complex interactions between an operator and a system (i.e., the HCIL) have properties and characteristics that are separate from the operator alone or the system alone, and the HCIL can lead to many different types of faults that have many different underlying causes – some of which involve the fault being "induced" in the operator by outside forces. For example, an aircraft's hard landing may arise from within the operator (e.g., a pilot's early-stage Parkinson's disease that reduces their muscular coordination), from another person (e.g., someone shining a laser pointer into the pilot's eyes from the end of the runway), or from effects of the natural world (e.g., air turbulence that shakes a pilot's arm as they try to press a button on the instrument panel). Although these three faults are very different in terms of implications for design, they would all be placed in the same category in the Avizienis framework (i.e., "Operational/External/Human-made/Non-malicious/Non-deliberate/Accidental" operator faults). To address this gap, we need to broaden the dimensions that characterize faults. In this paper we focus only on operational faults (leaving aside the development faults), and expand the dimensions of *System boundary* and *Phenomenological cause*.

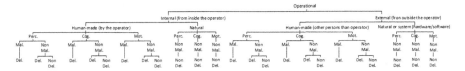

Fig. 2. Overview of the taxonomy of faults focusing on the HCI Loop.

We expand the *System boundary* dimension to add the HCIL as a conceptual location for faults that should be considered separately from Avizienis et al.'s categories of "internal to the system" and "external to the system." We apply the idea of internal/external to divide HCIL-based faults into those that arise from inside the operator (see Fig. 3) and those that arise external to the operator (see Fig. 4).

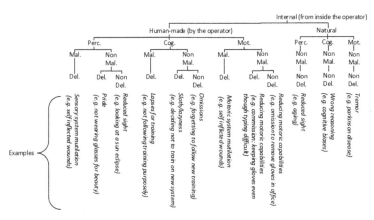

Fig. 3. Focus of the taxonomy on Internal faults (from inside the operator) with examples.

We next identify new levels for the *Phenomenological cause* dimension that explicitly recognize that when an operator is unable to perform task actions correctly, the cause may be human-made or from the natural world. When the fault is internal, human-made implies that it is within the operator; when external, human-made implies the action of another person. We then create a new dimension – *Human capability* – to characterize the human processing subsystem where the fault is located (see discussion of the human information processor in the previous section). The HCIL requires three main kinds of human ability (perception, cognition, and motor control) and faults in any of these can lead the operator to reach an error state.

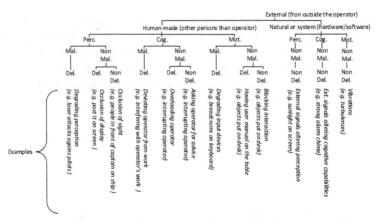

Fig. 4. Focus of the taxonomy on External faults (from outside the operator) with examples.

Finally, there are several other dimensions that play roles in our characterization of operator faults. We use the *Objective* (Malicious, Non-malicious), *Intent* (Deliberate, Non-deliberate), and *Persistence* (Persistent, Transitory) dimensions in a similar fashion to Avizienis and colleagues; however, the *Capability* dimension, which classifies faults as accidental or due to incompetence, focusses on the cause of the fault rather than its description. For this reason, we decided to leave it outside of our classification.

3.2 Operator Faults Arising Externally (From Outside the Operator)

Operator Faults Induced by the Natural World. This category can only have Non-malicious and Non-deliberate faults, because the source of these faults is the natural world, which does not have objectives or intents. There are fault types that affect each of the three human capabilities (perception, cognition, motor control), and it is important to note that some types of environmental phenomena may arise from the system itself rather than from weather, sunshine, or terrain (e.g., vibration may come from an aircraft's engines as well as from air turbulence). The main difference between system-based and non-system induced faults is in the operator's ability to control the system to reduce the phenomena (e.g., reduce engine power to reduce vibration); we discuss this further in Sect. 4 below.

Environment-Induced Perceptual Faults are caused by natural-world phenomena that reduce the operator's perception of the system. The primary senses of concern for interactive systems are sight, hearing, and touch. Example faults in this category include bright sunlight that "washes out" a display screen, reducing the operator's ability to see and interpret visual objects; vibration from air turbulence or a rough road that reduces both the operator's visual perception (e.g., tracking a moving object on a vibrating display) and tactile perception (e.g., receiving vibro-tactile alerts); or a noisy environment that reduces the operator's ability to hear alert sounds.

Environment-Induced Cognitive Faults are caused by phenomena that reduce the operator's cognitive capabilities – primarily memory and decision-making. Natural phenomena such as loud noises and bright flashing lights are known to cause problems for cognitive ability by saturating the brain's communication channels [34]. In addition, environmental conditions such as a low-oxygen atmosphere can have severe effects on cognitive ability, memory [36], and peripheral perception [35]. This demonstrates that environmental faults may alter operator performance on all three capabilities, but dividing these into three is relevant as some faults only alter one capability.

Environment-Induced Motor Faults involve natural phenomena that reduce motor abilities including movement precision, strength, or endurance. For example, air turbulence reduces the accuracy of a pilot's finger movement toward a touchscreen target; if the variance in the pilot's finger movement exceeds the system's tolerance (as determined by the size of the target) then failures in selecting targets can occur [23]. Similarly, reduced temperature can affect muscular control in an operator who needs to carry out precise hand movements or complex gestures [37].

Operator Faults Induced by Other People. This category involves another person acting in such a way that the operator's perceptual, cognitive, or motor abilities are compromised. Because the source is another human, these faults can vary in terms of *Objective* and *Intent*.

Other-Person-Induced Perceptual Faults are those in which another person's actions compromise the operator's sight, hearing, or touch. Malicious actions include, for example, shining a laser pointer into a pilot's eyes (preventing them from seeing a display [38]), or making loud noises when an operator needs to hear an auditory signal. The degree to which the operator's perception is compromised and the tolerance built into the HCIL will determine whether or not a failure can occur.

Non-malicious faults in this category can be either Deliberate or Non-deliberate. Non-deliberate actions are extremely common: these could involve a person inadvertently standing in front of the operator (and thus occluding a display screen) or talking loudly to the operator (and thus preventing them from hearing an auditory signal). Deliberate but non-malicious actions in this category are less frequent, but still possible: for example, a person could stick a post-it note on a display to cover an annoying flashing alert (i.e., deliberately reducing perception of the display) without realizing that the operator will not perceive future alerts.

Other-Person-Induced Cognitive Faults are those in which another person compromises the operator's memory or decision-making ability. A Malicious and Deliberate action here could involve another person interrupting the operator to prevent proper decision-making. Non-malicious and Non-deliberate actions could include another person providing information to the operator at the exact time when the operator is trying to memorize something. Other types are less likely: e.g., it is unlikely that someone would deliberately compromise an operator's cognitive abilities without malice.

Other-Person-Induced Motor Faults are those in which another person reduces the operator's motor control. A Malicious and Deliberate action here could involve another person bumping the operator's arm to prevent them from targeting precisely. Non-malicious and Non-deliberate actions could include another person placing objects on a desk that get in the operator's way, or a child pulling on a parent's arm while the parent is trying to drive a car. Alternatively, an operator might Deliberately but Non-maliciously block another person's action (by grabbing their arm, for example) if they see that they are about to select an incorrect control (a fault would occur if the blocking results in the triggering of another incorrect control).

3.3   Operator Faults Arising Internally (From Inside the Operator)

This category involves faults that are not induced in the operator by external forces, but that arise from the operator him- or herself. These can still be categorized in terms of their effects on the operator's perception, cognition, and motor abilities.

Operator-Made Faults. Operator-made faults are those in which the operators compromise their own perceptual, cognitive, or motor abilities. These faults are most commonly Non-malicious, although rare cases involving malice are possible. Examples of *Operator-Made Perceptual Faults* include Non-malicious actions that are Deliberate (e.g., an operator not wearing their prescription glasses because of vanity, thereby reducing their visual acuity) or Non-deliberate (e.g., damaged hearing from listening to loud music). Malicious actions are rare (e.g., deliberate self-harm of the operator's eyes or ears).

Examples of Non-malicious *Operator-Made Cognitive Faults* include Deliberate actions (e.g., an operator skipping system training because of laziness) and Non-deliberate actions (e.g., an operator drinking or using drugs on the job, or an operator forgetting to carry out a training module). Again, malice is rare in this category (e.g., purposefully choosing to skip training or take a drug to impair cognition). *Operator-Made Motor Faults* can be Non-malicious and Deliberate (e.g., an operator wearing gloves even though they know this reduces their ability to type) or Non-deliberate (e.g., having long fingernails that reduce touch accuracy on touchscreens). Malicious and Deliberate actions (again rare) could involve self-mutilation of the hands or fingers needed to operate a system.

Faults in the Operator Induced by the Natural World. The natural world can also affect the operator's capabilities through natural processes that are internal to the operator. Aging, disease, fatigue, and other elements of the human condition can have substantial effects on perception, cognition, and motor control. As the natural world is the source of these faults, they are all Non-malicious and Non-deliberate. Examples of *Natural Perceptual Faults* include reduction in color perception due to color-vision deficiency (commonly called color blindness) or reduction in visual acuity because of age-related presbyopia; reduction in auditory capability is commonly caused by age-related deafness. Examples of *Natural Cognitive Faults* include well-known cognitive biases (e.g., "loss aversion" [39] in which people prefer to avoid losses rather than achieve equivalent gains) as well as age- or disease-related dementia and memory loss. Examples of *Natural Motor Faults* include reduction in touch accuracy due to conditions such as Parkinson's disease, or reduction in strength due to aging (e.g., the captain of Ethiopian flight ET302 requested the first officer to "Pull with me", applying a force of up to 110 lbs on the control column [49]).

It is important to note that these biases are not separated out in Avizienis et al.'s classification, even though they are of different types (information overload, lack of meaning, need for fast action, and decisions about what to remember), are numerous [41], and have strong safety implications (e.g., attention tunneling in aviation [40]).

4 Analysis of Gaps for Improving Dependability of the HCIL

The taxonomy presented above introduces new concepts and classes for the domain of operator faults, and the specific characteristics of many of these categories suggest ways in which the faults can be avoided, ameliorated, or repaired. In this section we consider four common mechanisms for improving dependability – fault removal, fault tolerance, fault prevention, and fault forecasting – and apply them to the taxonomy.

Many of the strategies described in the sections below arise from our basic characterization of interaction between an operator and a system as a communication of information with certain variance and tolerance (Sect. 2.2). Improvements to dependability can therefore focus on either increasing tolerance or reducing variability. On the input side, tolerance could be increased by making touchscreen buttons larger and using a more stable selection action such as a long press instead of a tap; variability could be reduced by training the operator to brace their hand on the display bezel. For output, the operator's visual acuity could be improved with corrective lenses, or the size and contrast of the text in an alert dialog could be increased to improve comprehensibility. While at the core of HCI discipline, systematically identifying design options with respect to the faults they address could lead to more dependable interactive systems.

4.1 Fault Prevention

Fault prevention involves preventing the introduction or occurrence of faults. In Avizienis et al., prevention of operational faults is not addressed (even though prevention of development faults is covered in section 5.1, p. 24). Prevention of operational faults (inside the operator) can be done by adapting input devices, output devices, interaction techniques and user interface so that they prevent faults from occurring. On the External side (Fig. 4) this can be done by removing interference from others, from the system, and from natural causes. Some solutions are beyond current technology (e.g. preventing turbulence in aircraft) or may add other problems (e.g., removing the first officer to reduce distraction would cause more problems when workload increases). On the Internal side (see Fig. 3), prevention can be accomplished through training (e.g. informing operators about cognitive biases and techniques for debiasing [44]) or through human augmentation (e.g. using night-vision goggles, although their use can induce new types of accidents [43]). As operator behavior is far from predictable, however, fault prevention techniques might fail and faults then have to be removed.

4.2 Fault Removal

Fault removal strategies attempt to reduce the number and severity of faults. The main type of fault removal for the HCIL is "preventive maintenance" which aims to uncover and remove faults before they cause errors (Avizienis, p. 28). However, different strategies will be needed in the different main categories of our taxonomy:

- *Internal/Operator-made faults* arise from actions taken by the operator, and are therefore best removed through organizational strategies (e.g., better enforcement of training, increased concern for operator mental health, and better understanding of conditions in the workplace that could lead operators to act in an unsafe manner).

- *Internal/Natural faults* must be removed by addressing the underlying natural cause. For example, faults caused by limits on ability due to aging or disease can be avoided both by treating conditions that are treatable (e.g., providing corrective lenses to operators who need them) and by accommodating reduced ability by increasing system tolerances (e.g., using brighter cockpit displays to accommodate the reduced night vision of an aging pilot population).
- *External/Human-made faults* involve the actions of other people, and so removal strategies are more difficult to prescribe. Regulations that limit access to the operators' workplace can assist with this category (e.g., not allowing the public near where operators are working, and ensuring that people who do have access are aware of the risks of interrupting or disrupting operators).
- *External/Natural faults* involve natural-world phenomena inducing faults in the operator. Removal strategies can focus either on reducing the effects of likely phenomena or on improving the operator's abilities during the phenomena. For example, the effects of turbulence could be mitigated by allowing pilots to fly to smoother air (reducing the phenomenon), or by teaching pilots to brace their hands while reaching for controls [18] or better control their movements during turbulence (improving operator abilities). Similarly, strategies could reduce sunlight or loud noise through filters or through technologies such as noise-cancelling headphones, or could increase the magnitude of the system's visual or auditory signals.

4.3 Fault Tolerance

Fault tolerance is the delivery of a correct service despite the occurrence of faults, and has several elements that are relevant to the HCIL, including error detection, recovery, and error handling. First, error detection in a human-computer system will often involve the operator rather than the system – that is, it is often only the operator who can determine that an input was erroneous. The design of an interactive system can assist the operator using well-known HCI strategies such as providing sufficient feedback to the operator to help them detect errors (e.g., mode errors in aircraft automation [42]), or providing "reasonableness checks" on input.

Second, HCIL-based recovery and error handling (i.e., mechanisms that eliminate errors from the interactive system state) can be based on the idea that input and output are a kind of communication between the operator and the system that occurs in a noisy channel. Telecommunications theory uses the idea of adding redundancy in order to preserve the signal, and a similar approach can provide fault tolerance in the HCIL. For example, in an aircraft cockpit where turbulence causes touchscreen errors, the human-system communication channel could add redundancy through command repetition or explicit confirmation. As in telecommunications, however, adding redundancy reduces the throughput of the system, and as a result, operator actions will take longer. Therefore, an important design principle is that the degree of redundancy should be adaptively matched to the amount of "noise" in the channel. In the case of turbulence, sun glare, or ambient sound, this could be accomplished using environmental sensors and models of the effects of these phenomena on the operator. In the context of interactive cockpits, self-checking interactive components have been proposed that migrate checking from the flight crew to a software component – a study of this system showed that dependability increased without degrading operator throughput [20].

4.4 Fault Forecasting

Predictive models are another type of fault forecasting that is critical to some of the strategies described above. These models provide a prediction of the likelihood that a physical phenomenon such as noise, sunlight, or turbulence will affect operator actions or perception; these predictions are critical because of the possibility of adapting the system to the magnitude or severity of the current phenomena. In addition, if techniques such as adding redundancy are used (see Sect. 4.2), models can help avoid situations where the system asks for more confirmation or repetition than is required by the environmental conditions. As an example, recruitment procedures of operators aim at detecting operators' capabilities in order to reduce likelihood of failures [45].

Experimental psychology is also an evolving field and previous knowledge can be overturned by new studies. For example, Wason [46] describes a study where a large majority were not able to deduce information correctly (philosophyexperiments.com//wason). A more recent study [47] showed that the abstract nature of the task was the limiting factor; concrete presentation of the same information removed the difficulty.

5 Discussion and Conclusion

We analysed our taxonomy in terms of the requirements identified by Hansman [54]: acceptability, completeness, standard terminology, determinism, mutual exclusiveness, repeatability, and unambiguity. We meet several of these requirements by using well-accepted foundations (i.e., the Avizienis framework and the standard HCI model of the human information processor); this improves **acceptability**, facilitates **completeness** (although further sub-divisions are possible), uses **standard terminology** that is familiar to researchers, and provides clear classification structures (**determinism**). We partially meet the requirements of **mutual exclusiveness**, **repeatability**, and **unambiguity**: the divisions in the taxonomy are clearly separated, but because many tasks involve multiple human capabilities, a phenomenon could affect multiple categories (e.g., turbulence can affect both perception and motor action); therefore, users of the taxonomy will need to separately consider effects on different human capabilities. In addition, it is often difficult to ascertain people's internal states (i.e., deliberateness and maliciousness may not be knowable). Finally, the **usefulness** of the taxonomy is in providing new ways to think about operator faults, which can lead to better analysis of incidents and improved designs. However, usefulness must be further determined as the taxonomy is used by the research and practitioner communities.

Although several taxonomies exist that cover different aspects of operator failures, these have not comprehensively explored the many ways in which operators fail while interacting with an interactive human-computer system. We expanded on Avizienis et al.'s fault taxonomy [6] to better characterize and explain operator faults, focusing on internal and external faults that induce error states inside the operator. Our new taxonomy explicitly recognizes that operators can be induced into error states, and separates out faults in the operator's perceptual, cognitive, and motor subsystems. These additions provided 24 types of operator faults that expand on the coverage of previous taxonomies. The framework highlights the fact that the some research contributions are able to address one type of fault (e.g., stabilizing touch interaction by bracing the hand on the display [48]) while triggering another type of fault (e.g., bracing with the hand on the display may cause other faults if the hand occludes the display content).

Our work provides new opportunities for future research. First, we will refine and validate the taxonomy by classifying existing incidents in consultation with domain experts and practitioners. Second, we will develop new adaptive fault-removal techniques for different environmental conditions such as ambient noise, vibration, and glare. Third, we will look more deeply into some of the fault categories by developing formal models of the operator's actions in the HCIL, and will further develop the idea of human-system interaction as communication in a noisy channel that can be improved through redundancy. Overall, our new taxonomy provides researchers and designers with a broad understanding of how and where operator faults can arise, and can improve the design of new interactive systems in complex environments. Our classification is able to integrate previous work in multiple domains such as medicine, psychology, and HCI, all of which contribute to the dependability of interactive systems.

References

1. Geske, R.: The Nall Report: General Aviation Accidents in 2015. AOPA Air Safety Institute (2015)
2. Boeing Corp.: Statistical Summary of Commercial Jet Airplane Accidents, Worldwide Operations 1959-2018
3. Sheikh Bahaei, S., Gallina, B., Laumann, K., Skogstad, M.R.: Effect of augmented reality on faults leading to human failures in socio-technical systems. In: 2019 4th International Conference on System Reliability and Safety (ICSRS), pp. 236–245. IEEE (2019)
4. Sheikh Bahaei, S., Gallina, B.: Augmented reality-extended humans: towards a taxonomy of failures – focus on visual technologies. In: European Safety and Reliability Conference (ESREL). Research Publishing, Singapore (2019)
5. Sheikh Bahaei, S., Gallina, S.: Towards assessing risk of safety-critical socio-technical systems while augmenting reality. In: International Symposium on Model-Based Safety and Assessment (IMBSA) (2019). (easyconferences.eu/imbsa2019/proceedings-annex/)
6. Avizienis, A., Laprie, J.C., Randell, B., Landwehr, C.: Basic concepts and taxonomy of dependable and secure computing. IEEE Trans. Dependable Secure Comput. 1(1), 11–33 (2004)
7. International Standard Organization: "ISO 9241–11" Ergonomic requirements for office work with visual display terminals (VDT) – Part 11 Guidance on Usability (1996)
8. ISO 9241–210 Ergonomics of Human-System Interaction Ergonomics of human-system interaction – Part 210: Human-centred design for interactive systems (2010)
9. W3C Web Accessibility Initiative. Web Content Accessibility Guidelines (WCAG) Overview. Web Accessibility Initiative (WAI). www.w3.org/WAI/standards-guidelines/wcag/
10. Davis, F.D.: Perceived usefulness, perceived ease of use, and user acceptance of information technology. MIS Q. 13(3), 319–340 (1989)
11. ISO/IEC 13407: Human-Centred Design Processes for Interactive Systems now integrated in ISO 9241 part 210 [8] (1999)

12. Gulliksen, J., Göransson, B., Boivie, I., Blomkvist, S., Persson, J., Cajander, Å.: Key principles for user-centred systems design. Behav. Inf. Technol. **22**(6), 397–409 (2003)
13. Gray, J.N.: Dependability in the Internet Era. In: High Dependability Computing Consortium Conference, Santa Cruz, CA, 7 May 2001
14. CS-25 – Amendment 17 - Certification Specifications and Acceptable Means of Compliance for Large Aeroplanes. EASA (2015)
15. Fayollas, C., Martinie, C., Palanque, P., Deleris, Y., Fabre, J., Navarre, D.: An approach for assessing the impact of dependability on usability: application to interactive cockpits. In: 2014 Tenth European Dependable Computing Conference, pp. 198–209 (2014)
16. Canny, A., Bouzekri, E., Martinie, C., Palanque, P.: Rationalizing the need of architecture-driven testing of interactive systems. In: Bogdan, C., Kuusinen, K., Lárusdóttir, M.K., Palanque, P., Winckler, M. (eds.) HCSE 2018. LNCS, vol. 11262, pp. 164–186. Springer, Cham (2019). https://doi.org/10.1007/978-3-030-05909-5_10
17. Bass, L., et al.: The arch model: Seeheim revisited. In: User Interface Developers' Workshop (1991)
18. Cockburn, A., Masson, D., Gutwin, C., Palanque, P., Goguey, A., Yung, M., Trask, C.: Design and evaluation of brace touch for touchscreen input stabilisation. Int. J. Hum. Comput. Stud. **122**(21–37), 7 (2019)
19. Navarre, D., Palanque, P., Basnyat, S.: A formal approach for user interaction reconfiguration of safety critical interactive systems. In: Harrison, M.D., Sujan, M.A. (eds.) SAFECOMP 2008. LNCS, vol. 5219, pp. 373–386. Springer, Heidelberg (2008). https://doi.org/10.1007/978-3-540-87698-4_31
20. Tankeu-Choitat, A., Navarre, D., Palanque, P., Deleris, Y., Fabre, J.-C., Fayollas, C.: Self-checking components for dependable interactive cockpits using formal description techniques. In: IEEE Pacific Rim Dependable Computing Conference, pp. 164–173 (2011)
21. Reason, J.: Human Error. Cambridge University Press, Cambridge (1990)
22. Card, S.K., Moran, T.P., Newell, A.: The model human processor: an engineering model of human performance. In: Handbook of Perception and Human Performance. Vol. 2: Cognitive Processes and Performance, pp. 1–35 (1986)
23. Cockburn, A., et al.: Turbulent touch: touchscreen input for cockpit flight displays. In: CHI, pp. 6742–6753 (2017)
24. Norman, D.A., Draper, S.W. (eds.): User-Centered System Design: New Perspectives on Human-Computer Interaction. Lawrence Earlbaum Associates, Hillsdale (1986)
25. Gould, I.D., Lewis, C.: Designing for usability: key principles and what designers think. Commun. ACM **28**(3), 300–311 (1985)
26. Cronel, M., Dumas, B., Palanque, P., Canny, A.: MIODMIT: a generic architecture for dynamic multimodal interactive systems. In: Bogdan, C., Kuusinen, K., Lárusdóttir, M.K., Palanque, P., Winckler, M. (eds.) HCSE 2018. LNCS, vol. 11262, pp. 109–129. Springer, Cham (2019). https://doi.org/10.1007/978-3-030-05909-5_7
27. Feiler, P.H., Gluch, D.P., Hudak, J.J.: The architecture analysis & design language (AADL): An introduction (No. CMU/SEI-2006-TN-011). CMU Software Engineering Inst. (2006)
28. Albinsson, P.A., Zhai, S.: High precision touch screen interaction. In: Proceedings ACM CHI Conference, pp. 105–112 (2003)
29. Olwal, A., Feiner, S.: Rubbing the fisheye: precise touch-screen interaction with gestures and fisheye views. In: Conference Supplement of UIST, pp. 83–84 (2003)
30. Diaper, D., Stanton, N.: The Handbook of Task Analysis for Human-Computer Interaction. Lawrence Erlbaum Associates, Mahwah (2003). ISBN 0-8058-4432-5
31. Fitt, P.M.: The information capacity of the human motor system in controlling the amplitude of movement. J. Exp. Psychol. **47**, 381–391 (1954)
32. Soukoreff, W., MacKenzie, S.: Towards a standard for pointing device evaluation, perspectives on 27 years of Fitts' law research in HCI. IJHCS **61**(6), 751–789 (2004)

33. Beaudouin-Lafon, M., Mackay, W.: Prototyping tools and techniques. In: The Human-Computer Interaction Handbook: Fundamentals, Evolving Technologies and Emerging Applications, pp. 1006–1031. L. Erlbaum Associates Inc., Mahwah (2002)
34. Irgens-Hansen, K., Gundersen, H., et al.: Noise exposure and cognitive performance: a study on personnel on board Royal Norwegian Navy vessels. Noise Health **17**(78), 320–327 (2015)
35. Ando, S., Yamada, Y., Kokubu, M.: Reaction time to peripheral visual stimuli during exercise under hypoxia. J. Appl. Physiol. **108**(5), 1210–1216 (2012)
36. Winder, R., Borrill, J.: Fuels for memory: the role of oxygen and glucose in memory enhancement. Psychopharmacology **136**(4), 349–356 (1998)
37. Goncalves, J., et al.: Tapping task performance on smartphones in cold temperature. Interact. Comput. **29**(3), 355–367 (2017)
38. Palakkamanil, M.M., Fielden, M.P.: Effects of malicious ocular laser exposure in commercial airline pilots. Can. J. Ophthalmol. **50**(6), 429–432 (2015)
39. Kahneman, D., Tversky, A.: Prospect theory: an analysis of decision under risk. Econometrica **47**(4), 263–291 (1979)
40. Wickens, C., Alexander, A.: Attentional tunneling and task management in synthetic vision displays. Int. J. Aviat. Psychol. **19**, 182–199 (2009)
41. The cognitive biases codex: 175 cognitive biases, 29 February 2020. https://medium.com/better-humans/cognitive-bias-cheat-sheet-55a472476b18
42. Sarter, N., Woods, D.: How in the world did we ever get into that mode? Mode error and awareness in supervisory control. Hum. Factors **37**, 5–19 (1995)
43. Johnson, C.W.: The role of night vision equipment in military incidents and accidents. In: Johnson, C.W., Palanque, P. (eds.) Human Error, Safety and Systems Development. IIFIP, vol. 152, pp. 1–16. Springer, Boston, MA (2004). https://doi.org/10.1007/1-4020-8153-7_1
44. Carney, D., et al.: Cognitive de-biasing strategies: a faculty development workshop for clinical teachers in emergency medicine. MedEdPORTAL J. Teach. Learn. Resour. **13**, 10646 (2017)
45. Carretta, T., Ree, M.: Pilot Candidate Selection Methods (PCSM): sources of validity. Int. J. Aviat. Psychol. **1994**(4), 103–117 (2000)
46. Wason, P.C.: Reasoning. In: Foss, B. (ed.) New Horizons in Psychology, pp. 135–151. Penguin Books, Harmondsworth (1966)
47. Griggs, R., Cox, J.: The elusive thematic-materials effect in Wason's selection task. Br. J. Psychol. **73**, 407–420 (1982)
48. Palanque, P., Cockburn, A., Désert-Legendre, L., Gutwin, C., Deleris, Y.: Brace touch: a dependable, turbulence-tolerant, multi-touch interaction technique for interactive cockpits. In: Romanovsky, A., Troubitsyna, E., Bitsch, F. (eds.) SAFECOMP 2019. LNCS, vol. 11698, pp. 53–68. Springer, Cham (2019). https://doi.org/10.1007/978-3-030-26601-1_4
49. Aircraft Accident Investigation Bureau Interim Report Interim Investigation Report of accident 737–8 MAX ET-AVJ, ET-302 (2020). www.aib.gov.et/wp-content/uploads/2020/documents/accident/ET-302-Interim-Investigation-Report-March-9-2020.pdf
50. Reason, J.: Generic Error-Modeling System (GEMS): a cognitive framework for locating common human error forms. New Technol. Hum. Error **63**, 63–83 (1987)
51. Norman, D.: Errors in human performance. University of California, San Diego, Report 8004, pp. 46 (1980)
52. Rasmussen, J.: Human errors. A taxonomy for describing human malfunction in industrial installations. J. Occup. Accid. **4**(2–4), 311–333 (1982)
53. Kang, K.C., Cohen, S.G., Hess, J.A., Novak, W.E., Peterson, A.S.: Feature-Oriented Domain Analysis (FODA) Feasibility Study. Technical Report CMU/SEI-90-TR-21 - ESD-90-TR-222. Carnegie-Mellon Univ Pittsburgh Pa Software Engineering Inst. (1990)
54. Hansman, S.: A taxonomy of network and computer attack methodologies. Comput. Secur. **24**, 31–43 (2003)

Author Index